# Principles of
# Macroeconomics

# About the Author

John B. Taylor is the Raymond Professor of Economics at Stanford University and the director of Stanford's Introductory Economic Studies Center. Professor Taylor is a renowned teacher. Each year he teaches the introductory economics course about which students are wildly enthusiastic. As described in *The Stanford Daily*, "Many students say this course was their best experience in the classroom." Professor Taylor is known for his clear explanations and for his novel teaching ideas, including appearances by his family and a spiritual visitation by the voice of Adam Smith. In recognition of his teaching talents, he has received the Hoagland Prize, presented annually to Stanford's most outstanding teacher of undergraduate students, and the Rhodes Prize for excellent teaching in introductory courses. Professor Taylor studied economics at Princeton and received his Ph.D. at Stanford. He has also taught at Columbia, Yale, and Princeton.

Professor Taylor has published over 100 research papers and several books on economics, including his frequently cited work on wage setting and expectations. His book *Macroeconomics* is a best-selling intermediate text. His articles have appeared in the *Wall Street Journal,* the *Los Angeles Times,* and the *New York Times.* He has appeared on TV and radio shows, including CNN's *Crossfire,* ABC's *Nightline,* PBS's *NewsHour,* and NPR's *Talk of the Nation.* A formula he devised in 1993—now widely referred to as the Taylor Rule—is frequently used to predict Federal Reserve decisions, and "has attracted widening interest in recent years in the financial markets, the academic community, and at central banks," according to Alan Greenspan, chair of the Federal Reserve.

Professor Taylor served as a member of the President's Council of Economic Advisers from 1989 to 1991, where he helped put together the economic forecasts and was a trade negotiator at the Uruguay Round. In 1991 he returned to Stanford and his first loves, teaching and research. He directed the Stanford Center for Economic Policy Research from 1994 to 1997 and is now a member of the California Governor's Council of Economic Advisers and the Congressional Budget Office's Panel of Economic Advisers.

John Taylor currently lives on the Stanford campus with his wife and two children.

# Principles of Macroeconomics

**second edition**

**John B. Taylor**
*Stanford University*

Houghton Mifflin Company    Boston    New York

Editor-in-Chief: Bonnie Binkert
Basic Book Editor: Ann West
Senior Project Editor: Margaret M. Kearney
Senior Production/Design Coordinator: Carol Merrigan
Senior Manufacturing Coordinator: Priscilla J. Abreu
Marketing Manager: Juli Bliss

COVER DESIGN: Harold Burch, Harold Burch Design, New York City

PHOTO CREDITS: **Chapter 1:** p. 18, AP/Wide World Photos; p. 20, B. Markel/Gamma Liaison. **Chapter 2:** p. 36, Hazel Hankin/Stock Boston; p. 39, The Bettmann Archive; p. 40, Amanda Merillo/Stock Boston; p. 47 (top left), Phillip J. Griffiths/Magnum, p. 47 (bottom left), Nathan Benn/Stock Boston, p. 47 (middle), C. Pedrick/The Image Works, p. 47 (right), Kindra Clineff/ The Picture Cube. **Chapter 3:** p. 59 (left), Roy Morsch/Stock Market, p. 59 (right), Bob Daemmrich/Stock Boston.

*(Credits continue following the index.)*

Printed in the U.S.A.

Library of Congress Catalog Card Number: 97-72554

ISBN: 0-395-87453-X

23456789-VH-01 00 99 98

# Brief Contents

# Contents

## Part 3  LONG-RUN FUNDAMENTALS AND ECONOMIC GROWTH  166

### Chapter 7  Unemployment and Employment  168

# Preface

The goal of this book is to present modern economics in a form that is intuitive, interesting, and useful for students who have had no prior exposure to this fascinating subject. When I took the introductory economics course in college way back in the 1960s, I found the course and the textbook (Paul Samuelson's) fascinating. People called 1960s-vintage economics the "new economics," because many new ideas, including those put forth by John Maynard Keynes, were being applied for the first time in public policy. But during the 1970s, the 1980s, and the 1990s, economics underwent another tremendous wave of change. Now at the end of the 20th century, economics places much greater emphasis on incentives, on expectations, on long-run fundamentals, on the use of experiments, on rich surveys of individual experiences, on the theory of institutions, and on the importance of stable, predictable economic policies. These new ideas are both interesting and of great relevance to individuals, to firms, and to governments as we start the 21st century. The world economy has also changed radically in the last thirty years with market economies now being the preferred choice of virtually all countries around the world and with billions of more people linked together through international trade. With these changes economics is now more fascinating and more relevant than ever.

## JOINING THE OLD WITH THE NEW

My strategy in developing the first edition of the textbook, published three years ago, was to give these changes a prominent, clearly explained place alongside the older parts of economics and thereby to make modern economics—with all its fascination and relevance—available to beginning students. The enthusiastic reaction of teachers and students to the first edition has validated this strategy. Teachers who have successfully taught from the first edition point to the clear demonstrations of how a market economy actually works, to the thorough explanation of why markets are efficient when incentives are right and inefficient when incentives are wrong, to the emphasis on long-run fundamentals, to the lively analysis and discussion of real-world public policy, and perhaps most crucial—and certainly the most gratifying to me—to the clear, intuitive explanation of basic economic principles through analogy, example, and user-friendly graphs and illustrations.

## DEVELOPING THE SECOND EDITION

My strategy in developing the second edition of the text was to produce a streamlined version of the first edition—with more efficient exposition, better organization, more visually effective page layouts, and with many new and updated real-world examples. Suggestions for the revision came from students in the introductory course I teach each year, from students and faculty who have used the book at many other colleges and universities, and from experts in specialized areas—such as experimental economics or international trade—whose advice we sought directly.

Armed with these suggestions we created a revised outline for the second edition. I then revisited every line of text, every graph, every box, every cartoon, and every photo, adding, deleting, or rewriting to streamline, clarify, and update. After faculty reviews of this draft and, of course, more editing and rewriting, the manuscript moved into production, during which layout—the size and placement of text, tables, and graphs on the page—became my paramount concern. One of the advantages of modern computer page-making techniques is that I could interact in real time with the production editor, experimenting with different layouts and making sure, for example, that the descriptions of the graphs in the text were placed at the most helpful positions relative to the graphs themselves. Though most time-consuming, this interaction was invaluable for making a user-friendly, visually efficient layout.

## Key Text Revisions: Streamlining, Updating, and Enhancing Intuition

A few examples of the changes I made in the second edition will show how the discussion was streamlined, made more intuitive, and updated. A detailed account of all the additions, deletions, and modifications is found in the transition guide in the Instructor's Resource Manual and on the web site (http://www.hmco.com/college).

Streamlining was acheived, for example, by reducing the preview of macroeconomic theory in the macroeconomic overview chapter; Chapter 5 now focuses more on a review of the key macroeconomic facts. I also shortened the appendix on growth accounting accompanying Chapter 9, "Technology and Economic Growth," and moved some of the explanatory material on growth accounting into a new box in Chapter 9. The chapter on economic growth around the world (Chapter 10 in the first edition) was moved toward the end of the book, leaving four chapters on long-run fundamentals and economic growth and the same number of chapters on economic fluctuations. The description of the Fed was moved into the long-run oriented chapter on the monetary system (Chapter 10), with the later chapter on monetary policy (Chapter 16) now focusing more on monetary independence. The chapters that develop the model of the recovery of the economy after a recession were consolidated into a single chapter (13) in order to better exploit the analogy with supply and demand curves. Chapter 14, "Toward Recovery and Expansion," uses the model developed in Chapter 13 to illustrate the path the economy takes toward recovery after a recession. A streamlined description of the Fed's behavior in response to inflation is contained in Chapter 13, while the more detailed description of different policies is covered in Chapter 16. I also increased the number of teaching options by making it possible for instructors to skip Chapter 12, "The Uncertain Multiplier," which discusses the multiplier calculations using the Keynesian Cross.

Examples of new material added to this edition include discussions of the new chain-weighted real GDP measures, the CPI bias problem, the world savings shortage, the new line-item veto authority used by President Clinton for the first time in 1997, pre-emptive monetary strikes, and, of course, all the new macroeconomic data and developments from the last three years.

## New, Improved Boxes

As we revised, added, or updated boxes, we gave many of them special designations—"Reading the News About . . ." or "Using Economics to Explain . . ."—in order to help students use the material more effectively. Among the many new or revised boxes you'll find coverage of interest rates and exchange rates (Chapter 8) and forecasting with econometric models (Chapter 11); you'll also find Reading the News boxes about price floors (Chapter 3), GDP each month (Chapter 6), the Fed (Chapter 13), and Big Mac purchasing power parity (Chapter 17), among many others.

### Enhanced Teaching and Learning Package

The package of teaching and learning aids (described below) has been completely revised with several new options. The teaching software has been expanded to match each chapter of the text. A web page is now available to provide additional help and information to both students and instructors. And a new series of teaching videos has been produced.

# A BRIEF TOUR

*Principles of Macroeconomics* is designed for a one-term course. I recognize that teachers use a great variety of sequences and syllabi, and I have therefore taken great pains to allow for alternative plans of coverage. International economic issues are considered throughout the text, with separate chapters on international economic policy.

**PART 1**
**Introduction to Economics and Its Foundations**

The basic workings of markets and the reasons they improve people's lives are the subjects of Part 1. Chapter 1 introduces the field of economics through a case study showing how economists observe and explain economic puzzles. Chapter 1 defines key terms and ideas, and Chapter 2 outlines the basic unifying themes of economics: scarcity, choice, and the production possibilities curve. The role of prices, the inherent international aspect of economics, the importance of property rights and incentives, and the difference between central planning and markets are some of the key ideas in these chapters. Chapters 3 and 4 cover the basic supply and demand model. I have tried to explain these basic ideas as fully and as clearly as I can, adding the extra sentence of clarification whenever it might help in understanding. The goal is to show how to use the supply and demand model and to learn to "think like an economist."

**PART 2**
**Introduction to Macroeconomics**

**PART 3**
**Long-Run Fundamentals and Economic Growth**

Part 2 begins the study of macroeconomics. Chapter 5 is an overview of the facts emphasizing that macroeconomics is concerned with the growth and the fluctuations in the economy as a whole. Chapter 6 shows how GDP and other variables are measured.

Response to the first edition's treatment of long-run issues before developing the theory of economic fluctuations was overwhelmingly positive, and the second edition takes that approach one step further by streamlining the coverage of economic growth from five to four chapters so as to allow for a speedier introduction to fluctuations. Part 3 thus begins with an analysis of how the level of unemployment in the economy as a whole is determined and goes on to explore the accumulation of capital and technological progress. Labor, capital, and technology are presented here as the fundamental determinants of the economy's growth path. One clear advantage of this approach is that it allows students to focus first on issues about which there is general agreement among economists and in which many of the deep policy problems facing us at the start of the 21st century lie: long-term growth. Moreover, this ordering helps the student better understand short-term economic fluctuations.

As shown in the four chapters of Part 4, the economy does fluctuate as it grows over time. Declines in production and increases in unemployment (characteristics of the recessions of the early 1980s and early 1990s) have not vanished from the landscape as the problems of long-term growth have come to the fore. Part 4 delves into the causes of these fluctuations and an analysis of why they end. It begins by explaining why shifts in aggregate demand may cause the economy to fluctuate and ends by showing that price adjustment plays a significant role in the end of recessions.

Countries have tried a variety of approaches to deal with economic growth and economic fluctuations. Part 5 examines these approaches to policy, about which there are many differing opinions. I have tried to explain these differences as clearly and as objectively as I can; there are also areas of agreement, which are stressed. Chapter 20 examines alternative approaches to converting economies from central planning to more market-oriented systems, a task that confronts a large segment of the world's population today. Part 5 also looks into the international aspects of policy, especially in Chapter 17 on international finance and Chapters 21 and 22 on international trade theory and policy.

**PART 4**
**Economic Fluctuations**

**PART 5**
**Macroeconomic Policy**

# PEDAGOGICAL FEATURES

The following pedagogical features are designed to help the student learn economics.

*Case studies within the text.* This feature uses real-world situations to help motivate economic ideas and models. Examples include health care in Chapter 1, a recent drought in the U.S. peanut market in Chapter 3, and setting national park fees in Chapter 4.

*Interesting economic puzzles to stimulate interest in economic models.* Most chapters begin with a description of real-world phenomena which economics can help to explain. Examples include the opportunity costs of college for Tiger Woods in Chapter 1 and the sharp rise in oil prices during the Persian Gulf War in Chapter 4.

*Integrating modern economic concepts* in the context of substantive economic problems rather than in separate chapters. This approach demonstrates the relevance of the new ideas and keeps the text to a manageable size. For example, time inconsistency is described in the context of particular economic policy problems.

*Brief reviews at the end of each major section* (about four per chapter) summarize the key points in abbreviated form as the chapter evolves; these reviews are useful for preliminary skim reading as well as for review.

*Boxes to give both current event and historical perspectives.* Many of the text's boxes explain how to decipher recent news stories about economic policy. Others examine the contributions of the great economists such as Adam Smith and Alfred Marshall, the history of great ideas, and key historical events.

*Functional use of full color* to distinguish between curves and to show how the curves shift dynamically over time. An example of the effective use of multiple colors can be found in the discussion of increasing opportunity costs in Chapter 2.

*Complete captions and small conversation boxes in graphs.* The captions and the small yellow-shaded conversation boxes, such as in the graph in the margin, make many of the figures completely self-contained. In some graphs, sequential numbering of these conversation boxes stresses the dynamic nature of the curves.

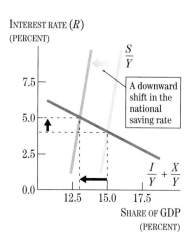

*Use of photos and cartoons to illustrate abstract ideas.*   Special care has gone into the selection of photos to illustrate difficult economic ideas such as inelastic supply curves or opportunity costs. Each text photo (many consisting of two or three parts) has a short title and caption to explain its relevance to the text discussion.

*Key term definitions* in the margin and a listing of the terms at the end of every chapter and appendix. There is also an alphabetized glossary at the end of the book.

*Questions for review* at the end of every chapter. These are tests of recall and require only short answers; they can be used for oral review or as a quick self-check.

*Problems,* an essential tool in learning economics, have been carefully selected and tested. An ample supply of these appear in every chapter and appendix. Some of these problems ask the reader to work out examples that are slightly different from the ones in the text; others require a more critical thinking approach. A second set of problems which parallels those at the end of each chapter has been developed for the second edition. Included in the accompanying test bank, this problem set is also available to instructors via the web site.

# A COMPLETE PACKAGE OF TEACHING AND LEARNING AIDS

The highly effective teaching and learning package prepared to accompany the text has been completely revised, updated, and expanded. It provides a full range of support for instructors and students.

*Study Guide.*   David Papell of the University of Houston and John Solow of the University of Iowa have prepared the study guide for the text. In my view, this study guide provides a wonderful learning opportunity that many students will value. Each chapter contains an overview, informal chapter reviews, and a section called "Zeroing In," which harnesses student intuition to explain the chapter's most important concepts. The study guide also provides ample means for practice in using the economic ideas and graphs introduced in each text chapter. A section called "Working It Out" provides worked problems that take students step by step through the analytical process needed to solve real-world applications of core concepts covered in the chapter. End-of-part quizzes offer students one last chance to test their retention of material before taking in-class exams.

*Taylor Tutorial and Simulation Software*.   A flexible, interactive computerized tutorial is available for students to review basic concepts covered in the text. A tutorial for each chapter in the text provides a second opportunity for students to review concepts and models and then to test themselves on what they've learned. A glossary and context-sensitive help are always available. The simulation component of the software includes over 60 years of data on more than 20 key economic indicators, allowing students to graph and compare various measurement instruments and print out their results.

*Test Bank.*   A reliable test bank is the most important resource for efficient and effective learning and teaching. A test bank to go along with the text has been prepared by Stuart Glosser of the University of Wisconsin, Whitewater, and myself. It contains more than 3,000 test questions—including multiple choice, true/false, short answer, and problems—many of which are based on graphs. The questions are coded for correct answer, question type, level of difficulty, and text topic. At the end of each test bank chapter is a set of problems that parallels the end-of-chapter problems from the text.

*Computerized Testing Program.*   A sophisticated and user-friendly program called ESA Test is available so that instructors can quickly create tests according to various selection criteria, including random selection. The program prints graphs as well as the text part of each question. Instructors can scramble the answer choices, edit questions, add their own questions to the pool, and customize their exams in various other ways. The program is available in Windows and Mac versions.

*Instructor's Resource Manual.*   Prepared by Wm. Stewart Mounts, Jr. of Mercer University, Denise Hixson of Midlands Technical College, and myself, the Instructor's Resource Manual provides both first-time and experienced instructors with a variety of additional resources for use with the text. Each chapter contains a brief overview, teaching objectives, key terms from the text, a section that orients instructors to the text's unique approach, and a suggested lecture outline with teaching tips that provide additional examples not found in the text and hints for teaching more difficult material. Discussion topics and solutions to end-of-chapter text problems are also provided.

*Overhead Transparencies.*   A set of full-color transparencies for all of the numbered figures used to describe the economic models or theories in the text is available for those who are using the text. I usually use two overhead projectors in class so that more than one figure or table can be shown simultaneously.

*Power Presentation Manager.*   This Windows-based software, developed by Houghton Mifflin, allows instructors to create customized lecture presentations that can be displayed on computer-based projection systems. The software, which includes a run-time version of Microsoft PowerPoint, makes available the figures, tables, and key equations from the text and also allows for access to laser disk sequences, instructors' own PowerPoint sets, and screens from other Windows-based software. With the Power Presentation Manager, instructors can quickly and easily integrate all these components—and create their own screens as well—to prepare a seamless classroom presentation with minimal in-class tinkering.

*Classroom Experiments: A User's Guide.*   As I mentioned previously, the text makes use of results from experimental economics to test models and to explain how markets work. I have regularly used experiments in my introductory economics classes—both small sections and large lectures—to illustrate how markets work, and it seems that more and more instructors are incorporating experiments into their classroom teaching. For those instructors who would like to do similar experiments, a lab manual has been prepared by Greg Delemeester of Marietta College and John Neral of Frostburg State University. Written with the first-time user in mind, the manual includes detailed step-by-step instructions for conducting 18 experiments in the classroom setting.

*Economics Video Series.*   This exciting teaching tool, which combines footage from my own classroom, animated charts and graphs, and additional narration, brings key economic ideas from the text to life. The video segments can be used as lecture launchers or as a review of material both inside and outside the classroom. The videos also serve as an introduction to some of the concepts that are unique to my text—such as the development of the aggregate demand and price adjustment graph.

***Web Site.*** The web site (http://www.hmco.com/college), developed to accompany this text, provides an extended learning environment for students and a rich store of teaching resources for instructors who are using the text. With materials carefully chosen to complement and supplement each chapter, students will find key economic links for every chapter as well as numerous opportunities to test their mastery of chapter content—including extended web-based assignments developed by John Kane of SUNY, Oswego. Another feature allows students and instructors to submit questions or comments about the text. Instructors will find a complete set of parallel questions matching the end-of-chapter problems from the text (with answers), economic and teaching resource links, teaching tips, and the opportunity to view and demo the teaching and student software components of the teaching package.

# ACKNOWLEDGMENTS

Completing a project like this is a team effort. I have had the chance to work with an excellent team of professionals at Houghton Mifflin. I worked closely with Bonnie Binkert, Ann West, and Margaret Kearney on this edition and I am grateful to them for their help and encouragement. I would also like to thank Priscilla Abreu, Juli Bliss, Patricia English, Carol Merrigan, Penny Peters, and Adrienne Vincent.

I am grateful to many of my colleagues at Stanford whom I consulted hundreds of times and to the Economics 1 students who used the book and gave me feedback that helped me determine when and where to add that extra sentence of explanation.

Many college teachers and researchers read all or part of the manuscript and gave very helpful comments that were incorporated into revisions. The book would not exist without the help of these reviewers, who are listed on the next page. In particular, I wish to thank David Figlio, Denise Hixson, and David Spencer, who reviewed the text for accuracy during the last stages of production.

My family deserves very special thanks for putting up with me and with the seemingly endless early morning phone calls and piles of manuscript, news clippings, reviews, galleys, and page proof scattered about the house as I worked on the second edition. This book is dedicated to my family.

John B. Taylor
Stanford, California

# REVIEWERS

Mark D. Agee
*Pennsylvania State University, Altoona*

Lee J. Alston
*University of Illinois*

Christine Amsler
*Michigan State University*

Charles Andrews
*Mercer University*

Dean Baim
*Pepperdine University*

Raymond S. Barnstone
*Northeastern University and
  Lesley College*

Kari Battaglia
*University of North Texas*

Klaus G. Becker
*Texas Tech University*

Valerie R. Bencivenga
*Cornell University*

Roger Bowles
*University of Bath*

Jozell Brister
*Abilene Christian University*

Paula Bracy
*University of Toledo*

Robert Brown
*Texas Technical University*

Robert Buchele
*Smith College*

Michael R. Butler
*Texas Christian University*

Richard Call
*American River College*

Leonard A. Carlson
*Emory University*

Michael J. Carter
*University of Massachusetts, Lowell*

Kenneth Chinn
*Southeastern Oklahoma State University*

Mike Cohick
*Collin County Community College*

Eric D. Craft
*University of Richmond*

William F. Chapel
*University of Mississippi*

Marcelo Clerici-Arias
*Stanford University*

Stephen L. Cobb
*University of North Texas*

Kathy L. Combs
*California State University, Los Angeles*

Joyce Cooper
*Boston University*

Steven Craig
*University of Houston*

Michael A. Curme
*Miami University*

Ward S. Curran
*Trinity College*

Audrey Davidson
*University of Louisville*

Joseph Daniels
*Marquette University*

Gregg Davis
*Marshall University*

Gregory E. DeFreitas
*Hofstra University*

Mary E. Deily
*Lehigh University*

David N. DeJong
*University of Pittsburgh*

David Denslow
*University of Florida*

Enrica Detragiache
*Johns Hopkins University*

Michael Devereux
*University of British Columbia*

Michael Dowd
*University of Toledo*

Douglas Downing
*Seattle Pacific University*

Dean Dudley
*United States Military Academy*

Mary E. Edwards
*St. Cloud State University*

David Figlio
*University of Oregon*

Gerald Friedman
*University of Massachusetts, Amherst*

Edwin T. Fujii
*University of Hawaii*

Mary Gade
*Oklahoma State University*

Janet Gerson
*University of Michigan*

J. Robert Gillette
*University of Kentucky*

Donna Ginther
*Southern Methodist College*

Mark Glick
*University of Utah*

Stuart M. Glosser
*University of Wisconsin, Whitewater*

Phil Graves
*University of Colorado, Boulder*

Paul W. Grimes
*Mississippi State University*

Lorna S. Gross
*Worcester State College*

Shoshana Grossbard-Shechtman
*San Diego State University*

Alan Haight
*Bowling Green State University*

David R. Hakes
*University of Northern Iowa*

Greg Hamilton
*Marist College*

David Hansen
*Linfield College*

Mehidi Harian
*Bloomsburg University*

Richard Harper
*University of West Florida*

Mitchell Harwitz
*State University of New York, Buffalo*

Mary Ann Hendryson
*Western Washington University*

James B. Herendeen
*University of Texas, El Paso*

Pershing J. Hill
*University of Alaska, Anchorage*

Denise Hixson
*Midlands Technical College*

Gail Mitchell Hoyt
*University of Richmond*

James M. Hvidding
*Kutztown University*

Beth Ingram
*University of Iowa*

Joyce Jacobsen
*Wesleyan University*

Syed Jafri
*Tarleton State University*

David Jaques
*California Polytech University, Pomona*

John Jascot
*Capital Community Technical College*

Allan Jenkins
*University of Nebraska, Kearney*

David Johnson
*Wilfred Laurier University*

Charles W. Johnston
*University of Michigan, Flint*

Nake Kamrany
*University of Southern California*

John Kane
*State University of New York, Oswego*

Manfred Keil
*Claremont McKenna College*

Elizabeth Kelly
*University of Wisconsin, Madison*

Kristen Keith
*University of Alaska*

John Klein
*Georgia State University*

Harry T. Kolendrianos
*Danville Community College*

Margaret Landman
*Bridgewater State College*

Philip J. Lane
*Fairfield University*

William Lang
*Rutgers University*

William D. Lastrapes
*University of Georgia*

Jim Lee
*Fort Hays State University*

Lawrence A. Leger
*Loughborough University*

David Li
*University of Michigan*

Susan Linz
*Michigan State University*

John K. Lodewijks
*University of New South Wales*

R. Ashley Lyman
*University of Idaho*

Craig MacPhee
*University of Nebraska, Lincoln*

Michael Magura
*University of Toledo*

Robert A. Margo
*Vanderbilt University*

John D. Mason
*Gordon College*

Robert McAuliffe
*Babson College*

Henry N. McCarl
*University of Alabama, Birmingham*

Laurence C. McCulloch
*Ohio State University*

Rob Roy McGregor
*University of North Carolina, Charlotte*

Richard McIntyre
*University of Rhode Island*

Gaminie Meepagala
*Howard University*

Douglas Morgan
*University of California, Santa Barbara*

Micke Meurs
*American University*

Khan A. Mohabbat
*Northern Illinois University*

Norma Morgan
*Curry College*

W. Douglas Morgan
*University of California, Santa Barbara*

Wm. Stewart Mounts, Jr.
*Mercer University*

Vai-Lam Mui
*University of Southern California*

David C. Murphy
*Boston College*

Ronald C. Necoechea
*Ball State University*

Hong V. Nguyen
*University of Scranton*

Rachel Nugent
*Pacific Lutheran University*

Anthony Patrick O'Brien
*Lehigh University*

William C. O'Connor
*Western Montana College*

Eliot S. Orton
*New Mexico State University*

David Papell
*University of Houston*

Walter Park
*American University*

Charles Parker
*Wayne State College*

James Payne
*Eastern Kentucky University*

E. Charles Pflanz
*Scottsdale Community College*

William A. Phillips
*University of Southern Maine*

Glenn J. Platt
*Miami University*

Charles Plott
*California Institute of Technology*

Lidija Polutnik
*Babson College*

David L. Prychitko
*State University of New York, Oswego*

Salim Rashid
*University of Illinois, Urbana-Champaign*

Margaret A. Ray
*Mary Washington College*

Geoffrey Renshaw
*University of Warwick*

John Ridpath
*York University*

Greg Rose
*Sacramento City College*

B. Peter Rosendorff
*University of Southern California*

Robert Rossana
*Wayne State University*

Marina Rosser
*James Madison University*

Kartic C. Roy
*University of Queensland*

Daniel Rubenson
*Southern Oregon State College*

Jeffrey Rubin
*Rutgers University*

Robert S. Rycroft
*Mary Washington College*

Jonathan Sandy
*University of San Diego*

Jeff Sarbaum
*State University of New York, Binghamton*

Gary Saxonhouse
*University of Michigan*

Edward Scahill
*University of Scranton*

James Byron Schlomach
*Texas A&M University*

Torsten Schmidt
*University of New Hampshire*

Thomas J. Shea
*Springfield College*

William J. Simeone
*Providence College*

Michael Smitka
*Washington & Lee University*

Ronald Soligo
*Rice University*

John L. Solow
*University of Iowa*

Clifford Sowell
*Berea College*

Michael Spagat
*Brown University*

David Spencer
*Brigham Young University*

J. R. Stanfield
*Colorado State University*

Ann B. Sternlicht
*University of Richmond*

Richard Stevenson
*Liverpool University*

James Stodder
*Rensselaer Polytechnic Institute*

Leslie S. Stratton
*University of Arizona*

Robert Stuart
*Rutgers University*

James Swoffard
*University of South Alabama*

Bette Lewis Tokar
*Holy Family College*

Paul Turner
*University of Leeds*

Gerald R. Visgilio
*Connecticut College*

Manhar Vyas
*University of Pittsburgh*

William V. Weber
*Eastern Illinois University*

Karl Wesolowski
*Salem State College*

Joseph Wesson
*State University of New York, Potsdam*

Geoff Whittam
*University of Glasgow*

Kenneth P. Wickman
*State University of New York, Cortland*

Catherine Winnett
*University of Bath*

Jennifer P. Wissink
*Cornell University*

Simon Wren-Lewis
*University of Strathclyde*

Peter R. Wyman
*Spokane Falls Community College*

Ali Zaker Shahrak
*University of Santa Clara*

# Principles of
# Macroeconomics

second edition

# part

1

# Introduction to Economics and Its Foundations

A market economy is a social system in which most goods and services produced by people are sold to other people in markets at freely determined prices. But what exactly is a market? And how are prices determined? Does a market economy improve people's lives? If so, why, and by how much compared with other economic systems, such as the economies of primitive societies where little was bought or sold in markets, or those in modern societies where buying and selling has been severely restricted in some way? These are the most fundamental questions of economics and they are addressed in the first four chapters of the book. To answer these questions you must learn to "think like an economist."

Chapters 1 and 2 together define economics and present the first inklings of how economists think. In

PRICE

CHOICE

QUANTITY

SCARCITY

SUPPLY

DEMAND

Chapter 1 we show how economists observe and explain economic facts. In Chapter 2 we delineate three unifying themes of economics: *scarcity* of time or resources, *choices* among several alternative ends, and the *interaction* of people in using the resources to achieve the ends. In Chapters 3 and 4 we reveal a one-hundred-year-old model—called the supply and demand model—which economists still use every day to explain how markets work.

These ideas and models are of great use to economists working for the government and for private business firms. When economists object to government controls on prices, they have these models in mind. When they argue that restrictions on the imports of foreign goods will cost consumers dearly, they use the supply and demand model to calculate the cost. When

economists make recommendations for improving the operation of government or firms, they think about how markets provide incentives; they sometimes find ways for government or organizations to mimic the market. Once you understand the models you can use them to help form and defend your own ideas on these important issues.

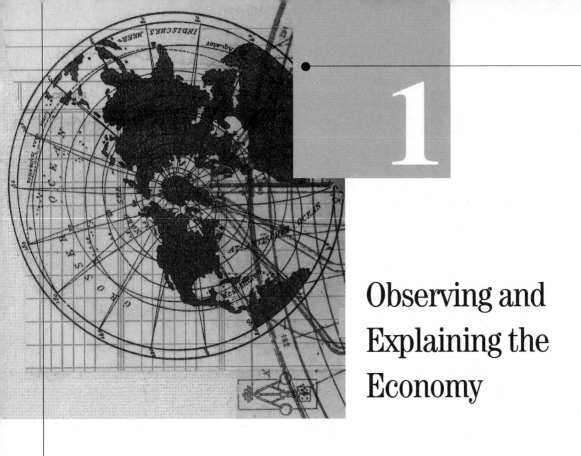

# 1

# Observing and Explaining the Economy

This is a true story. In the spring of 1996, a 19-year-old college sophomore, who had just finished taking introductory economics, was faced with a *choice:* to continue college for an additional two years or to devote full time to a job. The job was being a professional golfer on the pro tour—a job for which the sophomore was uniquely qualified, having won three U.S. amateur titles. Doing both college and the pro tour was not an option because time is *scarce:* With only 24 hours in the day, he simply did not have time to do both. For this sophomore, completing college had a great cost: not only the two years of college expenses, but also the foregone tournament winnings and advertising endorsements (over $40 million) that a successful pro golf career would bring. The golfer—his name is Tiger Woods—made a choice. He became a pro. By the fall of 1996 he was selected Sportsman of the Year by *Sports Illustrated,* and in April 1997 he stunned the golfing world with a record-setting win of the venerable Masters Tournament—winning nearly half a million dollars.

More than anything else, economics is about such choices: whether to go to college or get a job after high school, to take economics or biology, to invest in one stock or another, to take one job or another, to go to work or stay home with children, or even whether to buy a cup of coffee at the student union or at a stylish café down the street. Economics is also about how to make good collective decisions as citizens of a community, state, or country. Decisions about what sort of taxes should be levied, whether bridges should be free or have tolls, or whether citizens of other countries should be allowed to trade freely with and migrate to your country are all informed by economics. Whether it is Tiger Woods, you, your best friend, your teacher, the president of a large firm, or even the president of the United States, the economic principles underlying the decisions are the same. Economics helps individuals and societies make choices about the challenges and opportunities they face.

The world faces a variety of economic challenges and opportunities as we move from the twentieth to the twenty-first century. Smaller improvements in living standards—a trend that started in the 1970s—are leaving many people in the current generation little better off than their parents, if better off at all. The gap between the wages of low-skilled and high-skilled workers has widened. Aside from a few notable exceptions in east Asia, many less-developed countries have not significantly reduced the gap between themselves and the more developed countries, such as the United States, in the last 50 years. People worry about losing their jobs to foreign workers in an increasingly global economy.

Yet, if we look around the world, we see tremendous economic opportunities. Political revolutions—symbolized by the tearing down of the Berlin Wall in 1989—have freed billions of people from tight government controls on their economies. Advances in information and transportation technologies have opened up new markets to sell and buy goods. Experience with a great inflation in the 1970s has taught us important lessons about how and why to keep inflation low, complementing the lessons about unemployment taught earlier by the Great Depression of the 1930s.

How we—workers, students, parents, consumers, retirees, politicians, voters—approach these economic challenges and opportunities will depend on our knowledge of how the economy works. If our economic knowledge is sound and if we apply it well, we can transform the challenges and opportunities into genuinely improved outcomes. Fifty years from now, historians will look back to the turn of the century to determine why the first decades of the twenty-first century were so good, or so bad. They will study how people applied their economic knowledge to decisions concerning jobs, education, child-rearing, consumption, retirement, and the role of government.

The purpose of this book is to introduce you to the field of economics and to help you understand the eco-

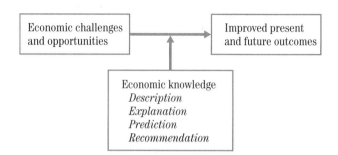

nomic challenges and opportunities you face as an individual and as a participant in the world economy. The objective is not to peek passively but to analyze actively. Economics is a way of thinking. It entails accurately *describing* economic events, *explaining* why the events occur, *predicting* under what circumstances such events might take place in the future, and *recommending* appropriate courses of action. To make use of economics, you will want to learn to do the describing, the explaining, and even the predicting and recommending yourself; that is, to reason and to think like an economist.

In answer to the question "What is economics?" a wisecracking economist once said, "It's what economists do." To get us started in our study of economics, this chapter examines two of the main things economists do: documenting and quantifying observations about the economy and developing and using models of how the economy works.

# OBSERVATIONS: WHAT ECONOMISTS ENDEAVOR TO EXPLAIN

Just as physicists try to explain the existence of black holes in outer space or biologists try to explain why dinosaurs became extinct, economists try to explain puzzling observations and facts about the economy. Many observations come from everyday life. You might want to begin your study of economics by asking questions about economic observations—from your own experience, from recent news stories, from your history or political science courses. Perhaps some of your questions might be on topics like these:

▶ Why did health-care spending increase so rapidly compared to the rest of the U.S. economy in the last 20 years?

▶ Why did the price of health care increase more than most other prices?

► Why has the price of a college education also been increasing rapidly?

► Why have the wages of college-educated people increased much more rapidly than the wages of high school dropouts since the 1970s?

► What caused the Great Depression of the 1930s?

► Why is the average income of people in the United States about 30 times higher than that of people in China?

► Why is unemployment much higher in Europe than in the United States?

All these questions are based on observations about the economy. Some, like rising college tuition, are fairly obvious and are based on casual observation. But in order to answer such questions, economists, like physicists or biologists, need to systematically document and quantify their observations and look for patterns. If we can establish the date when dinosaurs became extinct, then we might test our hunch that a cataclysmic event such as an asteroid hitting the earth may have caused their extinction. To illustrate how economists document and quantify their observations, let us briefly focus on the first two of the preceding questions, the ones concerning health care and the economy.

## Documenting and Quantifying Observations: A Case Study

Rising health-care spending and prices are more than a curiosity. The more a society spends on health care, the less it can spend on other things. Concerns about rising health-care spending have led to major proposals for changing how health care is provided and paid for in the United States. Throughout the 1990s, health care has been a major political issue. For example, debates about how to slow rising spending on Medicare—a government health-care program for the elderly—raged during the 1996 presidential and congressional elections. Let's see how the facts about health-care spending are put together.

In order to determine whether health-care spending has increased relative to the rest of the economy, as stated in the first question, we need a measure of health-care spending and a measure of the size of the overall economy.

### GDP, Health Care, and the Health-Care Share

**gross domestic product (GDP):** a measure of the value of all the goods and services newly produced in an economy during a specified period of time.

The most comprehensive available measure of the size of an economy is the **gross domestic product (GDP).** For the United States, GDP is the total value of all products made in the United States during a specified period of time, such as a year. GDP includes all newly made goods, such as cars, trucks, shoes, airplanes, houses, and telephones; it also includes services, such as education, rock concerts, and health care. To measure the total value of all products made in the economy, economists add up all the dollars that people spend on the products.

How large is GDP in the United States? In 1995, it was $7,246 billion, or about $7.2 trillion. We can compute GDP in any year, and the question about health-care spending and the size of the economy requires that we look at the economy over time. In 1977, GDP was $2,027 billion. Column (1) of Table 1.1 provides a 20-year history of GDP.

**economic history:** the study of economic events and the collection of economic observations from the past.

In order to document observations and look for patterns, economists usually need to look back at some historical period and see what happened. The study of economic events of the past is called **economic history.** Economic historians frequently go back much more than 20 years to obtain observations. For example,

TABLE 1.1
**GDP and Health-Care Spending, 1977–1996**

| Year | (1) GDP | (2) Health-Care Spending | (3) Health-Care Share of GDP (percent) |
|------|---------|--------------------------|----------------------------------------|
| 1977 | 2,027 | 123 | 6.1 |
| 1978 | 2,291 | 140 | 6.1 |
| 1979 | 2,558 | 158 | 6.2 |
| 1980 | 2,784 | 181 | 6.5 |
| 1981 | 3,116 | 213 | 6.8 |
| 1982 | 3,242 | 239 | 7.4 |
| 1983 | 3,515 | 268 | 7.6 |
| 1984 | 3,902 | 294 | 7.5 |
| 1985 | 4,181 | 322 | 7.7 |
| 1986 | 4,422 | 346 | 7.8 |
| 1987 | 4,692 | 381 | 8.1 |
| 1988 | 5,050 | 429 | 8.5 |
| 1989 | 5,439 | 477 | 8.8 |
| 1990 | 5,744 | 538 | 9.4 |
| 1991 | 5,917 | 586 | 9.9 |
| 1992 | 6,244 | 647 | 10.4 |
| 1993 | 6,550 | 697 | 10.6 |
| 1994 | 6,931 | 739 | 10.7 |
| 1995 | 7,246 | 784 | 10.8 |
| 1996 | 7,576 | 816 | 10.8 |

*Note:* GDP and health-care spending are measured in billions of dollars.
*Source:* U.S. Department of Commerce.

100 times column 2 divided by column 1

Robert Fogel, an economic historian who won the Nobel Prize in economics in 1993, has gone back over 300 years to collect data on nutrition and health, partly to better understand rising health-care spending today. As Fogel stated in his Nobel lecture, "Uncovering what actually happened in the past requires an enormous investment in time and effort."[1] Although covering a relatively short period, the observations shown in Table 1.1 are enough to illustrate how economists quantify their observations.

Economists frequently use graphs to present data like those shown in Table 1.1. For example, Figure 1.1 plots the data on GDP from column (1) of Table 1.1. The vertical axis is measured in billions of dollars; the horizontal axis is measured in years. For example, the point at the extreme lower left in Figure 1.1 represents GDP of $2,027 billion (on the vertical axis) in the year 1977 (on the horizontal axis). The points are connected by a line, which helps us visualize the steadily growing GDP during this period.

Now let us consider health-care spending, which includes payments for hospital services, lab tests, nursing homes, visits to the doctor or dentist, drugs, hearing aids, and eyeglasses. By adding up all spending on health care, we get $784 billion in 1995. This amount is about three times as large as the entire automobile industry, including cars, trucks, and parts.

1. Robert W. Fogel, "Economic Growth, Population Theory, and Physiology: The Bearing of Long-Term Processes on the Making of Economic Policy," *American Economic Review,* June 1994, p. 389.

**FIGURE 1.1**
**Gross Domestic Product (GDP) in the United States, 1977–1996**

GDP is the total dollar value of newly produced goods and services. It can be measured by adding up what people spend on everything from health care to cars. For each year from 1977 to 1996, GDP is plotted; the line connects all the points.

*Source:* U.S. Department of Commerce.

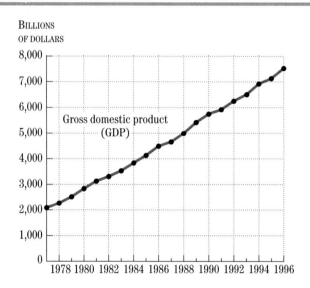

**FIGURE 1.2**
**Spending on Health Care in the United States, 1977–1996**

Health-care spending is the dollar value of payments for hospitals, doctors, dentists, nursing homes, drugs, and other items that provide medical care. Health care is one part of GDP.

*Source:* U.S. Department of Commerce.

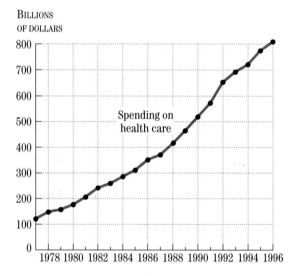

**FIGURE 1.3**
**Health-Care Spending as a Percent of GDP**

Each point in the graph is the ratio of spending on health care from Figure 1.2 to GDP from Figure 1.1, measured as a percent. For example, in 1995, health-care spending was $784 billion and GDP was $7,246 billion. The ratio is 784/7,246 = .108, or 10.8 percent.

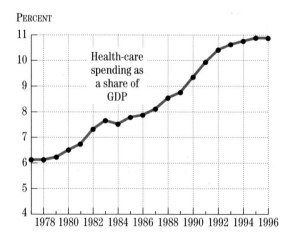

Health-care spending from 1977 to 1996 is listed in column (2) of Table 1.1 and is plotted in Figure 1.2. Figures 1.1 and 1.2 show that both GDP and health-care spending have grown since 1977. One way to assess the growth of health-care spending compared to spending on all goods and services is to look at health-care spending as a share, or percentage, of GDP. For example, health-care spending in 1995 was $784 billion; GDP was $7,246 billion. Thus, the share (in percentage terms) of GDP going to health care was

$$\frac{\text{Health-care spending}}{\text{GDP}} \times 100 = \begin{array}{l} \text{health-care spending} \\ \text{as a share of GDP} \end{array}$$

$$\frac{784}{7,246} \times 100 = 10.8 \text{ percent}$$

Column (3) of Table 1.1 performs this calculation for all years from 1977 to 1996. Again, you can observe a pattern by plotting the shares, as in Figure 1.3. Health-care spending has been rising as a percent of GDP—or relative to the size of the economy, although it has recently started to slow down. Although both GDP and health-care spending have been increasing, health-care spending has been increasing more quickly, at least until recently. We have now quantified the observation about rising health-care spending. Now let us go on to consider the second question about health care and see whether the price of health care has risen compared with the price of other goods and services in the economy.

### Overall Price Level, Health-Care Price, and Relative Price

Column (1) of Table 1.2 shows a measure of the average price of all the goods and services in GDP. Economists gather this information from surveys of prices of individual goods and services. They average these prices, giving greater weight to the prices of items on which more is spent. This average, plotted in Figure 1.4, is called the **overall price level.** A quick glance at the figure shows the increasing trend in the overall price level. There is a tendency for all prices to rise over time. The general increase in prices over time is called **inflation.** The **inflation rate** is defined as the percentage increase in the overall price level from one year to the next. The inflation rate has never fallen below zero during these years; in other words, the price level has never declined.

**overall price level:** an average of the prices of all goods and services with greater weight given to items on which more is spent.

**inflation:** an increase in the overall price level.

The tendency for the overall price level to rise over time affects our measure of GDP. Economists correct GDP for the rise in the overall price level and get a measure called **real GDP.** Real GDP can be computed by dividing GDP by the overall price level. Real GDP increases much less rapidly than GDP.

**inflation rate:** the percentage increase in the overall price level from one year to the next.

Having examined the overall price level, let us now determine whether the increase in the price of health care is greater than the increase in the overall price level. Column (2) of Table 1.2 shows a measure of the price of health care from lab tests to drugs. It is an average of the prices of all the items we included in our measure of health-care spending. Figure 1.5 plots the price of health care; like the overall price level, it has increased.

**real gross domestic product (real GDP):** a measure of the value of all the goods and services newly produced in a country during some period of time, adjusted for inflation.

Now, to determine whether the price of health care has increased more or less rapidly than the overall price level, we look at the relative price of health care. The **relative price** is a measure of health-care prices compared with the average prices of all goods and services. It is computed by dividing the health-care price by the overall price level:

**relative price:** the price of a particular good compared to the price of other goods.

$$\begin{array}{l} \text{Relative price} \\ \text{of health care} \end{array} = \frac{\text{health-care price}}{\text{overall price level}}$$

**FIGURE 1.4**
**The Overall Price Level in the United States**

The overall price level in the economy is like an average of prices of all goods and services in GDP. The overall price level has risen every year from 1977 to 1996.

*Source:* U.S. Department of Commerce.

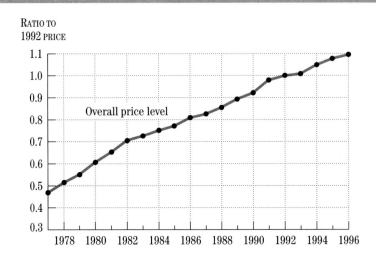

**FIGURE 1.5**
**The Price of Health Care**

The average price of health care has increased sharply since the 1970s, although the increase has slowed somewhat in the 1990s.

*Source:* U.S. Department of Commerce.

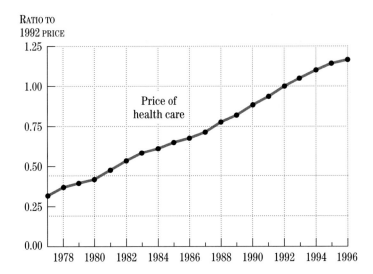

**FIGURE 1.6**
**Relative Price of Health Care**

The figure shows the ratio of the price of health care from Figure 1.5 to the overall price level from Figure 1.4. Health-care prices have risen more rapidly than the overall price level in most years. Hence, the relative price of health care has increased.

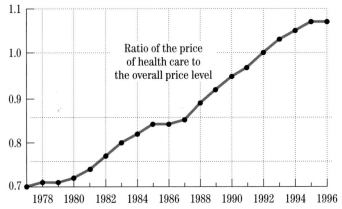

TABLE 1.2
**The Overall Price Level and the Price of Health Care**

| Year | (1)<br>Overall<br>Price Level | (2)<br>Health-Care<br>Price | (3)<br>Relative<br>Health-Care<br>Price |
|------|------|------|------|
| 1977 | 0.474 | 0.331 | 0.70 |
| 1978 | 0.510 | 0.363 | 0.71 |
| 1979 | 0.553 | 0.394 | 0.71 |
| 1980 | 0.604 | 0.436 | 0.72 |
| 1981 | 0.659 | 0.488 | 0.74 |
| 1982 | 0.701 | 0.541 | 0.77 |
| 1983 | 0.731 | 0.583 | 0.80 |
| 1984 | 0.759 | 0.623 | 0.82 |
| 1985 | 0.784 | 0.656 | 0.84 |
| 1986 | 0.806 | 0.678 | 0.84 |
| 1987 | 0.831 | 0.709 | 0.85 |
| 1988 | 0.861 | 0.764 | 0.89 |
| 1989 | 0.897 | 0.829 | 0.92 |
| 1990 | 0.936 | 0.892 | 0.95 |
| 1991 | 0.973 | 0.944 | 0.97 |
| 1992 | 1.000 | 1.000 | 1.00 |
| 1993 | 1.026 | 1.059 | 1.03 |
| 1994 | 1.050 | 1.105 | 1.05 |
| 1995 | 1.075 | 1.146 | 1.07 |
| 1996 | 1.097 | 1.170 | 1.07 |

*Note:* The prices in columns (1) and (2) are given as a ratio to the price in 1992. This year is arbitrary: Using another year would not change the patterns of the relative price.
*Source:* U.S. Department of Commerce.

Column 2 divided by column 1

The relative price of health care is shown in column (3) of Table 1.2 and is plotted in Figure 1.6. Although the prices of all goods have increased on average, the price of health care has risen more rapidly in most years. Thus, we have quantified the second observation about health care: The price of health care has increased relative to the overall price level.

## Interpreting the Observations

We have developed two economic variables to quantify our observations about health care in the United States. These variables are (1) the share of health-care spending in GDP and (2) the relative price of health care. An **economic variable** is any economic measure that can vary over a range of values. How have these two variables been related? Are there interesting patterns? How do we interpret the patterns?

Figure 1.7 shows how the relative price of health care and the health-care share of GDP have been related. Each point in the figure corresponds to a relative price and a health-care share taken from the last columns of Table 1.1 and Table 1.2. The relative price is on the vertical axis and the share of health care in GDP is on the horizontal axis.

**economic variable:** any economic measure that can vary over a range of values.

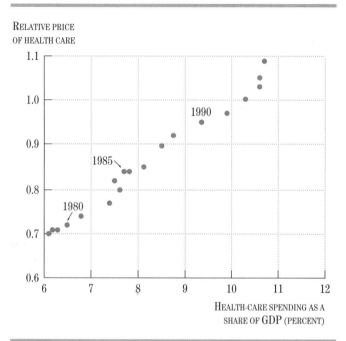

RELATIVE PRICE
OF HEALTH CARE

**FIGURE 1.7**
**Relative Price of Health Care versus Health-Care Spending Share**
The figure plots pairs of points: the relative price of health care on the vertical axis and health-care spending as a share of GDP on the horizontal axis. The observations come from the last columns of Table 1.1 and Table 1.2.

**correlation:** the degree to which economic variables are observed to move together: If they move in the same direction there is positive correlation; if they move in opposite directions there is negative correlation.

**causation:** a relation of cause and effect between variables in which one variable is a determinant of another variable.

*Based on facts*

**controlled experiments:** empirical tests of theories in a controlled setting in which particular effects can be isolated.

*zoom-nonsense*

The points in Figure 1.7 trace out a close **correlation:** As the relative price of health care has increased, so has spending on health care as a share of GDP. Two variables are correlated if they tend to move up or down around the same time. There is a *positive correlation* if the two variables move in the same direction: When one goes up, the other goes up. The share of health-care spending in GDP and the relative price of health care are positively correlated.

Two variables are negatively correlated if they tend to move in opposite directions. If we had observed that the lower relative prices of health care were associated with higher spending shares, then there would have been a *negative correlation.*

### Correlation versus Causation

Just because there is a correlation between two variables does not mean that one caused the other. There is a difference between *causation* and *correlation.* Correlation means that one event is usually observed to occur along with another. For example, high readings on a thermometer occur when it is hot outside. **Causation** means that one event brings about another event. But correlation does not imply causation. For example, the high reading on the thermometer does not cause the hot weather even though the high reading and the hot weather are correlated. In this example, we know that the causation goes the other way around: Hot weather causes the reading on the thermometer to be high.

More to the point of economics, if you look at the correlation in Figure 1.7, you might be tempted to say that the higher price of health care caused health-care spending to rise. But Figure 1.7 alone does not permit us to make such a conclusion about causation. The figure shows a correlation. Because we know a little about how thermometers work and the effects of the weather on temperature, we can draw a conclusion about causation. Similarly, we need to know more about how health care is produced and the effects of the price of health care on health-care spending before we can make statements about causality.

### Controlled Experiments

In many sciences—certainly psychology, medicine, and biology—investigators perform **controlled experiments** to determine whether one event causes another event. An example of a controlled experiment is the clinical trial of new drugs. New drugs are tested by trying them out on two groups of individuals. One group gets the drug; the other group gets a placebo (a pill without the drug). If the experiment results in a significantly greater number of people in the group taking the drug being cured than in the control group not taking the drug, then investigators conclude that the drug causes the cure.

Unfortunately, such controlled experiments are rare in economics. In the case of health-care prices and health-care spending, we cannot go back and repeat the years from 1977 to 1996 with a different health-care price and see what happens. True, we could look at other countries' experience, or we could look at the experience of different states within the United States. Economists use such comparisons to help determine causation. For example, we could look at one state in which the price of medical care increased and one in which it did not. We could then look at the health-care spending in each state to see if higher prices caused health-care spending to increase. But, unfortunately, no two countries or states are alike in all respects. Thus, attempting to control for other factors is not as easy as in the case of clinical trials.

### Experiments in Economics: A New Trend

In recent years economists have adapted some methods of experimental science and have begun to conduct economic experiments in laboratory settings that are similar to the real world. The experiments can be repeated, and various effects can be controlled for. **Experimental economics** is a growing area of economics. The findings of experimental economics have affected economists' understanding of how the economy works. Experiments in economics also provide an excellent way to *learn* how the economy works, much as experiments in science courses can help one learn about gravity or the structure of plant cells. But because it is difficult to replicate real-world settings exactly in such experiments, they have not yet been applied as widely as the clinical or laboratory experiments in other sciences.

**experimental economics:** a branch of economics that uses laboratory experiments to analyze economic behavior.

### Faulty Data

Economic data are not always accurate. People sometimes do not understand the survey questions, are too busy to fill them out carefully, or do not have the correct information. Hospitals reporting data on health-care prices, for example, may not take account of changes in the quality of health care. When people purchase medical care, the quality of the service provided can vary widely over time and from doctor to doctor.

If the quality of health care is improving, then the higher relative prices we have observed might partly reflect better service rather than an increase in the price of the same service. The actual price of health care might have increased less rapidly if we measured the improved quality, such as reduced chances of serious stroke or depression because of better drugs.

### The Behavior of People Underlying the Observations

Interpreting economic observations requires that one look behind the data to the behavior of the people whose economic decisions generate the data—for example, the people who consume health care (health-care consumers) and the people who produce health care (health-care producers).

Economists often group the people who consume goods and services into *households* (see Figure 1.8). A household is an individual or a group of individuals who share the same living quarters. For example, a household could be a group of recent college graduates sharing an apartment, a divorced person living alone, a family with four children, or a single retiree. Every individual in an economy belongs to a household, and each household must make decisions about the products and services it consumes.

**FIGURE 1.8**

**A Circular Flow Diagram**

This diagram shows how spending in general, and spending on health care in particular, equals production in general, and production of health care in particular. Buying and selling of goods and services takes place in the product market. The inputs to production—from tractors to magnetic resonance imagers—are supplied by households, either as workers or owners. Buying and selling take place in the labor and capital markets.

Producers of goods and services are often referred to as *organizations,* which include firms and governments (see Figure 1.8). A private hospital, a health maintenance organization (HMO), or a small group practice of doctors are examples of firms producing health care. Governments also produce goods and services, such as national defense, police, education, and, occasionally, health care, but they serve other functions as well—such as the establishment and maintenance of laws and law enforcement. Government can play an important role in influencing economic decision-makers through the laws it sets on taxing and spending, but it is also one of the main tasks of economics to determine what role the government itself should play as a producer and consumer of goods in the economy.

Figure 1.8 also illustrates the working of markets. Households buy goods and services in markets. A **market** refers to an arrangement through which exchanges of goods or services between people take place. For example, HMOs produce health-care services and households purchase the health-care services in the health-care market, shown in the box labeled *product market* at the bottom of Figure 1.8.

Households also supply their **labor** to the firms who employ them; the buying and selling take place in the labor market, also shown in Figure 1.8. For example, a doctor or nurse may be employed by an HMO and receive wages in return. Households also supply other resources to firms—such as machines, land, and equipment—either by owning shares in the firms, renting equipment to the firms, or lending the firms funds to buy equipment. Resources, such as machines, used by firms to produce goods and services are called **capital.** In the health-care industry, capital includes such items as x-ray machines, hospital beds, and doctors' offices. For example, a young couple may rent out the first floor of their house as a doctor's office. They receive rent in return. Capital and labor are also called **inputs** or **factors of production** because they are used to produce goods and services.

**market:** an arrangement by which economic exchanges between people take place.

**labor:** the number of hours people work in producing goods and services.

**capital:** the factories, improvements to cultivated land, machinery, and other tools, equipment, and structures used to produce goods and services.

**inputs or factors of production:** labor, capital, and other resources used in the production of goods and services.

## Review

▶ Economists endeavor to explain facts and observations about the economy, but it is not always easy to establish what the facts are. Obtaining the relevant economic facts requires a study of economic history and surveys of firms and individuals. To establish patterns, it is necessary to carefully organize and present the information obtained, either in tables or graphs.

▶ GDP is a measure of all the goods and services produced in a country during a period of time. GDP is measured by adding up what people spend. The production of a type of good or service—such as health care—can be measured in the same way as GDP.

▶ Correlation does not imply causation. Because controlled experiments are rare in economics, establishing causation is more difficult than in other sciences.

▶ Recent advances in experimental economics are improving this situation.

▶ Economic observations are not always accurate. For example, the quality of a service such as medical care can be difficult to measure.

▶ Looking at the individual behavior of firms, households, and governments is an important part of interpreting economic observations.

# ECONOMIC MODELS

In order to explain economic facts and observations, one needs an economic theory, or a *model*. An **economic model** is an explanation of how the economy or a part of the economy works. In practice, most economists use the terms *theory* and *model* interchangeably, although sometimes the term *theory* suggests a general explanation whereas the term *model* suggests a more specific explanation. The term *law* is also typically used interchangeably with the terms *model* or *theory* in economics.

**economic model:** an explanation of how the economy or part of the economy works.

### What Are Economic Models?

Economic models are always abstractions, or simplifications, of the real world. They take very complicated phenomena, such as the behavior of people, firms, and governments, and simplify them, much like a model of a building used by architects is an abstraction, or simplification, of the actual building. Some models can be very detailed; others are just broad abstractions. Be sure to remember that the model and the phenomenon being explained by the model are different.

Do not be critical of economic models simply because they are simplifications. In every science, models are simplifications of reality. Models are successful if they explain reality reasonably well. In fact, if they were not simplifications, they would be hard to use effectively. Economic models differ from those in the physical sciences because they endeavor to explain human behavior, which is complex and often unpredictable. It is for this reason that the brilliant physicist Max Planck said that economics was harder than physics.

Economic models can be described with words, with numerical tables, with graphs, or with algebra. To use economics, it is important to be able to work with these different descriptions. Figures 1.9 and 1.10 show how models can be illustrated with graphs. By looking at graphs, we can see quickly whether the model has an inverse or direct relationship. If a model says that one variable varies inversely

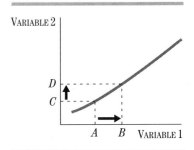

**FIGURE 1.9**
**A Model with Two Positively Related Variables**
The upward-sloping line shows how the variables are related. When one variable increases from *A* to *B*, the other variable increases from *C* to *D*. If one variable declines from *B* to *A*, the other variable declines from *D* to *C*. We say that variable 1 is positively related to variable 2, or that variable 1 varies directly with variable 2.

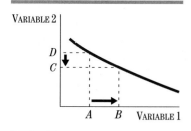

**FIGURE 1.10**

**A Model with Two Negatively Related Variables**

When one variable increases from *A* to *B,* the other variable decreases from *D* to *C.* Likewise, when one variable decreases from *B* to *A,* the other variable increases from *C* to *D.* We say variable 1 is negatively related to variable 2, or that variable 1 varies inversely with variable 2.

**positively related:** a situation in which an increase in one variable is associated with an increase in another variable; also called *directly related.*

**negatively related:** a situation in which an increase in one variable is associated with a decrease in another variable; also called *inversely related.*

with the other, this means that if the first variable rises, then the second falls. If a model says that one variable varies directly with another, this means that if one variable rises, the other also rises. In economics, the expression "is positively related to" is frequently used in place of the phrase "varies directly with," which is more common in other sciences. Similarly, the expression "is negatively related to" is frequently used in place of "varies inversely with."

In Figure 1.9, two variables—perhaps a relative price variable and a spending variable—are shown to be **positively related.** In other words, when variable 1 increases from *A* to *B,* variable 2 increases from *C* to *D* by the specific amount given by the curve. Likewise, when variable 1 decreases from *B* to *A,* variable 2 decreases from *D* to *C.* In Figure 1.10, a model with two variables that are **negatively related** is shown. Here, when variable 1 increases from *A* to *B,* variable 2 decreases from *D* to *C.* Likewise, when variable 1 decreases from *B* to *A,* variable 2 increases from *C* to *D.* Models have *constants* as well as variables. The constants in the models in Figures 1.9 and 1.10 are the positions and shapes of the curves.

### An Example: A Model with Two Variables

Figure 1.11 shows an example of a model describing how doctors employed in a health maintenance organization provide physical examinations. The model states that the more doctors who are employed at the HMO, the more physical exams can be given. The model is represented in four different ways: (1) with words, (2) with a numerical table, (3) with a graph, and (4) with algebra.

On the lower right of Figure 1.11, we have the verbal description: more doctors, more physical exams, but with additional doctors increasing the number of exams by smaller amounts, presumably because the diagnostic facilities at the HMO are limited; for example, there are only so many rooms in the HMO available for physical exams.

On the upper left, we have a table with numbers showing how the number of examinations depends on the number of doctors. Exactly how many examinations are given by each number of doctors is shown in the table. Clearly this table is much more specific than the verbal description. Be sure to distinguish between the meaning of a table that presents a model—like the table in Figure 1.11—and a table that presents data—like Table 1.1. They look similar, but one represents observations about the real world and the other is a model of the real world.

On the upper right, we have a curve showing the relationship between doctors and physical examinations. The curve shows how many exams each number of doctors can perform. The points on the curve are plotted from the information in the table. The vertical axis has the number of examinations; the horizontal axis has the number of doctors. The points are connected with a line to help visualize the curve.

Finally, in the lower left we show the doctor-examination relationship in algebraic form. In this case the number of exams is equal to the square root of the number of doctors times 20. If we give a symbol (*y*) for the number of exams and (*x*) for the number of doctors, the model looks a lot like the equations in an algebra course.

All four representations of models have advantages and disadvantages. The advantage of the verbal representation is that we usually communicate to people in words, and if we want our economic models to have any use we need to communicate with people who have not studied economics. However, the verbal representation is not as precise as the other three. In addition to the verbal analysis, in this book we will focus on the tabular and graphical representations rather than on the algebraic descriptions.

*table – таблица*

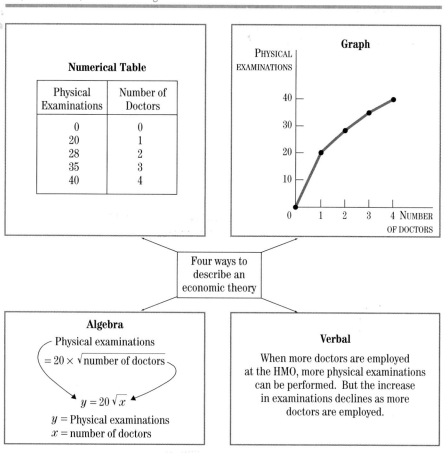

**FIGURE 1.11**
**Economic Models in Four Ways**
Each way has advantages and disadvantages; this book focuses mostly on verbal, graphical, and numerical tables, but occasionally some algebra will help to explain things.

## Prediction and the Ceteris Paribus *Assumption*

Prediction is one of the most important uses of models. For example, using the model in Figure 1.10, we can predict that if variable 1 rises from *A* to *B,* then variable 2 will fall from *D* to *C.* Using the HMO model for physical exams, we might predict that more doctors at the HMO will increase the number of physicals that can be given. Economists use models to predict variables ranging from GDP next year to the price of medical care in the year 2000.

In order to use models for prediction, economists use the assumption of *ceteris paribus,* which means "all other things equal." For example, the prediction that variable 2 will fall from *D* to *C* assumes that the curve in Figure 1.10 does not shift: The position of the curve when variable 1 is at *A* is *equal* to the position of the curve when variable 1 is at *B.* If other things were not equal—if the curve shifted—then we could not predict that variable 2 would fall from *D* to *C* when variable 1 rose from *A* to *B.* Similarly, predicting that more doctors can produce more physical exams assumes that there is no power outage that would cause the diagnostic equipment to stop operating.

*ceteris paribus:* all other things being equal; refers to holding all other variables constant or keeping all other things the same when one variable is changed.

## Microeconomic Models versus Macroeconomic Models

There are two main branches of economics: microeconomics and macroeconomics; thus, there are both microeconomic models and macroeconomic models.

# Using Economics to Explain Gender Pay Gaps

Is there a gender pay gap in the United States? Although many people speak generally about the difference between the average pay of women and men in this country, labor economists such as Francine Blau of Cornell University and June O'Neill, formerly at Baruch University and now director of the Congressional Budget Office, have confirmed the existence of a significant gender pay gap—but one that has narrowed in recent years. Women earned 60 percent as much as men earned on average in 1980, but by 1990, women's wages were on average 71 percent that of men.

In order to explain the gender pay gap, labor economists look at the evidence and apply models. Such models indicate that the pay gap is due either to differences in the qualifications of workers (schooling or experience) or to discrimination. According to Francine Blau, "A large body of evidence . . . suggests that both gender differences in qualifications and labor market discrimination as conventionally measured play a role in explaining gender earnings differences. . . . Precisely determining the relative importance of each factor is difficult, however."[*]

Determining the relative importance of qualifications versus discrimination is crucial in court cases involving gender discrimination, in which women bring suit against firms for illegally discriminating. Such cases also illustrate how economics can be used in a partisan as well as a scientific way. Consider, for example, *Stender v. Lucky Stores Inc.,* a recent court case in which a California grocery store chain, Lucky Stores, was sued for discriminating against female workers.

Economists were called as expert witnesses for both sides. Labor economist John Pencavel testified for the plaintiffs, the women who brought the suit. He found that women at Lucky earned between 76 percent and 82 percent as much as Lucky's male workers earned. Pencavel found that women were regularly placed in jobs that paid less than jobs given male coworkers, although there was no significant difference between the education and experience of the workers. There was little difference in the wages of the male and female workers within each type of job; but some jobs paid more than others and women happened to be assigned to the lower-paying jobs.

Joan Haworth, another labor economist, was an expert witness for the defendant, Lucky Stores. She reported survey evidence showing that Lucky's assignment of women and men to different jobs reflected differences in the work preferences of men and women. Thus, Lucky justified its job assignments by arguing that there was a gender difference in attitudes toward work. Lucky argued that its employment policies were based on observed differences in the career aspirations of male and female employees. For example, one manager at Lucky testified that women were more interested in cash register work and men were more interested in floor work.

After weighing the facts and economic arguments, Judge Marilyn Hall Patel decided the case in favor of the plaintiffs. Although male and female employees received equal pay for equal work, she concluded that Lucky's employment policies

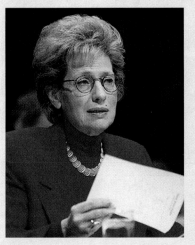

*Labor economist June O'Neill, Director of the Congressional Budget Office, testifies before Congress in 1997.*

involved discrimination. Judge Patel wrote: "The court finds defendant's explanation that the statistical disparities between men and women at Lucky are caused by differences in the work interests of men and women to be unpersuasive."[†]

The decision is a landmark because of the economic analysis that showed that discrimination could exist even if men and women were being paid the same wage for equal work. Of course, not all sex discrimination cases are decided in favor of the plaintiffs. But whoever wins a given case, economics is almost always a key consideration in the judge's decision.

[*]Francine Blau, "Gender and Economic Outcomes: The Role of Wage Structure," *Labour,* Vol. 7, 1993, pp. 73–92.

[†]*West's Federal Supplement,* Vol. 803 (St. Paul, Minn.: West Publishing Company, 1993), pp. 259–337.

**Microeconomics** studies the behavior of individual firms and households or specific markets like the health-care market or the college graduate market. It looks at variables such as the price of a college education or the reason for increased wages of college graduates. Microeconomic models explain why the price of gasoline varies from station to station or why there are discount airfares.

**Macroeconomics** focuses on the whole economy—the whole national economy or even the whole world economy. It tries to explain the changes in GDP over time rather than the changes in a part of GDP like health-care spending. It looks at questions such as what causes the overall price level to rise year after year, why many more workers are unemployed in Europe than in the United States, or why the Great Depression of the 1930s occurred.

**microeconomics:** the branch of economics that examines individual decision-making at firms and households and the way they interact in specific industries and markets.

**macroeconomics:** the branch of economics that examines the workings and problems of the economy as a whole—economic growth, inflation, unemployment, and economic fluctuations.

## The Use of Existing Models

Because economics has been around for a long time, there are many existing models that can be applied to explain observations or make predictions that are useful to decision-makers. Much of what economists do in practice, whether in government or business or universities, is use models that are already in existence.

The models are used in many different types of applications, from determining the effects of discrimination in the workplace to evaluating the gains from lower health-care prices. Frequently the models are applied in new and clever ways.

## The Development of New Models

Like models in other sciences, economic models change and new models are developed. Many of the models in this book are much different from the models in books published 40 years ago. New economic models evolve because some new observations cannot be explained by existing models.

The process of the development of new models or theories in economics proceeds much like any other science. First one develops a *hypothesis,* or a hunch, to explain a puzzling observation. Then one tests the hypothesis by seeing if it predicts well in explaining other observations. If the hypothesis passes this test, then it becomes accepted. In practice, however, this is at best a rough description of the process of scientific discovery in economics. Existing models are constantly being re-examined and tested. Some economists specialize in testing models; other specialize in developing them. There is an ongoing process of creating and testing of models in economics.

## Review

▶ Economists use economic models to explain economic observations. Economic models are similar to models in other sciences. They are abstractions, or simplifications, of reality, and they have variables and constants. But economic models are different from models in the physical sciences because they must deal with human behavior. Models can be represented verbally, with numerical tables, with graphs, and with algebra.

▶ New economic models are developed in part because existing models cannot explain facts or observations.

# USING ECONOMICS FOR PUBLIC ECONOMIC POLICY

**market economy:** an economy characterized by freely determined prices and the free exchange of goods and services in markets.

**command economy:** an economy in which the government determines prices and production; also called a centrally planned economy.

**mixed economy:** a market economy in which the government plays a very large role.

**positive economics:** economic analysis that explains what happens in the economy and why, without making recommendations about economic policy.

**normative economics:** economic analysis that makes recommendations about economic policy.

**Council of Economic Advisers:** a three-member group of economists appointed by the president of the United States to analyze the economy and make recommendations about economic policy.

One purpose of increasing our knowledge about the economy is to improve people's lives. People have used economic ideas to help reduce the likelihood of another Great Depression, to use scarce resources more efficiently, and to increase living standards. Your knowledge of economics will help you make better personal decisions about education, employment, and investments.

Ever since the birth of economics as a field—around 1776, when Adam Smith published the *Wealth of Nations*—economists have been concerned and motivated by a desire to improve the economic policy of governments. In fact, economics was originally called *political economy.* Much of the *Wealth of Nations* is about what the government should or should not do to affect the domestic and international economy.

Adam Smith argued for a system of *laissez faire*—little government control—where the role of the government is mainly to promote competition, provide for national defense, and reduce restrictions on the exchange of goods and services. Karl Marx, in contrast, argued in the nineteenth century against a laissez-faire approach. Marx's ideas led to a view that the government should essentially own and control all production. Partly as a result of these different views, two widely different types of economic systems existed for much of the twentieth century: **market economies,** where the vast majority of prices are free to vary, and **command economies,** where the vast majority of prices are determined by the central government. Command economies are also called *centrally planned* economies. The centrally planned economies of the former Soviet Union, Eastern Europe, and China can be traced to Marx's ideas. Today the debate about the role of government continues. Most countries have rejected the command economy and have moved toward market economies. But in many modern market economies, the government plays a large role, and for this reason such economies are sometimes called **mixed economies.** How great should the role of government be in a market economy? Should it provide health-care services? Should it react to the ups and downs in the economy? These are some of the questions we address in this book.

## Positive versus Normative Economics

In debating the role of government in the economy, economists distinguish between positive and normative economics. **Positive economics** is about what is; **normative economics** is about what should be. For example, positive economics endeavors to explain why the Great Depression occurred. Normative economics aims to develop and recommend policies that will prevent another Great Depression. In general, normative economics is concerned with making recommendations about what the government should do—whether it should control the price of electricity or health care, or whether it should aim for a zero inflation rate or a 4 percent inflation rate. Economists who advise governments spend much of their time doing normative economics. For example, in the United States the president's **Council of Economic Advisers** has legal responsibility for advising the president about which economic policies are good and which are bad.

Positive economics can also be used to explain *why* governments do what they do. For example, why did the U.S. government control airfares and then stop? Why were tax rates cut in the 1980s and then increased in the 1990s? Positive analysis of

**Economist Janet Yellen**

In 1997 economist Janet Yellen became the chair of the Council of Economic Advisers, which gives advice to the President of the United States on all economic policy matters.

government policy requires a mixture of both political science and economic science, with a focus on what motivates voters and the politicians they elect.

## Economics as a Science versus a Partisan Policy Tool

Although economics, like any other science, is based on facts and theories, it is not always used in a purely scientific way.

In political campaigns, economists put arguments forth in favor of one candidate, emphasizing the good side of their candidate and de-emphasizing the bad side. In a court of law, one economist will help a defendant—making the best case possible—and another economist might help the plaintiff—again, making the best case possible. In other words, economics is not always used objectively. A good reason to learn economics for yourself is to see through fallacious arguments.

But economics is not the only science that is used in these two entirely different modes. For example, there is currently a great controversy about the use of biology and chemistry to make estimates of the costs and benefits of different environmental policies. This is a politically controversial subject, and some on both sides of the controversy have been accused of using science in nonobjective ways.

## Economics Is Not the Only Factor in Policy Issues

Although economics can be very useful in policy decisions, it is frequently not the only factor. For example, national security sometimes calls for a different recommendation on a policy issue than one based on a purely economic point of view. Although most economists recommend free exchange of goods between countries, the U.S. government restricted exports of high-technology goods such as computers during the cold war because defense specialists worried that the technology could help the military in the former Soviet Union, and this was viewed as more important than the economic argument. There are still heavy restrictions on trade in nuclear fuels for fear of the proliferation of nuclear weapons.

## Review

▶ Economic theory can be used to make better economic decisions. Improving government policy decisions has long been a purpose of economics.

▶ The most basic economic policy questions concern the general role of government in a market economy.

# CONCLUSION: A READER'S GUIDE

In this chapter, we have discussed how economic models can be used to answer important questions. But we have not answered the questions. To do so, we need the models themselves. In the following chapters, we will present the models. As you read more about economic models in these chapters, the following brief guide may prove useful. It brings together many of the ideas raised in this chapter.

*First, economics—more than other sciences—requires a mixture of verbal and quantitative skills.* Frequently those who come to economics with a good background in physical science and mathematics find the mix of formal models with more informal verbal descriptions of markets and institutions unusual and perhaps a little difficult. If you are one of these students, you might wish for a more cut-and-dried, or mathematical, approach.

In contrast, those who are good at history or philosophy may find the emphasis on formal models and graphs difficult and might even prefer a more historical approach that looks more at watershed events and famous individuals and less at formal models of how many individuals behave. If you are one of these students, you might wish economic models were less abstract.

In reality, however, economics is a mixture of formal modeling, historical analysis, and philosophy. If you are very good at math and think the symbols and graphs of elementary economics are too simple, think of Max Planck's comment about economics and focus on the complexity of the economic phenomena that these simple models and graphs are explaining. Then when you are asked an open-ended question about government policy that does not have a simple yes or no answer, you will not be caught off guard. Or if your advantage is in history or philosophy, you should spend more time honing your skills using models and graphs. Then when you are asked to solve a cut-and-dried economic problem with an exact answer requiring graphical analysis, you will not be caught off guard.

*Second, the scope of economics is very wide.* When your friends or relatives hear that you are taking economics, they might ask you for advice about what stock to buy. Economists' friends and relatives are always asking them for such advice. But economics alone offers no recommendations about the success of particular companies. Rather, economics gives you some tools to obtain information about companies and to analyze them yourself, perhaps to become an investment adviser.

Economics will also help you answer questions about whether to invest in the stock market or in a bank or how many stocks to buy. But the scope of economics is much, much broader than the stock market or banks, as the questions at the start of the chapter indicate. In fact, the scope of economics is even wider than these examples. Economists use their models, or theories, to study environmental pollution, crime, discrimination, and who should have the right to sue whom.

*Third, there is less economic controversy than you may think.* Watching economists debate issues on television or reading their opinions in a newspaper or magazine certainly gives the impression that they rarely agree. There are major controversies in economics, and we will examine these controversies in this book. But when people survey economists' beliefs, they find a surprising amount of agreement.

Why, then, the popular impression of disagreement? Because there are many economists, and one can always find some economist with a different viewpoint. When people sue other people in court and economics is an issue, it is always possible to find economists who will testify on each side, even if 99 percent of economists would agree with one side. Similarly, television interviews or news shows want to give both sides of public policy issues. Thus, even if 99 percent of economists agree with one side, it is possible to find at least one on the other side.

Economists are human beings with varying moral beliefs and different backgrounds and political views that are frequently unrelated to economic models. For example, an economist who is very concerned about the importation of drugs into the United States might appear to be more willing to condone a restriction on coffee exports, which might give Colombia a higher price for its coffee to offset a loss in revenue from cocaine. Another economist who might feel less strongly about drug imports may argue strongly against such a restriction on coffee. But if asked about restrictions on trade in the abstract, both economists would probably argue for government policies that prevent them.

*Fourth, and perhaps most important, the study of economics is an intellectually fascinating adventure in its own right.* Yes, economics is highly relevant, and it affects people's lives. But once you learn how economic models work, you will find that they are actually fun to use. And they would be just as much fun if they were not so relevant. Every now and then, just after you have learned about a new economic model, put the book down and think of the economic model independent of its message or relevance to society, perhaps like you would an enjoyable movie. In this way, too, you will be learning to think like an economist.

# KEY POINTS

**1.** Economics provides explanations of certain economic observations in a way that can be used to make decisions.

**2.** Economics is useful for personal, business, and government policy decisions.

**3.** Observations or facts about the economy are sometimes not easy to establish.

**4.** Spending on health care and the price of health care provides a good example of how economists document the facts and explain them with models.

**5.** Economic models are abstractions, or simplifications, of reality.

**6.** Economic models, like models in other sciences, can be described with words, with tables, with graphs, or with

mathematics. All four ways are important and complement one another.

**7.** Much of economics uses existing models. Such models have been developed over the last 200 years and are used by individuals, businesses, and government.

**8.** Sometimes the facts require that economists develop new models.

**9.** Improving economic policy has been a goal of economists since the time of Adam Smith.

**10.** Decisions about the role of government in areas from airfares to health care are influenced by economic analysis.

# KEY TERMS

gross domestic product (GDP)
economic history
overall price level
inflation
inflation rate
real GDP
relative price
economic variable
correlation
causation

controlled experiments
experimental economics
market
labor
capital
inputs or factors of
    production
economic model
positively related
negatively related

*ceteris paribus*
microeconomics
macroeconomics
market economy
command economy
mixed economy
positive economics
normative economics
Council of Economic Advisers

# QUESTIONS FOR REVIEW

**1.** How do the economic challenges and opportunities around the world in the 1990s differ from those of the 1940s?

**2.** Why do economists need to document and quantify observations about the economy?

**3.** What is the most comprehensive available measure of the size of an economy?

**4.** What is the overall price level? What is inflation?

**5.** What is meant by a relative price?

**6.** How do economic models differ from the economic phenomena they explain?

**7.** Why doesn't correlation imply causation?

**8.** What is the difference between a variable and a constant in economics?

**9.** What is the difference between positive and normative economics?

**10.** How do economists use the *ceteris paribus* assumption?

# PROBLEMS

**1.** Which of the following issues are microeconomic, and which are macroeconomic?
   a)  The overall unemployment rate
   b)  A tax that affects workers in the auto industry
   c)  Inflation
   d)  Prices of agricultural commodities
   e)  Real GDP

**2.** Identify whether the following policy statements are positive or normative. Explain.
   a)  "The government fought inflation during the early 1980s because it felt the inflation was damaging potential long-term economic growth."
   b)  "The government should cut taxes in order to stimulate GDP."
   c)  "Increases in consumer spending improved the Japanese economy last year, which indicates stronger growth of real GDP for next year."
   d)  "Balancing the federal budget would be good for the economy."

**3.** Interpret the data on housing spending in the table below by filling in the blanks.
   a)  What has happened to housing spending as a share of GDP over this 30-year period? How does this differ from the figures for health care in Tables 1.1 and 1.2?
   b)  What has happened to the relative price of housing over this period? How does this compare to the change in the relative price of health care over this period?

**4.** Draw a diagram like Figure 1.8 for the market for movies and give examples of capital, labor, and firms in that market. Show how there is a complete circular flow of funds and goods in the economy as a whole.

**5.** Why is it typical for economists to make the *ceteris paribus* assumption when making predictions?

**6.** Interpret the observations on food spending in the table at the bottom of the page by filling in the blanks.
   a)  What has happened to spending on food as a share of GDP over this 30-year period? How does this differ from the figures for health care in Tables 1.1 and 1.2?
   b)  What has happened to the relative price of food over this period? How does this compare to the change in the relative price of health care over this period?

**7.** What is the difference between the overall price level and relative price? Which information is more useful if you are interested in the change in spending on a particular good? Which measure is more useful if you are interested in inflation?

**8.** Indicate whether you expect positive or negative correlation for the following pairs of variables. What is required to show causation?
   a)  Sunrise and crowing roosters
   b)  Price of theater tickets and number of theatergoers
   c)  Purchases of candy and purchases of Valentine's Day cards

**Problem 3**

| Year | GDP (billions of dollars) | Spending on Housing | Housing as a Share of GDP | Overall Price | Housing Price | Relative Housing Price |
|------|------|------|------|------|------|------|
| 1960 | 526.6 | 48.2 | ——— | 0.233 | 0.234 | ——— |
| 1970 | 1,035.6 | 94.0 | ——— | 0.306 | 0.285 | ——— |
| 1980 | 2,784.2 | 255.2 | ——— | 0.604 | 0.524 | ——— |
| 1990 | 5,743.8 | 586.3 | ——— | 0.936 | 0.985 | ——— |

**Problem 6**

| Year | GDP (billions of dollars) | Spending on Food | Food as a Share of GDP | Overall Price | Food Price | Relative Food Price |
|------|------|------|------|------|------|------|
| 1960 | 526.6 | 82.3 | ——— | 0.233 | 0.229 | ——— |
| 1970 | 1,035.6 | 143.8 | ——— | 0.306 | 0.301 | ——— |
| 1980 | 2,784.2 | 355.4 | ——— | 0.604 | 0.636 | ——— |
| 1990 | 5,743.8 | 634.5 | ——— | 0.936 | 0.951 | ——— |

# Acquiring an Eye for Economics: Reading and Understanding Graphs

Frances M. James worked in the Executive Office of the President for more than thirty years, serving under seven presidents, from Harry Truman to Jimmy Carter. Her job was to make sure the economic statistics used by each president and his Council of Economic Advisers were accurate and were presented clearly and meaningfully. Her skills were rare and valuable. She could look at a table with hundreds of numbers and quickly see whether something was wrong. "There is a minus sign missing," or, "It's billions not millions," or, "You must have confused Austria's GDP with Australia's GDP" are the kinds of things she would say. Such skills are hard to acquire, and Frances admired people who had taken the time to acquire them. She called the skill "having a nose for numbers."

But because most people do not have such a highly developed sense for deciphering columns of numbers, economists rely on graphs to make visual pictures of a table of numbers or a formula. Developing an eye for economics as represented in graphs is easier than developing a nose for numbers in tables. Graphs help us see correlations, or patterns, in economic observations. Graphs and diagrams are also useful for understanding economic models. They help us see how variables in the model behave. They help us describe assumptions about what firms and consumers do.

This appendix reviews the rudiments of analytical geometry that are used to create graphs for representing observations and models.

# REPRESENTING OBSERVATIONS WITH GRAPHS

Most economic graphs are drawn in two dimensions, like the surface of this page, and the graphs are constructed using a **Cartesian coordinate system.** The idea of Cartesian coordinates is that pairs of observations on variables can be represented in a plane by designating one axis for one variable and the other axis for the other variable. Each point, or coordinate, on the plane corresponds to a pair of observations.

## Time-Series Graphs

In many instances, we want to see how a variable changes over time. For example, many people are interested in changes in the federal debt—all the outstanding borrowing of the federal government that has not yet been paid back. Table 1A.1 shows six observations of the U.S. federal debt in billions of dollars. The observations are for every 10 years and are taken from the budget of the U.S. government; the observation for the year 2000 is based on a government projection. Because there are so few observations in Table 1A.1, it is easy to graph them by hand, and we have done so in Figure 1A.1. The graph in Figure 1A.1 is called a **time-series graph** because it plots a series—that is, several values of the variable—over time. When there are many observations, as in Table 1.1, economists use computers to plot the graphs automatically. Figure 1.1 was plotted by computer.

Observe the scales on the horizontal and vertical axes in Figure 1A.1. The six years are put on the horizontal axis, spread evenly from the year 1950 to the year 2000. For the

**TABLE 1A.1**
**U.S. Federal Government Debt**

| Year | Debt (billions of dollars) |
|------|---------------------------|
| 1950 | 219 |
| 1960 | 237 |
| 1970 | 283 |
| 1980 | 709 |
| 1990 | 2,410 |
| 2000 | 4,873 |

*Source: Budget of the U.S. Government, Fiscal Year 1993; The Economic and Budget Outlook,* Congressional Budget Office, September 1993.

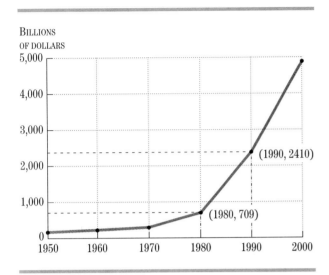

**FIGURE 1A.1**

**U.S. Federal Debt**

Each point corresponds to a pair of observations—the year and the debt—from Table 1A.1.

vertical axis, one needs to decide on a scale. The range of variation for the debt in Table 1A.1 is very wide—from a minimum of $219 billion to a maximum of $4,873 billion. Thus, the range of from $0 to $5,000 billion on the vertical axis in Figure 1A.1 is wide enough to contain all these points.

Now observe how each pair of points from Table 1A.1 is plotted in Figure 1A.1. The point for the pair of observations for the year 1950 and the debt of $219 billion is found by going over to 1950 on the horizontal axis, then going up to $219 billion and putting a dot there. The point for 1960 and $237 billion and all the other points are found in the same way. In order to better visualize the points, they can be connected with lines. These lines are not part of the observations; they are only a convenience to help eyeball the observations. The points for 1980 and 1990 are labeled with the pair of observations corresponding to Table 1A.1, but in general there is no need to put in such labels.

Now look at the pattern of points in Figure 1A.1. Some people feel that the pattern looks like a hockey stick. It is striking. The long handle of the hockey stick is the sharp increase in the debt in the 1980s and 1990s. The part of the hockey stick that you hit the ball or puck with represents slower increases in the debt in the earlier years. But the debt has increased throughout the period in the graph.

One could choose different scales than in Figure 1A.1, and if you plotted your own graph from Table 1A.1 with-

**FIGURE 1A.2**

**Stretching the Debt Story in Two Ways**

The points in both graphs are identical to Figure 1A.1, but by stretching or shrinking the scales the problem can be made to look either less alarming or more alarming.

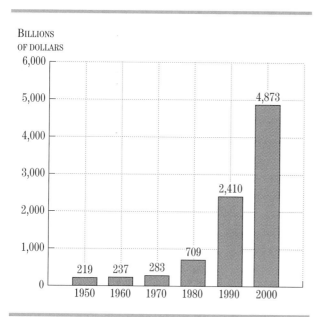

**FIGURE 1A.3**
**U.S. Federal Debt in Bars**
The observations are identical to
those in Figure 1A.1

**TABLE 1A.2**
**U.S. Federal Debt as a Percent of GDP**

| Year | Debt (percent of GDP) |
|------|------------------------|
| 1950 | 82.5 |
| 1960 | 46.8 |
| 1970 | 28.7 |
| 1980 | 26.8 |
| 1990 | 44.2 |
| 2000 | 55.7 |

*Source:* U.S. Department of Commerce and Table 1A.1.

out looking at Figure 1A.1, your scales would probably be different. The scales determine how much movement there is in a time-series graph. For example, Figure 1A.2 shows two ways to stretch the scales to make the increase in the debt look either more alarming or less alarming. The diagram at the right looks even more like a hockey stick. But the diagram at the left looks less worrisome. So as not to be fooled by graphs, therefore, it is important to look at the scales and think about what they mean.

As an alternative to time-series graphs with dots connected by a line, the observations can be shown on a bar graph, as in Figure 1A.3. Some people prefer the visual look of a bar graph, but as is clear from a comparison of Figures 1A.1 and 1A.3, they provide the same information.

The debt as a percent of GDP is given in Table 1A.2 and graphed in Figure 1A.4. Note that this figure makes the debt look a lot different than the first one. For one thing, the line declines, reaches a minimum, and then begins to increase. As a percent of GDP, the debt fell from the end of the World War II (when it was very large because of the war debt) until around 1980. It increased again during the 1980s. As a percent of GDP, the debt is now less than after World War II, but it is still growing. When we consider the debt as a percentage of GDP, the recent increase appears less alarming. But that does not mean the increase is not a problem.

The scale in Figure 1A.4 for the debt as a percentage of GDP is from 0 to 90 percent. This leaves some wasted space at the bottom and the top of the graph. To eliminate this space and have more room to see the graph itself, we can start the range near the minimum value and end it near the maximum value. This is done in Figure 1A.5. Note, however, that cutting off the bottom of the scale could be misleading to people who do not look at the axis. In particular, 0 percent is no longer at the point where the horizontal and vertical axis intersect. To warn people about the missing part of the scale, a little cut is sometimes put on the

**FIGURE 1A.4**
**U.S. Federal Debt as a Percent of GDP**
Each point corresponds to a pair of observations from Table 1A.2.

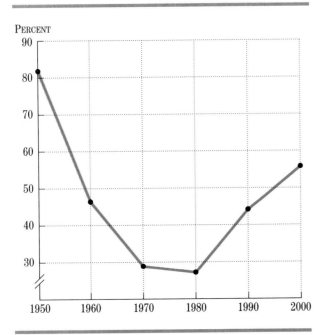

**FIGURE 1A.5**
**A Stretched-Scale Look at Debt as a Percent of GDP**
To alert the reader that the bottom part of the axis is not shown, a break point is sometimes used, as shown here.

**TABLE 1A.3**
**Interest Rate and Federal Debt as a Percent of GDP**

| Year | Debt (percent of GDP) | Interest Rate (percent) |
|---|---|---|
| 1950 | 82.5 | 1.2 |
| 1960 | 46.8 | 2.9 |
| 1970 | 28.7 | 6.5 |
| 1980 | 26.8 | 11.5 |
| 1990 | 44.2 | 7.5 |
| 2000 | 55.7 | 4.5 |

*Source:* Federal Reserve Board and Table 1A.2.

axis, as shown in Figure 1A.5, but you have to look carefully at the scale.

## Time-Series Graphs Showing Two or More Variables

So far we have shown how a graph can be used to show observations on one variable over time. What if we want to see how two or more variables change over time together? Suppose, for example, we want to look at how observations on debt as a percentage of GDP compare with the interest rate the government must pay on its debt. The two variables are shown in Table 1A.3.

The two sets of observations can easily be placed on the same time-series graph. In other words, we could plot the observations on the debt percentage and connect the dots and then plot the interest rate observations and connect the dots. If the scales of measurement of the two variables are much different, then it might be hard to see each, however. For example, the interest rate ranges between 4 and 12 percent; it would not be very visible on a graph going all the way from 0 to 100 percent, a range that is fine for the

debt percentage. In this situation, a **dual scale** can be used, as shown in Figure 1A.6. One scale is put on the left-hand vertical axis and the other scale is put on the right-hand vertical axis. With a dual-scale diagram, it is very important to be aware of the two scales. In this book we will emphasize the different axes in dual-scale diagrams by the color line

**FIGURE 1A.6**
**Comparing Two Time Series with a Dual Scale**
When two variables have different scales, a dual scale is useful. Here the interest rate and the debt as a percent of GDP are plotted from Table 1A.3.

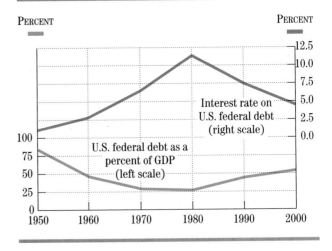

segment at the top of each vertical axis. The color line segment corresponds to the color of the curve plotted using that scale, as in Figure 1A.6.

## Scatter Plots

Finally, two variables can be usefully compared with a **scatter plot.** The Cartesian coordinate method is used, as in the time-series graph, except that we do not put the year on one of the axes; rather, the horizontal axis is used for one of the variables and the vertical axis for the other variable. We do this for the debt percentage and the interest rate in Figure 1A.7. The interest rate is on the vertical axis and the debt percentage is on the horizontal axis. For example, the point at the upper left is 26.8 percent for the debt as a percent of GDP and 11.5 percent for the interest rate.

Note that this scatter plot reveals a negative correlation between the debt percentage and the interest rate. Recall that a negative correlation is when the points in a scatter plot tend to decline as you move from left to right. Note that this negative correlation is also apparent in a different way in Figure 1A.6 in which the debt percentage fell as the interest rate rose over time and then rose as the interest rate fell over time.

Remember that such a correlation does not imply causation or that there is an economic relation between the two variables. In particular it would be a serious mistake to conclude from Figure 1A.7 that there is a negative causal relationship between the debt ratio and the interest rate. The observed correlation could be caused by a third variable—such as inflation—that is affecting both the debt percentage and the interest rate.

## Pie Charts

Time-series graphs, bar graphs, and scatter plots are not the only visual ways to observe economic data. For example, the *pie chart* in Figure 1A.8 is useful for comparing percentage shares for a small number of different groups or a small number of time periods. In this example, the pie chart is a visual representation of how the industrial countries produce more than half of the world's GDP while the developing countries produce 34 percent and the former communist countries in Eastern Europe and the former Soviet Union, now in transition toward market economies, produce about 11 percent.

**FIGURE 1A.7**
**Scatter Plot**

Interest rate and debt as a percent
of GDP are shown.

INTEREST RATE
ON FEDERAL DEBT
(PERCENT)

DEBT AS A PERCENT OF GDP

**FIGURE 1A.8**
**Pie Chart Showing the Shares of
the World's GDP**

The pie chart shows how the world's
GDP is divided up into (1) the
industrial countries, such as the
United States, Germany, and Japan,
(2) the developing countries, such
as India, China, and Nigeria, and
(3) countries in transition from
communism to capitalism, such as
Russia and Poland.

*Source:* International Monetary Fund.

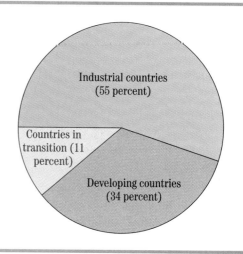

Industrial countries
(55 percent)

Countries in
transition (11
percent)

Developing countries
(34 percent)

# REPRESENTING MODELS WITH GRAPHS

Graphs can also represent models. As with graphs showing observations, graphs showing models are usually restricted to curves in two dimensions.

## Slopes of Curves

Does a curve slope up or down? How steep is it? These questions are important in economics as in other sciences. The **slope** of a curve tells us how much the variable on the vertical axis changes when we change the variable on the horizontal axis by one unit.

The slope is computed as follows:

$$\text{Slope} = \frac{\text{change in variable on vertical axis}}{\text{change in variable on horizontal axis}}$$

In most algebra courses, the vertical axis is usually called the $y$-axis and the horizontal axis is called the $x$-axis. Thus,

the slope is sometime described as

$$\text{Slope} = \frac{\text{change in } y}{\text{change in } x} = \frac{\Delta y}{\Delta x}$$

where the Greek letter $\Delta$ (delta) means "change in." In other words, the slope is the ratio of the "rise" (vertical change) to the "run" (horizontal change).

Figure 1A.9 shows how to compute the slope. In this case, the slope declines as the variable on the $x$-axis increases.

Observe that *the steeper the curve, the larger the slope.* When the curve gets very flat, the slope gets close to zero. Curves can either be upward-sloping or downward-sloping. If the curve slopes up from left to right, as in Figure 1A.9, it has a **positive slope,** and we say the two variables are positively related. If the curve slopes down from left to right, it has a **negative slope,** and we say the two variables are negatively related. Figure 1A.10 shows a case where the slope is negative. When $x$ increases by 1 unit ($\Delta x = 1$), $y$ declines by 2 units ($\Delta y = -2$). Thus, the slope equals $-2$; it is negative. Observe how the curve slopes down from left to right.

**FIGURE 1A.9**
**Measuring the Slope**

The slope between two points is given by the change along the vertical axis divided by the change along the horizontal axis. In this example, the slope declines as $x$ increases. Since the curve slopes up from left to right, it has a positive slope.

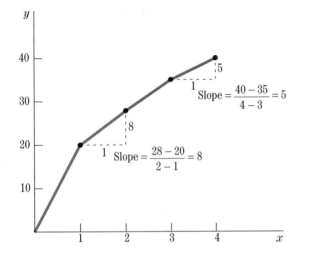

**FIGURE 1A.10**
**A Relationship with a Negative Slope**

Here the slope is negative: $(\Delta y)/(\Delta x) = -2$. As $x$ increases, $y$ falls. The line slopes down from left to right. In this case, $y$ and $x$ are inversely, or negatively, related.

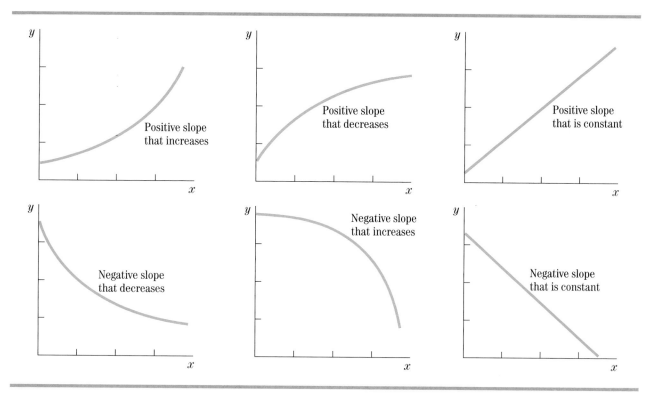

**FIGURE 1A.11**
**Six Types of Relationships**
In the top row, the variables are positively related. In the bottom row, they are negatively related.

If the curve is a straight line, then the slope is a constant. Curves that are straight lines—as in Figure 1A.10—are called **linear.** But economic relationships do not need to be linear, as the example in Figure 1A.9 makes clear. Figure 1A.11 shows six different examples of curves and indicates how they are described.

## Graphs of Models with More Than Two Variables

In most cases, economic models involve more than two variables. For example, the number of physical examinations could depend on the number of nurses as well as the number of doctors. Or the amount of lemonade demanded might depend on the weather as well as on the price.

Economists have devised several methods to represent models with more than two variables with two-dimensional graphs. Suppose, for example, that the relationship between $y$ and $x$ in Figure 1A.10 depends on third variable $z$. For a given value for $x$, larger values of $z$ lead to larger values of $y$. This example is graphed in Figure 1A.12. As in Figure 1A.10, when $x$ increases, $y$ falls. This is a **movement along**

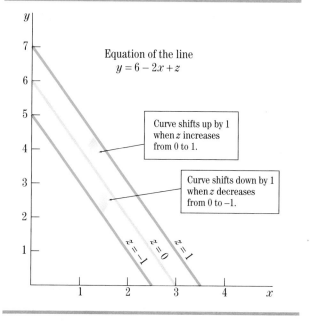

**FIGURE 1A.12**
**A Third Variable Shifts the Curve**
In order to represent models with three variables ($x$, $y$, and $z$) on a two-dimensional graph, economists distinguish between movements along the curve (when $x$ and $y$ change, holding $z$ unchanged) and shifts of the curve (when $z$ changes).

the curve. But what if $z$ changes? We represent this as a **shift of the curve.** An increase in $z$ shifts the curve up; a decrease in $z$ shifts the curve down.

Thus, by distinguishing between shifts and movements along a curve, economists represent models with more than two variables in only two dimensions. Only two variables ($x$ and $y$) are shown explicitly on the graph, and when the third ($z$) is fixed, changes in $x$ and $y$ are movements along the curve. When $z$ changes, the curve shifts. The distinction between "movements along" and "shifts of" curves will come up many times in this book.

# KEY TERMS AND DEFINITIONS

**Cartesian coordinate system:** a graphing system in which ordered pairs of numbers are represented on a plane by the distances from a point to two perpendicular lines, called axes.

**time-series graph:** a graph that plots a variable over time, usually with time on the horizontal axis.

**dual scale:** a graph that uses time on the horizontal axis and different scales on left and right vertical axes to compare the movements in two variables over time.

**scatter plot:** a graph in which points in a Cartesian coordinate system represent the values of two variables.

**slope:** refers to a curve and is defined as the change in the variable on the vertical axis divided by the change in the variable on the horizontal axis.

**positive slope:** a slope of a curve that is greater than zero, representing a positive or direct relationship between two variables.

**negative slope:** a slope of a curve that is less than zero, representing a negative or inverse relationship between two variables.

**linear:** a situation in which a curve is straight, with a constant slope.

**movement along the curve:** a situation in which a change in the variable on one axis causes a change in the variable on the other axis, but maintains the position of the curve.

**shift of the curve:** a change in the position of a curve usually caused by a change in a variable not represented on either axis.

# QUESTIONS FOR REVIEW

**1.** What is the difference between a scatter plot and a time-series graph?

**2.** Why are dual scales sometimes necessary?

**3.** What is the advantage of graphs over verbal representations of models?

**4.** What does a curve with a negative slope look like?

**5.** What is the difference between a shift in a curve and a movement along a curve?

# PROBLEMS

**1.** The table at the right presents data on the debt to GDP ratio and interest rates in the United Kingdom.
   a) Construct a time-series plot of the ratio of government debt to GDP.
   b) Construct a time-series plot of the interest rate.
   c) Construct a scatter plot of the debt ratio and the interest rate.

| Year | Debt to GDP Ratio | Interest Rate |
|------|-------------------|---------------|
| 1984 | 47.3 | 9.9 |
| 1985 | 46.1 | 10.8 |
| 1986 | 45.0 | 10.5 |
| 1987 | 42.0 | 4.8 |
| 1988 | 35.7 | 10.0 |
| 1989 | 30.4 | 13.9 |
| 1990 | 28.7 | 14.8 |
| 1991 | 30.3 | 11.5 |
| 1992 | 35.6 | 9.5 |
| 1993 | 41.1 | 6.6 |

*Source:* Organization for Economic Cooperation and Development.

**2.** The following table presents data on U.S. turkey production and prices.

| Year | Turkey Production (billions of pounds) | Price per Pound |
|------|---------------------------------------|-----------------|
| 1985 | 3.7 | 49.1 |
| 1986 | 4.1 | 47.1 |
| 1987 | 4.9 | 34.8 |
| 1988 | 5.1 | 38.6 |
| 1989 | 5.5 | 40.9 |
| 1990 | 6.0 | 39.4 |

*Source: Statistical Abstract of the United States, 1993.*

a) Construct a time-series plot of turkey production in the United States.

b) Construct a time-series plot of the price of turkey per pound.

c) Construct a scatter plot of turkey production and turkey prices.

**3.** The following table shows the number of physical examinations given by doctors at an HMO with three different-size clinics: small, medium, and large. The larger the clinic, the more patients the doctors can handle. (Observe that the small clinic is exactly like Figure 1.11.)

| Exams per Small Clinic | Exams per Medium Clinic | Exams per Large Clinic | Number of Doctors |
|------------------------|-------------------------|------------------------|-------------------|
| 0 | 0 | 0 | 0 |
| 20 | 30 | 35 | 1 |
| 28 | 42 | 49 | 2 |
| 35 | 53 | 62 | 3 |
| 40 | 60 | 70 | 4 |

a) Show the relationship between doctors and physical exams given with *three* curves where the number of doctors is on the horizontal axis and the number of examinations is on the vertical axis.

b) Describe how the three relationships compare with one another.

c) Is a change in the number of doctors a shift or a movement along the curve?

d) Is a change in the size of the clinic a shift or a movement along the curve?

# Scarcity, Choice, and Economic Interaction

Boiled down to its essence, economics is the study of (1) the choices people make when there is a scarcity of resources, and (2) the economic interactions of people with other people when they make these choices. By exploring this brief definition, we can learn much about economics and about how economists think.

**Scarcity** is a situation where people's wants exceed their resources. People always face a scarcity of something, usually time or income. Scarcity implies that people must make a **choice**—to forego, or to give up, one thing in favor of another. For example, a college student who chooses to work during the school year has less time for studying, rollerblading, watching television, or something else. A college, with a given amount of tuition receipts or government grants, must choose between spending more on language instruction or more on mathematics instruction. A government, with a given amount of tax receipts, must choose between spending more on crime prevention or more on education. The people of a country, with a given amount of resources, must choose between spending more on health care or more on other things. Scarcity is a fact of economic life for individuals, for families, for colleges, for governments, for whole economies, and even for the whole world. Scarcity is pervasive, and it forces us to pick and choose.

**Economic interaction** between people occurs when they trade or exchange goods or services with each other. For example, a college student buys education services from a college in exchange for tuition. A teenager sells labor services to Taco Bell in exchange for cash. Within a family, one spouse may agree to cook every day in exchange for the other spouse's doing the dishes every day. Within a university, workers at the university-owned copy center may provide copy services so that the faculty can give students lecture outlines.

As these examples indicate, economic interactions can occur either within an organizational structure, such as a university or a family, or in a market. Interactions *within* **organizations** include the cooking-washing arrangement between members of a family or the use of a university-owned copier, rather than a Kinko's copier, by faculty for lecture handouts. Interactions that take place *outside* of organizations take place in markets. Recall that a **market** is simply an arrangement where buyers and sellers can interact with each other. Interactions in markets include the buying and selling of a college education, of the labor services of Taco Bell workers, or of the copy services of firms like Kinko's. There are many other markets where economic interaction takes place, from the New York Stock Exchange to a local flea market.

Economic interaction, like scarcity and choice, is a fact of economic life. But economic interactions can make our lives much better. How an economy is set up to handle such interactions determines how well the economy as a whole works in providing for the well-being of the people in the economy.

In this chapter we look at the ways in which economists portray scarcity and choice for individuals and for whole economies. We show how people benefit from economic interactions, whether they occur within organizations or in markets. Many of the ideas and terms defined in this chapter will be used and studied in more detail in later chapters.

**scarcity:** the situation in which the quantity of resources is insufficient to meet all wants.

**choice:** a selection among alternative goods, services, or actions.

**economic interaction:** exchanges of goods and services between people.

**organization:** a human structure, such as a family, firm, government, or college, through which people may exchange goods and services.

**market:** an arrangement by which economic exchanges between people take place.

# SCARCITY, CHOICE, AND INTERACTION FOR INDIVIDUALS

It is easy to find everyday examples of how scarcity affects individual choices. A choice that may be on your mind when you study economics is how much time to spend on it versus other activities. If you spend all your time on economics, you might get 100 on the final exam, but that might mean you get a zero in biology. If you spend all your time on biology, then you might get 100 in biology and a zero in economics. Most people resolve the choice by balancing out their time to get a decent grade in both subjects. If you are premed, then biology will probably get more time. If you are interested in business, then more time on economics might be appropriate.

Now let us apply this same idea to two economic problems: individual choices about what goods to *consume* and individual choices about what goods to *produce*. For each type of economic problem, we first show how scarcity forces one to make a choice; we then show how people gain from interacting with other people.

## Consumer Decisions

Consider the choice made by a person deciding how much of a good or service to consume.

### *Scarcity and Choice for Individual Consumers*

Consider Maria, who loves both ballet and opera. Suppose Maria has $500 to spend on entertainment. The $500 limit on her spending is an example of a *budget constraint,* because Maria is limited to spending no more than this budgeted amount for

**Choice and Opportunity Cost**

Choice creates opportunity costs. In this photograph, Coca-Cola appears to be the next best alternative to milk. Thus, the opportunity cost of choosing milk is the foregone consumption of Coca-Cola.

**opportunity cost:** the value of the next-best foregone alternative that was not chosen because something else was chosen.

**gains from trade:** improvements in income, production, or satisfaction owing to the exchange of goods or services.

entertainment. Suppose the price of a season ticket to 20 ballet performances is $500, and the price of a season ticket to 20 opera performances is also $500. Hence, the scarcity of funds for entertainment forces Maria to choose between two alternatives: a season ticket to the ballet or a season ticket to the opera. The decision depends on her tastes. Although she loves both ballet and opera, we assume that, if forced by scarcity to make a choice, she will choose the season opera tickets. She would prefer to buy both season tickets, but she cannot afford it. She would prefer to go to half of the operas and half of the ballets, but that choice is not open to her.

Maria's decision is an example of an economic problem that all people face. A budget constraint forces them to make a choice between different items that they want. Such choices create opportunity costs. The **opportunity cost** of a choice is the value of the foregone alternative that was not chosen. The opportunity cost of the opera season ticket is the loss from not being able to buy the ballet season ticket. An opportunity cost occurs every time there is a choice. For example, the opportunity cost of going to an 8 A.M. class rather than sleeping in is the lost sleep from getting up early.

In many cases involving choice and scarcity, there are many more than two things to choose from. If you choose vanilla ice cream out of a list of many possible flavors, then the opportunity cost is the loss from not being able to consume the *next best* flavor, perhaps strawberry. In addition to extending their choices, people may be able to increase the amount they have to spend by working more; then the opportunity cost is less leisure time. But the structure of the situation is much the same as Maria's choice.

Now, Maria is not the only consumer. Consider Adam, who also has $500 to spend. Adam also loves both ballet and opera. But he likes ballet slightly more than opera. If forced to make a choice between the season tickets, he will choose to buy season tickets to the ballet. His decisions are shaped by scarcity just as Maria's are: Scarcity comes from the budget constraint; he must make a choice, and there is an opportunity cost for each choice.

### Gains from Trade

Now let us consider the possibility of economic interaction between Maria and Adam. Suppose that Maria and Adam can trade with each other. Maria decides to trade half (10) of her opera tickets for half (10) of Adam's ballet tickets, as shown in Figure 2.1. Through such a trade, both Maria and Adam can improve their situation. There are **gains from trade** because the trade reallocates goods between the two individuals in a way they both prefer. Trade occurs because Maria is willing to exchange 10 opera tickets for 10 ballet tickets, and Adam is willing to exchange 10 ballet tickets for 10 opera tickets. Because trade is mutually advantageous for both Maria and Adam, they will voluntarily do so if they are able to. In fact, if they did not gain from the trade, then neither would have bothered to make the trade.

### Improvements Through Reallocation

This trade is an example of an economic interaction in which a reallocation of goods through trade makes both parties better off. There is no change in the total quantity of goods produced. The number of ballet and opera performances has remained the same. Trade simply reallocates existing goods.

The trade between Maria and Adam is typical of many economic interactions we will study in this book. Thinking like an economist in this example means recognizing that a voluntary exchange of goods between people must make them better off. Many economic exchanges are like this, even though they are more complicated than the exchange of season tickets to the opera and the ballet. In some cases one party might gain much more than the other. Maria, for example, might bargain with Adam and get him to give up 90 percent of his tickets for only 10 percent of hers. If we saw Adam after such a transaction, he might seem pretty angry; but, to an economist, if Adam made a voluntary trade, then he gained from the trade.

## Producer Decisions

Now consider how scarcity, choice, and economic interaction might occur for people who produce goods. Again we consider an illustrative numerical example.

### *Scarcity and Choice for Individual Producers*

Although all people face limitations on what they are able to produce, not all people face the same limitations. Consider Emily, a poet, and Johann, a printer, who both face scarcity and must make choices. Because of differences in training, abilities, or inclination, Emily is much better at writing poetry than Johann, but Johann is much better at printing books, pamphlets, and greeting cards than Emily. Suppose that Emily and Johann cannot interact with each other; perhaps they live on different islands and cannot communicate.

If Emily writes poetry full time, she could produce 10 poems in a day; but if Emily wants to make and sell greeting cards with her poems in them, she must spend some time printing cards and thereby spend less time writing poems. However, Emily is not very good at printing cards; it takes her so much time to print a card during the day that she has time to write only 1 poem rather than 10 poems during the day.

If Johann prints full time, he can produce 10 different greeting cards in a day. However, if he wants to sell greeting cards, he must write a poem to put inside them. Johann is so poor at writing poems that in order to write only 1 poem a day, his production of greeting cards drops from 10 to 1 per day.

Here is a summary of the choices Emily and Johann face because of a scarcity of time and resources.

**Before Trade**

| *Maria* | *Adam* |
|---|---|
| 20 opera tickets | 20 ballet tickets |

**Two-way Trade**

10 opera tickets

Maria ⟷ Adam

10 ballet tickets

**After Trade**

| *Maria* | *Adam* |
|---|---|
| 10 opera tickets | 10 opera tickets |
| 10 ballet tickets | 10 ballet tickets |

**FIGURE 2.1**

**Gains from Trade Through a Better Allocation of Goods**

Without economic interaction, Maria has more opera tickets than she would like, and Adam has more ballet tickets than he would like. By trading 10 ballet tickets for 10 opera tickets, they can both arrive at a more satisfactory situation.

|  | **Emily, the Poet** | | **Johann, the Printer** | |
|---|---|---|---|---|
|  | Write Full Time | Write and Print | Print Full Time | Write and Print |
| Cards | 0 | 1 | 10 | 1 |
| Poems | 10 | 1 | 0 | 1 |

If Emily and Johann could not interact, then each could produce only 1 greeting card with a poem on the inside. Alternatively, Emily could produce 10 poems without the cards and Johann could produce 10 cards without the poems, but then neither would earn anything. We therefore assume that when confronted with this choice, both Emily and Johann will each choose to produce 1 greeting card with a poem inside. In total, they produce 2 greeting cards.

### Gains from Trade

Now suppose that Emily and Johann can trade. Johann could sell his printing services to Emily, agreeing to print her poems into nice greeting cards. Then Emily could sell the greeting cards to people. Under this arrangement, Emily could spend all day writing poetry and Johann could spend all day printing. In total, 10 different greeting cards could be produced with the same time and effort as only 2 greeting cards when Emily and Johann could not trade.

Note how in this example the interaction took place in a market; Emily sold her poems to Johann or Johann sold his print jobs to Emily. Another approach would be for Emily and Johann to go into business together, forming a firm, Dickinson and Gutenberg Greetings, Inc. Then their economic interaction would occur within the firm, without buying or selling in the market.

Whether in a market or within a firm, the gains from trade are huge in this example. By trading, Emily and Johann can increase production of greeting cards by five times, from 2 cards to 10 cards. In fact, the gains are so large that Emily and Johann would be very likely to trade unless they were prevented from doing so.

### Specialization, Division of Labor, and Comparative Advantage

**specialization:** the situation in which a resource, such as labor, concentrates and develops efficiency at a particular task.

**division of labor:** the division of production into various parts in which different groups of workers specialize.

**comparative advantage:** a situation in which a person or country can produce one good more efficiently than another good in comparison with another person or country.

This example illustrates another reason economic interaction takes place and why there are gains from trade. Economic interaction allows for **specialization** by people in what they are good at. Emily specializes in poetry, and Johann specializes in printing. The example illustrates the idea of the division of labor. A **division of labor** occurs when some workers specialize in one task while others specialize in another task. They divide the overall production into parts, with some workers concentrating on one part (printing) and other workers concentrating on another part (writing). Adam Smith is usually given credit for developing the concept of division of labor; he placed great emphasis on it in the *Wealth of Nations.*

The poetry/printing example of Emily and Johann also illustrates another economic concept, **comparative advantage.** In general, a person or a group of people have a comparative advantage in producing one good relative to another good if they can produce that good with comparatively less time, effort, or resources than another person can produce that good. For example, compared with Johann, Emily has a comparative advantage in writing relative to printing. And compared with Emily, Johann has a comparative advantage in printing relative to writing. As this example shows, production can be increased if people specialize in the skill in which they have a comparative advantage.[1] That is, Emily specializes in writing and Johann in printing.

## Trade Within a Country versus International Trade

Thus far, we have said nothing about where Maria, Adam, Emily, or Johann live or work. They could all reside in the same country, but they could also reside in different countries. Emily could live in the United States; Johann, in Germany. If so,

---

1. Other examples will be explored in the chapter "The Gains from International Trade," where we will see that comparative advantage can also occur when one person is absolutely better at both activities.

# Adam Smith, 1723–1790

**BORN:**
Kircaldy, Scotland, 1723

**EDUCATION:**
M.A. degree, University of Glasgow, Scotland, 1740
Independent study, Oxford, 1741–1748

**JOBS:**
Independent study, Edinburgh, 1748–1751
Professor, University of Glasgow, 1751–1764
Tutor for a duke, traveling in Europe, 1764–1766
Independent study, Kircaldy, 1766–1776
Commissioner of Customs, Edinburgh, 1777–1790

**MAJOR PUBLICATIONS:**
*The Theory of Moral Sentiments,* 1759
*An Inquiry into the Nature and Causes of the Wealth of Nations,* 1776

In 1776, at the age of 53, Adam Smith published an amazing book that would eventually earn him the title "founder of modern economics." The *Wealth of Nations*—still relevant and widely quoted after 200 years—defined the landscape of economics. Its most revolutionary ideas, illustrated with hundreds of juicy examples, were that people's real incomes, rather than gold or silver, are the measure of a society's wealth and that real incomes would grow through the division of labor, trade, and the use of money.

What personal qualities enabled Smith to write such a classic? What does it take to start a whole new field? Clearly, Smith was bright. After all, he obtained a master's degree at age 17 at a time when few even went to college. But there were other factors that prepared Smith to write his great work. He spent 10 years in independent study, at Oxford and Edinburgh, before obtaining a job as a philosophy professor at the University of Glasgow, his alma mater. After about a dozen successful years at Glasgow, however, he resigned to follow a career path that would take him back to solitary study. In exchange for tutoring a young duke and traveling around Europe for two years, he was given a salary for life. After his tutoring job ended, Smith returned to the small town of his birth, Kircaldy, on the east coast of Scotland, and worked virtually alone for more than 10 years on economics. Thus, Smith spent nearly 25 years in independent study—observing facts, developing theories, imagining how to express the theories—a process that culminated in the *Wealth of Nations.* His intelligence and his love of independently pursuing ideas day after day, year after year are the sources of the *Wealth of Nations.*

Adam Smith is frequently associated with the idea that self-interest, rather than benevolence, should be the basis

of society. But an earlier book by Smith, *The Theory of Moral Sentiments,* focused on people's compassion for others, and there is a continuity between this earlier book and the *Wealth of Nations.* Smith recognized the need for cooperation, but reasoned that people's compassion diminishes as they become remote from others in distance, time, or family relationship; and the complexity of a modern economy—the division of labor and the need for resources from all over the world—increases these distances between people, creating the need for alternatives to benevolence. Smith reasoned that self-interest and markets provide that alternative. He wrote that people are

*. . . at all times in need of the co-operation and assistance of great multitudes. . . . The woolen coat, for example . . . is the produce of the joint labour of . . . [t]he shepherd, the sorter of the wool, the wool-comber or carder, the dyer, the scribbler, the spinner, the weaver, the fuller, the dresser, with many others. . . . [But man's] whole life is scarce sufficient to gain the friendship of a few persons . . . , and it is in vain for him to expect [help from] benevolence only. . . . It is not from the benevolence of the butcher, the brewer, or the baker, that we expect our dinner, but from their regard to their own interest. We address ourselves, not to their humanity but to their self-love, and never talk to them of our own necessities but of their advantages. [Man is] led by an invisible hand to promote an end which was no part of his intention. Nor is it always the worse for the society that it was no part of it. By pursuing his own interest he frequently promotes that of the society more effectually than when he really intends to promote it.*

*Source of quote:* Adam Smith, *Wealth of Nations* (New York: Modern Library, 1994), pp. 12, 15, 485.

**international trade:** the exchange of goods and services between people or firms in different nations.

when Emily purchases Johann's printing service, **international trade** will take place because the trade is between people in two different countries. Similarly, Maria could live in Detroit, Michigan, and Adam, in Windsor, Ontario. If so, their trade would also be international.

The gains from international trade are thus of the same kind as the gains from trade within a country. Either people can better satisfy their preferences for goods by trading (as in the case of Maria and Adam), or they can better utilize their comparative advantage (as in the case of Emily and Johann). In either situation there is a gain from trade.

## Multilateral Trade and the Need for a Medium of Exchange

Our examples have focused on the trade between only *two* people. But, in fact, thousands or even billions of people engage in trade. Such trade is called **multilateral trade,** rather than bilateral trade, because more than two parties participate.

**multilateral trade:** trade among more than two persons or nations.

Multilateral trade between people requires a medium of exchange to facilitate such trades. A **medium of exchange** is a generally acceptable item that people can buy and sell goods for. Money—paper currency or coin—is such a medium of exchange.

**medium of exchange:** an item that is generally accepted as a means of payment for goods and services.

Money facilitates trade by permitting people to exchange any good or service for money. The money can then be used to buy any other good or service—not only ballet or opera tickets—from anyone—not only Adam or Maria. Hence, money circulates among the buyers and sellers, facilitating the exchange of goods. Money is very handy when trade is multilateral.

### Different Money in Different Countries

**exchange rate:** the price of one currency in terms of another.

Different countries use different forms of money: dollars in the United States, yen in Japan, marks in Germany, pesos in Mexico, and so on. The use of different monies is a custom or tradition much like the use of different languages. But just as different languages create a need for translators so that people can communicate, different monies create a need for exchanging one currency for another so that people can trade. In other words, trade between countries requires that people exchange the currency of one country for that of another.

**Exchanging One Currency for Another**

Cash machines are one way to exchange currency.

### Exchange Rates

When Emily in the United States buys printing services from Johann in Germany, he will want to be paid in marks, but she will have dollars to pay. Thus, Emily will need to exchange her dollars for marks. The exchange rate tells us how many marks Emily can get for her dollars. The **exchange rate** is the price of one money in terms of another.

For example, if the dollar/mark exchange rate is 2 marks per dollar, then Emily could obtain 2 marks for each of her dollars when buying printing services from Johann. If the dollar/mark exchange rate fell to 1 mark per dollar, then Emily could obtain only 1 mark per dollar. If the exchange rate rose to 3 marks, she could get 3 marks per dollar.

Emily could exchange dollars for marks in many places: Most international airports offer travelers the opportunity to exchange dollars for several different currencies. There are also cash machines that change one currency into another. As long as there is a place where such exchanges can be carried out, people can trade goods and services in different countries, much as they can in the same country. However, the exchange rate can fluctuate from year to year or even day to day. Like most other prices, the exchange rate is determined by the forces of supply and demand. We will study supply and demand and their effect on prices in the next chapter.

## Review

▶ All individuals face scarcity in one form or another. Scarcity forces people to make choices. When there is choice, there is also an opportunity cost of not doing one thing because another thing has been chosen.

▶ People benefit from economic interactions—trading goods and services—with other people. Gains from trade occur because goods and services can be allocated in ways that are more satisfactory to people.

▶ Gains from trade also occur because trade permits specialization through the division of labor. People should specialize in the production of goods they have a comparative advantage in.

▶ Money facilitates trade. Because different countries use different monies, international trade requires people to exchange foreign money. The price of one country's money in terms of another country's money is the exchange rate.

# SCARCITY AND CHOICE FOR THE ECONOMY AS A WHOLE

Just as individuals face scarcity and choice, so does the economy as a whole. The total amount of resources in an economy—labor, land, capital, and technology—is limited. Thus, the economy cannot produce all the health care, crime prevention, education, or entertainment that people want. A choice must be made. Let us first consider how to represent scarcity and choice in the whole economy and then consider alternative ways to make the choices.

## Production Possibilities

To simplify things, let us suppose that production in the economy can be divided into two broad categories. Suppose the economy can either produce computers (mainframes, PCs, hand calculators) or movies (thrillers, love stories, mysteries, musicals). The choice between computers and movies is symbolic of one of the most fundamental choices individuals in any society must face: how much to invest in order to produce more or better goods in the future versus how much to consume in the present. Computers help people produce more or better goods. Movies are a form of consumption. Other pairs of goods could also be used in our example. Another popular example is guns versus butter, representing defense goods versus nondefense goods.

With a scarcity of resources such as labor and capital, there is a choice between producing some goods, such as computers, versus other goods, such as movies. If the economy produces more of one then it must produce less of the other. Table 2.1

**production possibilities:** alternative combinations of production of various goods that are possible, given the economy's resources.

gives an example of the alternative choices, or the **production possibilities,** for computers and movies. Observe that there are six different choices, some with more computers and fewer movies, others with fewer computers and more movies.

Table 2.1 tells us what happens as available resources in the economy are moved from movie production to computer production or vice versa. If resources move from producing movies to producing computers, then fewer movies are produced. For example, if all resources are used to produce computers, then 25,000 computers and zero movies can be produced, according to the table. If all resources are used to produce movies, then no computers can be produced. These are two extremes, of course. If 100 movies are produced, then we produce 24,000 computers rather than 25,000 computers. If 200 movies are produced, then computer production must fall to 22,000.

●————————————————

**TABLE 2.1**
**Production Possibilities**

|   | Movies | Computers |
|---|--------|-----------|
| A | 0      | 25,000    |
| B | 100    | 24,000    |
| C | 200    | 22,000    |
| D | 300    | 18,000    |
| E | 400    | 13,000    |
| F | 500    | 0         |

### Increasing Opportunity Costs

The production possibilities in Table 2.1 illustrate the concept of opportunity cost for the economy as a whole. The opportunity cost of producing more movies is the value of the foregone computers. For example, the opportunity cost of producing 200 movies rather than 100 movies is 2,000 computers.

An important economic idea about opportunity costs is demonstrated in Table 2.1. Observe that movie production increases as we move down the table. As we move from row to row, movie production increases by the same number: 100 movies. The decline in computer production between the first and second rows—from 25,000 to 24,000 computers—is 1,000 computers. The decline between the second and third rows—from 24,000 to 22,000 computers—is 2,000 computers. Thus, the decline in computer production gets greater as we produce more movies. As we move from 400 movies to 500 movies, we lose 13,000 computers. In other words, the opportunity cost, in terms of computers, of producing more movies increases as we produce more movies. Each extra movie requires a loss of more and more computers. What we have just described is called **increasing opportunity costs.**

**increasing opportunity cost:** a situation in which producing more of one good requires giving up producing an increasing amount of another good.

Why do increasing opportunity costs occur? You can think about it in the following way. Some of the available resources are better suited for movie production than computer production and vice versa. Workers who are good at building computers might not be so good at acting, for example, or moviemaking may require an area with a dry, sunny climate. As more and more resources go into making movies, we are forced to take resources that are much better at computer making and use them for moviemaking. Thus, more and more computer production must be lost to increase the production of movies by the same amount. Adding specialized computer designers to a movie cast would be very costly in terms of lost computers, and it might add little to movie production.

### The Production Possibilities Curve

**production possibilities curve:** a curve showing the maximum combinations of production of two goods that are possible, given the economy's resources.

Figure 2.2 is a graphical representation of the production possibilities in Table 2.1 that nicely illustrates increasing opportunity costs. We put movies on the horizontal axis and computers on the vertical axis of the figure. Each pair of numbers in a row of the table becomes a point on the graph. For example, point *A* on the graph is from row A of the table. Point *B* is from row B, and so on.

When we connect the points in Figure 2.2, we obtain the **production possibilities curve.** It shows the maximum number of computers that can be produced for each quantity of movies produced. Note how the curve in Figure 2.2 slopes downward and is bowed out from the origin. That the curve is bowed out indicates that the opportunity cost of producing movies increases as more movies are produced. As resources move from computer making to moviemaking, each additional movie means a greater loss to computer production.

The connection between increasing opportunity costs and the production possibilities curve is further illustrated in Figure 2.3. The opportunity costs are shown on the left of the figure. For example, the opportunity cost of producing 100 rather than zero movies is 1,000 computers (24,000 rather than 25,000). As these opportunity costs increase, the production possibilities curve declines more and more sharply, as shown on the right.

### Inefficient, Efficient, or Impossible?

The production possibilities curve shows the effects of scarcity and choice in the economy as a whole. Three situations can be distinguished in Figure 2.2, depending on whether production is in the shaded area, on the curve, or outside the curve.

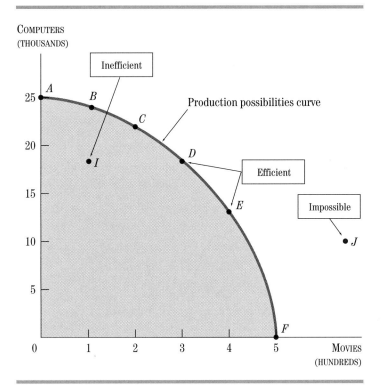

FIGURE 2.2
**The Production Possibilities Curve**
Each point on the curve shows the maximum amount of computers that can be produced when a given amount of movies is produced. The points with letters are the same as in Table 2.1 and are connected by smooth lines. Points in the shaded area inside the curve are inefficient. Points outside the curve are impossible. For the efficient points on the curve, the more movies that are produced, the fewer computers that are produced. The curve is bowed out because of increasing opportunity costs.

First, imagine production at point *I*. This point is inside the curve with 100 movies and 18,000 computers. But the production possibilities curve tells us it is possible with the same amount of resources to produce more computers, more movies, or both. For some reason, the economy is not working well at point *I*. For example, instead of using movie film, people may be taking still photos and then sticking them together with tape to make the movie. Points inside the curve, like point *I*, are *inefficient* because the economy could produce larger numbers of movies, as at point *D*, or a larger number of computers, as at point *B*. Points inside the production possibilities curve are possible, but they are inefficient.

Second, consider points on the production possibilities curve. These points are *efficient*. They represent the maximum amount that can be produced with available resources. The only way to raise production of one good is to lower production of the other good.

Third, consider points to the right and above the production possibilities curve, like point *J* in Figure 2.2. These points are *impossible*. The economy does not have the resources to produce those quantities.

### Economic Growth: Shifts in the Production Possibilities Curve

The production possibilities curve is not immovable. It can *shift* out or in. For example, the curve is shown to shift out in Figure 2.4. More resources—more labor, more capital, or more technology—shift the production possibilities curve out. A technological innovation that allowed one to edit movies faster would shift the curve outward. So would more moviemaking machinery: cameras, lights, studios.

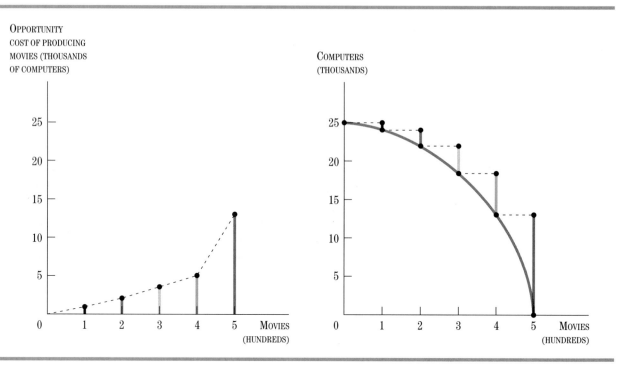

**FIGURE 2.3    Increasing Opportunity Costs and the Production Possibilities Curve**

As shown on the left, the opportunity cost of producing more movies increases with the number of movies produced. This is why the production possibilities curve declines more and more steeply and is bowed out from the origin. Each opportunity cost is designated by a different color, which is then shown along the production possibilities curve.

**FIGURE 2.4**
**Shifts in the Production
Possibilities Curve**

The production possibilities curve shifts out as the economy grows. The maximum amount of movies and computers that can be produced increases. Improvements in technology, more machines, or more labor permit the economy to produce more.

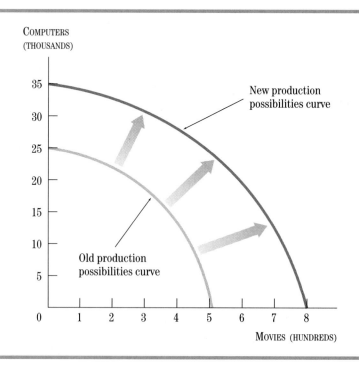

## Using Economics to Explain Educational Choice and Economic Growth

More education raises economic growth—the outward shift of the production possibilities curve over time. Why? Because job skills obtained in elementary school, high school, or college enable workers to produce more goods and services. Economists consider education a type of *human capital.*

What type of education—elementary school, high school, or college—has contributed most to the shift in the production possibilities curve in the twentieth century? You might guess that the answer is college, but according to Claudia Goldin, an economic historian at Harvard University: "Increased high school attendance, not that of college nor elementary school, was responsible for the enormous increase in the human capital stock during this century."*

High school graduation rates rose dramatically from only 5 percent in 1910 to 65 percent in 1960, and the high school curriculum changed radically. In 1910, the typical high school focused on Latin and Greek, preparing most students for college. By the 1930s, high schools were teaching courses more useful for getting a job. The English curriculum was expanded. Vocational courses were introduced.

But why did so many more teenagers go to high school? Child labor laws and compulsory schooling laws might seem to be the obvious answer, but "evidence is mounting that legal change was not the spur it appears to be," according to Goldin's research, because most of these laws were passed or strictly enforced only after high school enrollment rates rose. Similarly, it appears that advertising campaigns including *The More You Learn the More You Earn* posters did not have much impact, according to Professor Goldin.

Changes in *opportunity cost* provide a better explanation. During the 1920s, the wages of those with a high school degree rose sharply compared to those without a high school degree. Increased mechanization and foreign immigrants reduced the demand for child and teenage labor, lowering the wage for those teenagers who dropped out of school. In other words, the opportunity cost of staying in school fell: A teenager would earn much less by dropping out of school and working than by graduating from high school. Thus, it is not surprising that many more teenagers chose to stay in high school, fueling economic growth for much of the century.

*Claudia Goldin, "How America Graduated from High School: 1910 to 1960," National Bureau of Economic Research, Working Paper No. 4762, June 1994.

---

When the production possibilities curve shifts out, more goods and services can be produced. When the economy's production increases, we say there is **economic growth.** The outward shift of the production possibilities curve, representing economic growth, need not be by the same amount in all directions. There can be more movement up than to the right, for example.

**economic growth:** an upward trend in real GDP, reflecting expansion in the economy over time; it can be represented as an outward shift in the production possibilities curve.

As the production possibilities curve shifts out, impossibilities are converted into possibilities. Some of what was impossible for the U.S. economy in 1970 is possible now. Some of what is impossible now will be possible in 2020, unless there is a complete halt to the growth of the economy. Hence, the economists' notion of possibilities is a temporary one. When we say that a certain combination of computers and movies is impossible, we do not mean "forever impossible" but only "impossible for a while."

### Scarcity, Choice, and Economic Growth

However, the conversion of impossibilities into possibilities is also an economic problem of choice and scarcity; if we do not invest in the future now—in machines, in education, in children, in technology—rather than consume everything, it is unlikely that economic growth will continue. If we take computers and movies as symbolic of investment and consumption, then choosing more investment will result in a larger outward shift of the production possibilities curve, as illustrated in

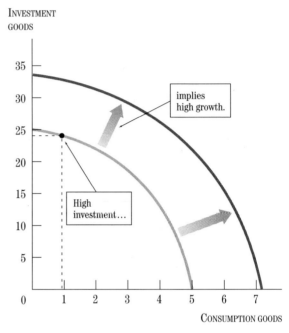

## FIGURE 2.5
### Shifts in the Production Possibilities Curve Depend on Choices

On the left, few resources are devoted to investment for the future; hence, the production possibilities curve shifts only a little over time. On the right, more resources are devoted to investment and less to consumption; hence, the production possibilities curve shifts out by a larger amount over time.

Figure 2.5. More investment in capital enables the economy to grow by a larger amount.

The production possibilities curve represents a tradeoff, but it does not mean that the economy is a *zero-sum game,* a term that means some people win only if others lose. First, it is not necessary for someone to lose in order for the production possibilities curve to shift out. When the curve shifts out, the production of both items increases. Although some people may fare better than others as the production possibilities curve is pushed out, no one necessarily loses. In principle, everyone can gain from economic growth. Second, if the economy is at an inefficient point (like point *I* in Figure 2.2), then production of both goods can be increased with no tradeoff. In general, therefore, the economy is more like a *positive-sum game*—one where everyone can win.

## Review

▶ The production possibilities curve represents the choices open to a whole economy when confronted by a scarcity of resources. With a scarcity of technology, labor, and capital, as more of one item is produced, less of another item must be produced. The opportunity cost of producing more of one item is the reduced production of another item.

▶ The production possibilities curve is bowed out because of increasing opportunity costs.

▶ Points inside the curve are inefficient. Points on the curve are efficient. Points outside the curve are impossible.

▶ The production possibilities curve shifts out as labor, capital, and technology increase.

▶ Outward shifts of the production possibilities curve or moves from inefficient to efficient points are the reasons why the economy is not like a zero-sum game, despite the existence of scarcity and choice.

# MARKET ECONOMIES, COMMAND ECONOMIES, AND PRICES

Although the production possibilities curve for the economy as a whole is a simplified representation of scarcity and choice, it enables us to discuss key questions about any economy.

## Three Questions

Economists typically focus on three essential questions or problems that every economy must find a way to solve, whether it is a small island economy or a large economy like the United States.

▶ *What* is to be produced: movies, computers, guns, butter, greeting cards, rollerblades, health care, or something else? In other words, where on the production possibilities curve should an economy be?

▶ *How* are these goods to be produced? In other words, how can an economy use the available resources so that it is not at an inefficient point inside the production possibilities curve.

▶ *For whom* are the goods to be produced? We know from our ballet/opera tickets example that the allocation of goods in an economy affects people's well-being. An economy in which Maria cannot trade her opera tickets for ballet tickets would not work as well as one in which such trades and reallocations were possible. Moreover, an economy in which some people get everything and others get virtually nothing is also not working well.

Broadly speaking, the *market economy* and the *command economy* are two alternative approaches to these questions. In a market economy, most decisions about what, how, and for whom to produce are made by individual consumers, firms, governments, and other organizations interacting in markets. In a command,

**The Three Fundamental Economic Questions**
Any economic system has to answer three questions: What goods and services should be produced—cars, televisions, or something else? How should these goods or services be produced—in what type of factory, and with how much equipment and labor? And for whom should these goods be produced?

or centrally planned, economy, most decisions about what, how, and for whom to produce are made by those who control the government, which, through a central plan, commands and controls what people do.

Centrally planned economies are much less common today than they were in the mid-twentieth century, when nearly half the world's population lived in centrally planned economies, including Eastern Europe, the former Soviet Union, and China.

In recent years, the people of these countries have been trying to convert their command economies into market economies. After many decades, they became disillusioned with the way in which their command economies were working. By comparison the market economies in Western Europe, the United States, and Japan worked much better: These economies were more productive and offered greater quality and more variety of goods and services to consumers.

### Key Elements of a Market Economy

Let us consider some of the key features of a market economy.

#### *Freely Determined Prices*

**freely determined price:** a price that is determined by the individuals and firms interacting in markets.

In a market economy, most prices—such as the price of computers or the price at which Maria and Adam trade ballet and opera tickets—are freely determined by individuals and firms. These **freely determined prices** are an essential characteristic of a market economy. In a command economy, most prices are set by government, and this leads to inefficiencies in the economy. For example, in the former Soviet Union, the price of bread was set so low that farmers had an incentive to feed the bread to the cows. Feeding bread to livestock is an enormous waste of resources. Livestock could eat plain grain. By feeding cows bread, farmers added the cost of the labor to bake the bread and the fuel to heat the bread ovens to the cost of livestock feed. This is inefficient, like point *I* in Figure 2.2.

In practice, not all prices in market economies are freely determined. For example, some cities control the price of rental apartments. We will look at these exceptions later. But the vast majority of prices are free to vary.

#### *Property Rights and Incentives*

**property rights:** rights over the use, sale, and proceeds from a good or resource.

Property rights are another key element of a market economy. **Property rights** give individuals the legal authority to keep or sell property, whether land, capital, or other resources. Property rights are needed for a market economy because they give people the ability to buy and sell goods. Without property rights, people could take whatever they wanted without paying. People would have to devote time and resources to protecting their earnings or goods.

**incentive:** a device that motivates people to take action, usually so as to increase economic efficiency.

Moreover, by giving people the rights to the earnings from their work, as well as letting them suffer some of the consequences or losses from their mistakes, property rights provide **incentives.** For example, if an inventor cannot get the property rights to an invention, then the incentive to produce the invention is low or even nonexistent. Hence there would be few inventions and we would all be worse off. If there were no property rights, people would not have incentives to specialize and reap the gains from the division of labor. Any extra earnings from specialization could be taken away.

### Competitive Markets

Markets are competitive when there are many buyers and sellers and no single firm or group of firms dominates the market. When a market is dominated by a large firm, the outcome will most likely be inefficient. A single firm may be able to control the price, set it very high, and produce very little. With a high price, people will consume very little. Competitive markets mean that there are many milk companies or many automobile companies competing with each other.

### Freedom to Trade at Home and Abroad

Economic interaction is a way to improve economic outcomes, as the examples in the previous section indicate. Allowing people to interact freely is thus another necessary ingredient of a market economy. Freedom to trade can be extended beyond national borders to other economies.

International trade increases the opportunities to gain from trade. This is especially important in small countries, where it is impossible to produce everything. But the gains from exchange and comparative advantage also exist for larger countries.

### A Role for Government

Just because prices are freely determined and people are free to trade in a market economy does not mean there is no role for government. For example, in virtually all market economies, the government provides for defense and police protection. The government also helps establish property rights. But how far beyond that does it go? Should the government also address the "for whom" question by providing a safety net—a mechanism to deal with the individuals in the economy who are poor, who go bankrupt, who remain unemployed? Most would say yes, but what should the government's role be? As you will see, economics provides an analytical framework to answer such questions. In certain circumstances—called **market failure**—the market economy does not provide good enough answers to the "what, how, and for whom" questions, and the government has a role to play in improving on the market. However, the government, even in the case of market failure, may do worse than the market, in which case economists say there is **government failure.**

> **market failure:** any situation in which the market does not lead to an efficient economic outcome and in which there is a potential role for government.

> **government failure:** a situation in which the government makes things worse than the market, even though there may be market failure.

There is wide agreement among economists that the government has a role in keeping the overall price level stable in a market economy. A stable price level is necessary for a market economy to function well. Imagine how difficult it would be to set prices or decide what to buy if the overall price level rose by 50 percent one month and 100 percent the next month. There is also considerable agreement that the government has a role in keeping the overall economy stable and in preventing a repeat of the Great Depression of the 1930s or even less catastrophic increases in unemployment.

### The Role of Nongovernment Organizations

It is an interesting feature of market economies that many economic interactions between people take place in organizations—firms, households, universities—rather than in markets. Some economic interactions that take place in organizations could take place in the market. In some circumstances, the same type of interaction takes place in a firm and in a market simultaneously. For example, many large firms employ lawyers as part of their permanent staff. Other firms simply purchase the services of such lawyers in the market; if the firm wants to sue someone or is being sued by someone, it hires an outside lawyer to represent it.

Economic interactions in firms differ from the market. Staff lawyers inside large firms are usually paid annual salaries that do not depend directly on the number of hours worked or their success in the lawsuits. In contrast, outside lawyers are paid an hourly fee and a contingency fee based on the number of hours worked and how successful they are.

Economic interactions within organizations take place at transfer prices. If your economics teacher wants to use special audiovisual equipment, the economics department may have to pay a price—called a *transfer price*—to the university's audiovisual department. A **transfer price** is a price that one department of an organization must pay to receive goods or services from another department in the same organization. The transfer price is usually set by the managers of the organization. If the shipping department of a large firm wants to use a lawyer in the firm's legal department, it will probably be charged a fee. If those same transactions occurred in the market, they would take place at a price or wage determined in the market.

Incentives within an organization are as important as incentives in markets. If the lawyers on a legal staff get to keep some of the damages the firm wins in a lawsuit, the lawyers will have more incentive to do a good job. Some firms even try to create marketlike competition between departments or workers in order to give more incentives.

Why do some economic interactions occur in markets and others in organizations? Ronald Coase of the University of Chicago won the Nobel Prize for showing that organizations such as firms are created to reduce market **transaction costs**, the costs of buying and selling that include finding a buyer or a seller and reaching agreement about a price. When market transaction costs are high, we see more transactions taking place within organizations. For example, the firm might have a legal staff rather than outside lawyers because searching for a good lawyer every time there is a lawsuit is too costly. In a crisis, a good lawyer may not be available.

**transfer price:** a price that one department of an organization must pay to receive goods or services from another department in the same organization.

**transaction cost:** the cost of buying or selling in a market including search, bargaining, and writing contracts.

## Prices in Action: An Example

The previous discussion indicates that in market economies freely determined prices are important for determining what is produced, how, and for whom. In this section we examine the roles of prices in a market economy with an example demonstrating that (1) prices serve as *signals* about what should be produced and consumed when there are changes in tastes or changes in technology, (2) prices provide *incentives* to people to alter their production or consumption, and (3) prices affect the *distribution of income,* or who gets what in the economy.

Suppose that there is a sudden new trend for college students to ride bicycles more and drive cars less. How do prices help people in the economy decide what to do?

***Signals.***   First, consider how the information about the change in tastes is signaled to the producers of bicycles and cars. As people try to buy more bicycles, the price of bicycles rises. A higher price will signal that it is more profitable for firms to produce more bicycles. In addition, some bicycle components, like lightweight metal, will also increase in price. Increased lightweight metal prices signal that production should increase. As the price of metal rises, wages for metalworkers may increase. Thus, prices are a signal all the way from the consumer to the metalworkers that more bicycles should be produced. This is what is meant by the expression "prices are a signal."

It is important to note that no single individual knows the information that is transmitted by prices. Any economy is characterized by limited information, where people cannot know the exact reasons why prices for certain goods rise or fall. Hence, it is rather amazing that prices can signal this information.

***Incentives.*** Now consider how prices provide incentives. A higher price for bicycles will increase the incentives for firms to produce bicycles. Because they receive more for each bicycle, they produce more. If there is a large price increase and it continues, new firms may enter the bicycle business. In contrast, the reduced prices for cars signals to car producers that production should decrease.

***Distribution.*** How do prices affect the distribution of income? On the one hand, the workers who find the production of the good they make increasing because of the higher demand for bicycles will earn more. On the other hand, income will be reduced for those who make cars or who have to pay more for bicycles. Local delivery services that use bicycles will see their costs increase.

## Review

▶ The market economy and the command economy are two alternative systems for addressing the questions any economy must face: what to produce, how to produce, and for whom to produce.

▶ A market economy is characterized by several key elements, such as freely determined prices, property rights, and freedom to trade at home and abroad.

▶ For a market economy to work well, markets should be competitive and the government should play a role, including keeping the overall price level and the overall economy stable.

▶ Prices are signals, they provide incentives, and they affect the distribution of income.

# CONCLUSION

This chapter and Chapter 1 have given a broad overview of economics. In Chapter 1, we saw how economists document and quantify observations about the economy. We also saw that models—abstract simplifications of how the economy works—are used to explain observations and make predictions useful for decision-making in government, business, and everyday life.

In this chapter, we have learned about certain common characteristics of economic models and about how economists think, based on scarcity, choice, and interaction. We've looked at the three essential questions an economy must solve: what and how to produce and for whom. Now we are ready to actually do some economics. In the next chapter, we consider the most famous and frequently used model in economics: the basic supply and demand model.

# KEY POINTS

**1.** Economics is the study of how people make choices when there is a scarcity of resources or time, and how people who make choices interact with each other.

**2.** Economic interactions occur in markets and in organizations.

3. Scarcity leads to choice, and choice leads to opportunity costs.

4. Trade leads to gains because it allows goods and services to be reallocated in a way that improves people's well-being and because it permits people to specialize in what they are relatively good at.

5. The production possibilities curve summarizes the tradeoffs in the whole economy due to scarcity. Economic production is efficient if the economy is on the production possibilities curve.

6. The three basic questions that any economy must face

are what, how, and for whom production should take place.

7. A well-functioning market system involves free prices, property rights, competition, freedom to trade, and a role for government and nongovernment organizations.

8. If prices are set at the wrong levels by government, waste and inefficiency—such as feeding bread to livestock—will result.

9. Prices transmit signals, provide incentives, and affect the distribution of income.

10. In organizations, transfer prices affect incentives for different departments within the organization.

# KEY TERMS

scarcity
choice
economic interaction
organizations
market
opportunity cost
gains from trade
specialization
division of labor

comparative advantage
international trade
multilateral trade
medium of exchange
exchange rate
production possibilities
increasing opportunity costs
production possibilities curve
economic growth

freely determined prices
property rights
incentives
market failure
government failure
transfer price
transaction costs

# QUESTIONS FOR REVIEW

1. How do scarcity, choice, and economic interaction fit into the definition of economics?

2. Why does scarcity imply a choice among alternatives?

3. Why does choice create opportunity costs?

4. What is the difference between economic interaction in markets and in organizations?

5. Why is there a gain from trade even if total production of goods and services does not change?

6. How can specialization lead to a gain from trade?

7. What is the principle of increasing opportunity costs?

8. What are the key ingredients of a market economy?

9. What are the three basic questions any economic system must address?

10. What are the three roles of prices?

# PROBLEMS

1. Suppose you must divide your time between studying for economics and studying for biology. To make things simple, suppose there are only two choices. Suppose that the time and the grades on the finals are as follows:

| Fraction of Time on Economics | Economics Grade | Biology Grade |
| --- | --- | --- |
| 100 | 100 | 0 |
| 80 | 97 | 40 |
| 60 | 90 | 75 |
| 40 | 75 | 90 |
| 20 | 40 | 97 |
| 0 | 0 | 100 |

a) Draw a production possibilities curve for the economics grade versus the biology grade.
b) What is the opportunity cost of increasing the time spent on economics from 80 percent to 100 percent? From 60 percent to 80 percent?
c) Are there increasing opportunity costs from spending more time studying economics? What about biology? Explain why this is the case using examples from your own study experience.

2. A small country produces only two goods, cars and cookies. Given its limited resources, this country has the following production possibilities:

| Cars | Cookies |
|------|---------|
| 0 | 100 |
| 20 | 90 |
| 40 | 70 |
| 60 | 40 |
| 80 | 0 |

a)  Draw the production possibilities curve.
b)  Suppose the production of cars requires the use of large machinery and the production of cookies uses mostly labor. Show the change in the production possibilities curve when the number of machines increases but the amount of labor stays constant.

**3.** Suppose two countries have the production possibilities curve shown in Figure 2.2, where computers represent investment and movies represent consumption. However, one country chooses a combination that has more investment goods than the other country. How do you think the production possibilities curves of these two countries will differ 50 years from now?

**4.** Suppose that you are president of the student government, and you have $10,000 for guest speakers for the year. Spike Lee costs $10,000 per appearance. Former economic advisers to the government charge $1,000 per lecture. Hence, you cannot have both Spike Lee and the former economic advisers. Explain the economic problem of choice and scarcity in this case. What issues would you consider in arriving at a decision?

**5.** Compare two countries. In one country, the government sets prices and never adjusts them. In the other country, the government adjusts prices daily, endeavoring to allocate resources to consumers to satisfy their tastes. Are either of these a market economy? Why or why not?

**6.** Suppose there is a drought in Australia that causes a severe decline in the production of wheat and raises the price of wheat in the United States. Explain how this change in the price signals information to farmers, provides incentives to farmers in the United States, and affects the distribution of income.

**7.** Look at Figure 2.2 and compare points *I* and *D*. What is the opportunity cost of moving from *I* to *D?* What are some ways that the economy can move out of the inefficient area inside the production possibilities curve?

**8.** Suppose one country is more efficient at producing airplanes and another at producing computers. Should these two countries specialize and trade with each other? Why? Explain how specialization and trade is a positive-sum game.

**9.** Suppose Robert and Jennifer can produce the following combinations of apple pie and computer programs in a day:

| Robert | | Jennifer | |
|--------|---|----------|---|
| Pies | Programs | Pies | Programs |
| 0 | 5 | 0 | 8 |
| 1 | 4 | 1 | 6 |
| 2 | 3 | 2 | 4 |
| 3 | 2 | 3 | 2 |
| 4 | 1 | 4 | 0 |
| 5 | 0 | 5 | 0 |

a)  If Robert is currently producing 2 pies and Jennifer is currently producing 2 pies, then how many computer programs do they each produce? What is the total production of pies and computer programs between them?
b)  Is it possible to increase the total production of pies and computer programs? Give an example of how they can change production to increase the total.
c)  If they can increase total production, will there be gains from trade when they specialize and trade between themselves?

**10.** Consider a production possibilities curve showing the tradeoff a country faces in producing consumption goods (butter) and military equipment (guns). As the government decides to move production toward guns, there are increasing opportunity costs. Why?

**11.** "When you look at the economies in the United States, Europe, or Japan, you see most of the ingredients of a market economy. For example, consider bicycles. Prices in the bicycle market are free to vary; people have property rights to the bicycles they buy; many people sell bicycles; many bicycles sold in the United States, Europe, and Japan come from other countries; the government regulates bicycle use (no bicycles on the freeways, for example); and bicycle production takes place within firms with many workers." Replace bicycles with another good or service of your choosing in the previous quotation and comment on whether the sentence is still true.

**12.** Allison will graduate from high school next June. She has ranked her three possible postgraduation plans in the following order: (1) work for two years at a consulting job in her home town paying $20,000 per year, (2) attend a local community college for two years with tuition and expenses of $5,000 per year, and (3) travel around the world tutoring a rock star's child for pay of $5,000 per year. What is the opportunity cost of her choice?

**13.** Compare the opportunity cost of one more year of school versus working for one year for a (1) high school graduate, (2) college graduate, and (3) medical school graduate.

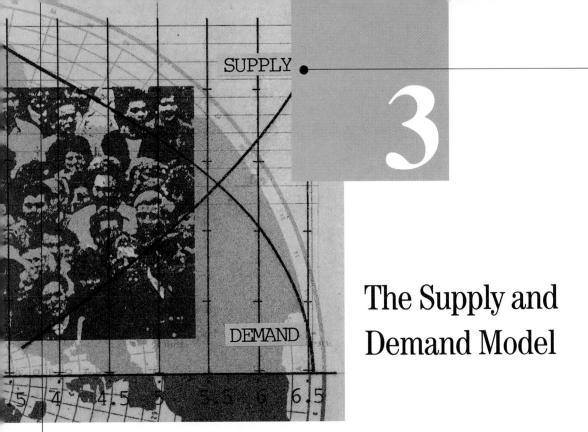

SUPPLY

DEMAND

# 3

# The Supply and Demand Model

Prices are both the lifeblood and the nervous system of a market economy. By transmitting vital information and providing incentives, prices enable a market economy to adjust to change and to thrive. But how are prices determined? What caused the price of health care to rise? What caused the price of computers to fall? What determines the price at which people buy or sell gasoline, electronic goods, printing services, or foreign currencies? The purpose of this chapter is to show how to find the answers to such questions.

To do so, we need to construct a model—a simplified description of how a market economy works. The model economists use to explain how prices are determined in a market economy is called the *supply and demand model.* This model describes how particular markets—such as the health-care market or the computer market—work. It

consists of three elements: *demand,* describing the behavior of consumers in the market; *supply,* describing the behavior of firms in the market; and *market equilibrium,* connecting supply and demand and describing how consumers and firms interact in the market.

Economists like to compare the supply and demand model to a pair of scissors. Demand is one blade of the scissors. Supply is the other. Either blade alone is incomplete and virtually useless; but when the two blades of a pair of scissors are connected to form the scissors, they become an amazingly useful, yet simple, tool. So it is with supply and demand.

In this chapter, we first describe each of the three elements of the model. We then show how to use the model to answer a host of questions about price determination in a market economy.

# DEMAND

To an economist, the term *demand*—whether the demand for health care or the demand for computers—has a very specific meaning. **Demand** is a relationship between two economic variables: (1) *the price of a particular good,* and (2) *the quantity of the good consumers are willing to buy at that price during a specific time period,* all other things being equal. For short, we call the first variable the **price** and the second variable the **quantity demanded.** The phrase *all other things being equal,* or *ceteris paribus,* is appended to the definition of demand because the quantity consumers are willing to buy depends on many other things besides the price of the good; we want to hold these other things constant, or equal, while we examine the relationship between price and quantity demanded.

Demand can be represented either numerically with a table or graphically with a curve. In either case, demand describes how much of a good consumers will purchase at each price. Consider the demand for bicycles in the United States. An example of the demand for bicycles is shown in Table 3.1. Several prices for a typical bicycle are listed in the first column of the table, ranging from $140 to $300. Of course, there are many kinds of bicycles—mountain bikes, racing bikes, children's bikes, and inexpensive one-speed bikes with cruiser brakes—so you need to think about the price of an average, or typical, bike.

Listed in the second column of Table 3.1 is the quantity demanded (in millions of bicycles) each year in the United States at the price in the first column. This is the total demand in the bicycle market. For example, at a price of $180 per bicycle, consumers would buy 11 million bicycles. That is, the quantity demanded would be 11 million bicycles each year in the United States, according to Table 3.1.

Observe that, as the price rises, the quantity demanded by consumers goes down. If the price goes up from $180 to $200 per bicycle, for example, the quantity demanded goes down from 11 million to 9 million bicycles. On the other hand, if the price goes down, the quantity demanded goes up. If the price falls from $180 to $160, for example, the quantity demanded rises from 11 million to 14 million bicycles.

The relationship between price and quantity demanded in Table 3.1 is called a **demand schedule.** This relationship is an example of the law of demand. The **law of demand** says that the higher the price, the lower the quantity demanded in the market; and the lower the price, the higher the quantity demanded in the market. In other words, the law of demand says that the price and the quantity demanded are negatively related, all other things being equal.

## The Demand Curve

Figure 3.1 represents demand graphically. It is a graph with the price of the good on the vertical axis and the quantity demanded of the good on the horizontal axis. It shows the demand for bicycles given in Table 3.1. Each of the nine rows in Table 3.1 corresponds to each of the nine points in Figure 3.1. For example, the point at the lower right part of the graph corresponds to the first row of the table, when the price is $140 and the quantity demanded is 18 million bicycles. The resulting curve showing all the combinations of price and quantity demanded is the **demand curve.**

**demand:** a relationship between **price** and **quantity demanded.**

TABLE 3.1
**Demand Schedule for Bicycles**
(millions of bicycles per year)

| Price | Quantity Demanded |
| --- | --- |
| $140 | 18 |
| $160 | 14 |
| $180 | 11 |
| $200 | 9 |
| $220 | 7 |
| $240 | 5 |
| $260 | 3 |
| $280 | 2 |
| $300 | 1 |

**demand schedule:** a tabular presentation of demand showing the price and quantity demanded for a particular good, all else being equal.

**law of demand:** the tendency for the quantity demanded of a good in a market to decline as its price rises.

**demand curve:** a graph of demand showing the downward-sloping relationship between price and quantity demanded.

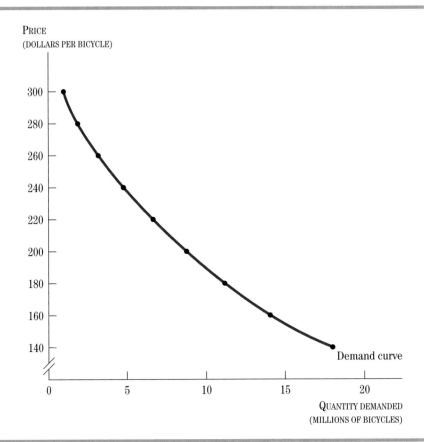

| Price | Quantity Demanded |
|-------|-------------------|
| $140  | 18 |
| $160  | 14 |
| $180  | 11 |
| $200  | 9  |
| $220  | 7  |
| $240  | 5  |
| $260  | 3  |
| $280  | 2  |
| $300  | 1  |

**FIGURE 3.1**
**The Demand Curve**

The demand curve shows that the price of a good and the quantity demanded by consumers are negatively related. The curve slopes down. For each price, the demand curve gives the quantity demanded, or the quantity that consumers are willing to buy at that price. The points along the demand curve for bicycles shown here are the same as the pairs of numbers in Table 3.1.

It slopes downward from left to right because the quantity demanded is negatively related to the price. To remember that the *d*emand curve slopes *d*ownward, think of the *d* in *demand*.

Why does the demand curve slope downward? The demand curve tells us the quantity demanded by all consumers. If the price of bicycles falls, then some consumers who previously found the price of bicycles too high may decide to buy a bicycle. The lower price of bicycles gives them an incentive to buy bicycles rather than other goods. It is important to remember that when economists draw a demand curve, they hold constant the price of other goods: running shoes, rollerblades, motor scooters, etc. When the price of bicycles falls, bicycles become more attractive to people in comparison with these other goods. As a result, the quantity demanded rises when the price falls. Conversely, when the price of bicycles rises, some people may decide to buy rollerblades or motor scooters instead of bicycles. As a result, the quantity demanded declines when the price rises.

## Shifts in Demand

Now price is not the only thing that affects the quantity of a good that people buy. The weather, people's concerns about the environment, or the availability of bike lanes on roads can influence people's decisions to purchase bicycles, for example. The quantity of bicycles bought might increase if a climate change brings on an extended period of dry weather. Because people would enjoy riding their bicycles

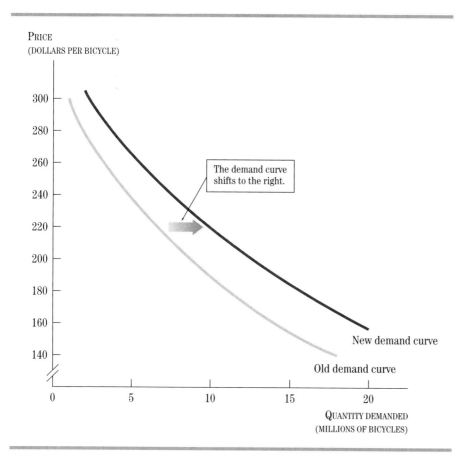

PRICE
(DOLLARS PER BICYCLE)

The demand curve
shifts to the right.

New demand curve

Old demand curve

QUANTITY DEMANDED
(MILLIONS OF BICYCLES)

**FIGURE 3.2**
**A Shift in the Demand Curve**
The demand curve shows how the quantity demanded of a good is related to the price of the good, all other things being equal. A change in one of these other things—the weather or people's tastes, for example—will shift the demand curve as shown in the graph. In this case the demand for bicycles increases; the demand curve for bicycles shifts to the right.

more in dry weather, more bicycles would be purchased at any given price. Or perhaps there is a health trend leading people to get exercise by riding bicycles rather than driving their cars. This would also lead to more purchases of bicycles.

The demand curve is drawn assuming all other things equal, except the price of the good. A change in any one of these other things, previously assumed equal, will shift the demand curve. An increase in demand shifts the demand curve to the right. A decrease in demand shifts the demand curve to the left. This is illustrated in Figure 3.2. The lightly shaded curve labeled "old demand curve" is the same as the demand curve in Figure 3.1. The arrow shows how this curve has shifted to the right to the more darkly shaded curve labeled "new demand curve." Thus, Figure 3.2 shows that the demand curve for bicycles shifts to the right. When the demand curve shifts to the right, more bicycles are purchased than before at any given price. For example, before the shift in demand, a $200 price led to 9 million bicycles purchased. But when the demand curve shifts to the right because of drier weather, that same price leads to 13 million bicycles purchased. The demand curve would shift to the left if a climate change to wetter weather reduced people's purchases of bicycles at any given price.

There are many reasons the demand curve may shift. Most of them can be categorized into several sources: *consumers' preferences, consumers' information, consumers' incomes, the number of consumers in the population, consumers' expectations of future prices,* and *the price of related goods.* Let us briefly consider each source of shifts in demand.

### Consumers' Preferences

In general, a change in people's tastes or preferences for a product compared to other products will change the amount of the product they purchase at any given price. The physical fitness craze leading to an increase in the demand for bicycles is an example. Other examples of changes in preferences that cause shifts in demand for other goods and services include an increase in the demand for over-the-counter cold remedies when the weather turns wet and chilly in the winter, an increase in the demand for taxis on rainy days, and a decline in the demand for travel on subways because of increasing concerns about crime.

### Consumers' Information

A change in information relating to a product can also cause the demand curve to shift. For example, when people learned about the dangers of smoking, the demand for cigarettes declined. Similarly, information about the effects of cholesterol may have reduced the demand for beef and increased the demand for chicken. The demand curve for chicken shifted to the right. The demand curve for beef shifted to the left.

### Consumers' Incomes

**normal good:** a good for which demand increases when income rises and decreases when income falls.

**inferior good:** a good for which demand decreases when income rises and increases when income falls.

If people's incomes change, then their purchases of goods usually change. An increase in income increases the demand for most goods. For example, higher incomes increase the demand for eating out, for cars, for movies. A decline in income reduces the demand for these goods. Goods for which demand increases when income rises, or for which demand decreases when income falls, are called **normal goods** by economists.

However, the demand for some goods—such as one-speed bicycles or day-old bread—may decline when income increases. Such goods are called **inferior goods** by economists. The demand for inferior goods declines when people's income increases because they can afford more attractive goods, such as fresh bread or 15-speed bicycles. But whether goods are normal or inferior, the demand for them usually shifts when consumers' incomes change.

### Number of Consumers in the Population

Demand is a relationship between price and the quantity demanded by *all* consumers in the market. If the number of consumers increases, then demand will increase. If the number of consumers falls, then demand will decrease. For example, the number of teenagers in the U.S. population expanded sharply in the late 1990s. This increases the demand for *Seventeen* magazine, for rollerblades, for Clearasil, and for other goods that teenagers tend to buy. As the number of older people in the population increases in the early part of the twenty-first century, the demand for nursing homes is expected to increase.

### Consumers' Expectations of the Future

If people expect the price of a good to increase, they will want to buy it before the price increases. Conversely, if people expect the price to decline, they will purchase less and wait for the decline. One sees this effect of expectations of future price changes often. "We better buy before the price goes up" is a common reason for purchasing items during a clearance sale. Or, "Let's put off buying that bicycle until the postholiday sales."

In general, it is difficult to forecast the future, but sometimes consumers know quite a bit about whether the price of a good will rise or fall, and they react accordingly. Thus, demand increases if people expect the *future* price of the good to rise. And demand decreases if people expect the *future* price of the good to fall.

### Prices of Closely Related Goods

A sharp decrease in the price of motor scooters or rollerblades will decrease the demand for bicycles. Why? Because buying these related goods becomes relatively more attractive than buying bicycles. Motor scooters or rollerblades are examples of substitutes for bicycles. A **substitute** is a good that provides some of the same uses or enjoyment as another good. Butter and margarine are substitutes. In general, the demand for a good will increase if the price of a substitute for the good rises, and the demand for a good will decrease if the price of a substitute falls.

On the other hand, a sharp increase in the cost of bicycle helmets—another good closely related to bicycles—will decrease the demand for bicycles, especially if there is a law that requires that bicycle riders, but not rollerbladers, wear helmets. A bicycle helmet is an example of a good that is a complement to a bicycle. In general, a **complement** is a good that tends to be consumed together with another good. Coffee and sugar are complements. The demand for a good (sugar) increases if the price of a complement (coffee) decreases, and the demand for a good (sugar) decreases if the price of a complement (coffee) increases.

**Substitutes and Complements**
Butter and margarine are examples of substitutes; they have similar characteristics. For example, margarine can be substituted for butter on toast. A *rise* in the price of butter will *increase* the demand for margarine. Hot dogs and hot dog buns are examples of complements; they tend to be consumed together. A *rise* in the price of hot dogs will *decrease* the demand for hot dog buns.

**substitute:** a good that has many of the same characteristics and can be used in place of another good.

**complement:** a good that is usually consumed or used together with another good.

## Movements Along versus Shifts of the Demand Curve

We have shown that the demand curve can shift, and we have given many possible reasons for such shifts. In using demand curves, it is very important to distinguish *shifts* of the demand curve from *movements along* the demand curve. This distinction is illustrated in Figure 3.3.

A *movement along* the demand curve occurs when the quantity demanded changes due to a *change in the price of the good.* For example, if the price of bicycles rises, causing the quantity demanded by consumers to fall, then there is a movement along the demand curve. A movement along the demand curve for bicycles occurs when the quantity demanded changes from point *A* to point *B* or from point *A* to point *C* in Figure 3.3. At point *A* the price is $200 and the quantity demanded is 9 million. At point *B* the price is $220 and the quantity demanded is 7 million. If the quantity changes because the price changes, economists say there is a *change in the quantity demanded.*

A *shift* of the demand curve, on the other hand, occurs if there is a change due to *any source except the price.* When the demand curve shifts, economists say there is a *change in demand.* Remember, the term *demand* refers to the entire curve or schedule relating price and quantity demanded, while the term *quantity demanded* refers to a single point on the demand curve. You should be able to tell whether any

## FIGURE 3.3
### Shifts versus Movements Along the Demand Curve

A *shift* in the demand curve occurs when there is a change in something (other than the good's own price) that affects the quantity of a good consumers are willing to buy. An increase in demand is a shift to the right of the demand curve. A decrease in demand is a shift to the left of the demand curve. A movement along the demand curve occurs when the price of the good changes, causing the quantity demanded to change as, for example, from point *A* to points *B* or *C*.

economic event causes (1) a change in demand or (2) a change in the quantity demanded; or, equivalently, (1) a shift in the demand curve or (2) a movement along the demand curve.

## Review

▶ Demand is a relationship between the price of a good and the quantity people will buy at each price, all other things equal. The demand curve slopes down. The price and the quantity demanded are negatively related.

▶ When the price of a good changes, the quantity demanded changes and we have a movement along the demand curve.

▶ When something other than the price changes and affects demand, there is a shift in the demand curve or, simply, a change in demand.

# SUPPLY

**supply:** a relationship between **price** and **quantity supplied.**

Whereas demand refers to the behavior of consumers, supply refers to the behavior of firms. The term *supply*—whether it is the supply of health care or computers— has a very specific meaning for economists. **Supply** is a relationship between two variables: (1) *the price of a particular good,* and (2) *the quantity of the good firms are willing to sell at that price,* all other things the same. For short, we call the first variable the **price** and the second variable the **quantity supplied.**

Supply can be represented with a numerical table or a graph. An example of the supply of bicycles is shown in Table 3.2. Listed in the first column of Table 3.2 is the price of bicycles; the range of prices is the same as for the demand schedule in Table 3.1. The second column lists the quantity supplied (in millions of bicycles) in the entire market by bicycle-producing firms at each price. For example, at a price of $180, the quantity supplied is 7 million bicycles. Observe that as the price increases, the quantity supplied increases, and that as the price decreases, the quantity supplied decreases. For example, if the price rises from $180 to $200, the quantity supplied increases from 7 to 9 million bicycles. The relationship between price and quantity supplied in Table 3.2 is a **supply schedule.** This relationship is an example of the law of supply. The **law of supply** says that the higher price, the higher the quantity supplied, and the lower the price, the lower the quantity supplied. In other words, the law of supply says that the price and the quantity supplied are positively related.

## The Supply Curve

We can represent the supply schedule in Table 3.2 graphically by plotting the price and quantity supplied on a graph, as shown in Figure 3.4. The scales of each axis in

**supply schedule:** a tabular presentation of supply showing the price and quantity supplied of a particular good, all else being equal.

**TABLE 3.2**
**Supply Schedule for Bicycles**
(millions of bicycles per year)

| Price | Quantity Supplied |
| --- | --- |
| $140 | 1 |
| $160 | 4 |
| $180 | 7 |
| $200 | 9 |
| $220 | 11 |
| $240 | 13 |
| $260 | 15 |
| $280 | 16 |
| $300 | 17 |

**FIGURE 3.4**
**The Supply Curve**
The supply curve shows that the price and the quantity supplied by firms in the market are positively related. The curve slopes up. For each price on the vertical axis, the supply curve shows the quantity that firms are willing to sell along the horizontal axis. The points along the supply curve for bicycles match the pairs of numbers in Table 3.2.

**law of supply:** the tendency for the quantity supplied of a good in a market to increase as its price rises.

**supply curve:** a graph of supply showing the upward-sloping relationship between price and quantity supplied.

Figure 3.4 are exactly the same as those in Figure 3.1, except that Figure 3.4 shows the quantity supplied, whereas Figure 3.1 shows the quantity demanded. Each pair of numbers in Table 3.2 is plotted as a point in Figure 3.4. The resulting curve showing all the combinations of prices and quantities supplied is the **supply curve.** Note that the curve slopes upward: $280 represents a high price, and there the quantity supplied is high—16 million bicycles. If the price is down at $160 a bicycle, then firms are willing to sell only 4 million bicycles.

Why does the supply curve slope upward? Imagine yourself running a firm that produces and sells bicycles. If the price of the bicycles goes up, from $180 to $280, then you can earn $100 more for each bicycle you produce and sell. Given your production costs, if you earn more from each bicycle, you will have a greater incentive to produce and sell more bicycles. If producing more bicycles increases the costs of producing each bicycle, perhaps because you must pay the bike assembly workers a higher wage for working overtime, the higher price will give you the incentive to incur these costs. Other bicycle firms will be thinking the same way. Thus, firms are willing to sell more bicycles as the price rises. Conversely, the incentive for firms to sell bicycles will decline as the price falls. Basically, that is why there is a positive relationship between price and quantity supplied.

## Shifts in Supply

The supply curve is drawn assuming all other things equal, except the price of the good. If any one of these other things change, then the supply curve shifts. For example, suppose a new machine is invented that makes it less costly for firms to produce bicycles; then firms would have more incentive at any given price to produce and sell more bicycles. Supply would increase; the supply curve would shift to the right.

Figure 3.5 shows how the supply curve for bicycles would shift to the right because of a new cost-reducing machine. The supply curve would shift to the left when there is a decrease in supply. Supply would decrease, for example, if bicycle-producing firms suddenly found that their existing machines became too hot and had to be oiled with an expensive lubricant each time a bicycle was produced. This would raise costs, lower supply, and shift the supply curve to the left.

Many things can cause the supply curve to shift. Most of these can be categorized by the source of the change in supply: *technology, the price of goods used in production, the number of firms in the market, expectations of future prices,* and *government taxes, subsidies, and regulations.* Let us briefly consider the sources of shifts in supply.

### Technology

Anything that changes the amount a firm can produce with a given amount of inputs to production can be considered a change in technology. Because of new discoveries and ideas for improving production, technology usually gets better over time. Better bicycle-making machinery is an example. Another example is the rapid improvement in the technology for producing computers. These technological improvements increase supply and shift the supply curve to the right.

Droughts, earthquakes, and terrorists' bombing of factories also affect the amount that can be produced with given inputs. A drought that reduces the amount of wheat that can be produced on a farm in the Midwest or a freeze that reduces the number of oranges yielded by trees in Florida orchards are examples. Because such

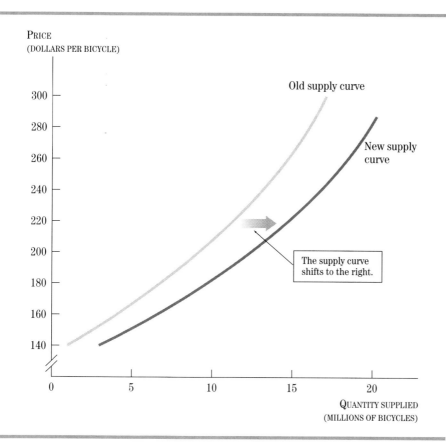

PRICE
(DOLLARS PER BICYCLE)

Old supply curve

New supply curve

The supply curve shifts to the right.

QUANTITY SUPPLIED
(MILLIONS OF BICYCLES)

**FIGURE 3.5**
**A Shift in the Supply Curve**
The supply curve is a relationship between the quantity supplied of a good and the price of the good, all other things being equal. A change in one of these other things (other than the good's price) will shift the supply curve as shown in the graph. In this case the supply of bicycles increases; the supply curve for bicycles shifts to the right.

events change the amount that can be produced with a given amount of inputs, they are similar to changes in technology, though these examples reduce rather than increase supply. In these cases, the supply curve shifts to the left.

### The Price of Goods Used in Production

If the prices of the inputs to production—raw materials, labor, or capital—increase, then it becomes more costly to produce goods, and firms would produce less at any given price; the supply curve would shift to the left. For example, if the price of fertilizer rises, then the cost of growing corn will rise, and the supply of corn will decrease. On the other hand, if the price of an input, such as fertilizer, falls, supply increases and the supply curve shifts to the right.

### The Number of Firms in the Market

Remember that the supply curve refers to *all* the firms producing the product—all the corn farmers, for example. If the number of firms increases, then more goods will be produced at each price; supply increases, and the supply curve shifts to the right. For example, as more firms entered the overnight package delivery service in the 1980s and 1990s, the supply increased.

A decline in the number of firms would shift the supply curve to the left. For example, the number of drive-in movie theaters has declined sharply over the last 30 years; hence the supply curve has shifted.

### Expectations of Future Price

If firms expect the price of the good they produce to rise in the future, then they will hold off selling at least part of production until the price rises. For example, farmers in the United States who anticipate an increase in wheat prices because of political turbulence in Russia may decide to store more wheat in silos and sell it later, when the price rises. Thus, expectations of *future* price increases tend to reduce supply. Conversely, expectations of *future* price decreases tend to increase supply.

### Government Taxes, Subsidies, and Regulations

The government has the ability to affect the supply of particular goods produced by firms. For example, the government imposes taxes on firms to pay for such government services as education, police, and national defense. These taxes increase firms' costs and reduce supply. The supply curve shifts to the left when a tax on what firms sell in the market increases.

    The government also makes payments—subsidies—to firms to encourage the firms to produce certain goods. Many farms now receive subsidies to produce certain food products. Such subsidies have the opposite effect of taxes on supply. An increase in subsidies reduces firms' costs and increases the supply.

**FIGURE 3.6**

**Shifts versus Movements Along the Supply Curve**

A *shift* in the supply curve occurs when there is a change in something (other than the price) that affects the amount of a good firms are willing to supply. An increase in supply is a shift to the right of the supply curve. A decrease in supply is a shift to the left of the supply curve. A movement along the supply curve occurs when the price of the good changes, causing the quantity supplied by firms to change; for example, from point *D* to points *E* or *F*.

Governments also regulate firms. In some cases, such regulations can change the firms' costs of production and thereby affect supply. For example, when the government requires that firms install safety features on their products, the cost of producing the products rises, and thus supply declines.

### Movements Along versus Shifts of the Supply Curve

Figure 3.6 compares *shifts* of the supply curve with *movements along* the supply curve. A *movement along* the supply curve occurs when a change in price causes a change in the quantity supplied. Economists then say there is a *change in the quantity supplied,* as, for example, when the quantity supplied changes from point *D* to point *F* or from point *D* to point *E* in Figure 3.6.

A *shift* of the supply curve occurs if there is a change due to *any source except the price.* When the supply curve shifts, economists say there is a *change in supply.* The term *supply* refers to the entire supply curve. The term *quantity supplied* refers to a point on the supply curve. As we will soon see, it is important to be able to tell whether a change in something causes (1) a change in supply or (2) a change in the quantity supplied; or, equivalently, (1) a shift in the supply curve or (2) a movement along the supply curve.

## Review

▶ Supply is a positive relationship between the price of a good and the quantity supplied of the good by firms. The supply curve slopes upward because higher prices give firms more incentive to produce and sell more.

▶ When the quantity supplied changes because of a change in price, we have a movement along the supply curve. Other factors—such as technology, the number of firms, and expectations—affect supply. When these determinants change, the supply curve shifts.

# MARKET EQUILIBRIUM: COMBINING SUPPLY AND DEMAND

Thus far, we have examined consumers' demand for goods in a market and firms' supply of goods in a market. Now we put supply and demand together to complete the supply and demand model. When consumers buy goods and firms sell goods, they interact in a market and a price is determined. Recall that a market does not need to be located at one place; the U.S. bicycle market consists of all the bicycle firms that sell bicycles and all the consumers who buy bicycles.

Although it may sound amazing, no single person or firm determines the price in the market. Instead the market determines the price. As buyers and sellers interact, prices might go up for a while and then go down. Alfred Marshall, the economist who did the most to develop the supply and demand model in the late nineteenth century, called this process the "higgling and bargaining" of the market. The assumption underlying the supply and demand model is that, in the give and take of the marketplace, prices adjust until they settle down to a level where the quantity supplied by firms equals the quantity demanded by consumers. Let's see how.

# Overview of Supply and Demand

### SUPPLY

Supply describes firms.

The supply curve looks like this:

### Law of Supply

| Price and quantity supplied are positively related. |
| --- |

### Movements along supply curve occur

| when price rises and quantity supplied rises |
| --- |
| or |
| when price falls and quantity supplied falls. |

### Shifts in supply are due to:

**Technology** (new inventions)

**Number of firms in market**

**Price of goods used in production** (inputs such as fertilizer, labor)

**Government taxes, subsidies, regulations** (commodity taxes, agricultural subsidies, safety regulations)

**Expectations of future prices** (firms will sell less now if prices are expected to rise; for example, farmers may store goods to sell next year)

### DEMAND

Demand describes consumers.

The demand curve looks like this:

### Law of Demand

| Price and quantity demanded are negatively related. |
| --- |

### Movements along demand curve occur

| when price rises and quantity demanded falls |
| --- |
| or |
| when price falls and quantity demanded rises. |

### Shifts in demand are due to:

**Preferences** (nice weather or fitness craze changes tastes)

**Number of consumers in market**

**Price of related goods** (both substitutes, like butter and margarine, and complements, like coffee and sugar)

**Consumers' income** (normal goods versus inferior goods)

**Expectations of future prices** (consumers will buy more now if prices are expected to rise in the future)

**Consumers' information** (about cholesterol or smoking, for example)

## Determination of the Market Price

To determine the market price, we combine the demand relationship between the price and the quantity demanded with the supply relationship between the price and the quantity supplied. We can do this using either a table or a diagram. First consider Table 3.3, which combines the demand schedule from Table 3.1 with the supply schedule from Table 3.2. The price is in the first column, the quantity demanded by consumers is in the second column, and the quantity supplied by firms is in the third column. Observe that the quantity consumers are willing to buy is shown to

| Price | Quantity Demanded | Quantity Supplied | Shortage, Surplus, or Equilibrium | Price Rises or Falls |
|-------|-------------------|-------------------|-----------------------------------|----------------------|
| $140 | 18 | 1 | Shortage = 17 | Price rises |
| $160 | 14 | 4 | Shortage = 10 | Price rises |
| $180 | 11 | 7 | Shortage = 4 | Price rises |
| $200 | 9 | 9 | Equilibrium | No change |
| $220 | 7 | 11 | Surplus = 4 | Price falls |
| $240 | 5 | 13 | Surplus = 8 | Price falls |
| $260 | 3 | 15 | Surplus = 12 | Price falls |
| $280 | 2 | 16 | Surplus = 14 | Price falls |
| $300 | 1 | 17 | Surplus = 16 | Price falls |

**TABLE 3.3**
**Finding the Market Equilibrium**

Quantity supplied equals quantity demanded.

decline with the price, while the quantity firms are willing to sell is shown to increase with the price. In order to determine the price in the market, consider each of the prices in Table 3.3.

### Finding the Market Price

Pick a price in Table 3.3, any price. Suppose the price you choose is $160. Then the quantity demanded by consumers (14 million bicycles) is greater than the quantity supplied by the firms (4 million bicycles). In other words, there is a shortage of $14 - 4 = 10$ million bicycles. A **shortage** is a situation where the quantity demanded is greater than the quantity supplied.[1] With a shortage of bicycles, the price will quickly rise above $160; firms will charge higher prices, and consumers who are willing to pay more than $160 for a bicycle will pay higher prices to firms. Thus, $160 cannot last as the market price. Observe that as the price rises above $160, the quantity demanded falls, and the quantity supplied rises. Thus, as the price rises, the shortage begins to decline. If you choose any price below $200, the same thing will happen: There will be a shortage and the price will rise. The shortage disappears only when the price rises to $200, as shown in Table 3.3.

**shortage:** the situation in which quantity demanded is greater than quantity supplied.

Now pick a price above $200. Suppose you pick $260. Then the quantity demanded by consumers (3 million bicycles) is less than the quantity supplied by firms (15 million bicycles). In other words, there is a surplus of 12 million bicycles. A **surplus** is a situation in which the quantity supplied is greater than the quantity demanded.[2] With a surplus of bicycles, the price will fall: Firms that are willing to sell bicycles for less than $260 will offer to sell at lower prices to consumers. Thus, $260 cannot be the market price either. Observe that as the price falls below $260, the quantity demanded rises and the quantity supplied falls. Thus, the surplus declines. If you choose any price above $200, the same thing will happen: There will be a surplus and the price will fall. The surplus disappears only when the price falls to $200.

**surplus:** the situation in which quantity supplied is greater than quantity demanded.

Thus, we have shown that for any price below $200, there is a shortage and the price rises; while for any price above $200, there is a surplus and the price falls. What if the market price is $200? Then the quantity supplied equals the quantity demanded; there is neither a shortage nor a surplus, and there is no reason for the

1. *Excess demand* is another term for *shortage.*
2. *Excess supply* is another term for *surplus.*

**equilibrium price:** the price at which quantity supplied equals quantity demanded.

**equilibrium quantity:** the quantity traded at the equilibrium price.

**market equilibrium:** the situation in which the price is equal to the equilibrium price and the quantity traded equals the equilibrium quantity.

price to rise or fall. This price of $200 is therefore the most likely prediction of the market price. It is called the **equilibrium price** because at this price the quantity supplied equals the quantity demanded, and there is no tendency for price to change. There is no other price for which quantity supplied equals quantity demanded. By looking at all the other prices, you will see that there is either a shortage or a surplus, and there is a tendency for the price to either rise or fall.

The quantity bought and sold at the equilibrium price is 9 million bicycles. This is the **equilibrium quantity.** When the price equals the equilibrium price and the quantity bought and sold equals the equilibrium quantity, we say there is a **market equilibrium.**

Our discussion of the determination of the equilibrium price shows how the market price coordinates the buying and selling decisions of many firms and consumers. We see that the price serves a *rationing function;* that is, the price alleviates shortages: A higher price reduces the quantity demanded or increases the quantity supplied when necessary to eliminate a shortage. Similarly, a lower price increases the quantity demanded or decreases the quantity supplied when there is a surplus. Thus, both shortages and surpluses are eliminated by the forces of supply and demand.

### Two Predictions

By combining supply and demand, we have completed the supply and demand model. The model can be applied to many markets, not just the example of the bicycle market. One prediction of the supply and demand model is that *the price in the market will be the price for which the quantity supplied equals the quantity demanded.* Thus, the model provides an answer to the question of what determines the price in the market. Another prediction of the model is that *the quantity bought and sold in the market is the quantity for which the quantity supplied equals the quantity demanded.*

## Finding the Equilibrium with a Supply and Demand Diagram

The equilibrium price and quantity in a market can also be found with the help of a graph. Figure 3.7 combines the demand curve from Figure 3.1 and the supply curve from Figure 3.4 in the same diagram. Observe that the downward-sloping demand curve intersects the upward-sloping supply curve at a single point. At that point of intersection, the quantity supplied equals the quantity demanded. Hence, the *equilibrium price occurs at the intersection of the supply curve and the demand curve.* The equilibrium price of $200 is shown in Figure 3.7. At that price, the quantity demanded is 9 million bicycles and the quantity supplied is 9 million bicycles. This is the equilibrium quantity.

If the price were lower than this equilibrium price, say $160, then the quantity demanded would be greater than the quantity supplied. There would be a shortage and the price would begin to rise, as shown in the graph. On the other hand, if the price were above the equilibrium price, say $260, then there would be a surplus, as shown in the graph, and the price would begin to fall. Thus, the market price will tend to move toward the equilibrium price at the intersection of the supply curve and the demand curve. We can calculate exactly what the equilibrium price is on the graph by drawing a line over to the vertical axis. And we can calculate the equilibrium quantity by drawing a line down to the horizontal axis.

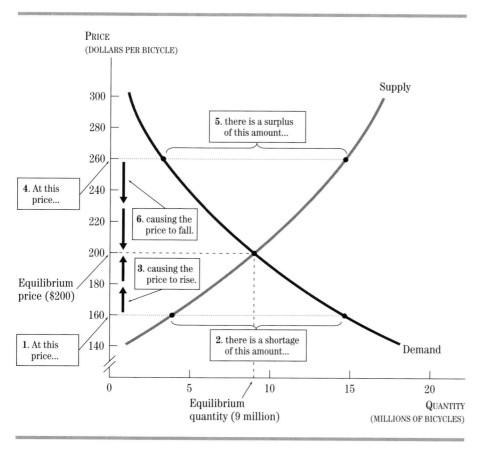

**FIGURE 3.7**
**Equilibrium Price and Equilibrium Quantity**
When buyers and sellers interact in the market, the equilibrium price is at the point of intersection of the supply curve and the demand curve. At this point, the quantity supplied equals the quantity demanded. The equilibrium quantity is also determined at that point. At a higher price, the quantity demanded will be less than the quantity supplied; there will be a surplus. At a lower price, the quantity demanded will be greater than the quantity supplied; there will be a shortage.

## A Change in the Market

In order to use the supply and demand model to explain or predict changes in prices, we need to consider what happens to the equilibrium price when there is a change in supply or demand. We first consider a change in demand and then a change in supply.

### Effects of a Change in Demand

Figure 3.8 shows the effects of a shift in the demand curve for bicycles. Suppose that a shift occurs because of a fitness craze that increases the demand for bicycles. The demand curve shifts to the right, as shown in graph (a) in Figure 3.8. The demand curve before the shift and the demand curve after the shift are labeled the "old demand curve" and the "new demand curve," respectively.

If you look at the graph you can see that something must happen to the equilibrium price when the demand curve shifts. The equilibrium price is determined at the intersection of the supply curve and the demand curve. With the new demand curve, there is a new intersection and, therefore, a new equilibrium price. The equilibrium price is no longer $200 in Figure 3.8(a). It is up to $220 per bicycle. Thus, the supply and demand model predicts that the price in the market will rise if there is an increase in demand. Note also that there is a change in the equilibrium

**FIGURE 3.8**

**Effects of a Shift in Demand**

When the demand increases, as in graph (a), the demand curve shifts to the right. The equilibrium price rises, and the equilibrium quantity also rises. When demand decreases, as in graph (b), the demand curve shifts to the left; the equilibrium price falls, and the equilibrium quantity also falls.

**(a) Increase in Demand**

**(b) Decrease in Demand**

quantity of bicycles. The quantity of bicycles sold and bought has increased from 9 million to 11 million. Thus, the equilibrium quantity has increased along with the equilibrium price. The supply and demand model predicts that an increase in demand will raise both the price and the quantity sold in the market.

We can use the same method to find out what happens if demand decreases, as shown in graph (b) in Figure 3.8. In this case, the demand curve shifts to the left. At the new intersection of the supply and demand curve, the equilibrium price is lower and the quantity sold is also lower. Thus, the supply and demand model predicts that a decrease in demand will lower the price and lower the quantity sold in the market.

Note in these examples that when the demand curve shifts, it leads to a movement along the supply curve. First, the demand curve shifts to the right or to the left. Then there is movement along the supply curve because the change in the price affects the quantity of bicycles firms will sell.

### Effects of a Change in Supply

Figure 3.9 shows what happens when there is a change in the market that shifts the supply curve. In graph (a) of Figure 3.9 we show the effect of an increase in supply, and in graph (b) we show the effect of a decrease in supply.

When the supply curve of bicycles shifts to the right, there is a new equilibrium price, which is lower than the old equilibrium price. In addition, the equilibrium quantity rises. Thus, the supply and demand model predicts that an increase in the supply of bicycles—perhaps because of better technology in bicycle production—will lower the price and raise the quantity of bicycles sold.

When the supply curve of bicycles shifts to the left, the equilibrium price rises, as shown in graph (b) of Figure 3.9, and the equilibrium quantity falls. Thus, the model predicts that anything that reduces supply will raise the price of bicycles and lower the quantity of bicycles produced.

Table 3.4 summarizes the results of this analysis of shifts in the supply and demand curve.

### When Both Curves Shift

The supply and demand model is easiest to use when something shifts either demand or supply but not both. However, in reality, it is possible for something or several different things to simultaneously shift both supply and demand. To predict whether the price or the quantity rises or falls in such cases, we need to know whether demand or supply shifts by a larger amount. Dealing with the possibility of simultaneous shifts in demand and supply curves is important in practice, as we show in the next section.

| Shift | Effect on Equilibrium Price | Effect on Equilibrium Quantity |
|---|---|---|
| Increase in demand | Up | Up |
| Decrease in demand | Down | Down |
| Increase in supply | Down | Up |
| Decrease in supply | Up | Down |

**TABLE 3.4**
**Effects of Shifts in Demand and Supply Curves**

**FIGURE 3.9**

**Effects of a Shift in Supply**

When supply increases, as in graph (a), the supply curve shifts to the right; the equilibrium price falls and the equilibrium quantity rises. When supply decreases, as in graph (b), the supply curve shifts to the left; the equilibrium price rises and the equilibrium quantity falls.

**(a) Increase in Supply**

**(b) Decrease in Supply**

## Review

▶ When firms and consumers interact in a market, a price is determined by the market.

▶ The supply and demand model predicts that the price is found at the intersection of the supply and demand curves. This price is called the equilibrium price.

▶ At this price, the quantity supplied equals the quantity demanded, and there is no tendency for the price to change.

▶ A shift in the demand curve or the supply curve will change the equilibrium price and the equilibrium quantity. By considering changes in supply or demand, the model can be used to explain or predict price changes.

# USING THE SUPPLY AND DEMAND MODEL: A CASE STUDY

Economists use the supply and demand model both to explain past observations about prices and to predict what would happen to prices under different scenarios. The hypothetical example of the bicycle market has been useful for defining and explaining general features of the supply and demand model. But now we want to show how to apply the model in real-world situations. In real-world applications, economists have to decide exactly what goods are included in the market and the time period for the application. To illustrate the application of the supply and demand model, we look in detail at some actual events in a specific market—the peanut market in the United States.

## Explaining and Predicting Peanut Prices

To apply the supply and demand model to the peanut market, we need to know a little about where peanuts are produced and consumed. Figure 3.10 shows that most peanuts are produced on farms in the southeastern part of the United States. The biggest peanut-producing state is Georgia, but peanuts are also produced in Alabama, Florida, North Carolina, Texas, Oklahoma, and Virginia. The United States produces about 4 billion pounds of peanuts. Georgia produces over 1.8 billion of that 4 billion.

The demand for peanuts comes from consumers all over the United States. People from California to Maine eat peanuts and peanut butter. The U.S. government uses peanut butter in the school lunch program. In addition, Canadians buy U.S. peanuts. In sum, about 4 billion pounds of U.S.-produced peanuts are consumed each year in the United States and Canada.

Figure 3.11 shows a supply and demand model for peanuts. The model is an accurate description of the peanut market based on many observations over the years. You can see that the demand curve for peanuts is downward sloping. In the diagram, prices range from $.20 a pound all the way to $1.80 a pound for raw shelled peanuts. As you can see, when the price for peanuts is high, the quantity demanded is low. The supply curve shows that at a higher price farmers will want to produce more peanuts. The equilibrium price is shown to be $.60 a pound, and the equilibrium quantity about 4 billion pounds. These are close to the actual price and quantity of peanuts in early 1990.

**FIGURE 3.10**
**Peanut Production in the United States**

Most peanuts are produced in the Southeast. Hence, a drought in the Southeast will have a big effect on the supply of peanuts. The information in this map for 1989 is important for establishing that the 1990 drought did indeed shift the supply curve of peanuts to the left.

*Source:* U.S. Department of Agriculture.

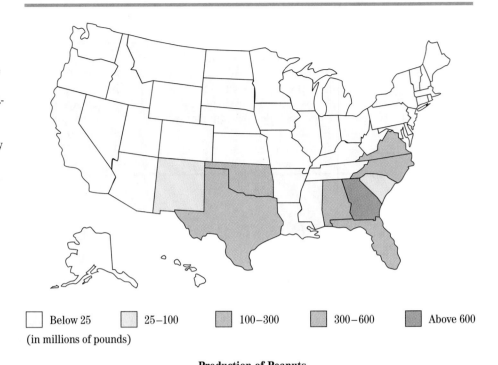

| Below 25 | 25–100 | 100–300 | 300–600 | Above 600 |

(in millions of pounds)

**Production of Peanuts**

| State | Quantity (million pounds) | Share of Total (percent) |
|---|---|---|
| Alabama | 538 | 13.5 |
| Florida | 215 | 5.4 |
| Georgia | 1,850 | 46.3 |
| New Mexico | 44 | 1.1 |
| North Carolina | 370 | 9.3 |
| Oklahoma | 211 | 5.3 |
| South Carolina | 33 | .8 |
| Texas | 485 | 12.1 |
| Virginia | 246 | 6.2 |
| U.S. total | 3,992 | 100.0 |

### Drought in the Southeast

During 1990, there was a drought in the southeastern part of the United States, where most of the peanuts are grown. The drought meant that supply declined. Production dropped sharply in Georgia, Alabama, and Florida. In the supply and demand model, we would show that drought by a shift to the left in the supply curve for peanuts, as shown in Figure 3.12.

As you can see in Figure 3.12, the equilibrium price rises. In fact, the price of peanuts in the drought of 1990 did rise from about $.60 a pound to about $1.25 a pound. Thus, the supply and demand model can explain the rise in the peanut price.

Quite understandably, this price rise forced some hard choices on people who consume a lot of peanuts. Poor people tend to eat more peanut butter than rich people, so the price change affected the distribution of income. Further, the U.S.

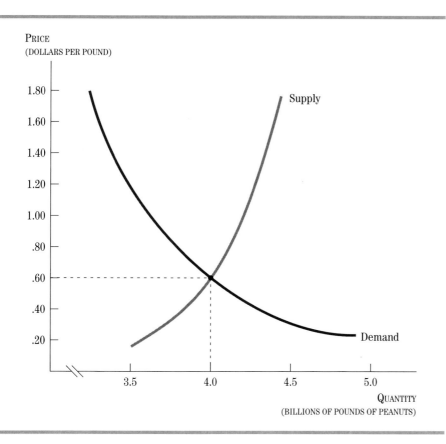

**FIGURE 3.11**
**Supply and Demand for Peanuts**
The quantity refers to the number of pounds produced in the United States. The price is the average price of raw peanuts in the United States.

Department of Agriculture (USDA) school lunch program that provides meals for poor children in the United States had to stop buying peanut butter because it got so expensive.

Thus, the price performed its three roles. The higher price lowered the quantity demanded by providing incentives for people to choose some other food. It transmitted information about the effects of the drought in the Southeast all over the country. It also affected the distribution of income because people who buy peanuts and peanut butter had less to spend on other things.

### A Change in the Foreign Peanut Quota?

Although the market responded to the drought as predicted, the higher price made life difficult for some consumers. Was there anything to be done? Could the supply and demand model help in deciding what to do? Could it predict what would happen under various courses of action?

Believe it or not, the U.S. government prohibits virtually any imports of peanuts into the United States from other countries. There is a law limiting the amount of imported peanuts to a small quantity: about 1.7 million pounds, compared to the nearly 4 billion pounds consumed. This limit is called a **quota.** The United States allows only about a quarter of 1 percent of its peanut consumption to come from foreign countries.

**quota:** a governmental limit on the quantity of a particular good sold or imported.

**FIGURE 3.12**
**Effects of a Drought in the Southeast**

The drought reduces the supply of peanuts. Hence, the supply curve shifts to the left, raising the equilibrium price of peanuts and lowering the equilibrium quantity. The supply and demand model explains the observed increase in the price of peanuts.

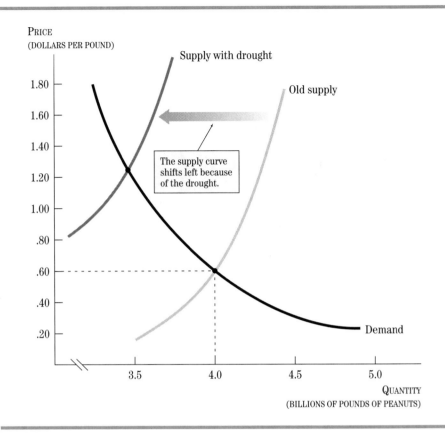

One simple way to lower the price would be to allow more foreign peanuts to come into the United States from Argentina, China, and other peanut-growing countries. In fact, the supply and demand model predicts that the price would fall if the quota was increased.

Allowing more foreign peanuts into the United States would shift the supply curve of peanuts to the right, as shown in Figure 3.13. That would lower the equilibrium price. For the size of the rightward shift in the diagram, the price would go down to about $.75 a pound, which would have helped the peanut consumers who were being hurt by the drought.

However, that is not what happened in 1990. The United States has a formal process to determine whether or not more foreign peanuts can be brought into the country. A committee, the International Trade Commission (ITC), decides whether the peanut farmers might be harmed by the lower price caused by such foreign peanuts. In 1990 it took many months for the ITC to make the decision. A majority of the commissioners determined that peanut farmers would not be affected a great deal if the U.S. government allowed more peanuts in. Economists who work for the ITC used a supply and demand model just like the one in Figure 3.13 to analyze the situation and make a recommendation to increase the quota. But others—including the peanut growers and some members of Congress—claimed there was no reason to increase the quota. They argued that the demand for peanuts had decreased after

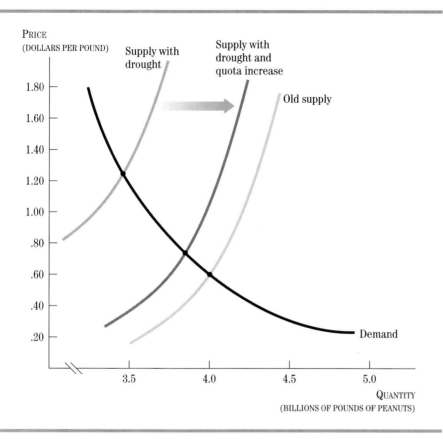

**FIGURE 3.13**
**Predicted Effects of an Increase in the Peanut Quota**
The supply and demand model can also be used to predict what would happen if more peanuts were allowed to enter the United States from abroad. The increase in supply would shift the supply curve to the right. The equilibrium price of peanuts would fall. Hence, the model predicts that increasing the quota would lower the price of peanuts and thereby tend to offset the effects of the drought.

the drought and that an increase in the supply of foreign peanuts was unnecessary. One peanut growers' group was quoted as saying, "Demand for peanut butter and peanut products will be less this year because the USDA has drastically reduced its purchases of peanut products."[3] Such statements confuse shifts of the demand curve and movements along the demand curve. As shown in Figure 3.12, the drought led to a movement along the demand curve because higher peanut prices forced people to reduce the quantity demanded. But this was not a decline in demand. Rather, consumers reduced the quantity demanded because the price was so high.

These debates led to delays. By the time the quota increase came, in July 1991, it was too little and too late. Ultimately, only about 16 million extra pounds of peanuts were imported. The supply and demand model predicts that such a small increase in supply will reduce the price only a small amount. Although the ultimate result may have been disappointing, the 1990 drought and peanut quota increase provide an excellent case study of how the supply and demand model is used in practice both to explain observations about prices and to make useful predictions about prices.

3. *Peanuts,* U.S. International Trade Commission Publication 2369, March 1991, p. A-70.

# Reading the News About Supply and Demand

The following news account describes the situation in the peanut market after the drought of 1990. Observe how the supply and demand model corroborates ① the size of the price increase and the reason for the price increase, ② the effects on the price of increasing peanut imports by 300 million pounds, and ③ the typical rationalization on the part of growers that there was no reason to increase the quota because "supply was sufficient," while not mentioning that it was the doubling of prices that brought the quantity demanded down to equal the lower quantity supplied.

## Peanuts could sell for peanuts again

### By John Schmeltzer

Peanut butter, that staple of the American school lunch menu that all but disappeared last fall when peanut prices soared, may soon make a comeback, industry leaders say.

In recent months, prices for shelled peanuts more than doubled on the wholesale level, to $1.25 a pound from 60 cents a pound—a move that prompted the Department of Agriculture to substitute cholesterol-rich cheese in the school lunch program for the cholesterol-free peanut butter.

Analysts said the peanut shortfall was caused by severe import restrictions and last year's drought in the Southeast.

Peanut butter, which had been selling in the grocery store for about $3 for a 28-ounce jar, quickly skyrocketed to more than $4.

"You can import pistols but not peanuts," said James Mack on Wednesday, referring to restrictions that all but set quotas for how many goobers each U.S. peanut farmer is allowed to produce each year. Mack is general counsel for the Peanut Butter and Nut Processors Association.

---

'You can import pistols but not peanuts.'

—James Mack,
Peanut Butter and
Nut Processors Association

---

But processors say they expect a decision in as little as two weeks by President Bush on a temporary lifting of import restrictions, which would allow as much as 300 million pounds of peanuts to be imported between now and July 31. The temporary relaxation has been recommended by the U.S. International Trade Commission.

Since the ITC recommendation last week, prices for shelled peanuts have fallen to about $1 a pound, according to Mack. He said if the ITC recommendation is adopted, prices will probably drop to about 75 cents a pound—still 25 percent higher than before last year's poor crop hit the market.

The ITC recommendation is being opposed by growers and congressional leaders, who maintain there is sufficient supply for the domestic market and say Mack's association only represents 30 percent of the producers, none of whom are the major manufacturers of brands such as Planters or Skippy.

Sen. Wyche Fowler Jr. (D-Ga.), in a letter signed by 11 other senators, argued that opening the door to increased imports could end up costing U.S. taxpayers because of price-support programs.

"We don't think the importation of peanuts is necessary" said Emery Murphy, assistant executive director of the Georgia Peanut Commission. "We're certain there will be adverse effects to the industry and the government."

The nut processors association has been joined in its efforts to lift the import ban by the Consumer Alert Advocate Fund, whose president, Barbara Keating, said slow action by the government already has cost consumers $553 million.

# Review

▶ The supply and demand model can be used in practical applications to explain price changes in many markets. It can also be used to predict what will happen to prices when certain actions—such as increasing a quota—are taken.

▶ In applying the model, economists consider shifts of the supply curve or the demand curve. In the case study of the drought, the supply curve for peanuts shifted.

# INTERFERENCE WITH MARKET PRICES

Thus far we have used the supply and demand model in situations in which the price is freely determined without government control. But many times throughout history, and around the world today, governments have attempted to control market prices. The usual reason is that government leaders were not happy with the outcome of the market, or they were pressured by groups who would benefit from price controls.

**Price controls** were used widely by the U.S. government during World War II and again in the early 1970s. Price controls now exist in certain housing markets, agriculture markets, and labor markets in the United States. What are the effects of this government interference in the market? The supply and demand model can help answer this question.

> **price control:** a government law or regulation that sets or limits the price to be charged for a particular good.

## Price Ceilings and Price Floors

In general there are two broad types of government price controls. Controls can stipulate a **price ceiling,** or a maximum price, at which a good can be bought and sold. For example, the United States government controlled oil prices in the early 1970s, stipulating that firms could not charge more than a stated maximum price of $5.25 per barrel of crude oil; the equilibrium price was well over $10 per barrel at this time. Some cities in the United States have price controls on rental apartments. Landlords are not permitted to charge a rent higher than the maximum stipulated by the **rent control** law in these cities. Price ceilings are imposed by governments because of complaints that the market price is too high. The purpose is to help the consumers who must pay the prices. For example, rent controls exist in order to help people who must pay rent. However, as we will see, price controls have harmful side effects that can end up hurting those consumers the law is apparently trying to help.

> **price ceiling:** a government price control that sets the maximum allowable price for a good.

> **rent control:** a government price control that sets the maximum allowable rent on a house or apartment.

Government price controls can also stipulate a **price floor,** or a minimum price. Price floors are imposed by governments in order to help the suppliers of goods and services. For example, the U.S. government requires that the price of sugar not fall below a certain amount in the United States. In the labor market, the U.S. government requires that firms pay workers a wage no less than a minimum, called the **minimum wage.**

> **price floor:** a government price control that sets the minimum allowable price for a good.

> **minimum wage:** a wage per hour below which it is illegal to pay workers.

## Shortages and Related Problems Resulting from Price Ceilings

If the government prevents firms from charging more than a certain amount for their products, then a shortage is likely to result, as illustrated in Figure 3.14. When the maximum price remains below the equilibrium price on the market, there is a persistent shortage; sellers are unwilling to supply as much as buyers want to buy. This is illustrated for the general case of any good in the top graph in Figure 3.14 and for the specific case of rent control in the bottom graph.

"I always wondered how the government set milk prices."

**FIGURE 3.14**

**Effects of a Maximum Price Law**

The top diagram shows the general case when the government prevents the market price from rising above a particular maximum price, or sets a price ceiling below the equilibrium price. The lower diagram shows a particular example of a price ceiling, rent controls on apartment units. The supply and demand model predicts there will be a shortage. The shortage occurs because the quantity supplied is less than consumers are willing to buy at that price. The shortage leads to rationing, black markets, or lower product quality.

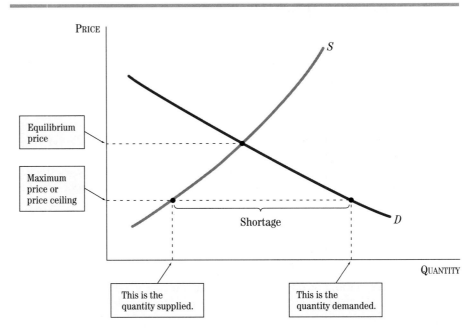

**The General Case of a Price Ceiling**

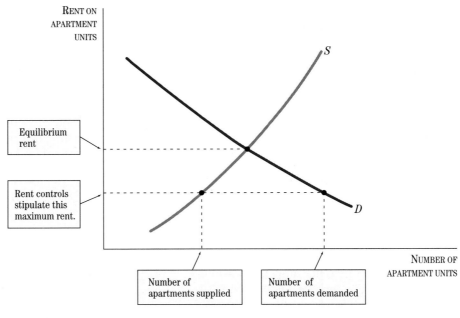

**The Case of Rent Control**

### Dealing with Persistent Shortages

Because higher prices are not allowed, the shortage must be dealt with in other ways. Sometimes the government issues a limited amount of ration coupons to people to alleviate the shortage; this was done in World War II. The law required that people present these ration coupons at stores in order to buy goods. Thus, the total quantity demanded could not be greater than the amount of ration coupons. Alternatively, if there are no ration coupons, then the shortage might result in long waiting lines. In formerly centrally planned economies, long lines for bread were frequently observed because of price controls on bread. Sometimes black markets develop in which people buy and sell goods outside the watch of the government and charge whatever price they want. This typically happens in command economies. Black markets are also common in less-developed countries today when the governments in these countries impose price controls.

Another effect of price ceilings is a reduction in the quality of the good sold. By lowering the quality of the good, the producer can reduce the costs of producing it. Low-quality housing frequently results from rent control. By lowering the quality of the apartments—perhaps being slow to paint the walls or repair the elevator—landlords make the apartments shoddy and unattractive.

### Making Things Worse

Although the stated purpose of price ceilings is to help people who have to pay high prices, the preceding examples indicate how they can make things worse. Issuing ration coupons raises difficult problems about who gets the coupons. In the case of a price ceiling on gasoline, for example, should the government give more coupons to those who commute by car than to those who do not? More generally, who is to decide who deserves the coupons? Rationing by waiting in line is also a poor outcome. People waiting in line could be doing more enjoyable or more useful things. Similarly, black markets, being illegal, encourage people to go outside the law; they thereby lose their rights to protection in the case of theft or fraud. Lowering the quality of the good is also a bad way to alleviate the problem of a high price. This simply eliminates the higher-quality good from production; consumers and producers lose.

Paradoxically, price ceilings frequently end up hurting those they try to help. Many people who benefit from controls, for example, are not poor at all. If rent controls reduce the supply of apartments, they make less housing available for everyone.

## Surpluses and Related Problems Resulting from Price Floors

If the government imposes a price floor, then a surplus will occur, as shown in Figure 3.15. With the price above the equilibrium price, suppliers of goods and services want to sell more than people are willing to buy. Hence, there is a surplus. This is illustrated for the general case of any good in the top graph of Figure 3.15 and for the specific case of the minimum wage in the bottom graph.

How is this surplus dealt with in actual markets? In markets for farm products, the government usually has to buy the surplus and, perhaps, put it in storage; but buying farm products above the equilibrium price costs taxpayers money, and the higher price raises costs to consumers. For this reason, economists argue against

**FIGURE 3.15**
**Effects of a Minimum Price Law**

The top diagram shows the general case when the government prevents the market price from falling below a particular minimum price, or sets a price floor above the equilibrium price. The lower diagram shows a particular example when the price of labor—the wage—cannot fall below the minimum wage. The supply and demand model predicts that sellers are willing to sell a quantity greater than buyers are willing to buy at that price. Thus, there is a surplus of the good or, in the case of labor, unemployment for some of those who can be hired only at a lower wage.

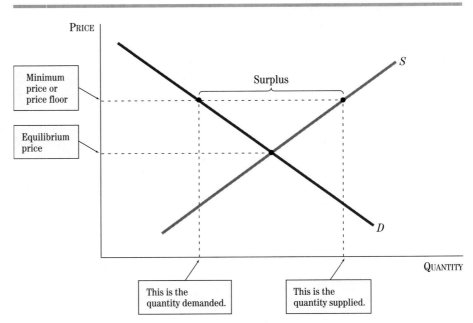

The General Case of a Price Floor

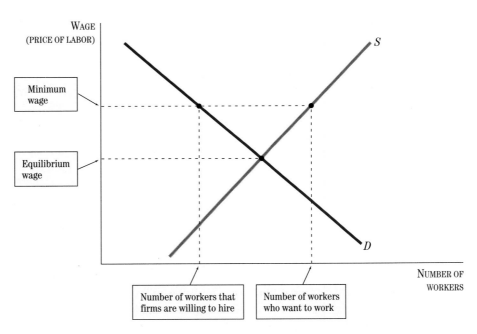

The Case of the Minimum Wage

# Reading the News about Price Floors

The following news report depicts the pressures that sometimes lead governments to try to interfere with the prices that emerge from markets. As the price of milk dropped in August 1991, legislation was introduced into the U.S. Congress to put a floor on the price. At the time the market price for milk was $11.47 per hundred pounds; the legislation would have put a floor on the price at a higher level, $13.09. Hence, if the legislation passed, the situation would be exactly like that in Figure 3.15. Consumers would have paid more for milk, and there would have been a milk surplus.

The article focuses on the hardships of milk farmers and their families, but it does not mention the cost to consumers. In this case the legislation did not pass. It is, therefore, an example where the government, through the political process, chose not to impose price controls, perhaps because of concerns about the harms from such controls, as illustrated in Figure 3.15.

*Source of article: Burlington Free Press,* March 23, 1991, pp. 1–2. Reprinted courtesy of the Burlington Free Press.

## Dairy price support defeat worries Vermont farmers

John Malcolm, Vermont's dairyman of the year, estimated the U.S. House defeat of milk price support legislation Thursday would cost him $10,000 this year, and would cost the state's economy $28 million.

"Anything is a lot of money," the Pawlet farmer said Friday. "We aren't even breaking even now."

Bulk prices for milk have dropped nearly 30 percent since August. Prices per hundred pounds of milk average $11.47, while the cost for Vermont farmers to produce that amount of milk averages $13.75. Leahy's plan would have temporarily fixed the price at $13.09.

Malcolm said he can keep farming for about a year with prices the way they are now, provided he makes cuts in equipment purchases. For some Vermont dairy families, the prospects are worse.

"We are just hanging on by a thread," said Helen Wilcox, who leases a farm in Alburg with her husband, Alvin. Of the couple's nine children, six are still at home, and the family has been selling bull calves for grocery money.

"I thought it was really sad," she said of the proposal's defeat, "because it would have helped drastically. . . . If (the price of milk) continues at $11.50,

we'll be out of farming by the year's end," she said.

"The Senate recognized that dairy farmers in virtually every state are suffering and acted to stop the hemorrhaging," Leahy, chairman of the Senate Agriculture Committee, said Friday. "This is a sad day for our nation's dairy farmers. The administration and House turned a deaf ear to their plight."

The Bush administration had threatened to veto the entire spending bill if it included the price support.

---

price floors on agricultural goods. As an alternative, the government sometimes reduces the supply by telling firms to plant fewer acres or to destroy crops, or by restricting the amount that can come from abroad. In the United States, the federal government uses acreage restrictions in the case of wheat and other grains; it also uses import restrictions in the case of sugar. But government requirements to keep land idle or even destroy crops are particularly repugnant to most people.

As we will see in more detail later in this book, the supply and demand model can also be applied to labor markets. In that case, the price is the price of labor, or the wage. What does the supply and demand model predict about the effects of a minimum wage? In the case of labor markets, a minimum wage can cause unemployment. If the equilibrium wage is below the minimum wage, then some workers would be willing to work for less than the minimum wage. But employers are not permitted to pay them less than the minimum wage. Therefore, there is an oversupply of workers at the minimum wage. The number of workers demanded is less than the number of workers willing to work; thus, the supply and demand model predicts that the minimum wage causes unemployment.

The minimum wage would have no effect if the equilibrium wage were above the minimum wage. The supply and demand model predicts that the minimum wage affects workers whose wages would be below the minimum. Thus, a minimum wage would be most likely to increase unemployment for teenage workers with very few skills if their wages would otherwise be below the minimum.

## Review

▶ Price ceilings cause persistent shortages, which, in turn, cause rationing, black markets, and a reduced quality of goods and services.

▶ Price floors cause persistent surpluses and unemployment, according to the supply and demand

model. In the case of price floors on agricultural products, the surpluses are bought by the government and put in storage. In the case of the minimum wage, the surpluses mean more unemployment for those who can only get jobs below the minimum wage.

## CONCLUSION

This chapter has shown how prices are determined in markets where buyers and sellers interact freely. The supply and demand model is used to describe how prices are determined in such markets. It is probably the most frequently used model in economics and has been in existence for over a hundred years in pretty much the same form as economists use it now.

The key idea behind the model is that the price is found by the intersection of the supply and demand curves. To apply the model in practice, we need to look for factors that shift either the supply curve or the demand curve. In the most successful applications of the supply and demand model, the factors that affect supply and demand can be separated.

In the next chapter we show how economists measure "how much" quantity supplied and quantity demanded change when the price changes in the supply and demand model. Then, in later chapters we will see how the supply and demand model fits into the common economic problem of scarcity and choice, as defined in the previous chapter. By doing so, we will be able to take a closer look at the basic questions economists face: what, how, and for whom to produce.

## KEY POINTS

**1.** Demand is a negative relationship between the price of a good and the quantity demanded by consumers. It can be shown graphically by a downward-sloping demand curve.

**2.** A movement along the demand curve occurs when a higher price reduces the quantity demanded or a lower price increases the quantity demanded.

**3.** A shift of the demand curve occurs when something besides the price causes the quantity people are willing to buy to change.

**4.** Supply is a positive relationship between the price of a good and the quantity supplied by firms. It can be shown graphically by an upward-sloping supply curve.

**5.** A movement along the supply curve occurs when a higher price increases the quantity supplied or a lower price decreases the quantity supplied.

**6.** A shift of the supply curve occurs when something besides the price causes the quantity firms are willing to sell to change.

**7.** The equilibrium price and equilibrium quantity are determined by the intersection of the supply curve and the demand curve where the quantity supplied equals the quantity demanded.

**8.** By shifting either the supply curve or the demand curve, observations on prices can be explained and predictions about prices can be made.

**9.** Price ceilings cause shortages, with the quantity supplied less than the quantity demanded. Shortages lead to rationing or black markets.

**10.** Price floors cause surpluses, with the quantity supplied greater than the quantity demanded.

# KEY TERMS

demand
price
quantity demanded
demand schedule
law of demand
demand curve
normal goods
inferior goods
substitute

complement
supply
quantity supplied
supply schedule
law of supply
supply curve
shortage
surplus
equilibrium price

equilibrium quantity
market equilibrium
quota
price control
price ceiling
rent control
price floor
minimum wage

# QUESTIONS FOR REVIEW

**1.** Why does the demand curve slope downward?

**2.** Why does the supply curve slope upward?

**3.** What is the difference between a shift in the demand curve and a movement along the demand curve?

**4.** What are four things that cause a demand curve to shift?

**5.** What are four things that cause a supply curve to shift?

**6.** What is the difference between a shift in the supply curve and a movement along the supply curve?

**7.** What are the equilibrium price and equilibrium quantity?

**8.** What happens to the equilibrium price if the supply curve shifts to the right and the demand curve does not shift?

**9.** What happens to the equilibrium price if the demand curve shifts to the right and the supply curve does not shift?

**10.** Do price ceilings cause shortages or surpluses? What about price floors? Explain.

# PROBLEMS

**1.** Consider the following supply and demand model of the world tea market (in billions of pounds).

| Price per Pound | Quantity Supplied | Quantity Demanded |
|---|---|---|
| $.38 | 1,500 | 525 |
| $.37 | 1,000 | 600 |
| $.36 | 700 | 700 |
| $.35 | 600 | 900 |
| $.34 | 550 | 1,200 |

a) Is there a shortage or a surplus when the price is $.38? What about $.34?

b) What are the equilibrium price and the equilibrium quantity?
c) Graph the supply curve and the demand curve.
d) Show how the equilibrium price and quantity can be found on the graph.

**2.** Consider the supply and demand model in problem 1. Suppose that there is a drought in Sri Lanka that reduces the supply of tea by 400 billion pounds. Suppose demand does not change.

a) Write down in a table the new supply schedule for tea.

b) Find the new equilibrium price and the new equilibrium quantity.

c) Did the equilibrium quantity change by more or less than the change in supply?

d) Graph the new supply curve, along with the old supply curve and demand curve.

e) Show the change in the equilibrium price and the equilibrium quantity on the graph.

**3.** Use the supply and demand model to explain what happens to the equilibrium price and the equilibrium quantity in the orange juice market in each of the following cases.

a) The *New England Journal of Medicine* issues a widely publicized report that says vitamin C cures cancer, and orange juice is the best source of vitamin C.

b) A freeze in Florida destroys half the orange crop.

c) There is a sudden inflow of cheap orange juice imports from South America.

d) A major orange juice producer finds lead contamination in some containers, and this finding makes the nightly news.

**4.** For each of the following markets, indicate whether the stated change causes a shift in the supply curve, a shift in the demand curve, a movement along the supply curve, and/or a movement along the demand curve.

a) The housing market: Consumers' incomes increase.

b) The camera market: The price of film goes up.

c) The sugar market: There is a drought in the sugar cane fields in Hawaii.

d) The milk market: The price of milk increases, and the amount of milk people are willing to buy declines.

e) The fast food market: The number of fast food restaurants in the area increases.

f) The video rental market: The number of consumers in the area decreases.

g) The ice cream market: The price of frozen yogurt falls.

**5.** Draw a supply and demand diagram to indicate the market for Japanese cars in the United States, with the equilibrium price and quantity labeled. Suppose the government imposes a strict restriction on the quantity of Japanese cars sold in the United States. Show what happens in this market if the quantity restriction is less than the equilibrium quantity. What will happen if the quantity restriction is greater than the equilibrium quantity?

**6.** Consider the market for apartments in a town. The price for apartments is the rent.

a) Sketch the demand curve and the supply curve for apartments.

b) How is the equilibrium rent determined?

c) If the town council imposes a binding rent control below the equilibrium price, equivalent to a price ceiling in this market, what happens to quantity supplied and quantity demanded? How does the total amount of rent paid change?

d) Economists frequently argue against rent control because of the incentives it gives to landlords. Explain why this interference in the market may provide bad incentives.

**7.** In many countries there are price floors for agricultural commodities. Draw a supply and demand diagram that shows the market for a commodity that has a price fixed greater than the market equilibrium price. Will there be a shortage or a surplus?

**8.** Why is it necessary for people to stand in line for days before the sale of concert tickets for the most famous performers? Is the price mechanism working properly? Why are scalpers present on these occasions?

**9.** Assuming that either supply or demand, but not both, change, indicate the direction and change in either supply or demand that must have occurred to produce the following:

a) A decrease in the price and quantity of apples

b) A decrease in the price of bananas with an increase in the quantity of bananas

c) An increase in the price and quantity of cars

d) An increase in the quantity of computers with a decrease in the price

**10.** Draw a supply and demand diagram for each of the following changes in the bicycle market and show what happens.

a) Rollerblades replace bicycles as the most popular form of transportation for young people.

b) Incomes of people who like to ride bicycles increase.

c) Technology for producing bicycles improves.

d) The cost of the metal alloy used in producing bicycles increases.

**11.** Determine which of the following four sentences uses the terminology of the supply and demand model correctly.

a) "The price of bicycles rose, and therefore the demand for bicycles went down."

b) "The demand for bicycles increased, and therefore the price went up."

c) "The price of bicycles fell, decreasing the supply of bicycles."

d) "The supply of bicycles increased, and therefore the price of bicycles fell."

**12.** a) Suppose you find out that an increase in the price of first-class postage leads to an increase in the demand for overnight delivery service and a decrease in the demand for envelopes. For which good is postage a complement and for which is it a substitute?

b) Suppose someone tells you that a decrease in the price of pizza caused an increase in the demand for beer. Is this what you would expect? Why?

c) Suppose an increase in the price of coffee caused no change in the demand for tea. What can you conclude from this information?

**13.** Suppose an increase in consumers' incomes causes a rightward shift in the demand for computers and a leftward shift in the demand for radios. Which good is normal, and which is inferior? Draw a supply and demand diagram for each to explain how the price will change in each of these markets.

**14.** Straight-line demand and supply curves can be represented by algebraic equations. Given the following algebraic expressions for supply and demand, calculate the equilibrium price and quantity by solving the two equations for $P$ and $Q$.

Supply: $Q = 5 + 2P$

Demand: $Q = 10 - 2P$

Suppose that, due to an increase in consumers' incomes, the demand curve shifts. That is, the new demand equation is:

$Q = 13 - 2P$

Calculate the new equilibrium price and quantity.

# 4

# Elasticity and Its Uses

It was August 1990. Iraq had just invaded Kuwait. Military experts were holding meetings in the White House and the Pentagon to assess U.S. military options. Unbeknown to most people, economic experts were also holding meetings, mainly in the White House and the Treasury building next to the White House. The economic experts were assessing the seriousness of the world economic situation in the aftermath of the invasion. Iraq's invasion of Kuwait had eliminated about 7 percent of the world's daily oil supply of 60 million barrels. With Saudi Arabia's oil fields threatened by further Iraqi aggression and with Iran also possibly entering the conflict, the world's oil supply could have been reduced by another 18 percent, bringing the total reduction in supply to about 25 percent.

The supply and demand model tells us that such a reduction in supply should increase the price of oil. But by how much? By a negligible 3 percent? By a devastating 300 percent? Or by something in between? And what if Nigeria and Venezuela could be persuaded to increase

their oil production? By how much would oil prices rise then? These were the questions the economists were being asked. And they had to come up with quick answers.

There is an elegant, but remarkably useful, economic concept called *elasticity* that economists use to help answer such questions. In economics, elasticity is a measure of how sensitive one variable is to another. In particular, it measures how sensitive the quantity of a good that people demand or that firms supply is to the price of the good.

In this chapter we focus on elasticity. We first show why elasticity is important for making calculations such as the effects of a decline in oil supply. We then provide a formula for elasticity and show how it is calculated. Elasticity can apply to both demand and supply, and we consider both throughout the chapter. We also explain how elasticity is used in many different ways, from assessing the economic impact of a military invasion to determining an appropriate entrance fee to a national park.

# THE PRICE ELASTICITY OF DEMAND

In general, *elasticity* is a measure of how sensitive one economic variable is to another economic variable. There are as many different types of elasticity as there are types of economic variables.

We first consider an elasticity called the price elasticity of demand. The price elasticity of demand is a measure of the sensitivity of the *quantity demanded* of a good to the *price* of the good. The "price elasticity of demand" is sometimes shortened to "elasticity of demand," the "demand elasticity," or even simply "elasticity," when the meaning is clear from the context. The price elasticity of demand always refers to a particular demand curve or demand schedule, such as the world demand for oil or the U.S. demand for bicycles. For a particular demand curve, all other things besides the price of the good being equal, the following relationships hold: As the price increases, the quantity demanded by consumers declines; as the price decreases, the quantity demanded by consumers increases. The price elasticity of demand is a measure of *how much* the quantity demanded changes when the price changes.

For example, when economists report that the price elasticity of demand for contact lenses is high, they mean that the quantity of contact lenses demanded by people changes by a large amount when the price changes. Or if they report that the price elasticity of demand for bread is low, they mean the quantity of bread demanded changes by only a small amount when the price of bread changes.

Before giving a formula for computing elasticity exactly, let us show intuitively why it is important to know how sensitive the quantity demanded is to the price, that is, to know a good's elasticity.

## The Importance of Knowing the Price Elasticity of Demand

We began this chapter with questions about how much the price of oil would rise if the oil supply were reduced. The price elasticity of demand gives us the answers. Figure 4.1 illustrates how. It compares a high elasticity with a low elasticity.

### *High versus Low Elasticity*

There are two graphs in Figure 4.1, each showing a different possible demand curve for oil in the world. We want to show why it is important to know which of these two demand curves is correct, or at least which one gives a better description of economic behavior in the oil market. Each graph has the price of oil on the vertical axis (in dollars per barrel) and the quantity of oil demanded on the horizontal axis (in millions of barrels of oil a day).

Both of the demand curves pass through the same point *A,* where the price of oil is $20 per barrel and the quantity demanded is 60 million barrels per day. But observe that the two different curves show different degrees of sensitivity of the quantity demanded to the price. In the top graph, where the demand curve is relatively flat, the quantity demanded of oil is very sensitive to the price; in other words, the demand curve has a high elasticity. For example, consider a change from point *A* to point *B* when the price rises by $2 from $20 to $22, or by 10 percent

**FIGURE 4.1**
**Comparing Different Price**
**Elasticities of Demand**
Both sets of axes have exactly the
same scale. In the top graph, the
quantity demanded is very sensitive
to the price; the elasticity is high.
In the bottom graph, the quantity
demanded is not very sensitive to
the price; the elasticity is low. Thus,
the same increase in price ($2, or
10 percent) reduces the quantity
demanded much more when the
elasticity is high (top graph) than
when it is low (bottom graph).

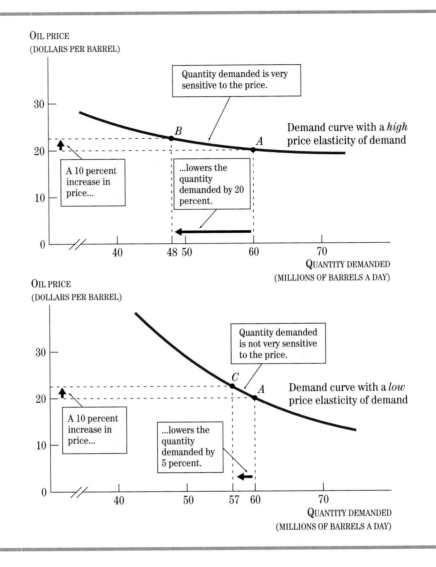

($2/$20 = .10, or 10 percent), and the quantity demanded falls by 12 million from
60 million to 48 million barrels a day, or by 20 percent (12/60 = .20 or 20 percent).

On the other hand, in the bottom graph the quantity demanded is not very sensitive to the price; in other words, the demand curve has a low elasticity. It is relatively steep. When the price rises by $2, or 10 percent, from point *A* to point *C,* the
quantity demanded falls by 3 million barrels, or only 5 percent. Thus, the sensitivity
of the quantity to the price, or the elasticity, is what distinguishes these two graphs.

### The Impact of a Change in Supply on the Price of Oil

Now consider what happens when there is a decline in supply in the world oil market. In Figure 4.2 we combine the supply curve for oil with the two possible
demand curves for oil from Figure 4.1. Initially the oil market is in equilibrium in
Figure 4.2; in both graphs the quantity demanded equals the quantity supplied. The

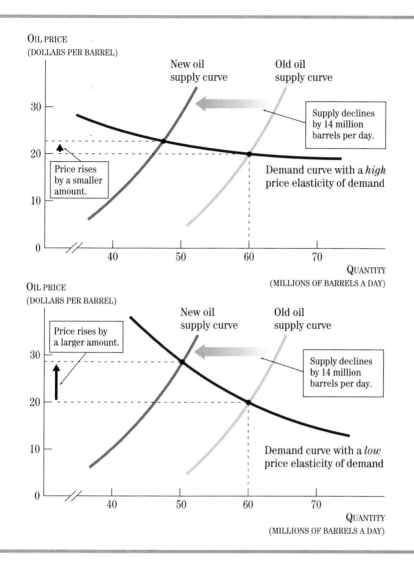

**FIGURE 4.2**
**The Importance of the Price Elasticity of Demand**
The impact on the oil price of a reduction in oil supply is shown for two different demand curves. The reduction in supply is the same for both graphs. When the price elasticity of demand is high (top graph), there is only a small increase in the price. When the price elasticity of demand is low (bottom graph), the price rises by much more.

equilibrium price is $20 per barrel and the equilibrium quantity is 60 million barrels per day, just like point *A* in Figure 4.1. A reduction in the supply of oil—perhaps because of the invasion of Kuwait by Iraq—is also shown. The exact same leftward shift in supply is shown in the top and bottom graphs of Figure 4.2.

Now, observe how the equilibrium price changes in the two graphs. Recall that this change is our prediction—using the supply and demand model—of what would happen to the price of oil if the supply declined. There is a huge difference in the size of the predicted price increase in the two graphs. In the top graph the oil price increases only a little. If the elasticity is very high, then only a small increase in the price is enough to get people to reduce their use of oil and thereby bring the quantity demanded down to a lower quantity supplied. On the other hand, in the bottom diagram the price rises by much more. Here the elasticity is very low, so that a large increase in price is needed to get people to reduce their use of oil and bring the quantity demanded down to quantity supplied.

Thus, in order to determine how much the price will rise in response to a shift in oil supply, we need to know the sensitivity of the quantity demanded to the price, or the elasticity of the demand curve.

## Definition of the Price Elasticity of Demand

**price elasticity of demand:** the percentage change in the quantity demanded of a good divided by the percentage change in the price of that good.

Having demonstrated the practical importance of elasticity, let us now show exactly how it is defined and measured. **Price elasticity of demand** is defined as the percentage change in quantity demanded divided by the percentage change in the price. That is,

$$\text{Price elasticity of demand} = \frac{\text{percentage change in quantity demanded}}{\text{percentage change in the price}}$$

We emphasize that the price elasticity of demand refers to a particular demand curve; thus the numerator of this formula is the percentage change in quantity demanded when the price changes by the percentage amount shown in the denominator. All the other factors that affect demand are held constant when we compute the price elasticity of demand.

For example, as we move from point *A* to point *B* in the top graph of Figure 4.1, the percentage change in the quantity demanded is 20 percent and the percentage change in the price is 10 percent. Hence, the elasticity is 2. Or consider the example in the bottom graph of Figure 4.1. As we move from point *A* to point *C* in the bottom graph, the percentage change in the quantity demanded is 5 percent while the percentage change in the price is 10 percent. Hence, the elasticity is 1/2. Thus, the formula gives us a quantitative measure of sensitivity. Rather than simply saying an elasticity is high or low, we can calculate its value. An elasticity of 2 is much greater than an elasticity of 1/2, and now we can compare these two with other values.

If we let the symbol $e_d$ represent the price elasticity of demand, then we can write the formula more compactly as

$$e_d = \frac{\Delta Q_d}{Q_d} \div \frac{\Delta P}{P} = \frac{\Delta Q_d / Q_d}{\Delta P / P}$$

where $Q_d$ is the quantity demanded, $P$ is the price, and $\Delta$ means "change in." Observe that to compute the percentage change in the numerator and the denominator, we need to divide the change in each variable ($\Delta P$ or $\Delta Q_d$) by the variable ($P$ or $Q_d$).

### The Minus Sign Is Implicit

Because the quantity demanded is negatively related to the price along a demand curve, the elasticity of demand is a negative number: When $\Delta P/P$ is positive, $\Delta Q_d / Q_d$ is negative. But when economists write or talk about elasticity, they usually ignore the negative sign and report the absolute value of the number. For example, a 10 percent *increase* in the price of oil *decreases* the quantity demanded by 20 percent; thus, $\Delta P/P = +.10$ and $\Delta Q_d / Q_d = -.20$, so that the ratio of $\Delta Q_d / Q_d$ to $\Delta P/P$ is $-2$. But economists would say that the price elasticity of demand for oil is 2 in this case. Because the demand curve always slopes downward, this nearly universal convention need not cause any confusion, as long as you remember it.

### The Advantage of a Unit-Free Measure

An attractive feature of the price elasticity of demand is that it does not depend on the units of measurement of the quantity demanded—whether barrels of oil or pounds of peanuts—or on the measure of price—whether in U.S. dollars or Mexican pesos. It is a **unit-free measure** because it uses *percentage changes* in price and quantity demanded. Thus, it provides a way to compare the price sensitivity of the demand for many different goods. It even allows us to compare the price sensitivity of cheap goods—like lard—with more expensive goods—like wool.

**unit-free measure:** a measure that does not depend on a unit of measurement.

For example, suppose that when the price of lard rises from 10 cents to 12 cents per pound, the quantity demanded falls from 20 tons to 19 tons: That is a decline of 1 ton for a 2 *cent* price increase.

In contrast, suppose that when the price of wool rises by $2, from $10 to $12 per pound, the quantity demanded falls by 1 ton, from 20 tons to 19 tons of wool. That would be a decline of 1 ton for a 2 *dollar* price increase.

Using these numbers, the price sensitivity of the demand for wool and lard might appear to be much different: 2 cents to get a ton of reduced purchases versus $2 to get a ton of reduced purchases. Yet the elasticities are the same. The percentage change in price is 20 percent in each case ($2/$10 = $.02/$.10 = .20, or 20 percent), and the percentage change in quantity is 5 percent in each case: 1 ton of lard/20 tons of lard = 1 ton of wool/20 tons of wool = .05, or 5 percent. Hence, the elasticity is 5/20 = 1/4 in both cases.

By looking at ratios of percentage changes, elasticity allows us to compare the price sensitivity of different goods regardless of the units for measuring either price or quantity. With hundreds of different currencies and hundreds of different units of measurement, this is indeed a major advantage.

### Elasticity versus Slope

The *elasticity of the demand curve* is not the same as the *slope of the demand curve*. The slope of the demand curve is defined as the change in price divided by the change in quantity demanded: $\Delta P / \Delta Q$. The slope is not unit free; it depends on how the price and quantity are measured. Thus, it is not a good measure of price sensitivity when we compare different goods.

To illustrate the difference between slope and elasticity, we show in Figure 4.3 a demand curve for lard and a demand curve for wool. The two demand curves have different slopes because the prices are so different. In fact, the slope of the wool demand curve is 100 times greater than the slope of the lard demand curve. Yet the elasticity is the same for the change from *A* to *B* for both demand curves.

## Terminology for Discussing Elasticities

Economists classify demand curves by the size of the price elasticities of demand, and they have developed a very precise terminology for doing so.

### Elastic versus Inelastic Demand

Goods for which the price elasticity is greater than 1 have an **elastic demand.** For example, the quantity of foreign travel demanded decreases by more than 1 percent when the price rises by 1 percent because many people tend to travel at home rather than abroad when the price of foreign travel rises.

**elastic demand:** demand for which price elasticity is greater than 1.

**FIGURE 4.3**
**Different Slopes and Same Elasticities**
The slope of the wool demand curve in the bottom graph is greater than the slope of the lard demand curve in the top graph. The price elasticity of demand for lard and wool from point *A* to point *B* is the same, however. From point *A* to point *B* the price rises by 20 percent and the quantity demanded decreases by 5 percent. Thus, the elasticity is 1/4 for both lard and wool at these points.

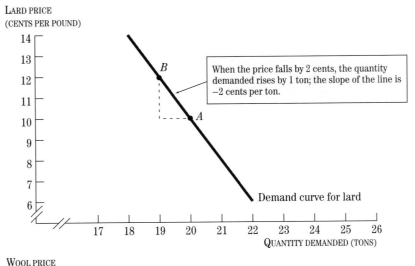

When the price falls by 2 cents, the quantity demanded rises by 1 ton; the slope of the line is −2 cents per ton.

When the price falls by 2 dollars, the quantity demanded rises by 1 ton; the slope of the line is −2 dollars per ton, or −200 cents per ton.

**inelastic demand:** demand for which the price elasticity is less than 1.

**unit elastic demand:** demand for which price elasticity equals 1.

**relatively elastic:** a situation in which the elasticity of one good is greater than the elasticity of another good.

Goods for which the price elasticity of demand is less than 1 have an **inelastic demand.** For example, the quantity of eggs demanded decreases by less than 1 percent when the price of eggs rises by 1 percent because many people do not want to substitute other things for eggs at breakfast.

A good with an elasticity of 1 is called **unit elastic.** This distinction between elastic demand, unit elastic demand, and inelastic demand depends solely on whether the elasticity is greater than 1, equal to 1, or less than 1.

### Relatively Elastic versus Relatively Inelastic Demand

Sometimes one wants to compare two elasticities, whether or not they are less than 1 or greater than 1. When doing so, economists frequently say a demand curve is **relatively elastic** compared with another demand curve if the elasticity of the first one is larger. For example, a good that has an elasticity of 1.8 is relatively elastic compared with a good with an elasticity of 1.2, or a good with an elasticity of .3 is relatively inelastic compared with a good with elasticity of .7. By using the modifier *relatively,* we are making a comparative statement that one price elasticity of demand is greater than another, regardless of whether it is less than 1 or greater than 1.

### Perfectly Elastic versus Perfectly Inelastic Demand

A demand curve that is vertical is called **perfectly inelastic.** Figure 4.4 shows a perfectly inelastic demand curve. The elasticity is zero because when the price changes, the quantity demanded does not change at all. No matter what the price, the same quantity is demanded. People who need insulin would have a perfectly inelastic demand for insulin. As long as there are no substitutes for insulin, they will pay whatever they have to in order to get the insulin.

A demand curve that is horizontal is called **perfectly elastic.** Figure 4.4 also shows a perfectly elastic demand curve. The elasticity is infinite. The perfectly flat demand curve is sometimes hard to imagine because it entails infinitely large movements of quantity for tiny changes in price. In order to better visualize this case you can imagine that the curve is tilted ever so slightly. The infinity case is extreme and is used to approximate demand curves with very high elasticities.

Table 4.1 summarizes the terminology about elasticities.

## Elasticities and Sketches of Demand Curves

After looking at Figure 4.1 or Figure 4.4, you might be tempted to say that demand curves that are very steep have a low elasticity, and demand curves that are very flat have a high elasticity. However, because the slope and the elasticity are such different concepts, we must be careful not to simply look at a steep curve and say it has a high elasticity. Recall, for example, that in Figure 4.3 we showed how different slopes can have the same elasticity. Moreover, as we show shortly, a curve with a constant slope has different elasticities at all points on the curve!

## Calculating the Elasticity with a Midpoint Formula

To calculate the elasticity, we need to find the percentage change in the quantity demanded and divide it by the percentage change in the price. As we have already illustrated with examples, to get the percentage change in the price or quantity, we need to divide the change in price ($\Delta P$) by the price ($P$), and the change in quantity ($\Delta Q_d$) by the quantity demanded ($Q_d$). But when price and quantity demanded

**FIGURE 4.4**
**Perfectly Elastic and Perfectly Inelastic Demand**
A perfectly inelastic demand curve is a vertical line at a certain quantity; the quantity demanded is completely insensitive to the price: No matter what happens to the price, the quantity demanded does not change. A perfectly elastic demand curve is a flat line at a certain price; an increase in price reduces the quantity demanded to zero; a small decrease in price raises the quantity demanded by a huge (literally infinite) amount.

**perfectly inelastic demand:** demand for which the price elasticity is zero, indicating no response to a change in price and therefore a vertical demand curve.

**perfectly elastic demand:** demand for which the price elasticity is infinite, indicating an infinite response to a change in the price and therefore a horizontal demand curve.

**TABLE 4.1**
**Terminology for Price Elasticity of Demand**

| Term | Value of Price Elasticity of Demand ($e_d$) |
|---|---|
| Perfectly inelastic | 0 (vertical demand curve) |
| Inelastic | Less than 1 |
| Unit elastic | 1 |
| Elastic | Greater than 1 |
| Perfectly elastic | Infinity (horizontal demand curve) |
| Good A is relatively elastic compared with good B. | Good A has a higher elasticity than good B. |

change, there is a question about what to use for $P$ and $Q_d$. Should we use the old price and old quantity demanded before the change, or should we use the new price and new quantity demanded after the change?

The most common convention economists use is a compromise between these two alternatives. They take the *average,* or the *midpoint,* of the old and new quantities demanded and the old and new prices. That is, they compute the elasticity using the following formula, called the *midpoint formula:*

$$\text{Price elasticity of demand} = \frac{\text{change in quantity}}{\text{average of old and new quantity}} \div \frac{\text{change in price}}{\text{average of old and new price}}$$

For example, if we use the midpoint formula to calculate the price elasticity of demand for oil when the price changes from \$20 to \$22 and the quantity demanded changes from 60 million to 48 million barrels a day, we get

$$\frac{60 - 48}{(60 + 48)/2} \div \frac{\$20 - \$22}{(\$20 + \$22)/2} = .2222 \div (-.0952) = -2.33$$

That is, the price elasticity of demand is 2.33 using the midpoint formula. In this case, this is close to the value of 2 we obtained by using the old price (\$20) rather than the average \$21 = (\$20 + \$22)/2, and the old quantity demanded (60) rather than the average quantity 54 = (60 + 48)/2.

## Revenue and the Price Elasticity of Demand

When people purchase 60 million barrels of oil at \$20 a barrel, they must pay a total of \$1,200 million (\$20 times 60 million). This is a payment to the oil producers and is the producers' revenue. In general, revenue is the price ($P$) times the quantity ($Q$), or $P \times Q$.

### The Two Effects of Price on Revenue

Because revenue is defined as price times quantity, an increase or a decrease in the price has an effect on revenue. However, there are two opposite effects. Consider an increase in the price. An increase in the price raises the payment per unit but also reduces the number of units. In other words, when the price increases, people pay more for each item and this increases revenue; but they buy fewer items, and this decrease in the quantity demanded reduces revenue. The elasticity determines which of these two opposite effects dominates.

Figure 4.5 illustrates how the price elasticity determines the effect of a price change on revenue for the special case of a demand curve that is a straight line. Look first at the demand curve shown in the top panel of Figure 4.5. Observe that the elasticity is greater than 1 on the left part of the demand curve and less than 1 on the right part of the demand curve.

Now look at the lower panel in Figure 4.5; it shows how revenue is related to price in the case of this same straight-line demand curve. Observe how revenue changes as the price increases. When the price elasticity is greater than 1—in the region on the left—an increase in the price will lower revenue. For example, an increase in the price from \$8 per unit to \$9 per unit reduces the quantity demanded from 4 units to 2 units and revenue falls from \$32 to \$18; the gain in revenue from the higher price per unit is offset by the loss in revenue from the decline in the number of units sold. However, when the price elasticity is greater than 1—in the

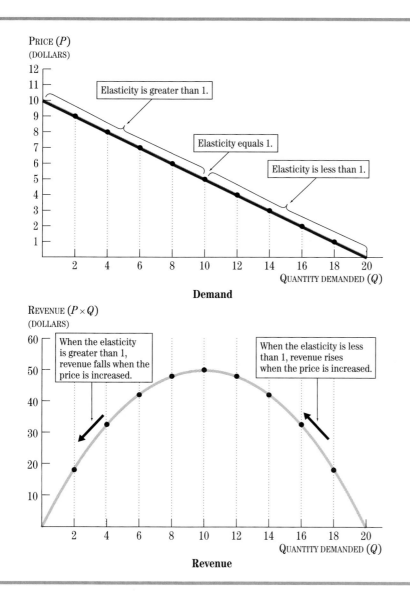

**FIGURE 4.5**
**Revenue and Elasticity of a Straight-Line Demand Curve**
Along the straight-line demand curve at the top, the price elasticity ranges from above 1 (to the left) to below 1 (to the right). When the price elasticity is greater than 1, an increase in the price will reduce revenue as shown in the lower panel.

region on the right—an increase in the price will raise revenue. For example, an increase in the price from $1 to $2 per unit reduces the quantity demanded from 18 units to 16 units and revenue rises from $18 to $32; in this case, the loss in revenue from the decline in number of units sold is not large enough to offset the gain in revenue from the higher price per unit.

Another illustration of the relationship between elasticity and revenue changes is found in Figure 4.6, which is a replica of Figure 4.1 with the scales changed to better illustrate the effects on revenue. We now know that the elasticity in the top graph is greater than 1 and the elasticity in the bottom graph is less than 1. We can see that the same price increase leads to a large decline in the quantity demanded when the elasticity is large and to a small decline in the quantity demanded when

**FIGURE 4.6**

**Effects of an Increase in the Price of Oil on Revenue**

These graphs are replicas of the demand curves for oil shown in Figure 4.1, with the scale changed to show the change in revenue when the price of oil is increased. An increase in the price has two effects on revenue, as shown by the gray- and pink-shaded rectangles. The increase in revenue (gray rectangle) is due to the higher price. The decrease in revenue (pink rectangle) is due to the decline in the quantity demanded as the price is increased. In the top graph, where elasticity is greater than 1, the net effect is a decline in revenue; in the bottom graph, where elasticity is less than 1, the net effect is an increase in revenue.

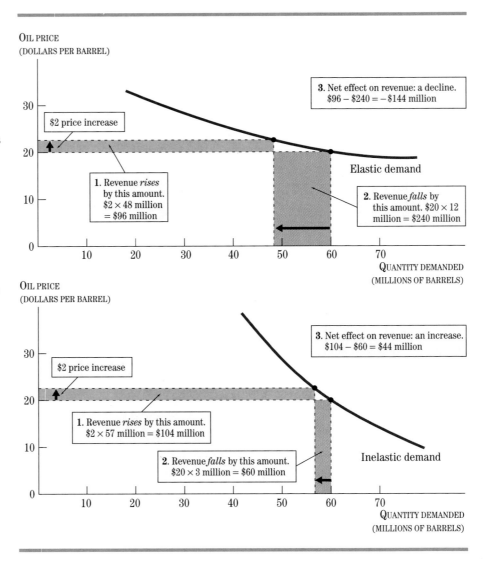

the elasticity is small. The two effects of a price increase are illustrated in the graphs. Revenue falls when the price is increased in the top graph and rises when the price is increased in the bottom graph.

Table 4.2 summarizes the relationship between revenue and the price elasticity of demand. Observe that an increase in price will raise revenue if the elasticity is less than 1 and will lower revenue if the elasticity is greater than 1.

## Differences in the Price Elasticity of Demand

Table 4.3 shows some price elasticities of demand obtained by observing patterns of prices and quantities for several different goods and services. The price elasticity of demand for jewelry, for example, is 2.6. This means that for each percentage increase in the price of jewelry, the quantity demanded will fall by 2.6 percent. Compared with other elasticities, this is large. The price elasticity for alcoholic bev-

| Elasticity Is | Terminology | Effect of a Price Increase on Revenue | Effect of a Price Decrease on Revenue |
|---|---|---|---|
| Less than 1 | Inelastic | Revenue increases | Revenue decreases |
| 1 | Unit elastic | No change in revenue | No change in revenue |
| Greater than 1 | Elastic | Revenue decreases | Revenue increases |

**TABLE 4.2**
**Revenue and the Price Elasticity of Demand**

erages is also large. On the other hand, the price elasticity for eggs is very small. For each percentage increase in the price of eggs, the quantity of eggs demanded falls by only .10 percent. The elasticity for gasoline is also low.

Why do these elasticities differ? Several factors affect elasticity.

**TABLE 4.3**
**Estimated Price Elasticities of Demand**

| Type of Good or Service | Price Elasticity |
|---|---|
| Eggs | .1 |
| Gasoline | .2 |
| Shoes | .9 |
| Foreign travel | 1.2 |
| Alcoholic beverages | 1.5 |
| Jewelry | 2.6 |

### The Degree of Substitutability

A key factor is whether there are good substitutes for the item in question. Can people easily find a substitute when the price goes up? If the answer is yes, then the price elasticity will be high. Foreign travel has a very high elasticity because there is a reasonably good substitute: domestic travel.

On the other hand, the low price elasticity for eggs can be explained by the lack of good substitutes. As many egg fans know, these items are unique; synthetic eggs are not good substitutes for many people. Hence, the price elasticity of eggs is small. People will continue to buy them even if the price rises a lot.

The degree of substitutability depends in part on whether a good is a necessity or a luxury. Necessities cannot easily be substituted for and thus have a smaller price elasticity. Food is a necessity and tends to have a lower price elasticity than luxury items like jewelry.

### Big-Ticket versus Little-Ticket Items

If a good represents a large fraction of people's income, then the price elasticity will be high. If the price of foreign travel doubles, many people will not be able to afford to travel abroad. On the other hand, if the good represents a small fraction of income, the elasticity will be low. For example, if the price of eggs doubles, most people can still afford to buy as many eggs as before the price rise. This is another reason why the price elasticity of the demand for foreign travel is larger than the price elasticity of the demand for eggs.

### Temporary versus Permanent Price Changes

If a change in price is known to be temporary, the price elasticity of demand will tend to be high because many people can easily shift their purchases either later or earlier. For example, suppose a fabric and sewing machine store announces a discount price to last only one day. Then people will shift their purchase of the fabric or sewing machine they were thinking about buying to the sale day.

On the other hand, if the price cut is permanent, the price elasticity will be smaller. People who expect the price decrease to be permanent will not find it advantageous to buy sooner rather than later.

### Long-Run versus Short-Run Elasticity

Frequently the price elasticity of demand is low immediately after a price change but then increases after a period of time has passed. In order to analyze these changes, economists distinguish between the *short run* and the *long run*. The short run is simply a period of time before people have made all their adjustments or changed their habits; the long run is a period of time long enough for people to make such adjustments or change their habits.

Many personal adjustments to a change in prices take a long time. For example, when the price of gasoline increases, people can reduce the quantity demanded in the short run only by driving less and using other transportation more. This might be inconvenient or impossible. In the long run, however, when it comes time to buy a new car, they can buy a more fuel-efficient one. Thus, the quantity of gasoline demanded falls by larger amounts in the long run than in the short run. In fact, the long-run price elasticity of the demand for gasoline is more than twice the short-run elasticity.

Habits that are difficult to break also cause differences between short-run and long-run elasticity. Even a large increase in the price of tobacco may have a small effect on the quantity purchased because people cannot break the smoking habit quickly. But after a period of time, the high price of cigarettes may encourage them to break the habit. Thus, the long-run elasticity for tobacco is higher than the short-run elasticity.

## Elasticities Related to Shifts in Demand

**income elasticity of demand:** the percentage change in quantity demanded of one good divided by the percentage change in income.

Before moving on to supply, we briefly compare the price elasticity of demand with some other elasticities related to demand. Recall that the price elasticity of demand refers to movements along the demand curve. We emphasized in the previous chapter the difference between a shift in the demand curve and a movement along the demand curve. A *shift* in the demand curve occurs when there is a change in the quantity people are willing to buy due to a change in anything except the price; for example, a change in income, the price of other goods, or expectations will shift the demand curve.

The concept of elasticity can be applied to changes in the quantity consumers are willing to buy caused by changes in variables other than price. These elasticities must be distinguished from the price elasticity of demand. The **income elasticity of demand** is the percentage change in the quantity of a good demanded at any given price divided by a percentage change in income. That is,

$$\text{Income elasticity of demand} = \frac{\text{percentage change in quantity demanded}}{\text{percentage change in income}}$$

For example, if incomes rise by 10 percent and, as a result, people purchase 15 percent more health care at a given price, the income elasticity of health care is 1.5. Table 4.4 lists some income elasticities of demand for several different goods and services.

As discussed in Chapter 3, the demand for most goods increases when people's incomes increase. If you have more income, your demand for movies will probably

**TABLE 4.4**
**Estimated Income Elasticities of Demand**

| Type of Good or Service | Income Elasticity |
|---|---|
| Food | .3 |
| Beer | .4 |
| Wine | 1.0 |
| Automobiles | 1.2 |
| Air travel | 6.0 |

increase at each price. Recall that a normal good is a good or service whose demand increases as income increases. But every good is not a normal good; if the demand for a good declines when income increases, the good is called an inferior good. The income elasticity of demand for an inferior good is negative and is reported as a negative number by economists.

Another type of elasticity relating to shifts in the demand curve is the **cross-price elasticity of demand,** which is defined as the percentage change in the quantity demanded divided by the percentage change in the price of another good. For example, an increase in the price of rollerblades would *increase* the quantity demanded of bicycles at every price as people shift away from rollerblading to bicycle riding. Rollerblades are a substitute for bicycles. A cross-price elasticity can also go in the other direction. An increase in the price of bicycle helmets may *reduce* the demand for bicycles. Recall that bicycle helmets and bicycles are complements. For a complement, the cross-price elasticity of demand is negative.

**cross-price elasticity of demand:** the percentage change in the quantity demanded of one good divided by the percentage change in the price of another good.

## Review

▶ The price elasticity of demand is a unit-free number that tells us how sensitive the quantity demanded is to the price. It is defined as the percentage change in the quantity demanded divided by the percentage change in the price.

▶ The elasticity also helps determine how much of a price increase will occur as a result of a shift in supply, and how much revenue will change when the price rises.

▶ Horizontal demand curves have infinite price elasticity. Vertical demand curves have zero price elasticity. Most products have a price elasticity between these two extremes.

▶ The size of the price elasticity of demand depends on the availability of substitutes for the item, whether the item represents a large fraction of income, and whether the price change is temporary or permanent. There are also important differences between long-run and short-run elasticities.

# THE PRICE ELASTICITY OF SUPPLY

Knowing how sensitive the quantity supplied is to a change in price is just as important as knowing how sensitive the quantity demanded is. The price elasticity of supply measures this sensitivity. Recall that supply describes the behavior of those who produce goods. A high price elasticity of supply means that producers raise their production by a large amount if the price increases. A low price elasticity of supply means that producers raise their production only a little if the price increases. Let us briefly see why knowing this elasticity is important.

## Why the Price Elasticity of Supply Is Important

Figure 4.7 shows two different supply curves for coffee. The horizontal axis shows the quantity of coffee supplied around the world in billions of pounds; the vertical axis shows the price in dollars per pound of coffee. For the supply curve in the top graph, the quantity supplied is very sensitive to the price; the price elasticity of supply is high. For the supply curve in the bottom graph, the price elasticity of supply is much lower.

**FIGURE 4.7**
**Comparing Different Price Elasticities of Supply**

In the top graph, the quantity supplied is much more sensitive to price than in the bottom graph. The price elasticity of supply is greater between points $A$ and $B$ at the top than between points $A$ and $C$ at the bottom.

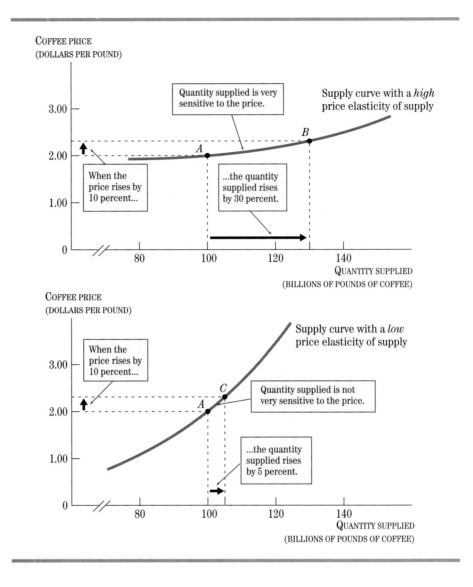

The price elasticity of supply is important for finding out the response of price to shifts in demand. This is shown in Figure 4.8, where the demand for coffee declines, perhaps because of concerns about the effect of the caffeine in coffee or because of a decrease in the price of caffeine-free substitutes for coffee. In any case, if the price elasticity of supply is high, as in the top graph, the price does not change as much as when the price elasticity of supply is low, as in the bottom graph. With a high price elasticity, a small change in price is enough to get firms to bring the quantity supplied down to the lower quantity demanded.

**price elasticity of supply:** the percentage change in quantity supplied divided by the percentage change in price.

## Definition of the Price Elasticity of Supply

The price elasticity of supply can be calculated in much the same way as the price elasticity of demand. The **price elasticity of supply** is defined as the percentage

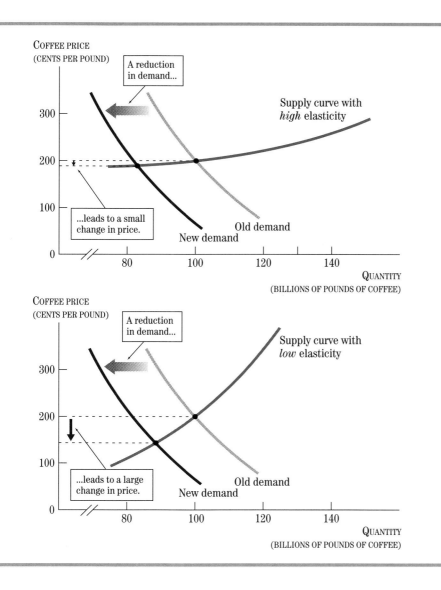

**FIGURE 4.8**
**Importance of Knowing the Price Elasticity of Supply**
When demand changes, the price will also change. If the price elasticity of supply is high, there will be a small change in price. If the price elasticity of supply is low, there will be a large change in price.

change in the quantity supplied divided by the percentage change in the price. That is,

$$\text{Price elasticity of supply} = \frac{\text{percentage change in quantity supplied}}{\text{percentage change in the price}}$$

The price elasticity of supply refers to movements of price and quantity supplied on a given supply curve, all other things being equal. Sometimes the "price elasticity of supply" is simply called the "supply elasticity" for short. If we let the symbol $e_s$ be the price elasticity of supply, then

$$e_s = \frac{\Delta Q_s}{Q_s} \div \frac{\Delta P}{P} = \frac{\Delta Q_s/Q_s}{\Delta P/P}$$

where $Q_s$ is the quantity supplied and $P$ is the price. The price elasticity of supply is a positive number because the price and quantity supplied are positively related.

**FIGURE 4.9**
**Perfectly Elastic and Perfectly Inelastic Supply**
When the quantity supplied is completely unresponsive to the price, the supply curve is vertical and the price elasticity of supply is zero; this case is called perfectly inelastic supply. When the quantity supplied responds by large amounts to a price change, the supply curve is horizontal; economists then say supply is perfectly elastic.

PRICE

Perfectly inelastic supply

Perfectly elastic supply

QUANTITY SUPPLIED

**perfectly elastic supply:** supply for which the price elasticity is infinite, indicating an infinite response of quantity supplied to a change in price and thereby a horizontal supply curve.

**perfectly inelastic supply:** supply for which the price elasticity is zero, indicating no response of quantity supplied to a change in price and thereby a vertical supply curve.

All of the attractive features of the price elasticity of demand apply to the price elasticity of supply. The price elasticity of supply is a unit-free measure. It differs from the slope. It does not depend on how the price or quantity is measured.

As in the case of demand, there can be **perfectly elastic supply** or **perfectly inelastic supply,** as shown in Figure 4.9. The vertical supply curve is perfectly inelastic; it has zero elasticity. Such supply curves are not unusual. For example, there is only one *Mona Lisa*. A higher price cannot bring about a higher quantity supplied, not even one more *Mona Lisa.* But the supply of most goods is not vertical. Higher prices will encourage coffee producers to use more fertilizer, hire more workers, and eventually plant more coffee trees. Thus the quantity supplied increases when the price rises.

The horizontal supply curve is perfectly elastic. In this case the price does not change at all. It is the same regardless of the quantity supplied. It is easier to understand the horizontal supply curve if you view it as an approximation to a supply curve that is *nearly* horizontal, one with a very high elasticity. Then only a small increase in price brings forth a huge increase in the quantity supplied by firms.

**Perfectly Inelastic Supply**
The *Mona Lisa* is an example of a good with a perfectly inelastic supply. The supply curve is vertical because no matter how high the price, no more *Mona Lisas* can be produced. However, the demand to see the *Mona Lisa* is *not* perfectly inelastic; raising the price of admission charged by the Louvre Museum in Paris would reduce the number of people coming to see the painting.

## Review

▶ The price elasticity of supply is a unit-free measure of how sensitive the quantity supplied is to the price. It is defined as the percentage change in the quantity supplied divided by the percentage change in the price.

▶ The price elasticity of supply is useful for determining how much prices will change when there is a change in demand.

# APPLICATIONS OF ELASTICITY

We began the chapter by discussing a wartime application of the price elasticity of demand. Having defined elasticity for both demand and supply, let us now finish reviewing that wartime application and also apply elasticity to some everyday economic problems.

## The Size of the Oil Price Increase

As stated in the introduction to this chapter, the 1990 military invasion of Kuwait by Iraq reduced the world oil supply by 7 percent. Economists estimated that the price elasticity of demand for oil was about .1 percent (that is, $e_d = .1$). Thus, with this small elasticity, they predicted that the oil price would rise by a large amount—about 70 percent. (Here's the calculation, using the symbols in the definition of the price elasticity of demand on page 92: $\Delta P/P = \Delta Q_d/Q_d \times 1/e_d = .07 \times 10 = .70$, or 70 percent.) In fact, the actual rise in the price of oil in 1990 *was* large, even larger than 70 percent: The price of oil rose from $17 per barrel in July 1990 to $36 in October 1990, or about 112 percent. (The larger than predicted price increase may have been due to worries that Iraq would also invade Saudi Arabia and reduce the oil supply even further.)

   Hence, the oil supply and demand analysis helped explain the price effects of the reduction in oil supply. This economic model—showing that a huge oil price increase could be caused by the 7 percent reduction in oil supply—was a factor in the decision by the United States and its allies to send troops to the Middle East to halt the Iraqi invasion of Saudi Arabia and to eventually force Iraq out of Kuwait.

## Setting National Park Fees

In 1994, the federal government proposed to increase the fees charged at national parks, from Yosemite to Yellowstone to the Great Smoky Mountains. It estimated that an increase in fees would raise revenue that could then be used to make repairs and improve facilities at the parks. However, an increase in fees could reduce the use of parks—decrease the quantity demanded—as you have seen. If the demand was elastic, then the higher fees would reduce revenue.

   Why did the government estimate that revenue would go up? For one thing, a survey found that most users of parks had incomes in excess of $50,000 per year. Hence, park fees—even the higher ones—are a relatively small part of their income. In this way, the federal government figured that the elasticity of demand is less than one.

# Alfred Marshall, 1842–1924

**BORN:**
Bermondsey (south of London), England, 1842

**EDUCATION:**
Cambridge University, graduated 1865

**JOBS:**
Professor, University College, Bristol, 1877–1883
Fellow, Oxford University, 1883–1885
Professor of political economy, Cambridge University, 1885–1908

**MAJOR PUBLICATIONS:**
*Principles of Economics,* 1890
*Money, Credit and Commerce,* 1923

Alfred Marshall was the first economist to define the powerful unit-free concept called elasticity, for which other economists are eternally grateful. The great economist John Maynard Keynes said, "I do not think Marshall did economists any greater service." Marshall defined elasticity in a remarkable book, *Principles of Economics,* published in 1890, when he was 48 years old. Here is how Marshall put it:

*The* elasticity of demand *in a market is great or small according as the amount demanded increases much or little for a given fall in price, and diminishes much or little for a given rise in price.*

Marshall's *Principles of Economics* contains many other innovations. The book was used in advanced economics courses for many decades; the economist Milton Friedman was still assigning the book to his students at the University of Chicago in the 1970s.

Why was the book so popular? It demonstrated the tremendous usefulness of the supply and demand model, in which the effects of economic policies are analyzed in a diagram by shifting supply or demand curves and considering their elasticities. Curiously, Marshall chose to make his diagrams the size of postage stamps and place them in small-print footnotes!

Marshall's *Principles of Economics* was not the first book to use demand or supply curves. Nearly 20 years earlier, in 1871, W. Stanley Jevons published a book of similar ideas. But more than anyone else, Marshall developed the supply and demand diagram into a powerful tool for analyzing real-world problems. Many economists credit Marshall with developing the *style* of economic reasoning that is routinely followed in applied economics work today. Marshall taught economists how to think like economists.

What was Alfred Marshall like? He spent much of his life as a professor, lecturing regularly and holding frequent office hours at his home. He trained a whole generation of economists, including John Maynard Keynes. For enjoyment, he loved to hike in the Alps in the summer. He lectured about the material in his *Principles of Economics* many years before the book was published, and he waited until he was over 80 to publish his major work on macroeconomics, which he had lectured about in his 30s! Many have wondered about the reasons for "Marshall's delay," looking into his personal life for answers.

Marshall was born south of London to a family that was not particularly well-off; his father was a dominating figure and forbade Alfred to study mathematics, which Marshall loved but his father did not understand. Rather than go to Oxford, where his father wanted him to go, Marshall went to Cambridge and financed his education with a loan from one of his uncles.

Marshall did not decide to become an economist until after college. The reason for his choice? He said he saw economics as a way to help the poor and unfortunate in society.

Marshall was the greatest economist of the neoclassical school of the late 19th and early 20th century. The neoclassical school maintained most of the principles of the classical school founded by Adam Smith, but improved on them with the supply and demand model and its underlying foundation.

Marshall's simple, yet broad, definition of economics has itself become a classic. To Marshall,

*Political Economy or Economics is a study of mankind in the ordinary business of life; it examines that part of individual and social action which is most closely connected with the attainment and with the use of the material requisites of wellbeing.*

*Source of quotes:* Alfred Marshall, *Principles of Economics,* 8th ed. (New York: Macmillan, 1920), pp. 1, 102.

### Taxes and Labor Supply

One of the most important supply curves is the supply curve of an individual's or a family's labor. Just as a firm decides how much to produce at each price of the good it sells, workers may decide how much to work at each price (wage) of the good they sell (labor). For example, a freelance editor may decide whether to take on a book-editing job depending on how high a wage the book publisher offers. At a very low wage, the editor may decide that there are better things to do than edit the book. At a higher wage, the editor may take the job—or even two jobs if the wage gets high enough. Thus, there is a labor supply curve for book-editing services.

A major source of revenue for the government is income taxes on the wages earned from working. The higher the tax rate, the less the worker can take home and, therefore, the less labor will be supplied. A higher tax rate increases the amount collected from each hour worked, but if fewer hours are worked as a result of the tax, then tax revenues may go down. The key factor is the labor supply elasticity—the percentage change in the quantity of labor supplied divided by the percentage change in take-home wage. If labor supply has a very low elasticity, then a higher tax rate will increase tax revenue. On the other hand, if labor supply has a very high elasticity, then a higher tax will decrease revenue.

## Review

▶ Demand and supply elasticities help make decisions in government, business, and in our personal lives. Knowing the size of the elasticity is essential.

▶ Many decisions depend simply on whether the price elasticity of demand is greater or less than 1. Others depend on the elasticity of supply.

# CONCLUSION

In this chapter we have provided a quantitative basis for the supply and demand model. We have seen that *how much* the equilibrium price and quantity change in response to a change in supply and demand depends on the elasticity of the supply and demand curves. Armed with these elasticities, we can predict what will happen to prices after a drop in the supply of a good. We can also predict what will happen to prices after a change in demand. And we can predict whether revenue will increase or decrease when prices, fees, or taxes are cut or raised.

Distinguishing between movements along and shifts of the curves, knowing the importance of the elasticity, and describing in words what happens when the intersection of the curves change are all important parts of economic thinking.

# KEY POINTS

**1.** Elasticity is a measure of the sensitivity of one economic variable to another. For example, the price elasticity of demand measures how much the quantity demanded changes when the price changes.

**2.** The price elasticity of demand is the percentage change in the quantity demanded divided by the percentage change

in price. It refers to changes in price and quantity demanded along the demand curve, all other things being equal.

**3.** Elasticity is a unit-free measure.

**4.** Demand is elastic if the price elasticity of demand is greater than 1 and inelastic if the price elasticity of demand is less than 1.

**5.** When the elasticity is greater than 1, an increase in the price reduces the quantity demanded by a percentage greater than the percentage increase in the price, thereby reducing revenue. When the elasticity is less than 1, an increase in the price reduces the quantity demanded by a percentage less than the percentage increase in the price, thereby increasing revenue.

**6.** The elasticity of demand for a good depends on whether the good has close substitutes, whether its value is a large or small fraction of total income, and the time period of the change.

**7.** If a good has a low price elasticity of demand, then a change in supply will cause a big change in price. Con-

versely, if a good has a high price elasticity of demand, then a change in supply will cause a small change in price.

**8.** The price elasticity of supply is defined as the percentage change in the quantity supplied divided by the percentage change in the price.

**9.** In the short run, the price elasticity of supply is very low. In the long run, the price elasticity of supply is higher.

**10.** If a good has a low price elasticity of supply, then a change in demand will cause a big change in price. Conversely, if a good has a high price elasticity of supply, then a change in demand will cause a small change in price.

# KEY TERMS

| | | |
|---|---|---|
| price elasticity of demand | relatively elastic | price elasticity of supply |
| unit-free measure | perfectly inelastic demand | perfectly elastic supply |
| elastic demand | perfectly elastic demand | perfectly inelastic supply |
| inelastic demand | income elasticity of demand | |
| unit elastic demand | cross-price elasticity of demand | |

# QUESTIONS FOR REVIEW

**1.** Why is the price elasticity of demand a unit-free measure of the sensitivity of the quantity demanded to a price change?

**2.** What factors determine whether the price elasticity of demand is high or low?

**3.** What is the difference between the price elasticity of demand, the income elasticity of demand, and the cross-price elasticity of demand?

**4.** Why is the price elasticity of demand useful for finding the size of the price change that occurs when supply shifts?

**5.** What is the difference between elastic and inelastic demand?

**6.** For what values of the price elasticity of demand do increases in the price increase revenue?

**7.** What is the slope of a perfectly elastic supply curve?

**8.** Why is the price elasticity of demand lower in the short run than in the long run?

**9.** Why is price elasticity of supply lower in the short run than in the long run?

**10.** What is the income elasticity of demand?

# PROBLEMS

**1.** Assume that demand can be characterized by a perfectly elastic demand curve. How will the price change as the supply curve shifts? Why does it behave in this way? How does total revenue change as the supply curve shifts?

**2.** Suppose a city government decides that it wants to increase revenue by raising the price of parking tickets.

 a) When government officials increase the price of a ticket from $40 to $50, they are surprised that their revenue actually falls. What happened? What does this say about the responsiveness of people to the price of illegal parking? Is it elastic or inelastic?

 b) Suppose the city government collects the following data:

| Price of Parking Ticket | Number of Tickets per Week |
|---|---|
| $10 | 100 |
| $20 | 80 |
| $30 | 60 |
| $40 | 40 |
| $50 | 20 |

Calculate revenue for each price-quantity combination. At what point does the demand for illegal parking go from the inelastic to the elastic portion of the curve? Use the midpoint formula for computing elasticities.

c) Given the preceding data, what ticket price will maximize the revenue received from parking tickets?

**3.** What does it mean for the supply curve to be perfectly inelastic? How does revenue change as the demand curve shifts?

**4.** Compare a market where supply and demand are very (but not perfectly) inelastic to one where supply and demand are very (but not perfectly) elastic. Suppose the government decides to impose a price floor $1 above the equilibrium prices in each of these markets. Compare, diagrammatically, the surpluses that result. Explain the difference between these two cases.

**5.** Using the following data for a demand curve, calculate the price elasticity of demand between a price of $9 and $10, and between $4 and $5. Use the midpoint formula.

| Price | Quantity Demanded |
|---|---|
| 10 | 10 |
| 9 | 20 |
| 8 | 30 |
| 7 | 40 |
| 6 | 50 |
| 5 | 60 |
| 4 | 70 |
| 3 | 80 |

a) Since this is a linear demand curve with a constant slope, why does the elasticity change?

b) At what point is price times quantity maximized? What is the elasticity *at that point?*

**6.** Use the following data to calculate the price elasticity of supply for the price between $7 and $8, and between $3 and $4. Use the midpoint formula. How does supply elasticity change as you move up the supply curve?

| Price | Quantity Supplied |
|---|---|
| 2 | 10 |
| 3 | 20 |
| 4 | 30 |
| 5 | 40 |
| 6 | 50 |
| 7 | 60 |
| 8 | 70 |
| 9 | 80 |

**7.** Suppose that the demand for cigarettes is very inelastic. If the government imposes a tax per pack of cigarettes, it is equivalent to the supply curve shifting up vertically by the

amount of the tax. Show this in a diagram. If the demand is perfectly inelastic, by how much does the price, including the tax, increase? Why?

**8.** Calculate the cross-price elasticity for the following goods. Are they substitutes or complements?

a) The price of movie theater tickets goes up by 10 percent, causing the quantity demanded for video rentals to go up by 4 percent.

b) Computer prices fall by 20 percent, causing the quantity demanded of software to increase by 15 percent.

c) The price of apples falls by 5 percent, causing the quantity demanded of pears to fall by 5 percent.

d) The price of ice cream falls by 6 percent, causing the quantity demanded of frozen yogurt to fall by 1 percent.

**9.** Given the following income elasticities of demand, would you classify the following goods as luxury, necessity, or inferior goods?

a) Potatoes: elasticity = 0.5

b) Pinto beans: elasticity = −0.1

c) Bottled water: elasticity = 1.1

d) Video cameras: elasticity = 1.4

**10.** In 1992, the federal government placed a tax of 10 percent on goods like luxury automobiles and yachts. The boat-manufacturing industry had huge declines in orders for boats and laid off many workers, whereas the reaction in the auto industry was much milder. (The tax on yachts was subsequently removed.) Explain this situation using two supply and demand diagrams. Compare the elasticity of demand for luxury autos with that for yachts based on the experience with the luxury tax.

**11.** The following data on world coffee production from 1985 to 1987 come from the *CRB Commodity Year Book.*

| | Production (millions of bags) | Price (dollars / pound) |
|---|---|---|
| 1985 | 96 | 1.42 |
| 1986 | 80 | 2.01 |
| 1987 | 103 | 1.09 |

a) Plot the observations on a scatter diagram with price on the vertical axis and production on the horizontal axis.

b) Assume that production equals the quantity demanded around the world and that the coffee demand curve did not change between 1985 and 1987. First, calculate the price elasticity of demand for 1985 to 1986 using the midpoint formula. Next, calculate the same elasticities from 1986 to 1987. Would you say the demand for coffee is elastic or inelastic?

c) If the two calculations in part (b) differ by much, explain why.

# 2 part

# Introduction to Macroeconomics

In the last 100 years the amount of goods and services that each person can produce on average has grown by more than five times in the United States. This *economic growth* is the single most important reason for improvements in living standards. Economic growth provides the means for people to reduce poverty and to achieve a better life. However, temporary fluctuations in production—such as the Great Depression of the 1930s or the much milder downturn in the early 1990s—sometimes interrupt this growth and cause great hardship. During such *economic fluctuations* people lose their jobs, poverty increases, and incomes fall until the economy returns to its upward growth path.

Patent No. 24,458,807

Interest
Rate

1990    1995

Whereas economists use the supply and demand model and other microeconomic models to explain the behavior of firms and consumers in particular markets—the markets for bicycles, telephones, wheat—they use macroeconomic models to explain economic growth and fluctuations. When economists build macroeconomic models, they must look at the whole economy, which represents the sum of many individual markets.

With these two chapters we begin to take a look at the whole economy. In Chapter 5 we examine the history of the ups and downs in the U.S. economy, paying particular attention to national income, unemployment, inflation, and interest rates. We also provide an overview of macroeconomic models of growth and fluctuations. In Chapter 6 we examine how production of goods and services in the whole economy is measured, laying down basic principles for defining saving and the accumulation of capital.

These two chapters will serve as preparation for the discussion of long-run economic growth in Part 3 and fluctuations in total production and employment in Part 4.

# 5

# A Preview of Macroeconomics

Macroeconomics is the study of how the economy as a whole grows and changes over time. It explains the miracles of economic growth: why, for example, young Americans living at the end of the twentieth century could choose to work only two months of the year, take a ten-month vacation each year, and still consume the same amount that their great-great-grandparents consumed 100 years ago. Macroeconomics also explains the dilemmas of economic growth: why a long-term economic slowdown that began in the mid-1970s is leaving many of these same young Americans no better off than their parents. Macroeconomics explains the dilemma of over 25 percent unemployment in the 1930s, and—another miracle—why we have not seen such high unemployment since. It explains why even in a good year about 5 percent of the workers are unemployed in the United States. Macroeconomics also explains why inflation—the mysterious increase in the price of virtually everything in the economy—caused a $100-a-month apartment in the 1950s to rent for $500 a month in the 1990s.

Macroeconomics concentrates on the *whole* economy—the whole national economy or even the whole world economy—rather than on particular parts of the economy, such as the health-care industry or the electronics industry. Determining what is produced and who gets it is closer to the subject of microeconomics than macroeconomics. Think of the economy as a pizza pie. Macroeconomics focuses on the size of the pie: Why does the size of the pie increase over the long haul? Why does the size shrink occasionally (a medium shows up when you ordered a large)? What can we do to increase the size of the pie and prevent it from shrinking occasionally?

Macroeconomics is important to you and your future. Your first job will be harder to find if unemployment is high. And if inflation picks up again, it may wipe out most of your savings. On a brighter note, increased economic growth would mean a better future for you, help alleviate poverty, and even provide funds to clean up the environment.

Good government policy can provide for high economic growth, low unemployment, and low inflation. But bad economic policy can lower growth and cause both high inflation and high unemployment. Macroeconomics is essential for determining what is good economic policy and how to achieve it.

This chapter first summarizes the recent historical performance of the economy, highlighting key facts to remember. It then gives a very short preview of the macroeconomic theory designed to explain these facts. The theory will be developed in Parts 3 and 4, and, along with the facts, will provide a basis for making decisions about economic policy.

# ECONOMIC OUTPUT OVER TIME

**Real gross domestic product** is the place to begin describing the subject matter of macroeconomics. You will recall from Chapter 1 that gross domestic product (GDP) is the total value of all goods and services produced in the economy during a specified period of time, such as a year or a quarter. The adjective *real* means that the measure of production is adjusted for the general increase in prices over time. This general increase in prices is called *inflation*. Although real GDP is not a perfect measure of how much is produced—for example, it does not include the value of a home-cooked meal or a garage painted by a do-it-yourselfer, and it does not subtract out pollution or environmental damage—it is the most comprehensive measure economists have to determine how the economy is doing. Real GDP is also called *output* or *production*.

Figure 5.1 shows the changes in real GDP over the last 40 years in the United States. When you look at real GDP over time, as in Figure 5.1, you notice two simultaneous patterns emerging. Over the long term, increases in real GDP demonstrate an upward trend, which economists call long-term **economic growth.** In the short term, there are **economic fluctuations**—more transient increases or decreases in real GDP. These short-term fluctuations in real GDP are also called **business cycles.** The difference between the long-term economic growth trend and the economic fluctuations can be better seen by drawing a relatively smooth line between the observations on real GDP. Such a smooth trend line is shown in Figure 5.1. Sometimes real GDP fluctuates above the trend line and sometimes it fluctuates below the trend line. In this section we look more closely at these two patterns: economic growth and economic fluctuations.

## Economic Growth: The Relentless Uphill Climb

The large increase in real GDP shown in Figure 5.1 means that each year in the 1990s people in the United States produce a much greater amount of goods and services than they did 30 or 40 years ago. Improvements in the well-being of individuals in any society cannot occur without such increases in real GDP. To get a better measure of how individuals benefit from increases in real GDP, we consider average production per person, or *real GDP per capita.* Real GDP per capita is real GDP divided by the number of people in the economy. It is the total of all food, clothes, cars, houses, CDs, concerts, education, computers, etc., per person. When real GDP per capita is increasing, then the well-being—or the standard of living—of individuals in the economy, at least on average, is improving.

**real gross domestic product (real GDP):** a measure of the value of all the goods and services newly produced in a country during some period of time, adjusted for inflation.

**economic growth:** an upward trend in real GDP, reflecting expansion in the economy over time.

**economic fluctuations:** swings in real GDP that lead to deviations of the economy from its long-term growth trend.

**business cycles:** short-term fluctuations in real GDP and employment.

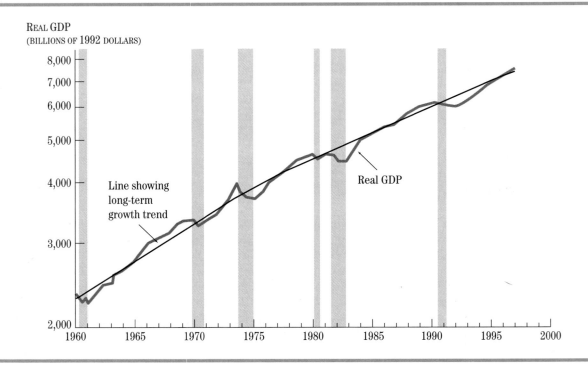

**FIGURE 5.1**

**Economic Growth and Fluctuations During the Last 40 Years**

Real GDP has tripled in the last 40 years. The trend in growth is shown by the black line. Real GDP is now more than $3 trillion higher than it was 40 years ago. At the same time, the economy has fluctuated up and down as it has grown, with six recessions—marked by the vertical shaded bars—and six subsequent recoveries since 1960.

*Source:* U.S. Department of Commerce.

### The Economic Growth Record

How much economic growth has there been during the last 40 years in the United States? The annual *economic growth rate*—the percentage increase in real GDP each year—provides a good measure. On the average for the last 40 years, the annual economic growth rate has been about 3 percent. This may not sound like much, but it means that real GDP has more than tripled in the last 40 years. The United States now produces $3 trillion more goods and services than it did in the 1950s. The increase in production in the United States since the early 1960s is larger than what Japan and Germany now produce together. It is as if all the production of Japan and Germany—what is made by all the workers, machines, and technology in these countries—were annexed to the U.S. economy, as illustrated in Figure 5.2.

How much has real GDP *per capita* increased during this period? Because the U.S. population increased by about 100 million people during this period, the increase in real GDP per capita has been less dramatic than the increase in real GDP, but it is impressive nonetheless. The annual growth rate of real GDP per capita is the percentage increase in real GDP per capita each year. It has averaged about 1.7 percent per year. Again, this might not sound like much, but it has meant that real GDP per capita doubled from about $10,000 per person in the 1950s to about $20,000 per person in the 1990s. That extra $10,000 per person represents increased opportunities for travel, VCRs, housing, washing machines, aerobics classes, health care, antipollution devices for cars, and so on.

To be sure, not everyone benefited by the same amount from this increased average production per person; some did not benefit at all. And perhaps the production could be used for better purposes. Some feel that Americans spend too much

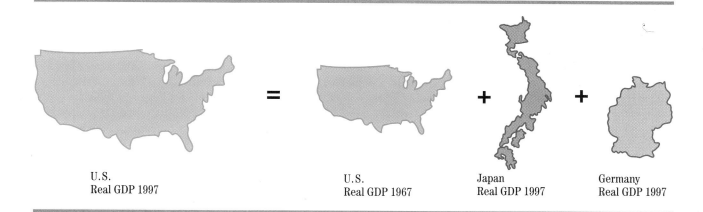

U.S.
Real GDP 1997

U.S.
Real GDP 1967

Japan
Real GDP 1997

Germany
Real GDP 1997

on health care and gasoline and not enough on child care and the criminal justice system.

### The Economic Growth Slowdown

Long-term growth was more rapid in the period from the 1950s to the 1970s than it was from the 1970s to the 1990s. Economic growth in the former period was about 3½ percent per year, but in the latter period, it slowed to 2½ percent per year. A similar slowdown in economic growth also occurred in many other countries. This decline in economic growth means a loss of $1 trillion a year that might have been spent on other things, including cars, houses, better roads and bridges, aid to the poor, or environmental cleanup. If economic growth had remained at 3½ percent per year, real GDP would have been $1 trillion higher now than it is. This decline in economic growth is a problem because it slows improvements in economic well-being. But although we lament that we could have done better, we should not ignore that we have done as well as we have.

Over long spans of time, small differences in economic growth—even less than 1 percent per year—can transform societies. For example, economic growth in the southern states was only a fraction of a percent greater than in the North in the 100 years after the Civil War. Yet this enabled the South to rise from a real income per capita about half that of the North after the Civil War to about the same as the North today. Economic growth is the reason that Italy has caught up and even surpassed the United Kingdom in real GDP per capita; 100 years ago Italy had a real GDP per capita about half that of the United Kingdom. Economic growth is also key to improvements in the less-developed countries in Africa, Asia, and Latin America. Because economic growth has been lagging in many of these countries, real GDP per capita is considerably less than in the United States.

### Economic Fluctuations: Temporary Setbacks and Recoveries

Clearly, real GDP grows over time, but every now and then real GDP stops growing, falls, and then starts increasing rapidly again. These ups and downs in the economy—that is, economic fluctuations or business cycles—can be viewed in Figure 5.1.

**FIGURE 5.2**
**Visualizing Economic Growth**
Over the last 30 years, production in the U.S. economy has increased by more than the total current production of the Japanese and German economies combined. It is as if the United States annexed Germany and Japan.

*Source:* International Monetary Fund.

*cnag*
**recession:** a decline in real GDP that lasts for at least six months.

**peak:** the highest point in real GDP before a recession.

*кормящ пагоиба*

**trough:** the lowest point of real GDP at the end of a recession.

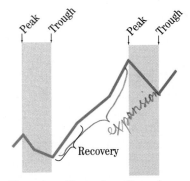

Recession   Expansion   Recession

Two of these business cycles, one in the mid-1970s and the other in the early 1990s, are blown up for closer examination in Figure 5.3. As these two examples illustrate, no two business cycles are alike. The pattern of real GDP varies considerably. However, certain phases are common to all business cycles. These common phases are sketched in the margin. When real GDP falls, economists say there is a **recession;** a rule of thumb says that the fall in real GDP must last for a half year or more before it is considered a recession. The highest point before the start of the recession is called the **peak.** The lowest point at the end of a recession is called the **trough,** a term that may cause you to imagine water accumulating at the bottom of one of the dips.

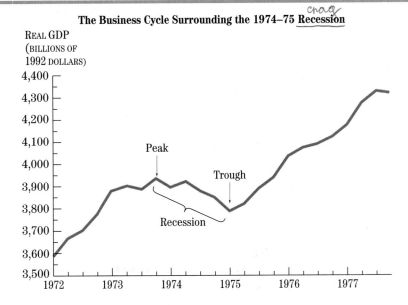

**FIGURE 5.3**

**The Phases of Business Cycles**

Although no two business cycles are alike, they have common features, including the four phases—*peak, recession, trough,* and *expansion,* which lasts until the next peak. The early part of the expansion is called the *recovery.* Note that the 1973–1975 recession was larger and deeper than the 1990–1991 recession.

*Source:* U.S. Department of Commerce.

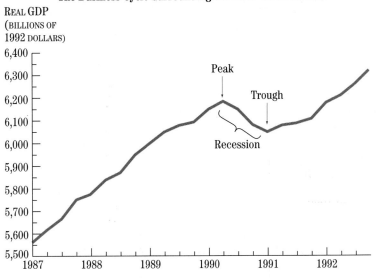

*nogouba* *kapbemo* *bepxyuuka*

The period between recessions—from the trough to the next peak—is called an **expansion.** The early part of an expansion is usually called a **recovery** because the economy is just recovering from the recession.

The peaks and troughs of the six recessions since 1960 are shown by vertical bars in Figure 5.1. The shaded areas represent the recessions. The area between the shaded bars shows the expansions. The dates of all peaks and troughs back to 1920 are shown in Table 5.1. The average length of each business cycle from peak to peak is five years, but it is clear from Table 5.1 that business cycles are not regularly occurring ups and downs, like sunup and sundown. Recessions occur irregularly. There were only 12 months between the back-to-back recessions of the early 1980s, while 58 months of uninterrupted growth occurred between the 1973–1975 recession and the 1980 recession. The recession phases of business cycles also vary in duration and depth. The 1980 recession, for example, was not nearly as long or as deep as the 1973–1975 recession.

The 1990–1991 recession was one of the shortest recessions in U.S. history, and it was followed by a very long expansion. Before that recession, economic growth occurred almost uninterrupted for most of the 1980s from the trough of the previous recession in November 1982 to a peak in July 1990. The 1980s and 1990s saw the first- and second-longest peacetime expansions in U.S. history.

Economists debate whether economic policies were responsible for the expansions of the 1980s and 1990s. We will examine these debates in later chapters. Another debate is the cause of the recession that began in 1990. The first month of recession occurred just after Iraq invaded Kuwait, causing a disruption in the oil fields and a jump in world oil prices. Some argue that this jump in oil prices was a factor in the recession. Others point to an increase in taxes in 1990.

**expansion:** the period between the trough of a recession and the next peak, consisting of a general rise in output and employment.

**recovery:** the early part of an economic expansion, immediately after the trough of the recession.

| Recession | | Duration of Recession (months from peak to trough) | Decline in Real GDP (percent from peak to trough) | Duration of Next Expansion (months from trough to peak) |
|---|---|---|---|---|
| Peak | Trough | | | |
| Jan 1920 | Jul 1921 | 18 | 8.7 | 22 |
| May 1923 | Jul 1924 | 14 | 4.1 | 27 |
| Oct 1926 | Nov 1927 | 13 | 2.0 | 21 |
| Aug 1929 | Mar 1933 | 43 | 32.6 | 50 |
| May 1937 | Jun 1938 | 13 | 18.2 | 80 |
| Feb 1945 | Oct 1945 | 8 | 11.0 | 37 |
| Nov 1948 | Oct 1949 | 11 | 1.5 | 45 |
| Jul 1953 | May 1954 | 10 | 3.2 | 39 |
| Aug 1957 | Apr 1958 | 8 | 3.3 | 24 |
| Apr 1960 | Feb 1961 | 10 | 1.2 | 106 |
| Dec 1969 | Nov 1970 | 11 | 1.0 | 36 |
| Nov 1973 | Mar 1975 | 16 | 4.9 | 58 |
| Jan 1980 | Jul 1980 | 6 | 2.5 | 12 |
| Jul 1981 | Nov 1982 | 16 | 3.0 | 92 |
| Jul 1990 | Mar 1991 | 8 | 1.4 | 78* |

**TABLE 5.1**
**Comparison of Recessions**

*As of September 1997.

*Source:* National Bureau of Economic Research.

*A Recession's Aftermath*

The economy usually takes several years to return to normal after a recession. Thus, a period of bad economic times always follows a recession while the economy recovers. Remember that economists define recessions as periods when real GDP is declining, not as periods when real GDP is down. Despite the technical definition, many people still associate the word *recession* with bad economic times. For example, although the 1990–1991 recession ended in March 1991, most people felt that bad economic times extended beyond March 1991 well into 1992, and they were right. But, technically speaking, the recession was over in March 1991, well before the effects of an improving economy were felt by most people.

**FIGURE 5.4**
**Growth and Fluctuations Throughout the Twentieth Century**
Economic growth has continued, but the size of economic fluctuations has diminished remarkably. Recent ups and downs are minuscule in comparison with the Great Depression.

*Source:* U.S. Department of Commerce.

*Recessions versus Depressions*

Recessions have been observed for as long as economists have tracked the economy. Some past recessions have lasted so long and were so deep that they are called *depressions*. There is no formal definition of a depression. A depression is a huge recession.

Fortunately, we have not experienced a depression in the United States for a long time. Figure 5.4 shows the history of real GDP for about 100 years. The most

REAL GDP
(BILLIONS OF 1992 DOLLARS)

noticeable decline in real GDP occurred in the 1929–1933 recession. Real GDP fell by 32.6 percent in this period. This decline in real GDP was so large that it was given its own designation by economists and historians—the *Great Depression.* The recessions of recent years have had much smaller declines.

Table 5.1 shows how much real GDP fell in the fifteen recessions since the 1920s. The 1920–1921 recession and the 1937–1938 recession were big enough to be classified as depressions, but both are small compared to the Great Depression. Real GDP also declined substantially after World War II, when war production declined.

Clearly, recent recessions are not even remotely comparable in severity to the Great Depression or the other huge recessions of the 1920s and 1930s. The 1990–1991 recession, for example, had only one-twentieth the decline in real GDP that occurred during the Great Depression. But because any recession rivets attention on people's hardship and suffering, there is always a tendency to view a current recession as worse than all previous recessions. Some commentators reporting on the 1990–1991 recession wondered whether it should be compared with the Great Depression. For example, in September 1992, Louis Uchitelle of the *New York Times* wrote, "Technically, the recession is over, but spiritually, it continues. . . . The question is, what to call these hard times. What has been happening in America since 1989 seems momentous enough to enter history as a major economic event of the 20th century."[1]

## Review

▶ Economic growth and economic fluctuations in real GDP occur simultaneously.

▶ Economic growth provides lasting improvements in the well-being of people. But recessions interrupt this growth.

▶ The Great Depression of the 1930s was a much larger downturn than recent recessions. It was about twenty times more severe than the 1990–1991 recession when measured by the decline in real GDP.

# JOBS, INFLATION, AND INTEREST RATES

As real GDP changes over time, so do other economic variables, such as employment and inflation. Looking at these other economic variables gives us a better understanding of the human story behind the changes in real GDP. They also provide additional information about the economy's performance—just as a person's pulse rate or cholesterol level gives information different from the body temperature. No one variable is sufficient. We start with a look at employment, productivity, and unemployment.

## Employment, Productivity, and Unemployment

When judging the success of an economy or the success of economic policies, many people look at how well the economy does in creating jobs. President Clinton set an economic policy goal of creating 8 million jobs in four years starting in 1993,

1. Louis Uchitelle, "Even Words Fail in This Economy," *New York Times,* September 8, 1992, p. C2.

and in his reelection campaign in 1996, he emphasized that this goal had been exceeded, with 10 million jobs created. President Reagan and President Bush pointed to the success of their economic policies by mentioning that 20 million jobs were created during the 1980s.

**labor productivity:** output per hour of work.

Although the number of jobs is important, so is the amount that each worker produces—what is called **labor productivity,** or sometimes simply *productivity.* More precisely, economists define labor productivity as real GDP per hour of work in the economy as a whole. As you will see, labor productivity is important because it ultimately determines how much workers are paid. Higher labor productivity leads to higher pay for work.

### The Record on Jobs and Productivity

What is the long-term record on jobs in the United States economy? By any measure, the record is impressive. About 65 million more people have jobs now in the United States than 40 years ago. That amounts to an average of 1.6 million more people working each year. Figure 5.5 shows this large growth—a doubling of employment (the number of people working), from about 65 million to 130 million people.

This increase in the number of people holding jobs represents the net effect of new jobs being created and old jobs being lost. In a growing economy, many jobs are destroyed as tastes change and firms go out of business. But because even more new jobs are created by new and expanding businesses, there is a *net increase* in the number of jobs.

A much greater fraction of the population is working now than was working 40 years ago, largely because more women are in the work force. Thus, the economy has been successful in creating jobs for a growing population as well as for the growing fraction of people who are working.

What is the record on labor productivity? The annual growth rate of labor productivity has averaged about 1.3 percent per year when measured by real GDP per

**FIGURE 5.5**

**Number of People Holding Jobs**

Employment in the United States has doubled during the last 40 years. During each recession, the number of people working declines and then increases during the expansion.

*Source:* U.S. Department of Labor.

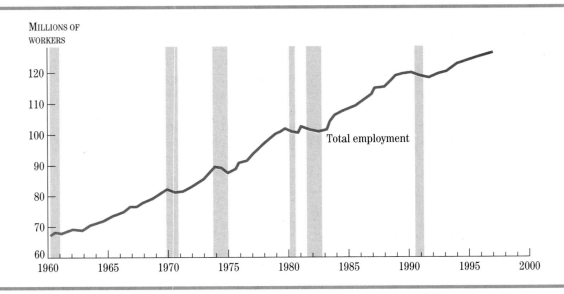

hour of work. However, just as there has been a slowdown in economic growth, there has been a slowdown in productivity growth over the longer term. Productivity growth averaged 2.0 percent from the 1950s to the 1970s and only 0.7 percent per year since then. Hence, the overall record on productivity growth is not as good as the record on job growth.

### *Unemployment During Recessions*

There are fluctuations in employment just as there are fluctuations in real GDP. In fact, the timing is nearly identical. Observe in Figure 5.5 that employment declines during recessions: Firms lay off workers in recessions, and it is difficult to find a job. But when real GDP starts to grow again during recovery periods, the number of jobs starts to increase again. The decline in the number of jobs during recessions is one of the reasons that recessions create severe hardship for people.

The fluctuations in employment may appear small and insignificant in Figure 5.5, but they are not insignificant if you lose your job. Workers who lose their jobs during recessions usually become unemployed. The **unemployment rate** is the number of unemployed people as a percentage of the labor force; the labor force consists of those who are either working or looking for work. Every time the economy goes into a recession, the unemployment rate rises because people are laid off and new jobs are difficult to find. The individual stories behind the unemployment numbers frequently represent frustration and distress.

Figure 5.6 shows what happens to the unemployment rate as the economy goes through recessions and recoveries. The increase in the unemployment rate during recessions is eventually followed by a decline in unemployment during the recovery. Note, for example, how unemployment rose during the recessions of 1969–1970 and 1973–1975. Around the time of the 1990–1991 recession, the unemployment rate rose from 5.1 percent to 7.8 percent.

Figure 5.7 shows how high the unemployment rate got during the Great Depression. It rose to over 25 percent; one in four workers was out of work. Fortunately, recent increases in unemployment during recessions have been much smaller. The unemployment rate reached 10.8 percent in the early 1980s, the highest level since World War II.

**unemployment rate:** the percentage of the labor force that is unemployed.

### FIGURE 5.6
### The Unemployment Rate

The number of unemployed workers as a percentage of the labor force—the unemployment rate—increases during recessions because people are laid off and it is difficult to find work. Sometimes the unemployment rate continues to increase for a while after the recession is over, as in 1971 and 1991. But eventually unemployment declines during the economic recovery.

*Source:* U.S. Department of Labor.

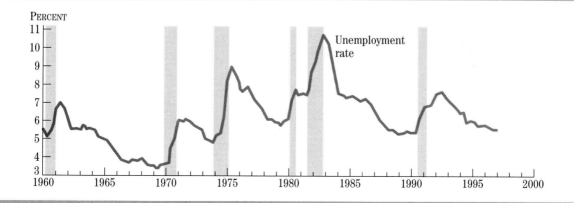

# Using Economics to Explain a Recession's Pain
## Around the Country

Although recessions, by definition, affect the whole economy, they have uneven effects on different regions. Some regions are hit at slightly different times and by different amounts. When the national recession is over, production and employment in certain regions of the country might still be falling.

The accompanying map shows the unemployment rate in each state of the United States in June 1992, a little over a year after the 1990–1991 recession ended. The national unemployment rate was 7.7 percent and coming down, but there was an enormous variety of unemployment experiences in different parts of the country. In California, Florida, Illinois, New York, New Jersey, Massachusetts, Michigan, Mississippi, and West Virginia, the unemployment rate was over 8.5 percent. But in several of the central and mountain states, the unemployment rate was less than 5.5 percent, below the national average in good times. Hence, while much of the country was still hurting from the recession, other parts had recovered.

The severity of the recession on California and New York may have had a significant impact on how people viewed the recession. For example, economic reporting about the recession may have depicted it as worse than it was for the economy as a whole, because many of the national media centers are in New York and California.

These regional differences also affect political strategy. When unemployment is high in a recession, people are less likely to vote for the incumbent; thus, states with very high unemployment rates might be given less attention when allocating scarce time and resources in a political campaign.

In the 1992 presidential election, which took place soon after the data shown on the map were collected, the incumbent president, George Bush, won only two of the nine states with unemployment over 8.5 percent. Bush lost in only two of the seven states with unemployment below 5.5 percent, and in both of these, Wisconsin and Iowa, he also lost in the 1988 election. Although the economy is not the only factor in elections, it seemed at least like a key factor in this case.

Why did high unemployment linger for so long in states like Massachusetts, California, and New York? One explanation helps us understand the causes of recessions. In the early 1990s, national defense expenditures were cut sharply. A large fraction of the California and Massachusetts economies produce military equipment. Hence, when national defense spending fell, employment in these regions fell sharply. There are other possible reasons. The California economy had an even stronger expansion than the rest of the national economy in the 1980s. This long expansion may have led to overbuilding, and when the expansion ended, people cut this back sharply. The construction business was particularly hard hit in this recession.

Another important example of regional differences is the Texas economy in the mid-1980s. While most of the national economy was expanding rapidly, the Texas economy went into a downturn because of a drop in the price of oil, a relatively large part of the Texas economy.

Similar regional differences exist in other countries. Unemployment has been higher in the south of Italy than in the north; and it has been higher in the north of the United Kingdom than in the south.

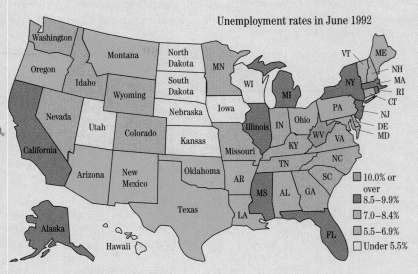

Unemployment rates in June 1992

10.0% or over
8.5–9.9%
7.0–8.4%
5.5–6.9%
Under 5.5%

*Source:* U.S. Department of Labor.

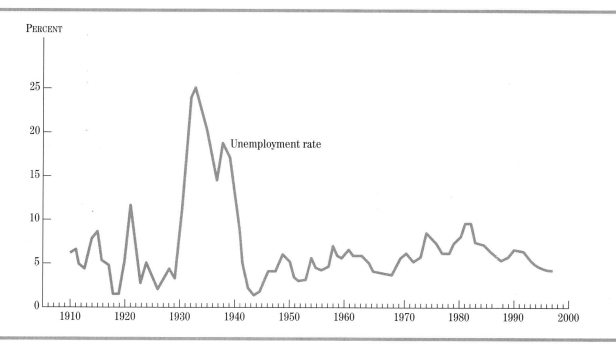

PERCENT

**FIGURE 5.7**
**Unemployment During the Great Depression**

The increase in unemployment in the United States during the Great Depression was huge compared with the increase in unemployment during more mild downturns in the economy. More than one in four workers were unemployed during the Great Depression.

*Source:* U.S. Department of Labor.

## Inflation

As output and jobs in the economy have grown and fluctuated over time, there have also been large changes in inflation, the general increase from year to year in the average price of goods and services. When inflation rises, people start to complain about how expensive everything is getting. When inflation gets very high, it begins to interfere with the workings of the economy because people and business firms find it difficult to determine the price of goods and services and worry about how much the price will change in the future. Thus low and stable inflation is considered a plus for an economy.

How does inflation actually behave? The **inflation rate** is the percentage increase in the average price of all goods and services from one year to the next. Figure 5.8 shows the inflation rate for the same 40-year period we have focused on in our examination of real GDP and employment. Clearly, a low and stable inflation rate has not been a feature of the United States during this period. There are several useful facts to note about the behavior of inflation.

First, inflation is closely correlated with the ups and downs in real GDP and employment: Inflation increased prior to every recession in the last 40 years and then subsided during and after every recession. We will want to explore whether this close correlation between the ups and downs in inflation and the ups and downs in the economy helps explain economic fluctuations.

Second, there are longer-term trends in inflation. For example, inflation rose from a low point in the mid-1960s to a high point of double-digit inflation in 1980. This period of persistently high inflation from the mid-1960s until 1980 is called the *Great Inflation.* The Great Inflation ended in the early 1980s, when the inflation rate declined substantially. Such a decline in inflation is called *disinflation.* (When inflation is negative and the average price level falls, economists call it *deflation.*)

**inflation rate:** the percentage increase in the overall price level over a given period of time, usually one year.

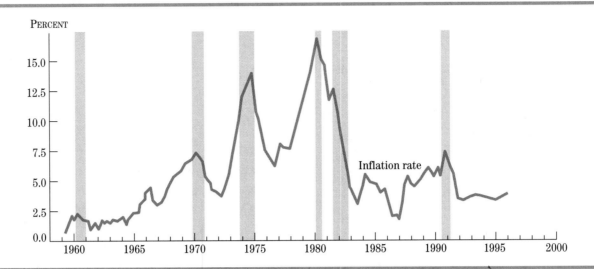

**FIGURE 5.8**
**The Ups and Downs in Inflation**
Inflation has increased before each recession and then declined during and immediately after each recession. In addition, a longer-term upward trend in inflation began in the mid-1960s and, after several ups and downs, reached a peak in 1980. In 1981–1983, America had a disinflation—a decline in the rate of inflation.
*Source:* U.S. Department of Labor (Consumer Price Index).

**interest rate:** the amount received per dollar loaned per year, usually expressed as a percentage (e.g., 6 percent) of the loan.

Third, judging by history, there is no reason to expect the inflation rate to be zero, even on average. Since the disinflation of the early 1980s, the inflation rate has remained around 3 or 4 percent in the United States.

Why does inflation increase before recessions? Why does inflation fall during and after recessions? What caused the Great Inflation? Why is inflation not equal to zero even in more normal times, when the economy is neither in recession nor in boom? What can economic policy do to keep inflation low and stable? These are some of the questions and policy issues about inflation addressed by macroeconomics.

## Interest Rates

The **interest rate** is the amount that lenders charge when they lend money, expressed as a percent of the amount loaned. For example, if you borrow $100 for a year from a friend and the interest rate on the loan is 6 percent, then you must pay your friend back $106 at the end of the year. The interest rate is another key economic variable that is related to the growth and change in real GDP over time.

### *Different Types of Interest Rates and Their Behavior*

There are many different interest rates in the economy: The *mortgage interest rate* is the rate on loans to buy a house; the *savings deposit interest rate* is the rate people get on their savings deposits at banks; the *Treasury bill rate* is the interest rate the government pays when it borrows money from people for a year or less; the *federal funds rate* is the interest rate banks charge each other on very short loans. Interest rates influence people's economic behavior. When interest rates rise, for example, it is more expensive to borrow funds to buy a house or a car, so many people postpone such purchases.

Figure 5.9 shows the behavior of a typical interest rate, the federal funds rate, during the last 40 years. First, note how closely the ups and downs in the interest rate are correlated with the ups and downs in the economy. Interest rates rise

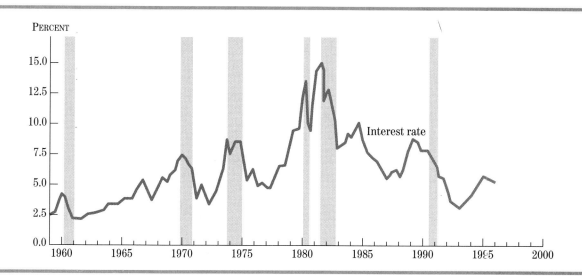

**FIGURE 5 9**
**The Ups and Downs in Interest Rates**

Interest rates generally rise just before a recession and then decline during and just after the recession. There was also a longer-term trend upward in interest rates in the 1960s and 1970s and a downward trend in the 1980s and 1990s. These longer-term trends are correlated with inflation, as shown in Figure 5.8. The interest rate shown here is the federal funds interest rate.

*Source:* Federal Reserve Board.

before each recession and then decline during and after each recession. Second, note that, like the inflation rate, there are longer-term trends in the interest rate. The interest rate rose from the mid-1960s until the 1980s. Each fluctuation in interest rates during this period brought forth a higher peak in interest rates. Then in the 1980s, the interest rate began a downward trend; each peak was lower than the previous peak. By the early 1990s, interest rates had returned to the levels of the 1960s.

### The Concept of the Real Interest Rate

As we will see, the trends and fluctuations in interest rates are intimately connected with the trends and fluctuations in inflation and real GDP. In fact, the longer-term rise in interest rates in the 1960s and 1970s was partly due to the rise in the rate of inflation. When inflation rises, people who lend money will be paid back in funds that are worth less because the average price of goods rises more quickly. To compensate for this decline in the value of funds, lenders require a higher interest rate. For example, if the inflation rate is 20 percent and you lend someone $100 for a year at 6 percent, then you get back $106 at the end of the year. However, the *average* price of goods you can buy with your $106 is now 20 percent higher. Thus, your 6 percent gain in interest has been offset by a 20 percent loss. It is as if you receive *negative* 14 percent interest: 6 percent interest less 20 percent inflation. The difference between the stated interest rate and the inflation rate is thus a better measure of the real interest rate. Economists define the **real interest rate** as the interest rate less the inflation rate people expect. The term **nominal interest rate** is sometimes used to refer to the interest rate on a loan, making no adjustment for inflation. For example, the real interest rate is 2 percent if the nominal interest rate is 5 percent and inflation is expected to be 3 percent (5 − 3 = 2). To keep the real interest rate from changing by a large amount as inflation rises, the nominal interest rate has to increase with inflation. Thus, the concept of the real interest rate helps us understand why inflation and interest rates have moved together. We will make much more use of the real interest rate in later chapters.

**real interest rate:** the interest rate minus the expected rate of inflation; it adjusts the nominal interest rate for inflation.

**nominal interest rate:** the interest rate uncorrected for inflation.

## Review

▶ The number of jobs has increased dramatically in the last 40 years as the population has grown and a greater percentage of the population has jobs.

▶ The number of jobs declines in recessions and rises during recoveries. The unemployment rate rises in recessions and falls during recoveries.

▶ Inflation and interest rates rise prior to recessions and then fall during and just after recessions.

▶ There was a longer-term increase in interest rates and inflation from the mid-1960s until the early 1980s. Interest rates and inflation have been lower again in the 1990s.

# MACROECONOMIC THEORY AND POLICY

Because strong economic growth raises living standards of people in an economy, and because increases in unemployment during recessions cause hardship, two goals of economic policy are to raise long-term growth and to reduce the size of short-term economic fluctuations. However, the facts—summarized above—about economic growth and fluctuations do not give economists a basis for making recommendations about economic policy. Before one can be confident about recommending a policy, one needs a coherent theory to explain the facts.

## Economic Growth Theory and Economic Fluctuation Theory

Macroeconomic theory is divided into two branches. *Economic growth theory* aims to explain the long-term upward rise of real GDP over time. Why does real GDP grow? Why does its growth slow down for long periods of time as it did in the mid-1970s? Will the long-term growth rate of real GDP pick up again? *Economic fluctuations theory* tries to explain the shorter-term fluctuations in real GDP. Economic growth theory and economic fluctuations theory combine to form *macroeconomic theory,* which explains why the economy both grows and fluctuates over time.

## Aggregate Supply and Long-Term Economic Growth

Economic growth theory starts by distinguishing the longer-term economic growth trend from the shorter-term fluctuations in the economy. This is not as easy as it may seem because the longer-term growth trend itself may change, as we have already seen from the long-term growth trend drawn in Figure 5.1. The trend line slows down in the mid-1970s. The growth trend could slow further or speed up in the future.

It will be useful to give a name to the upward trend line in real GDP shown in Figure 5.1. We will call it **potential GDP.** Potential GDP represents the long-run tendency of the economy to grow. Real GDP fluctuates around potential GDP. No one knows exactly where potential GDP lies and exactly what its growth rate is, but any trend line that has the same long-term increase as real GDP and intersects real GDP in several places is probably a good estimate.

Note that potential GDP as defined here and as used by most macroeconomists is not the maximum amount of real GDP. As Figure 5.1 shows, sometimes real GDP goes above potential GDP. Thus, potential GDP is more like the average or normal level of real GDP.

**potential GDP:** the economy's long-term growth trend for real GDP determined by the available supply of capital, labor, and technology. Real GDP fluctuates above and below potential GDP.

Economic growth theory postulates that the potential GDP of an economy is given by its **aggregate supply.** *Aggregate* means total. Aggregate supply is all goods and services produced by all the firms in the economy using the available labor, capital, and technology. **Labor** is the total number of hours workers are available to work in producing real GDP. **Capital** is the total number of factories, cultivated plots of land, machines, computers, and other tools available for the workers to use to produce real GDP. **Technology** is all the available know-how—from organizational schemes to improved telecommunications to better computer programming skills—that workers and firms can use when they produce real GDP. Labor, capital, and technology jointly determine aggregate supply.

### The Production Function

We can summarize the relationship between the three determinants and the aggregate supply of real GDP as:

Real GDP = $F$ (labor, capital, technology)

which we say in words as "real GDP is a function, $F$, of labor, capital, and technology." The function $F$ means that there is some general relationship between these variables. For this relationship, we assume that higher capital, higher labor, and higher technology all mean higher real GDP; and lower capital, lower labor, and lower technology all mean less real GDP. We call this relationship the **production function** because it tells us how much production (real GDP) of goods and services can be obtained from a certain amount of labor, capital, and technological inputs. A higher long-term economic growth rate for the economy requires a higher growth rate for one or more of these three determinants. A lower long-term economic growth rate may be due to a slower growth rate for one or more of these three determinants.

The production function applies to the entire economy, but we also have production functions for individual firms in the economy. For example, consider the production of cars. The car factory and the machines in the factory are the capital. The workers who work in the factory are the labor. The assembly-line production method is the technology. The cars coming out of the factory are the output. The production function for the economy as a whole has real GDP as output, not just cars, and all available labor, capital, and technology as inputs, not just those producing cars.

**aggregate supply:** the total value of all goods and services produced in the economy by the available supply of capital, labor, and technology (also called potential GDP).

**labor:** the number of hours people work in producing goods and services.

**capital:** the factories, improvements to cultivated land, machinery, and other tools, equipment, and structures used to produce goods and services.

**technology:** anything that raises the amount of output that can be produced with a given amount of labor and capital.

**production function:** the relationship that describes output as a function of labor, capital, and technology.

### Aggregate Supply and the Production Function

The theory of economic growth is based on the production function, which is a model of how labor ($L$), capital ($K$) and technology ($T$) jointly determine the aggregate supply of output in the economy. Here the workers at the automobile plant are part of the economy's labor (left), the tools that the workers are using to assemble the cars are the economy's capital (middle), and computer programming skills are part of the economy's technology (right), which raises the value of output for a given amount of labor and capital.

"That, in itself, is a breakthrough."

The production function can be written more compactly by introducing some symbols:

$$Y = F(L, K, T)$$

where the symbol $Y$ means real GDP, the symbol $L$ means labor, the symbol $K$ means capital, and the symbol $T$ means technology. This function tells us that an economy can increase its potential GDP by increasing labor ($L$), capital ($K$), and technology ($T$).

As we develop the theory of economic growth, we will consider each of these three determinants. But we can illustrate the use of the production function for explaining economic growth with what we have so far. For example, we noted earlier that the growth rate of real GDP slowed down in the 1970s. We now know that the slowdown must have been due to a slowdown of the growth of labor, capital, or technology. By the end of Chapter 9, we will be able to show that a large part, though not all, of the slowdown was due to technology.

## Government Policy for Long-Term Economic Growth

Most governments have been interested in finding ways to increase economic growth. Economic policies that aim to increase long-term economic growth are sometimes called *supply side policies* because they concentrate on increasing the growth of potential GDP, which is the aggregate supply of the economy.

### *Fiscal Policy*

Our preview of growth theory already tells us where policies to increase growth should focus: on increasing the available supply of labor, capital, and technology. The growth rate of capital depends on how much businesses invest in new capital each year. The amount that businesses choose to invest depends in part on the incentives they have to invest. We will see that the incentive to invest depends on the amount of taxing, spending, and borrowing by government. Hence, government policy can affect the incentive to invest and thereby stimulate long-term economic growth. Government policy concerning taxing, spending, and borrowing is called *fiscal policy.*

Labor supply also depends on incentives. In the case of labor, it is the incentive for firms to hire workers or for people to work harder or longer, or for workers who are not in the labor force to come into the labor force, or for people to retire later in life. Again, government policy toward taxing, spending, and borrowing affects these incentives.

Finally, technology growth can also be affected by government policy if the government gives incentives for researchers to invent new technologies or provides funds for education so workers can improve their skills and know-how.

### *Monetary Policy*

Keeping inflation low and stable is another part of government policy to stimulate long-term economic growth. We will see that the government has an important role to play in determining the inflation rate, especially over the long term, because the inflation rate in the long term depends on the growth rate of the money supply, which can be controlled by the government. Government policy concerning the money supply and the control of inflation is called *monetary policy.* The institution of government assigned to conduct monetary policy is the central bank. In the United States the central bank is the Federal Reserve System.

Why should low and stable inflation be part of an economic growth policy? An examination of inflation and economic growth in a number of countries indicates that inflation is negatively correlated with long-term economic growth. The reason for this negative correlation over the long term may be that inflation raises uncertainty and thereby reduces incentives to invest in capital or improve technology. The theory of economic growth tells us that lower capital growth and lower technological growth reduce economic growth.

## Economic Fluctuations Theory and Policy

Our review of the performance of the economy showed some of the hardships that come from economic fluctuations, especially the recessions and unemployment. Can government economic policy improve economic performance by reducing the size of the fluctuations? To answer these questions, we need a theory to interpret the facts of economic fluctuations.

The theory of economic fluctuations builds on the works of many economists—including John Maynard Keynes's 1936 book *The General Theory of Employment, Interest and Money;* Milton Friedman and Anna Schwartz's 1963 book *A Monetary History of the United States;* and a 1981 book, *Rational Expectations and Econometric Practice,* edited by Robert Lucas and Thomas Sargent.

### Aggregate Demand and Economic Fluctuations

The theory of economic fluctuations emphasizes fluctuations in the demand for goods and services as the reason for the ups and downs in the economy. Because the focus is on the sum of the demand for all goods and services in the economy— not only the demand for peanuts or bicycles—we use the term *aggregate demand.* More precisely, **aggregate demand** is the sum of demands from the four groups that contribute to demand in the whole economy: consumers, business firms, government, and foreigners. Originally, due to the influence of Keynes, the theory placed great emphasis on fluctuations in aggregate demand brought about by changes in demand by business firms. But Friedman and Schwartz argued that other parts of the economy, especially government, play a crucial role through adjustments in the money supply.

**aggregate demand:** the total demand for goods and services by consumers businesses, government, and foreigners.

According to this theory, the declines in real GDP below potential GDP during recessions are caused by declines in aggregate demand, and the increases in real GDP above potential GDP are caused by increases in aggregate demand. For example, the decrease in real GDP in the 1990–1991 recession may have been due to a decline in government demand. In fact, government military spending did decline sharply. Or the recession may have been due to a decline in demand by consumers as they learned about Iraq's invasion of Kuwait in August 1990, saw oil and gasoline prices rise, and worried about the threat of war.

Thus, a key assumption of the theory of economic fluctuations is that real GDP fluctuates around potential GDP. Why is this a good assumption? How do we know that the fluctuations in the economy are not due solely to fluctuations in potential GDP, that is, the economy's aggregate supply? The rationale for the assumption is that most of the determinants of potential GDP usually change rather smoothly. Clearly, population grows relatively smoothly. We do not have a sudden drop in the U.S. population every few years, nor is there a huge migration of people from the

United States during recessions. The same is true with factories and equipment in the economy. Unless there is a major war at home, we do not suddenly lose equipment or factories in the economy on a massive scale. Even the 1992 hurricane in Florida, the 1994 earthquake in California, or the 1997 flood in North Dakota, although devastating for those hit, took only a tiny fraction out of the potential GDP of the entire U.S. economy. Finally, technological know-how does not suddenly decline; we do not suddenly forget how to produce things. The steady upward movement of potential GDP thus represents gradual accumulations—growth of population, growth of capital, and growth of technology. However, although many economists place more emphasis on the role of aggregate demand in short-run economic fluctuations than on fluctuations in potential GDP, it is too extreme to insist that there are absolutely no fluctuations in potential GDP.

### *Macroeconomic Policy for Economic Fluctuations*

Macroeconomic policy has huge effects on economic fluctuations. In particular, fiscal and monetary policy can influence the size of the ups and downs in the economy just as they can influence economic growth. For example, an increase in government spending in a recession might increase aggregate demand and mitigate other forces that reduce aggregate demand. When we look at fiscal and monetary policy, we address such questions as: Is there something the government can do to improve the performance of the economy to prevent recessions from occurring? Can monetary policy prevent another Great Depression and perhaps even reduce the likelihood of all recessions? How can we avoid in the future another bout of high inflation like the Great Inflation?

## Review

▶ Economic growth theory concentrates on explaining the longer-term upward path of the economy.

▶ Economic growth depends on three factors: the growth of capital, labor, and technology.

▶ Government policy can influence long-term economic growth by affecting these three factors. To raise long-term economic growth, government fiscal policies can provide incentives for investment in capital, for research and development of new technologies, for education, and for increased labor

supply. A monetary policy of low and stable inflation can also have a positive effect on economic growth.

▶ Economic fluctuations theory assumes that fluctuations in GDP are due to fluctuations in aggregate demand.

▶ Monetary policy and fiscal policy can reduce the fluctuations in real GDP. Finding good rules for such policies is a major task of macroeconomics.

## CONCLUSION

This chapter started with a brief history of economic growth and fluctuations in the United States. Although this history mentioned specific individuals (presidents, economists, journalists), institutions (the government, the Federal Reserve System), and episodes (the Great Depression and the Great Inflation), the most important facts to remember are the patterns formed by the major economic variables. The key facts, therefore, are that economic growth provides impressive gains in the well-being of

---

## MACROECONOMIC FACTS

### Long-Term Economic Growth

1. Real GDP per capita growth has been spectacular over the last 75 years.
2. The number of jobs rose dramatically too.
3. Real GDP per capita growth slowed in the 1970s.
4. Productivity growth also slowed in the 1970s.
5. Inflation is negatively correlated with economic growth in many countries.

### Short-Term Economic Fluctuations

1. There have been 15 business cycles in 75 years, averaging 1 every 5 years.
2. Unemployment rose in every recession.
3. Inflation rose before recessions and fell during and after recessions.
4. Interest rates rose before recessions and fell during and after recessions.
5. The Great Depression was much worse than recent recessions.

---

## MACROECONOMIC THEORY

1. Long-term economic growth is due primarily to increases in aggregate supply.
   - Aggregate supply depends on the availability of labor, capital, and technology, whose relationship to one another is expressed by the production function.
   - Potential GDP gradually increases over time.

2. Short-term economic fluctuations are due primarily to fluctuations in aggregate demand.
   - Real GDP fluctuates around potential GDP.
   - Fluctuations in potential GDP play a smaller role.

---

## MACROECONOMIC POLICY

### To Increase Long-Term Growth

1. Fiscal policy should provide incentives to invest in capital, technology, and labor.
2. Monetary policy should keep inflation low and stable.

### To Reduce Short-Term Fluctuations

1. Fiscal and monetary policy should do no harm.
2. These policies should try to mitigate changes in aggregate demand.

---

individuals over the long term, that economic growth slowed down in the 1970s, that economic growth is temporarily interrupted by recessions, which have grown smaller in magnitude since the 1930s, that employment falls and unemployment rises in recessions, that all recessions end, that inflation rises before recessions and declines during and after recessions, and that interest rates also rise before recessions and then fall. These are the facts on which macroeconomic theory is based and about which macroeconomic policy is concerned. Remembering these facts not only helps you understand theory and make judgments about government policy, it prevents you from being fooled by people who try to distort economic history. Do not believe someone who tells you in the middle of the next recession—whenever it occurs—that it is the worst since the Great Depression—unless of course it is!

The connection between the facts, the theory, and the policy is shown schematically in Figure 5.10. After showing how we obtain the facts in the next chapter, we then go on to look at explanations for economic growth and economic fluctuations and proposals for macroeconomic policies.

**FIGURE 5.10**

**Macroeconomic Facts, Theory, and Policy**

This diagram summarizes some of the key ideas of macroeconomics that will be explored in later chapters. Looking through the diagram may help you see the forest of macroeconomics through the trees of facts and theory.

# KEY POINTS

**1.** Macroeconomics is concerned with economic growth and fluctuations in the whole economy.

**2.** The U.S. economy and many other economies have grown dramatically over the last 40 years. Long-term growth has slowed among the most advanced countries in the last 20 years.

**3.** Economists agree that economic growth occurs because of increases in labor, capital, and technological know-how.

**4.** Economic policies that provide incentives to increase capital and resources devoted to improving technology can raise productivity growth.

**5.** Economic fluctuations consist of recessions—when real GDP falls and unemployment increases—followed by recoveries—when real GDP rises rapidly and unemployment falls.

**6.** Recent recessions have been much less severe than the Great Depression of the 1930s, when real GDP fell by over 30 percent.

**7.** The unemployment rate is well above zero even when the economy is booming.

**8.** The most popular theory of economic fluctuations is that they occur because of fluctuations in aggregate demand.

**9.** Macroeconomic policies include monetary and fiscal policies that are aimed at keeping business cycles small and inflation low.

**10.** Economic growth theory and economic fluctuations theory combine to form macroeconomic theory, which explains why the economy grows and fluctuates over time.

# KEY TERMS

real gross domestic product (real GDP)
economic growth
economic fluctuations
business cycles
recession
peak
trough

expansion
recovery
labor productivity
unemployment rate
inflation rate
interest rate
real interest rate
nominal interest rate

potential GDP
aggregate supply
labor
capital
technology
production function
aggregate demand

# QUESTIONS FOR REVIEW

**1.** By how much did real GDP grow in the last 40 years?

**2.** What is the economic growth slowdown, and when did .it occur?

**3.** Why do bad economic times continue after recessions end?

**4.** Why does unemployment rise in recessions?

**5.** How many recessions have there been since the Great Depression?

**6.** How do the 1981–1982 and the 1990–1991 recessions compare?

**7.** What happens to inflation and interest rates immediately before, during, and after a recession?

**8.** What are the two broad branches of macroeconomic theory?

**9.** What are the three determinants of economic growth?

**10.** What is potential GDP?

**11.** What is aggregate demand?

**12.** What is the difference between monetary policy and fiscal policy?

# PROBLEMS

**1.** The chart at the top of the next page shows a business cycle that occurred in the United States in the early 1950s. The early 1950s were similar to the early 1990s in the sense that America was adjusting to the end of a war—World War II rather than the cold war, and to the return of a political party to the White House after a long absence—from Democrat to Republican rather than from Republican to Democrat. The economy expanded at a 2.5 percent growth rate in late 1951 and 1952, which appears to have been near the economy's potential growth rate. Draw in potential GDP and show the peak, recession, trough, and recovery phases of this business cycle. Compare this business cycle with the cycle in the early 1990s shown in Figure 5.3.

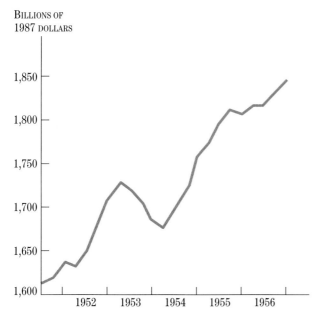

BILLIONS OF
1987 DOLLARS

*Source:* U.S. Department of Commerce.

INFLATION
(PERCENT)

*Source:* Organization for Economic Cooperation and Development.

**2.** Suppose the U.S. economy is currently at the trough of a business cycle. What is the relationship between real and potential GDP? Is it likely that real GDP will stay in this relative position for a long period of time (say, 10 years)? Explain briefly.

**3.** List several economic topics from this week's newspapers that are examples of macroeconomic issues. Which of the issues are related to economic growth, and which are related to economic fluctuations? Which are related to economic policy?

**4.** The following charts show the inflation rate for the four largest countries in Europe. Compare inflation in these countries with that in the United States as discussed in the chapter. Is a Great Inflation observable in the other countries? Which countries had the best inflation performances, and which had the worst? In which country would you expect interest rates to be lowest in 1976?

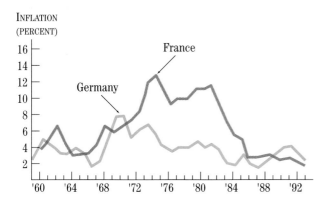

INFLATION
(PERCENT)

**5.** Using the following data from Great Britain, plot real GDP on the vertical axis and the year on the horizontal axis. Can you differentiate economic growth from economic fluctuations?

| Year | Real GDP (billions of pounds) | Rate of Unemployment (percent) |
|------|-------------------------------|--------------------------------|
| 1977 | 312 | 5.2 |
| 1978 | 324 | 4.9 |
| 1979 | 331 | 4.5 |
| 1980 | 324 | 6.1 |
| 1981 | 321 | 9.1 |
| 1982 | 325 | 10.4 |
| 1983 | 338 | 11.2 |
| 1984 | 343 | 11.4 |
| 1985 | 356 | 11.6 |
| 1986 | 370 | 11.8 |
| 1987 | 387 | 10.4 |
| 1988 | 404 | 8.2 |
| 1989 | 413 | 6.2 |
| 1990 | 417 | 5.9 |
| 1991 | 408 | 8.3 |
| 1992 | 404 | 10.1 |
| 1993 | 413 | 10.3 |
| 1994 | 429 | 9.3 |
| 1995 | 442 | 8.3 |
| 1996 | 455 | 8.1 |

a) Draw a line that shows the trend of potential GDP. Identify the years of the peaks, troughs, recessions, and expansions.

b) How does the timing of these business cycles compare with the U.S. business cycle shown in Figure 5.1?
c) Calculate the growth rate from 1989 to 1990 and from 1990 to 1991.
d) Calculate the average annual growth rate from 1977 to 1986 and from 1987 to 1996. (*Hint:* See the formula in the appendix to this chapter.) In which period was economic growth larger?
e) What relationship do you see between unemployment and real GDP?

**6.** Compare Figure 5.1 showing real GDP with Figure 5.5 showing employment for the same period in the United States. Describe how real GDP and employment are correlated over the long term and over the short term. Do employment and real GDP rise or fall over the long term? Explain why. Do they rise or fall during recessions? Try to explain why.

**7.** Suppose the annual rate of growth of real GDP per capita is 2 percent. How much will real GDP increase over a 10-year period? How much over a 50-year period? Answer the same questions for a growth rate of 1 percent. (*Hint:* See the formula in the appendix to this chapter.)

**8.** The shaded block in the following table shows the amount of output that can be produced using different combinations of capital and labor in a hypothetical economy with a particular technology. For example, 226 units of output are produced when 200 workers use 300 units of capital. The table is a numerical example of the production function described in the chapter. Hold capital constant at 300 while you increase labor. What happens to output? Now hold labor constant at 200 workers and raise the level of capital. What happens to output? Finally, what happens if you increase both capital and labor by the same amount?

|        | Labor |       |       |       |       |
|--------|-------|-------|-------|-------|-------|
|        | 100   | 200   | 300   | 400   | 500   |
| 100    | 100   | 162   | 216   | 264   | 309   |
| 200    | 123   | 200   | 266   | 325   | 380   |
| 300    | 139   | 226   | 300   | 367   | 429   |
| 400    | 152   | 246   | 327   | 400   | 468   |
| 500    | 162   | 263   | 350   | 428   | 500   |

(Capital labels the left column: 100, 200, 300, 400, 500)

**9.** Suppose there is a permanent decrease in the labor force. How does this affect the economy's potential GDP?

**10.** Suppose you had savings deposited in an account at an interest rate of 5 percent and your father tells you that he earned 10 percent interest 20 years ago. Which of you was getting the better return? Is that all the information you need? Suppose that the inflation rate in the United States was 12 percent 20 years ago and it is 3 percent now. Does this information change your answer? Be sure to use the concept of the real interest rate in your answer.

**11.** Suppose you have $1,000, which you can put in two different types of accounts at a bank. One account pays interest of 7 percent per year; the other pays interest at 1 percent per year plus the rate of inflation. Calculate the real return you will receive after 1 year if the inflation rate is 4 percent. Which account will you choose if you expect the rate of inflation to be 9 percent? Why?

**12.** Suppose people start retiring at a later age because of improved medical technology. How does this affect the economy's potential GDP? Why might the government want to encourage later retirement?

**13.** What factors can cause fluctuations in aggregate demand? Are these the same as the determinants of potential GDP? Why do economists think that changes in aggregate demand are the primary cause of short-term economic fluctuations?

**14.** What determines potential GDP? What factors could cause the growth rate of potential GDP to slow down? What economic policies can the government use to affect potential GDP?

**15.** What is the difference between increasing labor productivity and increasing real GDP? Why do governments want to pursue policies that improve labor productivity?

# The Miracle of Compound Growth

*Compound growth* explains why small differences in the annual economic growth rate make such huge differences to real GDP over time. This appendix explains this compounding effect and provides some simple formulas for computing growth rates with a hand calculator.

Compound growth works just like compound interest on a savings account. Compound interest is defined as the "interest on the interest" you earn in earlier periods. For example, suppose you have a savings account in a bank that pays 6 percent per year in interest. That is, if you put $100 in the account, then after one year you will get $100 times .06, or $6 in interest. If you leave the original $100 plus the $6—that is, $106—in the bank for a second year, then at the end of the second year you will get $106 times .06, or $6.36 in interest. The $.36 is the "interest on the interest," that is, $6 times .06.

At the end of the second year you have $100 + $6 + $6.36 = $112.36. If you leave that in the bank for a third year, you will get $6.74 in interest, of which $.74 is "interest on the interest" earned in the first two years. Note how the "interest on the interest" rises from $.36 in the second year to $.74 in the third year. Following the same calculations, the interest on the interest in the fourth year would be $1.15. After 13 years, "interest on the interest" is greater than the $6 interest on the original $100! As a result of this compound interest, the size of your account grows rapidly. At the end of 20 years it is $320.71; after 40 years your $100 has grown to $1,028.57.

This same idea applies to the growth of an economy. Suppose that real GDP is $100 billion, about the level of Taiwan's, and that the growth rate is 6 percent per year, about the Taiwan average in recent years. After one year, real GDP would increase $100 billion times .06, or by $6 billion. Real GDP rises from $100 billion to $106 billion. In the second year, real GDP increases $106 billion times .06, or by $6.36 billion. Real GDP rises from $106 billion to $112.36 billion. Continuing this way, here is how real GDP grows, rounding to the nearest $.1 billion:

| | Real GDP (billions) | | Real GDP (billions) |
|---|---|---|---|
| year 0 | $ 100.0 | year 20 | $ 320.7 |
| year 1 | $ 106.0 | year 30 | $ 574.3 |
| year 2 | $ 112.4 | year 40 | $1,028.6 |
| year 3 | $ 119.1 | year 50 | $1,842.0 |
| year 4 | $ 126.2 | year 60 | $3,298.8 |
| year 5 | $ 133.3 | year 70 | $5,907.6 |
| year 10 | $ 179.1 | | |

Thus, in less than the average life span, real GDP in Taiwan would increase by about 60 times and approach the current level of the United States.

There is a simple formula for computing these changes, which comes from multiplying 1.06 by the initial level year after year. For example, the level of real GDP after one year is $100 billion times .06 plus $100 billion, or $100 billion times 1.06; after two years, it is $106 billion times 1.06, or $100 billion times $(1.06)^2$. Thus, for *n* years the formula is

(Initial level) times $(1.06)^n$ = level at end of *n* years

where the initial level could be $100 in a bank, the $100 billion level of real GDP, or anything else. For example, real GDP at the end of 70 years in the table shown earlier is: $100 billion times $(1.06)^n$ = $100 billion times 59.076 = $5,907.6 billion, with *n* = 70. Here the growth rate (or the interest rate) is 6 percent. In general, the formula is:

(Initial level) times $(1 + g)^n$ = level at end of *n* years

where *g* is the annual growth rate, stated as a fraction: that is, 6 percent is .06. If you have a hand calculator with a key that does $y^x$, it is fairly easy to make these calculations, and if you try it you will see the power of compound growth.

When economists refer to average annual growth over time they include this compounding effect. The growth rate is computed by inverting the formula. That is, the growth rate, stated as a fraction, between some initial level and a level *n* years later is given by:

$$g = \left(\frac{\text{level at end of } n \text{ years}}{\text{initial level}}\right)^{1/n} - 1$$

For example, the growth rate from year 0 to year 20 in the table is:

$$g = \left(\frac{320.7}{100}\right)^{1/20} - 1$$
$$= (1.06) - 1$$
$$= .06$$

or 6 percent. Again, if your calculator has a key for $y^x$, you can make these calculations fairly easily. For a one-year growth rate, you simply need to divide the second year by the first and subtract 1 to get the growth rate. Problem 5 in Chapter 5 gives some exercises in computing growth rates.

You can use this formula to find how long it takes something to rise by a certain percentage. For example, to calculate how many years it takes something that grows at rate *g* to double, you solve $(1 + g)^n = 2$ for *n*. The answer is approximately *n* = .72/*g*. In other words, if you take 72 and divide it by the growth rate in percent, you get the number of years it takes to double the amount. This is called the *rule of 72*. If your bank account pays 7.2 percent interest, it doubles in 10 years.

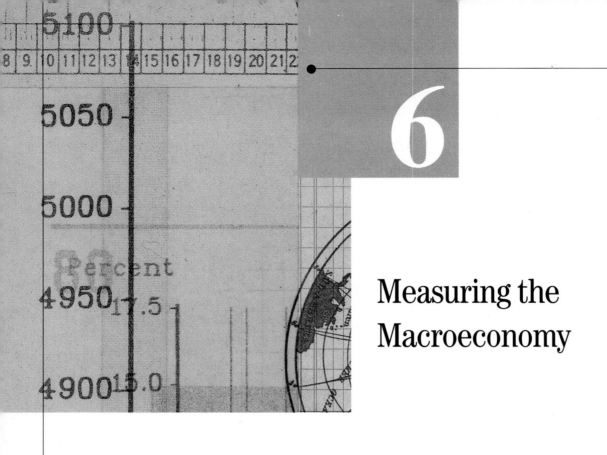

# 6

# Measuring the Macroeconomy

Whether they measure the performance of a quarterback, the weather patterns over the past 100,000 years, the severity of an earthquake, or the balance in your bank account, statistics are seldom interesting in their own right. Their value lies in the information we derive from them. Economic statistics contain valuable information about how the economy works. Every Monday the *Wall Street Journal* and other papers publish a list of the dates on which key statistics will be released during the week; when they are released, the data are headlines in many newspapers, frequently on the first page. In fact, if we use headlines as a gauge, economic statistics are as newsworthy as sports, politics, or weather statistics.

For those who run private business firms or government agencies, measuring the economy accurately is essential. Faulty economic statistics can lead to bad decisions. For example, many economists argue that overestimates of inflation cause the government to spend much more than it otherwise would. Bond and stock traders in New York, Tokyo, London, and everywhere else, glue their eyes to their computer terminals when a new government statistic measuring the course of the economy is about to be released. By buying or selling quickly in

reaction to the new information, they can make millions or avoid losing millions. Economists in the government likewise await economic statistics eagerly; the data will determine what fiscal and monetary policy actions they should recommend. In fact, top officials at the White House (including the president) find the data so important that they make sure they get them the night before they are released to the public.

To economists, economic measurement is interesting in its own right, involving clever solutions to intriguing problems. One of the first Nobel Prizes in economics was given to Simon Kuznets for solving some of these measurement problems. Economics students cannot help but learn a little about how the economy works when they study how to measure it, just like geology students cannot help but learn a little about earthquakes when they study how the Richter scale measures them.

In this chapter we examine how economists measure a country's production and the income that is generated from this production. We stated in the previous chapter that real gross domestic product (real GDP) is the most comprehensive measure we have of a country's production. But before measuring *real* GDP, we must show how to measure GDP itself. In the process of describing the measurement of GDP, we will observe several key relationships and interpret what these relationships mean.

# MEASURING GDP

To use GDP as a measure of production, we need to be precise about *what* is included in production, *where* production takes place, and *when* production takes place.

## A Precise Definition of GDP

*GDP is a measure of the value of all the final goods and services newly produced in a country during some period of time.* Let us dissect this definition to determine what is in GDP and what is not, as well as where and when GDP is produced.

▶ *What?* Only *newly produced* goods and services are included. That 10-year-old baby carriage sold in a garage sale is not in this year's GDP; it was included in GDP 10 years ago, when it was produced. Both *goods*—such as automobiles and new houses —as well as *services*—such as bus rides or a college education—are included in GDP.

▶ *Where?* Only goods and services produced *within the borders* of a country are included in GDP. Goods produced by Americans working in another country are not part of U.S. GDP; they are part of the other country's GDP. Goods and services produced by foreigners working in the United States are part of U.S. GDP. There is another measure, gross national product (GNP), which is like GDP except that it includes goods produced by Americans working abroad and excludes goods produced in America by foreigners.

▶ *When?* Only goods and services produced *during some specified period* of time are included in GDP. We always need to specify the period during which we are measuring GDP. For example, U.S. GDP in 1998 is the production during 1998. Production during a year is 365 times larger than production for a typical day.

Rounded off to the nearest billion, GDP, or total production, was $7,576 billion in the United States in 1996. Rounded off to the nearest trillion, GDP was $8 trillion. That is an average production of about $21 billion worth of goods and services a day for each of the 365 days during the year. GDP grew by about 5 percent from 1995 to 1996.

### Prices Determine the Importance of Goods and Services in GDP

GDP is a single number, but it measures the production of many different things, from apples to oranges, from car insurance to life insurance, from audio CDs to cassette tapes. How can we add up such different products? Is a CD more important than a tape? Each good is given a weight when we compute GDP and that weight is its *price*. If the price of a CD is greater than the price of a tape, then the CD will count more in GDP.

To see this, imagine that production consists entirely of CDs and tapes. If a CD costs $15 and a tape costs $5, then producing three CDs will add $45 to GDP while

**TABLE 6.1**
**Adding Up Unlike Products: Audio CDs and Cassette Tapes**

| 7 tapes<br>+3 CDs | $ 5 per tape<br>$15 per CD | $35 of tape production<br>+$45 of CD production |
|---|---|---|
| ? | | $80 of tape and CD production |

| To add up unlike products . . . | . . . we multiply by their prices to get the dollar value of each . . . | . . . and add together the dollar value of each to get the dollar value of the sum. |

producing seven tapes will add $35 to GDP. Thus, producing three CDs plus seven tapes adds $80 to GDP, as shown in Table 6.1.

Although this method of weighting by price might not appeal to you personally—you might like tapes more than CDs—it is hard to imagine anything more workable. In a market system, prices tend to reflect the cost and value of the goods and services produced. One of the great problems of measuring GDP in the former centrally planned economies such as the Soviet Union was that the price of goods was set by the government; thus, each item was given a weight that may have had little to do with its cost or value to individuals. Without market prices, measuring GDP in the former Soviet Union was difficult.

### Intermediate Goods Are Part of Final Goods

When measuring GDP, it is important not to count the same item more than once. This can occur if you are not careful. Consider bicycle tires. When you buy a $150 bicycle, the tires are considered part of the bicycle. Suppose the tires are worth $20. Then it would be a mistake to count the $20 value of the tires and the $150 value of the bicycle for a total value of $170. That would count the tires twice, which is called double counting. When a tire is part of a new bicycle, it is an example of an **intermediate good.** Intermediate goods are part of **final goods,** which by definition are goods that undergo no further processing. In this case, the final good is the bicycle. To avoid double counting, we never count intermediate goods; only final goods are part of GDP. If in a few years you bought a new $25 bicycle tire for your bicycle, then the tire would be a final good.

**intermediate good:** a good that undergoes further processing before it is sold to consumers.

**final good:** a new good that undergoes no further processing before it is sold to consumers.

### Three Ways to Measure GDP

Economists have three different ways to measure GDP. All give the same answer, but they refer to conceptually different activities in the economy and provide different ways to think about GDP. All three are important in the development of macroeconomic theory and are reported in the **national income and product accounts,** the official U.S. government tabulation of GDP put together by economists and statisticians at the U.S. Department of Commerce.

The first way measures the total amount that people *spend* on goods and services made in America. This is the *spending* approach. The second way measures the total *income* that is earned by all the workers and businesses that produce American goods and services. This is the *income* approach. By this measure, your income is a measure of what you produce. The third way measures the total of all the goods and services as they are *produced,* or as they are shipped out of the fac-

**national income and product accounts:** official government tabulation of the components of GDP and aggregate income.

tory. This is the *production* approach. Note that each of the measures considers the whole economy, and thus, we frequently refer to them as aggregate spending, aggregate income, or aggregate production, where the word *aggregate* means total. Let us consider each of the three approaches in turn.

## The Spending Approach

Typically, total spending in the economy is divided into four categories: *consumption, investment, government purchases,* and *net exports,* which equal exports minus imports. Each of the four categories corresponds closely to one of four groups into which the economy is divided: consumers, businesses, governments, and foreigners. Before considering each category and group, look at Table 6.2, which shows how the $7,576 billion of GDP in the United States in 1996 divided into the four categories.

### Consumption

The first category—**consumption**—includes purchases of final goods and services by individuals. Government statisticians who collect the data in most countries survey department stores, discount stores, car dealers, and other sellers to see how much consumers purchase each year ($5,152 billion in 1996, as given in Table 6.2). They count consumption as anything purchased by consumers. Consumption does not include spending by business and government. Consumer purchases may be big-ticket items such as a new convertible, an operation to remove a cancerous tumor, a new stereo, a weekend vacation, or college tuition, as well as smaller-ticket items such as an oil change, a medical checkup, a rose for a friend, a bus ride, or a driver's education class.

Consumption is a whopping 68 percent of GDP in the United States (See Figure 6.1). By comparison, consumption is 58 percent of GDP in Japan and 55 percent of GDP in Germany. Many consider the high consumption rate of Americans to be a serious economic problem because it represents less saving for the future than in other countries.

### Investment

The second item—**investment**—consists of purchases of final goods by business firms. When a business such as a pizza delivery firm buys a new car, economists consider that purchase as part of investment rather than consumption. The firm uses the car to make deliveries, which contributes to its production of delivered pizzas. Included in investment are all the new machines, new factories, and other tools that businesses use to produce goods and services. Purchases of intermediate goods that go directly into a manufactured product—such as the tire that is part of a bicycle—

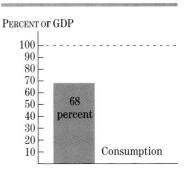

PERCENT OF GDP

**FIGURE 6.1**
**Consumption as a Share of GDP**
Consumption is 68 percent of GDP in the United States.

**consumption:** purchases of final goods and services by individuals.

**investment:** purchases of final goods by firms plus purchases of newly produced residences by households.

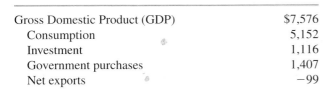

| Gross Domestic Product (GDP) | $7,576 |
|---|---|
| Consumption | 5,152 |
| Investment | 1,116 |
| Government purchases | 1,407 |
| Net exports | −99 |

*Source:* U.S. Department of Commerce.

**TABLE 6.2**
**Four Categories of Spending in 1996**
(billions of dollars)

**business fixed investment:** investment by firms in physical capital, such as factories and equipment.

**inventory investment:** a change in the stock of inventories from one date to another.

are not counted as investment. These items are part of the finished product—the bicycle, in this case—purchased by consumers. We do not want to count such items twice.

The new machines, factories, and other tools that are part of investment in any year are sometimes called **business fixed investment,** which amounted to $791 billion in 1996. There are two other items that government statisticians include as part of investment: inventory investment and residential investment.

**Inventory investment** is defined as the change in *inventories,* which are the goods on store shelves, on showroom floors, or in warehouses that have not yet been sold or assembled into a final form for sale. For example, cars on the lot of a car dealer are part of inventories. When inventory investment is positive, then inventories are rising. When inventory investment is negative, then inventories are falling. For example, if a car dealer has an inventory of 20 cars on September 30, gets 15 new cars shipped from the factory during the month of October, and sells no cars during the month, then the dealer's inventory will be 35 cars on October 31. Inventory investment is positive 15 cars, and inventory rises from 20 cars to 35 cars. If 22 cars are then sold during the month of November and there are no shipments from the factory, then the dealer's inventory will be 13 cars on November 30. Inventory investment is negative 22 cars, and inventory decreases from 35 cars to 13 cars.

Why is inventory investment included as a spending item when we compute GDP? The reason is that we want a measure of production. Consider the car example again. Car production rises by one car when a complete Jeep rolls out of the factory. But the Jeep is not usually instantaneously purchased by a consumer. First, the Jeep is shipped to the Jeep dealer, where it is put on the lot. If the government statisticians look at what consumers purchase, they will not count the Jeep because it has not been purchased yet. But if inventory investment is counted as part of investment spending, then the Jeep will get counted. That is why we include inventory investment in spending.

What happens when a consumer purchases the Jeep? Consumption will rise because the purchases of Jeeps have risen and the car dealer's inventory goes down by one car. Thus, inventory investment is negative one car. Adding one Jeep consumed to negative one Jeep of inventory investment gives zero, which is just what we want because there is no change in production.

In 1996 inventory investment throughout the economy was $14 billion. Some firms added inventories and others subtracted. Inventory investment tends to fluctuate up and down and therefore plays a big role in the business cycle.

The other part of investment that is not business fixed investment is **residential investment,** the purchase of new houses and apartment buildings. About $311 billion worth of housing and apartments were constructed in 1996. Although much of this was purchased by consumers rather than businesses, it is included in investment because it produces services: shelter and, in some cases, a place to relax and enjoy life.

Combining the three parts of investment, we find that investment was $1,116 billion in 1996: $791 billion of business fixed investment, $311 billion of residential investment, and $14 billion of inventory investment. Thus, investment was about 15 percent of GDP in 1996 (see Figure 6.2).

Note the special way the term investment is used in this discussion. To an economist, investment means the purchase of new factories, houses, or equipment. But in everyday language, investment usually refers to an individual putting away some funds for the future, perhaps in the stock market, such as "I'll invest in the stock market." Be sure to stay aware of this distinction.

**residential investment:** purchases of new houses and apartment buildings.

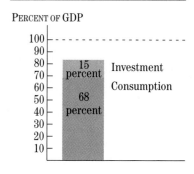

**FIGURE 6.2**
**Investment and Consumption as a Share of GDP**

Investment is a much smaller share of GDP than is consumption.

# Stocks and Flows

The distinction between inventories and inventory investment (the change in inventories) illustrates an important idea in economics. It is the distinction between *stocks* and *flows*. The amount of inventories at a firm *at a particular date* is a *stock*, while the change in inventories *during a particular period* between two dates is a *flow*. To remember the distinction, notice that the expression "to take stock" means adding up all the inventories on the shelves. If a car dealer has 35 cars on the lot at the close of business on October 31, we say the stock of inventory is 35 cars. If the stock increases to 40 cars by the close of business on November 30, then the flow of inventory investment is 5 cars during the month of November.

The economist's distinction between stocks and flows can be illustrated by picturing water flowing into and out of a lake, for example, the Colorado River flowing into and out of Lake Powell behind Glen Canyon Dam. When more water flows in than flows out, the stock of water in Lake Powell rises. Similarly, a positive flow of inventory investment raises the stock of inventory at a firm. And just as when more water flows out than flows in and the stock of water falls, negative inventory investment lowers the stock of inventory.

The distinction between stocks and flows can be made for other economic measures as well. The factories in America on December 31, 1998, are a stock. The investment in the number of factories during 1998 is a flow. The money in your checking account is a stock. The deposit you made last week is a flow.

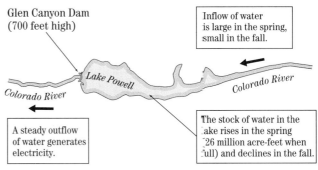

Glen Canyon Dam
(700 feet high)

Inflow of water is large in the spring, small in the fall.

*Lake Powell*

*Colorado River*

*Colorado River*

A steady outflow of water generates electricity.

The stock of water in the lake rises in the spring (26 million acre-feet when full) and declines in the fall.

## Government Purchases

The third category of spending—**government purchases**—is spending by federal, state, and local governments on new goods and services. Most spending by the U.S. government is for the military. At the state and local level, education, roads, and police dominate government purchases. Government purchases of goods and services were equal to $1,407 billion in 1996 (see Figure 6.3).

Not all government outlays are included in government purchases. A government welfare payment or retirement payment to an individual is not a purchase of a good or service; it is a *transfer payment* of income from the government to an individual. Transfer payments do not represent new production of anything, as would the purchase of a weapon or a new road or a new building. Because GDP measures the production of new goods and services, government outlays on transfer payments like social security, unemployment compensation, and welfare payments are excluded. Only purchases are counted because only these items represent something produced. Government outlays are purchases plus transfer payments.

**government purchases:** purchases by federal, state, and local governments of new goods and services.

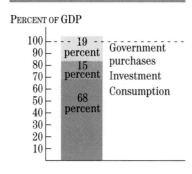

PERCENT OF GDP

**FIGURE 6.3**
**Government Purchases,**
**Investment, and Consumption as**
**a Share of GDP**
Government purchases as a share
of GDP are greater than investment
and less than consumption. When
the stacked bar goes above the 100
percent line, there are negative net
exports (a trade deficit), as shown
here. If the stacked bar stops below
the 100 percent line, there is a
trade surplus.

**net exports:** the value of exports
minus the value of imports.

**exports:** the total value of the
goods and services that people in
one country sell to people in other
countries.

**imports:** the total value of the
goods and services that people in
one country buy from people in
other countries.

**trade balance:** the value of exports
minus the value of imports.

## Net Exports

The final spending category is **net exports,** the difference between exports and imports. American **exports** are what Americans sell to foreigners, whether pharmaceuticals, computers, grain, or a vacation in Florida. American **imports** are what Americans buy from foreigners, whether cars, VCRs, shirts, or a vacation in France. Net exports are defined as exports minus imports. Net exports are a measure of how much more we sell to foreigners than we buy from foreigners. Another term for net exports is the **trade balance.** If net exports are positive, we have a trade surplus. If net exports are negative, we have a trade deficit. By these calculations, the United States had a trade deficit in 1996: $855 billion in exports and $954 billion in imports. Hence, net exports were a negative $99 billion, and appear in Table 6.2 as −$99 billion. The trade deficit got as high as $143 billion in 1987. The last time there was a trade surplus in the United States was in 1975, when it was $14 billion.

Why are net exports added in when computing GDP by the spending approach? There are two reasons. First, we included foreign goods in consumption and investment spending. For example, an imported Toyota purchased at a car dealer in the United States is included in consumption even though it is not produced in the United States. To measure what is produced in the United States, that Toyota must be deducted. Thus, imports must be subtracted to get a measure of total production in the economy. The second reason is that the exports Americans sell abroad are produced in the United States, but they are not counted in consumption or investment or government purchases in the United States. Thus, exports need to be added in to get a measure of production. Because, by definition, net exports are exports minus imports, adding net exports to spending is the same as adding in exports and subtracting out imports. Adding net exports to total spending kills two birds with one stone.

In 1996, the United States imported more than it exported, so the sum of consumption plus investment plus government purchases overstated what was produced in America. The sum of these three items exceeds GDP, as shown in Figure 6.3. In other words, GDP was $99 billion less than the sum of consumption plus investment plus government purchases.

## A Key Equation

The notion that we can measure production by adding up consumption, investment, government purchases, and net exports is important enough to herald with some algebra.

Let the symbol $C$ stand for consumption, $I$ for investment, $G$ for government spending, and $X$ for net exports. Let $Y$ stand for GDP because we use $G$ for government purchases. We will use these symbols many times again. The idea that production equals spending can then be written as

$$Y = C + I + G + X$$

This equation states, using algebraic symbols, that production, $Y$, equals spending: consumption, $C$, plus investment, $I$, plus government purchases, $G$, plus net exports, $X$ (meaning exports minus imports). In 1996 the values of these items (in billions of dollars) were:

$$7,576 = 5,152 + 1,116 + 1,407 + (-99)$$

This simple algebraic relationship plays a key role in later chapters.

## The Income Approach

The income that people earn producing GDP in a country provides another measure of GDP. To see why, first consider a simple example of a single business firm.

Suppose you start a driver's education business. Your production and sales of driver's education services in your first year is $50,000; this is the amount you are paid in total by 500 people for the $100 service. To produce these services, you pay two driving teachers $20,000 each, or a total of $40,000, which is your total cost because the students use their own cars. Your profits are defined as the difference between sales and costs, or $50,000 − $40,000 = $10,000. Now, if you add the total amount of income earned in the production of your driver's education service—the amount earned by two teachers plus the profits you earn—you get $20,000 + $20,000 + $10,000. This sum of incomes is exactly equal to $50,000 which is the same as the amount produced. Thus, by adding up the income of the people who produce the output of the firm, you get a measure of the output. The same idea is true for the country as a whole, which consists of many such businesses and workers.

To show how this works, look at each of the income items in Table 6.3. We first describe each of these items and then show that when we add the items up we get GDP.

### Labor Income

Economists classify wages, salaries, and fringe benefits paid to workers as **labor income,** signifying that it is payment to people for their labor. *Wages* usually refer to payments to workers paid by the hour; *salaries* refer to payments to workers paid by the month or year; and *fringe benefits* refer to retirement, health, and other benefits paid by firms on behalf of workers. As shown in Table 6.3, labor income was $4,449 billion in 1996.

**labor income:** the sum of wages, salaries, and fringe benefits paid to workers.

### Capital Income

Economists classify profits, rental payments, and interest payments as **capital income.** *Profits* include the profits of large corporations like General Motors or Exxon and also the income of small businesses and farms. The royalties an independent screenwriter receives from selling a movie script are also part of profits. *Rental payments* are income to persons who own buildings and rent them out. The rents they receive from their tenants are rental payments. *Interest payments* are

**capital income:** the sum of profits, rental payments, and interest payments.

| | |
|---|---:|
| Aggregate Income | $7,576 |
| Labor income (wages, salaries, fringe benefits) | 4,449 |
| Capital income (profits, interest, rents) | 1,588 |
| Depreciation | 853 |
| Indirect business taxes | 609 |
| Net income of foreigners | 9 |
| Statistical discrepancy | 68 |
| equals GDP | $7,576 |

**TABLE 6.3**
**Aggregate Income and GDP in 1996**
(billions of dollars)

*Source:* U.S. Department of Commerce.

income received from lending to business firms. Interest payments are included in capital income because they represent part of the income generated by the firms' production. Because many individuals pay interest (on mortgages, car loans, etc.) as well as receive interest (on deposits at a bank, etc.), interest payments are defined as the difference between receipts and payments. Table 6.3 shows that capital income was $1,588 billion in 1996, much less than labor income. Capital income is about one-third as large as labor income.

### Depreciation

**depreciation:** the decrease in an asset's value over time; for capital, it is the amount by which physical capital wears out over a given period of time.

**Depreciation** is the amount by which factories and machines wear out each year. A remarkably large part of investment that is part of GDP each year goes to replace worn-out factories and machines. Businesses need to replace depreciated equipment with investment in new equipment just to maintain productive capacity—the number of factories and machines available for use.

**net investment:** gross investment minus depreciation.

The difference between investment, the purchases of final goods by firms, and depreciation is called **net investment,** a measure of how much new investment there is each year after depreciation is subtracted. Net investment was $263 billion ($1,116 billion − $853 billion) in 1996, much smaller than the $1,116 billion in investment. Sometimes the $1,116 billion of investment, including depreciation, is called **gross investment.** The relationship between gross investment and net investment is thus

**gross investment:** the total amount of investment, including that which goes to replacing worn-out capital.

$$\text{Gross investment} - \text{depreciation} = \text{net investment}$$

The reason for the term *gross* in gross domestic product is that it includes gross investment, not only net investment. Another measure, called *net domestic product,* refers to gross domestic product less depreciation.

Profits and the other parts of capital income are reported to the government statisticians after subtracting out depreciation. But depreciation does represent part of GDP because the replacement of old equipment must be produced by someone. Thus, it is necessary to add in depreciation if we are to have a measure of GDP.

### Indirect Business Taxes

**indirect business taxes:** taxes, such as sales taxes, that are levied on products when they are sold.

**Indirect business taxes** consist mainly of sales taxes sent directly by businesses to the government. For example, the price of gasoline at the pump includes a tax that people who buy gasoline pay as part of the price and that the gasoline station sends to the government. When we tabulate total production in the United States by adding up the value of what people spend, we use the prices businesses charge for a specific good—such as gasoline. Part of that price includes a sales tax that is sent to the government and, like depreciation, is not included in firms' profits. Thus, capital income does not include the sales taxes paid by businesses to the government. But those taxes are part of the income generated in producing GDP. We therefore must add sales taxes to capital and labor income.

### Net Income of Foreigners

Foreigners produce part of the GDP in the United States. But their income is not included in labor income or capital income. For example, the salary of a Canadian hockey player who plays for the Pittsburgh Penguins and keeps his official residence as Canada would not be included in the U.S. labor income. But that income represents payment for services produced in the United States, which is part of U.S. GDP. We must add such income payments to foreigners for production in the United States because that production is part of GDP. Moreover, some of U.S. labor and capital income is earned producing GDP in other countries and to get a measure of income generated in producing U.S. GDP, we must subtract that out. For example, the salary of a U.S. baseball player who plays for the Toronto Blue Jays and keeps his official residence as the United States represents payment for services produced in Canada, which is not part of U.S. GDP. We must exclude such incomes paid for production in other countries. To account for both of these effects, we must add *net* income earned by foreigners in the United States—that is, the income earned by foreigners in the United States less what Americans earned abroad—to get GDP. In 1996, Americans earned less abroad ($223 billion) than foreigners earned in the United States ($232 billion); hence, in 1996 *net* income of foreigners was $9 billion as shown in Table 6.3.

**statistical discrepancy:** the discrepancy between calculations of GDP using the spending approach and the income approach due to unreported data or errors in data collection.

Table 6.3 shows the effects of adding up these five items. The sum is close but not quite equal to GDP. The discrepancy reflects errors made in collecting data on income or spending. The discrepancy has a formal name: the **statistical discrepancy.** In percentage terms the amount is small, less than 1 percent of GDP, considering the different ways the data on income and spending are collected. If we add in the statistical discrepancy, then we have a measure of *aggregate income* that equals GDP. From now on we can use the same symbol ($Y$) to refer to GDP or to aggregate income, because GDP and aggregate income amount to the same thing.

The yellow "pipes" in Figure 6.4 illustrate the link between aggregate income and aggregate spending. People earn income from producing goods and services, and they spend this income ($Y$) to buy goods and services ($C, I, G,$ and $X$).

$$\text{GDP} = \begin{matrix} \text{production} \\ \text{or} \\ \text{output} \end{matrix} = \text{income}$$

### National Income and Personal Income

In addition to aggregate income, there are two other measures of income that are sometimes used by economists. **National income** is the sum of labor income and capital income, as we have already defined them. Thus, this measure excludes the income earned to pay indirect business taxes, depreciation, and foreigners in the United States. Labor income is about 73 percent of national income and capital income is the remaining 27 percent. **Personal income** is a measure of the income paid directly to individuals. In addition to labor income, it includes transfer payments from the government to individuals and the part of capital income paid out to individuals in the form of dividends, interest, rent, and small business earnings.

**national income:** the sum of labor income and capital income.

**personal income:** income paid directly to individuals; includes labor income, transfer payments, and the part of capital income that is paid out to individuals.

## The Production Approach

The third measure of GDP adds up the production of each firm or industry in the economy. In order to make this method work, we must avoid the "double counting" problem discussed earlier. For example, if you try to compute GDP by adding new automobiles to new steel to new tires, you will count the steel and the tires that go into producing the new automobile twice. Thus, when we measure GDP by production, it is necessary to count only the **value added** by each manufacturer. Value added is the value of a firm's production less the value of the intermediate goods used in production. In other words, it is the value the firm adds to the intermediate inputs to get the final output. An automobile manufacturer buys the steel, tires, and

**value added:** the value of the firm's production minus the value of the intermediate goods used in production.

**FIGURE 6.4**

**The Circular Flow of Income and Expenditure**

This figure illustrates how aggregate expenditure equals aggregate income. First focus on the yellow "pipes." Starting at the bottom right part of the figure, consumption ($C$) is joined by government purchases ($G$), investment ($I$), and net exports ($X$) to sum to aggregate expenditures ($C + I + G + X$) on the left. At the top of the figure, this aggregate spending is received by firms that produce the goods and then pay out aggregate income ($Y$) to households in the form of rents, interest payments, and profits. The government takes in taxes and makes transfer payments in addition to government purchases.

The red pipes show the flows of saving as described in the section "Saving, Investment, and Net Exports." Private saving plus government saving add up to national saving ($S$). This saving then goes to finance investment by firms. If net exports are greater than zero, then some of the saving goes abroad.

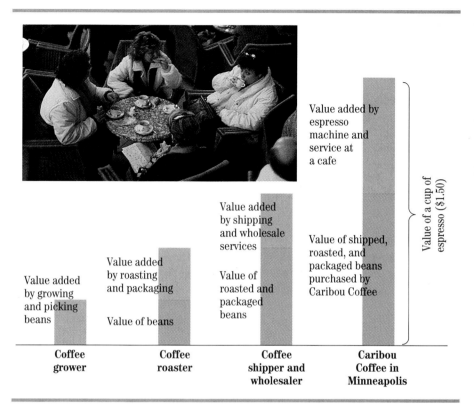

**FIGURE 6.5**
**Value Added in Coffee:**
**From Beans to Espresso**
By adding up the value added at each stage of production, from coffee bean growing to espresso making, we get a measure of the value of a cup of espresso. Double counting is avoided. Using the same procedure for the whole economy permits us to compute GDP by adding up production.

other inputs and adds value by assembling the car. When we measure GDP by production, we count only the value added at each level of production. Figure 6.5 shows how adding up the value added for each firm involved in producing a cup of espresso in the economy will automatically avoid double counting and give a measure of the final value of the cup of espresso when purchased at a coffeehouse or cafe. The same is true for the economy as a whole.

# Review

▶ Adding up all the spending—consumption, investment, government purchases, and net exports—in the U.S. economy gives a measure of total annual production—gross domestic product (GDP). Inventory investment is treated as part of investment spending to ensure that we get a measure of production. Net exports are added to ensure that imported goods in consumption are not counted as U.S. production and that U.S. exports are counted as U.S. production.

▶ The sum of labor income, capital income, depreciation, sales taxes, and net income paid to foreigners gives another measure of GDP.

▶ GDP can also be measured by adding up production, but with this method we must be careful not to double count. By adding up only the value added of each firm or industry, we automatically prevent double counting. Value added is the difference between a firm's sales and its payments for intermediate inputs to production.

# SAVING, INVESTMENT, AND NET EXPORTS

Armed with measures of aggregate spending, aggregate income, or aggregate production, economists often talk about a country's income or spending as if they were talking about a person's income or spending. Of course, the numbers are much larger for a country than for an individual. U.S. income of about $8 trillion is nearly unfathomable even compared with the income of the highest-paid movie stars or business executives. And, of course, the United States or any other country is not a person with one mind or set of plans. U.S. income and U.S. spending are simply the sums of incomes and spending of millions of individuals, even though we use single symbols like $Y$ to represent these enormous quantities.

Nevertheless, analogies between countries and individuals are useful, especially when discussing economic growth and change over time. In this section we define saving and show how to measure saving for an entire country, using the definitions of income and spending we have derived thus far. Measuring a country's saving will be important in our study of economic growth and fluctuations in later chapters.

For an individual, saving is defined as income less consumption. If you earn $20,000 in income during the year and spend $18,000 on consumption—food, rent, movies—by definition your saving is $2,000 for the year. But if your consumption is $23,000 for the year, then your saving is negative $3,000, and you will either have to take $3,000 out of the bank or borrow $3,000.

## The Definition of a Country's Saving

**national saving:** aggregate income minus consumption minus government purchases.

For a country, saving is defined the same way: by subtracting from the country's income what is consumed. For a country, however, there is also a government, and much (about 85 percent) of government purchases provide services that are like consumption—park services, police security services, and national defense services—rather than like investment, such as road building. Thus, **national saving** is defined as income less consumption and government purchases. That is,

National saving = income − consumption − government purchases

(An alternative definition would subtract only the part [85 percent] of government purchases that are clearly consumption.)

Using the symbol $S$ for national saving and the symbols already introduced for income $(Y)$, consumption $(C)$, and government purchases $(G)$, we define national saving as:

$$S = Y - C - G$$

Using the numbers from Table 6.2, national saving in 1996 was $1,017 = ($7,576 − $5,152 − $1,407), with all numbers in billions. Note that national saving, just like income, consumption, and government purchases, refers to a particular period of time, usually a year. National saving is what a country has left over in any one year for things other than consumption and government purchases.

## Saving Equals Investment plus Net Exports

Where does this national saving go? An important principle of macroeconomics is that the national saving of a country is used either to finance the country's investment in factories, equipment, and housing or to finance the net purchases of the country's goods by foreigners. Net purchases by foreigners are equal to the difference between exports and imports, or net exports. Just as a furniture store provides funds (in the form of a credit card loan) to purchasers of furniture, the country provides funds to foreigners for purchases of its exports over its imports.

We can prove this important principle by simply looking carefully at the definition of national saving. First, write down the equation

$$Y = C + I + G + X$$

which, as already discussed, states that income ($Y$) equals consumption ($C$) plus investment ($I$) plus government purchases ($G$) plus net exports ($X$). Next, subtract consumption ($C$) and government purchases ($G$) from the left-hand side of the equation to get national saving; this means you must also subtract consumption ($C$) and government purchases ($G$) from the right-hand side. Here is what the subtraction gives you:

$$Y - C - G = I + X$$
$$S = I + X$$

where we have substituted national saving ($S$) for ($Y - C - G$), on the left. Thus, in words we have shown that

National saving = investment + net exports

Using the numbers from Table 6.2, national saving in 1996 equaled $1,017 = $1,116 + (−$99), with all numbers in billions.

This remarkable result says that the saving by all the millions of individuals in a country must be equal to the investment in new factories, equipment, and housing in the country plus the excess of exports over imports—net exports. If the country does not trade with the rest of the world, national saving must exactly equal investment.

What is the explanation for this result? By definition, national saving is what a country has left over after consumption and government purchases. What is left over can be used for other things, and there are only two other types of things possible: (1) investment in new factories, equipment, and housing, or (2) providing funds to foreigners equal to any purchases they make (exports) over and above what they sell (imports), or net exports. When more is saved than is invested, the excess saving shows up as a trade surplus—net exports will be positive. However, when less is saved than is invested, net exports are negative—there is a trade deficit.

To give further insights into this relationship between national saving, investment, and net exports, it is useful to consider the behavior of individuals and firms.

### Saving by the Young, the Middle-Aged, and the Old

National saving is the sum of all saving in the economy. But some people are saving, some are not saving at all, and some even have negative saving, or *dissaving*. For example, when people are old they usually consume more than their income; they draw down their retirement savings. When people are middle-aged, they usually save for retirement—their income is greater than their consumption. And most young people save very little, or even dissave if they are able to borrow, perhaps from their friends or parents.

In most societies, there is a mixture of young, middle-aged, and old in the population. But the mixture is usually changing over time. National saving—the sum of everyone's saving—is affected by these changes. With the old tending to dissave, an increase in the number of old people in the society would therefore reduce the amount of national saving. For this reason, there is concern that national saving in the United States will decline as the post–World War II baby boom generation retires, starting around 2010.

### Government Saving

Because the government is part of the economy, any saving by the government is part of national saving. What do we mean by saving by the government? The difference between the government's receipts from taxes and the government's expenditures—called the government *budget surplus*—is government saving. When the surplus is negative there is a *budget deficit,* and the government dissaves. In recent years the U.S. federal government has been a dissaver; that is, it has taken in less in income through tax receipts than it has spent. When the government runs a budget deficit, it lowers national saving unless saving by individuals increases.

The red "pipes" in Figure 6.4 illustrate how government saving can contribute to national saving, which in turn equals investment plus net exports.

### People Saving and Investing

In general, the investing, exporting, and importing in the economy are not done by the same people who do the saving. Investment in factories and equipment in the economy is undertaken by firms. Investment in housing is done by individuals. Exporting and importing, which constitute net exports, are done by both firms and individuals. Saving is undertaken by other individuals as they save for retirement or other future events. Dissaving occurs if the government runs a budget deficit. There are some exceptions, where the same individuals do both the saving and investing. For example, you might decide to build your own house over a number of years. Each year you could use your savings to invest in part of the house. But typically investors and savers are different individuals.

Nevertheless, the link between national saving, investment, and net exports is maintained as millions of firms, individuals, and people in government go about their daily lives. There is a different story for everyone. Individuals who save might put their savings into a bank, and the bank in turn might lend out the funds to a firm that then uses the funds for investment in equipment. Or the bank might lend the money to another individual to build a house, or it might lend the funds to a firm in another country; that firm could use the funds to buy U.S. goods (exports).

The important point is that all these millions, even billions, of individual actions must adhere to the principle that national saving equals investment plus net exports.

# Review

▶ For an individual, saving equals income minus consumption. For the United States, national saving is defined as income minus consumption minus government purchases. Government purchases are subtracted because many of them provide consumptionlike services to individuals.

▶ National saving always equals investment plus net exports. When national saving is less than investment, there is a trade deficit. When national saving is greater than investment, there is a trade surplus.

# REAL GDP AND NOMINAL GDP

Economists use GDP to assess how the economy is changing over time. For example, they might want to know how rapidly the production of goods and services has grown and what that implies about economic growth in the future. However, the dollar value of the goods and services in GDP is determined by the price of these goods and services. Thus, an increase in the prices of all goods and services will make measured GDP grow, even if there is no real increase in the amount of production in the economy. Suppose, for example, that the prices of all goods in the economy double and that the number of items produced of every good remains the same. Then the dollar value of these items will double even though physical production does not change. A $10,000 car becomes a $20,000 car, a $7 haircut becomes a $14 haircut, and so on. Thus, GDP will double as well. At the other extreme, if the prices of all goods are cut in half, then measured GDP will fall by half even if there is no change in the number of items produced. Clearly, GDP is not useful for comparing production at different dates when there are increases in all prices. Although the examples of doubling or halving of all prices are extreme, we do know from Chapter 5 that there is a tendency for prices on the average to rise over time—a tendency that we have called inflation. Thus, when there is inflation, GDP becomes an unreliable measure of the changes in production over time.

## Adjusting GDP for Inflation

**Real GDP,** as we discussed in Chapter 5, is a measure of production that corrects for this inflation. To emphasize the difference between GDP and real GDP, we will define **nominal GDP** as what has previously been referred to as GDP.

**real gross domestic product (real GDP):** a measure of the value of all the goods and services newly produced in a country during some period of time, adjusted for inflation.

**nominal GDP:** gross domestic product without any correction for inflation; the same as GDP; the value of all goods and services newly produced in a country during some period of time, usually a year.

### Computing Real GDP Growth Between Two Years

To see how real GDP is calculated, consider an example. Suppose that total production consists entirely of the production of audio CDs and cassette tapes and that we want to compare this total production in two different years: 1997 and 1998.

|       | 1997 | | 1998 | |
|-------|-------|----------|-------|----------|
|       | Price | Quantity | Price | Quantity |
| CDs   | $15   | 1,000    | $20   | 1,200    |
| Tapes | $ 5   | 2,000    | $10   | 2,200    |

Notice that the number of CDs produced increases by 20 percent and the number of tapes produced increases by 10 percent from 1997 to 1998. Notice also that the price of CDs is greater than the price of tapes, but both increase between the two years because of inflation. Nominal GDP is equal to the dollar amount spent on CDs, plus the dollar amount spent on tapes, or $25,000 in 1997 and $46,000 in 1998, a substantial 84 percent increase.

Nominal GDP in 1997 = $15 × 1,000 + $ 5 × 2,000 = $25,000

Nominal GDP in 1998 = $20 × 1,200 + $10 × 2,200 = $46,000

Clearly, nominal GDP is not a good measure of the increase in production: Nominal GDP increases by 84 percent, a much greater increase than the increase in either CD production (20 percent) or tape production (10 percent). Thus, failing to correct for inflation gives a misleading estimate.

To calculate real GDP we must use the *same* price for both years and, thereby, adjust for inflation. That is, the number of CDs and tapes produced in the two years must be evaluated at the same prices. For example, production could be calculated in both years using 1997 prices. That is,

Using 1997 prices, production in 1997 = $15 × 1,000 + $5 × 2,000 = $25,000

Using 1997 prices, production in 1998 = $15 × 1,200 + $5 × 2,200 = $29,000

Keeping prices constant at 1997 levels, we see that the increase in production is from $25,000 in 1997 to $29,000 in 1998, an increase of 16 percent.

However, production can also be calculated in both years using 1998 prices. That is,

Using 1998 prices, production in 1997 = $20 × 1,000 + $10 × 2,000 = $40,000

Using 1998 prices, production in 1998 = $20 × 1,200 + $10 × 2,200 = $46,000

Keeping prices constant at 1998 levels, we see that the increase in production is from $40,000 in 1997 to $46,000 in 1998, an increase of 15 percent.

Observe that the percentage increase in production is slightly different (16 percent versus 15 percent) depending on whether 1997 or 1998 prices are used. Such differences are inevitable, because there is no reason to prefer the prices in one year to those of another year when controlling for inflation. Economists arrive at a single percentage by simply *averaging* the two percentages.[1] In this example, they would conclude that the *increase in real GDP from 1997 to 1998 was 15.5 percent,* the average of 16 percent and 15 percent.

This 15.5 percent increase in real GDP is much less than the 84 percent increase in nominal GDP and much closer to the actual increase in the number of CDs and tapes produced. By adjusting for inflation in this way, real GDP gives a better picture of the increase in actual production in the economy.

### A Year-to-Year Chain

This example shows how the growth rate of real GDP between the two years 1997 and 1998 is calculated in the case of two goods. The same approach is used for any other two years and more than two goods. To correct for inflation across more than two years, economists simply do a series of these two-year corrections and then "chain" them together. Each year is a link in the chain. For example, if the growth rate from 1998 to 1999 was found to be 13.5 percent, then chaining this together with the 15.5 percent from 1997 to 1998 would imply an average annual growth rate of 14.5 percent for the two years from 1997 to 1999. That is,

By chaining other years together, link by link, the chain can be made as long as we want.

---

1. A "geometric" average is used. The geometric average of two numbers is the square root of the product of the two numbers

### From the 1992 Base Year to Other Years

To obtain real GDP in any one year, we start with a *base year* and then use these growth rates to compute GDP in another year. The base year is a year when real GDP is set equal to nominal GDP. Currently, 1992 is the base year for government statistical calculations of GDP in the United States. Thus, real GDP in 1992 and nominal GDP in 1992 are the same: $6,244 billion.

To get real GDP in other years economists start with the base year and use the real GDP growth rates to find GDP in any other year. Consider 1993. The growth rate of real GDP in 1993—calculated using the methods just described for the entire economy—is 2.27 percent. Thus, real GDP in 1993 was $6,386, or 2.27 percent greater than $6,244 billion. The $6,386 billion is 1993 real GDP measured in 1992 dollars. To emphasize that this number is calculated by chaining years together with growth rates, economists say that real GDP is measured in "chained 1992 dollars," a term that frequently appears in newspaper reports about real GDP.

### Real GDP versus Nominal GDP over Time

Figure 6.6 compares real and nominal GDP over a 15-year period. Observe that for the 1992 base year, real GDP and nominal GDP are equal. However, by 1996 real GDP reached about $6.9 trillion with nominal GDP at $7.6 trillion. Thus, just as in the example, real GDP increased much less than nominal GDP. For the years prior to 1992, real GDP is more than nominal GDP because 1992 prices were higher than prices in earlier years. From Figure 6.6 you can see that nominal GDP would give a very misleading picture of the U.S. economy.

## The GDP Deflator *— reduce the inflation*

Nominal GDP grows faster than real GDP because of inflation. The greater the difference between nominal GDP growth and real GDP growth, the greater is the inflation. If there were a deflation, with prices falling, then nominal GDP would increase less than real GDP. Hence, a by-product of computing real GDP is a measure of the rate of inflation.

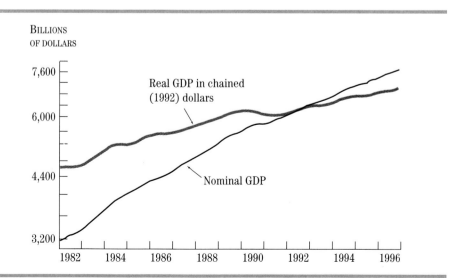

BILLIONS OF DOLLARS

Real GDP in chained (1992) dollars

Nominal GDP

7,600
6,000
4,400
3,200

1982   1984   1986   1988   1990   1992   1994   1996

**FIGURE 6.6**
**Real GDP versus Nominal GDP**
Real GDP increases much less than nominal GDP because real GDP is adjusted for rising prices. Most of the increase in nominal GDP is due to rising prices. The chart shows real GDP for the 1992 base year, when real GDP and nominal GDP are equal. Nominal GDP is below real GDP in earlier years because prices are generally lower before 1992.

*Source:* U.S. Department of Commerce.

# Reading the News About GDP Each Month

Near the end of every month, newspaper stories appear in most papers around the country (indeed, around the world) about the latest GDP measurement for the United States. The stories are generated by a release of data about GDP by economic statisticians at the U.S. Department of Commerce, where the national income and product accounts are tabulated.

Often the story appears on the first page of the newspaper with a big headline, as did the following story from the *New York Times* of October 31, 1996. Similar stories appeared in all the major newspapers, including the *Wall Street Journal*. Frequently the president of the United States or a high administration official comments on what the data mean for the economy, as did President Clinton's advisers in the story reproduced here. And because 1996 was an election year, presidential candidate Bob Dole also commented on the data.

The discussion of GDP in this chapter should give you the information

you need to read and understand these articles and to judge whether the headline, the reporter's interpretation of the GDP data, and the public official's comments make sense. The article reproduced here reported a slowdown for the economy, as reflected in its headline and general tone.

There are several points to keep in mind when reading news stories about GDP.

First, the measures of GDP are reported for each of the four quarters of the year. There is a news story each month because the data are revised twice. The first month after the quarter gives the first estimate of GDP; that is what is reported in the following article. In the second and third months, the estimates are revised as new data about the economy are obtained. Sometimes you have to read carefully to know whether what you are reading is a first-time report or a revision.

Second, the GDP measure for a quarter of a year represents the aggregate

production during the quarter, but the amount of production is stated at an *annual rate* to make the magnitude comparable to the annual GDP measure. For example, GDP was reported to be $7,616 billion in the third quarter at an annual rate in the attached article, but, in reality, GDP during the quarter was only one-fourth of that.

Third, the GDP measures for each quarter are *seasonally adjusted.* Some seasons of the year always involve more production than other seasons, and these differences have little to do with where the economy is going. For example, the fourth quarter (October–December) usually involves more production in anticipation of the holidays. Seasonal adjustments try to take out these fluctuations so that they do not show up in the reported measures of GDP.

*Source of article:* "Economic Growth Retreats to 2.2%," by David E. Sanger, *The New York Times,* October 31, 1996. Copyright © 1996 by The New York Times Company. Reprinted by permission.

# ECONOMIC GROWTH RETREATS TO 2.2%

Refers to the growth rate of real GDP

## Experts Differ on How Long Slowdown Is Likely to Last

### By DAVID E. SANGER

WASHINGTON, Oct. 30 — In one of the last major indicators of the country's economic performance before the Presidential election, the Commerce Department today reported a sharp slowdown in economic growth in the third quarter of the year, but no sign of a revival of even modest inflation.

Today's news, that the growth rate fell to 2.2 percent in the third quarter, from 4.7 percent in the second, did not come as a surprise. Most economists had expected that the economy would cool off considerably. But they differ on whether this is the beginning of a longer downturn or a brief slowing of an expansion that can be sustained well into next year.

Both sides in that debate could pick out evidence from numbers reported today to support their arguments: Growth in personal spending by consumers slowed to a near standstill, but companies continued to buy equipment at a remarkable pace, a sign that they expect continued good times.

There was little question, however, that the combination of slower growth and continued low inflation wiped out the fears prevalent three months ago that the Federal Reserve would be forced to raise short-term interest rates.

And the figures put the economy on a path to grow 2.8 percent for the year, by most estimates — well ahead of what both Democrats and Republicans expected early in the year.

*continued*

# Reading the News About GDP Each Month *(continued)*

Not surprisingly, both campaigns seized on today's numbers to bolster their sharply conflicting assessments of the nation's economic health. Commerce Secretary Mickey Kantor, carefully plucking out figures on the growth of the private economy, which exclude government spending, argued that the economy was growing faster than "in the so-called go-go 80's."

"We're in the midst of a balanced, sustained economic expansion that is delivering the goods for the American people," he said.

But Bob Dole, campaigning in Tennessee, referred to an economy that "is barely afloat," and said, "if this is a recovery, I can hardly wait for the recession." His staff compared today's numbers with those of the first quarter of 1993 — when Mr. Clinton was inaugurated and when the economy was climbing out of recession with growth at a rate of more than 4 percent — to support its argument that Mr. Clinton had been a lucky bystander to good times rather than a contributor to the economy's success. . . .

The biggest surprise in the figures was the paltry growth in consumer spending: a mere four-tenths of a percent at an annual rate. In the first half of the year the rate was closer to 3.5 percent. . . .

Inventories also increased sharply in the third quarter, suggesting that some of the G.D.P. gains were attributable to goods that were being produced but not yet consumed.

Buying habits historically wax and wane, so it is difficult to determine how much the spending slowdown really means. But the caution of consumers was in sharp contrast to the continued enthusiasm of American businesses, which spent 19 percent more than a year ago on equipment, largely computers, and built factories at a pace suggestive of a far more healthy expansion. . . .

One area that saw a significant downturn was exports, which until now have spurred the economy. Exports were up only six-tenths of a percent. Some of that slowdown is understandable: the United States economy has grown far faster than Europe's or Japan's, meaning that the country is in a position to take in more goods while demand for American exports lags. But it is an inconvenient turn of events for the Clinton Administration, which has made the export boom a centerpiece of its economic message. . . .

Data included in the gross domestic product for the third quarter of 1996 follow, with all dollar amounts in billions at seasonally adjusted annual rates. Percentage changes are from the previous quarter at seasonally adjusted annual rates.

*Different interpretations of the data in a presidential election campaign*

*Chained refers to the year-by-year method of estimating real GDP.*

*Some of the key components of spending are discussed here*

Nominal GDP

Real GDP

GDP deflator

| Current Prices | Last Quarter | Pct. Chg. |
|---|---|---|
| **Gross Domestic Product** | $7,616.0 | +3.8 |
| **Consumption** | 5,164.1 | +1.9 |
| **Business investment** | 801.6 | +15.2 |
| **Inventory change** | 42.4 | N.A. |
| **Housing** | 311.7 | −3.1 |
| **Net exports** | −115.7 | N.A. |
| **Government** | 1,412.0 | +0.9 |
| **Memo: Final sales*** | 7,573.7 | +2.0 |

### Chained 1992 Dollars

| | Last Quarter | Pct. Chg. |
|---|---|---|
| **Gross Domestic Product** | $6,929.7 | +2.2 |
| **Consumption** | 4,692.8 | +0.4 |
| **Business investment** | 776.6 | +14.7 |
| **Inventory Change** | 39.6 | N.A. |
| **Housing** | 277.4 | −5.8 |
| **Net exports** | −132.2 | N.A. |
| **Government** | 1,273.7 | −1.4 |
| **Memo: Final sales*** | 6,389.6 | +0.3 |
| **G.D.P. price deflator** | | +1.6 |
| **G.D.P. chain-weighted price index** | | +1.9 |

*G.D.P. less inventory change.
N.A. Data Not applicable.
*Source: Commerce Department*

**GDP deflator:** nominal GDP divided by real GDP; it measures the level of prices of goods and services included in real GDP relative to a given base year.

More precisely, if we divide nominal GDP by real GDP, we get the **GDP deflator,** a measure of the **price level,** which is the level of all the prices of the items in real GDP. That is,

$$\text{GDP deflator} = \frac{\text{nominal GDP}}{\text{real GDP}}$$

Here the GDP deflator is defined so that its value in the base year, such as 1992, is 1.00. (Sometimes it is scaled to equal 100 in the base year by multiplying by 100.)

**price level:** the average level of prices in the economy.

The reason for the term *deflator* is that to get real GDP we can deflate nominal GDP by dividing it by the GDP deflator. That is,

$$\text{Real GDP} = \frac{\text{nominal GDP}}{\text{GDP deflator}}$$

The percentage change in the GDP deflator from one year to the next is a measure of the rate of inflation.

## Other Inflation Measures

**consumer price index (CPI):** a price index equal to the current price of a fixed market basket of consumer goods and services in a base year.

There are other measures of inflation. A frequently cited one is based on the **consumer price index (CPI),** which is the price of a fixed collection—a "market basket"—of consumer goods and services in a given year divided by the price of the same collection in some base year. For example, if the market basket consists of one CD and two tapes, then the CPI for 1998 compared with the 1997 base year in the previous example would be

$$\frac{\$20 \times 1 + \$10 \times 2}{\$15 \times 1 + \$5 \times 2} = \frac{40}{25} = 1.60$$

The CPI inflation rate is the percent change in the CPI; it measures how fast the prices of the items in the basket increase in price.

Using a fixed collection of goods and services in the CPI is one of the reasons economists think the CPI overstates inflation. When the price of goods rises, the quantity demanded should decline; when the price falls, the quantity demanded rises. Thus, by not allowing the quantities to change when the price changes, the CPI puts too much weight on items with rising prices and too little weight on items with declining prices. The result is an overstatement of inflation.

In 1996, a group of economists appointed by the U.S. Senate and chaired by Michael Boskin of Stanford University, found that the government, by adjusting expenditures according to this overstated CPI, was spending billions of dollars more than it would with a correct CPI. Hence, getting the economic statistics right makes a big difference.

**chain weighted price index:** a price index using a changing basket of goods and services computed just as real GDP is computed.

Recently another measure of the average price of all goods and services in GDP has been developed. It is called the **chain weighted price index.** Unlike the CPI, it is not based on a fixed quantity of goods and services in some base year. Rather, the quantities in the index change each year, and the percentage changes in the index are chained together, just as in the calculation of real GDP. Moreover, the chain weighted price index includes consumption, investment, and government purchases, not just consumption. The chain weighted price index is usually mentioned as a measure of inflation in news reports about GDP.

Figure 6.7 shows how measures of inflation using the GDP deflator and the CPI compare. The general inflation movements are similar. The CPI is more volatile, however.

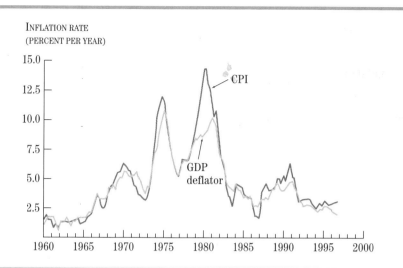

INFLATION RATE
(PERCENT PER YEAR)

**FIGURE 6.7**
**Comparison of Measures of Inflation**

Measuring inflation with either the CPI or the GDP deflator shows the rise in inflation in the 1960s and 1970s and the lower inflation in the 1980s and early 1990s. The CPI is more volatile: It bounces around more. (The inflation rate is based on yearly percent changes in the stated variable.)

*Source:* U.S. Department of Commerce.

Although these three measures of prices provide the main statistics for inflation, there are still other measures. The producer price index (PPI), for example, measures the prices of raw materials and intermediate goods as well as the prices of final goods sold by producers. Services are excluded from the PPI, however. Raw materials prices—oil, wheat, copper—are sometimes watched carefully because they give early warning signs of increases in inflation.

## Review

▶ Real GDP corrects nominal GDP for inflation. Real GDP measures the production of goods and services in the dollars of a given base year, such as 1992.

▶ Real GDP is a better measure of changes in the physical amount of production in the economy than is nominal GDP.

▶ The GDP deflator is a measure of the price level in the economy. It is defined as the ratio of nominal GDP to real GDP. The percentage change in the GDP deflator from year to year is a measure of the inflation rate.

# SHORTCOMINGS OF THE GDP MEASURE

Although GDP is the best measure of overall production we have, it is deficient in several ways. First, there are revisions to GDP that can change the assessment of the economy. Second, GDP omits some production. Third, the production of goods and services, even on a per person or per capita basis, is only part of what affects the quality of life.

## Revisions in GDP

Government statisticians obtain data on GDP from surveys of stores and businesses, and even income tax data from the Internal Revenue Service. Not all of the data are collected quickly. Data on sales at stores and large firms come in within a month; exports and imports take several months. Some income tax data are reported only once a year. Information about small firms comes in even more slowly.

For this reason, the statistics on GDP are frequently revised as new data come in. Every few years there is a big revision and the base year for computing real GDP is changed. For those who use the GDP data to make decisions, either in business or government, faulty data on GDP, which are apparent only when the data are revised, can lead to mistakes. Revisions of GDP are inevitable and occur in all countries.

## Omissions from GDP

Most of the production that is omitted from GDP either does not occur in a formal market or government statisticians have a difficult time measuring it. Examples are work done in the home, illegal commerce, and quality improvements in goods.

### Home Work and Production

Much of the production that people do at home—making dinner or a sweater, changing the car oil or a baby's diapers, cutting the grass or the kids' hair—is productive activity, but it is not included in GDP because the transactions are not recorded in markets where statisticians measure spending. Such production would be included in GDP if people hired and paid someone else to do any of these things.

Note that some home production is included in GDP. If you run a mail order or telemarketing business out of your home and pay taxes on your income, then this production is likely to be counted in GDP.

Government statisticians try to estimate some home production of final goods and include it in GDP. For example, if a person owns a house, the house provides services in the form of a place to live, eat, sleep, and entertain. An estimate of the value of these services is part of consumption even though there is no visible spending on them each year.

### Leisure Activity

Much leisure activity is not included in GDP even though it may be enjoyable. Going to the beach or hiking in the mountains more often and working less might be something you decide to do as your income increases. If people start taking Friday afternoons off, GDP will go down but the level of well-being may increase. The consumption of leisure is omitted from GDP unless it involves a purchase in the market such as a movie or a ballgame ticket.

### The Underground Economy

A large amount of production is not counted in GDP because it is purposely hidden from the view of the government. Illegal activity—growing marijuana in the California coastal range, selling pharmaceuticals not yet approved by the Food and Drug Administration—is excluded from GDP, because no one wants to report this activity to the government. People who get cash payments—perhaps in the form of tips at hotels or restaurants—may not report them in order to avoid taxes, and these are not counted either. If people do not report interest on a loan to a friend or relative, this is also omitted from GDP.

The sum of all the missing items is referred to as the *underground economy.* Estimates of the size of the underground economy are understandably uncertain. They range from about 10 percent of GDP in the United States to about 25 percent in Italy to over 40 percent in Peru.

The underground economy makes GDP a less useful measure of the size of an economy, and we should be aware of it when using GDP. But the underground economy does not render GDP a useless measure. It is unlikely that the underground economy grows much more or much less rapidly than the rest of the economy. Changes in laws can increase or decrease the incentives to produce outside the legal market economy, but these are unlikely to be large enough to change estimated growth rates of GDP by much. For example, the reduction of taxes in the United States in the 1980s encouraged more people to report more of their incomes to the government, and this increased both reported incomes and tax receipts. But it did not seem to have a major impact on the measurement of GDP.

### Improved Products

Our measure of GDP sometimes misses improvements in the quality of goods and services. For example, a personal computer made in 1988 looks similar to a personal computer made in 1998. Yet, the 1998 computer is vastly superior; it can do computations much faster and store much more information. If personal computers in GDP are valued by their price times their number, then GDP will vastly understate the amount of production in terms of storage and speed.

In recent years, government statisticians have tried to measure the improved performance of computers and include this in GDP. However, the same problem exists for many other goods, from medical care, where microscopic surgery allows for knee surgery unheard of 20 years ago, to ski boots, which are far more comfortable than they were 20 years ago.

## Other Measures of Well-Being

In the previous chapter, we described how improvements in the well-being of individuals in a society cannot occur without increases in real GDP per capita. However, even if real GDP per capita did include production in the underground economy, the value of home production, and all the improvements in goods and services, it would not alone serve as a measure of individual well-being. There are many other important aspects of the well-being of individuals: a long and healthy life expectancy, a clean environment, a small chance of war, crime, or the death of a child. The production of goods and services in a country can affect these other things, and indeed be affected by them, but it is not a measure of them.

### Vital Statistics on the Quality of Life

Consider what has happened to some other measures of well-being as real GDP per capita has grown. During the last 40 years, we have seen life expectancy in the United States increase from about 69 years in the 1950s to 76 years in the 1990s.

This compares with a life expectancy of only 47 years in the early part of this century. Infant mortality has also declined, from about 2.6 infant deaths per 100 live births in the mid-1950s to .9 in the mid-1990s. In the early part of this century, infant mortality in the United States was 10 deaths for every 100 live births. The fraction of women who die in childbirth has also declined. So by some of these important measures, the quality of life has improved along with real GDP per capita.

But there are still serious problems and room for gains; as death rates from car accidents, heart disease, and stroke have decreased, death rates among young people from AIDS, suicide, and murder have been rising. Also of serious concern is the increasing percentage of children who live in poverty. Thus, the impressive gain in real GDP per capita has been correlated with both gains and losses in other measures of well-being.

### Environmental Quality

A clean and safe environment is also a factor in the quality of life. Through much of the twentieth century, environmental pollution has increased as real GDP has grown. In the United States, Europe, and Japan in the last 40 years, however, some forms of pollution have been declining. For example, emissions of carbon monoxide, sulfur dioxide, and other air pollutants have declined. Part of the reason for these declines is that an increasing part of U.S. GDP has been devoted to reducing pollution. In the 1990s, about 2 percent per year of GDP has been spent on reducing pollution, from antipollution devices on cars to water-treatment plants.

As in other measures of the quality of life, however, there is room for improvement. There is a great debate about how much of GDP should be spent on improving the environment, just like there is debate about how much should be spent on police to reduce crime or on the military to defend the country. But GDP itself does not provide an indication of whether pollution or many of the other measures of the quality of life are improving or getting worse.

## Review

▶ Real GDP per capita is not without its own short-comings as an indicator of well-being in a society. Certain items are omitted—home production, leisure, the underground economy, and some quality improvements.

▶ There are other indicators of the quality of life, including vital statistics on mortality and the environment, that can be affected by GDP per capita but that are conceptually distinct and independently useful.

# INTERNATIONAL COMPARISONS OF GDP

As we showed earlier, GDP can be adjusted for inflation in order to make comparisons of production in different years. A more difficult problem is comparing GDP in different countries, where the prices of individual goods differ. Making accurate comparisons of GDP in different countries is important for economic policy. Politicians frequently compare economic performance of the United States with other countries in order to show what is right or wrong with current economic policies. In this section, we show how economists adjust GDP to make such comparisons. To illustrate the problem, consider comparing real GDP in the United States with Japan.

## The Problem with Using Market Exchange Rates for Comparisons

GDP in Japan was 470 trillion yen in 1994. In the United States, GDP was about $7 trillion in the same year. How do we compare these two numbers? One simple way would be to convert the yen to dollars using the exchange rate between yen and dollars in the foreign currency market. The market exchange rate in 1994 was about 100 yen per dollar. If we take the 470 trillion yen and convert it to dollars by dividing it by 100 yen per dollar, we get $4.7 trillion (470/100 = 4.7) as an estimate of GDP in Japan stated in dollars. The $4.7 trillion in Japan could then be compared with the $7 trillion in the United States. By this measure, Japanese production is approximately 67 percent of United States production—$4.7 trillion is 67 percent of $7 trillion. But is this comparison any good?

If we are interested in what a Japanese person can buy in Japan compared with what an American can buy in the United States, the answer is no. The prices of goods are much different in the two countries and the exchange rate is not a good guide to these price differences. Consider an example: Big Mac hamburgers sold by McDonald's. In fact, for those who trade in foreign currency markets, Big Macs are a favorite example; prices of Big Macs in different countries are printed in many magazines and newspapers. A Big Mac hamburger in Japan costs about 450 yen. If we convert that to dollars using the 1994 exchange rate, the cost of the Big Mac in dollars would be about $4.50 (450/100 = 4.50). But a Big Mac in the United States does not cost nearly that much; it costs about $2.50. Thus, the exchange rate overstates the price of Big Macs in Japan and, for the same reasons, overstates the value of GDP in Japan.

## Purchasing Power Parity Exchange Rates

To account for these price differences, economists use an adjusted exchange rate that better reflects the different prices in the different countries. An exchange rate that makes Big Macs in Japan and the United States cost about the same would be 180 yen per dollar. Then a 450 yen hamburger in Japan would translate into about $2.50 (450/180 = 2.50). This exchange rate would make the power of yen and dollars to purchase Big Macs the same in both countries. For this reason, 180 yen per dollar is called the **purchasing power parity exchange rate.** In reality, purchasing power parity exchange rates are computed using the prices of thousands of goods, not only Big Macs. More formally, the purchasing power parity exchange rate between the yen and the dollar is the number of yen required to buy the same amount of goods that can be bought with a dollar. Of course, purchasing parity exchange rates can be similarly defined and measured for French francs, German marks, and any other currency.

**purchasing power parity exchange rate:** an exchange rate such that the prices of similar goods in different countries are the same when measured in the same currency.

Let us compare U.S. and Japanese GDP, using 180 yen per dollar as the purchasing power parity exchange rate. The 470 trillion yen Japanese GDP now translates into $2.6 trillion, much less than the $4.7 trillion first estimated. According to this estimate, Japanese GDP is closer to 40 percent of U.S. GDP than to 67 percent.

### *Reversals of International Rankings*

The difference this conversion makes for GDP per capita is even more striking. GDP per capita in Japan translated into dollars using the market exchange rate is $31,000, *greater* than the $25,000 GDP per capita in the United States. But if we make the translation using the purchasing power parity exchange rate, GDP per capita in Japan is $17,000, *less* than in the United States. Thus, depending on which exchange rate you use, it is possible to rank the United States either higher or lower than Japan. In fact, because the yen/dollar market exchange rate fluctuated so much in the 1980s and 1990s—it fell from 250 yen per dollar to 100 yen per dollar—it is possible to show that the United States rapidly fell behind Japan. At 250 yen per dollar, Japanese GDP per capita would be $12,000; at 130 yen per dollar it would be $24,000. Clearly, this increase does not mean that the Japanese rapidly overtook America or that America fell rapidly behind.

Despite the difficulties in measuring the purchasing power parity exchange rate, most economists feel that it gives a much better international comparison than the market exchange rate.

## Review

▶ Comparing GDP in different countries is difficult because the prices are so different. Purchasing power parity is a method to compare GDP that takes into account the difference in prices.

▶ Serious mistakes about the relative performance of different countries can be made if market exchange rates are used for comparisons.

# CONCLUSION

In this chapter we have shown how to measure the size of an economy in terms of its GDP. In the process, we have explained that income, spending, and production in a country are all equal, that a country's saving equals its investment plus its net exports, and that GDP can be adjusted to make comparisons over time or between countries.

Given this information, we can now proceed to develop a theory of why the economy—as measured by real GDP—grows and changes over time.

In conclusion, it is important to recall that aggregate income (or production or spending), the subject of our study, tells us much about the quality of life of people in a country but it does not tell us everything. As the economist-philosopher John Stuart Mill said of aggregate income in his *Principles of Political Economy,* first published in 1848: "The inquiries which relate to it are in no danger of being confounded with those relating to any other of the great human interests. All know that it is one thing to be rich, another to be enlightened, brave or humane . . . those things, indeed, are all indirectly connected, and react upon one another."[2]

2. John Stuart Mill, *Principles of Political Economy,* in *Reprints of Economic Classics,* ed. Augustus M. Kelley (New York: Bookseller, 1965), pp. 1–2.

# KEY POINTS

**1.** U.S. gross domestic product (GDP) is the total production of new goods and services in the United States during a particular period.

**2.** GDP can be measured by adding all spending on new goods and services in the United States. Changes in inventories and net exports must be added to spending.

**3.** GDP can also be measured by adding labor income, capital income, depreciation, sales taxes, and net income of foreigners. Except for a small statistical discrepancy, the income approach gives the same answer as the spending approach.

**4.** Value added is a measure of a firm's production. Value added is defined as the difference between the value of the production sold and the cost of inputs to production. GDP can be measured by adding the value added of all firms in the economy.

**5.** National saving in the United States is defined as income less consumption less government purchases. National saving must be equal to investment plus net exports.

**6.** Real GDP is a measure of production adjusted for inflation. It is the best overall measure of changes in the production of goods and services over time.

**7.** GDP is not without its shortcomings. It does not include production in the underground economy or much work done in the home. And it is only one of many measures of well-being.

**8.** To compare real GDP in different countries, the exchange rate must be adjusted for differences in prices in the different countries using purchasing power parity.

# KEY TERMS

intermediate good
final good
national income and product
  accounts
consumption
investment
business fixed investment
inventory investment
residential investment
government purchases
net exports

exports
imports
trade balance
labor income
capital income
depreciation
net investment
gross investment
indirect business taxes
statistical discrepancy
national income

personal income
value added
national saving
real GDP
nominal GDP
GDP deflator
price level
consumer price index (CPI)
chain weighted price index
purchasing power parity
  exchange rate

# QUESTIONS FOR REVIEW

**1.** Why do we add up total spending in order to compute GDP when GDP is supposed to be a measure of production?

**2.** Approximately what were the percentages of consumption, investment, government purchases, and net exports in GDP in 1996 in the United States? How do they compare with Japan and Germany?

**3.** Why is the sum of all income equal to GDP?

**4.** What is national saving? Why is it always equal to investment plus net exports?

**5.** Under what assumptions about net exports will an increase in national saving increase investment?

**6.** What is the significance of value added, and how does one measure it for a single firm?

**7.** Why are increases in nominal GDP not a good measure of economic growth?

**8.** Why is the production of meals in the home not included in GDP? Should it be?

**9.** Why is the purchase of a used car not included in GDP? Should it be?

**10.** Why do we add inventory investment to spending when computing GDP?

# PROBLEMS

**1.** Given the information in the table at the bottom of the page for three consecutive years in the U.S. economy, calculate the missing data.

**2.** Suppose the U.S. government is trying to bring underground activities into the legal economy so it can collect taxes on these activities.

    a) How is this campaign likely to affect the measure of GDP?

    b) Will this change in GDP reflect a change in well-being?

**3.** In market economies, prices reflect the value people place on goods and services, and therefore it makes sense to use them as weights when calculating GDP. In centrally planned economies, however, prices are controlled by the government instead of the market. Examine the following data for a centrally planned economy that subsequently frees prices:

| Good | Quantity | Controlled Price | Market Price |
|------|----------|------------------|--------------|
| Bread | 1,000 | $ 2 | $10 |
| Shirts | 500 | $20 | $15 |

    a) Calculate GDP under the controlled prices and under market prices, assuming the quantities do not change. Did governmentally set prices mean an under- or overvaluation of production on the whole?

    b) How do people value each good in relation to previously controlled prices?

**4.** Look at the two scenarios for monthly inventories and sales for a company producing TV dinners. In both scenarios, the company's sales are the same. In scenario A, the company maintains production at a constant level. In scenario B, the company adjusts production within the month to match sales.

    a) Calculate the inventory investment in each month and resulting stock of inventory at the beginning of the following month for both scenarios.

    b) Does maintaining constant production lead to greater or lesser fluctuations in the stock of inventory? Explain.

**Scenario A**

| Month | Start-of the-Month Inventory Stock | Production | Sales | Inventory Investment |
|-------|------------|------------|-------|------------|
| Jan. | 80 | 80 | 80 | _____ |
| Feb. | _____ | 80 | 60 | _____ |
| Mar. | _____ | 80 | 40 | _____ |
| Apr. | _____ | 80 | 100 | _____ |
| May | _____ | 80 | 80 | _____ |

**Scenario B**

| Month | Start-of the-Month Inventory Stock | Production | Sales | Inventory Investment |
|-------|------------|------------|-------|------------|
| Jan. | 80 | 80 | 80 | _____ |
| Feb. | _____ | 60 | 60 | _____ |
| Mar. | _____ | 40 | 40 | _____ |
| Apr. | _____ | 100 | 100 | _____ |
| May | _____ | 80 | 80 | _____ |

**5.** Suppose there are only three goods in the economy:

| Year | Good | Price | Quantity |
|------|------|-------|----------|
| 1997 | Apples | $1/lb. | 500 lbs. |
| | Bananas | $2/lb. | 250 lbs. |
| | Computers | $1,000 | 5 |
| 1998 | Apples | $1.50/lb. | 400 lbs. |
| | Bananas | $2.50/lb. | 200 lbs. |
| | Computers | $1,000 | 7 |

    a) Calculate nominal GDP for 1997 and 1998.

    b) Calculate the percentage change in GDP from 1997 to 1998 using 1997 prices and 1998 prices.

    c) Calculate the percentage change in real GDP from 1997 to 1998 using your answers from (b).

    d) What is the GDP deflator for 1998 if it equals 1.0 in 1997?

**Problem 1**

| Year | Nominal GDP (in billions of U.S. dollars) | Real GDP (in billions of 1992 dollars) | GDP Deflator (1992 = 100) | Inflation (percent change in GDP deflator) | Real GDP per Capita (in 1992 dollars) | Population (in millions) |
|------|------|------|------|------|------|------|
| 1990 | 5,743.8 | _____ | 93.6 | 4.3 | _____ | 249.9 |
| 1991 | | 6,079.0 | _____ | 4.0 | _____ | 252.7 |
| 1992 | _____ | _____ | 100.00 | _____ | 24,449 | 255.4 |

**6.** Use the following data for a South Dakota wheat farm:

| | |
|---|---|
| Revenue: | $1,000 |
| Costs: | |
| Wages and salaries | $ 700 |
| Rent on land | $ 50 |
| Rental fee for tractor | $ 100 |
| Seed, fertilizer | $ 100 |
| Pesticide, irrigation | $ 50 |

a) Calculate value added by this farm.

b) Profits are revenue minus costs. Capital income consists of profits, rents, and interest. Show that value added equals capital income plus labor income paid by the farm.

c) Suppose that, due to flooding in Kansas, wheat prices increase suddenly and revenues rise to $1,100 but prices of intermediate inputs do not change. What happens to value added and profits in this case?

**7.** Suppose the following data describe the economic activity in a country for 1998.

| Component of Spending | Value in Billions of Dollars |
|---|---|
| Consumption | 500 |
| Business fixed and residential investment | 100 |
| Inventory stock at the end of 1997 | 10 |
| Inventory stock at the end of 1998 | 50 |
| Depreciation | 15 |
| Government outlays | 250 |
| Government purchases | 200 |
| Total government tax receipts | 190 |
| Exports | 150 |
| Imports | 120 |
| Labor income | 450 |
| Capital income | 250 |
| Net income of foreigners | 20 |
| Sales taxes | 100 |

Given these data, calculate the following:

a) Inventory investment

b) Net exports

c) Gross domestic product

d) Statistical discrepancy

e) National saving

f) Government saving

Verify that national saving equals investment plus net exports.

**8.** In 1991, investment in Japan was about 146 trillion yen and the trade surplus was 8 trillion yen. How much was national saving in Japan? If the government had neither a budget surplus nor a budget deficit, how much was saving by consumers and businesses in Japan?

**9.** When Americans travel to developing countries, they usually find their dollars buy much more than in the United States.

a) If purchasing power parity exchange rates are used instead of market exchange rates, what is likely to happen to estimates of GDP per capita for these developing countries?

b) GDP per capita is an imperfect measure of production because it doesn't include home production. In countries where a garden plot provides a significant portion of the family's food, is production likely to be overstated or understated by looking at GDP? Why?

**10.** Prices of Big Macs in various countries have been used to illustrate the purchasing power parity (PPP) exchange rates between the countries.

a) Suppose the price of a Big Mac in Moscow is 11,000 rubles, and in the United States the price is $2.50. What would be the PPP exchange rate according to Big Mac prices?

b) A friend of yours comes back from Moscow and tells you that he received 5,800 rubles for every dollar he traded on the street near Red Square. How does this exchange rate compare to the Big Mac PPP you calculated?

c) Suppose Russian GDP was 1,130 billion rubles in 1997. The price of a Big Mac in Moscow was about 11,000 rubles, while the street exchange rate at the end of the summer was about 5,800 rubles per dollar. Assuming a $2.50 U.S. price for a Big Mac, calculate Russian 1997 GDP in dollars using the Big Mac PPP rate. Compare this with the GDP using the street market exchange rate for 1997.

# part

## 3

# Long-Run Fundamentals and Economic Growth

Economic growth has long been a subject of economic research. It was the major subject of Adam Smith's *Wealth of Nations*, published in 1776, just as the first great wave of economic growth was gaining steam. The phrase *wealth of nations* was used to describe the economic growth of a nation. Labor, capital, and technology all played a role in Adam Smith's writings, but it was not until the 1950s that economists developed a theory sophisticated enough to distinguish between and measure the relative effects of labor, capital, and technology on economic growth. This new line of research is ongoing.

The theory of economic growth is based on a few fundamental economic principles that are particularly applicable to long-run issues. These long-run fundamentals pertain to four key areas: (1) the determination of employment through the supply and demand for labor, (2) the determination of the interest rate and

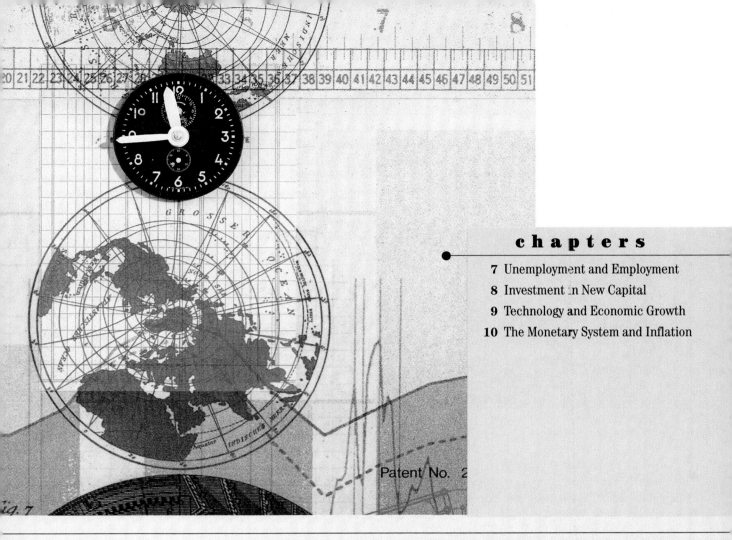

Patent No. 2

investment in the economy as a whole, (3) the production of technology through invention and innovation, and (4) the determination of the overall price level and inflation. The four chapters in this part of the book cover these four areas.

In Chapter 7 we look at what determines the number of jobs as well as the level of unemployment in the economy as a whole. In Chapter 8 we show how to determine the real interest rate and in doing so explain investment, saving, and capital accumulation. The level of well-being in an economy depends on the capital workers have to work with and on the growth of technology, including workers' skills. In Chapter 9 we illustrate how economists determine which factors are more important for economic growth. In Chapter 10 we examine the role of the monetary system in the economy and explain how the price level and inflation are determined in the long run.

There is considerable agreement among economists about the long-run macroeconomic principles discussed in these chapters. These principles address many of the deep problems the United States and other countries face at the end of the twentieth century, such as lower long-run economic growth than earlier in the century. The explanations for fluctuations in total production and employment—a more controversial but equally important topic—are discussed in the next part of the book, Chapters 11–14.

# 7

# Unemployment and Employment

Unemployment is where the macroeconomy touches people most intensely. When unemployment is low, it is easier for people to find satisfying, well-paying jobs. When unemployment is high, jobs are harder to find, and people may accept jobs that do not closely match their skills. Unemployment rises during recessions and declines during recoveries. But even during normal periods when the economy is growing smoothly—neither in recession nor in boom—unemployment remains well above zero. In 1997, for example, a full six years away from the previous recession, about 7 million people were unemployed in the United States. Seven million!

Unemployment in years like 1997 can be as painful and cause as much hardship to those who experience it as unemployment in recessions. Beyond the obvious hardship of economic loss, unemployment can have other, even more devastating effects on the people involved. If unemployment persists, people may fall into poverty. The lack of a job for a long time is hard on an individual's self-respect—and it can destroy families. Young people who are consistently unemployed may never learn marketable job skills and can become disillusioned about their hopes for the future. The rate of teenage unemployment is high—even in normal periods the unemployment rate for teenagers rarely dips below 15 percent—and is even higher for black teenagers—over 30 percent.

Aside from the individual and family hardships, there is another reason to be interested in the rate of unemployment. When more workers are unemployed, aggregate production in the economy is less than if those same workers were employed. That is, there is an underutilization of resources. In contrast, when employment is growing rapidly, the economy's production of goods and services is also growing rapidly, providing more resources to meet peoples' needs and wants.

This chapter examines unemployment, employment growth, and the effect of employment on the capacity of the economy to produce goods and services. It explains how unemployment is measured, and it examines the determinants of unemployment and the policy actions that can be taken to reduce unemployment.

# EMPLOYMENT AND UNEMPLOYMENT TRENDS

In this section we show how unemployment and employment are defined and measured, examine recent employment trends in the United States, and develop a comprehensive measure of labor input to production.

## Cyclical, Frictional, and Structural Unemployment

Figure 7.1 shows the unemployment rate and real GDP in the United States during a 15-year period that includes two recessions and two long expansions. Economists use the term **natural unemployment rate** to refer to the unemployment rate that exists when the economy is neither in a recession nor in a boom and real GDP is equal to potential GDP. Observe that the actual unemployment rate rises above the natural unemployment rate when the economy goes into a recession and real GDP falls below potential GDP. And the unemployment rate falls below the natural rate when the economy goes into a boom and real GDP rises above potential GDP. For example, as shown in Figure 7.1, the unemployment rate fell to 5 percent in 1989 as the economy boomed and then rose to over 7 percent when the economy went into a recession in 1991. Then the unemployment rate declined as real GDP moved closer to potential GDP in 1993 and 1994.

The increase in unemployment above the natural rate during and in the aftermath of recessions is called **cyclical unemployment** because it is related to the business cycle. For example, the increase in the unemployment rate from 1990 to 1992 was cyclical. The unemployment that exists in more normal times is due to a combination of **frictional unemployment** and **structural unemployment**. Frictional unemployment occurs as new workers enter the labor force and must look for work, or as workers change jobs for one reason or another and need some time to find another job. Most frictional unemployment is short lived. In contrast, some workers are unemployed for a long time, six months or more; they may have trouble finding work because they have insufficient skills, or their skills are no longer in demand because of a technological change or a shift in people's tastes toward new products. Such unemployment is called structural unemployment. The amount of frictional unemployment and structural unemployment in the economy is not a constant, so the natural unemployment rate may change over time. But such changes are more gradual and not directly related to business cycle fluctuations.

When economists use the term *natural* unemployment rate, they do not mean to say "okay" or "just fine," as when your doctor tells you that to have a higher temperature in the evening than in the morning is "natural." They simply mean that whenever the overall macroeconomy operates close to normal in the sense that real GDP is near potential GDP, the unemployment rate hovers around this natural rate.

The natural rate of unemployment appears to have been close to 5 percent in the 1950s. Some even claimed it was 4 percent. It increased slightly in the late 1960s and early 1970s. One possible reason for the increase was the influx of young baby boom workers into the labor force in the 1960s and 1970s. Young people tend to have higher unemployment rates than older people. There is a possibility that

**natural unemployment rate:**
the unemployment rate that exists in normal times, when there is neither a recession nor a boom and real GDP is equal to potential GDP.

**cyclical unemployment:**
unemployment due to a recession, when the rate of unemployment is above the natural rate of unemployment.

**frictional unemployment:**
short-term unemployment arising from normal turnover in the labor market, such as when people change occupations or locations, or are new entrants.

**structural unemployment:**
long-term unemployment due to structural problems such as poor skills or longer-term changes in demand or insufficient work incentives.

**FIGURE 7.1**
**Real GDP, Potential GDP, and the Unemployment Rate**

In periods like 1987 or early 1994 real GDP is equal to potential GDP and the unemployment rate is equal to the natural rate of unemployment, which appears to be somewhere around 6 percent. Note that when real GDP is above potential GDP, the unemployment rate is below the natural rate of unemployment; and when real GDP is below potential GDP, the unemployment rate is above the natural rate.

*Source:* U.S. Department of Commerce and U.S. Department of Labor.

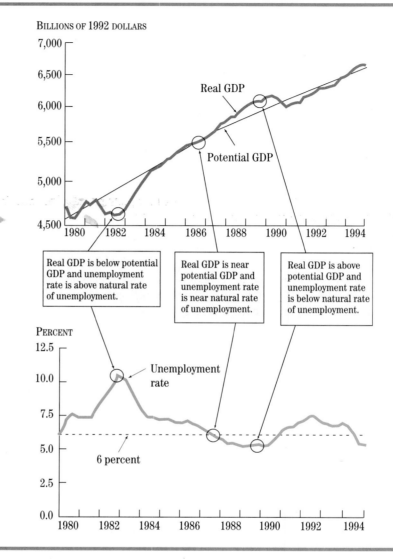

the natural rate is declining again as the labor force ages. Some economists believe that the natural rate fell to about 5.5 percent in the late 1990s, but it is unlikely to have fallen below 5 percent. It is important to remember that the natural unemployment rate is not a constant and that economists do not know its value precisely.

## How Is Unemployment Measured?

**current population survey:**
a monthly survey of a sample of U.S. households done by the U.S. Census Bureau; it measures employment, unemployment, the labor force, and other characteristics of the U.S. population.

**labor force:** all those who are either employed or unemployed.

Each month the U.S. Census Bureau surveys a sample of about 60,000 households in the United States. The survey is called the **current population survey.** By asking the people in the survey a number of questions, the Census Bureau determines whether each person 16 years of age or over is employed or unemployed. The **labor force** consists of all people 16 years of age and over who are either employed or unemployed.

### Who Is Employed and Who Is Unemployed?

To be counted as unemployed, a person must be looking for work, but not have a job. To be counted as employed a person must have a job, either a job outside the home—as in the case of a teaching job at a high school or a welding job at a factory—or a *paid* job inside the home—as in the case of a freelance editor or a telemarketer who works for pay at home. A person who has an *unpaid* job at home—for example, caring for children or working on the house—is not counted as employed. If a person is not counted either as unemployed or employed, then the person is not in the labor force. For example, a person who is working at home without pay and who is not looking for a paid job is considered not in the labor force.

    Figure 7.2 illustrates the definitions of employment, unemployment, and the labor force. Using 1996 as an example, it shows that out of a total population of 265.5 million, about 200.5 million were in the **working-age population,** people 16 years of age or over (and not in jail or a hospital unable to work). Of this 200.5 million, about 126.7 million were employed and about 7.2 million were unemployed; the remaining 66.6 million were of working age but not in the labor force.

> **working-age population:** persons over 16 years of age who are not in an institution such as a jail or hospital.

### The Labor Force and Discouraged Workers

Judging who should be counted in the labor force and who should not be counted is difficult. For example, consider two retired people. One decided to retire at age 65 and is now enjoying retirement in Florida. The other was laid off from a job at age 55 and, after looking for a job for two years, got discouraged and stopped looking, feeling forced into retirement. You may feel that the second person, but not the first, should be counted as unemployed. However, according to the official statistics, neither is unemployed; they are not in the labor force because they are not looking for work. In general, workers, such as the second retired worker, who have left the labor force after not being able to find a job are called *discouraged workers.*

    Defining and measuring the labor force is the most difficult part of measuring the amount of unemployment. In 1994 a slight change in the way the questions were phrased in the current population survey revealed that many women who were working at home without pay were actually looking for a paid job; as a result of the change in the question these women are now counted as unemployed rather than as out of the labor force. As a result of the change, the labor force and measured unemployment both rose.

### Part-Time Work

A person is counted as employed in the current population survey if he or she has worked at all during the week of the survey. Thus, part-time workers are counted as employed. The official definition of a **part-time worker** is one who works between 1 and 34 hours per week. About 11 percent of U.S. workers are employed part time.

> **part-time worker:** someone who works between 1 and 34 hours per week.

    There is a big difference between the percentage of men who work part time and the percentage of women who work part time. About 20 percent of women work part time while only about 7 percent of men work part time. Women give personal choice rather than unavailability of full-time jobs as a reason for part-time work more frequently than men do. About 29 percent of employed women who have children under 6 work part time.

    Because of part-time work, the average number of hours of work per worker each week is about 34 hours, less than the typical 40 hours a week.

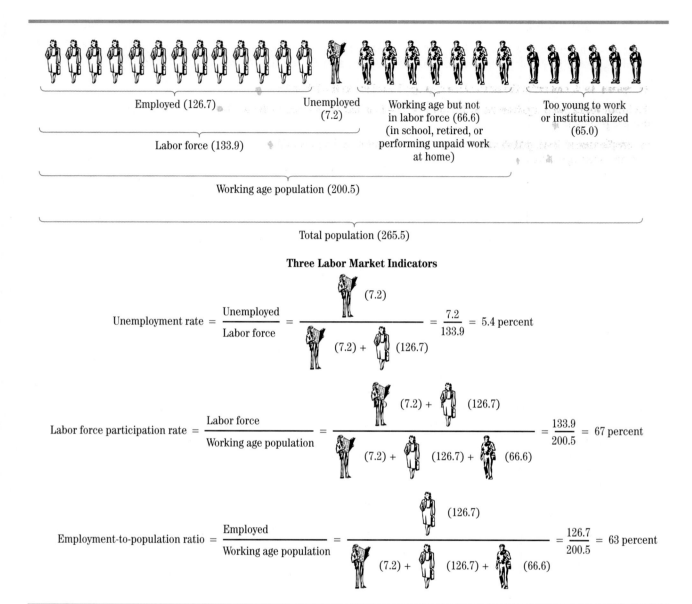

**FIGURE 7.2**

**Placing the Population into Labor Market Categories**

As shown at the top of this diagram, the total population is divided into four groups: employed, unemployed, working age but not in the labor force, and too young to work or institutionalized. Three key labor market indicators are then computed from these categories. For example, the unemployment rate is the number of unemployed divided by the number of people in the labor force. The employment-to-population ratio divides the number of employed workers by the working-age population. (The numbers in parentheses are millions and show statistics for 1996. Each pictograph represents approximately 10 million people.)

*Source:* U.S. Department of Labor.

## Comparing Three Key Indicators

Now let us examine the three key indicators of conditions in the labor market. These are

1. the **unemployment rate,** the ratio of unemployed workers to the labor force;

2. the **labor force participation rate,** the ratio of people in the labor force to the working-age population;

3. the **employment-to-population ratio,** the ratio of employed workers to the working-age population.

All three are measured in percent as shown in Figure 7.2. Both the unemployment rate and the labor force participation rate depend on the labor force, and therefore have the same measurement difficulties that the labor force does. Only the employment-to-population ratio does not depend on the labor force.

The shaded panel of Table 7.1 shows the behavior of these indicators from the mid-1970s to the mid-1990s. Note how the unemployment rate fluctuated around an average of about 6 percent during these years as the economy went through recessions in the early 1980s and early 1990s. The unemployment rate rose to about

**unemployment rate:** the ratio (usually expressed as a percentage) of unemployed workers to the labor force.

**labor force participation rate:** the ratio (usually expressed as a percentage) of people in the labor force to the working-age population.

**employment-to-population ratio:** the ratio (usually expressed as a percentage) of employed workers to the working-age population.

●━━━━━━━━━━━━━━━━

**TABLE 7.1**

**Recent History of Labor Market Indicators**

| Year | Population (millions) | Working-Age Population (millions) | Labor Force (millions) | Employed (millions) | Unemployed (millions) | Unemploy-ment Rate (percent) | Labor Force Participation Rate (percent) | Employ-ment-to Population Ratio (percent) |
|------|------|------|------|------|------|------|------|------|
| 1976 | 218.0 | 157.8 | 97.8 | 90.4 | 7.4 | 7.6 | 62 | 57 |
| 1977 | 220.2 | 160.7 | 100.7 | 93.7 | 7.0 | 7.0 | 63 | 58 |
| 1978 | 222.6 | 163.5 | 103.9 | 97.7 | 6.2 | 6.0 | 64 | 60 |
| 1979 | 225.1 | 166.5 | 106.6 | 100.4 | 6.2 | 5.8 | 64 | 60 |
| 1980 | 227.7 | 169.3 | 108.5 | 100.9 | 7.6 | 7.0 | 64 | 60 |
| 1981 | 223.0 | 171.8 | 110.3 | 102.0 | 8.3 | 7.5 | 64 | 59 |
| 1982 | 232.2 | 173.9 | 111.9 | 101.2 | 10.7 | 9.6 | 64 | 58 |
| 1983 | 234.3 | 175.9 | 113.2 | 102.5 | 10.7 | 9.5 | 64 | 58 |
| 1984 | 236.3 | 178.1 | 115.2 | 106.7 | 8.5 | 7.4 | 65 | 60 |
| 1985 | 238.5 | 179.9 | 117.2 | 108.9 | 8.3 | 7.1 | 65 | 61 |
| 1986 | 240.7 | 182.3 | 119.5 | 111.3 | 8.2 | 6.9 | 66 | 61 |
| 1987 | 242.8 | 184.5 | 121.6 | 114.2 | 7.4 | 6.1 | 66 | 62 |
| 1988 | 245.0 | 186.3 | 123.4 | 116.7 | 6.7 | 5.4 | 66 | 63 |
| 1989 | 247.3 | 188.1 | 125.6 | 119.0 | 6.6 | 5.3 | 67 | 63 |
| 1990 | 249.9 | 189.7 | 126.4 | 119.6 | 6.8 | 5.4 | 67 | 63 |
| 1991 | 252.7 | 191.3 | 126.9 | 118.4 | 8.5 | 6.7 | 66 | 62 |
| 1992 | 255.5 | 193.1 | 128.5 | 119.2 | 9.3 | 7.2 | 67 | 62 |
| 1993 | 258.2 | 195.0 | 129.5 | 120.8 | 8.7 | 6.7 | 66 | 62 |
| 1994 | 260.7 | 196.8 | 131.1 | 123.1 | 8.0 | 6.1 | 66 | 63 |
| 1995 | 263.0 | 198.6 | 132.3 | 124.9 | 7.4 | 5.6 | 67 | 63 |
| 1996 | 265.5 | 200.5 | 133.9 | 126.7 | 7.2 | 5.4 | 67 | 63 |

*Source:* U.S. Department of Labor, Bureau of Labor Statistics.

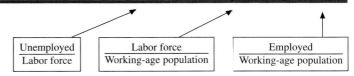

| $\dfrac{\text{Unemployed}}{\text{Labor force}}$ | $\dfrac{\text{Labor force}}{\text{Working-age population}}$ | $\dfrac{\text{Employed}}{\text{Working-age population}}$ |

**FIGURE 7.3**

**Employment-to-Population Ratio for Men, Women, and Everyone**

The percentage of working-age women who work outside the home has increased steadily since the 1950s. At the same time, the percentage of working-age men who work outside the home has declined, until the late 1970s, when it leveled off. Since then the total employment-to-population ratio has increased. There are declines in all three ratios during recessions.

*Source:* U.S. Department of Labor.

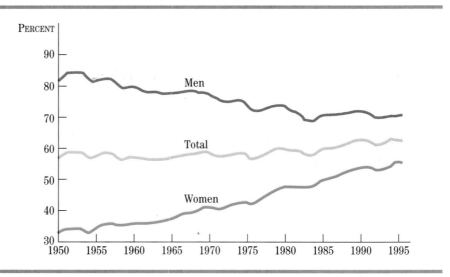

10 percent in 1982 after the 1981–1982 recession. In the absence of these business cycle fluctuations, the unemployment rate was about 6 percent. This indicates that the natural unemployment rate was about 6 percent during this period.

Table 7.1 shows a steady rise in the labor force participation rate, from 62 percent of the labor force in the mid-1970s to 67 percent of the labor force in the mid-1990s. This increase is mainly due to more women entering the labor force, a trend that has been going on since the 1950s. In the early 1950s about 30 percent of women were in the labor force, but now about 60 percent are. Possible explanations for this trend include reduced discrimination, increased opportunities and pay for women, the favorable experience of many women working for pay during World War II, and the women's movement, which emphasized the attractiveness of paid work outside the home.

The employment-to-population ratio fluctuates as real GDP fluctuates, but there is an important longer-term trend. The employment-to-population ratio has increased from about 57 percent in 1976 to about 63 percent in 1996. The employment-to-population ratio is higher than it has been at any time in U.S. history. In this sense the U.S. economy is creating more jobs now than at any time in its history. How does one explain this? Again, the rising percentage of women who are employed is a major factor, as shown in Figure 7.3.

## Aggregate Hours of Labor Input

As we have seen, some people work part time. Others work full time; some work overtime. For these reasons, the number of people employed is not a good measure of the labor input to production in the economy. For example, consider two typists who both work half time; one works 4 hours in the morning and the other works 4 hours in the afternoon, both 5 days a week. Together they work as much as one full-time typist; to say that the labor input of these two typists is twice as much as the labor input of one full-time typist would be an obvious mistake. Rather, their combined labor input is the same as one full-time typist: 40 hours a week.

This example shows why economists consider the number of hours people work rather than the number of people who work when they measure labor input to production, whether it is typists at a firm or workers in the whole economy. Thus, the most comprehensive measure of labor input to the production of real GDP is the total number of hours worked by all workers, or **aggregate hours.** The number of aggregate hours of labor input depends on the average number of hours of work for each person and the number of people working.

**aggregate hours:** the total number of hours worked by all workers in the economy in a given period of time.

### Effects of Unemployment on Labor Input

How does a change in the unemployment rate change the amount of labor input to production? Consider an example. Suppose that the rate of unemployment rises to 10 percent from 6 percent. With a labor force of 134 million this would lower the number of employed workers by about 5 million $[(.10 - .06) \times 134 = 5]$. Thus, an increase in the unemployment rate clearly reduces labor input.

### Case Study: CEA Forecasts of Future Aggregate Hours

The first row of Table 7.2 shows the growth rate of aggregate hours during the recent past and the near future. The information is taken from the 1997 *Economic Report of the President* and illustrates how aggregate hours are analyzed and projected by the Council of Economic Advisers (CEA), the group responsible for preparing the economic report and making economic forecasts for the president.

Observe in the second row of Table 7.2 that the growth of the working-age population slowed down in the 1990s to about 1 percent per year. This is the main reason the growth of aggregate hours also slowed down, as shown in the first row of Table 7.2.

How fast are aggregate hours likely to grow in the future? The President's Council of Economic Advisers predicts that the growth rate of aggregate hours during the late 1990s and early twenty-first century will be 1.2 percent per year, as shown in Table 7.2. It arrived at this estimate by considering three factors. Let us consider each in turn.

First, the CEA predicts that the growth rate of the working-age population will be *1.0 percent per year.* At least for the next 10 years there is little uncertainty about the growth of the working-age population because most of this population is already born and the number of people likely to immigrate can be estimated from U.S. limits on immigration.

Second, the CEA predicts that the employment-to-population ratio will increase slightly, contributing about *.2 percent per year* to the growth of aggregate hours.

| | 1973–1990 | 1990–1996 | 1996–2003 |
|---|---|---|---|
| Growth rate of aggregate hours | 1.7 | 1.4 | 1.2 |
| Growth rate of working-age population | 1.5 | 1.0 | 1.0 |

**TABLE 7.2**
**Growth Rates of Aggregate Hours and Working-Age Population**
(percent per year)

*Source: Economic Report of the President,* 1997, Table 2–3, p. 86.

Third, the CEA predicts that there will be little or no change in the number of hours per worker; in other words the CEA estimates that this will contribute *0 percent per year* to the growth of aggregate hours. The growth in the number of hours per worker slowed down in recent years, partly because of the increase in part-time work in the economy. However, the CEA predicts that this slowdown will end and the hours per worker will remain steady.

Adding this all up (1.0 percent + .2 percent + 0 percent), the CEA forecasts that aggregate labor input will grow by 1.2 percent per year in the next few years.

## Review

▶ Unemployment and employment in the United States are measured by a current population survey.

▶ Only working-age people can be unemployed, according to the official definition of unemployment, and to be counted as unemployed you have to be looking for work.

▶ The unemployment rate in the United States has averaged about 6 percent in the last 30 years, but the actual unemployment rate has fluctuated around this average. The unemployment rate in the absence of cyclical increases or decreases in unemployment is called the natural unemployment rate.

▶ The term *natural* in natural unemployment rate does not mean good or even satisfactory. The natural rate of unemployment is not a constant. It was around 5 percent in the 1950s and may return to 5 percent in the future.

▶ The employment-to-population ratio has risen in the 1970s and 1980s. More women have been entering the labor force since the early 1950s. Average hours worked per worker have declined.

▶ Aggregate hours is the most comprehensive measure of labor input. It is expected to grow by about 1.2 percent per year in the near future.

# THE NATURE OF UNEMPLOYMENT

Having examined the aggregate data, let us now look at the circumstances of people who are unemployed. There are many reasons people become unemployed, and their experiences with unemployment vary widely.

## Reasons People Are Unemployed

We can divide up the many reasons people become unemployed into three broad categories. People are unemployed because they have either *lost their previous job* (**job losers**), *quit their previous job* (**job leavers**), or *just entered the labor force to look for work* (**new entrants**).

### Job Losers

**job losers:** people who are unemployed because they lost their previous job.

**job leavers:** people who are unemployed because they quit their previous job.

**new entrants:** people who are unemployed because they just entered the labor force and are still looking for work.

Among the people who lost their jobs in a typical recent year was a vice president of a large bank in New York City. When the vice president's financial services marketing department was eliminated, she lost her job. After three months of unemployment that were spent searching for work and waiting for responses from her letters and telephone calls, the former vice president took a freelance job, using her expertise in bank accounts to advise clients. Within a year, she was making three times her former salary.

**Three Reasons People Are Unemployed**

At any given time, people are unemployed for one of three reasons: They lost their job and are looking for another job (left), they quit their previous job and are still looking for a new job (middle), or they just entered the labor force and are unemployed while looking for work (right).

The vice president's unemployment experience, although surely trying for her at the time, had a happy ending. In fact, you might say that the labor market worked pretty well. At least judging by her salary, she is more productive in her new job. Although one job was destroyed, another one—better, in this case—was created.

This transition from one job to another is part of the dynamism of any free market economy. The economist Joseph Schumpeter called this dynamism *creative destruction,* referring to the loss of whole business firms as well as jobs when new ideas and techniques replace the old. Creative destruction means that something better is created as something else is destroyed. In this case, a better job was created when another job was destroyed. On average, about 5 percent of jobs are destroyed each year by plant closings, bankruptcies, or downsizing of firms. In 1996 that amounted to about 6 million jobs destroyed. On balance, for an economy with growing employment more jobs are created than are destroyed. In 1996 enough jobs were created that on balance, employment increased by nearly 2 million jobs. But unemployment, at least part of it, is a by-product of these changes.

Many people who lose their job are probably not as lucky as the woman in our story. Among the unemployed in the 1990s were middle-aged engineers let go by McDonnell Douglas after many years of employment. Finding a new job is difficult for such workers because their skills are specific to a particular firm. The loss of such a job not only has disastrous effects on their incomes, but it can have psychological effects. It may mean that their children cannot go to college, or that they must sell their house. Unemployment compensation provides some relief—perhaps about $200 a week until it runs out. In many cases, though, this is well below what these workers were earning. Until they find a new job, they are obviously part of the millions of unemployed. Some may wait until a comparable job comes along; others may accept a lower-paying job. For example, one worker laid off from McDonnell Douglas took a job installing new kitchens at half the pay.

People may lose their jobs even when the economy is not in a recession. On average, about half of all unemployed workers are unemployed because they lost their job for one reason or another. The economy is always in a state of flux, with some firms going out of business or shrinking and other firms starting up or

**FIGURE 7.4**
**Unemployment According to Previous Job Status**

On average, about half of unemployment consists of people who lost their jobs, either temporarily or permanently. The rest consists of people who left their jobs to look for another job or who were previously out of the labor force. The number of unemployed who are job losers increases in recessions and decreases in booms.

*Source:* U.S. Department of Labor.

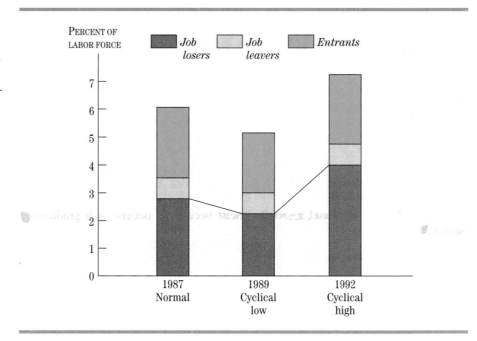

**job vacancies:** positions that firms are trying to fill, but for which they have yet to find suitable workers.

expanding. Tastes change, new discoveries are made, and competition improves productivity and changes the relative fortune of firms and workers.

**Job vacancies** are the jobs firms are trying to fill. Job vacancies and unemployment exist simultaneously. Unfortunately, many job vacancies require different skills, are in another part of the country, or are at lower wages than the skills, location, or former salaries of unemployed workers. This is especially true during periods of great change such as in the 1990s, when defense spending fell rapidly. Workers skilled at one job may be unemployed while firms cannot find workers with other skills.

The number of unemployed workers who have lost their job increases during recessions, when the unemployment rate is cyclically high, and declines in booms, when the unemployment rate is cyclically low, as shown in Figure 7.4. The main reason is that it is more difficult to find a new job in a recession, when fewer firms are hiring, than in a boom, when many firms are hiring. Figure 7.4 shows that increases and decreases in the number of unemployed workers who have lost their job is the only component of unemployment that moves up and down significantly during the business cycle. The proportion of people who are job leavers and new entrants is fairly constant.

### *Job Leavers*

Some estimate that on average American workers change jobs every three or four years. Many of these job changes occur when people are young: Young workers are finding out what they are good at or what they enjoy or are rapidly accumulating skills that give them greater opportunities. A small part of unemployment—about 1 percentage point—consists of people who quit their previous job to look for another job. While they are looking for work they are counted as unemployed.

There is very little increase in unemployment due to quits in recessions. Why? Two opposing forces net out to little change. In a recession, when unemployment is high, fewer workers quit their job because they fear being unemployed for a long period of time. This reduces quit unemployment, but the lower number of job vacancies makes finding a job more difficult and raises unemployment.

### New Entrants and Re-entrants

Figure 7.4 also shows that a large number of the unemployed workers in any year have just entered the work force. If you do not have a job lined up before you graduate, there is a good chance that you will be unemployed for a period of time while you look for work following graduation. In fact, there is a huge increase in unemployment each June when millions of students enter the labor force for the first time. This is called **seasonal unemployment** because it occurs each graduation "season." In contrast, unemployment is relatively low around the holiday season, when many businesses hire extra employees. Government statisticians smooth out this seasonal unemployment to help them see other trends in unemployment, so the newspaper reports on the unemployment rate rarely mention this phenomenon.

Some unemployed workers are re-entering the labor force. For example, a young person may decide to go back to school and then re-enter the labor force afterward. Others might choose to drop out of the labor force for several years to take care of small children at home—a job that is not counted in the employment statistics.

Some new entrants to the labor force find it very difficult to find a job. They remain unemployed for long periods of time. In fact, although the hardships of people who lose their jobs are severe, the hardships for many young people who seem to be endlessly looking for work are also severe.

**seasonal unemployment:** unemployment that varies with the seasons of the year due to seasonal fluctuations in supply or demand for labor.

**FIGURE 7.5**

**Unemployment by Duration**

On average, about half of unemployment is very short term—less than 5 weeks. Longer-term unemployment increases in recessions and decreases in booms along with total unemployment.

*Source:* U.S. Department of Labor.

## Long-Term versus Short-Term Unemployment

The hardships associated with unemployment depend on its duration. Figure 7.5 shows how the unemployment rate divides up according to how long the unemployed workers have been unemployed. On average, about half of unemployment is very short term, less than 5 weeks. A market economy encompassing 265 million people exercising free choice could not possibly function without some very short-term unemployment as people changed jobs or looked for new opportunities.

Another 35 percent of unemployed workers have been unemployed for more than 5 weeks but less than 6 months, leaving about 15 percent of unemployed workers who have been unemployed for more than 6 months—the truly long-term unemployed. Although the number of short-term unemployed does not vary much over the business cycle, the number of long-term unemployed increases dramatically in recessions and falls during booms.

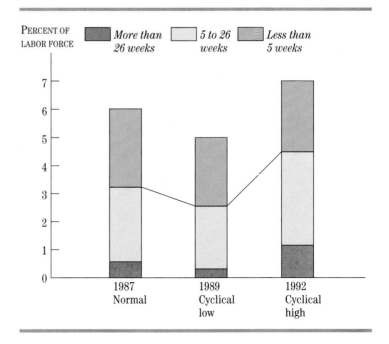

Each month—usually the first Friday of the month—the U.S. Department of Labor releases information about employment and unemployment in the previous month. There is a major news article about the report in most newspapers. The following article is a typical example. You should be able to find the terms discussed in this article in the text.

There is one frequent point of confusion in the monthly reports. The current population survey of *house-holds* provides data on employment. However, there is another way the government gets data about employment: by asking *firms* directly about how many workers they employ in the so-called *payroll* or *establishment survey*.

The establishment survey is always released with the household survey each month, and this is the cause for confusion, as illustrated in the article below: Although employment rose by a large amount in the household survey, it only rose by a small amount in the payroll survey. This is why the headline mentioned a skewed picture. Over short periods of time the establishment survey is a better measure, but over the longer term—a year or more—the current population survey is better because it captures employment at new firms or self-employment.

*Source of article:* Yi-Hsin Chang, "Jobless Rate Skews Picture of Labor Market." Reprinted by permission of *The Wall Street Journal,* © 1994 Dow Jones Company, Inc. All rights reserved worldwide.

# Jobless Rate Skews Picture of Labor Market

Big Drop Overstates Trend; Payroll Rise Suggests More Moderate Growth

## ECONOMY

By YI-HSIN CHANG
*Staff Reporter of* THE WALL STREET JOURNAL

WASHINGTON – May's big drop in the unemployment rate to 6% from 6.4% from April overstates the rate at which the job market is improving.

Labor Department officials said the more moderate rise of employment recorded in its separate survey of business payrolls – which grew by 191,000 jobs last month – is probably a more accurate gauge of the economy. That number suggests the economy is growing at a moderate, but not excessive, rate.

Katharine G. Abraham, commissioner of the Bureau of Labor Statistics, said the sharp decline in the unemployment rate "probably overstates what's going on." . . .

The White House called a news conference to boast of the figures, but some analysts were concerned that the continued sizable increases in average hourly earnings might be a harbinger of inflation.

"There's a distinct possibility that inflation could worsen as the unemployment rate falls below 6%," said Michael Penzer, senior economist at Bank of America in San Francisco, who believes the natural rate of unemployment is 6%. When the unemployment rate falls below the natural rate – a number economists can't seem to agree on – companies sometimes have difficulty finding the workers they need, which could lead to higher prices.

But Audrey Freedman, an economist at Audrey Freedman & Associates, said she didn't see a threat of inflation because she believes the natural rate of unemployment is closer to 5%. . . .

Labor Secretary Robert Reich said the economy was in good shape for the summer. "This is good news for college graduates and even for high school graduates who face the best job markets in years."

Here the administration emphasizes the good news.

Here the natural unemployment rate is discussed, illustrating uncertainty about its level.

A very large decline for one month . . .

but . . .

Data from current population survey

Data from payroll or establishment survey

Demographic data

**EMPLOYMENT**
Here are excerpts from the Labor Department's employment report. The figures are seasonally adjusted.

| | May 1994 | April 1994 |
|---|---|---|
| | (millions of persons) | |
| **Civilian labor force** | 130.8 | 130.7 |
| Civilian employment | 122.9 | 122.3 |
| Unemployment | 7.9 | 8.4 |
| **Payroll employment** | 112.8 | 112.7 |
| **Unemployment:** | (percent of labor force) | |
| All civilian workers | 6.0 | 6.4 |
| Adult men | 5.2 | 5.6 |
| Adult women | 5.4 | 5.6 |
| Teen-agers | 18.3 | 19.9 |
| White | 5.2 | 5.6 |
| Black | 11.5 | 11.8 |
| Black teen-agers | 39.9 | 36.2 |
| Hispanic | 9.5 | 10.8 |

| | Unemployment Rates | |
|---|---|---|
| | 1991 | 1996 |
| Females over 19 | 5.7 | 4.8 |
| Males over 19 | 6.4 | 4.6 |
| Experienced persons | 6.6 | 5.2 |
| All persons | 6.8 | 5.4 |
| Blacks | 11.1 | 9.3 |
| Male teens, 16–19 | 19.8 | 18.1 |
| Female teens, 16–19 | 17.5 | 15.2 |
| Black male teens, 16–19 | 36.3 | 36.9 |
| Black female teens, 16–19 | 36.0 | 30.3 |

**TABLE 7.3**
**Unemployment Rates for Different Demographic Groups**
(percent of labor force for each group)

*Source:* U.S. Department of Labor.

## Unemployment for Different Groups

Regardless of how one interprets the numbers, certain groups of workers experience very long spells of unemployment and suffer great hardships as a result of the difficulty they have finding work. Table 7.3 shows the unemployment rates for several different demographic groups in the United States in two years, 1991 and 1996.

Unemployment is lowest for adult men and women. But unemployment is very high for teenagers. To some extent this is due to more frequent job changes and the period of time required to find work after graduating from school. But many teenagers who are looking for work have dropped out of school and are therefore unskilled and have little or no experience. Their unemployment rates are extremely high, especially for young minorities. The unemployment rate is between 30 and 40 percent for black teenagers. Thus, even when there is good news about the overall unemployment rate, the news may remain bleak for those with low skills and little experience. The overall unemployment rate does not capture the long-term hardships experienced by certain groups.

## Review

▶ People become unemployed when they lose their job, quit their job, or decide to enter the labor force to look for a job. In a market economy, job loss occurs simultaneously with job creation.

▶ Quitting a job is the least likely reason that people are unemployed. Losing a job or looking for work after some time out of the labor force are more likely reasons to be unemployed. In a recession, job loss becomes the most common reason to be unemployed.

▶ Many unemployed people have been unemployed for a very short period of time. This frictional unemployment is probably not very harmful and is a necessary part of any market economy.

▶ But about 15 percent of unemployed people have been unemployed for 6 months or more, even in normal times. Long-term unemployment increases dramatically in recessions.

▶ Teenagers and minorities in the United States have very high unemployment rates, even in boom years.

# DETERMINATION OF EMPLOYMENT AND UNEMPLOYMENT

The most logical place to look for an explanation of employment and unemployment is in the economist's standard tool kit: supply and demand.

### Labor Demand and Labor Supply

**labor demand curve:** a downward-sloping relationship showing the quantity of labor firms are willing to hire at each wage.

**labor supply curve:** the relationship showing the quantity of labor workers are willing to supply at each wage.

**real wage:** the nominal wage adjusted for inflation. It is calculated by dividing the wage by the price level.

Figure 7.6 shows a labor demand curve and a labor supply curve. On the vertical axis is the price of labor (wage) and on the horizontal axis is the quantity of labor supplied or demanded. In a labor market, the **labor demand curve** describes the behavior of firms, indicating how much labor they would demand at a given wage. The **labor supply curve** describes the behavior of workers, showing how much labor they would supply at a given wage. The *wage,* usually measured in dollars per hour of work, is the price of labor. To explain employment in the whole economy, it is best to think of the wage relative to the average price of goods. In other words, the wage on the vertical axis is the **real wage,** which we define as:

$$\text{Real wage} = \frac{\text{wage}}{\text{price level}}$$

Firms consider the wages they must pay their workers in comparison with the price of the product they sell. The workers consider the wage in comparison with the price of goods they buy. Thus, in the whole economy, it is the real wage that affects the quantity of labor supplied and demanded.

The labor demand curve slopes downward because the higher the real wage, the less labor firms demand. A lower real wage gives firms an incentive to hire more workers.

**FIGURE 7.6**
**Labor Supply, Labor Demand, and Equilibrium Employment**
The intersection of the labor supply curve and the labor demand curve determines equilibrium employment and the real wage.

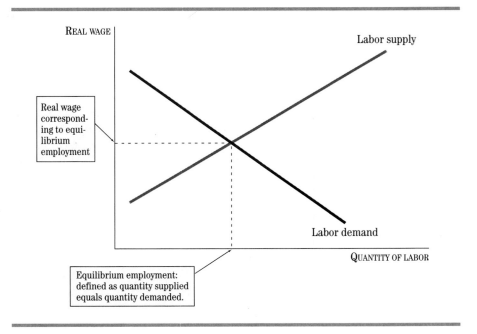

REAL WAGE

Labor supply

Real wage corresponding to equilibrium employment

Labor demand

QUANTITY OF LABOR

Equilibrium employment: defined as quantity supplied equals quantity demanded.

The labor supply curve slopes upward, showing that the higher the wage, the more labor workers are willing to supply. A higher real wage gives workers more incentive to work or to work longer hours.

Like any market, we would predict that the amount of labor traded—the number of workers employed—should be at the intersection of the labor demand curve and labor supply curve, as shown in Figure 7.6. The intersection also determines the equilibrium real wage that brings the quantity supplied into equality with the quantity demanded.

## Case Study: Explaining Long-Term Employment Trends

Our review of employment trends in the United States in recent decades showed that the proportion of people working in the population has increased. The labor supply and demand analysis provides an explanation for this increase.

Throughout the post–World War II period, real wages have been rising, though since the mid-1970s the trend has slowed. Thus, we have a combination of an increased real wage and an increased proportion of the population working. This pattern is consistent with a shift in the labor demand curve and movement along the labor supply curve as shown in Figure 7.7.

As described by the upward-sloping supply curve, the higher wages could be attracting more people into the work force. In fact, as wages have increased, there has been an especially large increase in the percentage of women in the work force. But what could have caused this movement along the supply curve? And why would it have been especially strong for women?

One possibility is that the growth of the service industries—medical, legal, retail trade, telecommunications, transportation—caused an especially large increase in the demand for women. Economists have found that the labor supply of women is more sensitive to changes in the wage than men. Thus, the increase in labor demand in service industries could explain the especially large rise in the employment-to-population ratio for women as well as the increase in the real wage.

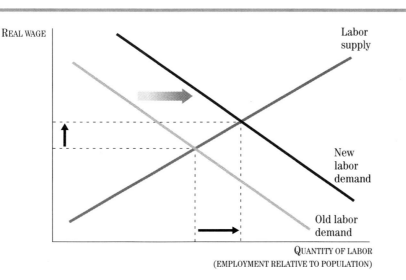

**FIGURE 7.7**

**Explaining the Increase in the Employment-to-Population Ratio**

One explanation for the rise in the employment-to-population ratio in recent decades is a shift in the labor demand curve, which would raise both the real wage and employment. For this purpose, interpret the horizontal axis as employment relative to the population.

Although the labor supply and demand analysis can explain this phenomenon, other factors also may have played a role, such as laws prohibiting discrimination and the women's movement. The point here is to show that the supply and demand model fits the facts.

Many other employment trends can be explained by the labor supply and labor demand analysis. The reduction in labor force participation of older men because of earlier retirement, for example, can be explained by the increased retirement pay due to private pensions and social security through which the government supports the elderly. Higher retirement payments make retirement more attractive compared to work and thus reduce labor supply.

## Why Is the Unemployment Rate Always Greater than Zero?

Despite its usefulness in explaining employment trends, the supply and demand model must be modified if it is to explain unemployment. Having read about unemployment in this chapter, do you see something wrong with the picture in Figure 7.6? It seems inconsistent with the discussion of unemployment. With the quantity of labor supplied equal to the quantity of labor demanded, as in Figure 7.6, there seems to be no unemployment. The intersection of the supply and demand curves seems to predict a market situation that is contrary to the facts. Hence, in order to use the basic supply and demand analysis to explain why unemployment is greater than zero in the real world, we need to modify the story.

Economists have developed two different explanations that adapt the standard labor supply and demand analysis to account for unemployment. Though quite different, the explanations are complementary. In fact, it is essential to use both simultaneously if we are to understand unemployment. Some economists tend to emphasize one over the other, and this frequently turns discussions of the labor market into debates. We will refer to the two explanations as **job rationing** and **job search.**

### Job Rationing

**job rationing:** a reason for unemployment in which the quantity of labor supplied is greater than the quantity demanded because the real wage is too high.

**job search:** a reason for unemployment in which uncertainty in the labor market and workers' limited information requires people to spend time searching for a job.

The job-rationing story has two parts. One is an assumption that *the wage is higher than what would equate the quantity supplied with the quantity demanded.* There are several reasons why this might be the case, but first consider the consequences for the labor supply and demand diagram. Figure 7.8 shows the same labor supply and demand curves as shown in Figure 7.6. However, in Figure 7.8 the wage is higher than the wage that would equate the quantity of labor supplied with the quantity of labor demanded. At this wage the number of workers demanded by firms is smaller than the number of workers willing to supply their labor at that wage.

The other part of the job-rationing story tells us how to determine the number of workers who are unemployed. This part of the story assumes that the number of workers employed equals the number of workers demanded by business firms. When the wage is too high, firms hire a smaller number of workers, and workers supply whatever the firms demand. Figure 7.8 shows the resulting amount of employment as point A on the labor demand curve at the given wage. With employment equal to the number of workers demanded, we see that the number of workers willing to supply their labor is greater than the number of workers employed; the excess supply therefore results in unemployment. The amount of unemployment measured in the horizontal direction is shown in the diagram.

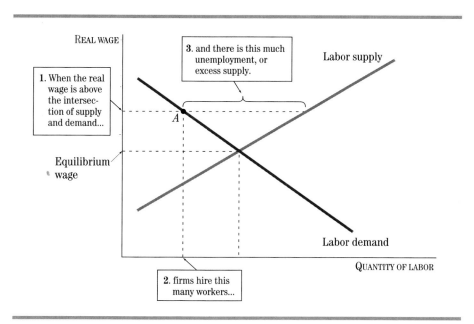

Real Wage

1. When the real wage is above the intersection of supply and demand...

3. and there is this much unemployment, or excess supply.

Labor supply

*A*

Equilibrium wage

Labor demand

2. firms hire this many workers...

Quantity of Labor

**FIGURE 7 8**
**Excess Supply of Labor and Unemployment**
The supply and demand curves are exactly as in Figure 7.6. Here, however, the real wage is too high to bring the quantity supplied into equality with the quantity demanded. The number of workers employed is given by point *A* on the demand curve, where the real wage is above the equilibrium wage. At this higher real wage, the quantity supplied is greater than the quantity demanded—a situation we can think of as unemployment.

This is a situation where workers would be willing to take a job at the wage that firms are paying, but there are not enough job offers at that wage. In effect the available jobs are rationed, for example, by a first-come-first-served rule or by seniority. It is as if, when enough workers are hired, the firms close their hiring offices and the remaining workers stay unemployed. If the wage were lower, then the firm would hire more workers, but the wage is not lower.

In most markets a situation of excess supply brings about a reduction in the price, or in this case the wage. Thus, if this explanation of unemployment is to work in practice, there has to be a force at work to prevent the wage from falling. If the theory is to be helpful in explaining unemployment, then the force has to be permanent, not only at work in a recession. Why doesn't the wage fall when there is an excess supply of workers?

Economists propose three key reasons to explain why the wage might be always too high to bring the quantity of labor demanded into balance with the quantity of labor supplied.

1. *Minimum wages.* Most countries have a legal **minimum wage,** or lowest possible wage, that employers can pay their employees. In the United States, the minimum wage is $5.15 per hour. A minimum wage could cause unemployment to be higher than it otherwise would be, as shown on the diagram in Figure 7.8: Employers would move down and to the right along their labor demand curve and hire more workers if the wage were lower.

One of the reasons teenage unemployment is high (as shown in Table 7.3) may be related to the minimum wage. Because many teenagers are unskilled, the wage firms would be willing to pay them is low. A minimum wage, therefore, may price them out of the market and cause them to be unemployed.

2. *Insiders versus outsiders.* Sometimes groups of workers—**insiders,** who have jobs—can prevent the wage from declining. If these workers have developed skills unique to the job, or if there is legislation preventing their firing without significant legal costs, then they have some power to keep wages up. Labor unions

**minimum wage:** a wage per hour below which it is illegal to pay workers.

**insider:** a person who already works for a firm and has some influence over wage and hiring policy.

**outsider:** someone who is not working for a particular firm, making it difficult for him or her to get a job with that firm although he or she is willing to work for a lower wage.

**efficiency wage:** a wage higher than that which would equate quantity supplied and quantity demanded set by employers in order to increase worker efficiency, for example, by decreasing shirking by workers.

may help them keep the wage higher than it would otherwise be. One consequence of the higher wage is to prevent the firm from hiring unemployed workers—the **outsiders**—who would be willing to work at a lower wage. This is a common explanation for the very high unemployment in Europe, and the theory has been developed and applied to Europe by the Swedish economist Assar Lindbeck and the British economist Dennis Snower.

3. *Efficiency wages.* Firms may choose to pay workers an **efficiency wage**—an extra amount to encourage them to be more efficient. There are many reasons why workers' efficiency or productivity might increase with the wage. Turnover will be lower with a higher wage because there is less reason for workers to look for another job: They are unlikely to find a position paying more than their current wage. Lower turnover means lower training costs. Moreover, workers might not shirk as much with a higher wage. This is particularly important to the firm when jobs are difficult to monitor. With efficiency wages, workers who are working are paid more than the wage that equates the quantity supplied with the quantity demanded. When workers are paid efficiency wages, unemployment will be greater than zero.

### Job Search

We now turn to the second explanation that modifies the standard labor supply and demand analysis. The labor market is constantly in a state of flux, with jobs being created and destroyed and people moving from one job to another. The demand for one type of work falls and the demand for another type of work increases. Labor supply curves also shift.

In other words, the labor market is never truly in the state of rest conveyed by the fixed supply and demand curves in Figure 7.6. But how can we change the picture? Imagine labor demand and labor supply curves that constantly bounce around. The demand for labor, the supply of labor, and the wage would be different every period. Figure 7.6 would be in perpetual motion. Mathematicians use the adjective *stochastic* to describe this constant bouncing around. Economists apply the term *stochastic* to models of the labor market that are in perpetual motion. Rather than a fixed equilibrium of quantity and a fixed wage, there is a *stochastic equilibrium.* This stochastic equilibrium in the labor market is a way to characterize the constant job creation and job destruction that exist in the economy. People enter the work force, move from one job to another, lose their jobs, or drop out of the labor force. Wages change, inducing people to enter or re-enter the market. Figure 7.9 is a schematic representation of the flows of workers in and out of the labor market.

In a stochastic equilibrium, at any point in time people will be searching for a job. Many who do so will be unemployed for some time. They lost their job, quit their job, or came back to the job market after an absence from work. One of the reasons they remain unemployed for a while is that they find it to their advantage not to accept the first job that comes along. Rather, they wait for a possibly higher-paying job. While they wait they are unemployed.

## Policy Implications

The theories of employment and unemployment that have been discussed above have implications for how economic policies affect the amount of employment and the unemployment rate.

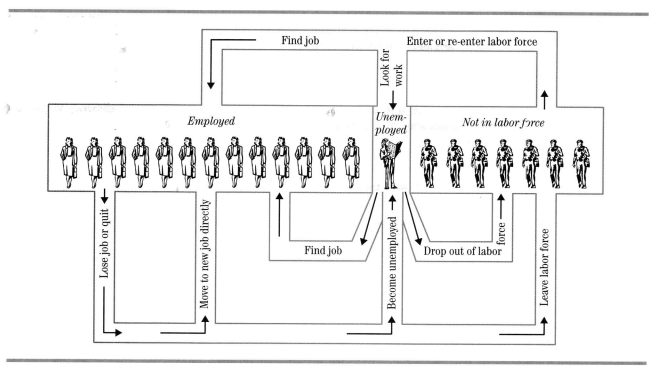

Find job

Enter or re-enter labor force

Look for work

Employed

Unem-ployed

Not in labor force

Lose job or quit

Move to new job directly

Find job

Become unemployed

Drop out of labor force

Leave labor force

### The Effects of Taxes

Consider first a tax on labor. An example of such a tax is a *payroll tax* that is collected in proportion to the workers' pay. In the United States there is a payroll tax to finance social security. A payroll tax can be paid either by the worker or by the firm, but its effects are the same.

Figure 7.10 shows the effect in the case where the tax is paid by the firm. The labor demand curve shifts down by the amount of the tax. For example, suppose a firm would employ 100 workers at $11 per hour without a tax. If there was a $1 tax, then the firm would demand 100 workers at a lower wage of $10. In either case the firm would be paying $11 per hour and would demand the same number of workers, but in one case the wage is $10 and in the other it is $11.

The effect of the tax is to lower employment, as shown in Figure 7.10. Thus, labor taxes reduce employment. Conversely, reducing labor taxes, or at least keeping them from rising, has a positive effect on employment.

### Policies to Reduce the Natural Unemployment Rate

Both the job-rationing model and the job-search model have implications for how public policy can reduce the natural rate of unemployment. We already mentioned how a very high minimum wage could increase unemployment. Conversely, a lower minimum wage for young workers could reduce unemployment. And if information about jobs is increased through job-placement centers or improved communication about the labor market, we would expect unemployment from job search to go down.

**FIGURE 7.9**
**Labor Market Flows**

The labor market is constantly in a state of flux, as people lose jobs, quit jobs, find jobs, and get in and out of the labor force. Most people pass through the unemployment box for a short period, but among the unemployed, some have not held jobs for a long time.

## Reading the News About European Unemployment

The following article from the *Economist* magazine gives a European perspective on unemployment. It begins by noting that the very high unemployment in Europe is not cyclical due to a recession but has persisted for many years. (See the bar chart showing the unemployment rate in several European countries and the United States in 1996.)

The *Economist* argues that it would be a mistake for the United States to follow European labor market policies such as a high minimum wage and generous unemployment benefits.

Most of the arguments in the article are consistent with either job rationing or job search.

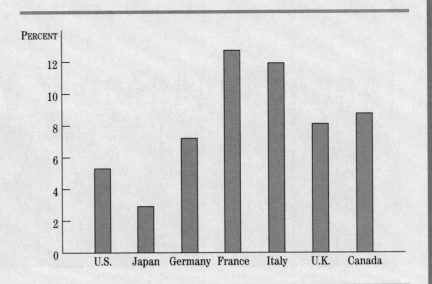

## Doleful

**Europe does indeed provide America with useful lessons about unemployment—about the policies to be avoided, not adopted**

If the jobs of labour ministers and labour economists were tied to the success of their policies, most of them would be joining the 35m people—8.5% of the workforce—in the rich world's still-lengthening unemployment queues . . .

Unemployment in the [European] Community averages 12% of the labour force, compared with less than 7% in America. Worse still, almost half of Europe's jobless have been on the dole for more than a year; in America the equivalent figure is only 11%. It is even more striking that, while the number of American jobs has almost doubled since 1960, EC employment has risen by a paltry 10%. . . .

These figures suggest that Europe has more to learn from America than the other way around. . . . Europe's generous social-security benefits give the unemployed little incentive to seek work. Minimum wages, intended to protect the low-paid, instead cost young workers their jobs. France's minimum wage was increased sharply in the 1980s, to more than 50% of average earnings; America's has fallen to about 30%. It is no coincidence that a quarter of France's people under 25 years of age are unemployed, roughly twice the share in America.

Employers' social-security contributions and other non-wage costs add, on average, an extra 30% to wage costs in the EC (almost 50% in Germany). As with everything else, higher prices mean less demand—in this case, the demand of employers for workers. . . .

So look not to Europe for answers. . . . In the long term, the way to create more well-paid jobs in both America and in Europe is through better education and training. But this takes time. In the short term, there is no substitute for flexible wages.

*Source of article:* "Doleful," *Economist,* October 9, 1993, p. 17. Copyright © 1993 The Economist Newspaper Group, Inc. Reprinted with permission. Further reproduction prohibited.

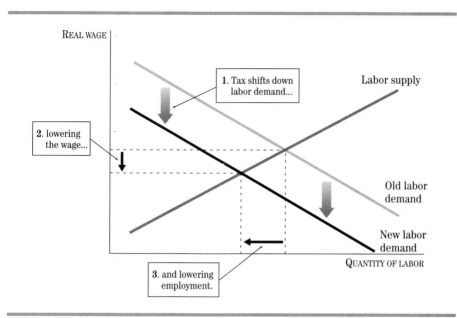

**FIGURE 7.10**
**Effects of a Payroll Tax**
A tax on labor lowers the labor demand curve by the amount of the tax because employers must pay more for workers. The new equilibrium has a lower wage and less employment.

Unemployment compensation, paid to workers who have been laid off from their job, also affects job search. Unemployment compensation enables workers to spend more time looking for a job or to hold out for a higher-paying job. But in the United States unemployment compensation does not last forever. In normal times it runs out after 26 weeks, and the evidence shows that many people stop searching and take a job just when their unemployment compensation runs out. Clearly, unemployment compensation not only helps mitigate the hardships associated with unemployment, it allows people more time to search. But as a by-product, unemployment compensation increases unemployment. In Europe, for example, generous unemployment benefits have been linked to persistent high unemployment. Thus, not allowing unemployment compensation to be paid for very long periods probably reduces unemployment.

# Review

▶ The supply and demand for labor is the starting point for explaining long-term employment trends. The intersection of supply and demand curves determines the amount of employment, and shifts in demand can explain why the employment-to-population ratio has increased.

▶ But the basic supply and demand theory needs to be modified to account for unemployment. Economists use two approaches, job rationing or job search, to explain why unemployment occurs.

▶ Job rationing occurs when the wage is too high. Unemployment can be interpreted as the difference between the quantity supplied and the quantity demanded at that high wage. Wages can be too high because of minimum-wage laws, insiders, or efficiency wages.

▶ Job search is another reason for unemployment. It takes time to find a job and people have an incentive to wait for a good job.

# CONCLUSION

Our analysis of aggregate employment and unemployment has put the spotlight on two different roles of labor. In one role, labor is simply an input to the production of real GDP. We showed that aggregate hours of all workers is the most comprehensive measure of labor input. We also showed that forecasts of the growth of aggregate hours in the future depend on forecasts of the growth rate of population, the employment-to-population ratio, and hours per worker.

In its other role, labor is the people doing the work. In this role the study of labor looks at the problems people face when they lose their job, decide to enter the labor force, or take a part-time job. It also looks at the effects of minimum wages and unemployment compensation on unemployment, at the serious problems that high rates of unemployment seem to cause (as evidenced by Europe in the 1980s and 1990s), and at the reasons why more women have entered the labor force in the past several decades.

In the next two chapters we consider the other inputs to production—capital and technology. But labor will continue to appear in these two different roles. For example, we will study human capital—education and training—both as something that raises the efficiency of labor in producing real GDP and as something that affects people and about which they make purposeful choices.

# KEY POINTS

**1.** Unemployment data are collected in the monthly current population survey.

**2.** A person is unemployed if he or she is old enough to work, is looking for work, but does not have a job.

**3.** Unemployment is never zero in a market economy, even during booms. In normal times the unemployment rate in the United States has been somewhere around 6 percent, although this number is not a fixed constant and could change in the future.

**4.** The employment-to-population ratio has risen in the United States during recent decades, and the average number of hours each worker works has declined.

**5.** Aggregate hours of work by all workers is the most comprehensive measure of labor input to producing real GDP.

**6.** People are unemployed for three reasons: They have lost their job, they have quit their job, or they have just entered the labor force.

**7.** The labor supply and labor demand curves can be used to explain trends in employment in the economy.

**8.** Unemployment can be explained by both job rationing, in which the wage is too high to equate supply and demand, and by job search, in which unemployed people look for work.

**9.** Economic policies, such as exemptions for teenagers from the minimum-wage laws, time limits on unemployment compensation, or the provision of information about job openings to reduce job search time, can reduce the natural unemployment rate.

# KEY TERMS

natural unemployment rate
cyclical unemployment
frictional unemployment
structural unemployment
current population survey
labor force
working-age population
part-time worker
unemployment rate

labor force participation rate
employment-to-population ratio
aggregate hours
job losers
job leavers
new entrants
job vacancies
seasonal unemployment
labor demand curve

labor supply curve
real wage
job rationing
job search
minimum wage
insiders
outsiders
efficiency wage

# QUESTIONS FOR REVIEW

**1.** How is the working-age population defined?

**2.** How do economists define unemployment, and how do they measure how many people are unemployed?

**3.** What is the definition of the labor force?

**4.** What happened to the employment-to-population ratio from the late 1970s to the mid-1990s?

**5.** What is the difference between frictional and structural unemployment?

**6.** What factors determine the amount of labor input— aggregate labor hours—to producing real GDP?

**7.** Why isn't the unemployment rate equal to zero in normal times?

**8.** What fraction of unemployment is due to job loss, job quits, and new entrants in normal times?

**9.** What is the difference between unemployment due to job rationing and unemployment due to job search?

**10.** What do we mean by a stochastic equilibrium in the labor market?

**11.** What three economic policies would reduce the rate of unemployment in normal times?

# PROBLEMS

**1.** Which of the following people would be unemployed according to official statistics? Which ones would *you* define as unemployed? Why?

   a) A person who is writing a book at home while seeking a permanent position on a newspaper

   b) A full-time student

   c) A recent graduate who is looking for a job

   d) A person who just wants to sit in front of the television all day

   e) A worker who quits his job because he thinks the pay is insufficient

   f) A teenager who gets discouraged looking for work and stops looking

**2.** The following table shows the demand and supply of labor at different hourly wages (in dollars).

| Demand for Labor | | Supply of Labor | |
|---|---|---|---|
| Wage/Hour | Quantity | Wage/Hour | Quantity |
| 6 | 100 | 6 | 60 |
| 7 | 90 | 7 | 70 |
| 8 | 80 | 8 | 80 |
| 9 | 70 | 9 | 90 |
| 10 | 60 | 10 | 100 |
| 11 | 50 | 11 | 110 |

   a) Draw the supply and demand of labor.

   b) What is the wage and the quantity of labor at equilibrium?

   c) Suppose the government passes a minimum-wage law and nobody can earn less than $10 per hour. What would the new quantity of labor in the market be? Show what happens graphically. Who gains and who loses from this law?

**3.** a) Suppose the government decided to eliminate the minimum wage. What is likely to happen to the wages of unskilled workers in an area where the cost of living is very low? What is likely to happen to the wages of highly skilled computer programmers? Will this change in government policy significantly reduce unemployment? Why or why not?

   b) Now suppose instead that the government changes unemployment benefits so that they end after two weeks. What is likely to happen to the unemployment rate? Will this change in government policy lead to an increase in labor productivity? Why or why not?

**4.** In 1994 the *New York Times* computerized its help-wanted advertising, allowing people who were looking for work to put résumés on file with the paper. Then, whenever a person saw an interesting job ad, the résumé would be sent to the prospective employer by computer. Here is part of the *New York Times* advertisement for the service, which is called FasTrak.

---

### ALL YOU DO IS . . .

1. Mail us your résumé.

2. Then, just keep up with the employment ads in the *New York Times* beginning January 9.

3. Anytime you see a FasTrak job that interests you, simply call the FasTrak phone number and punch in the code assigned to that particular job.

4. Your résumé will be sped to that employer via computer!

---

What would you predict this new service would do to the unemployment rate? Use one of the theories in this chapter to explain why unemployment will not be eliminated. What if the service became universally available in all parts of the country?

**5.** Suppose you own and run a bicycle repair shop with several employees. You decide to use your facilities at home to manage your business rather than hang around the bike shop while you do the books. You are surprised to discover that the productivity of your business falls. What happened? If you decide to keep your office at home, what will you have to do to increase the productivity of your business back to its previous level? If this same phenomenon is true of all businesses, then why may there be job rationing?

**6.** Use a supply and demand diagram to show the possible reduction in teenage unemployment from a lower minimum "training" wage for workers under 20 years of age. For what reasons might older, unskilled workers complain about such a policy?

**7.** Use the theories of job rationing and job search to try to explain why the natural rate of unemployment in the United States is below that in France. What can the French government do to try to remedy this situation? Might these remedies be politically unpopular?

**8.** Suppose in the year 2003 the economy is in "normal" times and the unemployment rate is 6 percent in the United States.

a) If the working-age population is 205 million and the total labor force is 135 million, how many people are unemployed?

b) What is the labor force participation rate in the year 2003?

c) What change has occurred in the labor force participation rate since 1996? Give one reason this change might have occurred.

d) What is the employment-to-population ratio? How has it changed since 1996?

**9.** Suppose that the natural rate of unemployment in the year 2003 has increased to 7 percent.

a) If the total labor force is 135 million, then how many people are unemployed?

b) If the situation is the same as in previous years, approximately how many of those people are job losers?

c) Approximately how many of them have been unemployed for less than five weeks?

d) If the population is 205 million, then what has happened to the employment-to-population ratio over the previous 6 years?

**10.** Average weekly hours per worker have fallen in the United States, as shown in the following table:

| Year | Average Weekly Hours per Worker | Employment-to-Population Ratio |
|------|--------------------------------|-------------------------------|
| 1960 | 38.6 | 56.1% |
| 1970 | 37.1 | 57.4% |
| 1980 | 35.3 | 59.2% |
| 1990 | 34.5 | 62.7% |

*Source:* U.S. Department of Labor.

a) What is the likely cause of the fall in the average weekly hours of work per worker?

b) If the employment-to-population ratio had remained constant over this period of time, what would have happened to the total hours of work per person in the United States?

**11.** Show that employment in the economy is equal to the working-age population times the labor force participation rate times (1 minus the unemployment rate) when both rates are measured as fractions. Use this equation to fill in the table below, which gives historical data for the United States. Calculate the employment-to-population ratio for 1950 and compare it with the figures given in Table 7.1. If the employment-to-population ratio for 1996 were the same as in 1950, what would total employment be in 1996, assuming the same 200.5 million for the working-age population?

**Problem 11**

| Year | Total Employment (millions) | Unemployment Rate (percent) | Labor Force Participation Rate (percent) | Working-Age Population (millions) |
|------|------------------------------|------------------------------|-------------------------------------------|------------------------------------|
| 1950 | _____ | 5.2 | 59.7 | 106.2 |
| 1960 | 67.6 | 5.4 | 60.0 | _____ |
| 1970 | 80.8 | _____ | 61.0 | 139.2 |

*Source:* U.S. Department of Labor.

**12.** The total employment in the economy is equal to the working-age population times (1 minus the unemployment rate) times the labor force participation rate.

    a) Using the data, fill in the table below showing how many employed people there were in the United States at the turn of each decade.

    b) Suppose the projection for the working-age population in the year 2020 for the United States is 255 million. If the unemployment rate and the labor force participation rate are the same in 2020 as they are in 1990, how much employment will there be?

    c) Using the same projection of 255 million for working-age population in 2020, calculate employment with an unemployment rate of 6 percent and a labor force participation rate of 60 percent. Do the same for a labor force participation rate of 70 percent. Which of these estimates do you think is more realistic? Why?

**13.** The age distribution of the population changes over time—in the United States, better health care and smaller family size in recent years means that there are increasingly larger proportions of people over age 16. At the same time, there is likely to be a decline in the labor force participation rate as baby boomers retire. Using the same method as in the previous question, calculate total employment and the employment-to-population ratio based on the scenario in the table below.

    a) Describe what happens to total employment and the employment-to-population ratio in this scenario.

    b) Is it possible that labor force participation falls so much that total employment falls? How low would the labor force participation rate have to be in 2010 for total employment to be lower than in 1990?

**Problem 12**

| Year | Total Employment (millions) | Unemployment Rate (percent) | Labor Force Participation Rate (percent) | Working-Age Population (millions) |
|------|------------------------------|------------------------------|-------------------------------------------|------------------------------------|
| 1970 | _____ | 4.8 | 61.0% | 139.2 |
| 1980 | _____ | 7.0 | 63.8% | 169.3 |
| 1990 | _____ | 5.4 | 66.6% | 189.7 |

*Source:* U.S. Department of Labor.

**Problem 13**

| Year | Unemployment Rate (percent) | Labor Force Participation Rate (percent) | Working-Age Population (millions) | Total Employment (millions) | Employment-to-Population Ratio |
|------|------------------------------|-------------------------------------------|------------------------------------|------------------------------|--------------------------------|
| 1990 | 5.5 | 66.4 | 188 | _____ | _____ |
| 2000 | 5.5 | 64.0 | 208 | _____ | _____ |
| 2010 | 5.5 | 62.0 | 230 | _____ | _____ |

*Source:* U.S. Department of Labor.

*Fig. 7*

# 8

# Investment in New Capital

A good way to get a view of the role of capital in the economy is simply to take a bus ride and stare out the window. If your ride is in the country you may see silos, barns, tractors, harvesters, fences, water towers, and irrigation systems. In the suburbs you may see shopping centers, airports, moving vans, high schools, amusement parks, and earth-moving equipment. Closer to the city you may see machine shops, warehouses, truck depots, oil storage tanks, pipelines, and electric power plants. As the bus pulls into a downtown bus terminal, you will see office buildings, taxicabs, hotels, and storefronts with copy machines, computers, and dry cleaning equipment. And all the time you are traveling on roads, over bridges, through tunnels, and, of course, in the bus.

Every one of these items, and many more, constitutes *capital*—the factories, machinery, and other productive resources used to produce the goods and services that make up the economy's real GDP. All this capital did not appear overnight. It gradually accumulated as people invested in new capital each year for many years.

Capital increases the amount of goods and services that each worker can produce. Thus, with more capital in

an economy, real GDP per hour of work—labor productivity—is higher. Simply increasing the amount of labor—the number of workers or the number of hours of work—increases real GDP, as we saw in the previous chapter, but it does not increase labor productivity. Increasing technological know-how also raises labor productivity because workers become more effective at using capital. Thus, capital and technology are the two key driving forces behind labor productivity growth and rising standards of living. In this chapter we look at capital. We examine technology in the next chapter.

If capital in the economy is to increase, there must be *investment* because capital is nothing other than the accumulation of past investment. Investment is one component of GDP, together with consumption, government purchases, and net exports. To determine how much GDP is devoted to investment, we work with the equation introduced in Chapter 6: GDP ($Y$) = consumption ($C$) + investment ($I$) + government purchases ($G$) + net exports ($X$). After describing how investment must compete with the other sources of spending, we will show how the interest rate is one of the factors that influences investment. We then show how the interest rate is determined, and, using this interest rate, we predict the share of GDP that goes to investment.

The theory developed in this chapter has many practical uses. For example, the president's Council of Economic Advisers (CEA) argues that an economic plan to reduce the budget deficit would "increase the share of domestic investment in GDP by about 1 percent," because it would lower the interest rate. "Lower interest rates . . . are the way the market accomplishes . . . expenditure switching," in this case, "away from consumption and government purchases toward investment," the CEA reasons. The CEA also predicts that an "increase in the share of investment in GDP of 1 percentage point would have a substantial effect on the capital-labor ratio"—the amount of capital that workers have to work with.[1] How do economists make such predictions? What underlies the CEA's reasoning? The theory developed in this chapter will allow you to answer such questions.

The theory applies more to the long run than to short-run economic fluctuations. For this reason, the Council of Economic Advisers was careful to note that its predicted rise in investment would take several years. The theory is also useful for explaining why the share of investment in GDP fell during the 1970s and 1980s in the United States, or why the increase in government spending in Germany in the 1990s led to higher interest rates in Germany.

# INVESTMENT AND THE ACCUMULATION OF PRODUCTIVE CAPITAL

Before we investigate what determines investment, we need to briefly review how investment is defined and consider how it increases the stock of capital over time.

## Gross Investment, Net Investment, and Increases in Capital

**Investment** ($I$) consists of the purchases of goods by businesses for use in production, as well as the purchases of new residences by households. Consider some examples. Investment occurs at large business firms, such as when Hewlett-Packard builds a new assembly plant in California or Ford Motor builds a Taurus factory in Georgia. Investment also occurs at start-up companies. The founders of Hewlett-Packard, William Hewlett and David Packard, purchased new equipment to construct their first electronic instrument product, the Model 200A, in Packard's garage. Sometimes entrepreneurs invest in new residential capital on a grand scale. Arthur Levitt built 17,000 houses in the potato fields of Long Island, New York, and sold them to returning veterans after World War II. But most residential capital is created on a much smaller scale, as when a family living in Levittown in 1998 puts in a new kitchen sink or converts the attic into a third bedroom.

These examples illustrate how investment increases capital. But there is an important difference between gross investment and net investment, as we discussed in Chapter 6. Investment in the preceding examples refers to *gross investment*—the actual amount of purchases of new goods by businesses each year. However, much of this new investment is going to replace old capital that is wearing out. The new

**investment:** purchases of final goods by firms plus purchases of newly produced residences by households.

1. *Economic Report of the President, 1994*, pp. 36, 83, 85.

### Investment and the Accumulation of Capital over Time

Starting with an existing capital stock—illustrated by the few small buildings in New York City at the time of the American Revolution—and adding investment each year, year after year—illustrated by the construction of new buildings in New York City—results in a higher level of capital—illustrated by the New York City skyline today.

assembly plant built by Hewlett-Packard may be replacing an old assembly plant that is being torn down. The increase in capital, then, is the value of the new assembly plant minus the value of the old assembly plant. Recall that the total amount of capital that wears out each year in the economy is called *depreciation*. Thus, it is only gross investment minus depreciation—or *net investment*—that adds to the total stock of capital in the economy. For example, $100 billion of net investment would be the difference between $770 billion gross investment and $670 billion in depreciation.

The total amount of capital in the economy increases each year by the amount of net investment during the year. More precisely:

$$\text{Capital at the end} \atop \text{of this year} \;=\; {\text{net investment} \atop \text{during this year}} \;+\; {\text{capital at the end} \atop \text{of last year}}$$

For example, if $10,000 billion is the value of all capital in the economy at the end of last year, then $100 billion of net investment during this year would raise the capital stock to $10,100 billion by the end of this year. This is a 1 percent increase in the capital stock. Figure 8.1 illustrates graphically, but with a different numerical example, how capital increases by the amount of net investment.

Although net investment is all that is added to the capital stock, the whole of gross investment must be produced and is thus part of real GDP. The economy's productive resources must be used to produce investment goods whether or not they are going to replace worn-out goods. When we use the symbol *I* for investment we always mean gross investment.

Keep in mind also that the new factories and machines that replace worn-out capital goods are frequently more efficient than old ones. For example, a new tractor may use less fuel than the old tractor it replaces. Thus, investment undertaken to replace an equal amount of worn-out capital, even though it does not raise the capital stock, may *improve* the existing capital stock. In fact, sometimes firms invest because they learn about an improved version of their old machine and want to acquire the new machine to improve productivity or the quality of production.

## Government Investment

Some investment is undertaken by government. Although government investment is not included in investment ($I$) as measured by the national income and product accounts, it increases the amount of capital used in producing GDP and, therefore, needs to be considered when studying the role of capital in economic growth.

### *Public Infrastructure Investment*

Part of government purchases ($G$) includes new highways, bridges, air-traffic control systems, courthouses, police cars, school buildings, water conservation projects, and computers to store patent and trademark information or process tax collections. Although not purchased by private firms or individuals, this type of capital is necessary for the provision of goods such as national defense, police protection, and education. Purchases of this type of capital are called **public infrastructure investment** because they add to the public infrastructure and thus contribute to the economy's productive potential. Public infrastructure investment is essential to the functioning of a modern economy. Without roads or highways for the transportation of goods, or without courts for the enforcement of laws, production would be much lower.

Public infrastructure investment increases the share of government purchases ($G$) in GDP, and the more GDP we devote to it, the less we have available to devote to something else, including the private investment that we defined by investment ($I$). Because investment ($I$) excludes public infrastructure investment, it is sometimes called *gross private domestic investment.*

### *Using Investment (I) in Practice*

Even though investment ($I$) may not be a completely inclusive measure of the investment that adds to capital and contributes to economic growth, it is a close approximation for most purposes. Moreover, the value of investment ($I$) can be adjusted if we truly want to know how much investment adds to growth. We can still use investment ($I$), as long as we are aware that the actual investment that contributes to growth may be slightly different. Thus, for the remainder of this chapter we focus on what determines investment ($I$).

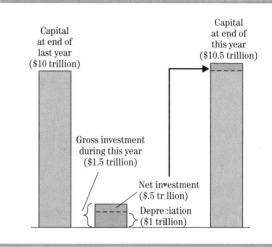

**FIGURE 8.1**

**Net Investment Increases Capital: An Example**

The figure illustrates how net investment—the difference between gross investment and depreciation—is added to the capital stock.

**public infrastructure investment:** purchases of capital by government for use as public goods, which add to the productive capacity of the economy.

## Review

▶ Much of gross investment replaces depreciating capital. Only net investment adds to the capital stock.

▶ New capital that replaces old capital frequently embodies improved methods and new ideas.

▶ Some capital accumulation is done under the heading of government purchases. Part of government purchases is public infrastructure investment, which adds to the productive capital of the economy.

# INVESTMENT AS A SHARE OF GDP

Investment is just one of the uses of GDP. We know that GDP is also used for consumption, government purchases, and net exports. Symbolically,

$$Y = C + I + G + X$$

where $Y$ equals GDP, $C$ equals consumption, $I$ equals investment, $G$ equals government purchases, and $X$ equals net exports. This equation can help determine how much of GDP is devoted to investment.

## The Investment Share versus the Other Shares of GDP

**investment share:** the proportion of GDP that is used for investment; equals investment divided by GDP, or $I/Y$.

The **investment share** of GDP is the proportion of GDP that is used for investment. The investment share of GDP is defined as investment ($I$) divided by GDP, or $I/Y$. When studying investment, economists frequently concentrate on the investment share of GDP. Sometimes the investment share is called the *investment rate*. For example, when the Council of Economic Advisers writes that the "investment rate is 13 percent," it means that $I/Y = .13$, or 13 percent.

As long as GDP is growing along with potential GDP and there is no recession that reduces GDP, an increase in the investment share means more investment and therefore a greater increase in capital. Because our focus in this chapter is on the long term rather than on short-term economic fluctuations, we concentrate on periods when GDP is close to potential GDP and look at what determines investment share. An increase in the share of GDP devoted to investment means an increase in the capital stock relative to GDP.

**consumption share:** the proportion of GDP that is used for consumption; equals consumption divided by GDP, or $C/Y$.

We can define the other shares of GDP analogously: $C/Y$ is the **consumption share,** $X/Y$ is the **net exports share,** and $G/Y$ is the **government purchases share.** We can also establish a simple relationship between the investment share and the other shares of spending in GDP by taking the equation $Y = C + I + G + X$ and dividing both sides by $Y$. This simple division gives us a relationship that says the sum of the shares of spending in GDP must equal 1. Writing that algebraically yields:

**net exports share:** the proportion of GDP that is equal to net exports; equals net exports divided by GDP, or $X/Y$.

$$1 = \frac{C}{Y} + \frac{I}{Y} + \frac{G}{Y} + \frac{X}{Y}$$

**government purchases share:** the proportion of GDP that is used for government purchases; equals government purchases divided by GDP, or $G/Y$.

If we use the shares that existed in 1996 (see Table 6.2), we get:

$$1 = \frac{5,152}{7,576} + \frac{1,116}{7,576} + \frac{1,407}{7,576} + \frac{-99}{7,576}$$

$$1 = .680 + .147 + .186 + (-.013)$$

In other words, consumption accounted for 68.0 percent of GDP; investment for 14.7 percent of GDP; government purchases for 18.6 percent of GDP; and net exports, in deficit at negative $99 billion, accounted for about negative 1.3 percent of GDP. In this example from 1996, the sum of the four shares on the right equals 1. And, of course, this must be true for any year.

Figure 8.2 shows the four shares of spending in GDP for the last 65 years in the United States. A huge temporary fluctuation in the shares of spending in GDP occurred in World War II, when government spending on the military rose sharply.

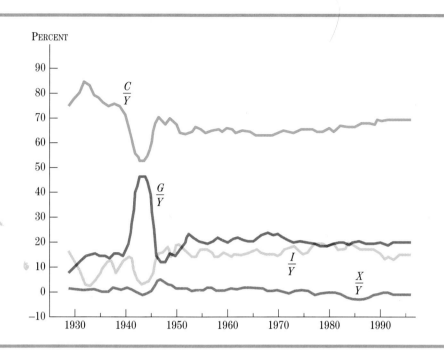

PERCENT

**FIGURE 8.2**
**History of Spending Shares in GDP**
The government purchases share rose sharply during World War II, and all three of the other shares declined. Since the mid-1950s, the changes in the shares have been much smaller. The consumption share rose, and net exports went from positive to negative.

*Source:* U.S. Department of Commerce.

Government purchases reached 50 percent of GDP, and the other three shares declined. Clearly, the movements in government spending as a share of GDP are a factor in determining the share of investment in GDP. Since World War II the shares have been much steadier. In recent years the consumption share has been higher than in the 1950s and 1960s and the net exports share has been negative as the United States has run trade deficits. (Recall that when net exports are negative, there is a trade deficit.)

## If One Share Goes Up, Another Must Go Down

The share of spending equation demonstrates a simple but important point: A change in one of the shares implies a change in one or more of the other shares. That the shares must sum to 1 means that an increase in any of the shares must entail a reduction in one of the other shares. For example, an increase in the share of spending going to government purchases must result in a decrease in the share going to one or more of the other components of spending. Similarly, in a budget-cutting era, decreases in the government purchases share must result in an increase in some other share, such as the investment share. One cannot have an increase in government purchases as a share of GDP, going from, say, 19 percent to 25 percent, without a decline in the share of either consumption or investment or net exports.

What determines the investment share as well as the other shares of GDP? What is the mechanism through which a change in one share—such as the government share of GDP—brings about a change in one of the other shares? Does the investment share change? Or do the consumption or net exports shares change? To answer these questions, we need to consider the interest rate.

## Review

▶ The share of investment in GDP determines how much new capital will be accumulated as the economy grows over time.

▶ Simple arithmetic tells us that the sum of all the shares of spending in GDP must equal 1.

▶ Thus, an increase in the share of GDP going to investment must be accompanied by a reduction in one or more of the other three shares—consumption, government purchases, or net exports.

# INTEREST RATES AND CONSUMPTION, INVESTMENT, AND NET EXPORTS

In this section we show that the interest rate affects all three of the components of spending done by the private sector: consumption, investment, and net exports. Each component competes for a share of GDP along with government purchases, and the interest rate is a key factor in determining the amount that people in the economy are willing to devote to each component.

## Consumption

If total consumption rises as a share of GDP, then the families and individuals in the economy on average raise their consumption relative to their income. For a family or an individual, saving is defined as income less consumption. Thus, if consumption increases, saving must decline for an individual or family with a given income. Because saving is used for future consumption, more consumption now means less consumption later.

However, if total consumption falls as a share of GDP, then families and individuals on average lower their consumption relative to their income. Therefore, they must save more. By saving more, they can consume more in the future. Less consumption now means more consumption later.

### Consumption and the Interest Rate

People's decision to consume more or less today and thus less or more tomorrow depends on a relative price, much like any other economic decision. The relative price is defined as the price of consuming today relative to the price of consuming tomorrow.

Changes in the interest rate will change the relative price. A higher interest rate will raise the price of consumption today relative to the price of consumption tomorrow because it will enable a family to get more for its saving (either a bigger, more enjoyable home improvement, a larger retirement fund, or more college education). Because a higher interest rate raises the price of consuming today rather than tomorrow, it should reduce consumption today. A lower interest rate lowers the price of consuming today and thereby increases consumption relative to income. Thus, consumption is negatively related to the interest rate.

Why does the interest rate affect the relative price of consumption today? If the interest rate is higher, that means that any saving will deliver more funds in the future, which can then be used for consumption in the future. A higher interest rate makes consuming today more expensive compared to the future because it makes the return on saving higher. At a 6 percent interest rate, you can put $100 in the bank and receive $106 at the end of the year, whereas at 2 percent interest you will get only $102 at the end of the year. The change in the interest rate from 2 percent to 6 percent raises the price of consuming $100 worth of goods today by $4. Of course, $4 might seem like a small amount compared to $100, but imagine saving for a long period of time, say for retirement or a college education for one's children, and that small difference in interest rates builds up to quite a bit.

Stated somewhat differently, a higher interest rate gives people more incentive to save for the future, whether for home improvements, retirement, or a college education. With more saving, there is less consumption. The decision to consume is really a decision to consume at one time (today) rather than at another time (tomorrow). A higher interest rate makes consuming at this time relatively more costly compared to consuming at a later time.

What is true for individuals on average will be true for the economy as a whole. Figure 8.3 shows how the consumption share is negatively related to the interest rate. For this example, when the interest rate is 4 percent, the share of consumption in GDP will be about 65 percent. If the interest rate increases to 8 percent, then the share declines to 64 percent. Alternatively, if the interest rate declines, the consumption share increases.

### Movements along versus Shifts of the Consumption Share Line

Observe that the relationship between the interest rate and consumption as a share of GDP in Figure 8.3 looks much like a demand curve. Like a demand curve, it is downward-sloping. And like a demand curve, it shows the quantity consumers are willing to consume at each interest rate. The interest rate is like a price: A higher price—that is, a higher interest rate—reduces the amount people will consume, and a lower price—that is, a lower interest rate—increases the amount of goods and services people will consume. When an increase in the interest rate leads to a decline in consumption, we see a *movement along* the consumption share line, as shown in Figure 8.3.

As with a demand curve, it is important to distinguish such movements along the consumption share line from *shifts of* the consumption share line. The interest rate is not the only thing that affects consumption as a share of GDP. When a factor other than the interest rate changes the consumption share of GDP, there is a shift in the consumption share line in Figure 8.3. For example, an increase in taxes on consumption—such as a national sales tax—would reduce the quantity of goods people would consume relative to their income. In other words, an increase in taxes on consumption would shift the consumption share line in Figure 8.3 to the left: Less would be consumed relative to

**FIGURE 8.3**
**The Consumption Share and the Interest Rate**
A higher interest rate lowers the amount of consumption relative to GDP. A higher interest rate discourages consumption and encourages saving.

INTEREST RATE ($R$)
(PERCENT)

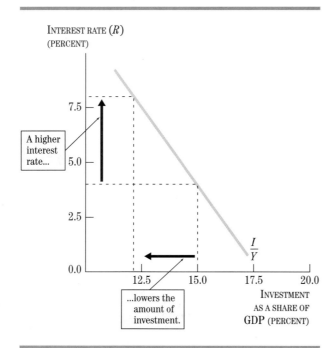

A higher interest rate...

...lowers the amount of investment.

7.5

5.0

2.5

0.0

12.5          15.0          17.5          20.0

$\frac{I}{Y}$

INVESTMENT
AS A SHARE OF
GDP (PERCENT)

**FIGURE 8.4**

**The Investment Share and the Interest Rate**

A higher interest rate lowers investment. The sensitivity of investment to the interest rate is greater than the sensitivity of consumption to the interest rate, as shown in Figure 8.3.

GDP at every interest rate. Conversely, a decrease in taxes on consumption would shift the consumption share line in Figure 8.3 to the right.

## Investment

A similar relationship exists for investment and interest rates. Figure 8.4 shows that there is a negative relationship between the interest rate and the investment share. For this example, when the interest rate rises from 4 percent to 8 percent, the investment share decreases from 15 percent to 12 percent. Economists have observed that investment is more sensitive than consumption to interest rates. Therefore, the line for $I/Y$ in Figure 8.4 is less steep than the line for $C/Y$ in Figure 8.3.

Why does this negative relationship exist in the case of investment? When businesses decide to invest, they frequently borrow the funds to buy the new machines and equipment or to build a new factory. The higher the interest rate, the more they must pay to borrow. Thus, higher interest rates discourage borrowing. Less borrowing means fewer purchases of new equipment. Investment projects that would be undertaken at lower interest rates are postponed or cancelled when interest rates rise. However, when interest rates fall, firms pay less to borrow. Thus, firms are willing to purchase more equipment or build factories that they would not build at higher interest rates.

Recall that investment also includes the purchases of new houses. Most people need to take out loans (mortgages) to purchase houses. When the interest rate on mortgages rises, people purchase fewer or smaller houses; when the interest rate falls, people purchase more or larger houses.

The negative relationship between investment as a share of GDP and the interest rate is observed in the economy for many years and it makes sense: A higher interest rate discourages investment, and a lower interest rate encourages investment.

Observe that the relationship between the investment share of GDP and the interest rate in Figure 8.4 looks like a demand curve. It is downward-sloping. The interest rate is like the price: A higher interest rate decreases the amount of investment firms will do, and a lower interest rate increases the amount of investment firms will do.

Other factors besides interest rates also affect investment; when these factors change, the investment share line in Figure 8.4 will *shift*. For example, an investment tax credit in which a firm's taxes are lowered if the firm buys new equipment would increase the amount that firms would invest at each interest rate. An investment tax credit would shift the investment share line in Figure 8.4 to the right: The investment that firms are willing to do as a share of GDP rises at a given interest rate. A change in firms' expectations of the future could also shift the investment share line; if firms feel that new computing or telecommunications equipment will lower their costs in the future, they will purchase the equip-

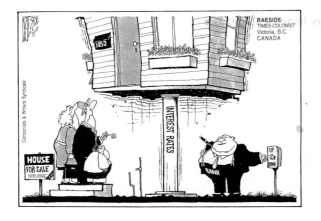

ment, thereby increasing their investment at a given interest rate; the investment share line will shift to the right. Conversely, pessimism on the part of firms about the benefits of investment could shift the line to the left.

## Net Exports

Net exports are also negatively related to the interest rate. As you can see in Figure 8.5, a negative relationship exists that is much like the relationship of consumption and investment to the interest rate. For this example, when the interest rate goes up, from 4 percent to 8 percent, net exports go from zero to about −4 percent of GDP. Remember that when net exports are negative there is a trade deficit.

The story behind this relationship is unfortunately somewhat more involved than for investment or for consumption. However, you may find the story more interesting because it includes the role of foreign exchange rates in determining exports and imports, as well as the relationship between interest rates and exchange rates. In any case, it is important to grasp the key features. The story has three parts. (Recall that foreign exchange rates were discussed in Chapter 2.)

### The Interest Rate and the Exchange Rate

Let us start with the relationship between the interest rate and the exchange rate. International investors must decide whether to put their funds in assets denominated in dollars—such as an account at a U.S. bank in New York City—or in assets denominated in foreign currencies—such as an account at a Japanese bank in Tokyo. If interest rates rise in the United States, then international investors are more interested in placing their funds in dollar-denominated assets. They can earn more by doing so. For example, suppose the interest rate paid on U.S. dollar deposits in New York rises and there is no change in the interest rates in Japan. Then international investors who are considering investing in Japanese yen versus U.S. dollars will start to shift their funds from Tokyo to New York in order to take advantage of the higher interest rate. As funds are shifted to the United States, the demand for dollar-denominated assets begins to increase. This increased demand puts upward pressure on the dollar exchange rate, and the exchange rate will rise. In other words, the higher interest rate will tend to bring about a higher level of the dollar exchange rate. For example, an increase in the interest rate in the United States might cause the dollar to increase from 100 yen per dollar to 120 yen per dollar. Conversely, a lower interest rate in the United States brings about a lower exchange rate for the dollar.

Thus, the interest rate and exchange rate are positively related. Such a relationship is confirmed by observing interest rates and exchange rates in the market over several years. When the interest rate increases compared to interest rates abroad, the exchange rate rises. See the box "Interest Rates and Exchange Rates," which discusses the significant rise of the U.S. dollar relative to the German mark in the mid 1980s when the U.S. interest rate rose.

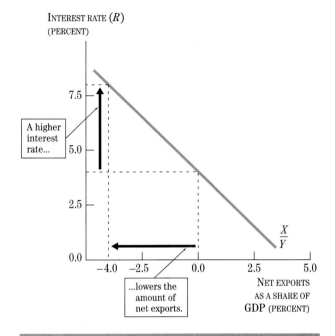

**FIGURE 8.5**
**The Net Exports Share and the Interest Rate**
A higher interest rate lowers net exports because it tends to raise the exchange rate. The higher exchange rate lowers exports and raises imports, thereby lowering net exports. When net exports are negative, there is a trade deficit. When net exports are positive, there is a trade surplus.

# Interest Rates and Exchange Rates

In general, an increase in interest rates in the United States is associated with an increase in the dollar exchange rate because higher interest rates attract the funds of international investors.

The exchange rate between the U.S. dollar and the German mark in the 1980s and 1990s shows how well the theory works. The purple line in this graph shows the exchange rate in marks per dollar from 1978 through 1991 with the scale on the right-hand axis. The dollar appreciated—more marks per dollar—from 1978 to 1984 and then depreciated with a few ups and downs in between.

The green line in the graph is the interest rate on U.S. Treasury bonds measured relative to the interest rate on German bonds. (That is, the figure shows the difference between the two interest rates.) The scale is on the left-hand axis.

As the U.S. interest rate rose compared to Germany, the value of the dollar rose relative to the German mark. Although the relationship is not perfect, the direction is clear. The same type of relationship is true for other currencies.

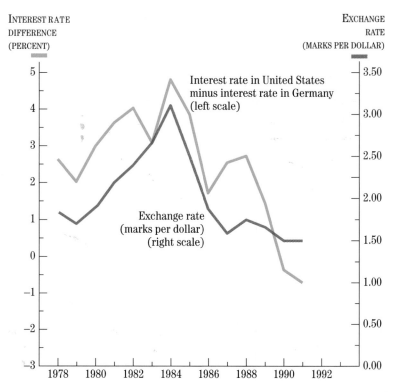

*Source:* Organization for Economic Cooperation and Development.

### The Exchange Rate and Net Exports

A higher dollar exchange rate brought about by a higher interest rate will tend to make imported goods to the United States more attractive because it makes these foreign goods cheaper. For example, the dollar exchange rate against the yen was relatively high at 250 yen per dollar in 1985 and comparatively low at 100 yen per dollar in 1994. When the exchange rate between the dollar and the yen was 250 yen per dollar in 1985, one could buy a kimono costing 25,000 yen for $100 (25,000/250). This was much cheaper than in 1994, when the exchange rate was 100 yen per dollar and the kimono cost $250 (25,000/100). Thus, a higher exchange rate increases the quantity demanded of imported goods.

In addition, the higher exchange rate makes U.S. exports less attractive because it makes American goods more expensive. For example, a $20,000 Jeep Cherokee cost 5 million yen in Japan in 1985 and only 2 million yen in 1994 because the dollar was higher in 1985. Thus, the exchange rate affects exports.

We have shown that a higher exchange rate means more imports and fewer exports. Since net exports are the difference between exports and imports, a higher exchange rate must mean that net exports are going down. Conversely, a lower exchange rate must mean that net exports are going up. To arrive at this result, we used a combination of some simple arithmetic that emphasizes net exports as the difference between exports and imports as well as an economic rationale that says both exports and imports should depend on the exchange rate.

### Combining the Two Relationships

Let us combine the two relationships. One relates the interest rate to the exchange rate and the other relates the exchange rate to net exports. Combining those two we get the relationship between the interest rate and net exports summarized below.

| Interest Rate | Exchange Rate | Net Exports |
|---|---|---|
| up $\longrightarrow$ | up $\longrightarrow$ | down |
| down $\longrightarrow$ | down $\longrightarrow$ | up |

If the interest rate goes up, then the exchange rate goes up and net exports go down. Thus, a higher interest rate reduces net exports. The link is the exchange rate, which is increased by the higher interest rate and which in turn makes net exports fall. Of course, all of this works in reverse too. If the interest rate goes down, then the exchange rate goes down and net exports go up. Thus, a lower interest rate increases net exports, because a lower interest rate means a lower exchange rate for the dollar, which stimulates U.S. exports and discourages imports.

By combining the relationships between the interest rate, the exchange rate, exports, and imports, we have derived the relationship between net exports as a share of GDP and the interest rate shown in Figure 8.5. Like the consumption share line and the investment share line, the net export line in the figure looks like a demand curve. It is downward-sloping. Changes in the interest rate lead to movements along the net export line in Figure 8.5. Changes in other factors—such as a shift in foreign demand for U.S. products—may cause the line to shift.

## Putting the Three Shares Together

We have shown that the consumption, investment, and net exports shares are all negatively related to the interest rate. Our next task is to determine the interest rate and, thereby, a particular value for each share. To determine the interest rate, we will require that the sum of these three shares equals what is left over after the government takes its share. This will ensure that all shares sum to 1.

## Review

▶ Consumption, investment, and net exports are negatively related to the interest rate.

▶ Higher interest rates raise the price of consumption this year relative to next year. This means fewer goods consumed this year.

▶ Business firms invest less when interest rates rise because higher interest rates raise borrowing costs.

▶ Higher interest rates raise the exchange rate and thereby discourage exports and encourage imports, leading to a decline in net exports.

▶ Other factors besides the interest rate may affect consumption, investment, and net exports. When one of these factors changes, the relationship between the interest rate and consumption, investment, or net exports shifts.

# DETERMINING THE EQUILIBRIUM INTEREST RATE

The interest rate affects the three shares (consumption, investment, and net exports) and therefore affects the sum of the three shares. This is shown by the downward-sloping line in diagram (d) of Figure 8.6. In diagram (d), an increase in the interest rate reduces the sum of the three shares of GDP.

## Adding the Nongovernment Shares Graphically

Note carefully how Figure 8.6 is put together and how the downward-sloping line in diagram (d) is derived. We have taken the graphs from Figures 8.3, 8.4, and 8.5 and assembled them horizontally in diagrams (a), (b), and (c) of Figure 8.6. The downward-sloping red line in diagram (d) is the sum of the three downward-sloping lines in diagrams (a), (b), and (c). It is the nongovernment share of GDP, or $NG/Y$, where $NG = C + I + X$ and as usual $Y$ is GDP. For example, when the interest rate is 4 percent, the line in diagram (d) shows that the nongovernment share—the sum of investment, consumption, and net exports as a share of GDP—is 80 percent; this is the sum of 65 percent for the consumption share, 15 percent for the investment share, and zero percent for the net exports share. Similarly, the other points in diagram (d) are obtained by adding up the three shares at other levels of interest rates. For example, at an interest rate of 5 percent, we see that the sum of the share of consumption, investment, and net exports is down to about 78 percent.

## The Share of GDP Available for Nongovernment Use

To determine the interest rate we must consider the fourth share: government. The share of GDP not used by the government is available for nongovernment use, that is, for either consumption, investment, or net exports. For example, if the government share is 22 percent of GDP, then the share available for nongovernment use is 78 percent. The sum of the consumption share, the investment share, and the net export share must equal 78 percent.

What brings this equality about? In a market economy, the government does not stipulate that consumption, investment, or net exports must equal 78 percent, or

**FIGURE 8.6**
**Summing Up Consumption, Investment, and Net Exports Shares**

Diagrams (a), (b), and (c) are reproductions of Figures 8.3, 8.4, and 8.5. For each interest rate, the three shares are added together to get the sum of shares shown in diagram (d). For example, when the interest rate is 4 percent, we get 65 percent for consumption share, 15 percent for investment share, and 0 percent for net exports, summing to 80 percent. The sum of the three nongovernment shares ($NG/Y$) is negatively related to the interest rate ($R$).

**(a) Consumption Share**

**(b) Investment Share**

**(c) Net Exports Share**

**(d) Nongovernment Share**

any other share of GDP. Instead, prices—in this case the interest rate—adjust to provide individual consumers or firms with the incentive to make the necessary adjustments. Recall from Chapter 2 that the price in a market serves as both a signal and an incentive to individuals. In a market economy as a whole, the interest rate adjusts to ensure equality between (1) the sum of investment, consumption, and net exports shares, and (2) the share of GDP available for investment, consumption, and net exports.

If the sum of consumption, investment, and net exports shares begins to rise above the share of GDP available after the government takes its share, then the interest rate will rise and will bring consumption, investment, net exports, or all three back down to what is available. Recall that a higher interest rate provides an incentive to people to reduce their consumption and for firms to reduce their investment. If the sum of consumption, investment, and net exports begins to fall below what was available, then the interest rate will fall, bringing the nongovernment shares up to what was available. Thus, in a market economy, changes in the interest rate bring consumption, investment, and net exports into equality with the amount of GDP available. Or, equivalently, changes in the interest rate ensure that the sum of all four shares of GDP is 1.

## Finding the Equilibrium Interest Rate Graphically

Figure 8.7 illustrates how the interest rate brings about the equality. Look first at diagram (d). In diagram (d), the share of GDP available for nongovernment use is indicated by the vertical line. The government share of spending is assumed not to depend on the interest rate but rather on public decisions made by voters and politicians about the role of government in the economy. This is why the share of GDP available for nongovernment use does not depend on the interest rate and why it is represented by a vertical line. In the case where government purchases are 22

**FIGURE 8.7**
**Determining the Equilibrium Interest Rate, Investment, and the Other Shares**
In this case, government purchases are assumed to be 22 percent of GDP. Mark the implied share available for nongovernmental uses of 78 percent in diagram (d). The equilibrium interest rate is determined at the intersection of the two lines in diagram (d). Given this interest rate, we can compute investment and the other shares of spending in GDP using diagrams (a), (b), and (c).

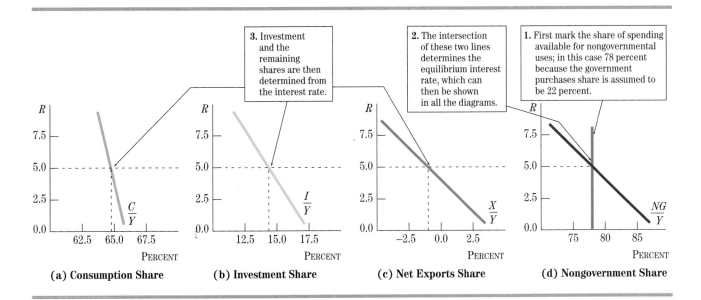

**(a) Consumption Share**   **(b) Investment Share**   **(c) Net Exports Share**   **(d) Nongovernment Share**

percent of GDP, the vertical line is at 78 percent, as shown in Figure 8.7 (d). If the government share were larger, we would draw the vertical line further to the left, showing that the share available for nongovernment use was smaller.

The sum of the three nongovernment shares is shown by the downward-sloping line in Figure 8.7 (d). This is the same line we derived in Figure 8.6 (d). At the intersection of this downward-sloping line and the vertical line, the sum of investment, consumption, and net exports is equal to the share that is available for nongovernment use. For example, when the share available is 78 percent, we see in diagram (d) of Figure 8.7 that the point of intersection occurs when the interest rate is 5 percent. This is the **equilibrium interest rate,** the interest rate that makes the sum of consumption, investment, and net export shares equal to the share of GDP available. It is also the interest rate for which the sum of all shares of GDP equals 1.

Once we determine the equilibrium interest rate, we can find each of the investment, consumption, and net exports shares. Each of these shares depends on the interest rate, as shown in diagrams (a), (b), and (c) of Figure 8.7. To determine each of the shares, simply draw a line across the three diagrams at the equilibrium interest rate. Then in diagram (a) we find the consumption share, in diagram (b) the investment share, and in diagram (c) the net exports share.

### Analogy with Supply and Demand

Observe that the intersection of the two lines in diagram (d) of Figure 8.7 is much like the intersection of a demand curve and a supply curve. The red downward-sloping line—showing how the sum of investment, consumption, and net exports is negatively related to the interest rate—looks just like a demand curve. The blue vertical line—showing the share of GDP available for consumption, investment, and net exports—looks like a vertical supply curve. The intersection of the two curves determines the equilibrium price—in this case the equilibrium interest rate in the economy as a whole. In the next section, we show how shifts in one or both of these two curves lead to a new equilibrium interest rate, much like shifts in supply and demand curves lead to a new equilibrium price.

### The Real Interest Rate in the Long Run

Having determined the equilibrium interest rate, it is important to mention once more that our analysis applies to the *long run*—perhaps three years or more—rather than to short-run economic fluctuations. It takes time for consumers and firms to completely respond to a change in interest rates.

Moreover, the interest rate in the analysis refers to the *real* interest rate, which, as defined in Chapter 5, is the interest rate on loans adjusted for inflation. The real interest rate is defined as the nominal interest rate less the expected inflation rate. If the inflation rate is low, there is little difference between the real interest rate and the nominal interest rate; but if inflation is high, there is a big difference and the real interest rate is a much better measure of the incentives affecting consumers and firms. An interest rate of 50 percent would seem high but would actually be quite low—2 percent in real terms—if people expected inflation to be 48 percent.

Broadly speaking, the analysis in this section shows that the real interest rate in the long run is determined by balancing people's demands for consumption, investment, and net exports with the available supply of goods and services in the economy.

**equilibrium interest rate:** the interest rate that equates the sum of consumption, investment, and net export shares to the share of GDP available for nongovernment use.

> ## Review
>
> ▶ The sum of consumption, investment, and net exports shares of GDP is negatively related to the interest rate, because each of the individual components is negatively related to the interest rate.
>
> ▶ The equilibrium interest rate is determined by the condition that the sum of the three nongovernment shares of GDP equal the share not used by government. Using the equilibrium interest rate, we can then find each of the nongovernment shares.

# IMPACTS ON THE INVESTMENT SHARE

Now let us use this theory to examine how the investment share—and thereby the accumulation of capital—is affected by changes in the economy. We consider a shift in government purchases and a shift in consumption. Both reflect possible economic policy decisions.

### A Change in Government Purchases

What happens when government purchases increase or decrease as a share of GDP? We know as a matter of arithmetic that some other share must move in a direction opposite to the government share. To find out what happens to investment we need to look at what happens to consumption and net exports too.

Suppose that the government share of GDP increases by 2 percent, perhaps as a result of an increase in defense spending, as in the early 1980s in the United States, or by an increased need for government infrastructure spending, as in the unification of Germany in the 1990s.

The effects of this change are shown in Figure 8.8. If government purchases as a share of GDP increase by 2 percent, then we know that the share of GDP available for nongovernmental use must *decrease* by 2 percent. Thus, in diagram (d) of Figure 8.8, we shift the vertical line marking the available share to the left by 2 percentage points. As Figure 8.8 (d) shows, there is now a new intersection of the two lines and a new higher equilibrium interest rate. The increase in the interest rate is the market mechanism that brings about a decline in consumption plus investment plus net exports as a share of GDP.

Diagram (d) of Figure 8.8, for example, shows that the new interest rate is 5 percent rather than 4 percent. That is, the interest rate has increased by 1 percentage point. Now we are prepared to answer the key question: What is the impact on investment?

To see the effect on investment share, we draw a horizontal line at 5 percent interest, as shown in Figure 8.8, and read off the implied amount of investment as well as consumption and net exports shares. According to the diagram, the share of consumption decreases by ¼ percent of GDP, the share of investment decreases by about ¾ percent of GDP, and the share of net exports decreases by about 1 percent of GDP. The sum is 2 percent, which is exactly the decrease in the share of government spending. It all adds up, and we have a particular prediction, not only about investment but also about consumption and net exports.

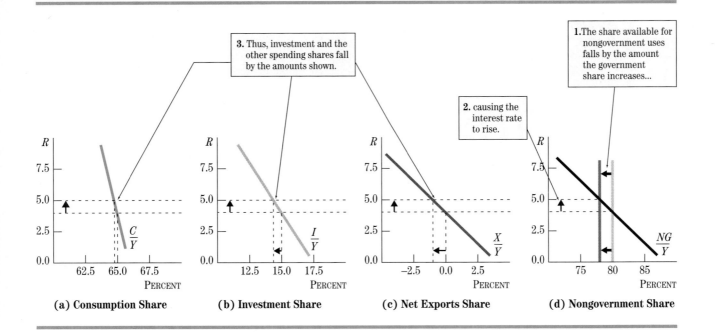

**(a) Consumption Share**          **(b) Investment Share**          **(c) Net Exports Share**          **(d) Nongovernment Share**

**FIGURE 8.8**

**The Effect of an Increase in Government Purchases**

If the government purchases share of GDP rises, then the share available for nongovernment uses must fall by the same amount. This causes a rise in interest rates, which reduces consumption, investment, and net exports as a share of GDP.

**crowding out:** the decline in private investment owing to an increase in government purchases.

The same process could work in reverse if we decreased government purchases as a share of GDP. In Figure 8.8, the interest rates would have to fall. To find out the effect on the other components of spending, we would draw a horizontal line at a lower interest rate. That would show us that investment would rise as a share of GDP, and so would consumption and net exports.

Sometimes the decline in investment due to an increase in government purchases is called **crowding out** because investment is "crowded out" by the government purchases. Thus, we have shown that an increase in government purchases as a share of GDP causes a crowding out of investment in the long run. However, because net exports and consumption also fall, the crowding out of investment is not as large as it would otherwise be. All these effects are summarized in Figure 8.8.

## Impact on Investment of a Shift in Consumption

Suppose that there is an increase in the amount people want to consume at every interest rate. Such a shift seems to have taken place in the United States from the early 1970s to the late 1980s. In 1973, the consumption share of GDP was 63 percent, and in 1989 it was 67 percent.

Economic policy changes can bring about such shifts. For example, in the late 1980s, Individual Retirement Accounts (IRAs), which allowed people to reduce their taxes if they saved for retirement each year, were virtually eliminated. The elimination of the lower tax on savings through IRAs may have been an inducement for many people to consume more and save less.

The impact of a shift in consumption—whatever its cause—is analyzed in Figure 8.9. The relationship between the interest rate and consumption shifts out in

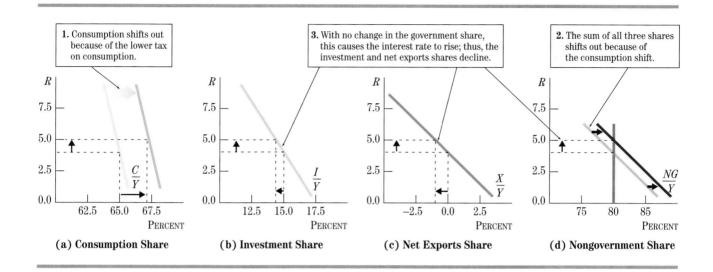

(a) Consumption Share

(b) Investment Share

(c) Net Exports Share

(d) Nongovernment Share

diagram (a); this causes the sum of investment, consumption, and net exports to shift out, as shown by the shift in the line in diagram (d).

The impact is an increase in the equilibrium interest rate and a decline in investment. However, because net exports decline, the impact on investment is much less than if net exports had not changed. The action of foreigners reduces substantially the effect of the increased consumption on capital formation.

The overall prediction of the effects of such a shift are very close to what has happened in the United States from the early 1970s to the late 1980s, as shown in Table 8.1. As the consumption share rose over this long period, the investment share and the net exports share fell. The government purchases share was unchanged. According to most estimates the real interest rate was higher in the 1980s than in the 1970s. Thus, the theory of investment put forth in this chapter explains the long-term trends in the shares of spending and interest rates very well under the assumption that there was a shift in consumption.

We can also investigate other policy changes. For example, what if there were an increase in the tax on consumption? In this case, the nongovernment share line in Figure 8.9 would shift to the left in diagram (d). Interest rates would fall and investment would rise; net exports would also rise. One of the reasons that taxes on consumption have been recommended by economists is that they would increase investment, as predicted by the theory.

**FIGURE 8.9**
**Effect of a Shift in Consumption**
If the amount of consumption relative to income rises at every interest rate—perhaps because of a tax change that reduces the tax on consumption—the interest rate will rise. Both investment and net exports decline.

|  | 1973 | 1989 |
|---|---|---|
| Consumption share | 63 | 67 |
| Investment share | 18 | 16 |
| Net exports share | 0 | -2 |
| Government purchases share | 19 | 19 |

**TABLE 8.1**
**Shares of GDP: 1973 and 1989**
(percent)

## Anticipation of Changes in Government Purchases

The theory of investment predicts that an increase in the government share of GDP will raise interest rates and thereby crowd out investment, net exports, and even consumption as a share of GDP. This graph shows how this actually happened in Germany in late 1989 and 1990 after the Berlin Wall fell and German unification was expected. The purple line shows that government purchases in Germany rose in mid-1990. The green line shows that interest rates also rose.

Notice that interest rates rose *before* the increase in government purchases. Most economists explained the increase in interest rates in late 1989 as due to anticipation of the increase in government purchases that would be needed for the expected reunification of Germany. This is an example of how expectations of the future can affect events in the present. The long-term interest rates on bonds reflect expectations of interest rates in the future because the bonds will not mature for many years.

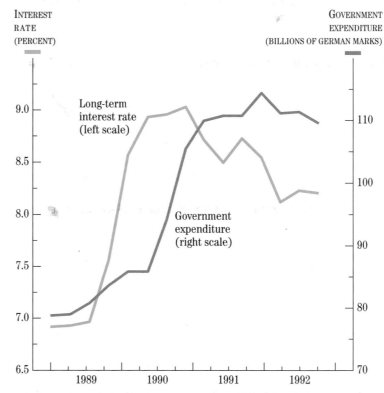

*Source:* Organization for Economic Cooperation and Development.

## Review

▶ The impact of a change in government spending on capital accumulation can be analyzed by looking at what happens to the interest rate and each component of GDP.

▶ An increase in the government spending share reduces the share available for nongovernment use

by exactly the same amount. This means that interest rates must rise. The rise in interest rates causes investment, consumption, and net exports to fall.

▶ An upward shift in consumption causes investment and net exports to fall and the interest rate to rise.

## THE SAVING INVESTMENT APPROACH

In Chapter 6, we derived a relationship showing that national saving equals investment plus net exports. This relationship provides an alternative approach to determine investment and the interest rate. The alternative gives exactly the same answers, but it provides additional insights because it focuses on saving, the flip side of consumption.

National saving ($S$) is defined as aggregate income minus consumption minus government purchases, or

$$S = Y - C - G$$

National saving must always be equal to investment plus net exports; that is,

$$S = I + X$$

Now we show that this relationship can be used to determine the interest rate and investment share.

## The National Saving Rate and the Interest Rate

The ratio of national saving to GDP is the **national saving rate.** If we divide each term in the definition of national saving by $Y$, we can write the national saving rate as 1 minus the share of consumption and government purchases in GDP. That is,

$$\frac{\text{National}}{\text{saving rate}} = 1 - \frac{\text{consumption}}{\text{share}} - \frac{\text{government}}{\text{purchases share}}$$

or

$$\frac{S}{Y} = 1 - \frac{C}{Y} - \frac{G}{Y}$$

We know that the consumption share ($C/Y$) depends on the interest rate. This equation tells us that the national saving rate also depends on the interest rate. In particular, the national saving rate is positively related to the interest rate because the consumption share is negatively related to the interest rate, as we showed earlier. In other words, when the interest rate rises, the consumption share falls, implying that the saving rate rises. The relationship between the national saving rate and the interest rate is shown in Figure 8.10.

The equation for $S/Y$ also shows that an increase in government share reduces saving at every interest rate; thus, the relationship between the national saving rate and the interest rate shifts to the left when the government share increases.

## Determination of the Equilibrium Interest Rate

If we divide both sides of the expression $S = I + X$ by $Y$, we get

$$\frac{S}{Y} = \frac{I}{Y} + \frac{X}{Y}$$

or, in other words, the national saving rate equals investment share plus net exports share. The terms on both sides of this equation depend on the interest rate. We can plot these two relationships in the same graph as Figure 8.10 to get a prediction of the equilibrium interest rate. This is done in Figure 8.11. The upward-sloping line in the figure shows the national saving

**national saving rate:** the proportion of GDP that is saved, neither consumed nor spent on government purchases; equals national saving ($S$) divided by GDP, or $S/Y$. It also equals 1 minus the consumption share minus the government purchases share of GDP.

**FIGURE 8.10**
**The National Saving Rate and the Interest Rate**
When the interest rate rises, national saving as a share of GDP rises because the consumption share falls. The sensitivity of the national saving rate to the interest rate is thought by most economists to be smaller than for the investment share.

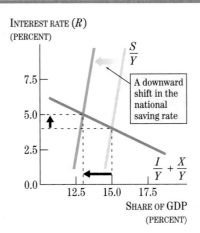

**FIGURE 8.11**
**Determining the Interest Rate Using the Saving Relationship**
The interest rate is determined at the point where national saving equals investment plus net exports, shown at the intersection of the two lines. The saving rate (and the sum of the investment and net exports shares) is shown on the horizontal axis.

**FIGURE 8.12**
**The Effect of a Downward Shift in the Saving Rate**
The effect is the same as the shift upward in the consumption share illustrated in Figure 8.9. The lower national saving rate raises interest rates and lowers the investment share and the net exports share.

rate. An increase in the interest rate causes the saving rate to rise. The downward-sloping line shows the sum of $I/Y$ and $X/Y$; this sum is negatively related to the interest rate.

At the intersection of the two lines in Figure 8.11, the national saving rate equals the investment share plus the net exports share. The intersection, therefore, determines the equilibrium interest rate. The interest rate is exactly the same as that in Figure 8.7, which is based on exactly the same relationships. The national saving rate is shown on the horizontal axis, and the investment share can be determined by subtracting the net exports share.

### Effect of a Downward Shift in the National Saving Rate

Now let us look at the same shift in consumption share considered in the previous section but with a focus on saving. An upward shift in the consumption share is equivalent to a downward shift in the saving rate. Thus, we shift the interest rate-saving rate relationship to the left in Figure 8.12, representing a downshift in the national saving rate. As shown in the figure, this leads to a higher interest rate and a lower share for investment and net exports. Hence the predictions are the same as the previous analysis in Figure 8.9. The decline in investment is less than the decline in the saving rate because net exports decline. (This is not shown in Figure 8.12.) If net exports fall by a large amount in response to the decline in the national saving rate, then investment does not change much at all.

## Review

▶ The national saving rate is an increasing function of the interest rate. The sum of the investment and net exports shares is a decreasing function of the interest rate. The equality of the national saving rate and the sum of the two shares determines the interest rate.

▶ A downward shift in the national saving rate lowers the investment share and raises the interest rate. It also lowers the net exports share. These are the same results caused by an increase in consumption; thus, an upward shift in the consumption share is equivalent to a downward shift in the saving rate.

# DETERMINATION OF GOVERNMENT'S SHARE OF GDP

Throughout this chapter we have said that government's share of GDP is determined by voters and politicians, and we looked at what impact a change in government share would have on investment and interest rates. A rise in the share of government purchases means that something else has to decline. A fall in the share of government purchases means that there is an opportunity for spending elsewhere. But what factors determine government's share?

## Arguments over the Appropriate Size of Government

Government has a significant role in the economy, a role that is most forcefully illustrated in the case of providing for goods such as national defense and police. Government also has a role in education, either by subsidizing education or by providing it directly. In most countries primary and secondary education comprises a large part of government purchases. College education in the United States is partly provided by the private sector, but there is also a very large public sector in college education.

Over the years there have been debates among economists and noneconomists alike about whether the United States or other economies devote too much or too little to public spending versus private spending. John Kenneth Galbraith of Harvard University supported the view in the 1950s and 1960s that the United States was not spending enough on public goods and was spending too much on private goods. In the 1980s the trend appeared to shift substantially, and people argued that too much was spent on public goods, especially on nondefense public goods. Indeed, this was part of the Reagan revolution and represents a view supported by economists such as Milton Friedman.

By the 1990s, the trend appeared to be moving back in the other direction. Economists began to emphasize that economic growth depends on government spending on public infrastructure. But there is a substantial difference of opinion in the United States about what the government's share of GDP should be. These differences of opinion have led to an intense political debate that promises to continue for years into the future.

### Size of Government and Economic Growth

This chapter has introduced an important macroeconomic factor to consider when assessing the appropriate size of government. Investment in new capital is affected by the size of government in the economy. Private investment is greater when purchases by the government are less. More investment spending raises productivity because there are more machines and factories for workers to work with. Higher government purchases are a negative for long-term growth on that account.

On the other hand, government spending is needed for the roads, education, and legal system that help produce economic growth. But even to the extent that government spending increases long-term growth, it reduces the share of GDP available for private investment. To the extent that consumption and net exports also shrink as government purchases increase, the effect on private investment is smaller.

Thus, there is a need for balance between government purchases and private investment. The mix will ultimately be determined in the political debate. This chapter provides some economic analysis, which is useful in that debate.

## Review

▶ Debates have raged for years about the appropriate size of the share of government purchases in the economy.

▶ A higher share for government means less private investment, and this could reduce economic growth.

▶ However, some government spending is essential for economic growth.

▶ Getting the right balance between government purchases and private investment is one of the most important jobs of a political system.

## CONCLUSION

In this chapter we have developed a theory that determines the equilibrium interest rate and the amount of investment in the whole economy. Because investment is only one of the uses of GDP, we needed to consider the other uses—consumption, government, and net exports—when we developed the theory.

For a given share of government purchases in GDP, the theory predicts the interest rate and the investment share as well as the consumption share and the net exports share. The theory can be used to analyze the impact on investment of a change in government purchases, a change in taxes, or a shift in consumption or saving. The theory applies to the economy in the long run as real GDP grows along the path of potential GDP.

The investment share of GDP determines how rapidly capital in the economy grows. With a higher investment share—or investment rate—the capital stock will grow more rapidly, and the amount of capital per worker will rise. With more capital to work with, workers will be able to produce more; in other words, productivity—real GDP per hour of work—will rise. Thus, understanding what determines investment is essential for understanding productivity growth. Here is how the

Council of Economic Advisers puts it: "The reasons for wanting to raise the investment share of GDP are straightforward: Workers are more productive when they are equipped with more and better capital, more productive workers earn higher real wages, and higher real wages are the mainspring of higher living standards. Few economic propositions are better supported than these—or more important."[2]

Productivity growth and rising living standards also depend on technological growth, which we turn to in the next chapter.

# KEY POINTS

**1.** The accumulation of capital through investment is one of two key ways that long-term growth of productivity—output per hour of work—occurs. The other is technology.

**2.** To raise capital relative to the GDP the share of investment in GDP must rise.

**3.** Over the long term, investment competes with consumption, government purchases, and net exports for a share of GDP.

**4.** Higher interest rates raise the price of consumption and lead to a reduction of consumption as a share of GDP.

**5.** Higher interest rates also reduce investment.

**6.** Higher interest rates lower net exports by causing the exchange rate to rise. A higher exchange rate reduces exports and raises imports.

**7.** An equilibrium interest rate is found by equating the sum of the consumption, investment, and net exports shares to the share of GDP available for nongovernment use.

**8.** An increase in government purchases crowds out the share of investment in GDP by raising interest rates. Consumption and net exports also fall, making crowding out of investment less severe.

**9.** The choice between private investment on the one hand and government purchases on the other affects long-term economic growth.

# KEY TERMS

| | | |
|---|---|---|
| investment | consumption share | equilibrium interest rate |
| public infrastructure investment | net exports share | crowding out |
| investment share | government purchases share | national saving rate |

# QUESTIONS FOR REVIEW

**1.** Why does an increase in investment share in GDP require a decrease in some other share?

**2.** What is the relationship between consumption and interest rates?

**3.** Why does investment fall when interest rates rise?

**4.** Why is there a relationship between the exchange rate and the interest rate?

**5.** How does the relationship between net exports and the exchange rate tie into the negative relationship between interest rates and net exports?

**6.** What determines the equilibrium interest rate?

**7.** Why should we care about achieving an increase in investment?

**8.** Are all investment goods accounted for in the investment component of GDP?

**9.** What is crowding out?

**10.** In what sense does the theory in this chapter apply to the long run rather than to short-run economic fluctuations?

2. *Economic Report of the President, 1994*, p. 36.

# PROBLEMS

**1.** Describe the long-run impact of a decline of defense spending by 1 percent of GDP on interest rates and on consumption, investment, and net exports as a share of GDP. Consider two different cases:
    a) No other changes in policy accompany the defense cut.
    b) The funds saved from the defense cut are used to increase government expenditures on roads and bridges.

**2.** Suppose that there is a technological improvement that makes capital last longer—that is, wear out at a slower rate. What happens to depreciation? For a fixed level of saving, what happens to gross and net investment in this case? Explain.

**3.** a) As government's share in GDP decreases, the nongovernmental share increases. Depict this in a diagram. What happens to interest rates?
    b) As interest rates fall, what change is there in the exchange rate? What happens to net exports in this case? Does this match your earlier picture?
    c) Suppose net exports are very sensitive to changes in interest rates. Does that mean a relatively big or relatively small change in net exports?

**4.** Suppose you have the following data for capital and investment in an economy:

| Year | Capital Stock on Jan. 1 | Depreciation | Gross Invest- ment | Net Invest- ment |
|---|---|---|---|---|
| 1993 | 1000 | ___ | 200 | ___ |
| 1994 | ___ | ___ | 310 | ___ |
| 1995 | ___ | ___ | 120 | ___ |
| 1996 | ___ | ___ | 200 | ___ |

    a) Assume that depreciation during any year is 10 percent of the January 1 level of the capital stock. Calculate the missing values in the table.
    b) Is depreciation of capital a stock or a flow variable? Explain. (*Hint:* See the box "Stocks and Flows" in Chapter 6.)
    c) Is net investment negative in any year? What does such a situation mean?

**5.** Suppose that the government wants to increase public infrastructure investment.
    a) If government purchases increase, what happens to government's share in total spending? Is there crowding out?
    b) Suppose instead that the government encourages private business to purchase the public infrastructure.

Where will it enter GDP? If government's share in spending is fixed, what happens to the other shares when this infrastructure is built?

**6.** Many people believe that the U.S. saving rate is too low. Suppose all private citizens save at a higher rate. Show what happens in this case in the savings and investment diagram where the $S/Y$ curve shifts. Now show the same situation in the $C/Y$, $I/Y$, and $X/Y$ diagrams. Which curve shifts? If government's share in GDP doesn't change, then what must happen to interest rates? Explain how this affects $X/Y$.

**7.** Draw two sets of diagrams like Figure 8.7 to depict two situations. In one set, draw investment and net exports being very sensitive to interest rates—that is, the $I/Y$ and $X/Y$ curves are very flat. In the other set, draw investment and net exports as insensitive to interest rates—that is, the $I/Y$ and $X/Y$ curves are nearly vertical. For the same increase in the government's share in GDP, in which set of diagrams will interest rates rise more? Why?

**8.** Suppose $C = 1,400$, $I = 400$, $G = 200$, $X = 0$.
    a) What is GDP? Calculate each component's share of GDP.
    b) Suppose government spending falls to 100 and GDP does not change. What is government spending's share of GDP now? What is the new nongovernment share?
    c) What happens to $C/Y$, $X/Y$, and $I/Y$? (Do not calculate anything—just give a direction.) Explain the mechanism by which each of these changes happens.

**9.** Using the diagram at the top of the next page, find the equilibrium interest rate when the government share is 20 percent. What is the investment share? Show what happens to all the variables if there is an upward shift in the investment relation because of a new tax policy that encourages investment.

**10.** Suppose the government institutes an investment tax credit so that at every level of the interest rate, businesses will invest a greater share of GDP. Show how this change will affect the interest rate and the shares of consumption and net exports in GDP, assuming that the share of government spending of GDP remains constant.

**11.** Suppose that there is a leftward shift in the $C/Y$ line due to higher consumption taxes, but at the same time, the government increases its share in GDP to maintain the same interest rate. Describe graphically how this affects each of the shares of GDP. If investment's share is the only thing that affects growth in this system, what will happen to growth as a result of this government policy?

**12.** Suppose the following equations describe the relationship between shares of spending in GDP ($Y$) and the inter-

**Problem 9**

(a) Consumption Share

(b) Investment Share

(c) Net Exports Share

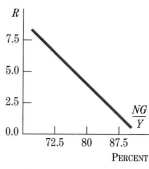

(d) Nongovernment Share

est rate ($R$), measured in decimal fractions (that is, $R = .04$ means that the interest rate is 4 percent).

$$\frac{C}{Y} = .65 - .25 (R - .04)$$

$$\frac{I}{Y} = .15 - .75 (R - .04)$$

$$\frac{X}{Y} = 0 - 1.00 (R - .04)$$

$$\frac{G}{Y} = .18$$

a) Use algebra to determine the values of the interest rate and the shares of spending in GDP.
b) Do the calculations again for a government share of 20 percent rather than 18 percent (that is, $G/Y = .20$).

**13.** Graph the relationships defined in problem 12 to scale in a four-part diagram like Figure 8.6. Use the diagram to analyze each of the following situations.

a) Suppose there is a decrease in the foreign demand for U.S. goods that changes the coefficient in the net exports share equation from 0 to $-.02$. What happens to the interest rate and the shares of consumption, investment, net exports, and government purchases in the United States?
b) Determine how an increase in taxes that reduces the coefficient in the consumption share equation from .65 to .63 would affect the interest rate and the shares of consumption, investment, net exports, and government purchases.
c) Suppose firms are willing to invest 20 percent rather than 15 percent of GDP at an interest rate of 4 percent. How would this affect the interest rate and the shares of spending in GDP?

**14.** Derive and draw the national saving rate-interest rate relation (as in Figure 8.10) from the information on consumption, government spending, and net exports used in problem 12. In the same graph, draw investment plus net exports as a share of GDP. Determine the equilibrium level of saving and the interest rate using this graph.

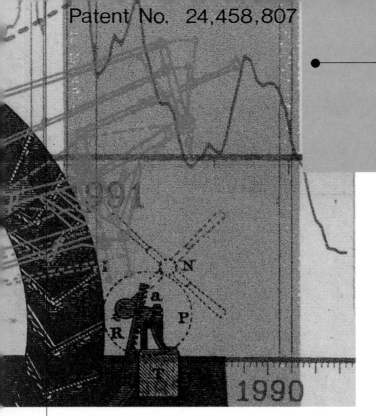

Patent No. 24,458,807

# 9

# Technology and Economic Growth

For most of human history there was no economic growth. True, vast quantities of wealth were amassed by kings and queens through conquest and exploitation; coliseums, pyramids, and great walls were constructed by millions of slaves; and great works of art were produced by talented individuals on all continents. But output per hour of work—the productive power of labor that determines the well-being of most people—grew hardly at all for thousands of years. Except for the ruling classes, people lived in extreme poverty.

This situation changed dramatically around the eighteenth century. Table 9.1 shows the growth rates of *output per hour of work,* or *productivity,* for different periods during the last 300 years. Observe that there was no growth in output per hour of work for most of the 1700s, much like the thousands of years before. Then, in the late 1700s and early 1800s—the period historians call the Industrial Revolution—economic growth began to pick up. Growth accelerated in the early 1800s and then rose to historically unprecedented levels in the twentieth century.

The increase in economic growth during the last 200 years has taken the average person's income in the advanced countries to a level never dreamed of in antiquity, except by the richest emperors and empresses. Although clearly dramatic to look at now, the growth rate

**TABLE 9.1**
**Economic Growth During the Last 300 Years**

| Period | The Growth Rate in Real GDP per Hour of Work (percent per year) |
|---|---|
| 1700–1785 | 0 |
| 1785–1820 | ½ |
| 1820–1890 | 1½ |
| 1890–1996 | 2¼ |

*Note:* In order to show productivity growth for the most advanced countries, rather than averaging over poorer countries and richer countries, the table reports growth for the country with the highest level of productivity in the given period: the Netherlands for the first period, the United Kingdom for the second, and the United States for the third and fourth periods.

*Source:* Angus Maddison, *Phases of Capitalist Development* (London: Oxford University Press, 1982); *Economic Report of the President,* 1997.

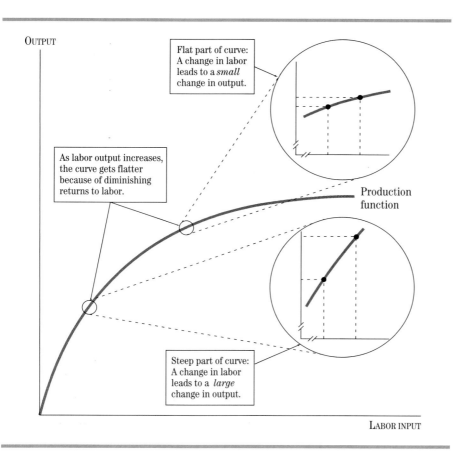

OUTPUT

Flat part of curve:
A change in labor
leads to a *small*
change in output.

As labor output increases,
the curve gets flatter
because of diminishing
returns to labor.

Production
function

Steep part of curve:
A change in labor
leads to a *large*
change in output.

LABOR INPUT

**FIGURE 9.1**
**A Theory Where Only Changes
in Labor Can Change Output**
The curve shows the production
function $Y = F(L)$ where $Y$ is output and $L$ is labor input (hours of
work). In this theory, capital and
technology are out of the picture.
With more labor working on a fixed
supply of land, there are diminishing returns, as shown by the curva-
ture of the production function.

cent in the United States today. Farm product and gross domestic product were
almost the same thing. Hence, agricultural examples such as the preceding one
were very fitting. Although the amount of farmland could be increased somewhat
by clearing more forests, the number of acres of land available for producing farm
goods was limited, especially in England, where many early economists lived. It
was not so unrealistic for them to think of labor as the only input to production that
could be increased. Moreover, they saw only small improvements in farming methods in Europe for thousands of years, so they can be excused for underestimating
the effects of capital and technology on output when they developed their economic
theories.

### Malthusian Predictions

One of the most influential ideas developed during this period was the pessimistic
Malthusian prediction about population and economic growth. Malthus emphasized
that workers and the population as a whole needed a certain amount of output to
survive or subsist. If output in the economy, which was largely farm output,
dropped below a certain amount, called the subsistence level, then people would
begin to die of starvation. This is illustrated in Figure 9.2. The axes of Figure 9.2
are the same as Figure 9.1. The line in Figure 9.2—called the **subsistence line**—
tells us how much output the population would need to subsist—to avoid starvation

**subsistence line:** a line
representing the minimum amount
of production the population needs
to survive or subsist.

**FIGURE 9.2**

**The Subsistence Line**

Along the subsistence line, output per worker is just equal to what it takes for people to live. For the example shown, subsistence is 50 units of output per worker, so that 20 workers need to produce 1,000 units to survive, 100 workers need to produce 5,000 units, and so on. Below subsistence, people die and labor input declines. Above the line, population and labor input rise.

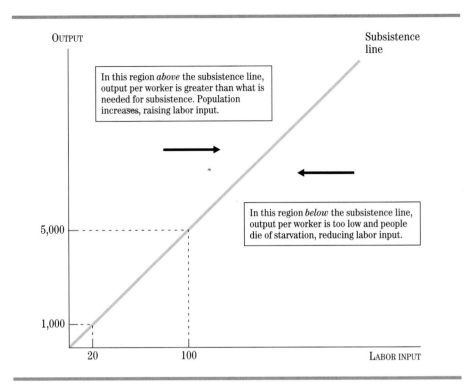

and death. A larger labor input corresponding to a larger population of workers requires more output to subsist; therefore, the line slopes upward. The subsistence level per worker—the minimum amount of output a worker and the worker's family would need to survive—is given by the slope of the subsistence line. For example, if it takes 50 units of output per worker to survive, then 100 workers require 5,000 units of output.

The subsistence line divides Figure 9.2 into two regions. Observe that in the region above the subsistence line, people have more than enough to survive. Malthus assumed that birthrates would increase and death rates would decline in this situation. Hence, the population and labor input would be increasing. This is shown by the arrow pointing to the right. In the region below the subsistence line, output is below the required amount; people do not have enough to live on, and starvation, health problems, and higher death rates reduce the population. Thus, the available labor input is declining, as shown by the arrow pointing to the left.

When the subsistence line is combined with the simple production function relating output to labor input, the Malthusian prediction about economic growth and population emerges. This is shown in Figure 9.3, which superimposes the subsistence line from Figure 9.2 on the production function from Figure 9.1. The amount of output for a particular amount of labor input is always given by the production function; that is, the economy is always at a point on the production function. If output is above the subsistence line, then there will be more output than people need to survive. In that case, the population of workers will grow, according to Malthus. An increase in the population will increase labor input and the economy will move back to the subsistence line. However, if output is below the subsistence line, then the labor input will decline and the economy will move back to the subsistence line.

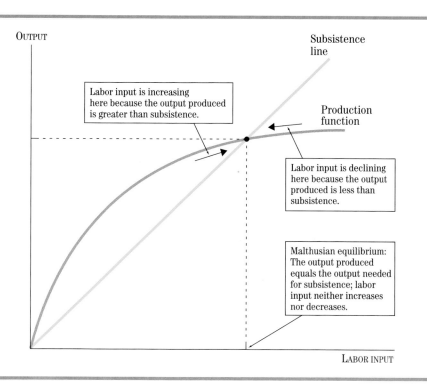

OUTPUT

Subsistence
line

Labor input is increasing
here because the output produced
is greater than subsistence.

Production
function

Labor input is declining
here because the output
produced is less than
subsistence.

Malthusian equilibrium:
The output produced
equals the output needed
for subsistence; labor
input neither increases
nor decreases.

LABOR INPUT

**FIGURE 9.3**
**A Malthusian Equilibrium**
There is only one equilibrium labor
input, as indicated on the diagram.
At a higher labor input, output will
fall below subsistence, reducing
the population and labor input.
At a lower labor input, output will
rise above subsistence, raising
birthrates and increasing the
population and labor input.

Thus, the Malthusian prediction is that real GDP will gravitate toward the subsistence level of output, limiting the well-being of all people—the workers and their children, their grandchildren, and so on for eternity. There is no long-term economic growth. The subsistence level of output is determined by the point of intersection of the production function and the subsistence line. This point is called a **Malthusian equilibrium** because the level of output given by the production function is exactly equal to the level of output needed for subsistence given by the subsistence line. Figure 9.3 shows the labor input corresponding to this Malthusian equilibrium.

Why is the Malthusian equilibrium a *stable* equilibrium? That is, why is there a tendency to move toward the equilibrium? If, starting at that equilibrium, the number of workers grew more rapidly, then output would not keep up and the economy would move into the starvation region; this would cause an automatic reduction in the labor input back to the equilibrium level. If, starting at that equilibrium, labor grew less rapidly, then output per worker would increase, which would stimulate population growth and again bring labor input back to the equilibrium level.

The Malthusian prediction was that the people of England would be forever limited to consuming a subsistence level of output. This prediction is called the **iron law of wages** because the total amount that workers could receive for their work—their wage—was limited to this subsistence amount. A science with that prediction and the associated world-view that most people would forever be struggling at the brink of starvation, with occasional bouts of hardship and mass starvation, seems to deserve the term *dismal science* it was given by the Scottish historian Thomas Carlyle. Malthus himself was less harsh when commenting on the theory,

**Malthusian equilibrium:** a situation in which production equals the subsistence level of output because population adjusts based on consumption of food.

**iron law of wages:** the prediction that wages will always tend to equal the subsistence level.

# Thomas Robert Malthus, 1766–1834

**BORN:**
Surrey, England 1766

**EDUCATION:**
Cambridge University, 1784–1788

**JOBS:**
Parson, Church of England, 1788–1804
Fellow, Cambridge University, 1793–1804
Professor of history and political economy, East India Company College,
   in Haileybury, England, 1805–1834

**MAJOR PUBLICATIONS:**
*An Essay on the Principle of Population as It Affects the Future Improvements of Society,* 1798; *Principles of Political Economy,* 1820

Thomas Robert Malthus, called Bob by his dad and Pop by his students, published his *Essay on the Principles of Population* anonymously when he was 32 years old. Very short—only 137 pages—and wonderfully written, this book had an enormous impact on economists, public officials, and even biologists. Its pessimistic idea—that workers would be forever limited to a bare subsistence with intermittent periods of starvation—immediately attracted wide attention and made Malthus famous for all time.

Malthus did not argue that the supply of farmland was completely fixed. He did insist, however, that even if the supply of farmland could be increased through forest clearing, its growth would be far less rapid than population growth. Malthus argued that population growth is geometric, but that the growth of farm production is arithmetic. Thus he wrote:

*. . . population, when unchecked, goes on doubling every twenty-five years, or increases in a geometrical ratio.
. . . the means of subsistence increases in an arithmetical ratio.*

*Let us now bring the effects of these two ratios together.*

*Taking the population of the world at any number, a thousand millions, for instance, the human species would increase in the ratio of 1, 2, 4, 8, 16, 32, 64, 128, 256, 512, etc. and subsistence as 1, 2, 3, 4, 5, 6, 7, 8, 9, 10, etc. In two centuries and a quarter, the population would be to the means of subsistence as 512 to 10: in three centuries as 4096 to 13; and in two thousand years the difference would be incalculable. . . .*

Malthus did not shy away from giving policy advice based on his theory. For example, he criticized Prime Minister William Pitt's "Poor Bill," which would have paid a small sum each week to workers with children.

*I confess, that before the bill was brought into Parliament, and for some time after, I thought that such a regulation*

*would be highly beneficial; . . . but further reflection on the subject has convinced me, that if . . . it tend[s] to increase population, without increasing the produce, . . . a day's labour will purchase a smaller quantity of provisions, and the poor therefore in general must be more distressed.*

Pitt was greatly influenced by Malthus's argument: After he heard the argument, he withdrew his support for the bill, arguing that helping the poor in this way would be futile and would only increase the population and lead to more suffering. For many years, the Malthusian prediction was cited as a reason not to give welfare to the poor.

Although Malthus used only elementary biology, his research helped stimulate one of the great discoveries in biology: Darwin's theory of evolution. Darwin wrote in his autobiography that he got the idea of natural selection while reading Malthus.

After Maltus wrote his famous *Essay,* he went on to a career as an economist with broad interests. He was the very first professor of economics (then called political economy) anywhere in the world. He was one of the classical economists, a friend and intellectual opponent of David Ricardo. We can use modern terminology to summarize their main difference: Malthus criticized Ricardo for ignoring short-run economic fluctuations and always focusing on the economy's long-run potential growth path; Ricardo criticized Malthus for ignoring the long-run growth path and always focusing on the short-run economic fluctuations. One can view the modern theory of economic growth and fluctuations described in this text as combining these two traditions.

*Source of quotes:* Thomas Robert Malthus, *An Essay on the Principle of Population as It Affects the Future Improvements of Society,* 1798, pp. 12–13, 50, in *The Works of Thomas Robert Malthus,* Vol. I, ed. E. A. Wrigley and D. Souden (London: William Pickering, 1986).

saying only that it had a "melancholy hue." But his depiction of the struggle for survival was one of unmistakable horror: "sickly seasons, epidemics, pestilence and plague advance in terrific array and sweep off their thousands and tens of thousands."[1]

Real GDP per worker was just beginning to grow rapidly as Malthus wrote (see Table 9.1). As growth continued, it gradually became clear that his dismal predictions were not coming true in England or in the other countries about which he wrote. In fact, the population was expanding, rather than stabilizing. Hence, the Malthusian prediction turned out to be wrong.

To be sure, starvation has not disappeared from the planet. Population growth in the underdeveloped parts of the world has frequently faced limited food supplies, resulting in struggles like those depicted by Malthus. And some twentieth-century writers, like Malthus, paint a bleak picture of the future—for example, in 1972 D. Meadows and others wrote *Limits to Growth,* which says that we are up against limited energy supplies and the only thing we can do is to stop economic growth. But since the problems of less-developed countries have occurred alongside a remarkable fiftyfold increase in living standards in the advanced countries, history suggests that there are non-Malthusian explanations for the Malthusian struggles we have observed in the less-developed countries. But what was missing from Malthus's theory? What can we add to the "labor only" theory to explain economic growth?

## Labor and Capital Only

One thing missing from the simple "output depends only on labor" story is capital—an input to production that can increase over time, if some of GDP is devoted to investment. With capital, the production function becomes $Y = F(L, K)$, where $K$ stands for capital. Output can be increased by using more capital, even if the amount of labor is not increased. Consider the vineyard example again. By buying a wheelbarrow to haul the fertilizer around the vineyard, the vineyard can produce more grapes with the same number of workers. More capital at the vineyard increases output. The same is true for the economy as a whole. By increasing the amount of capital in the economy, more real GDP can be produced with the same number of workers.

Figure 9.4 illustrates how more capital raises output. The axes are the same as Figure 9.1, and the curve again shows that more output can be produced by more labor. But, in addition, Figure 9.4 shows that if we add capital to the economy—by investing a certain amount each year—the relationship between output and labor shifts up: More capital provides more output at any level of labor input. To see this, pick a point on the horizontal axis, say point *A,* to designate a certain amount of labor input. Then draw a vertical line up from this point, such as the dashed line shown. The vertical distance between the curve marked "less capital" and the curve marked "more capital" shows how additional capital raises production.

The addition of capital to the growth model changes the Malthusian predictions. As the production function shifts up with more capital, the intersection of the production function and the subsistence line shifts out. Hence, it is possible for the population *and* labor input to increase, contrary to Malthus's prediction.

---

1. Thomas Robert Malthus, *An Essay on the Principle of Population as It Affects the Future Improvements of Society,* 1798, pp. ii, 52, in *The Works of Thomas Robert Malthus,* Vol. I, ed. E. A. Wrigley and D. Souden (London: William Pickering, 1986).

**FIGURE 9.4**
**Capital Becomes a Factor of Production**

The axes are just like those in Figure 9.1, but now if more capital is added to production, more output can be produced with the same labor input. For example, when labor input is at point *A,* more output can be produced with more capital.

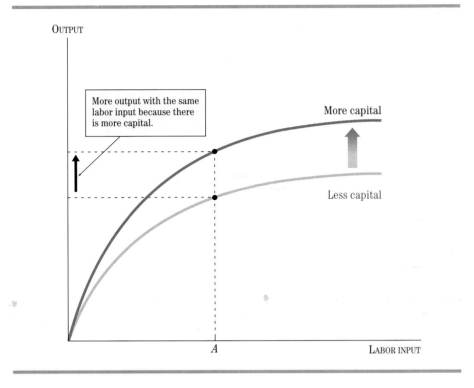

**FIGURE 9.5**
**Output Growing above Subsistence with Capital**

If capital grows along with labor input, output can remain above the subsistence line. Here labor input increases from *A* to *B,* the capital stock increases, and output moves away, rather than toward, the subsistence line, in contrast to Figure 9.3.

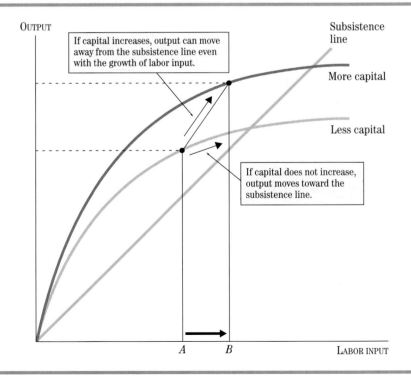

### Output Can Rise above Subsistence

Something more is possible: The population can continually increase while output rises above the subsistence level. This is shown in Figure 9.5, in which the production function is shifted up because of investment in more capital, while at the same time the labor input is increasing from point *A* to point *B* along the horizontal axis. With capital and labor increasing together, output rises above the subsistence level. In fact, output can grow along a line with a slope greater than the subsistence line.

Adding capital as an input to production prevents an economy from getting stuck in a Malthusian equilibrium with a stable population and output equal to subsistence. Population can grow and real GDP can grow above subsistence. By taking some production and using it for investment, the ratio of capital to labor can be increased. With each worker having more capital with which to work, output per worker is higher.

### Diminishing Returns to Capital

However, the addition of capital to the theory does not solve everything. If labor has diminishing returns, why would not capital? Figure 9.6 shows that there are *diminishing returns to capital* too. Each additional amount of capital—another wheelbarrow or another hoe—results in smaller and smaller additions to output. Hence, the gaps between the several production functions in Figure 9.6 get smaller and smaller as more capital is added. As more capital is added there is less ability to increase output per worker. Compare adding one wheelbarrow to the vineyard

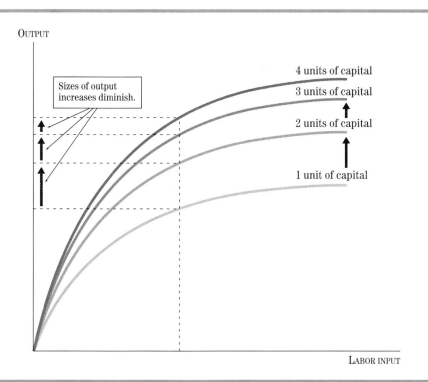

**FIGURE 9.6**
**Capital Has Diminishing Returns Also**

As capital per worker increases, each additional unit of capital produces less output. Thus, there is a limit to how much growth per worker additional capital per worker can bring.

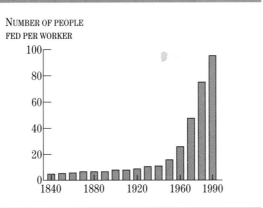

NUMBER OF PEOPLE
FED PER WORKER

**FIGURE 9.7**
**Food Output per Worker**

Farm productivity has risen dramatically. Simply adding more horse-drawn harvesting machines and threshers—the leading technology in 1840—would have led to diminishing returns and could not have produced this increased output. Technology—combines, gasoline-powered tractors, dry farming, etc.—was the key to sustained increases in output per worker.

*Source: Statistical Abstract of the United States and Historical Statistics of the United States.*

when there is already one with adding one wheelbarrow when there are already fifty. Clearly, the fifty-first wheelbarrow would increase farm output by only a minuscule amount, certainly much less than the second wheelbarrow. With a one-acre vineyard, there would not even be much room for the fifty-first wheelbarrow!

Diminishing returns to capital also occur for the economy as a whole. Thus, adding more capital per worker cannot raise real GDP per worker above some limit, and even getting close to that limit will require an enormous amount of capital. Investment would have to be such a large share of GDP that there would be little left for anything else. Thus, even with capital, the model yields a very pessimistic conclusion, not as devastating as Malthus's prediction, but not nearly as optimistic as the fiftyfold (and still counting) gain in productivity that we have observed. Eventually, growth in output per hour of work would stop. Economics still seems to deserve the nickname the "dismal science," even with capital.

Another way to prove that a model with capital and labor alone is not sufficient to explain the growth of productivity is to focus on one type of good, such as agricultural products. Figure 9.7 shows the increased farm output per worker in the past 150 years in the United States. Farm output per worker is measured by the number of people who could be fed on average by a single farm worker—the number of mouths fed per worker. Farm output per worker—a measure of labor productivity in agriculture—increased thirty times during this 150-year period—an average annual growth rate of productivity of 2¼ percent per year. Simply adding more of the type of capital goods available in 1840—for example, the horse-drawn grain harvesters or threshers—could not have produced this kind of growth. Increases in labor productivity required the increase in something else. We now know that "something else" is technology—for example, the invention of combines, which put harvesters and threshers together; the invention of gasoline-powered tractors; and the discovery of new methods of using farmland, such as the "dry farming" crop-rotation method for the plains of the United States.

Thus, labor and capital alone cannot explain the phenomenal growth in either farm output or real GDP during the last 200 years. We move on to the final step in our model construction and testing.

# Review

▶ An economic growth theory with capital and labor alone cannot account for the sustained increase in real GDP per hour of work that began in the late 1700s and continues today.

▶ Malthus predicted that output would forever hover around a subsistence level and that whenever the population increased, it would be forced back to an equilibrium level. Sustained increases in real GDP

per hour of work have contradicted Malthus's predictions.

▶ Adding capital to Malthus's theory can explain why real GDP can remain far above subsistence levels indefinitely, even with the population growing at a steady rate. However, it cannot explain the sustained *increases* in real GDP per hour of work that we have observed.

# LABOR, CAPITAL, AND TECHNOLOGY

When we add technology to capital and labor we have the modern theory of economic growth. The theory can be summarized symbolically by the familiar aggregate production function:

$$Y = F(L, K, T)$$

where $T$ now stands for technology. This function identifies labor, capital, *and* technology as inputs to production.

## What Is Technology?

Technology is the most difficult of the three inputs to production to define and envision. Technology is a form of knowledge; it includes the knowledge needed to produce agricultural products from baby food to wine, the knowledge to make industrial products from penicillin to satellites, the knowledge to produce services from rock concerts to heart transplants, even the knowledge of how to get oil and minerals out of the ground.

    **Technology** is defined as anything that raises the amount of real GDP that can be produced with a given amount of labor and capital. **Technological change** is simply the change in the existing technology between two dates. Technological progress is an improvement—an increase—in the technology, but since technology is usually increasing, the term *technological change* also usually means an improvement. Recall that real GDP is a measure that includes the quality of the goods produced (assuming that prices reflect quality) as well as the introduction of new products. Thus, technological progress also includes things that increase the quality and diversity of goods and services.

> **technology:** anything that raises the amount of output that can be produced with a given level of capital and labor.

> **technological change:** improvement in technology over time.

### Invention, Innovation, and Diffusion

Technological change occurs when new ideas are developed into new products that increase production, such as the steel plow, the harvester, the combine, the automobile, radar, the telephone, the computer, the airplane, lasers, and fiber optic cable. Economists distinguish between an **invention,** which is the discovery of new knowledge or a new principle, such as electricity, and **innovation,** in which the new knowledge is brought into application with a new product, such as the electric light bulb. Economists also distinguish between the innovation itself and the **diffusion** of the innovation throughout the economy, a process that involves advertising, marketing, and spreading the innovation to new uses, such as the use of the electric light bulb to create night shifts in factories.

    Thus, technology is much more than scientific knowledge. The discovery of DNA did not improve technology until it was applied to genetic engineering. The knowledge of mathematics made possible the invention and development of computers in the 1940s, a technology that has obviously improved productivity. Technology depends in part on scientific knowledge, and many people feel that science will become more and more important in future technological change.

    The sewing machine is a good illustration of invention, innovation, and diffusion. In 1847, "17 machines capable of mechanically forming a stitch had been invented," according to Ross Thompson, an economic historian. But only one of these, Elias Howe's sewing machine, developed into a commercially successful

> **invention:** a discovery of new knowledge.

> **innovation:** applications of new knowledge in a way that creates new products or significantly changes old ones.

> **diffusion:** the spreading of an innovation throughout the economy.

innovation. A Boston machinist turned entrepreneur, Howe tried to sell his invention. As he did so, he and others found out how to modify the invention to make it more useful and attractive to potential buyers. Soon the invention turned into a popular innovation used widely. Wide diffusion of the innovation occurred as others produced household versions of the sewing machine like the one marketed by the Singer Company. This story also illustrates that innovation and diffusion usually require the work of an entrepreneur who recognizes the potential of the invention.

### Organization and Specialization

Technology also includes how firms are organized. Better organization schemes can mean a smaller bureaucracy and more output per hour of work without the addition of capital. More efficient organization can improve the flow of information within a firm and thereby affect labor productivity. Better incentive programs that encourage workers to communicate their ideas to management, for example, increase productivity.

Henry Ford's idea of the assembly line greatly increased the productivity of workers. The assembly line enabled the car to come to the worker rather than have the worker go to the car. Thus, each worker could specialize in a certain type of activity; through specialization, productivity increased. The assembly line alone is estimated to have reduced the time it took a group of workers to produce a car from 12½ hours to ½ hour. Productivity increased and so did wages.

New technology can affect how labor and capital are used at a firm. Economists distinguish between *labor-saving* and *capital-saving* technological change. **Labor-saving technological change** means that fewer workers are needed to produce the same amount of output; **capital-saving technological change** means that fewer machines are needed to produce the same amount of output. An example of a labor-saving technological change would be the gasoline-powered tractor replacing a horse-drawn plow, enabling the same worker to plow many more acres. An example of a capital-saving technological change is the night shift. By bringing a crew of workers to work in a steel mill from 4 P.M. to midnight and another to work from midnight to 8 A.M., the same steel-making furnaces are three times as productive as when the working hours are only from 8 A.M. to 4 P.M.

Specialization of workers at a firm adds to productivity. Adam Smith emphasized the importance of specialization in his *Wealth of Nations;* his phrase **division of labor** refers to how a manufacturing task could be divided up among a group of workers, each of whom would specialize in a part of the job. His famous example was pin making. He described how a group of 10 workers could make 48,000 pins a day, an output per worker of 4,800 pins a day: "One man draws out the wire, another straightens it, a third cuts it, a fourth points it, a fifth grinds it at the top for receiving the head, . . ." and so on. Smith argued that one worker working alone could not produce even 20 pins, not even "two-hundred fortieth" of the productivity of each worker in the 10-person operation.

Because specialization permits workers to repeat the same task many times, their productivity increases, as in the old adage "practice makes perfect." Each time the task is repeated the worker becomes more proficient—a phenomenon economists call **learning by doing.** The commonsense principle of learning by doing is that the more one does something, the more one learns about how to do it. For example, as the number of airplanes produced of a particular type—say a DC-10—increases, the workers become more and more skilled at producing that type of airplane. Careful studies of aircraft production have shown that productivity increases

**labor-saving technological change:** a technological innovation that reduces the amount of labor needed to produce a given amount of output with a given amount of capital.

**capital-saving technological change:** a technological innovation that reduces the amount of capital needed to produce a given amount of output with a given amount of labor.

**division of labor:** dividing work into different tasks with groups of workers specializing in each task.

**learning by doing:** a situation in which workers become more proficient by doing a particular task many times.

by 20 percent for each 100 percent increase in output of a particular type of plane. This relationship between learning and the amount of production is commonly called the "learning curve." Learning is a type of technological progress.

### Human Capital

Many firms provide training courses for workers to increase their skills and their productivity. *On-the-job training* is a catchall term for any education, training, or skills a worker receives while at work.

Most workers receive much of their education and training before they begin working, whether in grade school, high school, college, or professional schools. Because increases in education and training can raise workers' productivity, such increases are considered another source of technological change.

The education and training of workers, called **human capital** by economists, is similar to physical capital—factories and equipment. In order to accumulate human capital—to become more educated or better trained—people must devote time and resources, much as a firm must devote resources to investment if physical capital is to increase.

**human capital:** accumulated education and training workers receive that increases their productivity.

The decision to invest in human capital is influenced by considerations similar to those that motivate a firm to invest in physical capital: the cost of the investment versus the expected return. For example, investing in a college education may require that one borrow the money for tuition; if the interest rate on the loan rises, then people will be less likely to invest in a college education. Thus, investment in education may be negatively related to the interest rate, much as physical investment is. This is one reason why, in order to encourage more education and thereby increase economic growth and productivity, the U.S. government provides low-interest loans to college students, making an investment in college more attractive. We will return to the government's role in education as part of its broader policy to increase economic growth later in the chapter.

## The Production of Technology: The Invention Factory

Technology is sometimes discovered by chance by a lone inventor and sometimes by trial and error by an individual worker. A secretary who experiments with several different filing systems to reduce search time or with different locations for the computer, the printer, the telephone, and the photocopier is engaged in improving technology around the office. Frequently, technological progress is better thought of as a continuous process with a small adjustment here and a small adjustment there that add up to major improvements over time.

But more and more technological change is the result of huge expenditures of research and development funds by industry and government. Thomas Edison's "invention factory" in Menlo Park, New Jersey, is one of the first examples of a large industrial laboratory devoted to the production of technology. It in turn influenced the development of many other labs, such as the David Sarnoff research lab of RCA. Merck & Co., a drug company, spends nearly $1 billion per year on research and development for the production of new technology.

HARRIS
USA

Cartoonists & Writers Syndicate

### Invention Factories

The amount of technology produced at Thomas Edison's invention factory (left) or at the research lab of a modern biotechnology firm like Cetus (right) can be explained by the laws of supply and demand. But technology is different from most private goods: If one person uses more technology, there is just as much available for others to use, and it is difficult to exclude people from using a new technology.

**patent:** a grant giving an inventor exclusive rights to use an invention for 17 years.

Edison's Menlo Park laboratory had about 25 technicians working in three or four different buildings. In the six years from 1876 to 1882, the laboratory invented the light bulb, the phonograph, the telephone transmitter, and electrical generators. Each of these inventions turned out to be a successful innovation that was diffused widely. For each innovation a **patent** was granted by the federal government. A patent indicates that the invention is original and that the inventor has the exclusive right to use it for 17 years. In order to obtain a patent for the rights to an invention, an inventor must apply to the Patent and Trademark Office of the federal government. Patents give inventors an inducement to invent. The number of patents granted is an indicator of how much technological progress is going on. Edison obtained patents at a pace of about 67 a year at his lab.

Edison's invention factory required both labor and capital input, much like factories producing other commodities. The workers in such laboratories are highly skilled, their own knowledge obtained through formal schooling or on-the-job training—human capital. A highly trained work force is an important prerequisite to the production of technology.

The supply of technology—the output of Edison's invention factory, for example—depends on the cost of producing the new technology, which must include the great risk that little or nothing will be invented, and the benefits from the new technology: how much Edison can charge for the rights to use his techniques for making light bulbs. Often inventive activity has changed as a result of shifts in the economy that change the costs and benefits. For example, increases in textile workers' wages stimulated the invention of the textile machines, because such machines then yielded greater profits.

### Special Features of the Technology Market

**nonrivalry:** the situation in which more people can consume a good without reducing the amount available for others to consume.

When viewed as a commodity that can be produced, technology has two special qualities that affect how much will be produced. The first is **nonrivalry.** This means that one person's use of the technology does not reduce the amount that another person can use. If one university uses the same book-filing system as another university, that does not reduce the quality of the first university's system. In contrast, most goods are rivals in consumption: If you drink a bottle of Coke, there is one less bottle of Coke around for other people to drink.

The second feature of technology is **nonexcludability.** This means that the inventor or the owner of the technology cannot exclude other people from using it. For example, the system software for Apple computers shows a series of logos and pull-down menus that can be moved around the screen with a mouse. The idea could easily be adapted for use in other software programs by other companies. In fact, the Windows program of Microsoft has similar features to the Apple software, but, according to the court that ruled on Apple's complaint that Microsoft was illegally copying, the features were not so similar that Microsoft could not use them.

**nonexcludability:** the situation in which no one can be prevented from consuming a good.

As the example of Apple and Microsoft shows, the legal system and the enforcement of **intellectual property laws** determine in part the degree of nonexcludability. Intellectual property laws provide for trademarks and copyrights as well as patents. These laws help inventors exclude others from using the invention without compensation. But it is impossible to exclude others from using much technology.

**intellectual property laws:** laws that protect ownership rights over ideas and inventions; includes patent laws, copyright laws, and trademark laws.

Thus, the technology may *spill over* from one activity to another. If your economics teacher invents a new way to teach economics on a computer, it might spill over to your chemistry teacher, who sees how the technology applies to a different subject. Sometimes spillovers occur because research personnel move from one firm to another. Henry Ford knew Thomas Edison and was stimulated to experiment on internal combustion engines by Edison. Hence, Edison's research spilled over to another industry, but Edison would find it very difficult to get compensation from Henry Ford even if he wanted to. Consider also the difficulty Malthus would have had trying to get compensation from Darwin for his ideas on natural selection (see the box on Malthus).

Because inventors cannot be fully compensated for the benefits their ideas provide to others, they might produce too little technology. The private incentives to invent are less than the gain from the inventions to society. If the incentives were higher—say through government subsidies to research and development—more inventions might be produced. Thus, there is a potential role for government in providing funds for research and development, both in industry and at universities. Before we consider this role, we must examine how to measure technological change in the economy as a whole.

# Review

▶ Technological change has a very broad definition. It is anything that increases production for a given level of labor and capital. Technological change has been an essential ingredient in the increase in the growth of real GDP per hour of work in the last 200 years.

▶ Technology can be improved by the education and training of workers—investment in human capital. Technology can also be improved through inventions produced in "invention factories" or industrial research laboratories, as well as by trial and error. In any case, the level of technology is determined by market forces.

▶ But technology exhibits nonrivalry in consumption and a high degree of nonexcludability. These are precisely the conditions in which there will be an underproduction of technology.

# GROWTH ACCOUNTING

Both technological change and capital formation cause real GDP per hour of work to grow. Is it possible to determine how much growth has been due to technology as distinct from capital? Surprisingly, the answer is yes. A significant recent development in economics has been a technique to measure quantitatively how important capital versus technology has been for growth in the economy as a whole. Robert Solow of MIT made the pioneering contribution and won the Nobel Prize for his innovation. In 1957 he published a paper called "Technical Progress and the Aggregate Production Function" that contained a simple mathematical formula. It is this formula—called the **growth accounting formula**—that enables economists to estimate the relative contributions of capital versus technology.

**growth accounting formula:** an equation that states that the growth rate of real GDP per hour of work equals capital's share of income times the growth rate of capital per hour of work plus the growth rate of technology.

## The Growth Accounting Formula

The growth accounting formula is remarkably simple. It can be written as follows:

$$\text{Growth rate of real GDP per hour of work} = \frac{1}{3}\left(\begin{array}{c}\text{growth rate of capital} \\ \text{per hour of work}\end{array}\right) + \left(\begin{array}{c}\text{growth rate} \\ \text{of technology}\end{array}\right)$$

The growth accounting formula can be derived from the aggregate production function. (The box on the next page contains a brief graphical explanation and the appendix to this chapter provides more details about the derivation.)

The two ingredients in the growth of real GDP per hour of work—the growth of *capital* and the growth of *technology*—are apparent in the formula. The growth accounting formula allows us to measure the importance of these two ingredients.

Here is how the formula works. The growth rates of real GDP per hour of work and capital per hour of work are readily determined from available data sources in most countries. Using the formula, we can express the growth rate of technology as follows:

$$\text{Growth rate of technology} = \left(\begin{array}{c}\text{growth rate of real} \\ \text{GDP per hour of work}\end{array}\right) - \frac{1}{3}\left(\begin{array}{c}\text{growth rate of capital} \\ \text{per hour of work}\end{array}\right)$$

Thus, the growth rate of technology can be determined by subtracting ⅓ times the growth rate of capital per hour of work from the growth rate of real GDP per hour of work. Consider an example. Suppose the growth rate of real GDP per hour of work is 2 percent per year. Suppose also that the growth rate of capital per hour of work is 3 percent per year. Then the growth rate of technology must be 1 percent per year: $2 - [(\frac{1}{3}) \times 3] = 1$. Thus, in the example, one-half of the growth of productivity is due to technological change and one-half to the growth of capital per hour of work.

Why is the growth of capital per hour multiplied by ⅓? The simplest reason is that economists view the production function for the economy as one in which output rises by only ⅓ of the percent by which capital increases. For example, a vineyard owner can estimate by what percent grape output will rise if the workers have more wheelbarrows to work with. If the number of wheelbarrows at the vineyard is increased by 100 percent and if the ⅓ coefficient applies to the vineyard, then grape production per hour of work will increase by 33 percent. In other words, this is a property of the grape production function. Statistical studies suggest that the ⅓ coefficient seems to apply to the production function in the economy as a whole.

Another reason for the ⅓ coefficient on capital growth is based on a basic principle of economics that inputs to production receive income according to their

# A Graphical Illustration of Growth Accounting

The growth accounting formula splits up the growth of productivity into two sources: the growth of capital per hour of work and the growth of technological change. The figure on the left below explains this split graphically through the familiar distinction between the shifts of and movements along curves. The figure shows the relationship between productivity ($Y/L$) and capital per hour of work ($K/L$). Higher capital per hour leads to more output per hour, as shown by the purple curves in the figure. Technological change shifts the purple curve up because, by definition, technological change is anything that raises productivity for a given level of capital per hour of work.

The purple curves in the figure are much like a production function except productivity ($Y/L$), rather than output ($Y$), is what is being explained. Hence, we call each purple curve in the figure a *productivity curve*. The production function and the productivity curve are perfectly compatible with each other, but one focuses on output and the other on output per hour of work.

Actual productivity increases in the economy are due to a combination of *movements along* the productivity curve, because of more capital per hour, and of *shifts* of the productivity curve, because of technological

change. The purpose of the growth accounting formula is to determine how much is due to movement along and how much is due to a shift. This is illustrated by two observations on productivity and capital per hour in two different years (year 1 and year 2). Observe how the increase in productivity from year 1 to year 2 is due partly to an upward shift of the productivity curve and partly to a movement along the curve.

This graphical approach can be applied to the productivity slowdown, as shown in the graph on the lower right. This graph focuses on the upper portion of three U.S. productivity curves corresponding to the three years, 1955, 1975, and 1995 (the lower portions are cut away for better visibility of the relevant parts of the curves).

Observe on the horizontal axis how productivity increased by a smaller percentage from 1975 to 1995 than it did from 1955 to 1975. Observe also that the curve shifts up by a much smaller amount from 1975 to 1995 than it does from 1955 to 1975. In fact, the productivity slowdown is almost entirely due to smaller shifts in the curve rather than to smaller percentage increases in capital per worker. This finding is also shown in Table 9.2

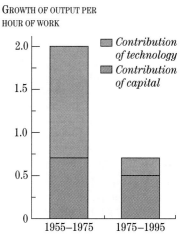

GROWTH OF OUTPUT PER
HOUR OF WORK

■ *Contribution of technology*
■ *Contribution of capital*

**FIGURE 9.8**
**The Role of Capital and Technology in the Growth of Productivity**

The slowdown in the growth rate of labor productivity is due both to capital and technology, but technology growth has slowed down by a larger amount, according to the growth accounting formula. (The data for the bar chart come from Table 9.2.)

*Source:* U.S. Department of Commerce.

contribution to production. If you look back at Table 6.3, you will find that capital income ($1,588 billion) plus depreciation ($853 billion) for the U.S. economy as a whole is about ⅓ of aggregate income ($7,576 billion). This provides statistical support for the ⅓ coefficient.

We should not give the impression, however, that economists know the coefficient on capital growth in the growth accounting formula with much precision. There is uncertainty about its size. It could be ¼ or even 5/12. In any case, the growth accounting formula is a helpful rule of thumb to assist policymakers in deciding what emphasis to place on capital versus technology when developing programs to stimulate economic growth.

## Case Studies: Using the Growth Accounting Formula

Before describing what economic policies can be put in place to improve technology, let us briefly examine quantitatively what the growth accounting formula tells us about the actual importance of technology in economic growth.

### *Productivity Slowdown in the United States*

Figure 9.8 and Table 9.2 show the breakdown between capital growth and technology growth during the productivity slowdown that began in the 1970s in the United States. Both capital growth and technology growth slowed down, but the slowdown in the growth of productivity seems to be largely due to a slowdown in the growth of technology.

The implication of this examination of the source of the productivity slowdown is that government policies to address the slowdown should pay particular attention to the slowdown in technological change due perhaps to insufficient research and development, education, rewards to inventors, or incentives to organize production efficiently.

### *Demise of the Soviet Union*

Table 9.3 shows the growth accounting formula applied to the former Soviet Union. It shows the high rates of growth in the Soviet Union in the 1970s and early 1980s, a time when many Americans were still worried about the Soviet Union overtaking the United States, recalling former Soviet Premier Nikita Khrushchev's highly publicized statement "We will bury you."

But as the table shows, most of that growth was due to increases in capital per worker and not to technological change. Such high rates of capital growth could not be maintained without severe burden on the people. Eventually the Soviet citizens

**TABLE 9.2**
**Accounting for the Productivity Growth Slowdown in the United States**
(The numbers are average annual growth rates.)

| Period | (1) Productivity Growth | (2) ⅓ Capital per Hour of Work | (3) Technology Growth |
|---|---|---|---|
| 1955–1975 | 2.0 | 0.7 | 1.3 |
| 1975–1995 | 0.7 | 0.5 | 0.2 |

*Source:* U.S. Department of Commerce and Bureau of Labor Statistics.

| Period | Productivity Growth | ⅓ Capital per Hour of Work | Technology Growth |
|--------|--------------------|-----------------------------|-------------------|
| 1971–1975 | 4.5 | 3.0 | 1.5 |
| 1976–1980 | 3.3 | 3.9 | −0.6 |
| 1981–1985 | 2.7 | 3.5 | −0.8 |

**TABLE 9.3**
**Growth Accounting in the Former Soviet Union**

*Source: A Study of the Soviet Economy,* International Monetary Fund, The World Bank, Organization for Economic Cooperation and Development, and European Bank for Reconstruction and Development, Paris, 1991, Table E.2, Volume 1, p. 100 and Table VI.I1, Volume 3, p. 370. (For technology growth, the average of upper and lower estimates are reported.)

complained that such a high share of their output was going to investment. They wanted the consumer goods that were being most visibly obtained in the market economies. One could have predicted problems and perhaps even the demise of the Soviet Union from an examination of the sources of growth.

### A Tale of Two Countries

The growth accounting formula can also be used to examine the very high-growth economies of East Asia. Consider Hong Kong and Singapore, for example. Both had approximately the same high rate of 5 percent per year productivity growth over the 1970s and 1980s. But, by applying the growth accounting formula, Alwyn Young of MIT found that there is an enormous difference in how important technological change was compared to the growth of capital per worker in the two countries. On the one hand, Hong Kong had a growth rate of technology that contributed almost 35 percent of the growth rate of output. Capital per worker contributed about 65 percent of growth. On the other hand, the growth accounting formula shows that Singapore had virtually no technological change during this period. It was generating the high growth rate solely through a very high growth rate of capital per worker.

Why the large difference in the role of technological change? Alwyn Young argues that the Singapore government encouraged firms to produce the very latest products. Perhaps this policy caused firms to switch too rapidly from one leading product to another and prevented them from learning to be more efficient in producing any given product. Hong Kong did not follow such a policy. Moreover, Hong Kong had a better-educated labor force, and this may have improved technology.

## Review

▶ With the growth accounting formula we can estimate the relative contributions of capital and technology to economic growth. In the growth accounting formula the weight given to capital growth is about ⅓, but it could be somewhat smaller or larger.

▶ The productivity slowdown in the United States during the last 20 years seems to be largely due to a slowdown in technology growth, although capital growth slowed down as well.

▶ Some countries depend more on capital for growth, and others depend more on technology.

# TECHNOLOGY POLICY

The growth accounting formula tells us that if economic policy is to help restore the higher productivity growth that existed before the productivity slowdown in the United States, it must provide incentives for, or remove disincentives to, technological progress. What policies might the United States pursue in order to improve technological progress?

## Policy to Encourage Investment in Human Capital

One policy is to improve education. A more highly trained work force is more productive. Better-educated workers are more able to make technological improvements. In other words, human capital can improve the production of technology. Hence, educational reform (higher standards, more local school autonomy, and school choice) as well as more funding would be ways to increase technological change. Some studies have shown that the U.S. educational system is falling behind other countries, especially in mathematics and science in the K–12 schools; hence, additional support seems warranted in order to raise economic growth.

## Policy to Encourage Research and Innovation

Today the United States and other advanced countries spend huge quantities on **research and development (R&D).** Some of the research supports pure science, but much of it is for applied research in engineering and medical technology. Figure 9.9 shows that about 2.6 percent of U.S. GDP goes to research and development. The government provides much of its R&D funds through research grants and contracts to private firms and universities through the National Science Foundation and the National Institutes of Health and through its own research labs. But private firms are the users of most of the research funds, as also shown in Figure 9.9.

The United States spends less on research and development as a share of GDP but more in total than the other countries. Total spending on research rather than spending as a share of GDP is a better measure of the usefulness of the spending if the benefits spill over to the whole economy.

During the cold war, much of U.S. research and development spending went for national defense. What should happen to those research dollars as overall defense spending has come down now that the cold war is over? Some argue that more civilian research should be supported. For many years the Defense Advanced Research Projects Agency (DARPA) funded research on computer networks and artificial intelligence. In 1993, the *D* in DARPA was dropped, signaling the new focus on civilian research. However, there is a debate about whether the government should directly support research in certain industries—say, computers or genetic engineering—at the expense of others. Such targeted technology policy is called *industrial policy.* Those who argue against it say that the private sector knows more than the government about which industries are promising for technological innovations.

**research and development (R & D):** activities designed to further scientific knowledge and develop new products.

**FIGURE 9.9**
**Research and Development Expenditures in the United States**
The United States devotes about 2.6 percent of its GDP to research and development. The funds come from the federal government and the private sector. Most of the R&D funds are used by private firms and universities.

*Source: Statistical Abstract of the United States.*

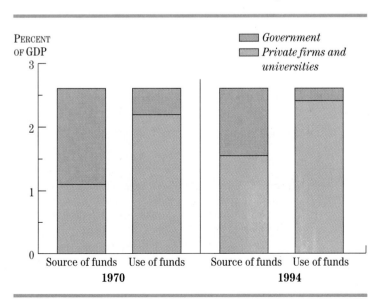

Increased government support for research and development regardless of industry can be achieved through tax credits. A *tax credit for research* allows firms to deduct a certain fraction of their research expenditures from their taxes in order to reduce their tax bill. This increases the incentive to engage in research and development. Another way to increase the incentive for inventors and innovators is to give them a more certain claim to the property rights from their invention. The government has a role here in defining and enforcing property rights, through patent laws, trademarks, and copyrights.

## Technology Embodied in New Capital

Although we have emphasized that capital and technology have two distinct effects on the growth rate of productivity, it is not always possible to separate them in practice. In order to take advantage of a new technology, it may be necessary to invest in new capital. Consider the Thompson Bagel Machine, invented by Dan Thompson, which can automatically roll and shape bagels. Before the machine was invented, bakers rolled and shaped the bagels by hand. According to Dan Thompson, who in 1993 was running the Thompson Bagel Machine Manufacturing Corporation, headquartered in Los Angeles, "You used to have two guys handshaping and boiling and baking who could turn out maybe 120 bagels an hour. With the machine and now the new ovens, I have one baker putting out 400 bagels an hour."[2] That is a productivity increase of over 500 percent! But the new technology is inseparable from the capital. In order to take advantage of the technology, bagel producers have to buy the machine as well as the new ovens to go with it.

Economists call this *embodied technological change* because it is embodied in the capital. An example of *disembodied technological change* would be the discovery of a new way to forecast the demand for bagels at the shop each morning so that fewer people would be disappointed on popular days and fewer bagels would be wasted on slack days. Taking advantage of this technology might not require any new capital.

The relationship between capital and technology has implications for technology policies. For example, policies that remove disincentives to invest might indirectly improve technology as they encourage investment in new, more productive equipment.

## Is Government Intervention Appropriate?

Any time there is a question about whether government should intervene in the economy, such as with the technology policies just discussed, the operation of the private market should be examined carefully. For example, we noted that incentives for technology production may be too low without government intervention. Certainly some research a business firm undertakes can be kept secret from others. In such cases, the firm may have sufficient incentive to do the research. But many research results are hard to keep secret. In that case, there is a role for government intervention in subsidizing the research. In general, policies to effect economic growth should be given the test for whether government intervention in the economy is necessary: Is the private market providing the right incentives? If not, can the government do better without a large risk of government failure? If the answers are "no" and "yes," respectively, then government intervention is appropriate.

2. *New York Times,* April 25, 1993.

## Review

▶ Policy proposals to increase productivity growth by providing incentives to increase technology include educational reform, research tax credits, increased funding for research, moving government support toward areas that have significant spillovers, and improving intellectual property laws to better define the property rights of inventors and extend them globally.

▶ Many technologies are embodied in new capital. Hence, policies to stimulate capital formation could also increase technology.

**FIGURE 9.10**
**Forecasting Potential GDP Growth: Now to 2003**
This figure shows the key ingredients that go into an actual forecast of potential GDP growth. Observe that within each bracket the percents add up to the total. In the upper left part of the figure, a coefficient of ⅓ in the growth accounting formula is assumed.

# CONCLUSION: IMPLICATIONS FOR POTENTIAL GDP

When we first examined the growth of the economy over time in Chapter 5, we noted the longer-term trend in real GDP. The long-run trend was called potential GDP. The growth of potential GDP depends on three factors: labor, which we studied in Chapter 7; capital, which we studied in Chapter 8; and finally technology, which we studied in this chapter.

To conclude our discussion of the three factors affecting economic growth, let us see how economists combine forecasts of labor growth, capital growth, and technology growth to project potential GDP growth in the future. For example, the president's Council of Economic Advisers forecasts potential GDP growth of 2.3 percent

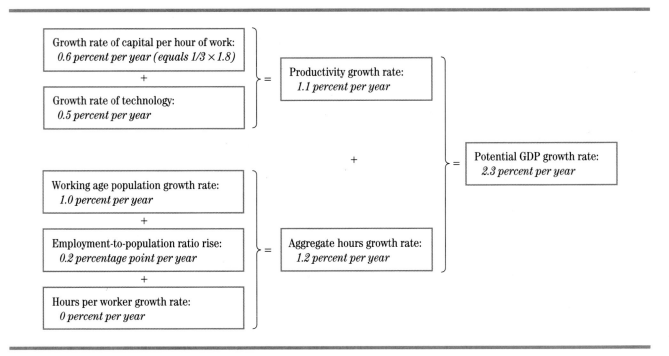

per year from now through the year 2003.[3] The assumptions that underlie this forecast are summarized in Figure 9.10. Observe that the 2.3 percent potential GDP growth rate is based on a growth rate of aggregate hours of 1.2 percent per year, as we discussed in Chapter 7, and a productivity growth rate of 1.1 percent per year. This estimate of productivity growth is less than in the 1950s and 1960s but greater than in the 1970s and 1980s. The growth rate of potential GDP is thus the sum of the growth rate of aggregate hours of work plus the productivity growth rate.

After discussing the monetary system in the next chapter, we will turn to the study of economic fluctuations around this potential GDP path.

# KEY POINTS

**1.** Technology, along with labor and capital, determines economic growth. Technological progress explains the growth wave that started in the late 1700s and enabled the developed countries to get rich.

**2.** Malthus's pessimistic growth prediction was wrong because it omitted the effects of capital and, more important, technology.

**3.** Technology is defined by economists to be much broader than "high-tech" products or inventions. Technology includes such things as better organizational structure for a firm and better education for workers as much as innovations like fiber optic cables.

**4.** As a commodity, technology has the special features of nonexcludability and nonrivalry.

**5.** Patent laws attempt to make technology more excludable and thereby increase the incentives to invest.

**6.** The growth accounting formula is itself a great invention that has enabled economists to better understand the role of technology in the economy.

**7.** Technology policy has the goal of offsetting disincentives to invest and innovate that exist in the private market.

**8.** Government support for education and research is a key part of a modern technology policy.

# KEY TERMS

| | | |
|---|---|---|
| diminishing returns | innovation | patent |
| subsistence line | diffusion | nonrivalry |
| Malthusian equilibrium | labor-saving technological change | nonexcludability |
| iron law of wages | capital-saving technological change | intellectual property laws |
| technology | division of labor | growth accounting formula |
| technological change | learning by doing | research and development (R&D) |
| invention | human capital | |

# QUESTIONS FOR REVIEW

**1.** Why did Malthus's predictions turn out to be wrong for England?

**2.** What is the essential difference between economic growth in the last 200 years and in the 2,000 years before that?

**3.** Why are economists so sure that technology played a big role in economic growth during the last 200 years?

**4.** Why does technology include different ways to organize a business firm?

**5.** How is technology produced?

**6.** What is the importance of nonrivalry and nonexcludability for technology?

**7.** Of what practical use is the growth accounting formula?

**8.** What is wrong with a growth policy that focuses on capital formation but not on technology?

**9.** What do intellectual property rights have to do with economic growth?

**10.** What is the rationale for government intervention in the production of technology?

3. *Economic Report of the President, 1997,* p. 86.

# PROBLEMS

**1.** Consider a country in which capital per hour of work from 1950 to 1973 grew by 3 percent per year and output per hour of work grew by about 3 percent per year. Suppose that from 1973 to 1991 capital per hour of work did not grow at all and output per hour of work grew by about 1 percent per year. How much of the slowdown in productivity (output per hour of work) growth was due to technological change? Explain. (Assume that the coefficient on capital in the growth accounting formula is ⅓.)

**2.** In Chapter 8, you learned that a decrease in government spending results, among other things, in an increase in investment in the long run. Suppose the capital stock is $1 trillion and a fall in government spending causes a $50 billion rise in investment. Determine the effect of the change in government purchases on long-run output growth using the growth accounting formula. (Assume that the coefficient on capital in the growth accounting formula is ⅓.)

**3.** The following table shows how output (shaded) depends on capital and labor (it is the same table as in problem 8, Chapter 5). Using the data in the table, draw the production function $Y = F(L)$, when the capital stock ($K$) is 100 and when it is 200. What do you observe? Now draw the same curve when the capital stock is 300 and 400. Do you observe any difference in the resulting increase in output? What do economists call this phenomenon?

|         | Labor |     |     |     |     |
|---------|-----|-----|-----|-----|-----|
|         | 100 | 200 | 300 | 400 | 500 |
| **100** | 100 | 162 | 216 | 264 | 309 |
| **200** | 123 | 200 | 266 | 325 | 380 |
| **300** | 139 | 226 | 300 | 367 | 429 |
| **400** | 152 | 246 | 327 | 400 | 468 |
| **500** | 162 | 263 | 350 | 428 | 500 |

(Capital is the row label.)

**4.** Using the table from problem 3, suppose the capital stock is 100 and the subsistence level is .8 units of output per unit of labor. How many units of labor will be employed in a Malthusian equilibrium? If the capital stock were 200, how many units would be employed? Draw a diagram to illustrate your answer.

**5.** Which of the following types of government spending are likely to help economic growth? Why?
   a) Military spending on advertising for recruits
   b) Military spending on laser research
   c) Funding for a nationwide computer network
   d) Subsidies for a national opera company
   e) Extra funding for educational programs

**6.** The former Soviet Union had high rates of economic growth, especially in the 1950s and 1960s, but could not maintain them. Why? What does this tell us about the limitations of capital and of government?

**7.** a) Suppose a country has no growth in technology, and capital and labor hours are growing at the same rate. What is the growth rate of real GDP per hour of work? Explain.
   b) Suppose that capital in the country described in part (a) continues to grow at its previous rate, technology growth is still zero, but growth in labor hours falls to half its previous rate. What happens to growth in real GDP per capita?

**8.** Suppose that in order to increase the rate of economic growth, the government is considering two options:
   1) A tax credit for research
   2) An increase in the life of patents
Write a one page memo presenting the economic case for either one of these two options over the other.

**9.** Identify the following as contributing to either capital, labor, or technological growth in the growth accounting equation:
   a) A business buys a computer.
   b) You take a course in computer programming.
   c) The government subsidizes joint research projects by Japanese and U.S. automakers to make more fuel-efficient cars.

**10.** Identify the following as either capital-saving or labor-saving technological change:
   a) A bagel baker buys a machine that rolls and shapes bagels automatically.
   b) An office reconfigures its computer network so more workers have access to the computers in the office.
   c) A university starts a summer program.

**11.** a) Draw a diagram for the Malthusian equilibrium, as in Figure 9.3, and explain the mechanism by which the economy gets to the equilibrium point.
   b) Instead of Malthus's assumption about population, assume that people choose how many children to have so that output is as far above the subsistence level as possible. How can you show this on the diagram? (*Hint:* Look at the point on the production function that has the same slope as the subsistence line.) Would this level of the population defy the dismal Malthusian prediction of people always living at the subsistence level?
   c) Suppose the subsistence level increases as a disease forces workers to eat more to stay alive. Show this situation on the diagram. What happens to the Malthusian equilibrium quantity of labor input?

**12.** If we incorrectly estimate the share of capital in income, it can affect our estimation of how large technological growth has been. Use the data from problem 1 to recalculate the change in output per hour of work when capital's share is ¼. Explain intuitively the difference in the importance of technology.

# Deriving the Growth Accounting Formula

Figure 9A.1 shows the relationship between productivity (*Y/L*) and capital per hour of work (*K/L*). Because of diminishing returns to capital, the line is curved: As capital per hour of work increases, the increased productivity that comes from additional capital per hour diminishes.

The curve in Figure 9A.1 is called a **productivity curve;** it can be represented in symbols as (*Y/L*) = *f(K/L)*, or productivity is a function of capital per hour of work.

An upward shift in the productivity function due to an increase in technological change is shown in Figure 9A.2.

For example, with capital per hour constant at point *A* in the figure, more technology leads to more productivity.

We can derive the growth accounting formula using this graph in much the same way as Robert Solow did in 1957. Productivity increases in the economy are due to a combination of *movements along* the productivity function, because of more capital per hour, and of *shifts* of the productivity function, because of technological change.

**FIGURE 9A.1**
**Productivity Curve**

Productivity, or output per hour of work, is shown to increase with the amount of capital that workers have, as measured by capital per hour of work. The productivity curve gets flatter as output per hour of work increases because of diminishing returns to capital.

**FIGURE 9A.2**
**A Shift in the Productivity Curve Due to Technology**

An increase in technology permits an increase in productivity even if there is no change in capital per hour of work. For example, if capital per hour of work stays at *A,* productivity increases when the productivity curve shifts up.

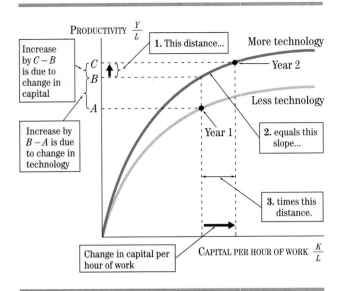

**FIGURE 9A.3**
**Growth Accounting with Capital**
**per Hour and Technology**
**Increasing**
Here a shift in the productivity curve and a
movement along the productivity curve due to
more capital per hour of work are combined.
Productivity increases. The part of the increase
due to capital and the part due to technological
change are shown in the diagram.

In Figure 9A.3, productivity and capital per hour in two
different years (year 1 and year 2) are shown. These could
be 1997 and 1998 or any other two years. In this example,
the growth rate of productivity is given by the increase in

productivity ($C$ minus $A$) divided by the initial level of productivity ($A$), or $(C - A)/A$. (The definition of the growth
rate of a variable is the change divided by the initial level.)
Observe in Figure 9A.3 how the increase in productivity
can be divided into the part due to technology ($B$ minus $A$)
and the part due to higher capital per worker hour ($C$ minus
$B$). Thus, we have

$$\underbrace{(C - A)/A}_{\substack{\text{Growth rate of} \\ \text{productivity}}} = \underbrace{(B - A)/A}_{\substack{\text{Growth rate} \\ \text{of technology}}} + \underbrace{(C - B)/A}_{\substack{\text{Term related to} \\ \text{capital per hour}}}$$

which is close to the growth accounting formula. To finish,
we need to examine the second term on the right. How does
this term relate to capital per hour of work? The boxes in
Figure 9A.3 show that $C - B$ equals the *change* in capital
per hour of work $\Delta(K/L)$ times the *slope* of the productivity
function. (The slope times the change along the horizontal
axis gives the changes along the vertical axis.) Let the symbol $r$ be the slope, which measures how much additional
capital increases output. Thus, $(C - B)/A$ is given by:

$$\frac{\Delta(K/L)r}{Y/L} = \frac{\Delta(K/L)}{(K/L)} r(K/Y)$$

The expression on the right is obtained by multiplying the
numerator and the denominator of the expression on the left
by $(K/Y)$. Now the term on the right is simply the growth
rate of capital per hour times $r(K/Y)$. The amount of
income paid to capital is $r$ times $K$ if capital is paid according to how much additional capital increases output. Aggregate income is given by $Y$. Thus, the term $r(K/Y)$ is the
share of capital income in aggregate income. As explained
in the text, $r(K/Y)$ is approximately $\frac{1}{3}$ in the United States.
Thus, the expression $(C - B)/A$ is the growth rate of capital
per hour of work times the share of capital income in
aggregate income. Thus, the growth accounting formula is
derived.

# KEY POINTS

**1.** The productivity curve describes how more capital per
hour of work increases productivity, or output per hour of
work.

**2.** The productivity curve shifts up if there is an increase in
technology.

**3.** The growth accounting formula is derived by dividing
an increase in productivity into (1) a shift in the productivity curve due to more technology, and (2) a movement
along the productivity curve due to more capital per worker.

# KEY TERM AND DEFINITION

**productivity curve:** a relationship stating the output per
hour of work for each amount of capital per hour of work in
the economy.

# QUESTIONS FOR REVIEW

**1.** What is the difference between the productivity curve and the production function?

**2.** What is the difference between a shift in the productivity curve and a movement along the curve?

**3.** Why does the share of capital income in total income appear in the growth accounting formula?

# PROBLEMS

**1.** Consider the following relation between productivity and capital per hour for the economy:

| Capital per Hour of Work ($K/L$) (dollars) | Output per Hour of Work ($Y/L$) (dollars) |
| --- | --- |
| 10 | 5 |
| 20 | 9 |
| 30 | 12 |
| 40 | 14 |
| 50 | 15 |

a) Plot the productivity curve.

b) Suppose in year 1, $K/L = 30$ and $Y/L = 12$, but in year 2, $K/L = 40$ and $Y/L = 14$. How much has technol-ogy contributed to the increase in productivity between the two years?

c) Suppose that between year 2 and year 3 the productivity curve shifts up by $1 at each level of capital per hour of work. If $K/L = 50$ and $Y/L = 16$ in year 3, how many dollars did capital contribute to productivity growth between year 2 and year 3? How much was the contribution as a fraction of the growth rate of capital per worker?

**2.** Suppose the production function $Y = f(K,L)$ is such that $Y$ equals the square root of the product ($K$ times $L$). Plot the production function with $Y$ on the vertical axis and $L$ on the horizontal axis for the case where $K = 100$. Plot the productivity curve with $Y/L$ on the vertical axis and $K/L$ on the horizontal axis.

# 10

# The Monetary System and Inflation

Working behind the scenes as the great drama of economic growth unfolds—with labor, capital, and technology in the leading roles—is the monetary system. The monetary system is the arrangement through which people carry out transactions with each other, whether buying or selling, saving or investing, borrowing or lending. Banks are part of the monetary system; they accept deposits, making it easier for people to lend, and they provide loans, making it easier for people to borrow; they channel funds from savers to investors; and they allow people to write checks on their deposits to make payments for goods and services, ranging from aircraft to photocopying. Coins and paper currency issued by governments are also part of the monetary system; these simple items also serve as a means of payment for goods and services. A well-functioning monetary system is essential for strong economic growth.

In this chapter we examine the monetary system. We first examine the role of coins, paper currency, and other forms of what we will define as money. We then consider commercial banks, one of the major providers of money. We will also consider the Federal Reserve System, the central bank of the United States, which has responsibility for controlling the amount of money in the economy. We will show that, in the long run, money is the cause of inflation, and inflation can influence economic growth. In doing so, we introduce a famous equation, called the quantity equation of money, which is, in the view of some economists, as fundamental for the monetary system as Einstein's equation $E = mc^2$ is for physics. We show how this equation provides a convenient way to organize one's thinking about the monetary system, inflation, and economic growth.

# WHAT IS MONEY?

**Tetradrachmas**

At the heart of the monetary system is **money.** Economists define money in a particular way. It is the part of a person's wealth that can be readily used for transactions, such as buying a lunch or selling a bicycle. Thus, money is anything that is generally accepted as payment for goods and services, not because it is inherently attractive or appealing, but because it can be used to pay for other goods and services. This definition of money is different from the more typical usage, which includes a person's total income or total wealth, as when we say, "She makes a lot of money," or "He has a lot of money." To an economist, money includes the dimes or quarters in a person's pocket but is not the amount the person earns each year.

## Commodity Money

Many items have been used for money throughout history. Salt, cattle, furs, tobacco, shells, and arrowheads have been used as money. Traces of their former use can still be found in our vocabulary. The word *salary* derives from the Latin word for salt and the word *pecuniary* derives from the Latin word for cattle. In World War II prisoner of war camps, cigarettes were used for money. On the island of Yap in the Pacific Ocean, huge stones weighing several tons were used for money. Throughout history the most common form of money has been metallic coins, usually gold, silver, or bronze. Gold coins were used as early as the seventh century B.C. in Lydia (now western Turkey). The Chinese were issuing bronze coins with a hole in the middle in the fifth century B.C., and in the fourth century the Greeks issued silver coins called tetradrachmas that had the goddess Athena on one side and her sacred animal, the owl, on the other. All these examples of money are commodities and are therefore called **commodity money.** Metals proved to be the most common form of commodity money because they could be divided easily into smaller units, are very durable, and could be carried around.

**money:** that part of a person's wealth that can be readily used for transactions; money also serves as a store of value and a unit of account.

**commodity money:** a good used as money that has some intrinsic value in a nonmonetary use.

When gold, silver, and other commodities were used as money, changes in the supply of the commodities would change their price relative to all other goods. An increase in the supply of gold would reduce the price of gold relative to all other goods or, alternatively stated, raise the price of all other goods in terms of the number of gold coins required to purchase them. Recall that an increase in the price of all goods is called inflation. Thus, increases in the supply of gold or any other commodity used as money would cause inflation to increase. Whenever there were huge gold discoveries, the price of gold fell and there were increases in inflation in countries that used gold as money. Thus, inflation was determined largely by the supply of precious metals. This relationship between the supply of money and inflation, which seems so clear in the case of commodity money, has persisted into modern times even though there are now many other forms of money. Before examining modern money, let us look carefully at the functions of money.

**Stone Money of Yap Island, Micronesia**

## Three Functions of Money

Money has three different functions: It is a medium of exchange, a unit of account, and a store of value. All three functions can be illustrated with the simple example of gold or silver coins.

### Medium of Exchange

**medium of exchange:** something that is generally accepted as a means of payment.

Money serves as a **medium of exchange** in that it is an item that people are willing to accept as payment for what they are selling because they in turn can use it to pay for something else they want. For example, in ancient times people received coins for their work and then used these coins to buy the goods and services they wanted.

The use of coins was a great technological improvement over **barter,** in which goods are exchanged only for other goods. Under a barter system, there is no single medium of exchange. Thus, under a barter system, if you make shoes and want to buy apples, you have to find an apple seller who needs new shoes. The disadvantage of a barter system is that it requires a rare **coincidence of wants** in which the person who wants to consume what you want to sell (shoes, for example) has exactly what you want to consume (apples, for example).

**barter:** trade in goods or services without the use of money.

**coincidence of wants:** a condition required for exchange in a nonmonetary system; to accomplish a trade, it is necessary to find someone who has what you want and who also wants what you have.

**store of value:** something that will allow purchasing power to be carried from one period to the next.

### Store of Value

Money also serves as a **store of value** from one period to another. For example, in ancient times people could sell their produce in September for gold coins and then use the coins to buy staples in January. In other words, they could store their purchasing power from one season to another.

Money is not the only thing that can provide a store of value. For example, rice or corn can also be stored from one season to the next. But if you are not a farmer with a large storage bin, money is a more convenient store of value.

### Unit of Account

**unit of account:** a standard unit in which prices can be quoted and values of goods can be compared.

Money also serves a third function, providing a **unit of account.** The prices of goods are usually stated in the units of money. For example, prices of shoes or apples in ancient Greece were stated in a certain number of tetradrachmas because people using these coins were familiar with that unit. Originally, units of money were determined by the weight of the metal. The British pound, for example, was originally a pound of silver; a penny was originally a pennyweight of silver—$\frac{1}{20}$ th of an ounce, or $\frac{1}{240}$ th of a pound. That terminology stuck even though, as we will see, modern money is unrelated to silver or any other metal.

To better understand the difference between the unit of account and the medium of exchange, it is helpful to find examples where they are based on different monies. For example, when inflation got very high in Argentina in the early 1990s, the prices of many goods were quoted in U.S. dollars rather than Argentine pesos, but people usually exchanged pesos when they bought or sold goods. Thus, the U.S. dollar was the unit of account while the medium of exchange was still the peso. But such cases are the exception; the unit of account and the medium of exchange are usually the same money.

## From Coins to Paper Money to Deposits

**paper money:** currency made of paper that has no intrinsic value.

Although coins and other commodity monies are improvements over barter, there are more efficient forms of money. Starting in the late eighteenth and early nineteenth century, **paper money** began to be used widely and supplemented or replaced coins as a form of money. Although there are a few examples where paper money was used earlier, it was at this time that it became generally recognized that paper money was easier to use and could save greatly on the use of precious metals.

Originally, the amount of paper currency was linked by law or convention to the supply of commodities. For example, the U.S. dollar was worth $22 per ounce of gold during the years before the Civil War. One reason for this link was the recognition that more money would cause inflation and that limiting the amount of paper money to the amount of some commodity like gold would limit the amount of paper money. Irving Fisher of Yale University, perhaps the most prolific and influential American economist of the early twentieth century, argued for linking paper money to commodities for precisely this reason. Many countries of the world linked their paper money to gold. They were on a **gold standard,** which meant that the price of gold in terms of paper money was fixed by the government. The government fixed the price by agreeing to buy and sell gold at that price. Occasionally, countries went off the gold standard—such as the United States during the Civil War. When this happened, the supply of paper money usually increased and inflation rose, just as when commodity money increased. The paper money issued during the Civil War was called *greenbacks.* During the years after the Civil War, the supply of greenbacks was reduced and the United States returned to the gold standard in 1879. The United States and most other countries went off the gold standard again during World War I. Today the United States and other countries have severed all links between their paper money and gold and apparently have no intention of returning. Governments now supply virtually all the coin and paper money—the two together are called **currency.**

**gold standard:** a monetary standard in which the value of paper money is linked to gold.

Though paper money was much easier to make and to use than coins, it too has been surpassed by a more efficient form of money. Today money consists mainly of **checking deposits,** or checkable deposits, at banks or other financial institutions. These are deposits of funds on which an individual can write a check to make payment for goods and services. The deposits serve as money because people can write checks on them. For example, when a student pays $100 for books with a check, the student's checking deposit at the bank goes down by $100 and the bookstore's checking deposit at its bank goes up by $100. Checking deposits are used in much the same way as when a student pays with a $100 bill, which is then placed in the store's cash register. The student's holding of money goes down by $100 and the store's goes up by $100. Such deposits are used by many people at least as a partial payment for coin or paper money. Writing checks to pay for goods has become more common than using currency.

**currency:** money in its physical form: coin and paper money.

**checking deposit:** an account at a financial institution on which checks can be written; also called checkable deposit.

## Alternative Definitions of the Money Supply

Today economists define the **money supply** as the sum of currency (coin and paper money) held by the public and deposits at banks. But there are differences of opinion about what types of deposits should be included.

**money supply:** the sum of currency (coin and paper money) held by the public and deposits at banks.

The narrowest measure of the money supply is called **M1.** The M1 measure consists mainly of currency plus checking deposits (travelers checks are also part of M1 but constitute less than 1 percent of total M1). The items in M1 have a great degree of *liquidity,* which means that they can be quickly and easily used to purchase goods and services.

**M1:** currency plus checking deposits plus travelers checks.

Many things that people would consider money, however, are not included in M1. For example, if you had no cash but wanted to buy a birthday gift for a relative, you could withdraw cash from your savings deposit. A **savings deposit** is a deposit that pays interest and from which funds can normally be easily withdrawn at anytime. In other words, a savings deposit is also liquid but not quite as liquid as a

**savings deposit:** an account at a financial institution that is very liquid but generally cannot be easily used for transactions.

**TABLE 10.1**
**Measures of Money in the United States, 1996**
(billions of dollars)

| | |
|---|---|
| Currency | 396 |
| M1: Currency plus checking deposits | 1,077 |
| M2: M1 plus time deposits, savings deposits, and other deposits on which check writing is limited or not allowed | 3,826 |

*Source:* Federal Reserve Board.

**time deposit:** an account at a financial institution that requires that the money be left in the account for a specified period of time.

**M2:** M1 plus savings, time, and limited checking deposits.

checking deposit. Similarly, **time deposits**—which require the depositor to keep the money at the bank for a certain time or else lose interest—are not as liquid as checking deposits, but it is possible to withdraw funds from them. Economists have created a broader measure of the money supply called **M2,** which includes all that is in M1 plus savings deposits, time deposits, and certain accounts for which check writing is very limited. Still broader concepts of the money supply can be defined, but M1 and M2 are the most important ones. Table 10.1 shows the total amounts of different definitions of the money supply for the whole U.S. economy in 1996.

Only about one-third of the M1 definition of the money supply is currency and only about one-tenth of the M2 definition is currency. There is disagreement among economists about whether the more narrowly defined M1 or the more broadly defined M2 or something else is the best definition of the money supply. There is probably no best definition for all times and all purposes. For simplicity, in the rest of this chapter we make no distinction between the Ms but simply refer to the money supply, M, as currency plus deposits.

## Review

▶ Commodity money—usually gold, silver, or bronze coins—originally served as the main type of money in most societies. Increases in the supply of these commodities would reduce their price relative to all other commodities and thereby cause inflation.

▶ Later, paper currency and deposits at banks became forms of money. Under the gold standard, the amount of paper currency was linked to gold. The

▶ United States and all other countries no longer link their money to any commodity, including gold.

▶ There are three roles for money—as a medium of exchange, as a store of value, and as a unit of account.

▶ The two main definitions of the money supply are M1 and M2.

# THE FED AND THE BANKS: CREATORS OF MONEY

**Federal Reserve System (the Fed):** the central bank of the United States, which oversees the creation of money in the United States.

We have seen that increases in the supply of commodity money such as gold would increase inflation. So would printing paper money by governments. But in today's world, money consists mainly of deposits. In the United States, the **Federal Reserve System,** nicknamed the "Fed," determines the supply of currency and the supply of deposits and is thus a most powerful institution. To understand how the Fed determines the supply of currency and deposits, we must first look at how the Fed works and at how banks accept deposits and make loans.

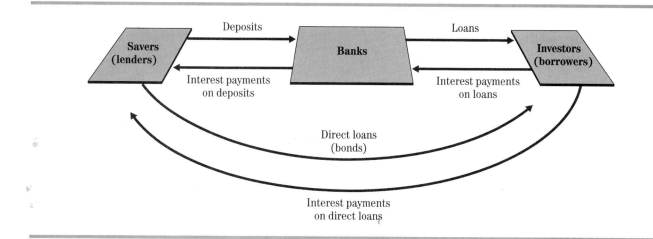

A **bank**—such as BankBoston or Wells Fargo Bank—is a firm that channels funds from savers to investors by accepting deposits and making loans. Figure 10.1 illustrates this function of banks. Banks are a type of *financial intermediary* because they "intermediate" between savers and investors. Other examples of financial intermediaries are credit unions and savings and loan institutions. Banks are sometimes called *commercial banks* because many of their loans are to business firms engaged in commerce. Banks accept deposits from people who have funds and who want to earn interest and then lend the funds to other individuals who want to borrow and who are willing to pay interest. A bank earns profits by charging a higher interest rate to the borrowers than it pays to the depositors.

## The Fed

The *central bank* of a country serves as a bank to other banks. In other words, commercial banks deposit funds at the central bank, and the central bank in turn makes loans to other commercial banks. We will see that the deposits of the commercial banks at the central bank are very important for controlling the money supply.

In the United States, the central bank is the Fed, which was established by the 1913 Federal Reserve Act and now consists of over 25,000 employees spread all over the country.

### Board of Governors

At the core of the Fed is the *Board of Governors of the Federal Reserve System,* or the Federal Reserve Board, consisting of seven people appointed to fourteen-year terms by the president of the United States and confirmed by the Senate. The Federal Reserve Board is located in Washington, D.C.

One of the governors is appointed by the president to a four-year term as chair of the board; this appointment also requires Senate confirmation and can be renewed for additional terms. Alan Greenspan was appointed to the chair by President Reagan in 1987 and reappointed by Presidents Bush and Clinton. Greenspan took over from Paul Volcker, who was appointed by President Carter in 1979 and reappointed by President Reagan in 1983.

**FIGURE 10.1**
**Channeling Funds from Savers to Investors**
Savers, those whose income is greater than consumption, can supply funds to investors in two ways: through banks (and other types of financial intermediaries) or by making direct loans, perhaps by buying bonds issued by a business firm. The banks earn profits by charging a higher interest on their loans than they pay on their deposits.

**bank:** a firm that channels funds from savers to investors by accepting deposits and making loans.

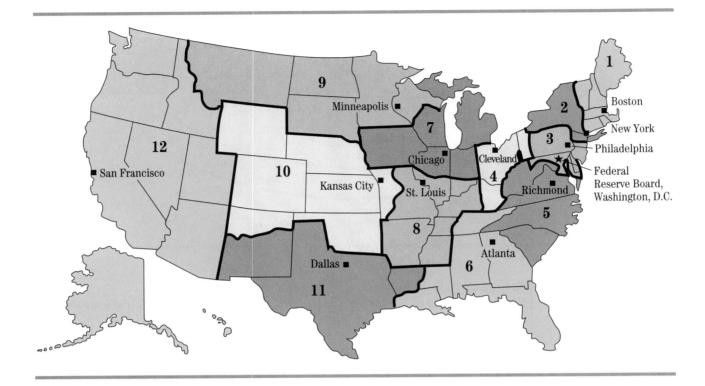

**FIGURE 10.2**
**The Twelve Districts and Fed Independence**
When the Fed was created by the Federal Reserve Act of 1913, the country was divided into twelve districts, each with a district Federal Reserve Bank. Each district bank is headed by a president who sits on the FOMC. Unlike the seven members of the Board of Governors, the presidents of the district banks are not selected by the president of the United States.

**Federal Open Market Committee (FOMC):** the committee, consisting of the seven members of the Board of Governors and the twelve presidents of the Fed district banks, that meets about eight times per year; only five of the presidents vote at any one time.

### The District Federal Reserve Banks

The Federal Reserve System not only includes the Federal Reserve Board in Washington but also twelve Federal Reserve Banks in different regions of the country. A map defining the regions is shown in Figure 10.2. For example, the district bank for the southeastern states is the Federal Reserve Bank of Atlanta, and the district bank for the western states is the Federal Reserve Bank of San Francisco. When the Federal Reserve was established by the Federal Reserve Act of 1913, the population density was more concentrated in the Midwest and the East than it is now. Hence, almost all of the Federal Reserve district banks are in the Midwest and the East. Missouri has two district banks, located in St. Louis and Kansas City. The Federal Reserve Bank of New York is particularly significant because the major financial markets are located in New York City, and responsibility for carrying out decisions made by the Fed is given to the New York Federal Reserve Bank.

The term *Fed* refers to the whole Federal Reserve System, including the Board of Governors in Washington and the twelve district banks. Each district bank is headed by a president who is chosen by commercial bankers and other people in the district and approved by the Board of Governors.

### The Federal Open Market Committee (FOMC)

The Fed makes decisions about the supply of currency and deposits through a committee called the **Federal Open Market Committee (FOMC).** The members of the FOMC are the seven governors and the twelve district bank presidents, but only five of the presidents vote at any one time. Thus, there are twelve voting members of the FOMC at any one time. The FOMC meets in Washington about eight times a

**FIGURE 10.3**

**The Structure of the Federal Reserve System**

Decisions about the money supply are made by the FOMC, which consists of the Fed governors and district Fed presidents.

year to decide how to implement monetary policy. Figure 10.3 shows the relationship between the FOMC, the Board of Governors, and the district banks.

Even though the chair of the Fed has only one vote among twelve on the FOMC, the position has considerably more power than that one vote might represent. Traditionally, the Fed has preferred to make decisions with a large degree of consensus, with only two or three dissenting votes. This consensus decision-making and the fact that the chair (1) has executive authority over the operations of the whole Federal Reserve System, (2) sets the agenda at the FOMC meetings, and (3) represents the Fed in testimony before Congress makes the position more powerful. Journalists in the popular press, writing about the Fed, usually act as if the chair has almost complete power over Fed decisions. Some view the chair of the Fed as the second most powerful person in America, after the president of the United States.

Now that we have described the Fed, let us examine the operation of banks and how they, along with the Fed, create money.

## The Balance Sheet of a Commercial Bank

A commercial bank accepts deposits from individuals and makes loans to others. To understand how a bank functions, it is necessary to look at its balance sheet, which shows these deposits and loans. Table 10.2 is an example of a balance sheet for a bank, called BankOne, that has $100 million in deposits, $70 million in loans, $20 million in bonds, and $10 million in reserves.

The different items are divided into *assets* and *liabilities*. An **asset** is something of value owned by a person or firm. A **liability** is something of value a person or a firm owes, such as a debt, to someone else. Thus a bank's assets are anything the bank owns or any sum owed by someone else to the bank. A bank's liability is anything the bank owes to someone else. People's *deposits* at banks are the main

**asset:** something of value owned by a person or a firm.

**liability:** something of value a person or firm owes to someone else.

**TABLE 10.2**
**Balance Sheet of BankOne**
(millions of dollars)

|  | Assets |  | Liabilities |  |
|---|---|---|---|---|
| Loans | 70 | Deposits | 100 | |
| Bonds | 20 | | | |
| Reserves | 10 | | | |

This is the initial situation. The ratio of reserves to deposits is .1.

**reserves:** deposits that commercial banks hold at the Fed.

**required reserve ratio:** the fraction of a bank's deposits that it is required to hold at the Fed.

**loan:** an interest-bearing asset to the bank that lends money to an individual or firm.

**bond:** a promise by a firm or government to pay a certain amount of money to the bondholder on a fixed date in the future.

liability of banks, as shown in Table 10.2. Certain assets, such as the bank's building or furniture, are not shown in this balance sheet because they do not change when the money supply changes. Also, when a bank starts up, the owners must put in some funds, called the bank's capital stock, which can be used in case the bank needs cash in an emergency. This asset is not shown in the balance sheet either.

Consider each of the assets shown in the balance sheet in Table 10.2. **Reserves** are deposits that commercial banks hold at the Fed, much like people hold deposits at commercial banks. Remember, the Fed is the bank for the commercial banks. Just as you can hold a deposit at a commercial bank, a commercial bank can hold a deposit at the Fed. Reserves are simply a name for these deposits by commercial banks at the Fed.

Under U.S. law, a commercial bank is required to hold reserves at the Fed equal to a fraction of the deposits people hold at the commercial bank; this fraction is called the **required reserve ratio.** In this example, reserves are equal to 10 percent of deposits (10/100 = .1), and we will assume for now that this is the required reserve ratio.

The two other assets of the bank are loans and bonds. **Loans** are made by banks to individuals or firms for a period of time; the banks earn interest on these loans. **Bonds** are a promise of a firm or government to pay back a certain amount after a number years. Bonds can be issued by entities with a good reputation for repayment—such as the U.S. government or a large corporation. After bonds are issued, they can be bought or sold, and banks sometimes buy such bonds, as BankOne has done in the example. For simplicity, we assume the bonds here are government bonds, issued by the U.S. government.

Observe how the bank channels funds from savers to investors. The bank's deposits come from the savings of individuals, while the loans are made to individuals or business firms who may use the funds for investment. Thus, the bank is receiving funds from people who are saving and lending to people who are investing. For example, if you save and deposit the funds in a bank, someone else in the economy uses the funds to invest (buy equipment at a business firm), or someone abroad gets a loan to buy goods made in the United States (exports). Consider how inefficient the process would be without banks (or other financial intermediaries). Small savers would have to look for people who wanted to borrow money to invest, a tedious job. Thus, banks make saving much more attractive. Without banks, both saving and investment would probably be lower.

## The Role of Banks in Creating Money

Because deposits at banks are a form of money, the banks play an important role in creating money. The Fed orchestrates this role. A link between the deposits at banks and the reserves at the Fed provides the key mechanism for the Fed to exert control over the amount of deposits at the commercial banks. To see this we first look at some examples and then show how this link between reserves and deposits works in the whole economy. To make the story simpler for now, we assume that everyone

| Assets | | Liabilities | |
|--------|----|-------------|-----|
| Loans | 70 | Deposits | 100 |
| Bonds | 10 | | |
| Reserves | 20 | | |

Note the effect of the Fed's purchase of bonds: Compared with Table 10.2, bonds are lower and reserves are higher in Table 10.3. The ratio of reserves to deposits is .2.

**TABLE 10.3**
**Balance Sheet of BankOne after Reserves Increase**
(millions of dollars)

uses deposits rather than currency for their money. (We will take up currency again in the next section.)

### Bank-by-Bank Deposit Expansion

To see how the Fed can change the deposit component of the money supply, let us examine a particular transaction in some detail. Suppose there is an increase in the amount of reserves BankOne holds at the Fed. The Fed can cause such an increase in reserves simply by buying something from BankOne and paying for it by increasing BankOne's reserves at the Fed. The Fed usually buys government bonds when it wants to increase reserves because banks have a lot of bonds. So let's assume that the Fed buys $10 million of government bonds from BankOne and pays for the bonds by increasing BankOne's reserves by $10 million. Thus, BankOne's holdings of bonds decline by $10 million, from $20 million to $10 million, and BankOne's reserves at the Fed increase by $10 million, from $10 million to $20 million. The balance sheet would then look like Table 10.3, a change from Table 10.2. The key point is that there are now $10 million more reserves in the economy than before the Fed purchased the government bonds from BankOne. The reserves are held by BankOne, but they will not be for long.

Recall that banks hold reserves equal to a certain fraction of their deposits, a fraction called the reserve ratio, which we are assuming is 10 percent in this example. But now, after the Fed's actions, BankOne has 20 percent of its deposits as reserves, or more than the required 10 percent. Because the reserves do not pay any interest, while loans and bonds do, the bank will have incentive to reduce its reserves and make more loans or buy more bonds.

Suppose BankOne decreases its reserves by making more loans; with the reserve ratio of .1, the bank can loan $10 million. Suppose the bank loans $10 million to UNO, a small oil company that uses the funds to buy an oil tanker from DOS, a shipbuilding firm. UNO pays DOS with a check from BankOne, and DOS deposits the check in its checking account at its own bank, BankTwo. Now Bank-Two must ask BankOne for payment; BankOne will make the payment by lowering its reserve account at the Fed and increasing BankTwo's reserve account at the Fed by $10 million. At the end of these transactions, BankOne's balance sheet is shown in Table 10.4.

Hence, after BankOne makes the loan and transfers its reserves to BankTwo, its reserves are back to 10 percent of its deposits. This is the end of the story for

| Assets | | Liabilities | |
|--------|----|-------------|-----|
| Loans | 80 | Deposits | 100 |
| Bonds | 10 | | |
| Reserves | 10 | | |

By making more loans, the bank reduces the ratio of reserves to deposits back to .1.

**TABLE 10.4**
**Balance Sheet of BankOne after It Makes Loans**

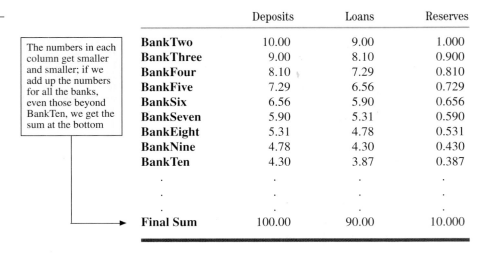

**TABLE 10.5**
**Deposit Expansion**
(millions of dollars)

The numbers in each column get smaller and smaller; if we add up the numbers for all the banks, even those beyond BankTen, we get the sum at the bottom

|  | Deposits | Loans | Reserves |
|---|---|---|---|
| **BankTwo** | 10.00 | 9.00 | 1.000 |
| **BankThree** | 9.00 | 8.10 | 0.900 |
| **BankFour** | 8.10 | 7.29 | 0.810 |
| **BankFive** | 7.29 | 6.56 | 0.729 |
| **BankSix** | 6.56 | 5.90 | 0.656 |
| **BankSeven** | 5.90 | 5.31 | 0.590 |
| **BankEight** | 5.31 | 4.78 | 0.531 |
| **BankNine** | 4.78 | 4.30 | 0.430 |
| **BankTen** | 4.30 | 3.87 | 0.387 |
| . | . | . | . |
| . | . | . | . |
| . | . | . | . |
| **Final Sum** | 100.00 | 90.00 | 10.000 |

BankOne, but not for the economy as a whole because BankTwo now has $10 million more in reserves and this is going to affect BankTwo's decisions. Let us see how.

Now BankTwo finds itself with $10 million in additional deposits and $10 million in additional reserves at the Fed. (Remember that deposits are a liability to BankTwo and the reserves are an asset; thus, assets and liabilities each have risen by $10 million.) However, BankTwo only needs to hold $1 million in reserves for the additional $10 million in deposits. Thus, BankTwo will want to make more loans until its reserves equal 10 percent of its deposits. It will lend out to other people an amount equal to 90 percent of the $10 million, or $9 million. The increase in deposits, loans, and reserves at BankTwo is shown in the first row of Table 10.5. This is the end of the story for BankTwo but not for the economy as a whole.

The people who get loans from BankTwo will use these loans to pay others. Thus, the funds will likely end up in yet another bank, called BankThree. Then, BankThree will find itself with $9 million in additional deposits and $9 million in additional reserves. BankThree will then lend 90 percent of the $9 million, or $8.1 million, as shown in the second row of Table 10.5. This process will continue from bank to bank. We begin to see that the initial increase in reserves is leading to a much bigger expansion of deposits. The whole process is shown in Table 10.5. Each row shows what happens at each bank. The sum of each column shows the change for the whole economy. If we sum the columns through the end of the process, we will see that deposits and thus the money supply increases by $100 million as a result of the $10 million increase in reserves. The increase in deposits is 10 times the actual increase in reserves! In reality, the whole process takes a short period of time (days rather than weeks) because banks adjust their loans and reserves very quickly.

### A Formula Linking Reserves and Deposits

It is no coincidence that the increase in deposits is 10 times the increase in reserves. With the reserve ratio equal to .1 for each bank in the economy, there is a formula linking reserves and deposits for the whole economy. It is given by

Reserves = (reserve ratio) × deposits

where reserves and deposits refer to the amount in the whole economy. If we divide both sides of this expression by the reserve ratio, we get

$$\text{Deposits} = \left(\frac{1}{\text{reserve ratio}}\right) \times \text{reserves}$$

Thus, any increase in reserves is multiplied by the inverse of the reserve ratio to get the increase in deposits. For example, if the $10 million change in reserves is multiplied by $(1/.1) = 10$, we get $100 million change in deposits, which is just what Table 10.5 shows in the detailed look at the expansion of deposits throughout the economy. This reasoning about what happens in the economy as a whole gives the same answer as the step-by-step analysis.

One could also analyze the effects of a decline in reserves using the same detailed examination of the process—or much more simply by using the formula linking reserves and deposits. A decrease in reserves occurs when the Fed sells bonds. For example, a decrease in reserves of $10 million would lead to a decrease in deposits by $100 million. Also, the relationship between deposits and reserves in the economy as a whole shows that there is nothing special about the detailed example; the same expansion would occur with more banks or fewer banks. Moreover, one could have started the example by assuming the Fed bought $10 million in government bonds from some person other than a bank. That person would deposit the check from the Fed in a bank and the process would play itself out just as in Table 10.5. In the end, the answer must be exactly the same: A $10 million increase in reserves leads to a $100 million increase in deposits.

## Review

▶ Banks serve two important functions in the monetary system: They help channel funds from savers to investors, and their deposits can be used as money.

▶ The Fed is a bank for the commercial banks. Commercial banks hold deposits, called reserves, at the Fed.

▶ The Fed includes a Board of Governors and twelve District Federal Reserve Banks. The Fed's Federal Open Market Committee makes decisions about the money supply.

▶ Banks create more deposits and thus more money when the Fed increases reserves. The deposits at banks increase by a multiple of the increase in reserves where the multiple depends inversely on the reserve ratio.

# HOW THE FED CONTROLS THE MONEY SUPPLY: CURRENCY PLUS DEPOSITS

We have now seen how the Fed, through an increase in reserves, can increase the amount of deposits, or, through a decrease in reserves, can reduce deposits. So far we have been ignoring currency. But the money supply includes currency as well as deposits. What determines the total money supply in the economy when currency is in the story? How does the Fed affect it? With currency in the picture, there are now three things to keep track of: deposits, reserves, and currency. We will find it useful to introduce some shorthand notation to keep track of all three.

## The Money Supply (*M*) and Bank Reserves (*BR*)

The supply of money is currency plus deposits. (Recall that we are not distinguishing between the different definitions of the money supply or different types of deposits.) If we let *CU* stand for currency and *D* stand for deposits, then

$$M = CU + D$$

or, in words, the money supply equals currency plus deposits.

We already know that commercial banks hold a fraction of their deposits at the Fed. Let *BR* represent the reserves the commercial banks hold at the Fed and let *r* be the reserve ratio. Then the relationship between reserves and deposits described in the previous section can be written using symbols as

$$BR = rD$$

or, in words, bank reserves equal the reserve ratio (*r*) times deposits (*D*). For example, if banks are required to hold 10 percent of their deposits as reserves at the Fed, then *r* = .1. Remember, reserves, held at the central bank by the commercial banks, are just like any other deposit, such as a checking deposit. For example, CitiBank, a commercial bank headquartered in New York City, holds a large amount of reserves at the Fed.

## Currency versus Deposits

Although currency and deposits are both part of the money supply, they have different characteristics. For some purposes, people prefer currency to checking deposits and vice versa. These preferences determine how much currency versus checking deposits is in the economy. If you want to hold more currency in your wallet because you find it is more convenient than a checking deposit, you just go to the bank and reduce your checking deposit and carry around more currency. If you are worried about crime and do not want to have much currency in your wallet, then you go to the bank and deposit a larger amount in your checking account. Thus, people decide on the amount of currency versus deposits in the economy. In Japan, where crime is less prevalent than in many other countries, people use much more currency compared to checking accounts than in other countries. Even Japanese business executives who earn the equivalent of $120,000 a year frequently are paid monthly with the equivalent of $10,000 in cash.

In order to determine the amount of currency versus deposits in the economy as a whole, we assume that people want to hold currency equal to a certain fraction of their deposits. More precisely, we assume that there is a ratio called the **currency to deposit ratio** that at any time describes how much currency people want to hold compared to their deposits. If people are happy holding an amount of currency equal to 40 percent of their deposits, then the currency to deposit ratio is .4. If deposits equal $700 billion and the currency to deposit ratio is .4, then currency would equal $280 billion and the money supply would equal $980 billion. Different individuals will have different tastes, but on the average, there will be an overall ratio of currency to deposits in the economy. That ratio depends on people's behavior, on custom, and, as already mentioned, on security in the community.

**currency to deposit ratio:** the proportion of currency that people in the economy want to hold relative to their deposits; it equals currency divided by deposits.

The ratio also depends on technology; for example, credit cards have reduced the currency to deposit ratio. Note, however, that credit cards are not money any more than a driver's license used for identification when cashing a check is money. Credit cards make more use of checking deposits relative to currency because people usually pay their credit card bills with a check.

At any given point in time, we can take the currency to deposit ratio as a fairly stable number. If the currency to deposit ratio is $k$, then we can write

Currency = (currency to deposit ratio) $\times$ deposits
$$= k \times \text{deposits}$$

Using the symbols we have already introduced, we can write this as

$$CU = kD$$

We now use this expression along with the previous two expressions for the money supply ($M$) and bank reserve ($BR$) to show how the Fed can control the money supply.

## The Money Multiplier

We saw that the Fed can change the amount of bank reserves by buying and selling bonds. We also saw that when the Fed increases reserves, deposits expand. If currency held by people is equal to $k$ times deposits, then currency will increase when deposits increase. Thus, by buying and selling bonds, the Fed can affect the supply of currency. The Fed can therefore control both currency and reserves. The sum of currency plus reserves is called the **monetary base** by economists. Because the Fed can control both currency and reserves it can control the monetary base. If we let $MB$ stand for the monetary base, then

$$MB = CU + BR$$

**monetary base:** currency plus reserves.

Table 10.6 shows the size of the monetary base in the U.S. economy in 1996.

We now want to derive a link between the monetary base $MB$ and the money supply $M$. That link can be used by the Fed to control the money supply. To derive the link we will use some algebra and equations just like the people at the Fed use. We can use the equation showing that the money supply equals currency plus deposits and the equation showing that currency is a certain fraction of deposits to get a relationship between the money supply and deposits. That is, substitute $CU = kD$ into the equation $M = CU + D$ to get $M = kD + D$, or

$$M = (k + 1)D$$

There is also the relationship that exists between bank reserves and deposits, $BR = rD$, which together with $CU = kD$ can be substituted into the equation $MB = CU + BR$ to get $MB = kD + rD$, or

$$MB = (k + r)D$$

Now, to find the link between $MB$ and $M$, divide $M$ by $MB$ and cancel out $D$ to get

$$\frac{M}{MB} = \frac{(k + 1)}{(r + k)}$$

We call this ratio, $(k + 1)/(r + k)$, the money multiplier. For example, suppose the reserve ratio $r$ is .1 and the currency to deposit ratio $k$ is .2, then the money

**TABLE 10.6**
**The Monetary Base for the United States, 1996**
(billions of dollars)

| | |
|---|---|
| Currency | 396 |
| Reserves | 57 |
| Monetary Base | 453 |

*Source:* Federal Reserve Board.

**FIGURE 10.4**

**The Inverted Monetary Pyramid**

The money supply, defined either as M1 or M2, is built on the monetary base. The money multiplier multiplies the monetary base to get either M1 or M2. These data are for the United States in 1996. The money multiplier for M1 is about 2.4 and for M2 it is about 8.4.

*Source:* Federal Reserve Board.

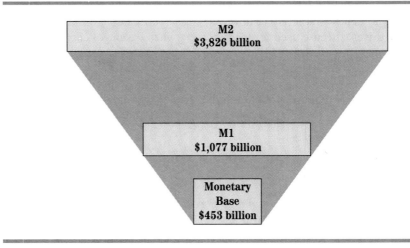

**money multiplier:** the multiple by which the money supply changes due to a change in the monetary base.

multiplier is $(.2 + 1)/(.1 + .2) = 1.2/.3 = 4$. An increase in the monetary base *MB* of $100 million would increase the money supply *M* by $400 million. This large increase is the reason for the term *multiplier*. In general, the **money multiplier** is the number you multiply the monetary base by to get the money supply.

To see how the money multiplier works in practice, suppose the Fed buys bonds so as to increase the monetary base by $1 billion; according to the money multiplier, the money supply in the economy should increase by $4 billion. The actual increase in the money supply occurs through a bank-by-bank process just like that shown in Table 10.5 with currency now changing as well. With currency in the story, the total effect on the money supply of a change in the monetary base is smaller than in Table 10.5 because people do not put all their money in banks. This reduces the amount of deposit expansion. Note that if $k = 0$, the case without currency, the money multiplier is 10 in this example. Thus, an increase in the monetary base of $10 million will increase money by $100 million, as in the previous section.

More important than the fact that the multiplier is greater than 1 is that it provides a link between the monetary base and the money supply in the economy. As long as the currency to deposit ratio and the reserve ratio do not change, the Fed can control the money supply by adjusting the monetary base. Remarkably, as illustrated by Figure 10.4, the whole money supply is built on the monetary base. Now let us look at the effects of changes in the money supply.

# Review

▶ The monetary base is the sum of currency plus bank reserves. The Fed can change the money supply—currency plus deposits—by adjusting the monetary base. A change in the monetary base changes the money supply by a multiple of the increase in the

monetary base. The multiple is called the money multiplier.

▶ The money multiplier depends on the reserve ratio and the currency to deposit ratio.

# MONEY GROWTH AND INFLATION

Because people use money to buy and sell goods and services, the total money supply in the economy and the total value of goods and services in the economy are closely related. In the economy as a whole, nominal GDP is the dollar value of all goods and services. Thus, we would expect to see a close relationship between the money supply and nominal GDP.

Consider first a simple example. Suppose that all of your transactions are with food-vending machines and video game machines. You will need money in your pocket to carry out your transactions. If you use the vending and video game machines ten times a day, you will need ten times more money in your pocket than if you use the machines once a day. Hence, ten times more transactions means ten times more money. If the prices for vending machine items and minutes on a video game double, then you will need twice as much money for each day's activities, assuming the higher price does not cure your habit. Hence, whether the volume of transactions increases because the real number of items purchased increases or because the price of each item increases, the amount of money used for transactions will rise. What is true for you and the machines is true for the whole population and the whole economy. For the whole economy, the number of transactions is closely related to nominal GDP. Nominal GDP can be expressed as the price level (the GDP deflator) times real GDP. Thus, nominal GDP increases if the price level rises or if real GDP rises. In either case the money supply needed for transactions rises.

## The Quantity Equation of Money

The relationship between money and nominal GDP in the economy as a whole can be summarized by the **quantity equation of money,** which is written:

Money supply × velocity = price level × real GDP

or

$$MV = PY$$

where $V$ is velocity, $P$ is the price level, and $Y$ is real GDP. Remember the right-hand side of this equation also equals nominal GDP. Velocity is computed by dividing nominal GDP by the money supply. That is,

$$V = \frac{\text{nominal GDP}}{M}$$

Thus, in 1996 velocity was about 7 with the money supply (M1) at $1,077 billion and nominal GDP at $7,576 billion. Thus, **velocity** is simply the term one multiplies the money supply by to get nominal GDP. If velocity were higher, the same money supply would permit more transactions—more nominal GDP. If velocity were lower, fewer transactions would be carried out with the same amount of money.

Note that *velocity* can be thought of as measuring how fast money is used. It is the number of times a dollar is used on average to make purchases of final goods and services. To see this, suppose an automatic teller machine is installed in the room with the vending machines and video games from the preceding example. Each morning you get cash from the automatic teller machine for your morning games, and each day at midday you could get cash from the machine to pay for your afternoon use of the games and vending machines; then you would need to

**quantity equation of money:** the equation relating the price level and real GDP to the quantity of money and the velocity of money: The quantity of money times its velocity equals the price level times real GDP; in terms of growth rates it states that money growth plus velocity growth equals inflation plus real GDP growth.

**velocity:** a measure of how fast money is turned over in the economy: Velocity equals nominal GDP divided by the money supply.

carry only half as much currency in your pocket as before they installed the auto-matic teller machines and you had to bring enough cash to last all day. From your perspective, therefore, the velocity of money doubles. As this example shows, velocity in the economy depends on technology and, in particular, on how efficient we are at using money.

If you look carefully at the preceding quantity equation of money, you see that if velocity is not affected by a change in money, then an increase in the money supply must lead to an increase in nominal GDP. In this sense, the money supply in the economy and nominal GDP are closely related. If real GDP is also not affected by a change in money, then an increase in the money supply will increase the price level. Higher rates of money growth would thus lead to higher inflation, just as in the case of commodity money at the start of the chapter.

A restatement of the quantity equation using growth rates leads to a convenient relationship between money growth, inflation, real GDP growth, and velocity growth. In particular,

Inflation + real GDP growth = money growth + velocity growth

For example, if the money supply growth is 5 percent per year, velocity growth is 0 percent per year, and real GDP growth is 3 percent per year, then this equation says that inflation is 2 percent per year. This growth rate form of the quantity equa-tion follows directly from the quantity equation itself; in general, the rate of growth of a product of two terms is approximately equal to the sum of the growth rates of the two terms. Thus, the growth rate of $M$ times $V$ equals the growth rate of $M$ plus the growth rate of $V$, and the growth rate of $P$ times $Y$ equals the growth rate of $P$ plus the growth rate of $Y$.

The quantity equation tells us that along a long-run economic growth path in which real GDP growth is equal to potential GDP growth, an increase in money growth by a certain number of percentage points will result in the long run in an increase in inflation of the same number of percentage points unless there is a change in velocity growth. Thus, higher money growth will lead to higher inflation in the long run. If velocity growth remains at zero, as in the previous example, and real GDP growth remains at 3 percent per year, then an increase in money growth by 10 percentage points, from 5 to 15 percent, will increase inflation by 10 percent-age points, from 2 to 12 percent.

Figure 10.5 shows the close relationship between money growth and inflation in the seven largest developed economies over a recent 20-year period. Money growth is plotted on the vertical axis and inflation on the horizontal axis. Each point represents a country. For countries with higher money growth, inflation has been higher. The line drawn through the points shows that inflation increases by about the same number of percentage points as money growth increases, as predicted by the quantity equation. Because the countries are close to this line, the quantity equation seems to work fairly well in predicting the relationship between money growth and inflation.

## Some Key Episodes in Monetary History

Figure 10.6 presents an overview of U.S. monetary history; it shows the U.S. price level during the past 200 years. Historical studies indicate that the supply of money has increased much more rapidly since World War II, and especially after the mid-1960s, than in any other period of similar length in U.S. history. This is why infla-tion has been worse, especially after the mid-1960s, as shown in Figure 10.6.

**FIGURE 10.5**
**The Relation Between Money Growth and Inflation**

As the data for these several coun-tries show, higher money growth is associated with higher inflation. The data pertain to the period 1973–1991 and are stated as the average percent per year.

*Source:* Organization for Economic Cooperation and Development.

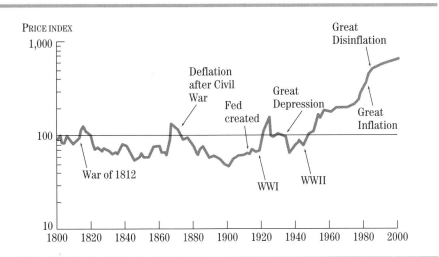

PRICE INDEX

*Labels on graph:*
Great Disinflation
Deflation after Civil War
Fed created
Great Depression
Great Inflation
War of 1812
WWI
WWII

**FIGURE 10.6**
**The Price Level in the United States, 1800–1996**

For much of U.S. history, the average price fluctuated around a stable level, though there were several periods of deflation, such as after the Civil War. Since World War II, and especially since the mid-1960s, rising prices—inflation—have been the rule. In the 1980s, there was a disinflation that reduced the inflation rate but did not bring it to zero.

*Source:* Historical Statistics of the United States.

Because the rate of increase in the price level is inflation, the upward movements of the line showing the price indicate periods of inflation. In the 150 years before World War II there was much less long-term inflation than there has been in recent years.

The United States experienced an even higher inflation during the Revolutionary War: The paper currency issued at the time, the Continental, lost so much value that the phrase "not worth a continental" became part of the language.

Why does inflation get so high? The most common reason is that the government prints money to pay for its expenditures. Countries with very high inflation have trouble raising revenues from taxes because it is easy for people to avoid taxes. These governments also do not have the credibility to borrow funds. Thus, the central bank starts printing money and letting the government use the money to pay for goods and services. As money growth increases, inflation rises. As inflation rises, people are not willing to hold as much money because it is losing its value, so the government has to print even more money.

Although printing money is not *now* a significant source of government financing for lower-inflation countries like the United States and Germany, there have been episodes in the past when both of these countries resorted to printing money to finance deficits. We mentioned the U.S. Revolutionary War. The hyperinflation in Germany was even worse. Inflation rose to over 100 percent per week.

A very high inflation is called *hyperinflation*. Hyperinflation occurred in Germany in 1923. The German government incurred huge expenses during World War I, and after the war, Germany lost all of its colonies, 10 percent of its population, and almost 15 percent of its main territory, which included much of the iron- and coal-producing areas.

Huge demands for war reparations from the victors in World War I compounded the problem. The budget deficit

**Hyperinflation and Nearly Worthless Money**

So much money was printed during the period of German hyperinflation that it became cheaper to burn several million German marks to cook breakfast—as this woman was doing in 1923—than to buy kindling wood with the nearly worthless money.

**FIGURE 10.7**
**German Hyperinflation of 1923**
The chart shows the weekly percent change in the price level in Germany in 1923. Inflation rose to truly astronomical levels for several months.

*Source:* J.P. Young, *European Currency and Finance*, Vol. 1 (Washington, D.C.: Government Printing Office, 1925), p. 503.

**50,000,000 German Mark
Reichsbank Note, 1923**

could be financed only by printing money, which finally gave way to the hyperinflation of 1923. Figure 10.7 shows the *weekly* increase in German prices. Shop owners closed their shops at lunchtime to change the prices. Workers were paid twice weekly. People would rush to the stores and buy everything they needed for the next few days. Firms also set up barter systems with their workers, exchanging consumer goods directly for labor.

The hyperinflation was caused by a huge increase in money growth. Everyone tried to get rid of cash as soon as possible, thus accelerating the inflationary process. Also, by the time the government received its tax revenue, it was not worth much because prices had risen sharply, and the budget deficit grew even greater. The government needed to print even more money. In the last months of hyperinflation more than 30 paper mills worked at full capacity to deliver paper currency. One hundred fifty printing firms had 2,000 presses running 24 hours a day to print German marks, and they could not keep up with the need for new notes. On November 15, 1923, an economic reform stabilized the inflation rate. By then, the German price level was 100 billion times what it was before the hyperinflation.

The German hyperinflation of 1923 is not a unique historical episode, and it is not necessarily linked to war, as the hyperinflation in the early 1990s in Argentina makes clear. In the mid-1990s, an inflation in Russia was also caused by the creation of too much money. Money growth is the cause of all hyperinflations.

# Review

- ▶ The money supply and the value of transactions in an economy are closely related. The quantity equation describes this relationship; it says that the money supply times velocity equals nominal GDP.

- ▶ Higher rates of money growth will eventually lead to higher inflation.

- ▶ A hyperinflation is a very high inflation.

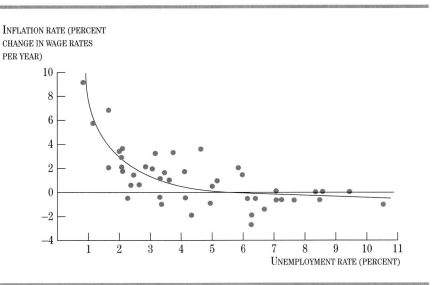

INFLATION RATE (PERCENT CHANGE IN WAGE RATES PER YEAR)

UNEMPLOYMENT RATE (PERCENT)

**FIGURE 10.8**
**A Replica of an Original Phillips Curve**

A.W. Phillips published this curve in a 1958 paper. The vertical axis measures inflation in terms of wages rather than prices, but the curve looks about the same with most measures of inflation. Each point represents one year. The curve drawn through the points had enormous influence and led many economists to argue that lower unemployment in normal times could be achieved by a higher inflation rate. But it did not work.

*Source:* A.W. Phillips, "The Relationship Between Unemployment and the Rate of Change of Money Wage Rates in the United Kingdom," from *Economica.* Copyright © 1958 by Basil Blackwell, Ltd. Used with permission. The data period is 1861–1913.

# INFLATION: EFFECTS ON UNEMPLOYMENT AND PRODUCTIVITY GROWTH

We have seen that inflation is related to money growth and that money growth is determined by the government, in particular, by the Fed. What effects does inflation have on the economy and, in particular, on the long-run growth of the economy? Two effects of inflation have been studied in great detail by economists: its effect on unemployment and its effect on the long-run growth of real GDP.

## Effects on Unemployment

In the late 1950s, the economist A. W. Phillips, then at the London School of Economics, published a paper showing that periods in British history with low unemployment were associated with high inflation and that periods with high unemployment were associated with low inflation.[1] In other words, if you place unemployment on the horizontal axis of a diagram and inflation on the vertical axis and plot pairs of observations from each year, you get a downward-sloping relationship. That relationship came to be called the **Phillips curve.** An original Phillips curve from Phillips's 1958 paper is shown in Figure 10.8.

The relationship led many to believe that lower unemployment could be achieved by having a higher inflation rate. In other words, the Phillips curve was taken to imply that there was a negative relationship between unemployment and inflation in the long run. However, basic economic reasoning—as first put forth in the late 1960s by economists Edmund Phelps and Milton Friedman—suggested otherwise.

**Phillips curve:** a downward-sloping relationship between inflation and unemployment; originally found by A.W. Phillips in data from the late 1800s and early 1900s.

1. A. W. Phillips "The Relationship Between Unemployment and the Rate of Change of Money Wage Rates in the United Kingdom," *Economica,* November 1958.

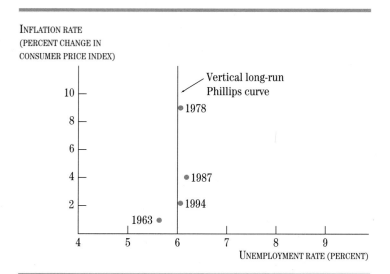

**FIGURE 10.9**
**The Modern View of the Long-Run Phillips Curve**

Economic theory and experience have shown that the Phillips curve is vertical in the long run. A higher inflation rate will not permanently lower the unemployment rate. The diagram shows four years in which real GDP is approximately equal to potential GDP. The points cluster around a line that is remarkably close to vertical.

*Source:* U.S. Department of Labor.

The hypothesis of Friedman and Phelps proved to be a remarkably accurate description of reality. They argued that the Phillips curve relationship between unemployment and inflation was only temporary. For example, suppose the central bank suddenly increases the rate of growth of the money supply and this causes a sudden increase in inflation. The rise in inflation might reduce the real wage (the wage divided by the price level) because wages might not adjust quickly enough to the higher inflation rate. The rate of unemployment would go down because firms would hire more workers at the lower real wage. But if the inflation persisted, people would begin to raise their expectation of inflation, and workers would soon demand higher wage increases to compensate for the lost purchasing power. These wage increases would raise the real wage again and the unemployment rate with it. Unemployment would return to normal. Thus, at best, the decline in unemployment would be temporary. In the long run, we would have a higher inflation rate, but the unemployment rate would remain at its natural rate.

According to Friedman and Phelps, therefore, the curve showing the relationship between inflation and unemloyment is vertical in the long run: that is, a higher inflation rate, as measured along the vertical axis of Phillips's diagram, would lead to about the same unemployment rate along the horizontal axis.

How well does this analysis of Friedman and Phelps describe the data in the long run? Figure 10.9 provides an answer. Four pairs of U.S. inflation and unemployment rates for four normal years when real GDP equals potential GDP are plotted. The points trace out a remarkably vertical curve, especially in comparison with the short-run curve in Figure 10.8. We have purposely only plotted points on the picture where real GDP is close to potential GDP because they exclude the economic fluctuations in the economy around potential GDP. But these points clearly show how the Phillips curve relationship between unemployment and inflation turned out to be wrong when applied to a situation of higher long-run inflation. Inflation did not lower the rate of unemployment. That there is no long-run tradeoff between inflation and unemployment has become a major principle of macroeconomics.

## Effects on Productivity Growth

The effects of inflation on economic growth occur through its effects on productivity growth. According to the growth accounting formula of Chapter 9, high rates of inflation will reduce productivity growth by reducing investment in physical and human capital and by reducing the rate of technological change. But why would inflation reduce investment or technological change? Part of the answer is that highly volatile inflation rates from year to year and increased volatility of relative prices are usually associated with higher inflation.

Recall that our discussion of investment in Chapter 8 showed that investment is negatively related to the interest rate. Higher interest rates reduce the attractiveness of new investment projects that do not have high enough returns. When inflation rates are high they are often volatile. Thus, high inflation increases uncertainty about the future returns from investment. A higher rate of inflation than expected would reduce the real cost of borrowing, and a lower rate of inflation than expected would increase the real cost of borrowing. Thus, by increasing uncertainty, high inflation could reduce investment; the resulting lower growth in the capital to labor ratio would thus reduce productivity growth.

Higher inflation could reduce the rate of technological change for similar reasons. Investment in human capital and in research and development—both factors in technological change—might therefore be lower.

Observations on economic growth in different countries indicate that inflation is negatively correlated with economic growth. How large are the effects? According to one recent estimate by Brian Motley, an economist who works at the Fed, a reduction in the inflation rate of 5 percentage points would increase the long-run growth rate of productivity by from .1 to .3 percent per year. If the larger estimate is correct, then reducing the inflation rate from 12 percent—close to where it was in the late 1970s—to 2 percent would raise productivity growth by .6 percentage points, nearly doubling the rate of the last 20 years. The estimate is uncertain, but even with the lower estimate the increase in growth associated with lower inflation would be substantial. Motley's results also indicate that there is relatively less improvement in lowering the inflation rate from 2 percent to 0 percent, a range where we have very little experience.

## Why Is Inflation Almost Always Greater than Zero?

If inflation does not lower unemployment and seems to be bad for long-term growth, then why is there inflation? If inflation can be reduced to zero simply by reducing money growth to the rate of real GDP growth less velocity growth, then why have governments not done it? What can we expect in the future?

### Printing Money to Finance Government Expenditures

One reason, which was discussed earlier, is that inflation is caused by printing money to finance government expenditures. In countries where tax collection is difficult and tax revenue has not been enough to cover government expenditure, printing money is a significant source of financing government spending. Effectively these countries use inflation as another tax, sometimes called the *inflation tax.*

However, this explanation does not apply to countries like the United States. In the United States the inflation tax is a minor source of revenue, and the Federal Reserve System is not in the business of lending funds directly to government.

### Bias in Measuring Inflation

In the 1990s inflation in the United States fell to around 3 percent for the first time in 25 years. But there is disagreement about whether it should be lowered further. Perhaps the main reason for not reducing inflation further is that many economists feel that inflation is measured with some upward bias and that when measured inflation is about 1 or 2 percent, actual inflation is essentially zero. One reason for the upward bias, discussed in Chapter 6, is that people tend to consume less of items that increase more rapidly in price.

It is hard to estimate how large this bias is, but 1 to 2 percent is a common view. If 2 percent is the bias, then the 3 percent inflation seen in America in the early 1990s was actually 1 percent, quite close to zero. Recall from Chapter 6 that a

Senate-appointed commission of economists, chaired by Michael Boskin of Stanford, concluded that the bias was about 1 percent.

### Concerns about Deflation or Disinflation

Another reason why zero inflation might not be the correct policy is that inflation is never perfectly steady. If zero is the average, then there will be some periods when inflation is negative, a situation of deflation. Historically, periods of deflation have been bad for the economy, and this raises concerns about deflation in the future.

Finally, even though low inflation may be good for long-term economic growth, the process of getting to low inflation from high inflation—a process called *disinflation*—may be costly to the economy. As we know from Chapter 5, periods when inflation *declines* are usually periods of high unemployment. If policymakers place a lot of emphasis on the short-run costs, they may be unwilling to make changes that provide benefits in the long run. We will take up this tradeoff between the long run and the short run in later chapters on economic fluctuations.

## Review

▶ The Phillips curve helped create the view that there was a long-run tradeoff between inflation and unemployment.

▶ Modern macroeconomic theory indicates that there is no such long-range tradeoff. Higher inflation does not reduce the unemployment rate in the long run.

▶ High inflation does seem to reduce economic growth.

▶ The need for countries to print money to finance government spending is one reason inflation is greater than zero.

▶ An upward bias in measures of inflation indicates that 1 or 2 percent measured inflation may be very close to zero.

## CONCLUSION

Money has fascinated economists for centuries. The famous quantity equation introduced in this chapter predates Adam Smith and was used by the economist-philosopher David Hume in the eighteenth century. Adam Smith placed money second only to the division of labor in the first chapters of the *Wealth of Nations*.

In this chapter we have seen how money and the whole monetary system fit into the theory of economic growth, helping to channel funds from savers to investors, providing an efficient way to exchange goods and services, and ultimately causing inflation, which in turn affects economic growth.

Although the role of money appears mysterious and has caused some great debates in economics and politics, most of the ideas presented in this chapter are relatively noncontroversial. The three functions of money, the deposit expansion process, the money multiplier, the technical ability of the central bank to control the monetary base, the fact that money is the cause of inflation in the long run, the conclusion that there is no long-run tradeoff between inflation and unemployment, and the belief that high inflation tends to lower productivity are things many economists now agree on.

Many of the controversies about money pertain to the short-run fluctuations in the economy and revolve around the effects changes in the money supply have on real GDP in the short run. After considering the reasons why real GDP may depart from potential GDP in the short run in the next two chapters, we will return to the relationship between money and the short-run fluctuations in the economy. When we do so we will make use of the analysis in this chapter that shows how the central bank controls the money supply.

# KEY POINTS

**1.** Commodity money, ranging from salt to gold coins, has been used in place of barter for many centuries. Now paper money and deposits are also part of money.

**2.** Money has three roles: a medium of exchange, a store of value, and a unit of account.

**3.** The quantity equation describes the relationship between money growth, real GDP growth, and inflation.

**4.** Higher money growth leads to higher inflation in the long run.

**5.** Commercial banks are financial intermediaries; their deposits are part of the money supply.

**6.** The central bank controls the money supply by changing the monetary base.

**7.** The central bank in the United States is the Federal Reserve System (the Fed).

**8.** The money multiplier tells us how much the money supply increases when the monetary base increases.

**9.** There is no long-run relationship between inflation and unemployment.

**10.** Inflation, at least at high levels, reduces long-run economic growth.

**11.** There is some disagreement about exactly how low inflation should be; few argue for inflation less than zero.

# KEY TERMS

| | | |
|---|---|---|
| money | money supply | reserves |
| commodity money | M1 | required reserve ratio |
| medium of exchange | savings deposit | loan |
| barter | time deposit | bond |
| coincidence of wants | M2 | currency to deposit ratio |
| store of value | Federal Reserve System (the Fed) | monetary base |
| unit of account | bank | money multiplier |
| paper money | Federal Open Market Committee | quantity equation of money |
| gold standard | (FOMC) | velocity |
| currency | asset | Phillips curve |
| checking deposit | liability | |

# QUESTIONS FOR REVIEW

**1.** What are some examples of commodity money?

**2.** What are the differences between the medium of exchange, store of value, and unit of account roles of money?

**3.** Why are bank deposits part of money but an expensive purse to put the money in is not?

**4.** Why does higher money growth cause inflation?

**5.** What is the quantity equation of money?

**6.** What is a bank?

**7.** How do banks create money?

**8.** What is the Fed, and how is the FOMC organized?

**9.** What is the money multiplier, and why does it depend on the required reserve ratio?

**10.** Why is the natural rate of unemployment unrelated to the inflation rate?

**11.** Why is the inflation rate rarely zero?

# PROBLEMS

**1.** Which of the following are money, and which are not? Explain.
   a) A credit card
   b) A dollar bill
   c) A check in your checkbook
   d) Funds in a checking account

**2.** State whether each of the following statements is true or false. Explain your answers in one or two sentences.
   a) The larger the reserve ratio at banks, the smaller the money multiplier.
   b) The Federal Reserve increases reserves by selling government bonds.
   c) The same money is always used as both a unit of account and a medium of exchange at any one time in any one country.
   d) When commodity money is the only type of money, a decrease in the price of the commodity serving as money is inflation.

**3.** Suppose that, before the invention of the automatic teller machine, people held currency equal to 20 percent of their bank deposits. If the required reserve ratio is 20 percent, what is the money multiplier? Now suppose that, after the invention of the ATM, people hold only 10 percent of the value of their deposits in currency. What is the money multiplier now? Explain how the change in the money multiplier occurs.

**4.** Sam sells his government bond and it is bought by the Fed. Sam receives $10,000, which he promptly deposits in his checking account at his bank.
   a) For simplicity, suppose that $k = 0$: People hold all their money in the bank. If the required reserve ratio is 10 percent for all bank deposits, how much of this new deposit will Sam's bank lend out?
   b) Sam's bank lends this money to Jason, who uses it to pay the contractor, Karen, who remodeled his kitchen. Karen deposits this money into her checking account at a different bank than Sam's. How much will be lent out by Karen's bank?
   c) This process of lending and relending will continue through the banking system until there is nothing left to lend. At that point, how much is the total increase in deposits created by Sam's initial $10,000?
   d) How will the total increase in deposits change from part (c) if $k > 0$? Why?

**5.** Every year you negotiate with your employer over your wage rate.
   a) Suppose you expect inflation to be 5 percent. If your wage is now $10 per hour, what new wage will keep your expected real wage unchanged?
   b) Your employer agrees to raise your wage by enough to keep your expected real wage constant. The employer

agrees with your expectation of inflation. But during the next year there is much lower inflation than expected—1 percent. What has happened to your real wage? How will your employer react to this?
   c) You manage to keep your job, but some of your coworkers are laid off. How will this affect the negotiations for next year's wages? What will have happened to your expectation of inflation?

**6.** Use the quantity equation in its growth form to answer the following:
   a) Suppose there is no change in velocity and that there is zero growth in output. If inflation is 30 percent per month, what must be the monthly growth rate of the money supply based on the quantity equation? Explain.
   b) Now suppose that inflation is still 30 percent per month but that output is falling at a rate of 5 percent per month. What must be the growth rate of money now?
   c) In this situation, why would workers want their employer to pay their monthly salary in weekly installments rather than once a month? What effect will increasing the frequency of pay have on the velocity of money?
   d) As the pace of inflation increases, people want to spend their money more quickly because it is losing value. Use the quantity equation to explain what effect this increase in velocity has on inflation.

**7.** Fill out the following table using the quantity equation:

| Year | Quantity of Money (M2) (billions of $) | Velocity | Real GDP (billions of 1992 $) | Price Level (GDP deflator 1992 = 100) |
|------|----------------------------------------|----------|-------------------------------|---------------------------------------|
| 1989 | 3,164 | ———— | 6,060 | 89.7 |
| 1990 | 3,282 | ———— | 6,139 | 93.6 |
| 1991 | 3,384 | ———— | 6,079 | 97.3 |

   a) Calculate the growth rates for each of the four variables between 1989 and 1990.
   b) Calculate nominal GDP for 1989 and 1990, and then calculate the growth rate of nominal GDP between 1989 and 1990. Compare this result with the sum of the growth rates of real GDP and the price level between those two years.
   c) The quantity equation of money in growth rates can be written as:

Growth in $M$ + growth in $V$ = growth in GDP + growth in $P$

Does the growth rate form of the quantity equation work for the time period from 1989 to 1990?

d) Compare the velocity in 1990 with velocity in 1991. Is this surprising? What are possible causes of this result?

**8.** Construct a balance sheet, with assets on the left and liabilities on the right, for two commercial banks (Combank and Mercbank) to show how banks create money. Assume that reserves are 10 percent of deposits and that people hold no currency—all their money is in their checking accounts.

a) Suppose Tony (a private citizen) sells a government bond that he owns back to the Fed and deposits all of the $10,000 sum into his account at Combank. Show how this creates both new assets and new liabilities for Combank.

b) How much of this new deposit can Combank lend out? Assume it lends this amount to Mark, who then deposits this amount in Mercbank. Show this on Mercbank's balance sheet.

c) Suppose a used car is bought with this loan. The former owner of the car, Leah, deposits the proceeds from the sale into her account at Combank. How much is this deposit? How much in new excess reserves are created when she makes this deposit?

d) This process of lending and relending creates money throughout the banking system. How much money (that is, in new deposits) has been created from the initial deposit of $10,000 due to the two subsequent loans?

e) Use the money multiplier for this example to calculate how much money will be created when the lending is allowed to continue forever.

**9.** Credit cards are not included in the money supply, but currency and deposits at banks are included. Explain why credit cards are excluded. (Hint: Credit cards are a form of identification that allows you to borrow.)

# 4 **part**

# Economic Fluctuations

During the Great Depression of the 1930s, the production of goods and services in the United States fell by one-third and many people lost their jobs and faced prolonged hardship. More recent economic downturns have been much milder, but they also have caused harm to people. Fortunately, recessions appear to have become less frequent, but there is no evidence that they have been eliminated. Hence, recessions persist as an economic problem, even as the problem of low long-term economic growth has risen in importance, as described in the four preceding chapters.

In the four upcoming chapters, we delve into the causes of recessions and examine the forces that cause each recession to end. In Chapter 11 we start to unveil the model of economic fluctuations. The main aim of Chapter 11 is to show why real GDP initially

Real GDP

steps away from potential GDP at the start of a recession or a boom. In Chapter 12 we define the multiplier, which determines the size of the initial steps of real GDP away from potential GDP. In Chapter 13 we examine the dynamic patterns of real GDP and inflation that occur as real GDP returns to potential GDP after a recession. We also complete the economic fluctuations model, and show that the model is based on a diagram similar to the basic supply and demand model. In Chapter 14 we look at how the economic fluctuations model developed in the preceding chapters is used to determine the path the economy takes toward recovery after a recession.

The ideas and models introduced in these chapters are used on a daily basis by economists in the world's capitals and financial centers. Economic forecasters in private firms and the government use models like these to forecast the growth of the economy over several years. Central bankers, who control the money supply in the United States and other countries, use these ideas to help them decide how much money to supply; their decisions have enormous impact on the economy. Economic advisers to the president of the United States or members of Congress use the models to determine how large the budget deficit will be and to decide whether a change in taxes is advisable; their decisions also have a great impact on the economy. The exciting thing about these models is that you can learn to use them in essentially the same way they are used by those making these momentous decisions about monetary and fiscal policy.

# 11

# The First Steps Toward Recession or Boom

Economic fluctuations are departures of the economy from its long-term growth trend. These departures include recessions, such as the ones that occurred in the United States, Japan, and the European countries in the early 1980s and again in the early 1990s. They also include booms, such as the ones that occurred in the same countries in the mid-1980s. Economic fluctuations—also called business cycles—have been a common occurrence in all economies at least since the great economic growth wave began 200 years ago, but they have changed over time. One notable difference is that they seem to have diminished in severity.

One recent economic fluctuation is brought into focus in Figure 11.1. A boom in 1988 and 1989 raised real GDP above potential GDP. A recession in 1990 lowered real GDP below potential GDP, and a recovery starting in 1991 brought real GDP back toward potential GDP by 1994. Our purpose now is to focus, as does Figure 11.1, on economic fluctuations.

Economic fluctuations occur simultaneously with long-term economic growth, as shown by the longer history in Figure 11.1. Real GDP has fluctuated around what might otherwise have been a steady upward-moving trend. Although no two economic fluctuations are alike—some are long, some are short, some are deep, some are shallow—they have common features. Perhaps the most important one is that the recessions and booms end, and real GDP eventually returns to a more normal long-run growth path.

Although recessions eventually end, they bring unemployment and hardship to many people. Booms can also cause harm. Inflation usually rises in booms. When inflation gets too high, it reduces long-term growth and frequently leads to subsequent recessions.

In this chapter, we look at the first steps the economy takes as it moves into a recession or a boom. In other words, we examine the initial, or short-run, increase or decrease of real GDP above or below potential GDP. We will show that the first steps of real GDP away from potential GDP are usually caused by changes in aggregate demand. Aggregate demand is the total amount consumers, businesses, government, and foreigners are willing to spend on all goods and services in the economy. In contrast, the growth of potential GDP is caused by increases in the available supply of inputs to production: labor, capital, and technology.

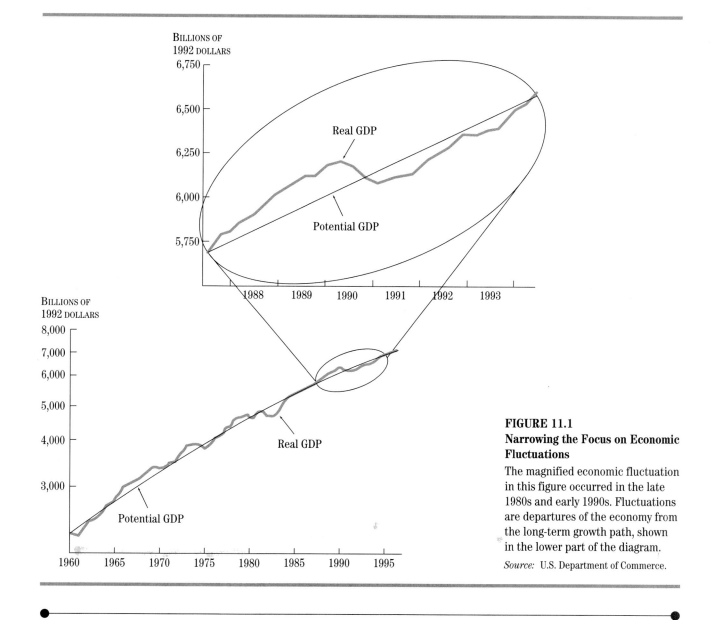

**FIGURE 11.1**
**Narrowing the Focus on Economic Fluctuations**
The magnified economic fluctuation in this figure occurred in the late 1980s and early 1990s. Fluctuations are departures of the economy from the long-term growth path, shown in the lower part of the diagram.

*Source:* U.S. Department of Commerce.

# CHANGES IN AGGREGATE DEMAND FIRST LEAD TO CHANGES IN OUTPUT

Figure 11.2 illustrates the essential idea used to explain economic fluctuations: that increases or decreases in real GDP that are above or below potential GDP occur largely because of increases or decreases in aggregate demand in the economy. Changes in aggregate demand occur when consumers, business firms, government,

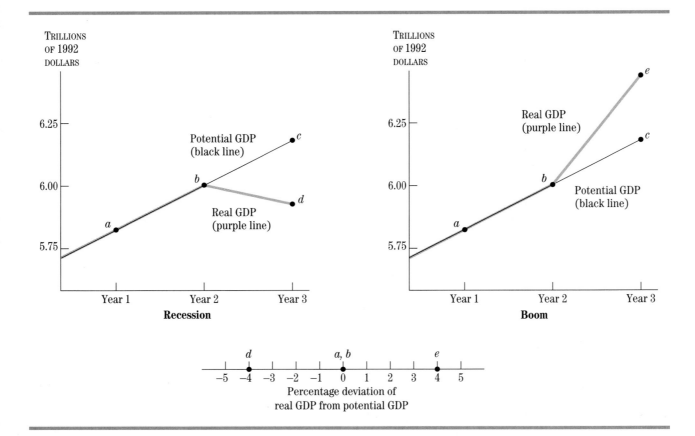

**Recession**

**Boom**

Percentage deviation of
real GDP from potential GDP

**FIGURE 11.2**
**The First Step of an Economic Fluctuation**

Potential GDP is shown by the black upward-sloping line in both diagrams. Points *a, b,* and *c* represent three different levels of potential GDP in three years. A recession is a downward departure of real GDP (shown in purple) from potential GDP, as illustrated by point *d* on the left. A boom is an upward departure of real GDP from potential GDP, as illustrated by point *e* on the right. The departures are explained by changes in aggregate demand. The line at the bottom shows the percent deviation of real GDP from potential GDP.

or foreigners expand or cut back their spending plans. Potential GDP in three years is marked by the points *a, b,* and *c* in Figure 11.2. These three values of potential GDP are part of the longer-term steady increase in potential GDP over time due to increases in the supply of labor and capital and improvements in technology. Potential GDP represents what firms would want to produce in "normal times," when the economy is neither in a recession nor in a boom. In normal times, real GDP is equal to potential GDP. Years 1 and 2 in Figure 11.2 are assumed to be normal years. However, year 3 is not a normal year. Point *d* in the left panel of the figure and point *e* in the right panel represent two alternative types of departures of real GDP from potential GDP that could occur in year 3: a recession and a boom.

In a boom, real GDP rises above potential GDP to a point like *e* in the right panel of Figure 11.2. Firms produce more in response to the increase in aggregate demand; they employ more workers, and unemployment declines. Eventually—this part of the story comes in later chapters—if demand for their products stays high, firms raise their prices, and real GDP returns toward potential GDP.

In a recession, all this works in reverse. Real GDP falls below potential GDP to a point like *d* in the left panel of Figure 11.2. Firms produce less and lay off workers. Unemployment rises. Eventually—again, this part of the story comes in later chapters—if demand stays low, firms begin to cut their prices, and real GDP moves back toward potential GDP. Thus, in both booms and recessions, changes in aggregate demand cause fluctuations in real GDP.

Economists frequently measure the departures of real GDP from potential GDP in percentages rather than dollar amounts. For example, if potential GDP is $6.20 trillion and real GDP is $6.45 trillion, then the percentage departure of real GDP from potential GDP is 4 percent: (6.45 − 6.20)/6.20 = .04. If real GDP were $5.95 trillion and potential GDP remained at $6.20 trillion, then the percentage departure would be −4 percent: (5.95 − 6.20)/6.20 = −.04. Percentages make it easier to compare economic fluctuations in different countries that have different sizes of real GDP. At the bottom of the two panels in Figure 11.2 is a horizontal line representing the size of the fluctuations in real GDP around potential GDP in each year.

Points *d* and *e* in Figure 11.2 represent the first steps of an economic fluctuation. These first steps occur in the short run.

## Production and Demand at Individual Firms

Why do firms produce more—bringing real GDP above *potential GDP*—when the demand for their products rises? Why do firms produce less—bringing real GDP below potential GDP—when the demand for their products falls? These questions have probably occupied economists' time more than any other in macroeconomics. Although more work still needs to be done, substantial improvements in economists' understanding of the issues have been made in the last 20 years.

**potential GDP:** the economy's long-term growth trend for real GDP determined by the available supply of capital, labor and technology. Real GDP fluctuates above and below potential GDP. (Ch. 5)

### *Normal Capacity Utilization and the Natural Unemployment Rate*

First consider some simple facts about how firms operate. In normal times, when real GDP is equal to potential GDP, most firms operate with some excess capacity so they can expand production without major bottlenecks. Small retail service businesses from taxi companies to dry cleaners can usually increase production when customer demand increases. Another taxi is added to a busy route and one of the drivers is asked to work overtime. One of the dry cleaning employees who has been working part time is happy to work full time. The same is true for large manufacturing firms. When asked what percent of capacity their production is in normal times, manufacturing firms typically answer about 80 percent. Thus, firms normally have room to expand production: In boom periods capacity utilization goes up to 90 percent or higher. If firms need more labor to expand production, they can ask workers to work overtime, call workers back from previous layoffs, or hire additional workers. With the unemployment rate equal to the *natural unemployment rate,* it is usually possible to find some workers to join the firm. That is why the unemployment rate drops below the natural unemployment rate in booms after real GDP rises above potential GDP.

**natural unemployment rate:** the unemployment rate that exists in normal times when there is neither a recession nor a boom and real GDP is equal to potential GDP. (Ch. 7)

In recessions, when demand declines, these same firms clearly have the capability to reduce production, and they do. In recessions, capacity utilization goes down to 70 percent or lower. Firms ask workers to stop working overtime, they move some workers to part time, or they lay off some workers. Some institute hiring freezes to make sure the personnel office does not keep hiring workers. That is why the unemployment rate rises above the natural unemployment rate in recessions when real GDP falls below potential GDP. For example, the unemployment rate rose to more than 7 percent when the 1990–1991 recession brought real GDP below potential GDP. We illustrated the relationship between the unemployment rate and the movements of real GDP relative to potential GDP in Figure 7.1, which is repeated in the margin to the right.

### Production and Employment Decisions at Actual Firms

Consider a typical service firm at the start of the 1990–1991 recession. Mayflower, the moving company named after the ship that moved the Pilgrims, found the demand for its moving and storage services growing rapidly in the boom of the late 1980s. The company expanded production by moving more households and, as a result, increased its employment from 6,800 workers in 1987 to 11,400 in 1989. In 1990, as the recession took hold, demand for Mayflower's services began to fall. The company reduced production—moved fewer households—and employment fell from 11,400 in 1989 to 10,900 in 1990, a decline of about 5 percent.

**Production Decisions by Actual Firms**

Individual firms—Mayflower moving services being just one example—raise production during booms when the demand for their goods or services rises, and lower production during recessions when the demand for their goods or services declines. These decisions by individual firms lead to fluctuations of real GDP above or below potential GDP.

Consider the example of a construction firm at about the same time. As is typical in recessions, construction was hit hard in the 1990–1991 recession. Trammell Crow, the real estate construction company based in Dallas, Texas, found the demand for its construction services fall off dramatically in 1990. Hence, the firm produced fewer of these services. It built fewer shopping malls and convention centers. Total square feet under construction by Trammell Crow fell from 44 million in 1989 to 27 million in 1990. Employment at Trammell Crow also fell from the year 1989 to 1990. Employment had expanded rapidly during the 1988–1989 boom. Thus, Trammell Crow is another example showing how fluctuations in demand cause a change in production.

## Why Changes in Demand Are Translated into Changes in Production

Economists apply theories of decision-making under uncertainty to explain the behavior of firms in such situations.

### Limited Information and Implicit Contracts

When a business firm notices an increase in demand for its products, it frequently does not know whether the increase in demand is temporary or permanent, or whether it is common to all firms in the economy or the industry. The firm is uncertain about the reasons for the change in demand for its products because it operates under **limited information.** In such a situation, the firm could raise its prices and thereby reduce the quantity demanded of its products and perhaps make greater short-term profits. But rather than raise its prices to limit the quantity demanded, the typical firm matches the increase in demand with more production.

If it is possible for the firm to expand production by increasing employment or the utilization of its capital, the firm is unlikely to raise prices right away. Raising prices may require costly changes in catalogues, menus, or advertising brochures. In a well-known study of prices of major magazines, Stephen Cecchetti of Ohio State University found that the price stays constant for many months or even years in the face of changes in demand for the magazines. Moreover, if the change in demand is temporary, raising prices might result in the firm losing some of its regu-

**limited information:** a situation in which firms have incomplete knowledge about some market conditions, such as whether a change in demand for their product is temporary or permanent or whether the change is due to a recession or boom in the whole economy.

lar customers. Kmart has a reputation as a low-price retailer. If it raises its prices in an unusually busy spring, it might lose its reputation. Wal-Mart might be the winner. Although Kmart, or other firms in similar situations, does not make any **explicit** price pledge or contract with its customers, economists describe the relationship between the firm and its customers as involving an **implicit contract.** It is as if the firm has an unwritten and unspoken promise with its customers not to change prices frequently.

For similar reasons, wages do not immediately rise, although the demand for labor increases. The firm does not want to pay new workers more, disrupt its pay scales, and perhaps lower the morale of its current employees. Pay scales are typically only changed once a year or less. Again, it is as if the firm has an implicit contract not to change wages at the drop of a hat. In some cases, union wage contracts that fix pay scales are negotiated only every three years.

"We figure it was HERE when the recession officially began."

Similarly, in a recession, when the firm finds the demand for its product declining, it may not know for a while whether the decline in sales is temporary, permanent, unique to itself, or a common feature in the economy. Hence, it will not cut prices immediately or reduce its employees' wages. When it is clear that the demand change is lasting and is occurring throughout the economy, then prices and eventually wages will begin to adjust.

The limited-information explanation for the finding that changes in demand get translated into changes in production and employment was incorporated into macroeconomic theory by Robert Lucas of the University of Chicago in the early 1970s. That limited information is not the whole story but appears to share a role with implicit contracts concerning prices and wages was incorporated into macroeconomic theory by other economists, such as Stanley Fischer of Massachusetts Institute of Technology and Edmund Phelps of Columbia University. Although there have been heated academic debates between those who use these two approaches, reality seems to combine limited information and implicit contracts. In fact, the preceding description of implicit contracts used the idea that firms have limited information. Sometimes economists use the term **nominal rigidities** to refer to inflexibilities in price and wage behavior that are implied by both theories.

**implicit contract:** an informal agreement between a firm and its customers or between a firm and its employees.

**nominal rigidities:** inflexibilities in wages and prices.

### A Graphical Illustration of the Typical Firm

Figure 11.3 illustrates how a change in demand gets translated into a change in the quantity produced at a typical firm. The firm's price is on the vertical axis and its production is on the horizontal axis. The firm faces a downward-sloping demand curve for its product. There are three downward-sloping demand curves: high, medium, and low, each corresponding to a different level of demand. Two types of assumptions for the behavior of the firm are illustrated: (1) the **sticky price assumption,** in which the firm does not immediately change its price when demand changes, and (2) the **flexible price assumption,** in which the firm raises its price immediately when demand increases and lowers its price immediately when demand falls. The ideas of limited information and implicit contracts imply that the firm will tend to change its price only after the change in demand is recognized as long-lasting.

**sticky price assumption:** an assumption that prices do not move quickly in response to a change in supply or demand; the assumption is used in the theory of economic fluctuations.

**flexible price assumption:** an assumption that prices adjust instantaneously in response to a change in supply or demand.

**FIGURE 11.3**
**Alternative Short-Run Responses of a Typical Firm to a Change in Demand**
The figure shows different demand curves for the firm's product: high, medium, and low. Two different production and price responses to the change in demand are also shown. With limited information or implicit contracts, the firm changes production by the amount of the change in demand. If the firm changes its production by a smaller amount, the price must change.

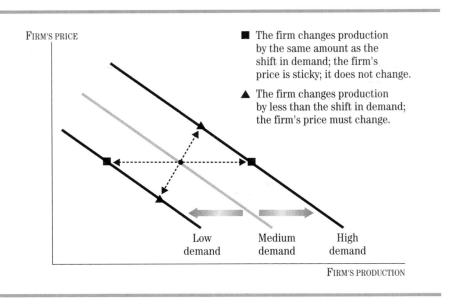

**real business cycle theory:**
a theory of macroeconomics that stresses that shifts in potential GDP are a primary cause of fluctuations in real GDP; the shifts in potential GDP are usually caused by changes in technology.

## Could Economic Fluctuations Also Be Due to Changes in Potential GDP?

Our discussion thus far of the production decisions of individual firms has shown why it is natural to identify fluctuations in real GDP with fluctuations in aggregate demand. To be sure, economic fluctuations also occur because of changes in potential GDP. For example, when agriculture was a much larger fraction of real GDP, drought and floods had more noticeable effects on real GDP. Although agriculture is currently a very small fraction of total production, the possibility that increases or decreases in potential GDP may still play a large role in economic fluctuations is a topic currently being examined by economists. Economic theories that emphasize changes in potential GDP as a source of economic fluctuations are called **real business cycle theories.** Most frequently changes in technology are assumed to be the reason for changes in potential GDP in real business cycle theories.

The factors that underlie potential GDP growth—population, capital, technological know-how—tend to evolve relatively smoothly. Population growth, for example, is much steadier than real GDP growth. We do not have a drop in the population every few years and a sudden spurt the next year. Slowdowns in population growth occur gradually over time as birthrates and death rates change. Similarly, although individual factories or machines may be lost in a hurricane or flood, this does not happen in such a massive way across the country that it would show up as large as a recession or a boom in the whole economy. Thus, the amount of capital changes slowly over time. Even technological change does not seem capable of explaining most fluctuations. It is true that some inventions and innovations raise productivity substantially in certain sectors of the economy over short periods of time. The impact on the whole economy is more spread out and gradual, however. Moreover, people do not suddenly forget how to use a technology. There do not seem to be sudden decreases in technological know-how. For these reasons, potential GDP usually tends to grow relatively smoothly over time, compared to the fluctuations in aggregate demand.

## Review

▶ Economic fluctuations are largely due to fluctuations in aggregate demand.

▶ When aggregate demand increases, firms first produce more; real GDP rises above potential GDP. Firms also hire more workers and the unemployment rate falls below the natural rate of unemployment. When aggregate demand decreases, firms produce less; real GDP falls below potential GDP. Unemployment rises above the natural rate of unemployment. After a period of time, real GDP returns to potential GDP.

▶ This type of behavior is observed by looking at individual firms. Limited information and implicit contracts, two important ideas developed by economists in the 1970s and 1980s, help explain this behavior.

▶ Short-run fluctuations in potential GDP also occur, but in reality most of the larger fluctuations in real GDP seem to be due to fluctuations of real GDP around a more steadily growing potential GDP.

*предсказывая*

# FORECASTING REAL GDP

To illustrate how we use the idea that changes in aggregate demand lead to short-run fluctuations in real GDP, we will focus on an important macroeconomic task: short-term economic forecasting of real GDP about one year ahead. To **forecast** real GDP, economic forecasters divide aggregate demand into its four key components: consumption, investment, government purchases, and net exports. Remember that real GDP can be measured by adding together the four types of spending: what people *consume,* what firms *invest,* what *governments purchase,* and what *foreigners purchase* net of what they sell in the United States. In symbols, we have

**forecast:** a prediction of an economic variable such as real GDP.

$$Y = C + I + G + X$$

In other words, real GDP ($Y$) is the sum of consumption ($C$), investment ($I$), government purchases ($G$), and net exports ($X$).

The preceding equation is a central tool of analysis used by economic forecasters at macroeconomic forecasting firms. These firms are hired by other businesses to forecast real GDP and related economic variables. (See the box "The Forecasting Industry.") Business decisions to hire new workers are frequently based on such forecasts. In addition, forecasting is part of the job of the Federal Reserve, the Congressional Budget Office (CBO), and the President's Council of Economic Advisers (CEA). These government agencies regularly make forecasts of where real GDP is headed in the short run. The Fed uses such forecasts to make decisions about how much money growth to provide. Each December the CEA develops a forecast for the following year that is used to prepare the president's budget proposals, which are submitted to Congress. The CBO then does its own analysis of the president's budget using another forecast. Similar organizations and firms exist in other countries.

## A Forecast for Next Year

Suppose that it is December 2004 and a forecast of real GDP ($Y$) is being prepared for the year 2005. Using the preceding equation, a reasonable way to proceed would be to forecast consumption for the next year, then forecast investment, then forecast government purchases, and, finally, forecast net exports. When forecasting each item, the forecaster would consider a range of issues: consumer confidence

# The Forecasting Industry

Short-term forecasting of real GDP—usually one year ahead—has become a major industry employing thousands of economists, statisticians, and computer programmers. Each month the *Blue Chip Economic Indicators* tabulates the forecasts of the top forecasters. A summary of 52 different forecasts of real GDP for 1994 made in November 1993 is shown in the table. Observe that the forecast is stated as the growth rate of real GDP for 1994 over 1993. The average (called the Blue Chip Consensus) was 2.8 percent. The highest forecasts are labeled "H," and the lowest forecasts are labeled "L." Virtually all the forecasters in this group use some version of the method of forecasting real GDP described in this chapter.

How accurate was the Blue Chip Consensus in 1994? We now know that the actual growth rate of real GDP was 3.5 percent, slightly above the 2.8 percent forecast; this is a rather typical margin of error for economic forecasting.

*Source:* Blue Chip Economic Indicators, Capitol Publications, Inc., November 10, 1993, p. 3.

---

### BLUE CHIP ECONOMIC INDICATORS

## 1994 Real GDP Consensus Estimate

**Percent Change 1994 From 1993 (Year-Over-Year)**

### NOVEMBER 1993
### Forecast for 1994

| | | | |
|---|---|---|---|
| Morgan Guaranty Trust Co. | 3.4H | Eggert Economic Enterprises, Inc. | 2.8 |
| UCLA Business Forecast | 3.4H | DuPont | 2.8 |
| Sears Roebuck & Co. | 3.4H | Comerica | 2.8 |
| Robert Genetski & Assoc., Inc. | 3.3 | CoreStates Financial Corp. | 2.8 |
| Morris Cohen & Associates | 3.3 | U.S. Trust Co. | 2.7 |
| Turning Points (Micrometrics) | 3.3 | PNC Bank | 2.7 |
| Bostonian Economic Research | 3.2 | SOM Economics, Inc. | 2.7 |
| Motorola, Inc. | 3.2 | National Assn. of Home Builders | 2.7 |
| Conference Board | 3.1 | Bank of America | 2.7 |
| Brown Brothers Harriman | 3.1 | Dun & Bradstreet | 2.6 |
| Prudential Securities | 3.1 | Morgan Stanley & Co. | 2.6 |
| Northern Trust Company | 3.1 | Nat'l. City Bank of Cleveland | 2.6 |
| NationsBanc Capital Markets, Inc. | 3.1 | U.S. Chamber of Commerce | 2.6 |
| Shawmut National Corp | 3.0 | Prudential Insurance Co. | 2.6 |
| Metropolitan Life Insurance Co. | 3.0 | Reeder Associates (Charles) | 2.6 |
| Chrysler Corporation | 3.0 | Cahners Economics | 2.5 |
| First Interstate Bancorp | 3.0 | Chase Manhattan Bank | 2.5 |
| General Motors | 3.0 | Bankers Trust Co. | 2.5 |
| Merrill Lynch | 3.0 | C. J. Lawrence, Inc. | 2.5 |
| Wayne Hummer & Co., Chicago | 2.9 | University of Michigan | 2.5 |
| Pennzoil Company | 2.9 | Arnhold & S. Bleichroeder | 2.4 |
| Ford Motor Co. | 2.9 | Evans Economics | 2.4 |
| Georgia State University | 2.9 | Econoclast | 2.0 |
| First National Bank of Chicago | 2.9 | Inforum - Univ. of Maryland | 1.7L |
| Mortgage Bankers Assn. of Amer. | 2.9 | Chemical Banking | 1.7L |
| Laurence H. Meyer & Assoc. | 2.9 | | |
| Fairmodel | 2.9 | **1994 Consensus: November Avg.** | **2.8** |

might affect consumption; business confidence might be a factor in investment; the mood of the country might be a factor in government purchases; and developments in foreign countries might affect the forecast for net exports. In any case, adding these four spending items together would give a forecast for real GDP for the year 2005. For example, one economist may forecast that $C = \$7,000$ billion, $I = \$900$ billion, $X = \$100$ billion, and $G = \$2,000$ billion. Then the forecast for real GDP is $\$10,000$ billion. If real GDP in 2004 is $\$9,700$, then the forecast would be for 3.1 percent growth for the year 2005. Forecasts are typically expressed as growth rates of real GDP from one year to the next.

Alternatively, the forecaster may be concerned about recessions in other countries and have a lower forecast for net exports, perhaps $X = \$50$ billion. This alternative and any others can be incorporated into the forecast of real GDP by using a different value for one of the components.

## A Conditional Forecast

The preceding forecast is prepared by making the best assumption about what is likely for government purchases and the other three components of spending. Another type of forecast—called a **conditional forecast**—describes what real GDP will be under alternative assumptions about the components of spending. For example, the president of the United States in the year 2004 might want the CEA or the CBO to estimate the effect of a proposal to change government purchases on the economy in 2005. A conditional forecast would be a forecast of real GDP conditional on this change in government purchases. A conditional forecast for real GDP can be made using similar methods. Let's see how.

**conditional forecast:** a prediction that depends on assumed values for government purchases, taxes, or some other variable that affects the forecast.

Suppose the proposal is to cut federal government purchases by $100 billion in real terms in one year. What is the effect of such a change in government purchases on aggregate demand in the short run? If the government demands $100 billion less, then firms will produce $100 billion less. A forecast conditional on a $100 billion spending cut would be $100 billion less for real GDP, or $9,900 billion. Again, we just add up $7,000 billion, $900 billion, $100 billion, and now $1,900 billion. Real GDP growth for the year is now forecast to be about 2.1 percent, conditional on the policy proposal.

The forecast is based on the equation that $Y = C + I + G + X$ and the idea that changes in aggregate demand cause real GDP fluctuations. Although simple, it is specific and substantive. For example, this same type of reasoning led economists to forecast an economic slowdown in the United States in the early 1990s due to the reduction in government defense spending occurring at that time. According to this method of forecasting, changes in aggregate demand are responsible for most of the short-run ups and downs in the economy. It is this explanation that most economic forecasters use when they forecast real GDP for one year ahead.

## Review

▸ The four components of spending can be added to make a forecast for real GDP. Making such a forecast is an important application of macroeconomics.

▸ Forecasts may be conditional on a particular event, such as a change in government purchases or a change in taxes.

# THE RESPONSE OF CONSUMPTION TO INCOME

In the forecasting example we assumed that none of the components—neither consumption, investment, nor net exports—change in response to the decline in government purchases. For example, consumption ($C$) was unchanged at $7,000 billion when we altered $G$ in our conditional forecast. But these components of spending are likely to change. Thus, something important is missing from the procedure for forecasting real GDP. To improve the forecast, we must describe how the components of aggregate demand—consumption, investment, or net exports— might change in response to other developments in the economy. We will eventually consider the response of consumption, investment, and net exports to many factors, including interest rates, exchange rates, and income. However, bringing all these factors into consideration at once is complicated, and we must start with a *simplifying assumption*. Here the simplifying assumption is that consumption is the only component of expenditures that responds to income, and that income is the only influence on consumption. Consumption is a good place to begin because it is by far the largest component. Before we finish developing a complete theory of economic fluctuations, we will consider the other components and the other influences. Let us begin by examining why consumption may be affected by income.

## The Consumption Function

**consumption function:** the positive relationship between consumption and income.

The **consumption function** describes how consumption depends on income. The notion of a consumption function originated with John Maynard Keynes, who wrote about it during the 1930s. Research on the consumption function has been intense ever since. For each individual, the consumption function says that the more income one has, the more one consumes. For the national economy as a whole, it says that the more income Americans have, the more Americans consume. For the world economy as a whole, it says that the more income in the world, the more people in the world consume. Table 11.1 gives a simple example of how consumption depends on income in the United States economy.

As you can see from the table, as income increases from 1,000 to 2,000, consumption increases as well from 1,600 to 2,200, and as income increases from 3,000 to 4,000, consumption increases from 2,800 to 3,400. More income means more consumption, but the consumption function also tells us *how much* consumption increases when income increases. Each change in income by 1,000 causes an increase in consumption by 600. The changes in consumption are smaller than the changes in income. Notice that, in this example, at very low levels of income, consumption is greater than income. If consumption were greater than income for a particular individual, that individual would have to borrow. At higher levels of income, when consumption is less than income, the individual would be able to save.

The consumption function is supposed to describe the behavior of individuals because the economy is made up of individuals. Consequently, it summarizes the behavior of all people in the economy with respect to consumption. The simple consumption function is not meant to be the complete explanation of consumption. Recall that it is based on a simplifying assumption.

**TABLE 11.1**
**An Example of the Consumption Function**
(billions of dollars)

| Consumption | Income |
|---|---|
| 1,600 | 1,000 |
| 2,200 | 2,000 |
| 2,800 | 3,000 |
| 3,400 | 4,000 |
| 4,000 | 5,000 |
| 4,600 | 6,000 |
| 5,200 | 7,000 |
| 5,800 | 8,000 |
| 6,400 | 9,000 |
| 7,000 | 10,000 |
| 7,600 | 11,000 |
| 8,200 | 12,000 |
| 8,800 | 13,000 |
| 9,400 | 14,000 |

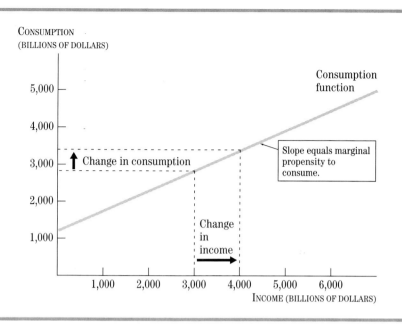

**FIGURE 11.4**
**The Consumption Function**
For the economy as a whole, more income leads to more consumption, as shown by the example of an upward-sloping consumption function in the figure. This represents the sum of all the individuals in the economy, many of whom consume more when their income rises. The graph is based on the numbers in Table 11.1.

### The Marginal Propensity to Consume

A concept related to the consumption function is the **marginal propensity to consume,** or **MPC** for short. The marginal propensity to consume measures how much consumption changes for a given change in income. The term *marginal* refers to the additional amount of consumption that is due to a change in income. The term *propensity* refers to the inclination to consume. By definition,

$$\text{Marginal Propensity to Consume (MPC)} = \frac{\text{change in consumption}}{\text{change in income}}$$

What is the MPC for the consumption function in Table 11.1? Observe that the change in consumption from row to row is 600. The change in income from row to row is 1,000; thus the MPC = 600/1,000 = .6. Although this is only a simple example, it turns out that the MPC is around that magnitude for the U.S. economy.

Figure 11.4 graphs the consumption function by putting income on the horizontal axis and consumption on the vertical axis. We get the upward-sloping line by plotting the pairs of observations on consumption and income in Table 11.1 and connecting them with a line. This line, which demonstrates that consumption rises with income, is the consumption function. Its slope is equal to the MPC. For this example, the MPC = .6. The graph shows that at low levels of income, consumption is greater than income, but at high levels of income, consumption is less than income.

### Which Measure of Income?

The consumption function is a straight-line relationship between consumption and income. Sometimes income in the relationship is measured by **aggregate income** (*Y*), which is also equal to real GDP, and sometimes by disposable income. **Disposable income** is the income that households receive in wages, dividends, and interest

**marginal propensity to consume (MPC):** the slope of the consumption function, showing the change in consumption that is due to a given change in income.

**aggregate income:** the total income received by all factors of production in the economy; also simply called "income."

**disposable income:** income that households have to spend after taxes have been paid and transfers from the government have been received.

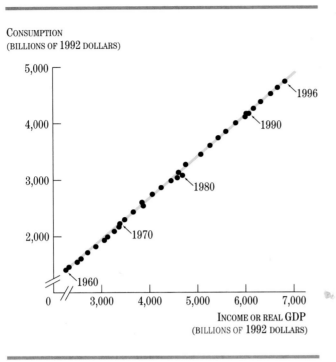

CONSUMPTION
(BILLIONS OF 1992 DOLLARS)

INCOME OR REAL GDP
(BILLIONS OF 1992 DOLLARS)

**FIGURE 11.5**
**Consumption versus Aggregate Income**

The graph shows the close relationship between consumption and aggregate income, or real GDP, in the U.S. economy. The points fall close to the straight line drawn in the diagram.

*Source:* U.S. Department of Commerce.

payments plus transfers they may get from the government minus any taxes they pay to the government. Disposable income is the preferred measure of income when one is interested in household consumption because this is what households have available to spend. But the consumption function for the whole economy looks similar for either aggregate income or disposable income because aggregate income and disposable income fluctuate and grow together. In the United States and most other countries, taxes and transfers are nearly proportional to income.

For the rest of this chapter, we will use aggregate income, or real GDP, as the measure of income in the consumption function. We put real GDP, or income (we drop the word *aggregate* in aggregate income), on the horizontal axis of the consumption function diagram, because real GDP and income are always equal. Figure 11.5 shows the actual relationship between consumption and income, or real GDP. Note, however, that when we consider an explicit change in taxes, we must take account of the difference between disposable income and income. (Remember, *income* means "aggregate income for the whole economy" in this chapter.)

## What about Interest Rates and Other Influences on Consumption?

Other factors besides income affect consumption. For example, you may recall from Chapter 8 that people's consumption is affected by the interest rate. Also, people's wealth—including their savings in a bank and their house—may affect their consumption. A person with a large amount of savings in a bank might consume a considerable amount even if the person's income in any one year is very low. Why have we not brought the interest rate or wealth into the picture here?

The answer is simple. To keep the analysis manageable at the start, we are putting the interest rate and other influences aside. We eventually return to consider the effects of interest rates and other factors on consumption. But during economic fluctuations, the effects of changes in income on consumption are most important, and we focus on these now.

## Review

▶ The consumption function describes the response of consumption to changes in income. The elementary consumption function ignores the effects of interest rates and wealth on consumption.

▶ The marginal propensity to consume (MPC) tells us *how much* consumption changes in response to a change in income.

▶ For the economy as a whole, the consumption function can be expressed in terms of aggregate income or disposable income. Aggregate income is always equal to real GDP. Here we use aggregate income.

# FINDING REAL GDP WHEN CONSUMPTION AND INCOME MOVE TOGETHER

Now let us use the consumption function to get a better prediction of what happens to real GDP in the short run when government purchases change. In other words, we want to improve the conditional forecast of real GDP when there is a change in government purchases, taking the consumption function into account. Again, as in the earlier example of forecasting, let us assume that government spending will decline by $100 billion next year. Our goal is to find out what happens to real GDP in the short run.

## The Logic of the Two-Way Link Between Consumption and Income

The consumption function is a relationship between consumption and income. But we also have another relationship between consumption and income: $Y = C + I + G + X$. Income is on the left-hand side of this identity because real GDP equals income. That is, $Y$ equals income as well as real GDP. The two relationships together will enable us to find out what happens to real GDP.

How? Think about it logically. The first attempt at our forecasting analysis said that a reduction in government spending is going to reduce real GDP. But now we see that something else must happen because consumption depends on income, and real GDP is equal to income. A reduction in government spending will reduce income. The consumption function tells us a reduction in income must reduce consumption.

Here is the chain of logic in brief:

1. A cut in government spending reduces real GDP.

2. Real GDP is income.

3. Thus, income is reduced.

4. Consumption depends on income.

5. Thus, consumption is reduced.

In sum, consumption will decline when we reduce government spending.

For example, when the government reduces defense spending, the firms that produce the defense goods find demand falling and they produce less. Some of the defense workers are either going to work fewer hours a week or be laid off. Therefore, they will receive a reduced income or no income at all. In addition, the profits at the defense firms will decline; thus, the income of the owners of the firms will decline. With less income, the workers and the owners will spend less; that is, their consumption will decline. This is the connection between government spending and consumption that we are concerned about: The change in government purchases reduces defense workers' income, which results in less consumption.

Consider a specific case study. This type of logic was applied by economists to estimate the impact of closing Fort Ord, the military base near Monterey Bay in California, on the Monterey economy. When the estimates were made, the base employed 3,000 civilians and 14,000 military personnel. Payroll was $558 million. Thus, closing the base would reduce incomes by as much as $558 million as these workers were laid off or retired. Although some workers might find jobs quickly elsewhere, there would be a decline in income that would result in a reduction in consumption by those workers. Using an MPC of .6, consumption would decline by $335 million (.6 times 558) if income was reduced by $558 million. This would tend to throw others in the Monterey area out of work as spending in retail and service stores declined. This would further reduce consumption, and so on. Although this case study refers to a small region of the entire country, the same logic applies to the economy as a whole.

## The 45-Degree Line

We can use a convenient graph to calculate how much income and consumption changes in the whole economy and thereby find out what happens to real GDP. In Figure 11.6 there is a line that shows graphically that income in the economy is equal to spending. That is, income ($Y$) equals spending ($C + I + G + X$). In Figure 11.6, income is on the horizontal axis and spending is on the vertical axis. All the points where spending equals income are on the upward-sloping line in Figure 11.6. The line has a slope of 1, or an angle of 45 degrees with the horizontal axis, because the distances from any point on the line to the horizontal axis and the vertical axis are equal. Along that line—which is called the **45-degree line**—spending and income are equal.

**45-degree line:** the line showing that aggregate expenditure equals aggregate income.

## The Aggregate Expenditure Line

**aggregate expenditure line:** the relation between the sum of the four components of spending ($C + I + G + X$) and aggregate income.

Figure 11.7 shows another relationship called the **aggregate expenditure line.** Like Figure 11.6, income or real GDP is on the horizontal axis, and spending is on the vertical axis. The top line in Figure 11.7 is the aggregate expenditure line. It is called the aggregate expenditure line because it shows how aggregate expenditure, or spending, depends on income. The four components that make up the aggregate expenditure line are consumption, investment, government purchases, and net exports. However, the aggregate expenditure line shows how these four components

**FIGURE 11.6**
**The 45-Degree Line**
This simple line is a graphical representation of the income equals spending identity. The pairs of points on the 45-degree line have the same level of spending and income. For example, the level of spending at $A$ is the same dollar amount as the level of income at $A$. Moreover, because income equals real GDP, we can put either income or real GDP on the horizontal axis.

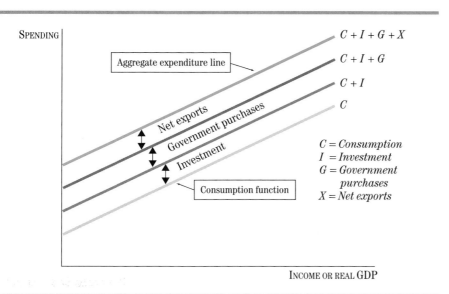

**FIGURE 11.7**
**Aggregate Expenditure Line**
By adding investment ($I$), government purchases ($G$), and net exports ($X$) to the consumption function, we build the aggregate expenditure line.

depend on income. It is this dependency of spending on income that is the defining characteristic of the aggregate expenditure line. Here is how the aggregate expenditure line is derived.

The consumption function is shown as the lowest line in Figure 11.7. It is simply the consumption function from Figure 11.4, which says that the higher income is, the more people want to consume. The next line above the consumption function in Figure 11.7 is parallel to the consumption function. This line represents the addition of investment to consumption at each level of income. It says investment is so many billions of dollars in the U.S. economy, and the distance between the lines is this amount of investment. For example, if investment equals $800 billion, the distance between the consumption function and this next line is $800 billion.

The reason the line is parallel to the consumption line is that we are starting our explanation by saying that investment does not depend on income. This simplifying assumption means that investment is a constant number, and the distance between the lines is the same regardless of income. We just add the same amount at each point.

The next line in Figure 11.7 adds in a constant level of government purchases. This next line is also parallel to the other lines because the increase at every level of income is the same. The distance between the lines represents a fixed level of government purchases, say $1,600 billion, at every level of income.

Finally, to get the top line in Figure 11.7, we add in net exports. For simplicity, we assume that net exports do not depend on income, an assumption that we will change soon. Thus, the top line is parallel to all the other lines. The top line is the sum of $C + I + G + X$. It is the aggregate expenditure ($AE$) line. The term *aggregate* is used because it refers to the whole economy. But the most important thing to remember about the $AE$ line is that it shows how the sum of the four components depends on income.

Before we can use the $AE$ line, we must know what determines its slope and what causes it to shift.

### The Slope of the AE Line

Observe in Figure 11.7 that the *AE* line is parallel to the consumption function. Therefore, the slope of the *AE* line is the same as the slope of the consumption function. We already know that the slope of the consumption function is the MPC. Hence, the slope of the *AE* line is also equal to the MPC.

Because the MPC is less than 1, the aggregate expenditure line is flatter (the slope is smaller) than the 45-degree line, which has a slope of exactly 1. This fact will soon be used to find real GDP.

### Shifts in the AE Line

The aggregate expenditure line can shift for several reasons. Consider first what happens to the aggregate expenditure line if government purchases fall because of a cut in defense spending. As shown in Figure 11.8, the *AE* line shifts downward in a parallel fashion. The *AE* line is simply the sum *C* + *I* + *G* + *X*. Because *G* is less at all income levels, the line shifts down. The aggregate expenditure line is lowered because the distance between the consumption function and the other lines declines (see Figure 11.7). The reverse of this, an increase in government purchases, will cause the aggregate expenditure line to shift up.

What happens to the aggregate expenditure line if investment falls? Investment, remember, is the gap between the first and second lines in Figure 11.7. If investment declines (as might happen if businesses get pessimistic about the future and invest less), then the aggregate expenditure line shifts downward. With less investment, the gap between the lines shrinks. The reverse of this, an increase in investment, will cause the aggregate expenditure line to shift up, as shown in Figure 11.8.

A change in net exports, perhaps because of a change in the demand for U.S. exports to other countries, will also shift the *AE* line. A downward shift in net exports lowers the *AE* line, and an upward shift in the net exports raises the *AE* line.

Finally, the aggregate expenditure line can also be shifted by changes in taxes. At any given level of income, an increase in taxes means people have less to spend,

**FIGURE 11.8**
**Shifts in the Aggregate Expenditure Line**

The aggregate expenditure line shifts down if (1) government purchases (*G*) fall, (2) investment (*I*) falls, (3) taxes (*T*) increase, or (4) net exports (*X*) fall. The aggregate expenditure line shifts up if (1) government purchases rise, (2) investment rises, (3) taxes are cut, or (4) net exports rise.

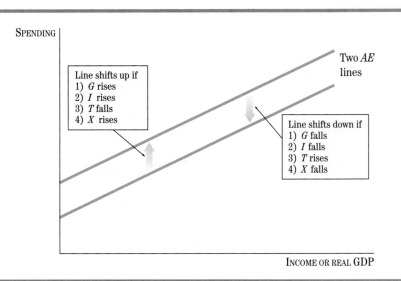

and this will cause people to consume less. Hence, the aggregate expenditure line shifts down when taxes rise. The reverse of this, a cut in taxes, causes the aggregate expenditure line to shift up. We will use the symbol $T$ to refer to taxes. For example, if $T = \$1,500$ billion, then people pay and the government receives $\$1,500$ billion in taxes.

## Determining Real GDP Through Spending Balance

Having derived the aggregate expenditure line and the 45-degree line, we can combine the two to find real GDP. Figure 11.9 shows how the aggregate expenditure line and the 45-degree line combine in one diagram. Observe that the two lines intersect. They must intersect because they have different slopes. Real GDP is found at the point of intersection of these two lines. Why?

Income and spending are always equal and the 45-degree line is drawn to represent this equality. Therefore, at any point on the 45-degree line, income equals spending. Moreover, income and spending must be on the aggregate expenditure line, because only at points on that line do people consume according to the consumption function.

If both relationships hold, that is, income and spending are the same (we are on the 45-degree line) and people's consumption is described by the consumption function (we are on the $AE$ line), then logically we must be at the intersection of these two lines. We call that point of intersection **spending balance.** The level of income determined by that point is just the right level to cause people to purchase an amount of consumption that—when added to investment, government purchases, and net exports—gives exactly the same level of income. We would not have spending balance at either a higher or lower level of income. The diagram in Figure 11.9 showing that the 45-degree line and the aggregate expenditure line cross is sometimes called the "Keynesian Cross" after John Maynard Keynes.

Table 11.2 provides an alternative way to determine spending balance. It uses a numerical tabulation of the consumption function rather than graphs. Aggregate

**spending balance:** the level of income or real GDP at which the 45-degree line and the aggregate expenditure line cross; also called equilibrium income.

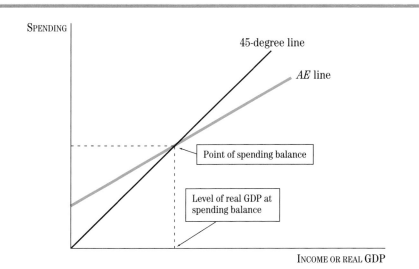

**FIGURE 11.9**
**Spending Balance**
Spending balance occurs when two relations are satisfied simultaneously: (1) income equals spending, and (2) spending equals consumption, which is a function of income, plus investment plus government purchases plus net exports. Only one level of income gives spending balance. That level of income is determined by the intersection of the 45-degree line and the $AE$ line.

**TABLE 11.2**
**A Numerical Example of Spending Balance**
(billions of dollars)

| Income or Real GDP | Aggregate Expenditure | Consumption | Investment | Government Purchases | Net Exports |
|---|---|---|---|---|---|
| 6,000 | 7,600 | 4,600 | 900 | 2,000 | 100 |
| 7,000 | 8,200 | 5,200 | 900 | 2,000 | 100 |
| 8,000 | 8,800 | 5,800 | 900 | 2,000 | 100 |
| 9,000 | 9,400 | 6,400 | 900 | 2,000 | 100 |
| 10,000 | 10,000 | 7,000 | 900 | 2,000 | 100 |
| 11,000 | 10,600 | 7,000 | 900 | 2,000 | 100 |
| 12,000 | 11,200 | 8,200 | 900 | 2,000 | 100 |
| 13,000 | 11,800 | 8,800 | 900 | 2,000 | 100 |
| 14,000 | 12,400 | 9,400 | 900 | 2,000 | 100 |

expenditure is obtained by adding the four columns on the right of Table 11.2. Consumption is shown to depend on income according to the same consumption function in Table 11.1. Observe that there is only one row where income equals aggregate expenditure. That row is where spending balance occurs. The row is shaded and corresponds to the point of intersection of the 45-degree line and the aggregate expenditure line in Figure 11.9.

Because the point of spending balance is at the intersection of two lines, we can think of it as an equilibrium, much as the intersection of a demand curve and a supply curve for wheat is an equilibrium. Because real GDP is not necessarily equal to potential GDP at this intersection, however, there is a sense in which the equilibrium is temporary; eventually real GDP will move back to potential GDP, as we will show in later chapters.

The point of spending balance is also an equilibrium in the sense that economic forces cause real GDP to be at that intersection. To see this, consider Table 11.2. As we noted, the shaded row corresponds to the intersection of the 45-degree line and the aggregate expenditure line: Income or real GDP equals aggregate expenditure. Suppose that income or real GDP were less than aggregate expenditure, as in one of the rows above the shaded row in Table 11.2. This would not be an equilibrium because firms would not be producing enough goods and services (real GDP) to satisfy people's aggregate expenditure on goods and services. Firms would increase their production, and real GDP would rise until it equaled aggregate expenditure. Similarly, if real GDP were greater than aggregate expenditure, as in one of the rows below the shaded row in Table 11.2, firms would be producing more than people would be buying. Hence, firms would reduce their production and real GDP would fall until it equaled aggregate expenditure.

## A Better Forecast of Real GDP

Now let us return to forecasting real GDP using these new tools. Recall the example of making a forecast of real GDP for the year 2005 (from the vantage point of December 2004), conditional on a proposed decline in government purchases of $100 billion. Our new tools will enable us to take account of the effect of this decline on consumption, which we had previously ignored in the simple forecast.

Figure 11.10 shows two *AE* lines. The top *AE* line is without the change in government purchases. In this case, $G = \$2,000$ billion, $C = \$7,000$ billion, $I = \$900$ billion, and $X = \$100$ billion, yielding income, or real GDP, of $10,000

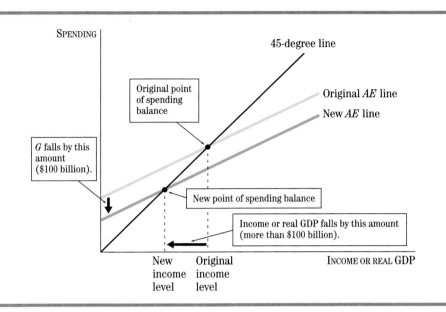

**FIGURE 11.10**
**From One Point of Spending Balance to Another**
The aggregate expenditure line shifts down because of a decline in government purchases. This shifts down the forecast for real GDP. A forecast of real GDP conditional on the decline in government purchases would therefore be lower.

billion. For the conditional forecast, we assume $G$ is cut by \$100 billion to \$1,900 billion. In Figure 11.10, that causes the $AE$ line to shift down to the "new" $AE$ line. Observe that the $AE$ line shifts down by \$100 billion—a parallel shift. This new $AE$ line cuts the 45-degree line at a lower point.

Logic tells us the economy will now operate at a different point of spending balance, where the aggregate expenditure line and the 45-degree line now intersect. Thus we move from one intersection to a new intersection as a result of the decline in the aggregate expenditure line. The new point of spending balance is at a lower level of real GDP.

We now have a prediction that real GDP will fall if government spending declines. Observe in Figure 11.10 that the decline in real GDP is larger than the \$100 billion decline in government purchases and, therefore, larger than the \$100 billion decline in real GDP in the simple forecast. The reason is that consumption has fallen as well as government purchases because income has declined. In Figure 11.10 the difference looks quite large. It is certainly large enough to influence a new administration's decision to reduce government purchases. The example and the application illustrate that it is not just for fun that we have derived the $AE$ line. It is an essential tool of the practicing macroeconomist.

# **Review**

▶ Spending balance occurs when the identity $Y = C + I + G + X$ and the consumption function relating $C$ to $Y$ hold simultaneously.

▶ Spending balance can be shown on a graph with the 45-degree line and the aggregate expenditure ($AE$)

line. The intersection of the two lines determines a level of income, or real GDP, that gives spending balance.

▶ A shift in the aggregate expenditure line brings about a new level of spending balance.

# Forecasting with Econometric Models

Economic forecasters use large mathematical models with hundreds of equations to help them forecast real GDP. Such models are called *econometric models*. They were first developed in the 1950s. Lawrence Klein of the University of Pennsylvania won a Nobel Prize for developing some of the first econometric models. Today, economists use high-speed computers to forecast real GDP with such models, but the basic ideas are no more difficult conceptually than those we use to find real GDP with the diagram of spending balance in this chapter. To see this, we show that finding real GDP through spending balance is equivalent to solving two equations. Once the idea is understood with two equations, the extension to hundreds of equations merely requires a computer.

The key idea behind spending balance is that two relationships, or equations, must hold simultaneously:

1. the consumption function relating income ($Y$) to consumption ($C$)

2. the income-spending identity relating income ($3$) to consumption ($C$)

Algebra provides a way to solve such relationships simultaneously. In the language of algebra, we have two equations in two unknowns.

The first equation is the consumption function. It can be written with algebra for the example given in Table 11.1 of the text as:

$$C = 1 + .6Y$$

where $C$ is consumption and $Y$ is income measured in trillions of dollars. For example, if $Y = \$5$ trillion, then $C = \$4$ trillion $[4 = 1 + (.6 \times 5)]$. Check to see that this is the fifth row of Table 11.1. Try some other values for $Y$.

The second equation is the income-spending identity. When investment ($I$) plus government purchases ($G$) plus net exports ($X$) equals $3 trillion, as in Table 11.2, the income-spending identity ($Y = C + I + G + X$) can be written as:

$$Y = C + 3$$

where we have set $I + G + X = 3$.

Spending balance occurs at the value of $Y$ that satisfies both equations.

To solve for $Y$ using algebra, first write the two equations next to each other:

$$C = 1 + .6Y$$
$$Y = C + 3$$

A two-equation model in two unknowns

Now substitute the first equation for $C$ into the right-hand side of the second:

$$1 + .6Y$$
$$Y = C + 3$$

to get

$$Y = 1 + .6Y + 3$$

Aggregate expenditure

Note that the right-hand side of this equation is aggregate expenditure. It shows explicitly that aggregate expenditure depends on income ($Y$), which is the essential idea behind the aggregate expenditure line. The left-hand side of the equation is income. Spending balance occurs when the left equals the right. Gathering all the terms in $Y$ together on the left-hand side gives

$$.4Y = 4$$

This tells you immediately that $Y = \$10$ trillion, which is the answer. Putting $Y = 10$ back into the consumption equation gives $C = 7$.

The value $Y = 10$ is the same answer as the one given in the shaded row of Table 11.2. It is also the same answer given by the intersection of the 45-degree line and the aggregate expenditure line.

Once one represents a model using algebra, it is possible to make interesting modifications. For example, to analyze the effect of taxes on their forecast, economists would change the consumption function to $C = 1 + .6(Y - T)$ where $T$ is taxes (say $T = \$.8$ trillion); the analysis would be similar.

Some people find algebra easier to work with than the numerical examples and the graphs. If you are one of those people, you can use this algebra to help you, but you should still learn the graphs and the numerical examples because that is how economic forecasters and other economists communicate their ideas to others.

# SPENDING BALANCE AND DEPARTURES OF REAL GDP FROM POTENTIAL GDP

We have shown how to compute a level of real GDP for the purpose of making short-term forecasts. This level of real GDP is determined by aggregate demand—consumption, investment, government purchases, and net exports. It is not necessarily equal to potential GDP, which depends on the supply of labor, capital, and technology. Thus, we can have real GDP departing from potential GDP, as it does in recessions and booms. Let's see how.

## Stepping Away from Potential GDP

Figure 11.11 illustrates how the first steps of a boom or a recession can be explained by shifts in the aggregate expenditure line. The left panel of the figure shows three different aggregate expenditure lines. Each line corresponds to a different level of government purchases or a different level of net exports or investment. The right panel of Figure 11.11—which is much like Figure 11.2—shows real GDP and potential GDP during a three-year period. There is a close connection between the left and right panels of Figure 11.11. The vertical axes are identical, and the points *c*, *d*, and *e* represent the same level of spending in both panels.

Observe how the three *AE* lines intersect the 45-degree line at three different levels of real GDP. Let us suppose that the middle *AE* line intersects the 45-degree line at a level of real GDP that is the same as potential GDP in year 3. This is point *c*. The other two *AE* lines generate the first step of a recession or a boom. The lower *AE* line represents a recession; real GDP at the intersection of this *AE* line and the

**FIGURE 11.11**

**Spending Balance and Departures of Real GDP from Potential GDP**
This figure shows how the levels of real GDP found through spending balance can explain the first steps of a recession or boom. The left panel shows spending balance for three *AE* curves; one (*c*) gives real GDP equal to potential GDP, a second (*e*) gives real GDP above potential GDP, and a third (*d*) gives real GDP below potential GDP. As shown in the right panel, two of these entail departures of real GDP from potential GDP.

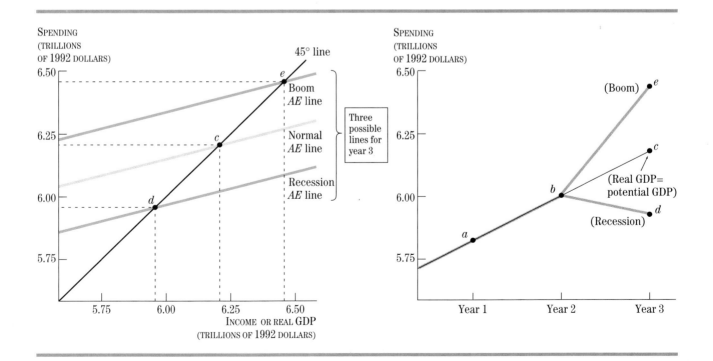

45-degree line (point *d*) is at a level below potential GDP and also below the level of real GDP in year 2. Thus, real GDP would decline from year 2 to year 3 with this aggregate expenditure line. On the other hand, the upper *AE* line corresponds to the first step of a boom. Real GDP at point *e* is above potential GDP in year 3.

By referring to these values of real GDP as the *first* steps of a boom or a recession, we are emphasizing that they are not the end of the story. We will see that there are forces in the economy that tend to bring real GDP back toward potential GDP. This calculation of real GDP gives only the short-run impact of changes in government spending, investment, net exports, or taxes.

### Starting Away from Potential GDP

Thus far we have shown how a shift in the *AE* line can bring the economy away from potential GDP when we start with real GDP equal to potential GDP. We could also have started our analysis with real GDP away from potential GDP.

For example, suppose that real GDP turns out to be below potential GDP in year 3 in Figure 11.11. If, in this situation, there is a further downward shift in the aggregate expenditure line, say because of a further decline in net exports, then real GDP could fall even further below potential GDP before there are sufficient forces to bring real GDP back toward potential. During the Great Depression in the 1930s, real GDP declined for several years in a row before starting to recover. Such successive declines could be explained by several successive shifts downward in the aggregate expenditure line.

Moreover, it is possible for the aggregate expenditure line in Figure 11.11 to shift back up from position *d* in year 3, say because of a change in government purchases, bringing real GDP back to potential GDP. For example, during World War II, government purchases increased for several successive years, and real GDP rose from below potential GDP to well above potential GDP during this period.

As these examples show, shifts in the aggregate expenditure line, for whatever reason, can explain many types of movements of real GDP around potential GDP.

## Review

▶ Shifts in the aggregate expenditure line can explain the departures of real GDP from potential GDP.

▶ When the aggregate expenditure line shifts down, real GDP declines, and, if it was previously equal to potential GDP, it will fall below potential GDP.

▶ Upward shifts in the aggregate expenditure line will bring real GDP above potential GDP.

▶ The aggregate expenditure line can shift for many reasons. Changes in taxes, government purchases, investment, and net exports will cause the *AE* line to shift.

## CONCLUSION

With this chapter we have begun to develop a theory of economic fluctuations. We have shown how economists explain departures of real GDP from potential GDP using the idea that these fluctuations are due to changes in aggregate demand. We used this explanation to make short-term forecasts of real GDP. The aggregate expenditure line—showing how the demand for consumption, investment, and net exports depends on income—and the 45-degree line are key parts of the forecasting process. However, our analysis thus far has made several simplifying assumptions. For example, the only thing people's consumption decisions respond to is a change in income.

In later chapters we show that consumption as well as investment and net exports respond to interest rates and inflation. The responses to interest rates and inflation will explain why real GDP returns to potential GDP in the long run.

# KEY POINTS

**1.** Economic fluctuations are temporary *deviations* of real GDP from potential GDP.

**2.** Employment and unemployment fluctuate with real GDP. Unemployment increases in recessions and decreases in booms.

**3.** The fluctuations in real GDP and potential GDP are mainly due to fluctuations in aggregate demand. Limited information and implicit contracts give a theoretical rationale for this fact, which appears to be an obvious feature of economic fluctuations when we look at individual firms and workers.

**4.** The idea that fluctuations in real GDP are mainly due to aggregate demand is used to find real GDP when making a short-term forecast.

**5.** Real GDP can be predicted on the basis of forecasts of consumption, investment, net exports, and government purchases. But these items depend on income and, thus, on the forecast of real GDP itself.

**6.** The consumption function describes how consumption responds to income.

**7.** The aggregate expenditure line is built up from the consumption function.

**8.** The 45-degree line tells us that expenditures equal income.

**9.** Combining the aggregate expenditure line and the 45-degree line in a diagram enables us to determine the level of income or real GDP.

**10.** The level of real GDP that gives spending balance changes when government spending changes. Real GDP will decline in the short run when government purchases are cut.

# KEY TERMS

| | | |
|---|---|---|
| limited information | real business cycle theory | aggregate income |
| implicit contract | forecast | disposable income |
| nominal rigidities | conditional forecast | 45-degree line |
| sticky price assumption | consumption function | aggregate expenditure line |
| flexible price assumption | marginal propensity to consume  (MPC) | spending balance |

# QUESTIONS FOR REVIEW

**1.** Why do theories of economic fluctuations focus on aggregate demand rather than potential GDP as the main source of the short-run economic fluctuations?

**2.** Why do theories of economic growth focus on potential GDP (with its three determinants) rather than aggregate demand as the main source of economic growth?

**3.** What is the role of implicit contracts in explaining why prices and wages are sticky?

**4.** Why does the unemployment rate rise above the natural unemployment rate when real GDP falls below potential GDP?

**5.** What is the normal rate of capacity utilization in manu-

facturing firms? What is the significance of this normal rate for explaining economic fluctuations?

**6.** What is a conditional forecast?

**7.** What accounting identity does the 45-degree line represent?

**8.** Why does the aggregate expenditure line have a slope less than 1?

**9.** Why do economic forecasters have to take into account the consumption function?

**10.** Why is real GDP given by the intersection of the 45-degree line and the aggregate expenditure line?

# PROBLEMS

**1.** Sketch a diagram with a 45-degree line and an aggregate expenditure line that describes macroeconomic spending balance. What factors determine how steep the aggregate expenditure line is? What macroeconomic relationship is described by the 45-degree line? Show on the diagram what will happen to the level of income if there is a rise in government purchases. Does U.S. income increase by more or by less than the upward shift in government purchases? Explain.

**2.** Describe what happens to the aggregate expenditure line in each of the following cases:

a) Government spending on highways rises.

b) The Chinese decide to spend $10 billion on aircraft built in the United States.

c) Firms become very pessimistic about the future.

d) A law is enacted requiring that the government pay $10,000 to anyone who builds a new house.

**3.** The following table shows the relationship between income and consumption in an economy.

| Income ($Y$) (in billions of dollars) | Consumption ($C$) (in billions of dollars) |
|---|---|
| 0 | 1,000 |
| 1,000 | 1,500 |
| 2,000 | 2,000 |
| 3,000 | 2,500 |
| 4,000 | 3,000 |
| 5,000 | 3,500 |
| 6,000 | 4,000 |
| 7,000 | 4,500 |

Assume that investment ($I$) is $500 billion, government purchases ($G$) are $300 billion, and net exports ($X$) are $200 billion.

a) What is the numerical value of the marginal propensity to consume?

b) Construct a table analogous to Table 11.2 for this economy. What is the level of income that gives spending balance in the economy?

c) For this level of income, calculate the level of national saving. Is national saving equal to investment plus net exports?

d) Sketch a diagram with a 45-degree line and an aggregate expenditure curve that describes the preceding relationships. Show graphically what happens to income when the government raises taxes.

**4.** Suppose government purchases will increase by $100 billion, and a forecasting firm predicts that real GDP will rise in the short run by $100 billion as a result. Would you say that forecast is accurate? Why? If you were running a business and subscribe to that forecasting service, what questions would you ask about the forecast?

**5.** Suppose that business executives are very optimistic, and they raise their investment spending. What happens to the $AE$ line? How will this affect real GDP? Sketch a diagram to demonstrate your answer.

**6.** Suppose that American goods suddenly become unpopular in Europe. What happens to net exports? How will this shift the $AE$ line? What happens to real GDP? Demonstrate this in a diagram.

**7.** Why are sticky prices important in explaining why changes in aggregate demand bring about large changes in production and real GDP? If firms have perfect (exact) information about whether changes in the demand for their products are temporary or permanent, will this increase or decrease the stickiness of prices? If all firms had perfect information, would there still be wide fluctuations of real GDP around potential GDP?

**8.** Suppose the information in the following table describes the economic situation in the United States at the end of 2004:

| Year | Real GDP (billions of 2004 dollars) | Potential GDP (billions of 2004 dollars) |
|---|---|---|
| 2002 | 9,613 | 9,613 |
| 2003 | 9,854 | 9,854 |
| 2004 | 10,100 | 10,100 |
| 2005 (optimistic forecast) | 10,600 | 10,353 |
| 2005 (pessimistic forecast) | 9,900 | 10,353 |

a) Graph real GDP over time, placing the year on the horizontal axis. Calculate the growth rate of real GDP between 2003 and 2004.

b) The optimistic forecast for the year 2005 is based on the possibility that businesses are optimistic about the economy. What will the growth rate of real GDP be if the optimistic forecast turns out to be true?

c) The pessimistic forecast is based on the possibility that businesses will be pessimistic about the economy. What will the growth rate of real GDP be if this forecast is correct?

d) What is the deviation (in terms of dollars and as a percentage) of real GDP from potential GDP in 2005 if the optimistic forecast is correct? What is the deviation (in terms of dollars and as a percentage) from potential GDP in 2005 if the pessimistic forecast is correct?

**9.** Given the following consumption function stated in algebraic form, calculate real GDP ($Y$) that results in spending balance in the economy:

$C = 100 + .5\,(Y - T)$
$I = 200$
$G = 200$
$X = 100$
$T = 200$

a) Suppose you find out that government purchases will increase to 300 next year. What is your forecast of real GDP for next year? Which way did the $AE$ line shift?
b) Suppose businesses are pessimistic about how the economy will do next year. They decide to decrease their spending on plant and equipment by 100. How will this shift the $AE$ line and by how much? What is the new level of real GDP?
c) Now suppose that the marginal propensity to consume is .6 instead of .5. How does this affect the level of real GDP at spending balance? Why?
d) Explain what happens when the government decides to increase taxes by $50 per person. Which way does the

$AE$ line shift? Why? How does this affect real GDP in the economy?
e) Suppose the government decides to increase taxes and government purchases by the same amount, that is, $T$ and $G$ both rise to 300. Calculate the new equilibrium $Y$ and compare it to the original equilibrium with $G = T = 200$. Why did $Y$ go up when both $T$ and $G$ rose by the same amount?

**10.** This problem incorporates taxes into the algebraic model described in the box "Forecasting with Econometric Models." Let the consumption function be given by

$C = 1 + .6(Y - T)$

where $T$ is taxes. Suppose $I + G + X = 3$. Everything is measured in trillions of dollars.

a) Find real GDP ($Y$) when $T = 1$.
b) Now increase $T$ to 1.2. What happens to $Y$ compared to part (a)?
c) Now decrease $T$ to .8. What happens to $Y$ compared to part (a)?
d) Using these results, explain how changes in taxes would affect one's short-term forecast of real GDP.

Potential GDP ⇨

⇦ Real GDP

# The Uncertain Multiplier — *Производитель*

How much does real GDP change in the short run when government purchases change, when taxes change, or when foreigners' demands for U.S. products change? Economists measure this change with the multiplier—the ratio of the change in real GDP to whatever is causing real GDP to change. If the economists at a forecasting firm report that the multiplier for a change in government purchases, for example, is 2, they mean that real GDP will change in the short run by twice as much as the change in government purchases. Another way to ask the opening question, then, is: How large is the multiplier?

We ended the last chapter with a partial answer when we showed that real GDP will depart from potential GDP in the short run when there is a change in government purchases. We showed that if consumption is positively related to income and if net exports are unrelated to income, then real GDP changes by more than the change in government purchases. In other words, the multiplier—in this case, the ratio of the change in real GDP to the change in government purchases—is greater than 1. In particular, we showed that a cut in government purchases of $100 billion would lead to a reduction in real GDP in the short run of more than $100 billion.

But there is considerable uncertainty about the exact size of the multiplier. DRI, a major forecasting firm, has put the multiplier for a change in government purchases in the United States at 2.1, meaning that a decrease in government purchases of $100 billion would decrease real GDP by $210 billion in the short run. Economists at the Federal Reserve Board put the multiplier at 1.7. The staff of the International Monetary Fund puts it at 1.2. Different assumptions about people's consumption behavior can lead to an even wider range of estimates of the size of the multiplier.

In this chapter we show how to measure the multiplier and we assess factors that affect its size. That the size of the multiplier is uncertain does not render it useless, and finding out why it is uncertain is far better than ignoring the multiplier. One way or another the multiplier must be taken into account in analyzing short-run fluctuations in real GDP, employment, and unemployment. Cuts in military purchases or a new federal program for construction of roads and bridges will have effects on the entire economy. Are the military cuts large enough to lead to a recession? Will the new construction program add too much to a booming economy? Assuming that such changes in government programs are good in the long run, how could we mitigate any adverse short-run effects on the economy?

For example, a decline in defense spending, made possible by the end of the cold war around 1989, was partly responsible for the slowdown in the U.S. economy in the early 1990s and is frequently mentioned as one of the possible causes of the recession that began in 1990. There was also a tax increase in 1990, aimed at reducing the U.S. budget deficit. Could the multiplier from this tax increase have been large enough to have caused the recession or made it worse? Should the tax increase have been delayed because of the recession? Or should the cuts in military spending have been delayed? To make judgments about when and by how much to change government programs, policymakers need to consider the short-run impact of changes in government purchases and taxes on real GDP. In other words, they need to consider the size of the multiplier.

# HOW TO FIND THE MULTIPLIER

We first show how to use graphs to find the multiplier. We make use of the 45-degree line and the aggregate expenditure line introduced in the previous chapter. We then derive the multiplier algebraically. Last, but not least, we describe in words how the multiplier actually works its way through the economy.

## A Graphical Derivation of the Multiplier

Figure 12.1 is a diagram like the one derived in the previous chapter with income or real GDP on the horizontal axis and spending on the vertical axis. The 45-degree line equates spending and income. There are two aggregate expenditure (*AE*) lines in Figure 12.1. Both *AE* lines show that aggregate expenditure in the economy—the sum of consumption plus investment plus government purchases plus net exports, or $C + I + G + X$—rises with income. Aggregate expenditure rises with income because consumption rises with income, according to the consumption function. We assume that the marginal propensity to consume is equal to .6. Thus, the slope of both aggregate expenditure lines is .6 in Figure 12.1.

### The Multiplier for a General Shift in the Aggregate Expenditure Line

Observe that one aggregate expenditure line is labeled "old" and the other is labeled "new." Our objective is to analyze the impact on real GDP of a shift in the aggregate expenditure line, that is, a shift from the "old" *AE* line to the "new" *AE* line. The upward-pointing black arrow shows the size of the shift in the aggregate expenditure line. Such a shift can occur because of a change in government purchases, a change in taxes, a change in investment, or a change in net exports.

Note that the "new" aggregate expenditure line intersects the 45-degree line at a different point of spending balance than the "old" aggregate expenditure line. At this new point of spending balance, the level of income, or real GDP, is higher than at the old point of spending balance. On the horizontal axis the black arrow pointing to the right shows this shift to a higher level of real GDP. Look carefully at the

**FIGURE 12.1**
**Graphical Calculation of the**
**Multiplier**
An upward shift in the *AE* line
raises real GDP in the short run by
a multiple of the shift in the *AE*
line. The multiplier can be found
graphically. It is the ratio of the
length of the black horizontal arrow
to the length of the black vertical
arrow.

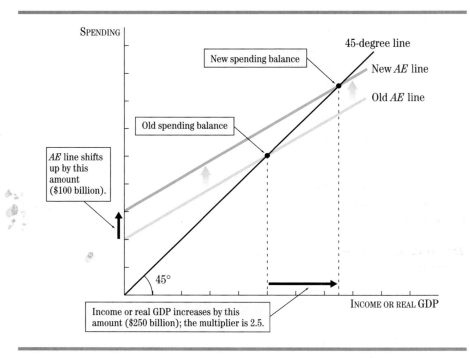

diagram to note the *size* of the change in real GDP along the horizontal axis and
compare it with the change in the aggregate expenditure line. Observe that the horizontal change is *larger* than the vertical change. This is due to the multiplier. In
fact, the term *multiplier* is used because the change in real GDP is a multiple of the
shift in the aggregate expenditure line.

**multiplier:** the ratio of the change
in real GDP to the shift in the aggregate expenditure line.

   In general, we define the **multiplier** as the ratio of the change in real GDP to
the shift in the aggregate expenditure line, regardless of the reason for the shift in
the aggregate expenditure line (whether it is due to a change in government purchases, a change in taxes, a change in investment, or a change in foreign demand).
That is, by definition,

$$\text{Multiplier} = \frac{\text{change in real GDP}}{\text{shift in the aggregate expenditure line}}$$

The multiplier is equal to the ratio of the length of the arrow along the horizontal
axis to the length of the arrow along the vertical axis in Figure 12.1. You can calculate the multiplier by measuring these lengths. Observe that for the aggregate
expenditure line with a slope of .6 drawn in Figure 12.1, the multiplier is 2.5.

   Note that the multiplier is greater than 1 in this example. Draw your own version of Figure 12.1 in order to convince yourself that as long as the aggregate
expenditure line is upward-sloping with a slope less than 1 (so that it is less steep
than the 45-degree line), the multiplier is greater than 1. The multiplier expresses a
key finding: A shift in the aggregate expenditure line results in a change in real
GDP in the economy greater than the shift in the aggregate expenditure line.

### Specific Cases of the Multiplier

The multiplier applies to anything that shifts the aggregate expenditure line. One
example is an increase in government purchases. An increase in government pur-

chases by $100 billion would shift the *AE* line up by $100 billion. This would increase real GDP by $250 billion if the multiplier for government purchases is 2.5. Another example would be a decrease in government purchases, which would shift the *AE* line down by the amount of the government purchases decrease. Thus, a $100 billion cut in government purchases would reduce real GDP by $250 billion in the short run if the multiplier is 2.5.

Another example is an increase in investment, which shifts the *AE* line. If there is a $20 billion increase in investment in new homes because of a new tax credit for first-time homebuyers, then the *AE* line will shift up by $20 billion, and real GDP rises by $50 billion if the multiplier is 2.5. Similarly, an increase in foreign demand for U.S. products shifts up the aggregate expenditure line.

The aggregate expenditure line will shift down if there is a drop in consumer confidence that leads people to consume less regardless of their income. This is called an *autonomous* change in consumption because it is independent of income. The *AE* line shifts down by the amount of the autonomous decline in consumption. The effect on real GDP is the multiplier times the shift in the *AE* line. Finally, there is the effect of income tax changes, a subject we take up later in the chapter.

## An Algebraic Derivation of the Multiplier

The multiplier also can be computed directly without using a diagram. To demonstrate this, let us focus again on a case where the MPC is .6. To be specific, we suppose that the particular reason for a change in the aggregate expenditure line is an increase in government purchases. Then the multiplier is the ratio of the change in real GDP to the change in government purchases. We already showed graphically that the multiplier was 2.5 when the MPC was .6. How do we get 2.5 with algebra? We need to consider the algebra that corresponds to the lines in the graphs.

As you know, the identity that income or real GDP ($Y$) equals consumption ($C$) plus investment ($I$) plus government purchases ($G$) plus net exports ($X$) can be written algebraically as

$$Y = C + I + G + X$$

To find the multiplier, we want to determine the impact of a *change* in government purchases on real GDP. That is, we want to find the change in $Y$ that occurs when $G$ changes. Any change in $Y$ must come either directly from a change in $G$ or indirectly from a change in $C$, $I$, or $X$, according to the preceding identity. Denote the change in any of these items by the Greek letter $\Delta$. Then we can write the identity in terms of changes:

$$\Delta Y = \Delta C + \Delta I + \Delta G + \Delta X$$

That is, the *change* in real GDP is equal to the *change* in consumption plus the *change* in investment plus the *change* in government purchases plus the *change* in net exports. Now consider each of the four terms on the right.

The change in government purchases ($\Delta G$) equals $100 billion. For convenience, to make things simple, we continue to assume that there is no change in investment or in net exports. In other words, we assume that neither responds to changes in income. Expressed in symbols, $\Delta I = 0$ and $\Delta X = 0$.

On the other hand, we have assumed a consumption function that tells us how much consumption changes when income changes. The consumption function we use for the algebraic calculation has an MPC of .6. Using algebra, we write $\Delta C = .6\Delta Y$. That is, the change in consumption equals .6 times the change in income; for example, if the change in income $\Delta Y = \$10$ billion, then the change in consumption $\Delta C = \$6$ billion if the MPC is .6.

Now let us take our ingredients:

1. $\Delta Y = \Delta C + \Delta I + \Delta G + \Delta X.$

2. The changes in investment and net exports are zero ($\Delta I = \Delta X = 0$).

3. The change in consumption is .6 times the change in income ($\Delta C = .6\Delta Y$).

Replacing $\Delta I$ with zero and $\Delta X$ with zero removes $\Delta I$ and $\Delta X$ from the right-hand side of the identity. Replacing $\Delta C$ with $.6\Delta Y$ in the same identity results in

$$\Delta Y = .6\Delta Y + \Delta G$$

Note that the term $\Delta Y$ appears on both sides of this equation. Gathering terms in $\Delta Y$ on the left-hand side of the equation gives

$$(1 - .6)\Delta Y = \Delta G$$

Dividing both sides by $\Delta G$ and by $(1 - .6)$ results in

$$\Delta Y/\Delta G = 1/(1 - .6)$$
$$= 1/.4$$
$$= 2.5$$

Thus, the change in income, or real GDP, that occurs when government purchases change, according to this calculation, is 2.5 times the change in government purchases. That is, $\Delta Y = 2.5\Delta G$. The number—2.5—is the multiplier. The calculations are summarized in Table 12.1. The algebraic calculation agrees with the graphical

---

**TABLE 12.1**

**Derivation of the Multiplier for MPC = .6**

The identity,

$$Y = C + I + G + X$$

when written in terms of changes, becomes

$$\Delta Y = \Delta C + \Delta I + \Delta G + \Delta X$$

We assume investment does not change,

$$\Delta I = 0$$

that net exports do not change either,

$$\Delta X = 0$$

and that consumption changes according to the equation

$$\Delta C = .6\Delta Y$$

Substituting $\Delta I$, $\Delta X$, and $\Delta C$ into the expression for $\Delta Y$ gives

$$\Delta Y = .6\Delta Y + \Delta G$$

Solving for $\Delta Y$ gives

$$\frac{\Delta Y}{\Delta G} = \frac{1}{1 - .6} = 2.5 \quad \text{(the multiplier)}$$

calculation. The $100 billion increase in government purchases is translated into a $250 billion increase in real GDP.

You can perform this same calculation for *any value* of the marginal propensity to consume (MPC), not just .6. To see this, again we focus on finding the change in income, or real GDP, associated with a change in government purchases. Assume that the change in investment and the change in net exports equal zero. The change in consumption equals the MPC times the change in income, where the MPC is any number. Using the same approach as in the case of MPC = .6 we find that the multiplier is

$$\frac{\Delta Y}{\Delta G} = \frac{1}{(1 - MPC)} \quad \text{(the multiplier)}$$

The algebraic derivation of the multiplier with a general value for the MPC is shown in Table 12.2; the derivation is similar to the case of MPC = .6.

An alternative algebraic way to write the multiplier uses the concept of the **marginal propensity to save (MPS).** The marginal propensity to save for a person is the additional amount that person saves when the person's income rises. Since an individual must either consume or save any additional income, the marginal propensity to consume (MPC) plus the marginal propensity to save (MPS) must equal 1. Thus, the MPS equals 1 − MPC. For example, if income increases by $100 and the MPC is .6, then consumption increases by $60 and saving must increase by $40. The MPS is .4.

The MPS can also be defined for the economy as a whole. Saving for the whole economy is defined as income (Y) minus consumption (C). Any increase in income that does not go to consumption must go to saving; as with an individual,

**marginal propensity to save (MPS):** the change in saving due to a given change in income; MPS = 1 − marginal propensity to consume (MPC).

---

Start with the identity

$$Y = C + I + G + X$$

and convert it to change form

$$\Delta Y = \Delta C + \Delta I + \Delta G + \Delta X$$

Substitute $\Delta I = 0$ and $\Delta X = 0$ and

$$\Delta C = MPC \times \Delta Y$$

into the change form of the identity to get

$$\Delta Y = MPC \times \Delta Y + \Delta G$$

Gather terms involving $\Delta Y$ to get

$$(1 - MPC) \times \Delta Y = \Delta G$$

Divide both sides by $\Delta G$ and by $1 - MPC$ to get

$$\frac{\Delta Y}{\Delta G} = \frac{1}{1 - MPC} \quad \text{(the multiplier)}$$

**TABLE 12.2**
**Derivation of the Multiplier for Any MPC**

MPC + MPS = 1 for the whole economy. Thus, we can replace 1 − MPC with MPS in the preceding expression for the multiplier. Doing so, we get

$$\frac{\Delta Y}{\Delta G} = \frac{1}{MPS}$$

Thus, the multiplier is equal to the inverse of the marginal propensity to save.

## Following the Multiplier Through the Economy

A third method to find the multiplier is to examine what happens when a change in government purchases winds its way through the economy. Such an economic narrative demonstrates how the multiplier works.

Assume that the government increases its military purchases, as it did in the early 1980s in the United States when President Reagan increased defense spending. In this example, the government increases purchases of jets and aircraft carriers. The immediate impact of the change in government purchases is an increase in production of jets and aircraft carriers. With an increase in demand, areospace and shipbuilding firms produce more, and real GDP rises. The initial increase in real GDP from an increase in government purchases of $100 billion is that same $100 billion. If the government is purchasing more jets, the production of jets increases. We call this initial increase in real GDP the *first-round* effect, which includes only the initial change in government purchases.

The first round is not the end of the story. A further increase in real GDP occurs when the workers employed in making the aircraft carriers and jets start working more hours and new workers are hired. As a result, the wage income workers get paid rises, and the profits made by the manufacturers increase. With both wage income and profit income rising, income in the economy as a whole rises by $100 billion. According to the consumption function, people will consume more. How much more? The consumption function tells us that .6 times the change in income, or $60 billion, will be the additional increase in consumption by the workers and owners of the defense firms. Real GDP rises by $60 billion, the increased production of the goods the workers and owners consume. This $60 billion increase in real GDP is the *second-round* effect. It is hard for anyone to know what the workers in the defense industry or the owners of the defense firms will start purchasing, but presumably it would be an array of goods: clothes, VCRs, movies, and restaurant meals. But with an MPC of .6, we do know they will purchase $60 billion more of these goods. The increase in production spreads throughout the economy. After this second round, real GDP has increased by $160 billion, the sum of $100 billion on the first round and $60 billion on the second round. This is shown in the first and second rows of Table 12.3.

The story continues. The workers who make the clothes, VCRs, and other goods and services for which there is $60 billion more in spending also have an increase in their income. Either they are no longer unemployed or they work more hours. Similarly, the profits of the owners of those firms increase. As a result, they consume more. How much more? According to the consumption function, .6 times the increase in their income. The increase in income outside of military production was $60 billion, so the increase in consumption must now be .6 times that, or a $36 billion increase. This increase is the *third-round* effect. As the increase permeates the economy, it is impossible to say what particular goods will increase in production, but we know that total production continues to increase. After three rounds, real GDP has increased by $196 billion, as shown in the third row of Table 12.3.

# The Origins of the Multiplier

John Maynard Keynes credited the idea of the multiplier to another British economist, R. F. Kahn. Kahn focused on the change in employment that would accompany a change in real GDP in a 1931 paper on the multiplier. Interestingly, Kahn's description of the multiplier began with a situation where real GDP is near potential GDP. In such a situation, Kahn wrote, "If investment increases, the production of consumption-goods must diminish by an equal amount."

But Kahn, like Keynes, did not write in times when real GDP was equal to potential GDP. He wrote during the Great Depression, a case of a departure from potential GDP. Under such conditions, he argued,

". . . for each man placed in primary employment, the number who receive secondary employment is $k + k^2 + k^3 + k^4 + \ldots = k/(1 - k)$."

For Kahn, $k$ was analogous to the marginal propensity to consume. By primary employment (of 1 man) he meant the first round of the multiplier process as described in this textbook; by secondary employment [of $k/(1 - k)$ men] he meant all the other rounds. Thus,

the value of Kahn's multiplier is $1 + k/(1 - k)$, which can be shown to equal $1/(1 - k)$, exactly the formula for the multiplier used in this chapter. But where does the long series involving $k$, $k^2$, $k^3$, and so on, which Kahn used to find the multiplier, come from?

Kahn observed that the impact on employment of successive rounds of the multiplier is like the terms in a geometric sum. A geometric sum, you may recall from your math courses, is a sum of terms each of which converges geometrically to zero. The terms in the sum are 1, $k$, $k^2$, $k^3$, $k^4$, $k^5$, and so on, where $k$ is less than 1. For example, if $k = .6$, the value of the MPC in the examples in the text, then the terms are 1, .6, .36, .216, .1296, .07776, and so on. Compare these terms with those in the second column of Table 12.3. Each shows the amount of the change in real GDP on each round of the multiplier. The geometric sum adds up all these rounds and gives the value of the multiplier.

*Source of quote:* R. F. Kahn, "The Relation of Home Investment to Unemployment," *Economic Journal*, June 1931.

---

The increase does not stop there. Another $36 billion more in consumption means that there is $36 billion more in income for people somewhere in the economy. This increases consumption further, by .6 times the $36 billion, or $21.6 billion. According to the column on the right of Table 12.3, the cumulative effect on real GDP is now up to $217.6 billion after four rounds. Observe how each new entry in the first column is added to the previous total to get the cumulative effect on real GDP.

| Round | Change in Real GDP | Cumulative Change in Real GDP |
|---|---|---|
| First round | 100.000 | 100.000 |
| Second round | 60.000 | 160.000 |
| Third round | 36.000 | 196.000 |
| Fourth round | 21.600 | 217.600 |
| Fifth round | 12.960 | 230.560 |
| . | . | . |
| . | . | . |
| . | . | . |
| After an infinite number of rounds | 0.000 | 250.000 |

**TABLE 12.3**
**A Numerical Illustration of the Multiplier Process**
(billions of dollars)

The story is now getting repetitive. We multiply .6 times $21.6 billion to get $12.96 billion. The total effect on real GDP is now $230.56 billion at the fifth round. In fact, we are already almost at $250 billion. If we kept on going for more and more rounds, we would get closer and closer to the $250 billion amount obtained from the algebra and graphs.

Hence, tracing out each round in the multiplier process gives the same answer as the other two approaches to finding the multiplier. It also shows why the multiplier is greater than 1. The repetitive flow of spending and income spreads throughout the economy, multiplying the initial increase in government purchases into increased spending and income for many others in the economy. Figure 12.2 gives a

**FIGURE 12.2**
**The Rounds of the Multiplier Process**

The height of each bar shows the cumulative impact on real GDP for each round of the multiplier. The dark part of each bar shows what is added to real GDP in each round. The top panel shows the rounds of spending when the marginal propensity to consume is .6, as in Table 12.3. The bottom panel shows the rounds of spending for a smaller MPC, equal to .4. In both cases, government purchases rise by $100 billion.

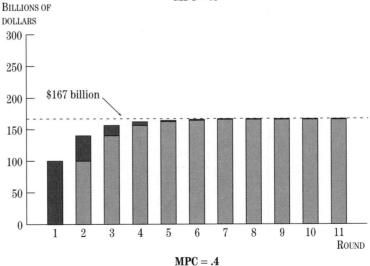

more visual perspective on the rounds of the multiplier. It shows in the bar chart in the top panel the same data presented in Table 12.3.

The successive rounds of the multiplier also occur when there is a decrease in government spending. Then the entries in Table 12.3 would decrease rather than increase. To test yourself, try following the multiplier through the economy after a *decrease* in military purchases of $100 billion.

In reality all the rounds of the multiplier occur very rapidly—getting close to the full value of the multiplier within a year or so. Thus, in looking at these rounds we are still considering what happens to real GDP in the short run, during the first step of real GDP away from potential GDP. Starting from a situation where real GDP equals potential GDP, an increase in military spending would raise real GDP above potential, and a decrease in military spending would lower real GDP below potential. In either case the multiplier tells us how large the change in real GDP will be.

## Review

▶ The multiplier is defined as the ratio of the change in real GDP to a shift in the aggregate expenditure line. In the case where the aggregate expenditure line shifts because of a change in government purchases, the multiplier is equal to the change in real GDP divided by the change in government purchases.

▶ The multiplier can be found using graphical methods, algebraic methods, or by summing up the rounds of the multiplier process. All three methods give the same answer, but each illustrates different aspects of the multiplier.

▶ After only a few rounds of the multiplier process, the final value of the multiplier is nearly reached.

# THE SIZE OF THE MULTIPLIER

What determines the size of the multiplier? Our graphical calculation of the multiplier indicates that the answer to this question can be found in the aggregate expenditure line, because the multiplier was derived from this line.

### The Multiplier and the Slope of the *AE* line

The left and right panels of Figure 12.3 show two different calculations of the multiplier. The calculations differ only in the slope of the aggregate expenditure line. The size of the upward shift in the aggregate expenditure lines is exactly the same in the two panels, but the left panel has aggregate expenditure lines that are relatively steep, while the right panel has aggregate expenditure lines that are relatively flat.

Observe the difference in the multiplier in the two panels. The shift in the *AE* line is the same in both graphs, but the increase in real GDP in the left panel is larger than the increase in real GDP in the right panel. Therefore, the multiplier is larger in the left panel. In the left panel the multiplier is 2.5. In the right panel it is 1.3.

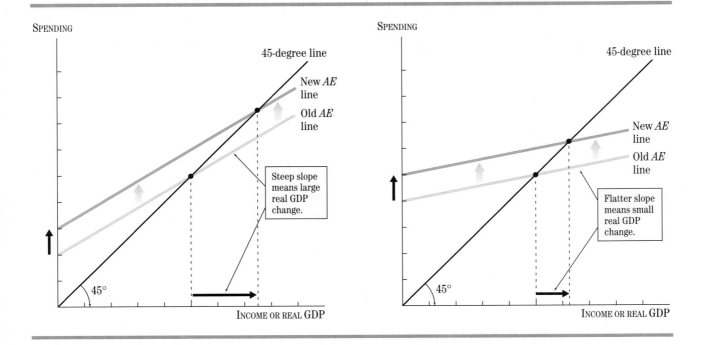

**FIGURE 12.3**
**The Multiplier and the Slope of the *AE* Line**

In the left panel the *AE* line is relatively steep. In the right panel the *AE* line is relatively flat. Observe that the multiplier is much larger in the left panel than in the right panel.

Figure 12.3 demonstrates that the multiplier is positively related to the slope of the aggregate expenditure line. Draw your own graphs with varying slopes of the aggregate expenditure line to convince yourself that the size of the multiplier depends on the slope of the *AE* line. The steeper the *AE* line, the larger the multiplier. The flatter the *AE* line, the smaller the multiplier.

## The Multiplier and the Marginal Propensity to Consume

The slope of the *AE* line is equal to the marginal propensity to consume. Thus, one interpretation of the relatively steep *AE* line in the left panel of Figure 12.3 is that the marginal propensity to consume is high compared to the marginal propensity to consume in the right panel. This implies that a relatively large marginal propensity to consume leads to a relatively large multiplier.

The formula for the multiplier that was derived earlier—showing that the multiplier is related to the marginal propensity to consume—confirms this. In particular, the size of the multiplier equals $1/(1 - MPC)$. For example, if the MPC is .6, then the multiplier is 2.5. If the MPC is .4, then the multiplier is $1/(1 - .4)$, or about 1.7. Lowering the MPC from .6 to .4 lowers the multiplier from 2.5 to 1.7. Therefore, if the MPC is lower, the multiplier is lower. And if the MPC is higher, the multiplier is higher. Thus, the algebra confirms the result that is illustrated graphically in Figure 12.3.

Is there any economic intuition behind the relationship between the multiplier and the marginal propensity to consume? Recall that in examining the rounds of the multiplier through the economy we found that the size of the second, third, and each subsequent round depended on the marginal propensity to consume. If the marginal propensity to consume is larger, then the increase in income from the first

# John Maynard Keynes, 1883–1946

**BORN:**
Cambridge, England, 1883

**EDUCATION:**
Cambridge University, graduated 1906

**JOBS:**
India Office, London, 1906–1909
Cambridge University, 1909–1915
British Treasury, 1915–1919
Cambridge University, 1919–1946

**MAJOR PUBLICATIONS:**
*The Economic Consequences of the Peace,* 1919; *A Tract on Monetary Reform,* 1923; *A Treatise on Money,* 1930; *The General Theory of Employment, Interest and Money,* 1936

John Maynard Keynes—the inventor of the marginal propensity to consume and of the broader idea that a decline in aggregate demand could bring the economy below its potential—was one of the greatest economists of all time, of similar stature to Adam Smith, David Ricardo, and Alfred Marshall. Keynes put forth the marginal propensity to consume and the multiplier in *The General Theory of Employment, Interest and Money*. Written in the midst of the Great Depression, it provided an explanation for a worldwide tragedy that prevailing economic theory—with its microeconomic emphasis, as represented by Marshall's *Principles of Economics*—hardly addressed. Keynes's ideas spread rapidly and had a lasting influence; referring to them as the "Keynesian revolution" is no exaggeration. Many elements of Keynes's theory are contained in this and the previous chapter of this text.

Much of the *General Theory* is difficult to read. As Keynes put it, "This book is chiefly addressed to my fellow economists." But Keynes's well-developed writing skills emerge in some of the less technical passages, especially those on speculation and expectations in financial markets.

The *General Theory* is a highly theoretical book with very little data. In fact, until Keynes demonstrated the importance of aggregate demand very little data were available on aggregate income, consumption, or investment. But Keynes did give factual evidence about the marginal propensity to consume and the multiplier. He recognized that existing aggregate data for Britain were not sufficiently accurate to estimate the marginal propensity to consume, so he provided estimates for the United States using preliminary data that were soon to be published for the first time by Simon Kuznets of Harvard University. Keynes writes:

*At present, however, our statistics are not accurate enough. . . . The best for the purpose, of which I am aware, are*

*Mr. Kuznets' figures for the United States . . . , though they are, nevertheless, very precarious. . . . If single years are taken in isolation, the results look rather wild. But if they are grouped in pairs, the multiplier seems to have been less than 3 and probably fairly stable in the neighbourhood of 2.5. This suggests a marginal propensity to consume not exceeding 60 to 70 per cent. . . .*

Note that Keynes's estimates of the MPC are very close to the example used in this chapter.

The *General Theory* was not Keynes's only book. Keynes gained notoriety in his thirties for a best-selling book called *The Economic Consequences of the Peace,* written in only two months during the summer of 1919. As an economic adviser to the British government, Keynes accompanied the prime minister to the Versailles Peace Conference in 1919 at the end of World War I. It was at that peace conference that the victors demanded heavy reparations from Germany, harming the German economy and thereby helping Hitler in his rise to power. In his 1919 book, Keynes predicted serious harm from the stiff reparations and ridiculed the heads of government at the conference, including his own prime minister, Lloyd George, and the American president Woodrow Wilson.

Keynes's *Tract on Monetary Reform* written in 1923 focused more on inflation than did the *General Theory*. Although Keynes has been criticized for not dealing with inflation in the *General Theory,* his earlier writings suggest that, if he had lived longer, he may have weighed in against the forces that led to the high inflation of the late 1960s and 1970s.

*Source of quote:* John Maynard Keynes, *The General Theory of Employment, Interest and Money,* first edition (1936), in *The Collected Writings of John Maynard Keynes,* Vol. VII (Cambridge: Cambridge University Press), pp. 154–155.

**TABLE 12.4**
**The MPC and the Multiplier**

| MPC | Multiplier $1/(1 - \text{MPC})$ |
|-----|-----------------|
| .25 | 1.33 |
| .30 | 1.42 |
| .35 | 1.54 |
| .40 | 1.67 |
| .45 | 1.82 |
| .50 | 2.00 |
| .55 | 2.22 |
| .60 | 2.50 |
| .65 | 2.86 |
| .70 | 3.33 |
| .75 | 4.00 |
| .80 | 5.00 |
| .85 | 6.67 |
| .90 | 10.00 |
| .95 | 20.00 |

round generates a larger increase in consumption on the second round, and so on. If each successive round is larger, then the multiplier is larger, because the multiplier comes from summing up all the rounds. In order to visualize this concept, look back at the bar charts in the top and bottom panels of Figure 12.2. The top panel, which we already considered, has an MPC of .6; the bottom panel has an MPC of .4. They show that the marginal propensity to consume determines the size of the multiplier.

### Uncertainty about the Size of the Multiplier

If there is uncertainty about the slope of the *AE* line or about the size of the MPC, then there is also uncertainty about the size of the multiplier. In order to see why, consider Table 12.4, which contains several different values of the MPC and the multiplier.

Uncertainty about the MPC might be described by a *range* of different values of the MPC. For example, if policymakers were uncertain about the MPC, they might say it was *around* .6, perhaps between .4 or .8, rather than exactly .6. According to Table 12.4, if the MPC is .8 rather than .6, then the multiplier is twice as large—5 rather than 2.5. If the MPC is .4, then the multiplier is 1.7. In reality, uncertainty about the size of the MPC in a given situation is one of the key reasons the multiplier itself is uncertain.

## Review

▶ The size of the multiplier is positively related to the slope of the *AE* line. The steeper the *AE* line, the larger the multiplier.

▶ The size of the multiplier is also positively related

to the marginal propensity to consume (MPC). The higher the MPC, the higher the multiplier.

▶ Uncertainty about the size of the MPC is a key reason that the size of the multiplier is uncertain.

# A KEY INTERNATIONAL ISSUE: NET EXPORTS DEPEND ON INCOME

Thus far we have made the simplifying assumption that net exports do not respond to income. However, another influence on the size of the multiplier is the response of net exports to income; it is time to incorporate this response into our analysis.

### How Do Net Exports Depend on Income?

To understand how the responsiveness of net exports to income affects the multiplier, we first need to consider how net exports depend on income. Recall that net exports are exports minus imports. To examine the effect of income on net exports, we first look at exports and then at imports.

### Exports

Exports are goods and services we sell to other countries—aircraft, pharmaceuticals, telephones. Do U.S. exports depend on income in the United States? No, not much. If Americans earn a little more or a little less, the demand for U.S. exports is not going to increase or decrease. What is likely to make the demand for U.S. exports increase or decrease is a change in income abroad—changes in income in Japan, Europe, or Latin America will affect demand for U.S. exports. U.S. exports will not be affected even if the United States has a recession. Of course, if Japan or Europe has a recession, that is another story. In any case, we conclude that U.S. exports are unresponsive to the changes in U.S. income.

### Imports

Imports are goods and services people in the United States purchase from abroad—automobiles, sweaters, vacations. Does the amount purchased of these goods and services change when our incomes change? Yes, because imports are part of consumption. Just as we argued that consumption responds to income, so must imports respond to income. Higher income will lead to higher consumption of both goods purchased in the United States and goods purchased abroad. That reasoning leads us to hypothesize that imports are positively related to income. The hypothesis turns out to be accurate when we look at observations on income and imports.

> **marginal propensity to import (MPI):** the change in imports because of a given change in income.

Figure 12.4 illustrates how higher income leads to higher imports. For example, if the slope of the line in Figure 12.4 is .2, then a rise of income in the United States by $10 billion raises imports by $2 billion. The effect of a change in income on imports is analogous to the marginal propensity to consume. When the MPC is .6, an increase in income by $10 billion leads consumption to rise by $6 billion. We are saying now that imports rise by .2 times the increase in income.

The **marginal propensity to import (MPI)** is the amount that imports change when income changes. Thus, the MPI is .2 in this example. The MPI is smaller than the MPC because most of the goods we consume when income rises are not imported. The United States imports less when U.S. income goes down and imports more when income goes up, but the changes are smaller than the change in consumption. For example, in the 1990–1991 recession when income in the United States fell, U.S. imports of cars from Japan declined, just as the consumption of cars produced in the United States declined. However, imports declined by a smaller amount than consumption.

### Net Exports

If exports are unrelated to income and imports are positively related to income, then net exports—exports less imports—must be negatively related to income. A numerical example of income, exports, imports, and net exports in Table 12.5 shows why. Income is shown in the

**FIGURE 12.4**
**Relationship Between Imports and Income**
The higher income is, the more foreign goods people want to buy. Thus, imports depend positively on income. The slope of the relationship is called the marginal propensity to import (MPI).

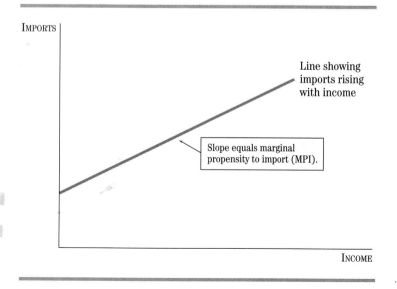

IMPORTS

Line showing imports rising with income

Slope equals marginal propensity to import (MPI).

INCOME

| Income | Exports | Imports | Net Exports |
|--------|---------|---------|-------------|
| 6,000 | 2,100 | 1,200 | 900 |
| 7,000 | 2,100 | 1,400 | 700 |
| 8,000 | 2,100 | 1,600 | 500 |
| 9,000 | 2,100 | 1,800 | 300 |
| 10,000 | 2,100 | 2,000 | 100 |
| 11,000 | 2,100 | 2,200 | −100 |
| 12,000 | 2,100 | 2,400 | −300 |
| 13,000 | 2,100 | 2,600 | −500 |
| 14,000 | 2,100 | 2,800 | −700 |

**TABLE 12.5**
**Net Exports and Income:**
**A Numerical Example**
(billions of dollars)

first column. Exports, in the second column, are assumed to be constant—$2,100 billion—or unresponsive to income. Imports, in the third column, rise with income with a marginal propensity to import of .2. Net exports, in the fourth column, are negatively related to income, simply because we subtract imports from exports to get net exports.

Note that net exports respond to income in the opposite direction as consumption. Consumption is positively related to income while net exports are negatively related to income. The amount by which net exports changes with income is the marginal propensity to import. Observe in the example that each $1,000 billion increase in income lowers net exports by $200 billion.

## The *AE* Line When Net Exports Depend on Income

How does this effect of income on net exports change our analysis? Table 12.6 shows how aggregate expenditure is determined when net exports depend on income. Net exports are shown in the far right column of the table. When net exports are added to consumption, investment, and government purchases, also shown in Table 12.6, we get aggregate expenditure. If you compare Table 12.6 with Table 11.2, you will see that aggregate expenditure rises less quickly with income. In Table 11.2 when net exports do not depend on income, aggregate expenditure increases by $600 billion for each $1,000 billion rise in income. In Table 12.6, aggregate expenditure rises by $400 billion for each $1,000 rise in income. Spending balance is achieved when real GDP is $10,000 billion.

**TABLE 12.6**
**Aggregate Expenditure When Net Exports Depend on Income**

| Income or Real GDP | Aggregate Expenditure | Consumption | Investment | Government Purchases | Net Exports |
|--------------------|-----------------------|-------------|------------|----------------------|-------------|
| 6,000 | 8,400 | 4,600 | 900 | 2,000 | 900 |
| 7,000 | 8,800 | 5,200 | 900 | 2,000 | 700 |
| 8,000 | 9,200 | 5,800 | 900 | 2,000 | 500 |
| 9,000 | 9,600 | 6,400 | 900 | 2,000 | 300 |
| 10,000 | 10,000 | 7,000 | 900 | 2,000 | 100 |
| 11,000 | 10,400 | 7,600 | 900 | 2,000 | −100 |
| 12,000 | 10,800 | 8,200 | 900 | 2,000 | −300 |
| 13,000 | 11,200 | 8,800 | 900 | 2,000 | −500 |
| 14,000 | 11,600 | 9,400 | 900 | 2,000 | −700 |

*Spending balance point* (handwritten annotation)

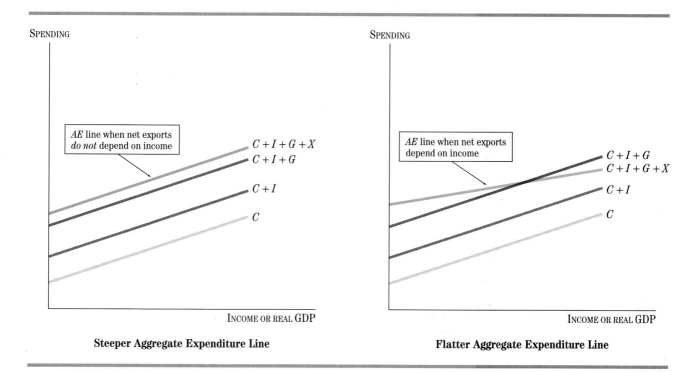

**Steeper Aggregate Expenditure Line**          **Flatter Aggregate Expenditure Line**

Figure 12.5 shows what happens graphically to the aggregate expenditure line when net exports depend on income. Compare the aggregate expenditure lines in both panels of Figure 12.5.

Note how the slope of the aggregate expenditure line is flatter when net exports depend on income. The reason is that the higher income, as shown in Table 12.6, results in the lower net exports. Recall that the aggregate expenditure line is built by adding up consumption, investment, government purchases, and net exports. Whereas investment and government purchases are still assumed to be unresponsive to income, net exports now depend on income. Thus, the higher income is, the less $X$ there is to add to $C + I + G$. In fact, as income gets very high, $X$ becomes negative, as shown in Table 12.5, so we must subtract dollars from $C + I + G$.

### Effects on the Size of Multiplier

Now we have an answer to the question about how net exports affect the multiplier. Recall that Figure 12.3 proved that the flatter the aggregate expenditure line, the smaller the multiplier. Thus, because the aggregate expenditure line is flatter with net exports depending on income, we know that the multiplier is smaller. We can think of the right panel of Figure 12.3 as corresponding to a situation where net exports respond to income; the $AE$ line is flatter and the multiplier is smaller. The responsiveness of imports to income makes the multiplier go down.

The intuitive reason that the multiplier is smaller when net exports respond to income is that some of the change in spending that occurs when income changes goes to goods and services produced abroad. In the case of an increase in military spending, for example, some of the increased income of defense workers is spent

**FIGURE 12.5**
**Net Exports and the Slope of the *AE* Line**

When net exports depend on income, the aggregate expenditure line is flatter. The reason is that net exports are high at low levels of income and low at high levels of income, as shown in Table 12.6.

The identity

$$Y = C + I + G + X$$

can be written in change form as

$$\Delta Y = \Delta C + \Delta I + \Delta G + \Delta X$$

We continue to assume that

$$\Delta I = 0$$

and

$$\Delta C = .6\Delta Y$$

But now the change in net exports is given by

$$\Delta X = -.2\Delta Y$$

Now put $\Delta I$, $\Delta C$, and $\Delta X$ into the identity to get

$$\Delta Y = .6\Delta Y + \Delta G - .2\Delta Y$$

Gather together the terms involving $\Delta Y$ to get

$$(1 - .6 + .2)\Delta Y = \Delta G$$

Dividing both sides by $\Delta G$, we get

$$\frac{\Delta Y}{\Delta G} = \frac{1}{1 - .6 + .2} = 1.7 \qquad \text{(the multiplier when MPI = .2)}$$

on Toyotas rather than Fords. A change in foreign production changes the income of workers in foreign countries, but not the workers at home. Thus, the multiplier process is partly cut off.

### How the Multiplier Depends on the MPI and the MPC

Table 12.7 shows how the multiplier can be computed with algebra in the case where the marginal propensity to consume is .6 and the marginal propensity to import is .2. The multiplier is reduced from 2.5 to about 1.7. Hence, making net exports respond to income affects the size of the multiplier significantly.

We can also show explicitly how the multiplier depends on the MPI along with the MPC. The derivation, which is much like that in Table 12.7, is shown in Table 12.8. The result is

$$\frac{\Delta Y}{\Delta G} = \frac{1}{1 - \text{MPC} + \text{MPI}}$$

For example, if MPC = .6 and MPI = .2, the multiplier is 1.7.

### The Rounds of the Multiplier When Net Exports Depend on Income

Let us now follow the multiplier through the economy when net exports depend on income using the example of an increase in defense spending. Table 12.9 provides the numerical example.

Start with

$$\Delta Y = \Delta C + \Delta I + \Delta G + \Delta X$$

Assume that

$$\Delta I = 0$$

and that

$$\Delta C = \text{MPC} \times \Delta Y$$

and that

$$\Delta X = - \text{MPI} \times \Delta Y$$

Putting the above expressions together we get

$$\Delta Y = (\text{MPC} \times \Delta Y) + \Delta G - (\text{MPI} \times \Delta Y)$$

and solving for the change in $Y$ we get

$$\frac{\Delta Y}{\Delta G} = \frac{1}{1 - \text{MPC} + \text{MPI}}$$

**TABLE 12.8**
**Derivation of the Multiplier for Any MPC and MPI**

We start with an increase in purchases of military equipment of $100 billion. This causes an increase in real GDP in the first round by the same amount as in Table 12.3, the case where net exports did not depend on income.

There is a difference in the second and later rounds, however. Those workers in the defense industries who are working more are going to spend more for clothes, cars, and other things. But now part of their increased spending falls on foreign goods, like Japanese cars. The increase in purchases on foreign goods lessens the increase in production in the United States because the higher demand is spread, for example, from Ford to Toyota. This lessens the increase in real GDP in the U.S. economy by $20 billion. Fewer workers in the U.S. automobile industry work longer hours or are hired when net exports respond to income because some of the increased spending goes abroad. Thus, at the end of the second round, real GDP has increased by $140 billion compared with $160 billion in Table 12.3. Note that in

| Round | Change in Real GDP | Change in Consumption | Change in Net Exports | Cumulative Change in Real GDP |
|---|---|---|---|---|
| First round | 100.000 | 0.000 | 0.000 | 100.000 |
| Second round | 40.000 | 60.000 | −20.000 | 140.000 |
| Third round | 16.000 | 24.000 | −8.000 | 156.000 |
| Fourth round | 6.400 | 9.600 | −3.200 | 162.400 |
| Fifth round | 2.560 | 3.840 | −1.280 | 164.960 |
| . | . | . | . | . |
| . | . | . | . | . |
| . | . | . | . | . |
| After an infinite number of rounds | 0.000 | 0.000 | 0.000 | 166.667 |

**TABLE 12.9**
**Multiplier Rounds with Net Exports**
(billions of dollars)

### Rounds of the Multiplier

These two rows of photos illustrate the initial two rounds of the multiplier. The top photo shows the first round: An increase in government purchases leads to increased production of aircraft. The photos in the second row illustrate the second round: Defense workers, whose incomes rise, will increase their consumption at retail stores (left), but some of this increased spending is on goods imported from abroad (right). These two rows of photos correspond to the first two rows of Table 12.9, but the multiplier process continues on and on for many more rounds.

**twin deficits:**  a term referring to a situation in which a government budget deficit and an international trade deficit occur simultaneously.

each round the effect on real GDP is reduced by the decrease in net exports. In the end, the increase in real GDP is about $167 billion, considerably less than the $250 billion in Table 12.3.

### The Impact on the Trade Deficit

An implication of net exports depending on income is that a change in government purchases—or any other shift in the *AE* line—affects the trade surplus or deficit. Recall that there is a trade surplus if net exports are positive and a trade deficit if net exports are negative.

Consider what happens to the trade surplus or deficit when government spending is cut in an effort to reduce the budget deficit. When we lower government purchases, income is reduced. This reduction of income causes imports to fall and, because net exports is defined as exports less imports, it causes net exports to rise, which will reduce the trade deficit. If there is a trade surplus, then it will increase the trade surplus.

Note also that lower government purchases will lower the budget deficit, which is defined as government receipts less government spending. The simultaneous occurence of a budget deficit and a trade deficit is sometimes called **twin deficits.** A lower budget deficit brought on by lower government purchases will lower the trade deficit.

## Does Investment Depend on Income Too?

In this section we have shown that net exports depend on income and examined the implications of this dependence. Now we have both consumption (*C*) and net exports (*X*) depending on income. But what about the other component of private spending, investment (*I*)? Doesn't investment depend on income too?

There are indeed several reasons why investment might depend on income. Recall that the purchases of new equipment and new factories used for production by businesses are included in investment. Businesses may be more willing to make such purchases if people's incomes are high and they can therefore expect to sell more products to people. Similarly, if people's incomes are low, businesses may be less willing to purchase new equipment because they expect that people will be spending less. Thus, investment, like consumption and net exports, probably depends on income, and many economists worry about this dependence when explaining economic fluctuations.

Incorporating the responsiveness of investment into the aggregate expenditure line would be no more difficult than incorporating the responsiveness of net exports, as we have done in this section. But doing so does not change the analysis in fundamental ways. The basic spending balance and multiplier story remains the same. For this reason, we do not formally incorporate the responsiveness of investment to income.

# Review

▶ U.S. exports to other countries are not affected by U.S. income. But U.S. imports from other countries depend positively on U.S. income. Thus, net exports—exports less imports—depend negatively on the level of income.

▶ The aggregate expenditure line is flatter with net exports depending on income.

▶ When net exports respond to income, the multiplier is smaller because the changes in income lead to spending on foreign goods.

▶ The marginal propensity to import and the size of the multiplier are negatively related.

# THE MULTIPLIER FOR A TAX CHANGE

Another government policy change in addition to increases or decreases in government purchases that can affect the economy in the short run is a change in taxes. There are many cases where government officials have cut taxes in order to increase real GDP. In the early days of his administration, for example, President Kennedy proposed tax cuts to increase real GDP and help the economy recover from a recession. What is the short-run impact on real GDP of a change in taxes? Suppose, for example, the newly elected president in December 2004 proposes a tax cut of $100 billion in the year 2005. What is the likely impact on real GDP?

Before assessing this impact, it is important to distinguish between a change in tax rates and a change in taxes, or tax revenue. The **tax rate** is the percentage of

**tax rate:** the percentage of income or the value of a good paid to the government in the form of taxes.

**tax revenue:** the total amount the government receives in the form of taxes; equals the tax rate times income (also simply called taxes).

your income that you are required to pay to the government. **Tax revenue** is the total amount the government gets. For example, if the tax rate is 20 percent and your income is $30,000, then the tax revenue the government gets from you is $6,000.

Changes in tax rates may affect people's incentive to work and, therefore, may raise or lower potential GDP. But changes in tax revenue—whether caused by a change in the tax rate or a refund or rebate of past taxes—can cause real GDP to depart from potential GDP in the short run. Changes in taxes have effects on people's income and, therefore, can affect their consumption. Our focus here is on the effects of changes in tax revenues on real GDP in the short run.

A change in tax revenue will affect disposable income. For example, a tax cut of $100 billion will increase disposable income by $100 billion throughout the economy. If people have more disposable income, their consumption will rise. According to the consumption function, consumption will rise by the marginal propensity to consume (MPC) times the increase in disposable income. Thus, in this example, if the MPC = .6, consumption will shift up by $60 billion. This is a shift up in consumption at every level of real GDP.

The effect of this upward shift in consumption can now be analyzed using the aggregate expenditure line and the 45-degree line. Figure 12.6 shows that the *AE* line will shift up by the MPC times the tax cut, or by $60 billion. It is an upward shift of the *AE* line because consumption is part of aggregate expenditure, and consumption shifts up at every level of real GDP.

The upward shift in the *AE* line has the same multiplier effect as the earlier shifts we considered. (To keep the algebra simple, we assume that net exports are unrelated to income, or MPI = 0. If the MPI were not zero, we would use the expression for the multiplier in the previous section.) The ratio of the increase in real GDP to the size of the upward shift in the *AE* line is given by $1/(1 - \text{MPC})$, just as before. Thus, the total effect on real GDP of the tax increase is

$$\text{Change in GDP} = \left( \frac{1}{1 - \text{MPC}} \right) \times \underbrace{\text{MPC} \times \text{change in taxes}}_{\text{Size of shift in } AE \text{ line}}$$

For example, if the MPC is .6 and the tax cut is $100 billion, then the impact on real GDP will be $2.5 \times .6 \times 100 = \$150$ billion.

Note that the impact on real GDP for the $100 billion tax cut is smaller than the impact of a $100 billion increase in government purchases. The reason is that the initial impact on the aggregate expenditure line is smaller: Only 60 percent of the $100 billion tax cut is spent by consumers, while 100 percent of the $100 billion government purchases increase is spent by government.

**balanced budget multiplier:** the ratio of the change in real GDP to a change in government purchases when the change in government purchases is matched by an equivalent change in taxes.

Because of the different impacts of taxes and spending, it is possible for the government to increase spending *and* tax revenue by the same magnitude and still increase real GDP. For example, suppose government purchases are increased by $100 billion and simultaneously taxes are raised by $100 billion so that the budget deficit neither rises or falls. According to our analysis, the spending increase will raise real GDP by $250 billion in the short run and the tax increase will lower GDP by $150 billion. The total increase in real GDP is thus $100 billion even though the budget deficit is unchanged. The **balanced budget multiplier** is defined as the ratio of the change in real GDP to a change in government purchases when that change is matched by a change in taxes.

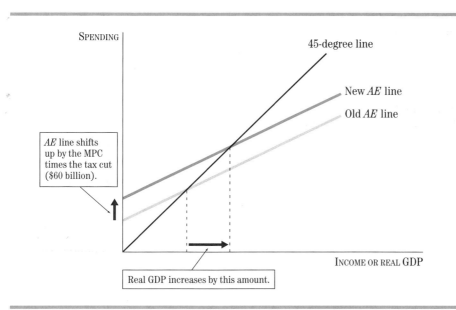

**FIGURE 12.6**
**The Multiplier for a Tax Cut**
A reduction in tax payments will raise disposable income at every level of real GDP. This will raise consumption and the *AE* line at every level of real GDP by the MPC times the tax cut. If required tax payments are reduced by $100 billion, the *AE* line will shift up by $60 billion. Then the multiplier goes to work.

## Review

▶ An increase in taxes reduces disposable income and thereby shifts the consumption function down. The downward shift in the consumption function equals the marginal propensity to consume times the tax increase.

▶ A cut in taxes works in reverse to raise consumption and real GDP.

▶ The total impact of a change in taxes on real GDP is less than the impact of a change in government purchases.

▶ It is essential to distinguish between taxes, or tax revenue, and tax rates. Tax revenue equals the tax rate times income. Tax rate changes affect potential GDP.

# THE FORWARD-LOOKING CONSUMPTION MODEL

Our analysis of the multiplier shows that it depends on the MPC. One reason there is uncertainty about the size of the multiplier is that the MPC seems to change in certain situations. Although the consumption function with a constant MPC gives an adequate prediction of people's behavior in many situations, it sometimes works very poorly. For example, the MPC turned out to be very small when taxes were cut in 1975; people saved almost the entire increase in disposable income that resulted from the tax cut. However, the MPC turned out to be very large for the tax cuts in 1981, only six years later; people saved very little of the increase in disposable income in that case.

**forward-looking consumption model:** a model that explains consumer behavior by assuming that people anticipate future income when deciding on consumption spending today.

**permanent income model:** a type of forward-looking consumption model that assumes that people distinguish between temporary changes in their income and permanent changes in their income; the permanent changes have a larger effect on consumption.

**life-cycle model:** a type of forward-looking consumption model that assumes that people base their consumption decisions on their expected lifetime income rather than on their current income.

**consumption smoothing:** the idea that, although their incomes fluctuate, people try to stabilize consumption spending from year to year.

**liquidity constraint:** the situation in which people cannot borrow to smooth their consumption spending when their income is low.

The **forward-looking consumption model** explains these changes in the MPC and identifies part of the uncertainty in the MPC. The forward-looking consumption model was developed independently and in different ways by two Nobel Prize-winning economists, Milton Friedman and Franco Modigliani. Friedman's version is called the **permanent income model,** and Modigliani's version is called the **life-cycle model.**

## Consumption Smoothing

The forward-looking model starts with the idea that people attempt to look ahead to their future income prospects when deciding how much to consume. They do not simply consider their current income. For example, if a young medical doctor decides to take a year off from a high-paying suburban medical practice to do community service at little or no pay, that doctor's income will fall below the poverty line for a year. But the doctor is unlikely to cut consumption to a fraction of the poverty level of income. Even if the doctor were young enough to have little savings, borrowing or taking out a home equity loan would be a way to keep consumption high and even buy an occasional luxury item. The doctor is basing consumption decisions on expected income for several years—making an assessment of a more permanent income, or a life-cycle income—not just for one year.

There are many other examples. Farmers in poor rural areas of Asia try to save something in good years so that they will be able to maintain their consumption in bad years. They try not to consume a fixed fraction of their income. In many cases the saving is in storable farm goods like rice.

As these examples indicate, instead of allowing their consumption to vary with their income, which may be quite erratic, most people engage in **consumption smoothing** from year to year.

## The MPC for Permanent versus Temporary Changes in Income

Once people estimate their future income prospects, they try to maintain their consumption at the same level from year to year. If their income temporarily falls, they do not cut their consumption by much; *the MPC is very small—maybe about .05— in the case of a temporary change in income.* But if they find out their income will increase permanently, they will increase their consumption a lot; *the MPC is very large—maybe .95—in the case of a permanent change in income.* For example, if a new fertilizer doubles permanently the rice yield of a rice farmer's land, we can expect that the farmer's consumption will about double.

The difference between the forward-looking consumption model and the simple consumption function is illustrated in Figure 12.7. In the right panel of Figure 12.7, income is expected to follow a typical life-cycle pattern: lower when young, higher when middle-aged, and very low when retired. However, consumption does not follow these ups and downs; it is flat. The left panel shows the opposite extreme of the standard consumption function with a fixed MPC. In that case people live well when middle-aged but have a tough time when young or old.

Occasionally some people are prevented from completely smoothing their income because they have a **liquidity constraint;** that is, they cannot get a loan to consume more than their income. Such liquidity constraints do not appear to be important enough in the economy as a whole to thwart the forward-looking model completely. Of course not all people try to smooth their income; some people like to go on binges, spending everything, even if the binge is followed by a long lull.

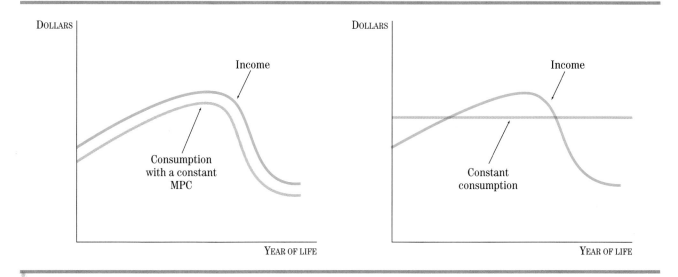

## Tests and Applications of the Forward-Looking Model

Observations on consumption and income for the economy as a whole indicate that the forward-looking model significantly improves our understanding of observed changes in the MPC. For example, economists have demonstrated that the measured MPC for the economy as a whole is lower for temporary changes in income that occur during recessions and booms than for more permanent increases in income that occur as potential GDP grows over time. Studies of thousands of individual families over time show that the individual MPC for temporary changes in income is about one-third of the MPC for permanent changes in income.

### *Permanent versus Temporary Tax Cuts*

The forward-looking model is also the most promising explanation for the low MPC during the tax cut of 1975. That tax cut was explicitly temporary, a one-time tax rebate, good for only one year. In contrast, the tax cut in the early 1980s was explicitly permanent and was expected to apply for many years into the future. The MPC was large in this case.

The effects of a permanent versus a temporary tax cut are illustrated using the aggregate expenditure line in Figure 12.8. The left panel shows the effects of a permanent tax cut. With a permanent tax cut, the MPC is high, so the shift in the aggregate expenditure line (the MPC times the tax cut) is big and the multiplier is big. For a temporary tax cut, shown in the right panel, the MPC is low, the shift in the aggregate expenditure line is small, and the multiplier is small. In estimating the effects of various tax proposals on the economy, economic forecasters take these changes in the MPC into account.

### *Anticipating Future Tax Cuts or Increases*

The forward-looking model changes our estimate of the impact of changes in taxes that are expected to occur in the future. For example, if people are certain of a tax cut in the future, they may begin to increase their consumption right away, before

**FIGURE 12.7**
**Two Extreme Forms of Consumption Behavior**
The right panel shows the future outlook of a young person or family described by the forward-looking model of consumption. The left panel shows the outlook of a young family with a constant MPC. The path of expected income (green line) is the same in both cases.

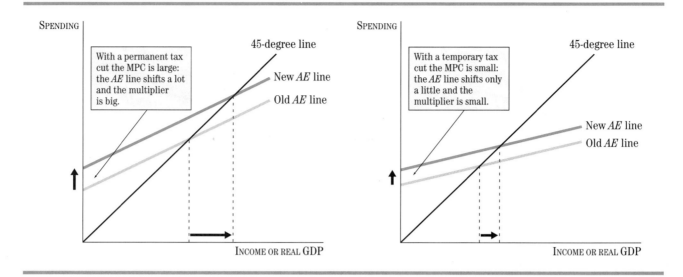

**FIGURE 12.8**

**A Temporary versus a Permanent Tax Cut**

The left diagram is for a permanent tax cut. Because people expect larger incomes over the long haul, the MPC is large, closer to 1. The right diagram is for a temporary tax cut. The MPC is small because people's long-term income has not changed much.

**rational expectations assumption:** the assumption that people forecast the future no better or no worse than economic forecasters.

the tax decreases. In this case the MPC is technically huge, because consumption increases with little or no observed change in current income. Conversely, they may reduce their consumption in anticipation of a tax increase.

It is difficult to know how large these effects are because we do not observe people's expectations of the future. Estimates based on the assumption that people forecast the future no better or no worse than economic forecasters—this is the **rational expectations assumption**—suggest that the effects are large and significant.

In situations where the expectations effects are obvious, we do see an impact. For example, in December 1992, after the 1992 presidential election when a tax increase became more likely, there was evidence that many people who could do so shifted their reported income for tax purposes from 1993 to 1992. But whether people held back their consumption in anticipation of future tax increases is difficult to say. In any case, because people's behavior is affected by their expectations of the future, attempts to estimate the impact of a policy proposal like a change in taxes need to take these expectations into account.

# Review

▶ The forward-looking consumption model helps explain why the MPC is sometimes large and sometimes small. It enables policymakers to better assess the impact of proposed policy changes.

▶ Most people try to smooth their consumption over time. They respond to expectations of future income as well as to current income when making consumption decisions.

▶ The MPC is smaller for temporary changes in income than for permanent changes in income. Hence, the multiplier for a temporary tax cut is less than for a permanent tax cut.

▶ Anticipations of future tax changes are also a factor in consumption decisions. Although expectations are difficult to measure, economists predicting the effects of policy changes must include the expectations of individuals and firms about the future.

# CONCLUSION

In this chapter we have shown how to find the size of the first step real GDP takes as it departs from potential GDP in the short run in response to several different events. The events we have described are increases or decreases in government purchases and increases or decreases in taxes. But the same approach can be used for anything that shifts the aggregate expenditure line: a change in investment, a change in net exports, or a shift in the consumption function.

The multiplier is the most common way economists describe how much real GDP changes in response to all these events. The size of the multiplier depends on the marginal propensity to consume. The size of the multiplier is uncertain because the marginal propensity to consume is uncertain. The forward-looking consumption model is an attempt to improve on the consumption function in order to reduce this uncertainty and better explain the departures of real GDP from potential GDP.

In this chapter we also allowed for net exports to depend on income, and in doing so brought key international factors into the theory of the fluctuations of real GDP that we have been developing.

But the theory of economic fluctuations is not yet finished. We have not yet begun to explain how and why real GDP returns to potential GDP in the long run. Our focus has remained on the short run in this chapter. The level of real GDP that gives spending balance is not a final equilibrium; it is not the end of the story. As explained in the next two chapters, spending balance itself automatically changes over time in response to economic forces. It is in these chapters that our story becomes dynamic—and where interest rates and inflation begin to play a formal role.

# KEY POINTS

**1.** The multiplier can be found in three ways: graphs with the 45-degree line, the aggregate expenditure line, and spending balance; algebra using the consumption function; and numerical summation of the successive rounds of spending and real GDP changes. All three ways show that the size of the multiplier is positively related to the marginal propensity to consume (MPC).

**2.** The formula for the multiplier is $1/(1 - MPC)$ or $1/MPS$, where MPS is the marginal propensity to save.

**3.** Uncertainty about the size of the multiplier can be traced to uncertainty about the size of the MPC.

**4.** Imports are positively related to income, and net exports are negatively related to income.

**5.** The size of the multiplier is negatively related to the marginal propensity to import.

**6.** The multiplier for tax changes is less than the multiplier for spending changes; part of a tax cut is saved.

**7.** The forward-looking consumption model explains why the MPC is low in some cases and high in others. It helps economists deal with the uncertainty in the multiplier.

**8.** The forward-looking consumption model also implies that anticipated changes in taxes affect consumption and are a further reason for uncertainty about the MPC. Although such effects have been observed, it is difficult to estimate their size in advance.

**9.** The rational expectations assumption, which suggests that people forecast the future no better or no worse than economic forecasters, is one method to make such estimates. With this assumption, the effects of anticipated tax changes on consumption are quite high.

# KEY TERMS

multiplier
marginal propensity to save (MPS)
marginal propensity to import (MPI)
twin deficits
tax rate

tax revenue
balanced budget multiplier
forward-looking consumption model
permanent income model
life-cycle model

consumption smoothing
liquidity constraint
rational expectations assumption

# QUESTIONS FOR REVIEW

**1.** What are the three ways to find the multiplier?

**2.** Why is the size of the multiplier positively related to the MPC?

**3.** To what degree is there uncertainty about the size of the multiplier for government purchases as judged by different economic forecasters?

**4.** Why is the size of the multiplier negatively related to the marginal propensity to import?

**5.** Why do imports depend on income while exports do not?

**6.** Why does real GDP change by a larger amount from changes in government purchases than from tax changes?

**7.** How does the forward-looking consumption model differ from the consumption function with a fixed MPC?

**8.** Why is the MPC for a temporary tax cut less than the MPC for a permanent tax cut? Are there examples that prove the point?

**9.** What is consumption smoothing?

**10.** Why do changes in future taxes that are anticipated in advance affect consumption?

# PROBLEMS

**1.** Using an aggregate expenditure/45-degree diagram show the following situations:

   a) The multiplier is greater than 1 and rises if the marginal propensity to consume rises.

   b) The multiplier for an economy when net exports respond to income is smaller than the multiplier for an economy when net exports do not resond to income.

   c) An increase in the budget deficit will increase the trade deficit.

Be sure to label the axes and lines and explain briefly the economic reasoning that underlies your argument.

**2.** The following table shows real GDP and imports in billions of dollars for an economy.

| Real GDP or Income | Imports |
|---|---|
| 2,000 | 400 |
| 3,000 | 500 |
| 4,000 | 600 |
| 5,000 | 700 |
| 6,000 | 800 |
| 7,000 | 900 |

Suppose that exports are equal to $700 billion.

   a) Construct a graph showing how imports depend on income.

   b) Construct a graph showing how net exports depend on income.

   c) If the level of real GDP that occurs at spending balance is $6,000 billion, will there by a trade surplus or deficit? What type of policy regarding government purchases would bring the trade deficit or trade surplus closer to zero?

   d) If the marginal propensity to consume is .6, what is the size of the multiplier?

**3.** The following numerical example shows how an economy's consumption and net exports depends on income:

| Real GDP or Income | Consumption | Net Exports |
|---|---|---|
| 100 | 80 | 30 |
| 200 | 160 | 20 |
| 300 | 240 | 10 |
| 400 | 320 | 0 |
| 500 | 400 | −10 |
| 600 | 480 | −20 |
| 700 | 560 | −30 |

   a) Find the marginal propensity to consume, the marginal propensity to save, the marginal propensity to import, and the multiplier.

   b) Suppose that $I = 60$ and $G = 50$ and taxes are zero. Find aggregate expenditures for each level of income listed in the table. What is the level of real GDP, consumption, and net exports where spending balance occurs? Is there a trade deficit or a trade surplus?

   c) Suppose that government purchases rise by 10. What happens to net exports?

**4.** Suppose that the marginal propensity to consume in a closed economy is estimated to be .6 but there is a 10 percent margin of error on either side. In other words, the MPC could be anywhere between .54 and .66. In what range will the multiplier lie? Quantify the range of impacts on real GDP of a $100 million increase in G. Do the same when the margin of error is 20 percent on either side of .6.

**5.** Suppose the marginal propensity to consume is .9 and that when income is zero, consumption is $100 billion. Assume $I = 200$, $G = 50$, $X = 0$, and $T = 50$.

   a) What would be the effect on income of a simultaneous increase in $G$ and $T$ of $10 billion? Why would income change at all?

b) Derive a multiplier that works for every case where the budget is balanced (that is, $G = T$).

**6.** Suppose Joe spends every additional dollar of income that he receives.

a) What is Joe's marginal propensity to consume? What does his consumption function look like?

b) Suppose that Jane spends half of each additional dollar of income that she receives. What is the slope of Jane's consumption function?

c) What differences in Joe's and Jane's incomes or jobs might explain the differences in their MPCs?

**7.** Plot values of the multiplier for different MPCs ranging from 0 to 1, putting the MPC on the horizontal axis and the multiplier on the vertical axis. What does it mean if the MPC is zero? What happens to the multiplier as the MPC approaches 1?

**8.** Given the following information, calculate the level of real GDP, which results in spending balance in the economy ($T$ is taxes or tax revenue).

$$C = 100 + .7 (Y - T)$$
$$I = 100$$
$$G = 200$$
$$T = 200$$
$$X = 50 - .1Y$$

a) What is the marginal propensity to consume in this example? What is the marginal propensity to save? What is the marginal propensity to import? How does the marginal propensity to import affect the slope of the *AE* line, compared to the same model without imports or exports?

b) What is the multiplier? Explain why this multiplier is smaller than when the marginal propensity to import is zero.

c) Is there a trade deficit or surplus?

d) Verify that saving equals investment plus net exports.

e) Suppose the net export equation is $X = 100 - .1Y$. Calculate a new equilibrium level of spending balance. Did this change affect the multiplier?

**9.** This problem examines what happens when taxes depend on income.

a) Use the equation $T = 100 + .2Y$ for taxes in the previous problem and determine the multiplier. What is the level of real GDP at spending balance now?

b) Suppose the government implements a new tax system with $T = 150 + .1Y$, rather than the one in part (a). What happens to the multiplier? What is the new level of real GDP at spending balance? Is the government budget in surplus or deficit?

**10.** Consider the following economy.

$$C = 100 + .8 (Y - T)$$
$$I = 100 + .1Y$$
$$X = 50 - .2Y$$
$$G = 200$$
$$T = 200$$

a) Solve for real GDP at spending balance. (Note that investment as well as consumption and net exports is responsive to income.)

b) Calculate national saving.

c) Now suppose that people start saving more of their income. In particular, the consumption function shifts down to $C = 25 + .8 (Y - T)$. What is the new level of real GDP? Calculate national saving now. How does this compare to your answer to part (b)?

d) Explain why national saving has declined despite the efforts of individuals to increase saving.

**11.** Each month a certain fraction of employees' pay is withheld and sent to the government as part of what is owed for personal income taxes. If the taxes owed for the year are less than the amount withheld, then a refund is sent early in the following year. Otherwise additional taxes must be paid by April 15. In 1992 the amount of income *withheld* was lowered by about $10 billion to increase consumption and real GDP and thereby speed recovery from the 1990–1991 recession. However, the amount of taxes owed was not changed. Discuss why the impact of this 1992 change would be smaller than a cut in taxes of $10 billion during 1992.

**12.** The following cartoon presents a puzzle: Increased consumption might be good for the economy and bad for the economy. By distinguishing between the long run (e.g., Chapter 8) and the short run in this chapter, explain this puzzle.

# Aggregate Demand and Price Adjustment

Why do recessions end? Why do booms end? Are there economic forces at work in market economies like that of the United States that bring real GDP back down toward potential GDP after a boom? Do these same forces work in a recession to halt the decline in real GDP and start a recovery, the period of relatively rapid growth that brings real GDP back up toward potential GDP? If such forces do exist, how fast can we expect them to work? Will recessions naturally end in one year or three years? Will recovery take three years or five years? These questions are important for economic policymaking.

To answer these questions, we need to construct an economic fluctuations model—a simplified description of how the whole economy adjusts over time after it moves away from potential GDP in a boom or in a recession. The purpose of this chapter is to construct, in graphical form, such an economic fluctuations model.

Although the economic fluctuations model pertains to the whole economy, it is analogous to the supply and demand model (Chapter 3), in which we used a graph to explain the behavior of particular markets such as the peanut market. Just as we presented the supply and demand model in a graph consisting of three elements:

▶ a *demand curve,*

▶ a *supply curve,* and

▶ an *equilibrium* at the intersection of the two curves,

we present the economic fluctuations model in a graph consisting of three elements:

▶ an *aggregate demand/inflation (ADI) curve,*

▶ a *price adjustment (PA) line,* and

▶ an *equilibrium* at the intersection of the curve and line.

The economic fluctuations model is based on ideas previously developed in this book. For example, in explaining the model we will use the idea that consumption, investment, and net exports depend negatively on the interest rate (Chapter 8), as well as the idea of spending balance (Chapter 11). We will also use observations of actual economic fluctuations presented in Chapter 5. One key observation—that fluctuations in inflation are closely associated with fluctuations in real GDP—is critical to this analysis. We observed in Chapter 5 that inflation typically increases just before a recession and subsides during and immediately after a recession as the recovery gets

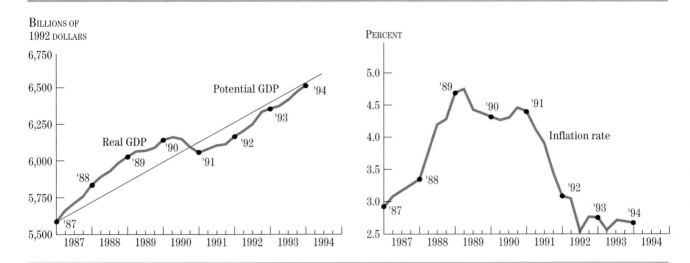

**FIGURE 13.1**
**Two Time-Series Graphs Showing Real GDP and Inflation from 1987 to 1994**
The economic fluctuation from 1987 through 1994 is shown in these diagrams. Inflation and real GDP appear to move together.

started. You can see this in Figure 13.1 for the case of the economic fluctuation that occurred from 1987 to 1994. The graph on the left shows real GDP fluctuating around potential GDP. The graph on the right shows inflation. Notice that in 1988 and 1989, when real GDP is above potential GDP (before the recession begins), the inflation rate is rising; during and after the recession, when real GDP is less than potential GDP (from 1991 to 1994), the inflation rate is declining.

Figure 13.2 summarizes this relationship, enabling us to monitor the movements of real GDP and inflation over time. Real GDP is shown on the horizontal axis and the inflation rate is shown on the vertical axis. Each dot on the graph corresponds to a pair of observations from the two time-series graphs in Figure 13.1. When the economy is in a boom or recovering from a recession, the points in Figure 13.2 are moving to the right. In a recession, the points are moving to the left. Increases in inflation are upward, while decreases in inflation are downward. The arrows drawn between the dots in Figure 13.2 show these movements. Follow the path of the arrows starting in 1987 and going all the way to 1994. For this period, the arrows form a circular pattern starting with low inflation (1987), moving toward higher inflation (1988–1989), and then moving into recession (1990–1991) and recovery (1992–1994).

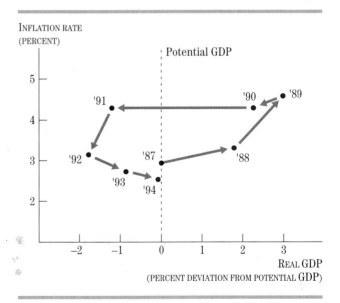

**FIGURE 13.2**
**Real GDP and Inflation Movements in a Single Diagram**
The dots represent real GDP and inflation rate points from Figure 13.1. Recessions are shown as leftward movements, and booms and recoveries as rightward movements.

*Source:* U.S. Department of Commerce.

**331**

The economic fluctuations model we develop in this chapter will help explain the pattern of these dots. We will do this much in the same way that we explained the pattern of price and quantity observations in the peanut or other microeconomic markets using supply and demand curves. In the microeconomic supply and demand model, the intersection of the *demand curve* and the *supply curve* gives us the *equilibrium* price and quantity. In the economic fluctuations model, the intersection of the

*aggregate demand/inflation* (*ADI*) *curve* and *the price adjustment* (*PA*) *line*—in a graph with the same axes used in Figure 13.2—gives us *equilibrium* real GDP and inflation.

We will start our construction of the economic fluctuations model by deriving the aggregate demand/inflation curve and then the price adjustment line. We will then show how their intersection determines real GDP and inflation.

# THE AGGREGATE DEMAND/ INFLATION CURVE

**aggregate demand/inflation (*ADI*) curve:** a line showing a negative relationship between inflation and the aggregate quantity of goods and services demanded at that inflation rate.

The **aggregate demand/inflation (*ADI*) curve** is a relationship between two economic variables: real GDP and the inflation rate. Real GDP is usually measured as percentage deviation from potential GDP, and the inflation rate is usually measured as the annual percentage change in the overall price level from year to year. Figure 13.3 shows an aggregate demand/inflation curve for the United States. Observe that inflation is measured on the vertical axis, that real GDP is measured on the horizontal axis, and that we have drawn a vertical dashed line to mark the point where real GDP equals potential GDP. The aggregate demand/inflation curve shows different combinations of real GDP and inflation. It is downward-sloping from left to right because real GDP is negatively related to inflation along the curve. The term *aggregate demand* is used because we interpret the movements of real GDP away from potential GDP as due to fluctuations in the sum (aggregate) of the demand for consumption, investment, net exports, and government purchases.

Why does the aggregate demand/inflation curve slope downward? We will answer this question and derive the curve in three steps. First, we show that there is a negative relationship between the interest rate and real GDP. Second, we show that there is a positive relationship between inflation and the interest rate. Third, we show that these two relationships imply that there is a negative relationship between real GDP and inflation, and that relationship is the aggregate demand/inflation curve. The following schematic chart shows how the three steps fit together.

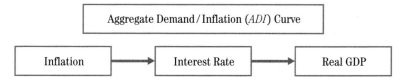

## Interest Rates and Real GDP

Consumption, investment, and net exports are all components of aggregate expenditure that are negatively related to the interest rate. Combining these components provides an explanation of the negative relationship between real GDP and the interest

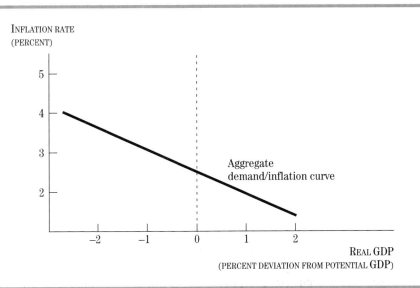

**FIGURE 13.3**
**The Aggregate Demand/Inflation Curve**
The aggregate demand/inflation curve shows that higher inflation and real GDP are negatively related.

rate. The negative effect of the interest rate on investment, net exports, and consumption is no different from the one discussed in Chapter 8 (pages 200-205). If you have already studied that chapter, the next few pages will serve as a brief review.

### Investment

Investment is the component of aggregate expenditure that is probably most sensitive to the interest rate. Recall that part of investment is the purchase of new equipment or a new factory by a business firm. Many firms must borrow funds to pay for such investments. Higher interest rates make such borrowing more costly. Hence, businesses that are thinking about buying a new machine and need to borrow funds will be less inclined to purchase such an investment good if interest rates are higher. The additional profits the firm might expect to earn from purchasing a photocopier or truck are more likely to be lower than the interest costs on the loan if the interest rate is high. Thus, higher interest rates reduce investment spending by businesses. Also, remember that part of investment is the purchase of new houses. Most people need to take out a mortgage in order to buy a house. Like any loan, the mortgage has an interest rate, and higher interest rates make mortgages more costly. Hence, with higher interest rates fewer people take out mortgages and buy new houses. Spending for new housing declines.

The same reasoning works to show why lower interest rates will increase investment spending: Lower interest rates reduce the cost of borrowing and make investment more attractive to firms and households.

To summarize, both business investment and housing investment decline when the interest rate rises, and they increase when the interest rate falls. At any time there are some firms or households deciding whether to buy a new machine or a new house, and they are going to be less inclined to buy such things when the interest rate is higher.

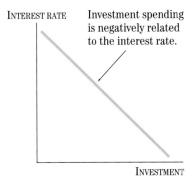

INTEREST RATE    Investment spending is negatively related to the interest rate.

INVESTMENT

### Net Exports

The negative relationship between net exports and the interest rate requires a somewhat more involved explanation than investment. The relationship exists because higher interest rates in the United States tend to lead to a higher dollar exchange rate and, in turn, a higher exchange rate reduces net exports.

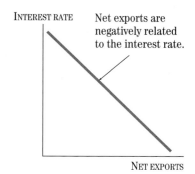

INTEREST RATE     Net exports are negatively related to the interest rate.

NET EXPORTS

   A higher interest rate in the United States compared with other countries raises the exchange rate because it increases the demand for U.S. dollar bank accounts and other assets that pay interest. That increased demand bids up the price of dollars; hence, the exchange rate—the price of dollars—rises. Now, with a higher exchange rate, net exports will be lower because U.S.-produced exports become more expensive to foreigners, who must pay a higher price for dollars, and imported foreign goods become cheaper for Americans, who can get more foreign goods for higher-priced dollars. With exports falling and imports rising, net exports—exports less imports—must fall. In sum, higher interest rates reduce net exports.

   The same reasoning works for lower interest rates as well. If the interest rate falls in the United States, then U.S. dollar bank accounts are less attractive compared with other countries such as Germany or Japan. This bids down the price of dollars, and the exchange rate falls. Now, with a lower exchange rate, net exports will be higher because U.S.-produced exports are less expensive to foreigners and imported foreign goods are more expensive for Americans. With exports rising and imports falling, net exports must rise. Thus, lower interest rates increase net exports.

   To summarize, there is a negative relationship between the interest rate and the exchange rate that works through the exchange rate as follows:

| Interest Rate | Exchange Rate | Net Exports |
|---|---|---|
| up $\longrightarrow$ | up $\longrightarrow$ | down |
| down $\longrightarrow$ | down $\longrightarrow$ | up |

If the interest rate goes up, then the exchange rate goes up, causing net exports to go down. If the interest rate goes down, then the exchange rate goes down, causing net exports to go up.

### Consumption

We have shown that two of the components of aggregate expenditure—investment and net exports—are sensitive to the interest rate. What about consumption?

   Although consumption is probably less sensitive to the interest rate than the other components, there is some evidence that higher interest rates encourage people to save a larger fraction of their income. As explained in Chapter 8, higher interest rates encourage people to save, because they earn more on their savings. Because more saving means less consumption, this implies that consumption is negatively related to the interest rate. However, most economists feel that the effect of interest rates on consumption is much less than on investment and net exports.

### Spending Balance

To summarize the discussion thus far, investment, net exports, and consumption are all negatively related to the interest rate. The overall effect of a change in interest rates on real GDP can now be assessed.

SPENDING

45-degree line

*AE* line with lower interest rate

*AE* line with higher interest rate

A higher interest rate lowers real GDP.

INCOME OR REAL GDP

**FIGURE 13.4**
**The Interest Rate, Spending Balance, and Real GDP**
A higher interest rate shifts the *AE* line down because consumption, investment, and net exports depend negatively on the interest rate. Thus, real GDP declines with a higher interest rate. Conversely, a lower interest rate raises real GDP.

Figure 13.4 shows the 45-degree line and two different aggregate expenditure (*AE*) lines corresponding to two different interest rates. Higher interest rates shift down the *AE* line because a higher interest rate lowers investment, net exports, and consumption, which are all part of aggregate expenditure.

Observe how the downward shift of the *AE* line leads to a new point of spending balance. The intersection of the *AE* line with the 45-degree line occurs at a lower level of real GDP. Note that real GDP is lower not only because the higher interest rate lowers investment, net exports, and consumption, but also because a decline in income will lower consumption further. Real GDP declines by the amount shown on the horizontal axis, which is larger than the downward shift in the *AE* line. *Thus, an increase in the interest rate lowers real GDP.*

What about a decline in the interest rate? A lower interest rate will raise the *AE* line. In that case, the *AE* line would shift up, and the point of spending balance at the intersection with the 45-degree line would be at a higher level of real GDP. *Thus, a decrease in the interest rate raises real GDP.*

In sum, we have shown that there is a negative relationship between the interest rate and real GDP.

Keep in mind that the *real* interest rate is a better measure of the effect of interest rates on investment, net exports, and consumption than the *nominal* interest rate because it corrects for inflation. Recall from Chapter 5 that the *real* interest rate equals the stated, or *nominal,* interest rate (on loans or mortgages) minus the expected inflation rate. For example, if the nominal interest rate is 13 percent and inflation has been at 10 percent and is expected to remain there, the real interest rate is 3 percent. When inflation is low and stable, the real and nominal interest rates do not differ much from each other. But when inflation rates are high, it is important to look at the real interest rate when examining the impact of interest rates on real GDP.

**Real interest rate =**

nominal − expected
interest rate   inflation rate.

## Interest Rates and Inflation

Now that we have seen why interest rates affect real GDP, let us proceed to the second step in our analysis. We want to show why a rise in inflation will increase the interest rate and thereby lower real GDP, or why a decline in inflation will decrease the interest rate and thereby raise real GDP.

### *Central Bank Interest Rate Policy*

The easiest way to see why the interest rate rises when the inflation rate increases is to examine the behavior of the central bank. We discussed the U.S. central bank—the Fed—in Chapter 10. The Fed and central banks in other countries typically follow policies in which they respond to an increase in the inflation rate by raising the interest rate. By far the most widely followed and analyzed decision by the Fed is its interest rate decision.

Why does the Fed raise the interest rate when the inflation rate rises? The inflation rate is ultimately the responsibility of the Fed, and the goal of controlling inflation requires that the central bank raise the interest rate when the inflation rate rises. Suppose that the economy starts into a boom and inflation starts to rise. If the central bank takes actions to raise the interest rate, then the higher interest rate will slow the growth of real GDP and cut off the boom. If the rise in the interest rate is high enough and soon enough, cutting off the boom in real GDP will then reduce inflationary pressures and bring inflation back down again.

The goal of controlling inflation also requires that the central bank lower the interest rate when inflation falls. Suppose that the economy starts to slow down and inflation starts to fall. If the central bank takes action to reduce the interest rate, then the lower interest rate will increase the growth of real GDP. If the decline in the interest rate is large enough and soon enough, the increase in real GDP will end the slowdown and the downward pressure on inflation will be cut off.

The data in Table 13.1 illustrate these actions of the Fed. For each inflation rate, an interest rate decision by the Fed is shown. For example, when inflation is 2 percent, the interest rate decision is 4 percent. When inflation rises to 4 percent, the interest rate decision by the Fed is 7 percent. Thus, when inflation rises, the central bank raises the interest rate, and when inflation falls, the central bank lowers the interest rate.

Note that the interest rate rises more than inflation rises in Table 13.1. The reason is related to the distinction between the nominal interest rate and the real interest rate. If an increase in the interest rate is to reduce real GDP, then the real interest rate must rise because real GDP depends negatively on the real interest rate, as described in the previous section. If the nominal interest rate rises by more than the expected inflation rate, then the real interest rate will rise and real GDP should decline. Thus, for the interest rate decisions in the table, the nominal interest rate rises by more than inflation as a way to get the real interest rate to rise. If, instead, the nominal interest rate rose by less than the increase in the inflation rate, then the real interest rate would not rise; rather, it would fall.

The behavior of the central bank illustrated in Table 13.1 is called a **monetary policy rule** because it describes the systematic response of the interest rate to inflation as decided by the central bank. For a given level of real GDP the central bank, as a rule, takes actions to raise the interest rate when inflation rises. Keep in mind that the central bank does not set interest rates by decree or by direct control. Governments sometimes do control the price of goods; for example, some city governments control the rents on apartments. The central bank does not apply such

---

**TABLE 13.1**

**A Numerical Example of Central Bank Interest Rate Policy**

| Inflation Rate | Interest Rate Decision |
|---|---|
| 0.0 | 1.0 |
| 1.0 | 2.5 |
| 2.0 | 4.0 |
| 3.0 | 5.5 |
| 4.0 | 7.0 |
| 5.0 | 8.5 |
| 6.0 | 10.0 |
| 7.0 | 11.5 |
| 8.0 | 13.0 |

---

**monetary policy rule:** a description of how much the interest rate or other instruments of monetary policy respond to inflation or other measures of the state of the economy.

controls to the interest rate. Rather it enters the markets in which short-term interest rates are determined by the usual forces of supply and demand. In the United States, the short-term interest rate the Fed focuses on is the interest rate on overnight loans between banks. It is called the **federal funds rate,** and the overnight interbank loan market is called the federal funds market. When the Fed wants to lower this interest rate, it supplies funds to this market. When it wants to raise the interest rate, it withdraws funds. This process is identical to the one the Fed uses to adjust bank reserves, as discussed in Chapter 10: It can supply funds by buying bonds and withdraw funds by selling bonds, a process that is illustrated with examples and case studies in Chapter 16.

**federal funds rate:** the interest rate on overnight loans between banks that the Federal Reserve influences by changing the supply of funds (bank reserves) in the market.

### A Graph of the Response of the Interest Rate to Inflation

Figure 13.5 represents the monetary policy rule graphically, using the information in Table 13.1. When the inflation rate rises, the nominal interest rate rises along the purple upward-sloping line. When the inflation rate declines, the nominal interest rate declines. The nominal interest rate must rise by more than the inflation rate if the *real* interest rate is to rise when inflation rises; this requires that the slope of the monetary policy rule line in Figure 13.5 be greater than 1. We illustrate that the slope is greater than 1 by drawing in a dashed line with a slope of 1. Observe that the dashed line intersects the vertical axis at 2 percentage points for the interest rate. Thus, for points along this dashed line, the difference between the nominal interest rate and the inflation rate is 2 percent; that is, the real interest rate is a constant 2 percent.

Most central banks have a **target inflation rate,** the inflation rate that the central bank tries to maintain on average over the long run. Because of various shocks to the economy, the central bank cannot control the inflation rate perfectly; sometimes the inflation rate will rise above the target inflation rate, and sometimes the inflation rate will fall below the target inflation rate. Some central banks, such as the Bank of England and the Reserve Bank of New Zealand, have explicit inflation targets. Other central banks, like the Fed or the German Bundesbank, have implicit target inflation rates that are not explicitly announced, but which can be assessed by observing central bank decisions over time. The target inflation rate for the Fed and the Bundesbank appears to be about 2 percent.

This 2 percent target inflation rate is shown in Figure 13.5. Observe that if the real interest rate is 2 percent, as in Figure 13.5, this target inflation rate implies that the average value of the nominal interest rate (the federal funds rate) will be about 4 percent. When the actual inflation rate rises above the target inflation rate of 2 percent, the Fed will raise the federal funds rate above the target of 4 percent.

**target inflation rate:** the central bank's goal for the average rate of inflation over the long run.

**FIGURE 13.5**
**A Monetary Policy Rule**
The monetary policy rule shows that the Fed lets the interest rate rise when inflation rises and lets the interest rate fall when inflation falls. The Fed's inflation target is assumed to be 2 percent. The dashed line has a slope of 1 and corresponds to a real interest rate of 2 percent. (The monetary policy rule is drawn using the information in Table 13.1.)

### A Simplifying Assumption

The behavior of the central bank described in this section provides the easiest explanation of the response of interest rates to inflation; but it is not the only possible explanation. Indeed, examples discussed in Chapter 16 show that the general upward-sloping relationship in Figure 13.5, which we call the monetary policy rule, is common to many different types of monetary policies, including policies in which the

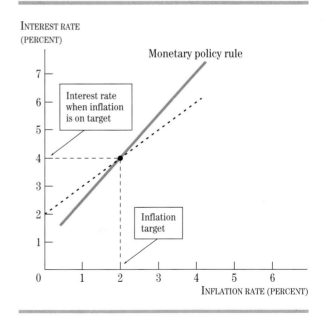

## Reading the News About the Fed

This front-page *New York Times* headline illustrates the great importance attached to central bank policy. The news article describes how the Fed took actions on March 25, 1997, to increase the interest rate because of concerns that inflation was rising. Similar headlines appeared in most of the newspapers in the country. The Fed decision was also widely reported on television and radio. In this case, the interest rate rose to 5.5 percent; it was 5.25 percent through much of 1996 and early 1997.

Because the rise in the inflation rate that brought about the Fed's interest rate decision was small, some analysts disagreed with the Fed's decision.

Observe how many of the terms and concepts used in this article are discussed in this chapter: Federal Reserve, federal funds rate, effect of interest rates on investment and consumption, goals of the Fed in restraining inflation, overnight loans between banks.

Note also how the article sounds as if the Fed controls interest rates by decree. In reality, the Fed does not literally set interest rates. Rather, it buys and sells government bonds and thereby influences the interest rate in the market.

# FEDERAL RESERVE LIFTS A KEY RATE; FIRST RISE SINCE '95

The Federal Reserve raised its short-term interest rate target—the Federal funds rate—for the first time since Feb. 1, 1995.

## UP QUARTER-POINT

Move to 5.5% Is Aimed At Checking Inflation —Stocks Weaken

**Yesterday:
Up 0.25 point
to 5.50%**

The Federal funds rate is raised to slow economic growth when the Fed wants to restrain inflation.

*Source: Associated Press*

Here the federal funds rate is defined.

Here the Fed's decision is described.

Here the effect of the higher interest rate on investment and consumption is mentioned.

**By Richard W. Stevenson**

WASHINGTON, March 25 — The Federal Reserve voted today to raise interest rates for the first time in more than two years, firing a warning shot at an inflationary threat that remained hidden over the horizon.

The central bank took one of the smallest steps it could, nudging up the more important of the two short-term rates it controls — the Federal funds target rate for overnight loans between banks — by a quarter of a percentage point, to 5.5 percent. In doing so, it was trying to keep the economy from growing so fast that it generates wage and price pressures strong enough to threaten the nation's six-year economic expansion.

Because banks tie their benchmark loan rates to the Federal funds rate, today's action will ripple through the economy, probably curbing investment and consumption somewhat by increasing the rates charged for many business and personal loans and for credit cards.

central bank keeps money growth constant, or adheres to a gold standard, or reacts to other variables in addition to inflation, such as real GDP. Although the position and shape of the monetary policy rule will differ for these different types of policies, the overall response of interest rates to inflation will be similar, and the story of economic fluctuations that we discuss in this chapter will be similar. Our reason for using this particular derivation of the monetary policy rule is that it is the easiest to explain and is a close approximation of the actual behavior of the Fed and other central banks today. In other words, it is a good *simplifying assumption.*

## Derivation of the Aggregate Demand/Inflation Curve

Thus far we have shown that the level of real GDP is negatively related to the interest rate and that the interest rate is positively related to the inflation rate through the central bank's policy rule. We now combine these two concepts to derive the aggregate demand/inflation (*ADI*) curve—the inverse relationship between the inflation rate and real GDP.

The chain of reasoning that brings about the aggregate demand/inflation curve can be explained by considering what would happen if the inflation rate rose. First, the interest rate would rise because the Fed raises the interest rate in response to a higher inflation rate. Next, the higher interest rate would mean less investment spending, a decline in net exports, and a decline in consumption. Lower investment spending occurs because investment is made more costly by the high interest rate. American goods become more expensive, and foreign goods become cheaper. Thus, net exports—exports minus imports—decline. We can represent this decrease in aggregate expenditure as a downward shift in the aggregate expenditure line. This leads to spending balance at a lower level of real GDP.

The opposite chain of events would occur if there were a fall in inflation below the target inflation rate. First, the Fed would lower the interest rate according to the monetary policy rule. The lower interest rate, in turn, would cause investment, net exports, and consumption to rise. Hence, the aggregate expenditure line would shift up, and the level of GDP would rise.

In sum, we see that when the inflation rate rises, real GDP decreases, and when the inflation rate falls, real GDP increases. In other words, there is a negative relationship between inflation and real GDP. When we graph this relationship in a diagram with real GDP on the horizontal axis and inflation on the vertical axis we get a downward-sloping curve like the one shown in Figure 13.3; this curve is the aggregate demand/inflation curve, which we have thus derived.

An alternative self-contained graphical derivation of the aggregate demand/inflation curve is provided in Figure 13.6; the figure traces through the chain of events following an increase in inflation, including the Fed interest rate increase according to its policy rule, the change in spending balance, and finally the decline in real GDP.

### Movements along the Aggregate Demand/Inflation Curve

Thus far, we have explained why the aggregate demand/inflation curve has a negative slope—that is, why higher inflation means lower real GDP. A *change in real GDP* due to a *change in inflation* is thus a *movement along* the aggregate demand/inflation curve. Recall that in microeconomics a similar movement along the demand curve occurs when a *change in the price* leads to a *change in quantity demanded.* When inflation rises and causes the Fed to raise the interest rate and real

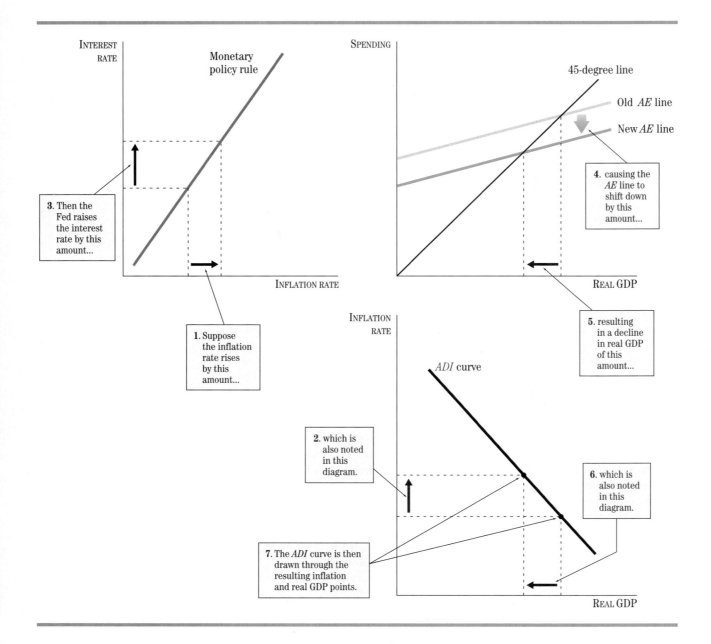

**FIGURE 13.6**
**Graphical Derivation of the Aggregate Demand/Inflation Curve**
When inflation rises, the central bank raises the interest rate and this lowers real GDP. Hence, we have the aggregate demand/inflation curve.

GDP declines, there is a movement up and to the left along the aggregate demand/inflation curve. When inflation declines and the Fed lowers the interest rate, causing real GDP to rise, there is a movement down and to the right along the aggregate demand/inflation curve.

### Shifts of the Aggregate Demand/Inflation Curve

Now the inflation rate is not the only thing that affects aggregate demand. Changes in government purchases, shifts in the *target* for monetary policy, shifts in foreign demand for U.S. exports, changes in taxes, and changes in consumer confidence,

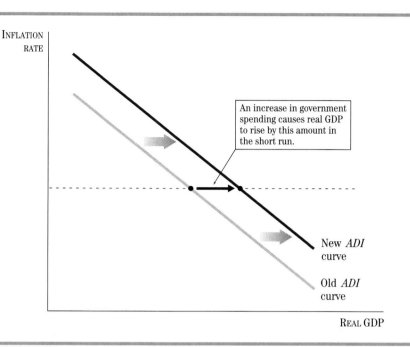

An increase in government
spending causes real GDP
to rise by this amount in
the short run.

New *ADI*
curve

Old *ADI*
curve

**FIGURE 13.7**
**How Government Purchases Shift
the Aggregate Demand/Inflation
Curve**
An increase in government purchases shifts the *ADI* curve to the
right. Real GDP rises by the same
amount at every level of inflation.

among other things, affect aggregate demand. When any of these factors changes
aggregate demand, we say there is a *shift* in the aggregate demand/inflation curve.
Let us briefly consider some of those sources of shifts in the aggregate demand/
inflation curve.

***Government Purchases***    Imagine that government purchases rise. We know from
our analysis of spending balance in the previous chapter that an increase in government purchases will increase real GDP in the short run. This increase in real GDP
occurs at any inflation rate: at 2 percent, at 4 percent, or at any other level. Now, if
real GDP increases at a given inflation rate, the aggregate demand/inflation curve
will shift to the right. This is shown in Figure 13.7. The new aggregate demand/
inflation curve will be parallel to the original aggregate demand/inflation curve
because no matter what the inflation rate is in the economy, the shift in government
purchases is going to have the same effect on real GDP. The same reasoning implies
that a decline in government spending shifts the aggregate demand/inflation curve
to the left.

***Changes in the Target Inflation Rate***    Now consider what happens if the Fed
shifts to a higher target inflation rate. Suppose that the previous target inflation rate
was 2 percent and the new target inflation rate is 4 percent. Figure 13.8 shows how
this shifts the monetary policy rule line outward toward higher inflation. Observe
that this will initially cause the interest rate to decline at every level of inflation. For
example, if the inflation rate was 2 percent before the change in policy, the interest
rate will drop from 4 percent to 3 percent, as shown in the diagram. These lower
interest rates will increase real GDP, and thereby shift the aggregate demand/
inflation curve out. The same reasoning implies that a lowering of the target inflation rate by the Fed will shift the monetary policy rule to the left, increase the interest rate, and shift the aggregate demand/inflation curve to the left.

**FIGURE 13.8**
**A Change in the Monetary Policy Rule**

A change in the policy rule to a higher inflation target initially implies a decline in the interest rate. The lower interest rate shifts up the *AE* line and increases real GDP in the short run. As a result, at a given inflation rate the *ADI* curve shifts to the right.

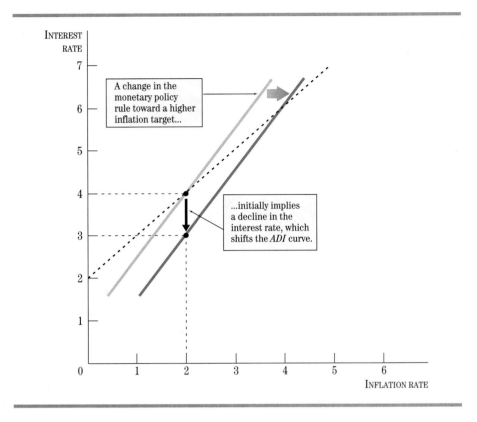

**FIGURE 13.9**
**Shifts in the Aggregate Demand/Inflation Curve**

Many things shift the *ADI* curve. For example, an increase in government purchases shifts the *ADI* curve to the right. A change in the monetary policy rule toward a higher inflation target shifts the *ADI* curve to the right. A decline in government purchases and a change in the monetary policy rule toward a lower inflation target shifts the curve to the left.

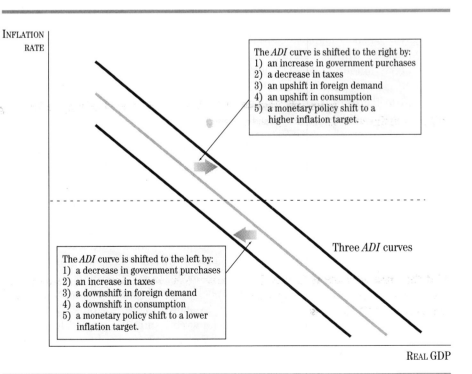

***Other Changes*** Any change in the economy (other than a change in the inflation rate) that shifts the aggregate expenditure line will also shift the aggregate demand/inflation curve. We considered many such possibilities in Chapter 11; their effects on the aggregate demand/inflation curve are shown in Figure 13.9. For example, an increase in the foreign demand for U.S. products will increase net exports, raise real GDP, and shift the aggregate demand/inflation curve to the right. A drop in consumer confidence that reduces the amount of consumption at every level of income will shift the aggregate demand/inflation curve to the left. Finally, an increase in taxes shifts the aggregate demand/inflation curve to the left, while a decrease in taxes shifts the aggregate demand/inflation curve to the right.

## Review

▶ The aggregate demand/inflation curve is an inverse relationship between inflation and real GDP.

▶ Investment, net exports, and consumption are negatively related to the interest rate. Hence, real GDP falls when the interest rate rises.

▶ When inflation increases, the central bank raises the interest rate, and this lowers real GDP. Conversely, when inflation falls, the central bank lowers the interest rate, and this raises real GDP. These are movements along the aggregate demand/inflation curve.

▶ The aggregate demand/inflation curve shifts to the right when the central bank changes its monetary policy rule toward more inflation and shifts to the left when the central banks changes its policy rule toward less inflation.

▶ Higher government purchases shift the aggregate demand/inflation curve to the right. Lower government purchases shift the aggregate demand/inflation curve to the left.

# THE PRICE ADJUSTMENT LINE

Having derived the aggregate demand/inflation curve and studied its properties, let us now look at the price adjustment line, the second element of the economic fluctuations model. The **price adjustment (*PA*) line** is a flat line showing the level of inflation in the economy at any point in time. Figure 13.10 shows an example of the price adjustment line in a diagram with inflation on the vertical axis and real GDP on the horizontal axis. For example, if the line touches 4 percent on the vertical axis, then it tells us that inflation is 4 percent.

The price adjustment line describes the economic behavior of firms and workers setting prices and wages in the economy. There are several important features about the slope and position of the price adjustment line.

**price adjustment (*PA*) line:** a flat line showing the level of inflation in the economy at a given point in time. It shifts up when real GDP is greater than potential GDP, and it shifts down when real GDP is less than potential GDP; it also shifts when expectations of inflation or raw materials prices change.

### The Price Adjustment Line Is Flat

That the price adjustment line is flat indicates that firms and workers adjust their prices and wages in such a way that the inflation rate remains steady in the short run as real GDP changes. Only after time does inflation change significantly and the price adjustment line move. In the short run, inflation stays at 4 percent, or wherever the price adjustment line happens to be, when real GDP changes.

In interpreting the price adjustment line, it is helpful to remember that it is part of a *model* of the overall economy and is thus an approximation of reality. In fact,

**FIGURE 13.10**
**Price Adjustment and Changes in Inflation**
In the top panel, real GDP is above potential GDP and inflation is rising; thus, the price adjustment line shifts up. In the bottom panel, real GDP is below potential GDP and inflation is falling; thus, the price adjustment line shifts down.

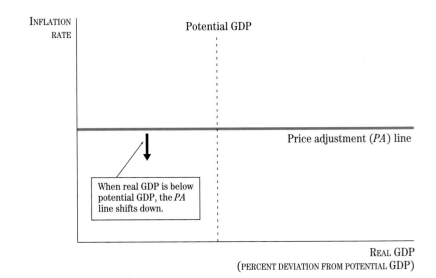

inflation does not remain *perfectly* steady, and the price adjustment line could have a small upward slope. But it is a good approximation to assume that the price adjustment line is flat.

There are two reasons why inflation does not change very much in the short run even if real GDP and the demand for firms' products changes: (1) expectations of steady inflation, and (2) staggered wage and price setting.

### *Expectations of Steady Inflation*

Expectations about the price and wage decisions of other firms influence a firm's price and wage decisions. For example, if the overall inflation rate in the economy has been hovering around 10 percent year after year, then a firm can expect that its competitors' prices will probably increase by about 10 percent per year, unless circumstances change. To keep prices near the competition, this firm will need to increase its price by about 10 percent each year. Thus, the inflation rate stays steady at 10 percent per year.

Wage adjustments also must be undertaken with expectations of the future. If firms and workers expect that workers at other firms will be getting large wage increases, then meeting the competition will require similar large wage increases. A smaller wage increase would reduce the wage relative to other workers. Many firms base their wage decisions on the wages paid by other firms to workers whose skills and experience are similar to their workers. If they see the wages at other firms rising, they will be more willing to increase wages.

Firms and workers also look to expectations of inflation when deciding on wage increases. In an economy with 10 percent inflation, wages will have to increase by 10 percent for workers just to keep up with the cost of living. Lower wage increases would result in a decline in workers' real wages.

### Staggered Price and Wage Setting

Not all wages and prices are changed at the same time throughout the economy. Rather, price setting and wage setting are staggered over months and even years. For example, autoworkers might negotiate three-year wage contracts in 1993, 1996, 1999, etc. Dockworkers might negotiate three-year contracts in 1994, 1997, 2000, etc. Bus companies and train companies do not adjust their prices at the same time, even though they may compete for the same riders. On any given day, we can be sure that there is a wage or price adjustment somewhere in the economy, but the vast majority of wages and prices do not change.

Staggered price and wage setting slows down the adjustment of prices in the economy. When considering what wage increases are likely in the next year, firms and workers know about the most recent three-year wage increase. For example, an agreement made by another firm to increase wages by 10 percent per year for three years into the future will affect the expectations of wages paid to competing workers in the future. This wage agreement will not change unless the firm is on the edge of bankruptcy and perhaps not even then. Hence, workers and firms deciding on wage increases will tend to match the wage increases recently made at other firms. Thus, price and wage decisions made today are directly influenced by price and wage decisions made yesterday.

As with many things in life, when today's decisions are influenced by yesterday's decisions, inertia sets in. The staggering of the decisions makes it difficult to break the inertia. Unless there is a reason to make a change—such as a persistent decline in demand or a change in expectations of inflation—the price increases or wage increases continue from year to year. The flat price adjustment line describes this inertia.

## The Price Adjustment Line Shifts Gradually When Real GDP Departs from Potential GDP

The price adjustment line does not always stay put; rather it may shift up or down from year to year. If real GDP stays above potential GDP, then inflation starts to rise. Firms see that the demand for their products is remaining high, and they begin adjusting their prices. If the inflation rate was 10 percent, then the firms will have to raise their prices by more than 10 percent if they want their relative prices to increase. Hence, inflation starts to rise. The price adjustment line is shifted upward to illustrate this rise in inflation; it will keep shifting upward as long as real GDP is above potential GDP.

However, if real GDP is below potential GDP, then firms will see that the demand for their products is falling off, and they will adjust their prices. If inflation was 10 percent, the firms will raise their prices by less than 10 percent—perhaps by 7 percent—if they want the relative price of their goods to fall. Hence, inflation falls. The price adjustment line is shifted down to illustrate this fall in inflation. Figure 13.10 shows the direction of these shifts.

If real GDP stays at potential GDP, neither to the left nor to the right of the vertical potential GDP line in Figure 13.10, then inflation remains unchanged. For example, in the absence of a recession or a boom, the inflation rate would remain steady year after year. This steady inflation is represented by an unmoving price adjustment line year after year.

The following is a shorthand summary of price adjustment in the economy as a whole:

Real GDP = potential GDP → inflation rate does not change (*PA* line does not shift)

Real GDP > potential GDP → inflation rate increases (*PA* line shifts up)

Real GDP < potential GDP → inflation rate decreases (*PA* line shifts down)

## Changes in Expectations or Commodity Prices Shift the Price Adjustment Line

Even if real GDP is at potential GDP, some special events in the economy can cause the price adjustment line to shift up or down. One important example is *shifts in expectations* of inflation. If firms and workers expect inflation to rise, then they are likely to raise wages and prices to keep pace with inflation. Thus, an increase in expectations of inflation will cause the price adjustment line to shift up to a higher inflation rate. And a decrease in expectations of inflation will cause the price adjustment line to shift down.

Another example is a change in commodity prices that affects firms' costs of production. For example, we will examine the effects on inflation of an oil price increase in the next chapter. By raising firms' costs, such an oil price increase would lead firms to charge higher prices, and the price adjustment line would rise, at least temporarily.

## Does the Price Adjustment Line Fit the Facts?

Are these assumptions about the price adjustment line accurate? Does inflation rise when real GDP is above potential GDP and fall when real GDP is below potential GDP? Figure 13.11 provides the relevant evidence. The points in the figure indicate the level of inflation and the percent deviation of real GDP from potential GDP for years when real GDP was more than 1 percent above or below potential GDP. (We only use deviations that are greater than 1 percent, because it is difficult to measure the deviations with better than 1 percent accuracy.) Up arrows indicate that inflation increased from the year before the labeled year.

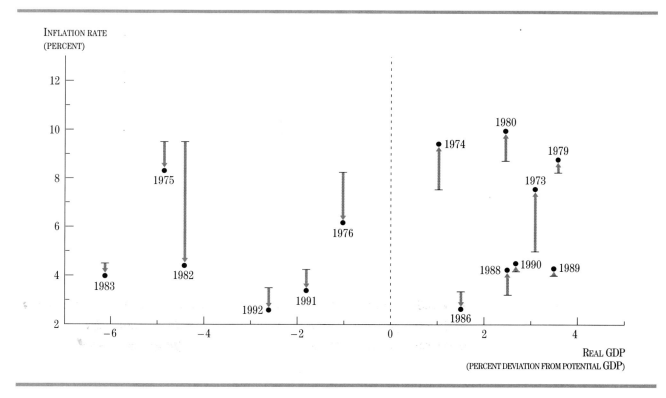

Down arrows indicate that inflation decreased. The length of the arrow is the size of the inflation increase or decrease.

Inflation declines when real GDP is less than—to the left of—potential GDP in Figure 13.11. The biggest decline in inflation occurred in 1982, when real GDP was far below potential GDP. When real GDP is greater than—to the right of—potential GDP, inflation is rising in the vast majority of cases. Figure 13.11 indicates that the theory of the price adjustment line shown in Figure 13.10 fits the facts very well.

**FIGURE 13.11**
**Declines and Increases in Inflation**
The data show that inflation falls when real GDP is below potential GDP; inflation rises when real GDP is above potential GDP.

*Source:* U.S. Department of Commerce.

# Review

▶ The price adjustment line, the second element of the economic fluctuations model, is a flat line showing the level of inflation in the economy at any point in time. The price adjustment line describes the economic behavior of firms and workers setting prices and wages in the economy.

▶ Firms do not change their prices instantaneously when the demand for their product changes. Thus, when aggregate demand changes and real GDP departs from potential GDP, the inflation rate does not immediately change; the price adjustment line does not shift in response to such changes in the short run.

▶ Staggered price setting tends to slow down the adjustment of prices in the economy as a whole.

▶ Over time, however, inflation does respond to departures of real GDP from potential GDP. This response can be described by upward and downward shifts in the price adjustment (*PA*) line over time.

# COMBINING THE AGGREGATE DEMAND/INFLATION CURVE AND THE PRICE ADJUSTMENT LINE

We have now derived two relationships—the aggregate demand/inflation curve and the price adjustment line—that describe real GDP and inflation in the economy as a whole. Both relationships can be combined to make predictions about real GDP and inflation.

Along the aggregate demand/inflation curve in Figure 13.3, real GDP and inflation are negatively related. This curve describes the behavior of firms and consumers as they respond to a higher interest rate caused by higher inflation. They respond by lowering consumption, investment, and net exports. This line presents a range of possible values of real GDP and inflation.

The price adjustment line in Figure 13.10, on the other hand, tells us what the inflation rate is at any point in time. Thus, we can use the price adjustment line to determine exactly what inflation rate applies to the aggregate demand/inflation curve. For example, if the price adjustment line tells us that the inflation rate for 2004 is 5 percent, then we can go right to the aggregate demand/inflation curve to determine what the level of real GDP will be at that 5 percent inflation rate. If the aggregate demand/inflation curve says that real GDP is 2 percent below potential GDP when inflation is 5 percent, then we predict that real GDP is 2 percent below potential GDP. The price adjustment line tells us the current location of inflation—and therefore real GDP—along the aggregate demand/inflation curve.

Figure 13.12 illustrates the determination of real GDP and inflation graphically. It combines the curve from Figure 13.3 with the price adjustment line from Figure 13.10. At any point in time, the price adjustment line is given as shown in Figure 13.12. The price adjustment line intersects the aggregate demand/inflation curve at a single point. It is at this point of intersection where inflation and real GDP are determined. The intersection gives an *equilibrium* level of real GDP and inflation. At that point we can look down to the horizontal axis of the diagram to determine the level of real GDP corresponding to that level of inflation. For ex-

**FIGURE 13.12**
**Determining Real GDP and Inflation**

Real GDP is determined at the intersection of the *ADI* curve and the *PA* line. All three panels have the same *ADI* curve and the same vertical line marking potential GDP. Three different levels of the *PA* line give three different levels of real GDP: less than, equal to, and greater than potential GDP.

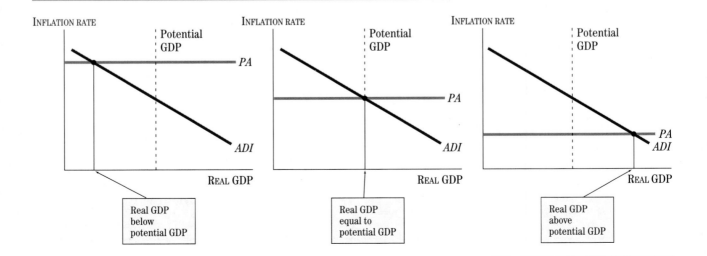

ample, the point of intersection in the left panel of Figure 13.12 might be when inflation is 5 percent and real GDP is 2 percent below potential GDP. The point of intersection in the right panel is at a lower inflation rate when real GDP is above potential GDP. The point of intersection in the middle panel of Figure 13.12 has real GDP equal to potential GDP.

As Figure 13.12 makes clear, the intersection of the price adjustment line and the aggregate demand/inflation curve may give values of real GDP that are either above or below potential GDP. But if real GDP is not equal to potential GDP, then the economy has not fully recovered from a recession, as on the left of Figure 13.12, or returned to potential GDP after a boom, as on the right. To describe dynamic movements of inflation and real GDP, we must consider how either the price adjustment line or the aggregate demand/inflation curve shift over time. That is the subject of the next chapter.

## Review

▶ In any year, the price adjustment line tells us what the inflation rate is. Using the aggregate demand/inflation curve we can then make a prediction about what real GDP is.

▶ The intersection of the aggregate demand/inflation curve and the price adjustment line gives a pair of observations on real GDP and inflation at any point in time.

## CONCLUSION

With the three elements of the economic fluctuations model—the aggregate/demand inflation curve, the price adjustment line, and their intersection—put together, we are now ready to use the model to explain the fluctuations of real GDP and inflation during recessions and booms. In reviewing the different elements it is useful to consider the scissors analogy mentioned in our discussion of the supply and demand model.

The aggregate demand/inflation curve is like one blade of the scissors. The price adjustment line is the other blade. Either blade alone is insufficient to explain economic fluctuations. Either blade alone is an incomplete story. But when the two blades of the scissors are put together to form a pair of scissors, they become a practical tool to explain the ups and downs in the economy. And compared to the complexity and vastness of the whole economy with millions of firms and consumers, this particular pair of scissors is amazingly simple.

## KEY POINTS

**1.** Along the aggregate demand/inflation (*ADI*) curve, real GDP is negatively related to inflation.

**2.** Investment, net exports, and consumption depend negatively on the interest rate. Hence, aggregate expenditure, which includes investment, net exports, and consumption, depends negatively on the interest rate.

**3.** An increase in the interest rate causes the aggregate expenditure line to shift down.

**4.** The level of real GDP at spending balance—the intersection of the aggregate expenditure line and the 45-degree line—depends negatively on the interest rate.

**5.** Central banks' actions to adjust the interest rate to maintain low inflation result in a relationship between interest rates and inflation. When inflation rises, the real interest rate rises. When inflation falls, the real interest rate falls.

**6.** The combined behavior of (1) the interest rate response to inflation and (2) the private sector adjusting spending in response to the interest rate generates an inverse relationship between real GDP and inflation—the aggregate demand/inflation curve.

**7.** Movements along the aggregate demand/inflation curve occur when inflation rises, causing the real interest rate to rise and real GDP to fall. Such movements along the curve also occur when inflation falls, the interest rate declines, and real GDP rises.

**8.** The aggregate demand/inflation curve shifts for many reasons, including a change in government purchases and a change in monetary policy to a different targe rate of inflation.

**9.** When adjusting prices, firms respond slowly to changes in demand and take account of expectations of inflation. So do workers when wages are being adjusted. As a result, inflation tends to increase when real GDP is above potential GDP and tends to decrease when GDP is below potential GDP.

**10.** The staggering of price and wage decisions tends to slow the adjustment of prices in the economy as a whole.

**11.** When combined with the aggregate demand/inflation curve, the price adjustment line provides us with a way to determine real GDP and inflation.

# KEY TERMS

aggregate demand/inflation (*ADI*) curve

monetary policy rule
federal funds rate

target inflation rate
price adjustment (*PA*) line

# QUESTIONS FOR REVIEW

**1.** How do we represent movements of inflation and real GDP in a single diagram?

**2.** Why are investment and net exports inversely related to the interest rate?

**3.** Why is real GDP inversely related to the interest rate in the short run?

**4.** Why does the interest rate rise when inflation begins to rise? Why may this rise be called a policy rule?

**5.** Why is real GDP inversely related to inflation in the short run? What is this relationship called?

**6.** What are examples of movements along the aggregate demand/inflation curve?

**7.** Why does a change in government purchases shift the aggregate demand/inflation curve to the right or left?

**8.** Why does a change in monetary policy shift the aggregate demand/inflation curve to the right or to the left?

**9.** Why does inflation increase when real GDP is above potential GDP?

**10.** What is the significance of expectations of inflation for price adjustment?

**11.** Why does staggered price setting slow down price adjustment in the economy?

# PROBLEMS

**1.** Which of the following statements are true, and which are false? Explain your answers in one or two sentences.
 a) A decrease in the U.S. interest rate will cause the dollar exchange rate to decline.
 b) The central bank typically lowers the interest rate when inflation rises.
 c) A higher interest rate leads to greater net exports because the higher interest rate raises the value of the dollar.
 d) Investment is positively related to the interest rate.

**2.** Suppose that European interest rates are very high relative to those in the United States, and the Fed decides to lower the interest rate as inflation falls in the United States. What effect will this have on the value of the dollar relative to European currencies? Will the U.S. net exports be higher or lower? Why?

**3.** Suppose that the Fed makes a mistake in its implementation of policy: It increases the interest rate while the economy is already going into a recession. What effect will this increase in the interest rate have on real GDP and inflation in the short run?

**4.** Suppose the United States reaches an agreement with Japan that increases U.S. exports to Japan but has no effect on the U.S. imports of Japanese goods. Which way will the aggregate expenditure line shift? Will this cause a shift in the aggregate demand/inflation curve? Sketch the effect of this change in a diagram. What will happen to U.S. real GDP in the short run?

**5.** State which of the following changes causes a shift of the aggregate demand/inflation curve and which ones are a movement along it.

   a) A shift to a higher inflation target in the monetary policy rule

   b) An increase in government purchases

   c) An economic boom in Japan

   d) Being thrifty becomes fashionable

   e) An increase in the German interest rate

   f) A surprise inflationary shock hits the economy

**6.** Suppose you could use a change in either government purchases or monetary policy to increase real GDP in the short run. How would each policy affect consumption, investment, and net exports in the short run? Why?

**7.** Suppose the Fed is considering the two different policy rules, shown in the following table. Graph the policy rules. What economic factors will the Fed consider when deciding which policy rule to follow?

| Inflation | Policy Rule 1 Interest Rate | Policy Rule 2 Interest Rate |
|---|---|---|
| 0 | 1 | 3 |
| 2 | 3 | 5 |
| 4 | 4 | 7 |
| 6 | 7 | 9 |
| 8 | 9 | 11 |

If the Fed is currently following policy rule 1 and then shifts to policy rule 2, which way will the aggregate demand/inflation curve shift? What reasons might the Fed have for changing its policy? What effect will this change have on real GDP?

**8.** Suppose the government implements a policy that subsidizes business investment. How will this affect the relationship between investment and the interest rate? How will the aggregate demand/inflation curve shift? What will happen to real GDP in the short run?

**9.** Suppose you have the following information on the Fed's and the Bundesbank's policy rules:

Fed interest rate = 1.5 (inflation rate − 2) + 2

Bundesbank interest rate = 1.2 (inflation rate − 2) + 3

   a) Graph these policy rules. If the inflation rate is 2 percent in both countries, what will be the interest rate in each country?

   b) Some argue that Germany has a much lower tolerance for inflation than the United States. Can you tell—either from the diagram or from the equations—whether this is true?

**10.** The following table gives a numerical example of an aggregate demand/inflation curve.

| Real GDP (percent deviation from potential GDP) | Inflation (percent per year) |
|---|---|
| 3.0 | 2.0 |
| 2.0 | 2.5 |
| 1.0 | 3.0 |
| 0.0 | 4.0 |
| −1.0 | 5.0 |
| −2.0 | 7.0 |
| −3.0 | 10.0 |

   a) Sketch the curve in a graph like Figure 13.3.

   b) What is the average rate of inflation in the long run?

   c) Suppose that the central bank increases the target inflation rate by 2 percent. What will happen to the average rate of inflation in the long run (assuming that potential GDP growth does not change)?

   d) Sketch a new aggregate demand/inflation curve corresponding to the new higher target inflation rate in part (c). How does the new curve compare to the old curve?

**11.** The following table gives a numerical example of a price adjustment line in the year 2000.

| Real GDP (percent deviation from potential GDP) | Inflation (percent per year) |
|---|---|
| 3.0 | 4.0 |
| 2.0 | 4.0 |
| 1.0 | 4.0 |
| 0.0 | 4.0 |
| −1.0 | 4.0 |
| −2.0 | 4.0 |
| −3.0 | 4.0 |

   a) Sketch the line in a graph like Figure 13.10.

   b) If real GDP is above potential GDP in the year 2000, will the price adjustment line shift up or down in the year 2001? Explain.

   c) In the same graph as part (a), sketch in the aggregate demand/inflation curve given in Problem 10. Find the equilibrium level of real GDP and inflation in the year 2000.

   d) Show what happens to the price adjustment line if there is a sudden increase in inflation expectations.

**12.** Compare and contrast the microeconomic supply and demand model with the macroeconomic model with a price adjustment line and the aggregate demand/inflation curve.

# Toward Recovery and Expansion

The economic fluctuations model is one of the most powerful models in economics. Versions of this model are employed by business economists making forecasts for their clients, by regional economists in state capitals looking at the impact of changes in federal laws, by policy economists in Washington analyzing the effects of the president's economic policy proposals, and by international economists working at organizations like the International Monetary Fund trying to determine the effect of tax or spending changes in hundreds of countries around the world.

Now we are ready to use the economic fluctuations model as explained graphically in the previous chapter. We will focus on using the model to determine the path the economy takes toward recovery after a recession. We examine how that recovery brings real GDP back to potential GDP, where it then can expand along with potential GDP until the next boom or recession. Knowing

the likely speed of the economy toward recovery after a recession is important for choosing the correct economic policy. For example, both President Bush and President Clinton made proposals to speed up the recovery from the recession in the early 1990s. But in both cases the proposals were rejected by Congress. Were the presidents correct, or was Congress correct? On what economic basis are such proposals made or rejected?

In this chapter, we also look at how real GDP and inflation change over time after a shift in monetary policy, either to lower inflation or to higher inflation. We examine boom-bust theories of the business cycle, where monetary policy first errs in causing a boom with higher inflation and then overreacts to the error and causes a recession. We also study the effect of world oil price shocks like those experienced in the 1970s and again in the 1990s.

# THE END OF RECESSIONS AND BOOMS

With the aggregate demand/inflation (*ADI*) curve and the price adjustment (*PA*) line as key elements of our model, we now examine the forces leading to a return of real GDP to potential GDP. To do so, we will focus on a particular example, a change in government purchases. In Chapter 11 we showed how a change in government purchases could push real GDP away from potential GDP in the short run. Now let us see the complete story.

## Real GDP and Inflation over Time

Suppose the government cuts military purchases permanently. We want to examine the effects of this decrease in government purchases on the economy in the short run (about one year), the medium run (two to three years), and the long run (four to five years and beyond). These three lengths of time represent the average duration of recessions and recoveries, but remember that no two economic fluctuations are exactly alike. Some are longer and some are shorter than these time spans. We use the term *short run* to refer to the initial departure of real GDP from potential GDP, *medium run* to refer to the recovery period, and *long run* to refer to when real GDP is nearly back to potential GDP.

Figure 14.1 shows the aggregate demand/inflation curve and the price adjustment line on the same diagram. The intersection of the aggregate demand/inflation

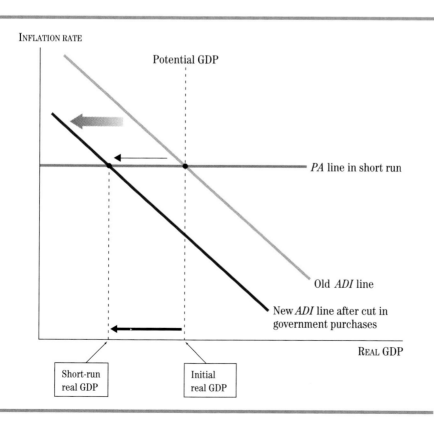

INFLATION RATE

Potential GDP

*PA* line in short run

Old *ADI* line

New *ADI* line after cut in government purchases

REAL GDP

Short-run real GDP

Initial real GDP

**FIGURE 14.1**
**Short-Run Effects of a Reduction in Government Purchases**
In the short run, the *PA* line does not move. Thus, in the short run, real GDP declines by the amount of the shift in the *ADI* curve, as noted on the horizontal axis.

curve and the price adjustment line determines a level of inflation and real GDP. Let us assume that we began with real GDP equal to potential GDP. Thus, the initial intersection of the aggregate demand/inflation curve and the price adjustment line occurs at a level of real GDP equal to potential GDP.

Now, recall from the previous chapter that a change in government purchases shifts the aggregate demand/inflation curve; in particular, a decline in government purchases shifts the aggregate demand/inflation curve to the left. Because the price adjustment line is flat, and because it does not move in the short run, a change in government purchases—shown by the shift in the aggregate demand/inflation curve from the "old" to the "new" in Figure 14.1—leads to a change in real GDP by the same amount as the shift in the aggregate demand/inflation curve. This is the short-run effect. The decrease in government purchases initially moves the aggregate demand/inflation curve to the left, and real GDP falls to the point indicated by the intersection of the price adjustment line and the new aggregate demand/inflation curve. At the new intersection real GDP is at a level below potential GDP.

Now consider what happens over time. The tendency for prices to adjust over time is represented by upward or downward shifts of the price adjustment line. Only in the short run does the price adjustment line stay put, reflecting the delay in the adjustment of price decisions. What is likely to happen over time when real GDP is below potential GDP? Inflation should begin to decline, because firms will increase their prices by smaller amounts. We represent a decline in inflation by shifting the price adjustment line down, as shown in Figure 14.2. The initial impact of the change in government spending took us to a point we label *SR,* for short run, in Figure 14.2. At that point, real GDP is lower than potential GDP. Hence, inflation will fall and the price adjustment line shifts down, as shown in the diagram. There is now a new point of intersection; we label that point *MR,* for medium run.

Note how real GDP has started to recover. At the point labeled *MR* in the diagram, real GDP is still below potential GDP but it is higher than the low (*SR*) point in the downturn. The reason real GDP starts to rise is that the lower inflation rate causes the central bank to lower the interest rate. The lower interest rate increases investment spending and causes net exports to rise. As a result, real GDP rises.

Because real GDP is still below potential GDP, there is still a tendency for inflation to fall. Thus, the price adjustment line continues to shift downward until real GDP returns to potential GDP. Figure 14.2 shows a third intersection at the point marked *LR* for the long run, where production has increased all the way back to potential GDP. At this point real GDP has reached long-run equilibrium in the sense that real GDP equals potential GDP. With real GDP equal to potential GDP, the price adjustment line stops shifting down. Inflation is at a new lower level than before the decline in government purchases, but at the final point of intersection in the diagram it is no longer falling. Thus, real GDP remains equal to potential GDP.

Note how successive downward shifts of the price adjustment line with intersections along the aggregate demand/inflation curve trace out values for real GDP and inflation as the economy first goes into recession and then recovers. In the short run, a decline in production comes about from the decrease in government spending; that

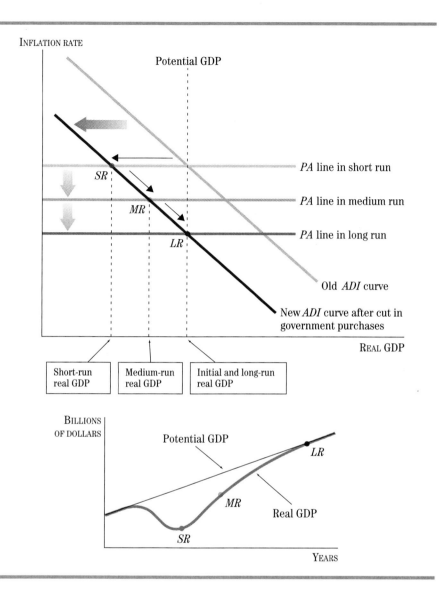

**FIGURE 14.2**
**Dynamic Adjustment after a Reduction in Government Purchases**
Initially, the reduction in government purchases shifts the *ADI* curve to the left. This reduces real GDP to the point labeled *SR*, or the short run. Then the *PA* line begins to shift down because real GDP is less than potential GDP. The *PA* line keeps shifting down until real GDP is back to potential GDP.

decline is followed by successive years of reversal as the economy recovers and real GDP returns to potential GDP. The behavior is shown in the sketch in the lower part of Figure 14.2. Thus, we have achieved one of the major goals of this chapter: showing how recessions end and recoveries take the economy back to normal.

## A More Detailed Report: Economic Behavior Behind the Scenes

It is possible to give a more detailed report on what happens to consumption, net exports, and investment during this temporary departure from, and return to, potential GDP. To do so, we need to bring in some of our supporting diagrams to examine the source of the movements in real GDP and inflation that we have already summarized with the aggregate demand/inflation curve and the price adjustment line diagram in Figure 14.2.

Figure 14.3 includes these supporting diagrams. At first glance, it may look complicated, but it simply includes information we discussed in Chapter 13. The diagram in the lower right panel is identical to that in Figure 14.2. Thus, we are still examining the decline in government purchases. The monetary policy rule describing the response of interest rates to inflation in the upper-left panel is identical to that of Figure 13.5. The upper-right panel is the familiar aggregate expenditure line and 45-degree line diagram. The small table in the lower left summarizes how each component of real GDP changes in the short run and the long run. The arrows in the table indicate what happens compared with what would have happened in the absence of change in government purchases. The path of the economy in the absence of the hypothetical change is called the **baseline.** The term *baseline* is commonly used in public policy discussions to refer to what would have happened if a contemplated policy action were not taken; the arrows in the table tell whether a variable is up or down relative to the baseline. In this case, the baseline for real GDP is potential GDP. Thus, a downward-pointing arrow in the real GDP column means real GDP is below potential GDP; an upward-pointing arrow means real GDP is above potential GDP.

**baseline:** the path of an economic variable that would occur without the policy change under consideration.

### Short Run

The decline in government spending gets things started. The aggregate expenditure (*AE*) line in the upper-right panel shifts down by the amount of the decrease in government spending. The new spending balance gives a lower level of real GDP. With lower income, people consume less. In the short run, investment does not change because interest rates have not yet changed, but net exports rise because the lower level of income in the United States means imports fall. That is, exports minus imports increase. This is all incorporated in the aggregate expenditure diagram.

The aggregate demand/inflation curve shifts to the left, and with no change in the price adjustment line, real GDP declines. This short-run effect is shown in the first row in the table. Real GDP and consumption are down *relative to the baseline.* Net exports are up *relative to the baseline.*

### Medium Run

Price adjustment takes us to the medium run. We do not know exactly how long this takes, but we suppose as an approximation that two or three years is the medium run. We know the decline in real GDP below potential GDP causes inflation to fall; thus, we shift the price adjustment line down.

With the lower rate of inflation the central bank reduces the interest rate. This is shown in the upper left of Figure 14.3. The lower interest rate means that the aggregate expenditure line is moving back up again. The level of real GDP giving spending balance increases. The intersection of the aggregate demand/inflation curve and price adjustment line is at a higher level of real GDP. This medium-run level of real GDP is still below potential GDP, however.

### Long Run

Now consider the long run, approximately four to five years. By this time real GDP has returned to potential GDP. Government spending is still lower than it was originally because we have assumed that this is a permanent decline in military

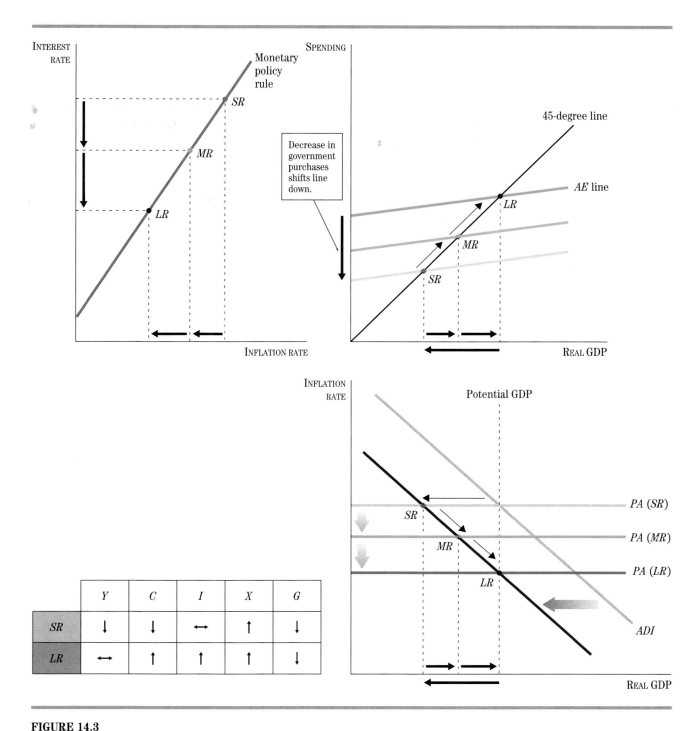

**FIGURE 14.3**

**More Detailed Analysis of a Reduction in Government Purchases**

The inflation–real GDP graph in the lower right diagram is the same as Figure 14.2. Also shown are the *AE* line, which shifts down by the amount government purchases are cut, and the monetary policy rule where interest rates fall as inflation falls. This decline in interest rates causes the *AE* line to move back up again. The arrows in the table keep track of the changes in the major variables relative to where they started.

**FIGURE 14.4**
**Increase in Long-Term Growth after a Recession Caused by a Decrease in Government Purchases**

A higher investment share of real GDP that results from the decline in government purchases leads to more capital and a higher growth of potential GDP. After the recession, real GDP will grow along, or fluctuate around, this higher growth path.

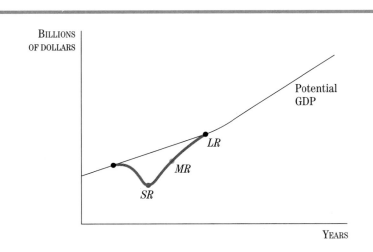

spending. Because real GDP is equal to potential GDP, aggregate income in the economy—which equals real GDP—is back to normal. Because income is back to normal, the effects of income on consumption and net exports are just what they would have been in the absence of the change in government purchases.

What about interest rates and their effect on consumption, investment, and net exports? We know that real GDP is back to potential GDP, so that the sum of consumption, investment, and net exports must be higher to make up for the decrease in government purchases. Interest rates must therefore remain lower. The summary table in Figure 14.3 shows consumption, investment, and net exports higher in the long run. We would expect that the consumption effects are small, however, because consumption is not very sensitive to interest rates. Most of the long-run impact of the decline in government purchases is to raise investment and net exports. The story is complete now. We have put all the pieces of the puzzle together.

To summarize, a decrease in government purchases has negative effects on the economy in the short run. Real GDP declines. Workers are laid off. Unemployment rises. In the long run, the economy is back to potential GDP, and consumption, investment, and net exports have gone up. In the long run, the decrease in government purchases permits greater private investment and more net exports. The increase in investment benefits long-run economic growth, as we know from Chapter 8; hence, the path of potential GDP over time has risen, and now real GDP is growing more quickly, as shown in Figure 14.4. In this sense, the decrease in government purchases is good for the long term despite its negative short-run effects.

## The Return to Potential GDP after a Boom

Surprisingly, the adjustment of real GDP back to potential GDP after a boom can be explained using the same theory. For example, suppose an increase in real GDP above potential GDP is caused by an increase in government purchases for new highway construction. Starting from potential GDP, the aggregate demand/inflation curve would shift to the right. Real GDP would increase above potential GDP in the short run.

With real GDP above potential GDP, however, firms start to adjust their prices; inflation begins to rise. We would represent that as an upward shift in the price adjustment line. In the medium run real GDP would still be above potential GDP, and inflation would continue to rise. Eventually, real GDP would go back to potential GDP and the boom would be over. Thus, we predict that real GDP goes back to potential GDP. However, in this case, because government purchases have risen, the new long-run equilibrium will have a higher interest rate, and the sum of consumption, investment, and net exports will be lower.

## Review

▶ With the price adjustment line and the aggregate demand/inflation curve, we can now explain both the initial steps of real GDP away from potential GDP and the return to potential GDP.

▶ In the short run a decline in government purchases, or any other change that shifts the aggregate demand/inflation curve to the left, will cause real GDP to fall below potential GDP.

▶ In the medium run, when the interest rate starts to fall, real GDP begins to increase again. Investment and net exports start to rise and partly offset the decline in government purchases.

▶ In the long run, real GDP returns to potential GDP. Interest rates are lower and consumption plus investment plus net exports have risen.

# CHANGES IN MONETARY POLICY

A large change in government spending is, of course, not the only thing that can temporarily push real GDP away from potential GDP. Changes in taxes, consumer confidence, or foreign demand can also cause recessions or booms. But a particularly important factor is a change in monetary policy.

Consider, for example, a change in monetary policy that aims to lower the rate of inflation. Suppose that the inflation rate is about 10 percent and a new head of the central bank is appointed who has the objective of reducing inflation. Suppose the aim is to reduce the inflation rate to 4 percent. A reduction in the inflation rate is called **disinflation. Deflation** means declining prices, or a negative inflation rate, which is different from a declining inflation rate. To be sure, the aim of policy in this example is not deflation.

**disinflation:** a reduction in the inflation rate.

**deflation:** a decrease in the overall price level, or a negative inflation rate.

Figure 14.5 shows the short-run, medium-run, and long-run impact of such a change in the monetary policy. The focal point of the figure is the lower-right diagram. The other panels play supporting roles to help us keep track of the details. The upper-left panel shows the change in monetary policy. A shift to a lower target inflation rate means a leftward shift or, equivalently, an upward shift, in the monetary policy rule line, as we discussed in Chapter 13.

With inflation initially at 10 percent, the Fed's new policy indicates the need to increase the interest rate. Hence, the initial effect of the lower target inflation rate is an increase in the interest rate. This increase in the interest rate is shown in the upper-left panel of Figure 14.5.

One effect of the increase in the interest rate is to lower investment. In addition, the higher interest rate causes the dollar to appreciate, and this tends to reduce

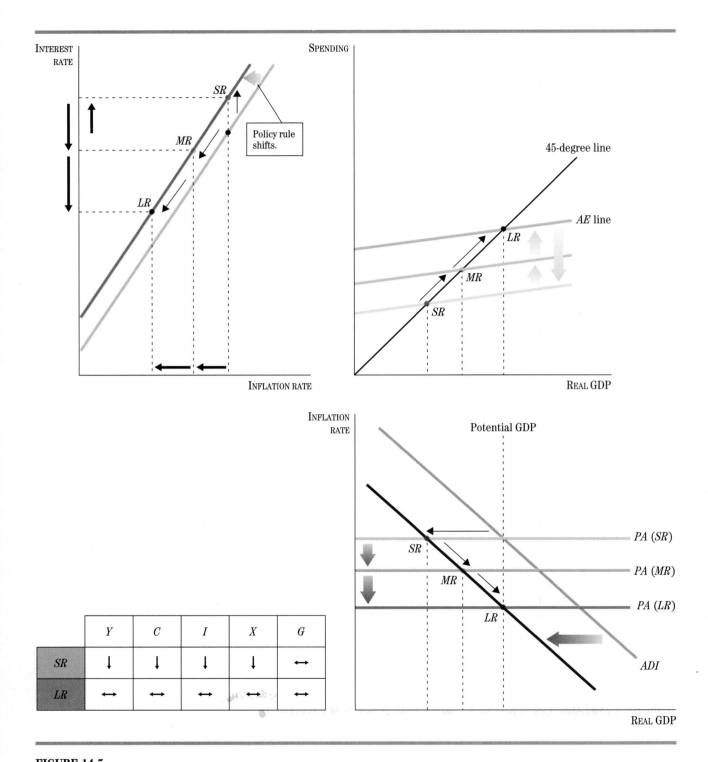

**FIGURE 14.5**
**Disinflation: A Transition to Lower Inflation**
The figure shows how a change in monetary policy to a lower target for inflation affects real GDP
over time. In the end, inflation is lower and real GDP is back to potential GDP.

net exports. The effect of the shift in investment and net exports is to shift the aggregate expenditure curve down and to reduce real GDP. The point labeled *SR* determines the new level of spending balance in the upper-right diagram and we therefore shift the aggregate demand/inflation curve, as shown in the lower-right diagram. Since prices are slow to adjust, we do not move the price adjustment line yet. Thus, inflation remains at 10 percent in the short run. The first row of the table summarizes the short-run effects. Note that consumption falls because real GDP is down and income is down. At this time things seem very grim. The short-run effect of the change to a new monetary policy is to cause real GDP to fall below potential GDP. If the disinflation is large enough, then this might mean a decline in real GDP, or a recession. If the disinflation is very small and gradual, then the decline in real GDP could result in a *temporary growth slowdown.* In a temporary growth slowdown, real GDP growth does not turn negative, as in a recession.

In any case, with real GDP below potential GDP, inflation will begin to decline. We show this in the lower-right diagram by moving the price adjustment line down. The lower price adjustment line, labeled *MR* for medium run, intersects the aggregate demand/inflation curve at a higher level of real GDP. Thus, the economy has begun to recover. The recovery starts because as inflation has come down, the Fed has begun to lower the interest rate. This is shown in the upper-left graph of Figure 14.5. As the interest rate declines, investment and net exports begin to rise again and the aggregate expenditure curve shifts up, as shown in the upper-right diagram.

However, at this medium-run situation, real GDP is still below potential GDP, so the inflation rate continues to decline. We show this in the diagram by shifting the price adjustment line down again. To make a long story short, we show the price adjustment line shifting all the way down to where it intersects the aggregate demand/inflation curve at potential GDP. Thus, in this long-run equilibrium, the economy has fully recovered, and the inflation rate is at its new lower target.

Note that the long-run equilibrium has consumption, investment, and net exports back to normal. However, inflation is changed, and it is lower. Moreover, with lower inflation the interest rate is also lower. It is interesting to note that to get this lower interest rate in the long run, the Fed first had to raise the interest rate, as shown in the upper-left graph in Figure 14.5.

The overall dynamic impacts of this change in monetary policy are very important. The initial impact of a monetary policy change is on real GDP. It is only later that the change shows up in inflation. Thus, there is a long lag in the effect of monetary policy on inflation.

Lower inflation would likely make potential GDP grow faster, perhaps because there is less uncertainty and productivity rises faster. If so, the return of real GDP to potential GDP will mean that real GDP is higher, and the long-run benefits of the disinflation to people in the economy may be great over the years. But such changes in the growth of real GDP will appear small in the span of years during which a disinflation takes place and will not change the basic story that a reduction in the rate of inflation, unless it is very gradual, usually results in a recession.

## The Volcker Disinflation

The scenario we just described is very similar to the disinflation in the United States in the early 1980s under Paul Volcker, the head of the Fed from 1979 to 1987. First, interest rates skyrocketed as the disinflation began. The federal funds interest rate

# Using Economics to Explain the Recovery from the Great Depression

The Great Depression was the biggest economic downturn in American history. There is simply no parallel either before or since. As shown in the figure, from 1929 to 1933, real GDP declined 35 percent. Between 1933 and 1937, real GDP rose 33 percent, then declined 5 percent in a recession in 1938. Real GDP increased by a spectacular 49 percent between 1938 and 1942. By 1942, real GDP had caught up with potential GDP, as estimated in the figure.

There is still much disagreement among economists about what caused the Great Depression, that is, the initial departure of real GDP from potential GDP. In their monetary history of the United States, Milton Friedman and Anna Schwartz argue that it was caused by an error in monetary policy, which implied a massive leftward shift in the aggregate demand/ inflation curve. Unfortunately, it took several years of continually declining real GDP, declining inflation, and even deflation before the errors in monetary policy were corrected.

Another explanation is that there was a downward shift in consumption and investment spending that lowered the aggregate expenditures. Peter Temin of MIT has argued that such a spending shift was a cause of the Great Depression.

But whatever the initial cause, there seems to be more consensus that monetary policy was responsible for the belated recovery from the Great Depression. Interest rates (in real terms) fell precipitously in 1933 and remained low or negative throughout most of the second half of the 1930s. These low interest rates led to an increase in investment and net exports. Christina Romer of the University of California at Berkeley estimates that without the monetary response "the U.S. economy in 1942 would have been 50 percent below its pre-Depression trend path, rather than back to its normal level."*

Could the recovery from the Great Depression be associated with an increase in government purchases or a reduction in taxes? Evidently not. Romer shows that government purchases and tax policy were basically unchanged until 1941, when government spending increased sharply during World War II. By that time the economy had already made up most of the Depression decline in real GDP relative to potential GDP.

*Christina Romer, "What Ended the Great Depression?" *Journal of Economic History,* Vol. 52, December 1992, pp. 757–784.

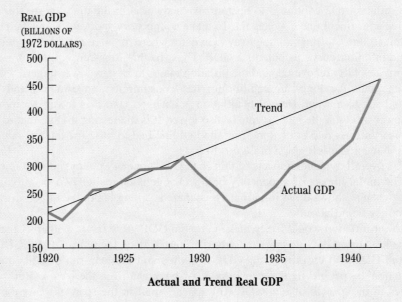

**Actual and Trend Real GDP**

went over 20 percent. By any measure, real GDP fell well below potential GDP in the early 1980s. Workers were laid off, the unemployment rate rose to 10.8 percent, investment declined, and net exports fell. Eventually, pricing decisions began to adjust and inflation began to come down. As inflation came down, the Fed began to lower the interest rate; the economy eventually recovered. In 1982, a recovery was under way and by 1985, the economy had returned to near its potential. The good news was that inflation was down from over 10 percent to about 4 percent, where it remained for several years before the economy entered a boom period in 1988. But that is another story.

## Reinflation

The opposite of disinflation might be called **reinflation,** an increase in the inflation rate caused by a change in monetary policy. This could be analyzed with our theory simply by reversing the preceding process, starting with a change in monetary policy to a higher target inflation rate. This would cause the aggregate demand/inflation curve to shift right. There would be a temporary boom, but eventually inflation would rise and cut off the boom.

Although it would be unusual for central bankers to explicitly admit they were raising the target inflation rate, there could be political pressures that would lead to less concern about inflation. In this way there would be an implicit rise in the target for inflation.

Reinflation is one way to interpret the increase in inflation in the United States and other countries in the 1970s. But there were other things going on at that time, including a quadrupling of oil prices as petroleum-exporting countries, many of which are located in the Middle East, banded together and formed a cartel. We consider oil price shocks in the next section.

**reinflation:** an increase in the inflation rate caused by a change in monetary policy.

## Review

▶ Disinflation is a reduction in inflation. It occurs when the central bank shifts monetary policy in the direction of a lower inflation target.

▶ According to the theory of economic fluctuations, disinflation has either a temporary slowing of real GDP growth or a recession as a by-product. A higher interest rate at the start of a disinflation lowers investment spending and net exports. This causes real GDP to fall below potential GDP. Eventually the economy recovers. Inflation comes down and so does the interest rate.

▶ The large disinflation in the early 1980s in the United States was accompanied by a recession, as predicted by the theory.

# THE CASE OF A PRICE SHOCK OR SUPPLY SHOCK

Shifts in the aggregate demand/inflation curve are called **demand shocks.** The change in government purchases and the change in monetary policy described in the previous two sections of this chapter are examples of demand shocks. However, shifts in the aggregate demand/inflation curve are not the only things that can push real GDP away from potential GDP. In particular, the price adjustment line can shift.

**demand shock:** a shift in one of the components of aggregate demand that leads to a shift in the aggregate demand/inflation curve.

## What Is a Price Shock?

**price shock:** a change in the price of a key commodity such as oil, usually because of a shortage, that causes a shift in the price adjustment line; also sometimes called a supply shock.

Shifts in the price adjustment line are called **price shocks.** A price shock usually occurs when a temporary shortage of a key commodity, or group of commodities, drives up prices by such a large amount that it has a noticeable effect on the rate of inflation. Oil price shocks have been common in the last 25 years. For example, oil prices rose sharply in 1974, in 1979, and again in 1990. After such shocks there have been declines in real GDP and increases in unemployment. Hence, they appear to move real GDP significantly, though temporarily, away from potential GDP.

Price shocks are sometimes called *supply shocks* in an attempt to distinguish them from demand shocks due to changes in government spending or monetary policy. However, a shift in potential GDP—rather than a shift in the price adjustment line—is more appropriately called a supply shock. Shifts in potential GDP—such as a sudden spurt in productivity growth due to new inventions—can, of course, cause real GDP to fluctuate. Recall that *real business cycle theory* places great emphasis on shifts in potential GDP. Although a price shock might be accompanied by a shift in potential GDP, it need not be. Here we are looking at departures of real GDP from potential GDP and thus focusing on price shocks.

**real business cycle theory:** a theory of macroeconomics that stresses that shifts in potential GDP are a primary cause of fluctuations in real GDP; the shifts in potential GDP are usually caused by changes in technology. (Ch. 11)

## The Effect of Price Shocks

How does our theory of economic fluctuations allow us to predict the effect of price shocks? The impact of a price shock can be illustrated graphically, as shown in Figure 14.6. In the case of a large increase in oil prices, for example, the price adjustment line will shift up to a higher level of inflation. Why? Because a large increase in oil prices will at first lead to an increase in the price of everything that

**FIGURE 14.6**
**A Price Shock**

Initially, inflation and the *PA* line rise because of a shock to oil or agricultural prices. This causes real GDP to fall. With real GDP below potential GDP, inflation begins to decline. As inflation declines, real GDP returns to potential GDP.

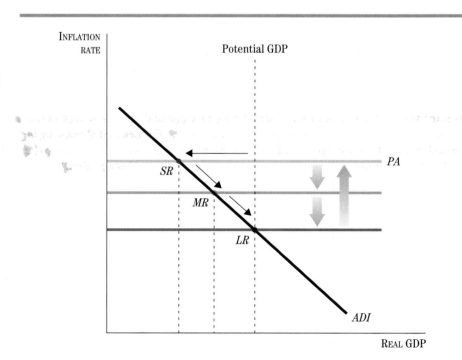

uses oil in production: home heating, gasoline, airplane fuel, airfares, plastic toys, and many other things. The overall price level is affected. As the price level rises, the price adjustment line, measuring inflation, must shift up.

The immediate impact of the shock is to lower real GDP as the intersection of the price adjustment line with the aggregate demand/inflation curve moves to the left. The reason this occurs is that interest rates rise, reducing investment spending and net exports.

With real GDP below potential GDP, however, the reduction in spending will put pressure on firms to adjust their prices. The lower prices bring about a lower rate of inflation. Thus, in the period following the rise of inflation, we begin to see a reversal. Inflation starts to decline. As inflation falls, interest rates begin to decline and the economy starts to recover again. If the central bank does not change its inflation target, the rate of inflation will return to where it was before the price shock started.

### Temporary Shifts in the Price Adjustment Line

In this analysis of the price shock, the central bank raises interest rates, and the resulting decline in real GDP exerts countervailing forces to reduce inflation. It is possible for some price shocks to have only a temporary effect on inflation. Such a temporary effect can be shown graphically as a rise followed by a quick fall in the price adjustment line. In such a situation—where the price shock would be expected to automatically reverse itself—it would be wise for the central bank to delay raising the interest rate. Then if the price shock only has a temporary effect on inflation, the decline in real GDP can be avoided. In reality, whenever there is a price shock there is a great debate about whether it will have a temporary or permanent effect on inflation. The debate is rarely settled until after the fact.

Price shocks can also occur when commodity prices fall. For example, in 1986 there was a decline in oil prices. This resulted in a temporary decrease in inflation and a rise in real GDP, exactly what would be predicted by the theory of economic fluctuations.

### Stagflation

An important difference between price shocks and demand shocks is that output declines while inflation rises in the case of a price shock. For demand shocks, inflation and output are positively related over the period of recession and recovery. The situation in which inflation is up and real GDP is down is called **stagflation.** As we have shown, price shocks can lead to stagflation.

**stagflation:** the situation in which high inflation and high unemployment occur simultaneously.

# Review

▶ A price shock is a large change in the price of some key commodity like oil. Such shocks can push real GDP away from potential GDP and lead to a recession.

▶ In the aftermath of a price shock, the interest rate rises. Eventually, with real GDP below potential GDP, inflation begins to come down and the economy recovers.

# COMBINING DIFFERENT SCENARIOS

The particular events or scenarios we have used thus far to illustrate the theory of economic fluctuations are isolated from each other. This has made it easier to explain what happens in the economy over time. However, in the real world, we rarely have one event occurring in isolation from others. Policymakers do not have the luxury of considering one event at a time. Fortunately, the economic fluctuations model is powerful enough to apply to such real-world situations. In this section, we show how.

## A Monetary Policy Change with a Government Purchases Change

The case of a decrease in government purchases discussed earlier is an important example of where it is useful to combine different scenarios. In particular, it calls for combining such a change in government purchases with a change in monetary policy. This is shown in Figure 14.7. The leftward shift in the aggregate demand/inflation curve due to reduction in government purchases is counteracted by a rightward shift in the aggregate demand/inflation curve due to monetary policy. If the change in monetary policy is by just the right amount, there will be no short-run impact on real GDP.

This type of shift requires a complex coordination of the central bank policy with the change in government purchases. In practice, this is difficult because the timing of the changes is uncertain—Congress could delay cutting purchases, for example, or the president might have trouble getting enough votes to pass the legislation needed to reduce government purchases. Or, a new president with different ideas could come into office. It was just this type of coordination problem that arose several times in the United States during the efforts to reduce government spending in the 1990s. Proposals to reduce government spending were made in

**FIGURE 14.7**

**Change in Monetary Policy to Accompany a Change in Government Purchases**

If the central bank uses an interest rate rule for monetary policy, then a reduction in government purchases that lowers interest rates in the long run will end up reducing inflation. The central bank can avoid the reduction in inflation by shifting its policy rule, as shown in the figure.

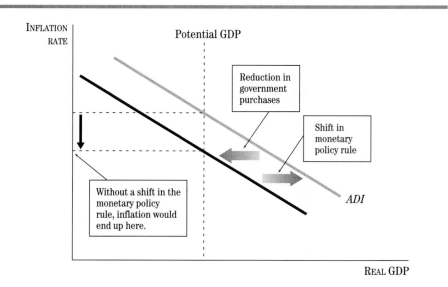

1990, 1993, and 1995. Each time the hope was that the Fed would adjust its monetary policy in a way consistent with a lower interest rate. This is an example of a combination of two scenarios: a reduction in government purchases and a change in monetary policy.

## Monetary Errors and Reversals: A Boom-Bust Cycle

Another case where combining different scenarios leads to a more realistic description of reality is called a **boom-bust cycle,** which is illustrated in Figure 14.8. In this case, the central bank first makes a mistake and lowers the interest rate too much. Political pressure might be behind such a development. In any case we know

**boom-bust cycle:** a business cycle caused by a monetary policy in which interest rates are initially too low, causing a boom, and there is a subsequent increase in interest rates, which causes a recession.

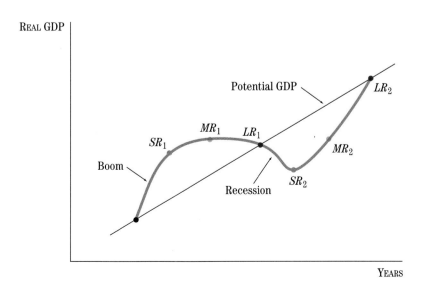

**FIGURE 14.8**
**A Complete Boom-Bust Cycle**
First, the central bank provides too much stimulus. The *ADI* curve shifts right, causing a boom. Inflation rises. Then the central bank notices the error and shifts the *ADI* curve back, causing a recession. Eventually, real GDP is brought to potential GDP. The short-run, medium-run, and long-run points for the boom and the recession are shown on both panels.

# Brief History of Thought on Price Adjustment

Price adjustment has played a key role in theories of economic fluctuations since the beginning of economics. In the late 1700s, while Adam Smith was still working on the *Wealth of Nations,* David Hume, the Scottish economist and philosopher, wrote about slow price adjustment as a reason for economic fluctuations. Hume wrote, ". . . by degrees the price rises, first of one commodity, then of another."* More than 150 years later, John Maynard Keynes argued in the 1930s that unemployment occurs because prices or wages do not adjust enough, though he also worried that too rapid reductions in wages could reduce consumption demand and make a recession worse. Fifty years after Keynes wrote, Milton Friedman argued that "prices are sticky,"[†] and that slow price and wage adjustment is the reason why the economy returns gradually to potential GDP in the long run.

Today economists still focus on the slow adjustment of prices. However, views about price adjustment have not been stagnant for 200 years. Especially in the last 25 years, practical experience and improved methods to deal with expectations, limited information, and implicit contracts have led to an improved understanding of the role of price adjustment in fluctuations.

The price adjustment line reflects this experience and improved methods. It is a graphical representation of the effects of slow price adjustment on economic fluctuations. Due to slow price adjustment, the price adjustment line is flat and does not shift in the short run. After the short run, however, prices do start to adjust and the curve shifts either down, as in Figure 14.2, or up.

An alternative graph—shown in this box—has also been used by economists to represent the slow adjustment of prices. In this alternative graph the overall price level—rather than the inflation rate—is on the vertical axis and real GDP is on the horizontal axis. Potential GDP is shown by a vertical dashed line. The upward-sloping curve in the graph shows different combinations of the overall price level and real GDP. Along the flat region of the curve, the overall price level does not change as real GDP increases. This represents a range of sticky prices; some authors call this range the "Keynesian range" because real GDP was well below potential GDP during the Great Depression when Keynes argued that in such circumstances the price level would not change much when real GDP changed. The range where the curve becomes vertical is sometimes called the "classical range" because

Keynes argued that classical economists such as Hume and Smith implicitly assumed that the economy was near potential and that prices would be flexible, rising rapidly if real GDP increased further.

The upward-sloping curve in this diagram is sometimes called an "aggregate supply curve." It is possible to combine this aggregate supply curve with a downward-sloping "aggregate demand curve," much like the price adjustment line is combined with the aggregate demand/inflation curve.

Although such an aggregate supply curve highlights Keynes's distinction between his own theory and those of the classical economists, it does not reflect the experience and methods of the last several decades. For example, it predicts that the price level will fall when real GDP falls below potential GDP; but in reality the price level rarely falls in this situation. Instead, the inflation rate falls, as described by downward shifts in the price adjustment line in Figure 14.2. Moreover, the "Keynesian" and "classical" ranges are not accurate characterizations of the history of economic thought because many of the classical economists as well as many of today's non-Keynesian economists assume that prices are sticky.

If you continue your study of economics, you will find that there are still other graphical approaches used by authors of more advanced textbooks in macroeconomics. Some authors draw an aggregate supply curve that is flat through its whole range, others argue that an aggregate supply curve does not exist, and still others avoid the use of such graphs entirely, using only microeconomic supply curves.

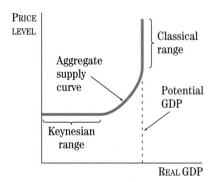

*David Hume: Writings on Economics,* ed. E. Rotwein (Madison, Wisc.: University of Wisconsin Press, 1955), p. 38.

[†]*Newsweek,* July 12, 1982, p. 64.

that such an error will cause a boom and a rise in inflation. The boom and the rise in inflation themselves might cause the central bank to see the error of its ways and to reverse its error. If so, the central bank will shift its policy again. This will then whipsaw the economy down, and a boom will quickly become a recession. Eventually the economy will recover from the recession, but the errors by the central bank—whether avoidable or unavoidable—have done damage. They have caused a complete economic fluctuation.

To illustrate a boom-bust cycle in Figure 14.8, we have patched two scenarios together. Scenario 1 is the mistaken shift in monetary policy that causes the aggregate demand/inflation curve to shift to the right with the reduction in interest rates causing the boom. Scenario 2 is the reversal, which causes the recession. Each scenario has a short run, a medium run, and a long run, as shown in the lower panel of Figure 14.8. Observe the path that real GDP would follow and how it corresponds to the points on the diagram.

Comparing the boom-bust cycle in Figure 14.8 with some actual economic fluctuations reveals a remarkable similarity. For example, compare the path of real GDP in Figure 14.8 with Figure 13.1 at the beginning of the previous chapter, which showed the economic fluctuations in real GDP and inflation in the United States economy from 1987 to 1994. This period fits into a boom-bust cycle very well.

## Review

▶ The real world is characterized by combinations of scenarios rather than by isolated scenarios.

▶ One combination of scenarios is a coordinated change in monetary policy when government purchases change. This raises issues about the coordination of government spending and monetary policies.

▶ Typically, mistakes in monetary policy have been followed by reversals that have led to boom-bust cycles. A boom scenario is followed by a bust scenario.

## CONCLUSION

Using the diagram with the aggregate demand/inflation curve and the price adjustment line, we can explain not only the first steps toward recessions and booms but also the recovery of the economy.

As we developed this model, we tested each piece of it. Each piece was shown to pass two tests: It fit the facts well, and it made economic sense. In conclusion, it is appropriate to ask how well the complete model fits the facts. How well does it explain actual behavior of real GDP and inflation in the economy? One basic test that the model passes is its consistency with the fact that inflation has remained greater than zero, year after year, without the price level declining even when real GDP returns to potential GDP after recessions. Any model that required the price level to fall in order for real GDP to return to potential GDP would be hopelessly wrong.

But the model also passes more stringent tests nearly as well. Figure 14.9 shows four actual patterns of fluctuations of real GDP and inflation. Each of the four episodes can be identified with a particular change in the economy that we

**FIGURE 14.9**
**Four Different Types of Economic Fluctuations**
Four different patterns of inflation and real GDP show the different types of economic fluctuations that can
be explained by the theory of economic fluctuations described in the text. (The number following the year
in the labeled points is the *quarter* of the year.)

have described in this chapter, either single scenarios or two spliced together. The episodes are labeled disinflation, boom-bust cycle, price shock, and reinflation. Although the pictures are not as smooth as in the theoretical diagrams, the theory works very well.

In the disinflation episode, real GDP falls below potential GDP and inflation declines, as would be predicted by a leftward shift of the aggregate demand/inflation curve followed by downward movement in inflation. The boom-bust cycle is easily explained by the combined monetary policy scenarios discussed in the previous section. In the price shock episode, inflation rises and real GDP declines, as would be predicted by an upward shift in the price adjustment line. In the reinflation episode, there is a boom and inflation rises, as would be predicted by the theory in the case of a demand shock.

The fact that real GDP returns toward potential GDP in the long run is also a test of the model because in reality all recessions and booms have ended. Real GDP appears to fluctuate around potential GDP rather than getting stuck forever in a boom or a recession. The tendency for real GDP to return toward potential GDP allows us to use the theory of long-run growth when discussing long-run trends in the economy. As the economy fluctuates, potential GDP gradually increases over time.

# KEY POINTS

**1.** An increase in government purchases temporarily causes a boom, but as prices adjust, real GDP returns to potential GDP.

**2.** A decline in government purchases temporarily reduces real GDP, but over time the economy recovers as prices adjust.

**3.** Shifts in monetary policy, including explicit attempts to disinflate or reinflate, cause real GDP to depart from potential GDP temporarily. But eventually real GDP returns to potential GDP and only the inflation rate is changed.

**4.** Price shocks can also cause recessions. A price shock that raises the inflation rate will cause the interest rate to rise and real GDP to fall.

**5.** If the Fed follows its monetary policy rule, then it will raise interest rates following a price shock, and eventually inflation will come back down.

**6.** If a price shock is clearly temporary, then the Fed should not change the interest rate.

**7.** Boom-bust cycles that appear common in the history of economic fluctuations can be explained by monetary policy errors followed by attempts to reverse the errors.

**8.** Shifts of the price adjustment line and aggregate demand/inflation curve trace out actual observations fairly closely. Thus, the economic fluctuations model works well, but, like most models in economics and elsewhere, it is not perfect.

# KEY TERMS

baseline
disinflation
deflation

reinflation
demand shock
price shock

stagflation
boom-bust cycle

# QUESTIONS FOR REVIEW

**1.** What causes the economy to recover after a recession? Does your answer depend on the cause of the recession?

**2.** What is the difference between the long-run and the short-run effects of a change in government spending?

**3.** What is disinflation, and how does the central bank bring it about?

**4.** What is reinflation, and what impact does it have on real GDP in the short run and long run?

**5.** What is a price shock, and why have price shocks frequently been followed by increases in unemployment?

**6.** What is the difference between a price shock and a supply shock?

**7.** Why do monetary policy errors seem to lead to boom-bust cycles?

**8.** When is it important to coordinate monetary policy with changes in plans for government spending?

**9.** In what ways is the economic fluctuations model discussed in this chapter consistent with real-world observations?

# PROBLEMS

**1.** Using the aggregate demand/inflation curve and the price adjustment line, describe what would happen to real GDP, consumption, investment, net exports, interest rates, and inflation in the short run, in the medium run, and in the long run if there were a permanent increase in government spending on highway construction. Be sure to provide an economic explanation for your results.

**2.** Suppose the central bank wants to revert to the original inflation rate before the increase in government spending in problem 1. How can it achieve its objective? Describe the proposed change in policy and its short-run, medium-run, and long-run effects on real GDP and inflation.

**3.** Using the aggregate demand/inflation curve and the price adjustment line, show what happens if the central bank reinflates the economy. Suppose the target inflation rate is changed from 2 percent to 5 percent. Consider the impact on the major components of spending in the short run, the medium run, and the long run.

**4.** The economy begins at potential GDP with an inflation rate of 4 percent. Draw this situation with an aggregate demand/inflation curve and a price adjustment line. Suppose there is a price shock that pushes inflation up to 6 percent in the short run, but the effect on inflation is viewed as temporary by the Fed. It expects the price adjustment line to shift back down by 2 percent next year, and in fact the price adjustment line does shift back down.

a) If the Fed follows its usual policy rule, where will real GDP be in the short run? How does the economy adjust back to potential?

b) Now suppose that since the Fed is sure that this inflationary shock is only temporary, it decides not to follow its typical policy rule but instead maintains the interest rate at its previous level. What happens to real GDP? Why? What will the long-run adjustment be in this case? Do you agree with the Fed's handling of the situation?

**5.** Use the following data to graph the aggregate demand/inflation curve:

| Inflation (percent) | Real GDP (billions of dollars) |
|---|---|
| 10 | 4,800 |
| 8 | 4,900 |
| 6 | 5,000 |
| 4 | 5,100 |
| 2 | 5,200 |

a) Suppose the current inflation rate is 4 percent, and potential GDP is $5,000 billion. Draw in the price adjustment line. What is the current deviation of real GDP from potential?

b) In the long run, what will the inflation rate be if there is no change in economic policy? Explain how this adjustment takes place.

**6.** Continuing from problem 5, suppose that after the long-run adjustment back to potential, the Fed changes its policy rule so that the inflation target is 4 percent but potential GDP remains at $5,000 billion. What type of monetary policy is the Fed undertaking? Use the following data to show the shift in the aggregate demand/inflation curve.

| Inflation (percent) | Real GDP (billions of dollars) |
|---|---|
| 10 | 4,700 |
| 8 | 4,800 |
| 6 | 4,900 |
| 4 | 5,000 |
| 2 | 5,100 |

a) How does the Fed accomplish this goal? What is the response of investment and net exports?

b) In the short run, what is the deviation from potential GDP?

c) How will the price adjustment line adjust in the medium and long run? Explain how this adjustment takes place.

**7.** Suppose that the GDP deflator in 2001 is 100, and in 2002 it is 105.

a) Suppose the economy is at potential GDP in 2001 and 2002. What is the rate of inflation in 2002?

b) Suppose instead that real GDP is below potential GDP in 2002. How is the adjustment back to potential made in this situation?

**8.** Suppose there are two countries that are very similar except that one has a much higher rate of money growth. They have identical potential GDP and are both at their long-run equilibrium. Draw this situation with an aggregate demand/inflation curve and a price adjustment line. Explain how these different equilibrium levels of inflation are possible. How do workers' and firms' expectations differ between the two countries?

**9.** Show in the shares of spending diagrams from Chapter 8 the effect of a decrease in government spending's share of GDP. Compare this case with the same situation using aggregate demand/inflation curves and price adjustment lines. Is the long-run effect the same in both models?

**10.** Recall from Chapter 13 that the Fed's policy rule shows different real interest rates for different levels of inflation.

> a) Graph the Fed's policy rule (as a solid line) along with that of a constant real interest rate (as a dashed line). What is the slope of the dashed line?
>
> b) Show the Fed's target rate of inflation on the graph.
>
> c) Recall from Chapter 8 that a permanent increase in government spending as a share of GDP will cause the real interest rate to rise. If the government permanently increases its spending share in GDP, what will happen in the policy rule diagram? How does the dashed line shift? Show the new long-run inflation and interest rate at the intersection of the monetary policy rule and the dashed line.
>
> d) Now suppose that the Fed insists on maintaining the level of inflation that existed prior to the increase in government purchases. What does the Fed have to do to force this disinflation? Which way will the policy rule shift? Show in your diagram that the real interest rate is still permanently higher after the long-run adjustment to this new monetary policy.

# 5

# Macroeconomic Policy

Using the macroeconomic theory developed in the previous two parts of the book, we now explore the fascinating world of macroeconomic policy in this last part. Macroeconomic policy, which includes both fiscal policy and monetary policy, has powerful effects on the economy.

Different countries have approached fiscal and monetary policy issues in various ways, and their approaches have changed over time. Some have successfully kept strict control over the government budget deficit. Others seem to have let the budget deficit grow out of control. As to monetary policy, some countries have given their central banks much independence; others require strict accountability. Some central banks are more concerned with the exchange rate than with the money supply; others focus on the money supply. As to policies that affect long-term growth, some countries have tax systems that

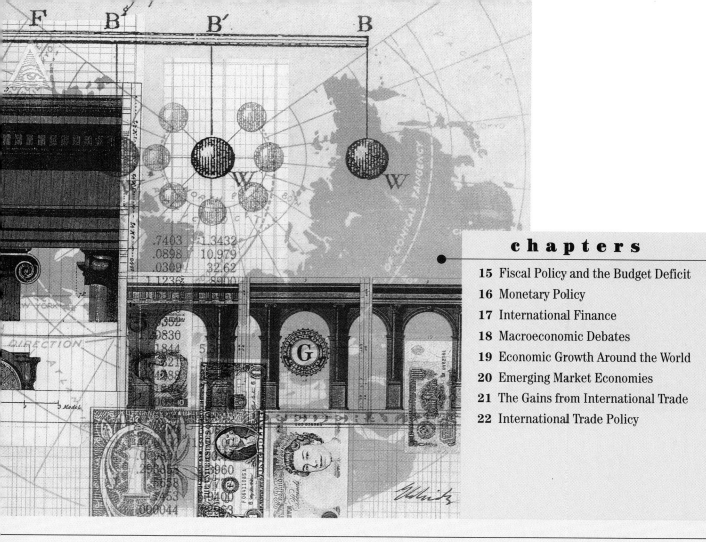

encourage saving, whereas others seem to tax saving at a higher rate than consumption. These six chapters examine the pros and cons of the different approaches to monetary and fiscal policy. There are great differences of opinion on these issues but there are also important areas of agreement.

In Chapter 15 we look at how fiscal policy decisions are made and examine alternative methods for assessing the effects of the budget deficit on the economy. In Chapter 16 we explore the reasons for central bank independence and study alternative proposals for the conduct of monetary policy. In Chapter 17 we extend the analysis of monetary and fiscal policy to global issues. In Chapter 18 we discuss macroeconomic debates. In Chapter 19 we focus on economic growth around the world. In Chapter 20 we apply the tools of economics to one of the most difficult policy problems in this age of emerging market economies: the

transition from central planning to a market system. In Chapter 21 we show that international trade between people in different countries is based on the same economic principles as trade between people in the same country. In Chapter 22 we investigate international trade policy—tariffs, quotas, trade agreements, and even trade wars.

From the disagreements between Malthus and Ricardo in the 1830s to the debates between Keynesians and monetarists in the 1960s to the disputes of the real business cycle school in the 1990s, macroeconomic policy issues have always been controversial. But macroeconomic models have had a great impact on economic policy outcomes. Exploring the policy issues in these chapters will prepare you for likely future debates over economic policy whether you are active in them or simply want to understand them as a citizen interested in the economic future of the world.

# Fiscal Policy and the Budget Deficit

15

Fiscal policy is much easier to define than to carry out. Two of the fiscal activities of government are *spending*—on national defense, road building, schools, or transfer payments—and collecting *taxes* to pay for this spending. When spending is greater than taxes, there is a budget deficit, which must be financed by government *borrowing,* a third fiscal activity. *Policy* refers to a plan of action by the government. Hence, **fiscal policy** is defined as the government's plans for spending, for taxes, and for borrowing to finance the budget deficit, if one exists.

In previous chapters, we showed that changes in government spending and taxes affect the economy. An increase in government purchases or a cut in taxes will increase real GDP in the short run. In this chapter, we examine whether fiscal policy can make use of these short-run effects to reduce the size of economic fluctuations. For example, a policy of cutting taxes in a recession might reduce unemployment by ending the recession early or quickening the pace of recovery from recession. We also examine problems that arise in formulating and carrying out fiscal policy and discuss why economists frequently disagree about fiscal policy.

We also showed in previous chapters that changes in government spending and taxes affect the economy in the long run. For example, a decrease in government purchases as a share of GDP will lower interest rates and thereby increase incentives to invest and perhaps raise economic growth. Can a fiscal policy for spending and taxes be designed to improve long-term economic growth? If so, what problems exist in carrying out such a policy?

In the past two decades government spending increased more than taxes in the United States and many other countries. As a result, budget deficits and government borrowing rose sharply. But what exactly is the effect of the debt? Is the deficit harmful? These questions are also addressed in this chapter.

There have been attempts in recent years to make fiscal policy work better—legally limiting the size of the deficit, capping spending, changing the balance of power between the legislative and the executive branches. Have these measures improved the situation? Other ideas have also been proposed—limiting the terms of elected officials, amending the Constitution to require a balanced budget, and restricting campaign contributions. Would these improve the situation?

Essential to answering questions about fiscal policy is a careful assessment of the government budget, which contains the plans for spending, taxes, and the deficit each year, and that is where we begin.

**fiscal policy:** the government's plans for spending, for taxes, and for borrowing.

# THE GOVERNMENT BUDGET: TAXES, SPENDING, THE DEFICIT, AND THE DEBT

The **federal budget** is the major summary document describing fiscal policy in the United States. The budget includes not only estimates of the deficit that get so much attention but also proposals for taxes and spending. Let's look at how the federal budget in the United States is put together.

**federal budget:** a summary of the federal government's proposals for spending, taxes, and the deficit.

## Setting the Annual Budget

In the United States, the president submits a new budget to Congress each year for the following fiscal year. The fiscal year runs from October to October. For example, *The Budget of the United States: Fiscal Year 1998* applied to spending and taxes from October 1, 1997, through September 30, 1998. It was submitted by President Clinton to Congress in early 1997. The president typically devotes part of

**The CEA and CBO**

The economic assumptions used for the federal budget are presented by the Council of Economic Advisers (CEA) in the *Economic Report of the President.* To assist the Senate and the House of Representatives in their deliberations on the president's fiscal policy proposals, the Congressional Budget Office (CBO) then does its own economic analysis, which is published each year in *The Economic and Budget Outlook.*

the State of the Union address to describing the budget and fiscal policy. Also at the start of each year, the *Economic Report of the President* is released, providing the economic assumptions underlying the budget prepared by the Council of Economic Advisers. The Congressional Budget Office makes its own economic assumptions. During the budget battles between President Clinton and the Congress in 1995, one of the main points of dispute was a discrepancy between the economic forecasts of the CEA and the CBO.

In putting together the federal budget, the president proposes many specific spending programs that fit into an overall philosophy of what government should be doing. President Bush proposed increased spending on scientific research and reduced spending on railroads, such as Amtrak. President Clinton proposed increased funding on training programs and reduced spending on defense. However, in any one year, most of the spending in the budget is determined by ongoing programs, which the president usually can do little to change. For example, payments of social security benefits to older people are a large item in the budget, but the amount of spending on social security depends on how many eligible people there are. If more people become eligible, then spending automatically goes up unless the social security law changes. Thus, in reality, the president can change only a small part of the budget each year.

### A Balanced Budget versus a Deficit or Surplus

Recall the difference between **tax rate** and **tax revenues** discussed in Chapter 12. For the income tax, if the average tax rate is 20 percent and income is $3,000 billion, then tax revenues are $600 billion.

Taxes to pay for the spending programs are also included in the budget. As part of the budget, the president may propose an increase or a decrease in taxes. *Tax revenues* are the total dollar amount the government receives from taxpayers each year. When tax revenues are exactly equal to spending, there is a **balanced budget.** When tax revenues are greater than spending, there is a **budget surplus.** When spending is greater than tax revenues, there is a **budget deficit,** and the government must borrow to pay the difference.

| Budget Deficit | Budget Balance | Budget Surplus |
|---|---|---|
| Tax revenues < spending | Tax revenues = spending | Tax revenues > spending |

**balanced budget:** a budget for which tax revenues equal spending.

**budget surplus:** the amount by which tax revenues exceed spending.

**budget deficit:** the amount by which government spending exceeds tax revenues.

There is no requirement in the United States that the president submit a balanced budget. Presidents Reagan, Bush, and Clinton all submitted budgets to Congress that did not balance. Rather, they were in deficit. There are many reasons why proposed budgets do not balance. For example, as we will discuss later in this chapter, if the economy is in recession, increasing taxes or lowering spending to balance the budget could make the recession worse.

### The Proposed Budget versus the Actual Budget

Keep in mind that the budget the president submits is only a *proposal.* The amount of tax revenues and spending, or expenditures, that actually occur during the fiscal year are much different from what is proposed. There are two main reasons for this difference.

First, the Congress usually modifies the president's budget, adding some programs and deleting others. Congress deliberates on the specific items in the president's budget proposal for months before the fiscal year actually starts. After the president's budget is debated and modified, it is passed by Congress. Only when the president signs the legislation is the budget enacted into law. Because of this congressional modification, the enacted budget is always different from the proposed budget.

Second, because of changes in the economy and other unanticipated events such as wars and natural disasters, the actual amount of spending and taxes will be different from what is enacted. After the fiscal year has begun and the budget has been enacted, various *supplementals* are proposed and passed. A supplemental is a change in a spending program or a change in the tax law that affects the budget in the current fiscal year. In addition, recessions or booms always affect tax revenue and spending to some degree.

Figure 15.1 shows the difference between proposed tax revenues, expenditures, and the deficit for the fiscal year 1991 budget (submitted in January 1990) and the actual tax revenues, expenditures, and deficit that occurred. The 1990–1991 recession was one reason why the difference was so large. In most years, the difference is smaller.

Figure 15.2 shows how the fiscal year 1997 budget moved from a proposal in early 1996 to enactment in late 1996 to completion in October 1997. The same **budget cycle** occurs every year. Because the whole cycle takes over two years, at any one time there are discussions about three budgets. For example, in September 1997, the budget for fiscal year 1997 was coming to a close, the budget for fiscal year 1998 was being considered by Congress, and the budget for fiscal year 1999 was being put together by the president's staff. The budget cycle does not always progress smoothly. In fiscal year 1996, President Clinton and the Congress did not settle on a budget until well into the fiscal year.

**budget cycle:** the more than two-year process in which the federal budget is proposed, modified, enacted, and implemented.

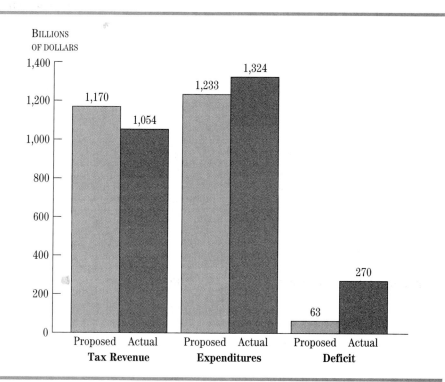

**FIGURE 15.1**
**The Difference Between the Proposed and the Actual Budget in a Recession Year (billions of dollars)**

When the fiscal year 1991 budget was submitted to Congress in early 1990, the 1991 deficit was forecast to be $63 billion. By the time the fiscal year was over—almost two years later—the deficit was $270 billion. Because of the 1990–1991 recession, tax revenues were smaller and spending was higher than in the proposed budget.

*Source: Economic Report of the President, 1990, Table C-76; Economic Report of the President, 1994, Table B-77.*

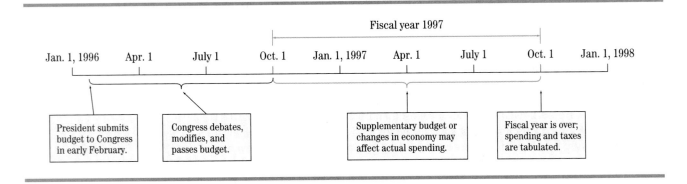

## FIGURE 15.2
**A Typical Budget Cycle: Fiscal Year 1997**

The budget cycle begins about one year before the fiscal year begins. After considering various spending and tax options, the president submits a budget proposal to the Congress in February. The cycle is not complete until the end of the fiscal year. By then, a new budget is being enacted.

## TABLE 15.1
**FY 1995 Federal Tax Revenues and Expenditures**
(billions of dollars)

| | | |
|---|---:|---:|
| Tax Revenues | 1,478 | |
| Personal Income | | 615 |
| Corporate Income | | 184 |
| Sales Taxes | | 91 |
| Payroll Taxes | | 588 |
| Expenditures | 1,640 | |
| Purchases | | 453 |
| Defense | | 302 |
| Other | | 151 |
| Transfers | | 958 |
| Interest | | 229 |
| Deficit | 162 | |

*Source: Economic Report of the President, 1997,* Table B-80.

## A Look at the Federal Budget

Table 15.1 contains summary totals from the federal budget for fiscal year 1995. The full budget, which is over 2,000 pages long, provides much more detail.

### The Deficit

Table 15.1 shows tax revenues ($1,478 billion) were less than expenditures ($1,640 billion), so there was a deficit ($162 billion). Budget deficits are common in the United States. The last year without a deficit was 1969.

### Taxes and Spending

The tax revenues of $1,478 billion include *personal income taxes* paid by individuals on their total income, *corporate income taxes* paid by businesses on their profits, *sales taxes* on items such as gasoline and beer, and *payroll taxes,* a percentage of wages paid by workers and their employers that supports government programs such as social security. Sales taxes are the smallest of the four components of total revenue, and corporate tax revenues are only slightly larger. Payroll taxes represent a large amount of revenues, nearly the same as personal income tax revenues. Payroll taxes have grown rapidly as a share of federal government revenues in recent years, while the other types of taxes have fallen in relative importance.

The expenditure side of the budget is divided into three basic classes of spending. One is called *purchases* of goods and services, the second is *transfer payments,* and the third is *interest payments.* Only purchases are included in the symbol $G$ that we have been using in the text. Purchases represent *new* production, whether postal trucks, federal courthouses, or food for military troops. If you look at total expenditures by the federal government, which is $1,640 billion, a surprisingly small fraction—less than 40 percent—is for the purchase of goods and services. Excluding military, it is only about 10 percent of all spending.

The remaining share of government expenditures consists of transfer payments and interest. The major transfer programs are social security payments to retired people, welfare payments to the poor, unemployment compensation to the unemployed workers, Medicare to older people, and Medicaid to poor people. Transfer payments are a much larger portion of the budget than purchases of goods and services. In other words, the amount that government absorbs in new production is considerably smaller than the amount it transfers to individuals.

Interest payments are what the federal government pays every year on its borrowing from that year and from previous years. The government pays interest on its borrowings just like anyone else. In fiscal year 1995 interest payments amounted to $229 billion, which is much larger than all nondefense federal government purchases. Total interest payments equal the interest rate multiplied by the amount of government debt outstanding. For example, the interest rate on federal government debt averaged 6 percent in 1995, and total outstanding debt was about $3,783 billion ($229 billion in interest payments is approximately .060 times $3,783 billion). If interest rates come down, then interest payments on the debt go down. Because the United States has such a large amount of outstanding debt, interest payments remain high even when interest rates are low.

### The U.S. Budget Deficit versus Other Countries

The United States is not the only country with a government deficit in recent years. Table 15.2 lists the deficits in many industrial countries in 1996, measured as a percentage of GDP. Greece had the largest deficit, and Japan had the smallest.

## The Federal Debt

It is important to distinguish between the *federal deficit* and the *federal debt.* The two are frequently mixed up in popular discussions. **Federal debt** is the total amount of outstanding loans that the federal government owes. The deficit, you will recall, is the yearly amount by which spending exceeds taxes. Each year the deficit adds to the debt. If the government runs a surplus, the debt comes down by the amount of the surplus.

Consider an example with thousands of dollars rather than trillions of dollars. Think of it in terms of a student, Sam, who graduates from college with a $14,000 outstanding loan. In other words, he has a debt of $14,000. Suppose the first year that he works his income is $30,000 but he spends $35,000. Sam's deficit is $5,000 and his debt rises to $19,000. Assume that in the second year of work, he has income of $35,000 and spends $38,000; his deficit is $3,000 and his debt rises to $22,000. Each year debt rises by the amount of his deficit. If in the third year Sam earns $40,000 and spends $33,000, then he has a surplus of $7,000. This would reduce his debt to $15,000.

The laws of accounting we apply to Sam also apply to Uncle Sam. The federal government's deficit of $162 billion in 1995 required that the government borrow that amount from individuals, businesses, or foreigners. As a result, the outstanding government debt increased by $162 billion during fiscal year 1995. Figure 15.3 shows the difference between debt and deficit in the United States since 1950.

### Long-Term and Short-Term Debt

The federal government borrows for both the short term and long term. With short-term borrowing, the government agrees to pay back the loan with interest in a short period of time, usually one year or less. Long-term government borrowing is for more than a year, up to 30 years. For example, in 1995 the federal government borrowed some funds long term and agreed to pay the loan back in the year 2025 at an interest rate of 7 percent.

The government borrows by selling government bonds. A **bond** is simply a contract (an IOU) that stipulates that the borrower will pay the person who owns

**TABLE 15.2**
**Deficits in Developed Countries, 1996**
(percentage of GDP)

| | |
|---|---|
| Greece | 10.0 |
| Sweden | 6.8 |
| Italy | 7.4 |
| Finland | 4.1 |
| United Kingdom | 2.4 |
| Spain | 3.9 |
| Canada | 3.5 |
| France | 3.7 |
| Australia | 3.9 |
| United States | 2.1 |
| Germany | 1.8 |
| Austria | 3.7 |
| Netherlands | 5.8 |
| Norway | 1.0 |
| Ireland | 2.5 |
| New Zealand | 1.6 |
| Japan | 0.9 |

*Source:* International Monetary Fund.

**federal debt:** the total amount of outstanding loans owed by the federal government.

**bond:** a financial contract that stipulates a specific repayment of principal plus interest on a loan at a given date in the future.

**FIGURE 15.3**

**The Deficit and the Debt**

When the deficit is zero, the debt does not change. When there is a deficit, the debt increases. When there is a surplus, the debt falls. Deficits and increasing debt have been the rule in recent years. The debt in 1950 was largely due to deficits during World War II.

*Source:* U.S. Department of Commerce; U.S. Department of the Treasury.

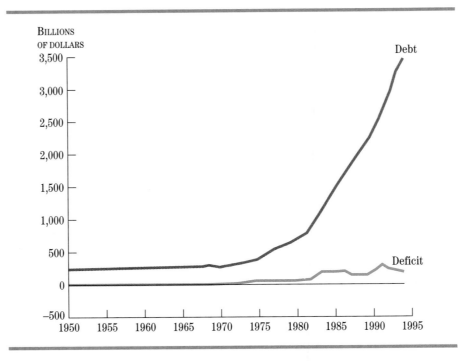

the bond a certain amount. The *maturity* of the bond is the number of years until the funds are paid back. For example, the government sells 30-year government bonds when it borrows funds for 30 years. It then uses the borrowed funds to pay for government spending in excess of tax revenues.

The average maturity on federal debt is about 6 years. Bonds that have a maturity of less than 1 year are called Treasury bills.

### The Debt to GDP Ratio

When looking at the debt and the deficit over time, it is important to consider the size of the economy. For example, a $3 trillion debt may not be much of a problem for an economy with a GDP of $10 trillion but could be overwhelming for an economy with a GDP of $1 trillion. An easy way to compare the debt to the size of the economy is to measure the debt as a percentage of GDP—the **debt to GDP ratio.** It is appropriate to consider the debt as a ratio to nominal GDP rather than real GDP because the debt is stated in current dollars just as nominal GDP is.

Figure 15.4 shows the behavior of the debt as a percentage of GDP in the United States since 1950. Note that the debt was a high percentage of GDP at the end of World War II because the U.S. government borrowed large amounts to finance its military expenditures during the war. The debt to GDP ratio fell until the mid-1970s, when it began to increase again. The debt to GDP ratio is a good overall gauge of how a government is doing in managing its fiscal affairs.

Note that the ratio of debt to GDP can stay constant when the deficit is greater than zero. This occurs when GDP grows as fast as the debt grows. For example, if GDP grows by 5 percent per year in current dollars, then the debt to GDP ratio will stay constant if the debt grows by 5 percent per year. If the outstanding debt is $3,000 billion, then a deficit of $150 billion would increase the debt by 5 percent

**debt to GDP ratio:** the total amount of outstanding loans the federal government owes divided by nominal GDP.

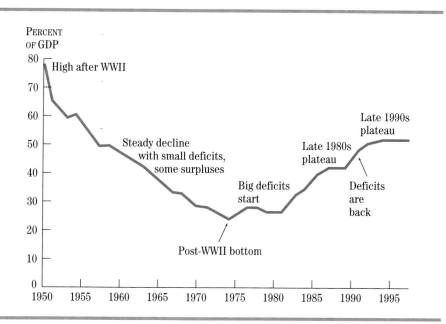

**FIGURE 15.4**
**Debt As a Ratio to GDP**
Relative to the size of GDP, the debt declined during the years after World War II. For the last 15 years, the debt has been rising as a ratio to GDP.

*Source:* U.S. Department of the Treasury.

(150/3000 = .05) and keep the debt to GDP ratio constant. If inflation rose by 5 percent per year so that GDP grew by 10 percent per year, then the deficit could be as large as $300 billion and the debt to GDP ratio would be constant. Robert Eisner, an economist at Northwestern University, emphasizes that the government's public infrastructure represents a public asset that can be viewed as a partial offset to the public debt.

## State and Local Government Budgets

Much of government spending and taxation in the United States occurs outside of the federal government, in state and local governments. Although fiscal policy usually refers to the plans of the federal government, it is the combined action of federal, state, and local governments that has an impact on the overall economy. For example, in the 1990–1991 recession, many states cut back on spending and raised taxes; both actions would tend to reduce real GDP in the short run, just as reduced spending and higher taxes at the federal level would. Taken as a whole, state and local governments are a large force in the economy. Table 15.3 shows that in 1995 state and local government expenditures were about 55 percent as much as federal government expenditures.

Most of the expenditures are for public schools, local police, fire services, and roads. Observe that state and local government *purchases* of goods and services are larger than federal government purchases, especially when national defense is excluded.

The state and local governments as a whole ran a surplus in 1995. By running surpluses for many years, state and local governments have accumulated assets—mostly U.S. government bonds—on which they earn interest. Thus, interest payments are negative in Table 15.3, indicating that these governments received interest income. Note, however, that the surplus for state and local governments as a whole masks the deficits that loomed in some states and some cities.

**TABLE 15.3**
**Combined Budgets of All State and Local Governments, 1995**
(billions of dollars)

| | | |
|---|---|---|
| Tax Revenues | 996 | |
| Expenditures | 901 | |
| Purchases | | 683 |
| Transfers | | 278 |
| Interest | | −60 |
| Surplus | 95 | |

*Source: Economic Report of the President, 1997,* Table B-83.

## Review

▶ In the United States, the president submits a budget to Congress giving proposals for spending, for taxes, and for the deficit. The actual budget is different from the proposed budget because of congressional modifications and unforeseen events like wars and recessions.

▶ A budget deficit occurs when spending is greater than tax revenues. Virtually all major countries have had large deficits in recent years.

▶ The debt differs from the deficit. When a government or an individual runs a deficit, the debt increases. Surpluses reduce the debt.

▶ It is appropriate to consider the debt in relation to the size of the economy by measuring it as a percentage of GDP.

▶ Federal government expenditures are larger than state and local government expenditures, but state and local government purchases are larger than federal government purchases.

# DISCRETIONARY AND AUTOMATIC COUNTERCYCLICAL FISCAL POLICY

Having seen how spending (purchases and transfers) and taxes fit together in the budget, let us now see whether plans for these—fiscal policy—can reduce the size of economic fluctuations.

## Impacts of the Instruments of Fiscal Policy

We showed in Chapters 11 through 14 how changes in government spending and taxes affect real GDP. We now show how these changes might bring real GDP closer to potential GDP. Government purchases, transfers, and taxes are called the *instruments* of fiscal policy because they are the variables that directly affect the economy.

### Changes in Government Purchases

We know that if there is a change in government purchases, real GDP will initially change by more than the change in government purchases. The exact amount depends on the size of the multiplier, which is uncertain, and depends on the marginal propensity to consume and the marginal propensity to import. If real GDP equaled potential GDP at the time of the change in government purchases, then real GDP will move away from potential GDP. Hence, a first lesson about fiscal policy is "do no harm." Erratic changes in government purchases can lead to fluctuations of real GDP away from potential GDP.

But suppose real GDP was already away from potential GDP. Then the change in government purchases could move real GDP closer to potential GDP. This is shown in Figure 15.5. In the top panel, real GDP starts out below potential GDP. An increase in government purchases shifts the aggregate demand/inflation curve to the right and moves real GDP back toward potential GDP. In the bottom panel, real GDP is above potential GDP, and a decrease in government purchases shifts the aggregate demand/inflation curve to the left, bringing real GDP back toward potential GDP. The important point is that a change in government purchases shifts the

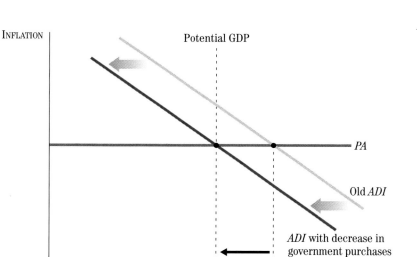

FIGURE 15.5
**Effect of a Change in Government Purchases**
If real GDP is below potential GDP, as in the top panel, an increase in government purchases, which shifts the *ADI* curve to the right, will move real GDP toward potential GDP. If real GDP is above potential GDP, as in the bottom panel, a decrease in government purchases will move real GDP toward potential. These are short-run effects.

aggregate demand/inflation curve from wherever it happens to be at the time of the change.

Now, these effects of government purchases are short term. Eventually, prices will adjust, and consumption, investment, and net exports will change and real GDP will return to potential GDP regardless of the change in government purchases. Nevertheless, as we will see, the short-run impacts of government purchases provide fiscal policy with the potential power to reduce the size of economic fluctuations.

A decrease in government purchases for defense is one example of a leftward shift in the aggregate demand/inflation curve. An increase in government purchases on roads and bridges works in the opposite direction. Because the changes in government spending affect investment, in the long run they may affect potential GDP. But for now, we focus on how they can move the economy closer to potential GDP.

### Changes in Taxes

A change in taxes also affects real GDP in the short run. At any given level of real GDP, people will consume less if there is a tax increase because they have less income to spend after taxes. They will consume more if there is a tax cut. In either case, the aggregate demand/inflation curve will shift. The top panel of Figure 15.6 shows how a tax cut will shift the aggregate demand/inflation curve to the right and push real GDP closer to potential GDP if it is below potential GDP. The bottom panel shows a tax increase reducing real GDP from a position above potential GDP. Again, these are short-term effects. Eventually prices will adjust and real GDP will return to potential GDP.

In the case of tax changes, the size of the effect on real GDP is more uncertain than in the case of a change in government purchases. Recall that a temporary cut

**FIGURE 15.6**

**Effects of a Change in Taxes**

A decrease in taxes shifts the *ADI* curve to the right and can move real GDP toward potential GDP, as in the top panel. An increase in taxes moves real GDP toward potential in the lower panel.

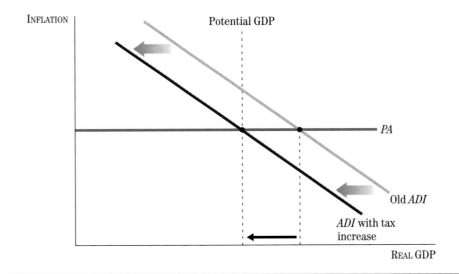

in taxes is unlikely to stimulate consumption by much, because the marginal propensity to consume is small. However, the marginal propensity to consume out of a permanent tax cut will be larger. In practice, people may be unsure how permanent a tax change will be.

Both increases and decreases in taxes can also affect potential GDP. For example, if an increase in tax rates causes some people to work less, then the labor supply will not be as large and potential GDP will be lower. But here our focus is on the departures of real GDP from potential GDP.

## Countercyclical Fiscal Policy

Because government spending and taxes affect real GDP in the short run, fiscal policy can, in principle, offset the impact of shocks that push real GDP away from potential GDP. Such use of fiscal policy is called **countercyclical policy,** because the cyclical movements in the economy are being "countered," or offset, by changes in government spending or taxes. Both booms and recessions can be countered, in principle. Recessions require cuts in taxes or increases in spending; booms require increases in taxes or cuts in spending.

Figure 15.7 shows what such a policy would ideally do. A possible recession in the year 2001 is shown, perhaps caused by a drop in foreign demand for U.S. products. Without any change in government purchases or taxes, the economy would eventually recover, as shown in the figure. But suppose that the government quickly cuts taxes or starts a road-building program. The hope is that this will raise real GDP, as shown in the figure, and hasten the return to potential GDP.

How would this work when prices are adjusting and the inflation rate is changing as well? Figure 15.8 provides the analysis. The recession is seen to be caused by the leftward shift in the aggregate demand/inflation curve. But the cut in taxes or increase in spending shifts the aggregate demand/inflation curve in the opposite direction. The aggregate demand/inflation curve shifts back to the right. If these countercyclical measures are timely enough and neither too small nor too large—

**countercyclical policy:** a policy designed to offset the fluctuations in the business cycle.

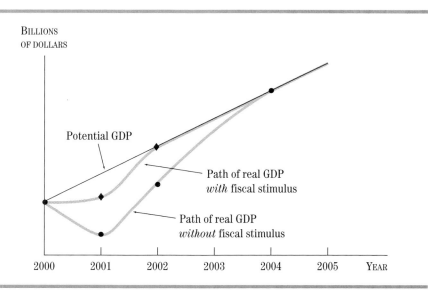

**FIGURE 15.7**
**Effect of a Well-Timed Countercyclical Fiscal Policy**
The figure shows a likely path of recovery from a recession caused by a decline in demand for U.S. products. A well-timed cut in taxes or increase in government purchases can reduce the size of the recession and bring real GDP back to potential GDP more quickly. The size of the economic fluctuation is smaller. The analysis is shown in Figure 15.8.

**FIGURE 15.8**
**Analysis of a Well-Timed Countercyclical Fiscal Policy**

A decline in demand—perhaps through a decrease in exports—shifts the *ADI* curve to the left. Without a countercyclical fiscal policy, real GDP recovers back to potential GDP, but a timely cut in taxes or increase in government purchases can offset the drop in demand and bring real GDP back to potential GDP more quickly.

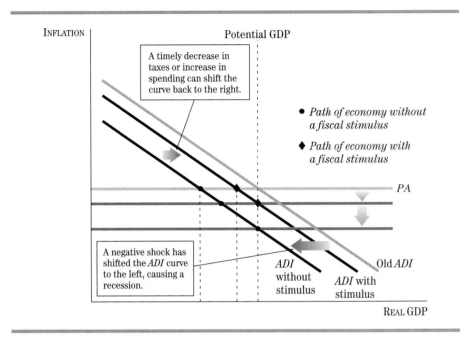

both big ifs—then the recession might be small and short lived. The example shows real GDP falling only slightly below potential GDP.

Figure 15.9 shows a less ideal case. Here government purchases are increased, but the response is too late. The increase occurs the year after the recession, during the recovery; it causes a boom.

Disagreements about the usefulness of fiscal policy boil down to an assessment of whether Figure 15.7 or Figure 15.9 is more likely. Let's first consider some examples.

**FIGURE 15.9**
**Effect of a Poorly Timed Fiscal Policy**

Here, in contrast to Figure 15.7, the fiscal stimulus comes too late, when the economy is already recovering. A boom is caused that could lead to inflation and perhaps another recession in later years.

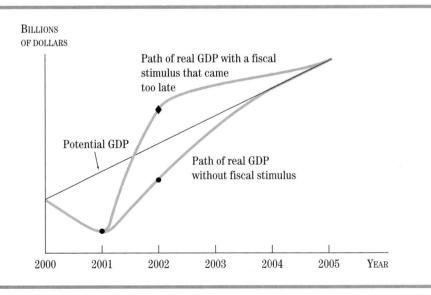

## Discretionary Changes in the Instruments of Fiscal Policy

**Discretionary fiscal policy** refers to specific changes in laws or administrative procedures, such as a change in an existing program to speed up spending, the creation of a new program (such as a new welfare program), or a change in the tax system (such as higher tax rates). These changes in the law are discretionary changes because they require action on the part of the Congress or the president.

**discretionary fiscal policy:** changes in tax or spending policy requiring legislative or administrative action by the president or Congress.

One of the most significant post–World War II discretionary fiscal policy actions was the 1964 tax cut, proposed by President John F. Kennedy and enacted after his death when Lyndon Johnson was president. The early 1960s were a period when real GDP was below potential GDP, and this large discretionary tax cut was a key factor in speeding the economic recovery. This cut in taxes also probably stimulated the growth of potential GDP and was therefore good for the long run.

Another example was the 1968 temporary income tax surcharge that raised tax rates. It was called a surcharge because 10 percent was added to any given tax rate. It was passed during the Vietnam War, when real GDP was above potential GDP. The aim was to bring real GDP back toward potential GDP. However, in this case, the boom continued. The tax increase came long after the boom had started. Perhaps because the surcharge was viewed as temporary, the marginal propensity to consume (MPC) was small and consumption did not change much.

Another large discretionary fiscal policy action was the Reagan tax cut of the early 1980s that lowered personal income tax rates by 25 percent. This tax cut helped the economy recover from the 1981–1982 recession. Like the Kennedy tax cut, this tax cut also probably raised the growth rate of potential GDP.

The impact of these examples of discretionary fiscal policy are neither as good as Figure 15.7 nor as bad as Figure 15.9. In none of these cases was the change in taxes speedy enough to offset a recession or a boom. The tax cuts came after the recessions and the tax increase came after the boom. At best, the tax cuts speeded up the recovery.

## Automatic Changes in the Instruments of Fiscal Policy

Taxes and spending also change automatically as well as by discretionary actions of government. Income tax revenues expand when people are making more and fall when people are making less. Thus, tax revenues respond automatically to the economy. Tax payments rise when the economy is in a boom and more people are working. Tax revenues fall when the economy is in a slump and unemployment rises.

These changes in tax revenues are even larger with a progressive income tax. A **progressive tax** system means that individual tax payments *rise* as a proportion of income as income increases. With a progressive tax, a person earning $100,000 per year pays proportionately more in taxes than a person earning $20,000 per year. Because of this progressive tax system, as people earn more, they pay a higher tax rate, and when they earn less, they pay a lower tax rate.

**progressive tax:** a tax system in which an individual's tax payments rise as a proportion of income as the individual's income rises.

Parts of government spending also change automatically. Unemployment compensation, through which the government makes payments to individuals who are unemployed, rises during a recession. When unemployment rises, so do payments to unemployed workers. Social security payments also increase in a recession because people may retire earlier if job prospects are bad. Welfare payments rise in a recession because people who are unemployed for a long period of time may qualify for welfare. As poverty rates rise in recessions, welfare payments increase.

**automatic stabilizers:** automatic tax and spending changes that occur over the course of the business cycle that tend to stabilize the fluctuations in real GDP.

These automatic tax and spending changes are called **automatic stabilizers** because they tend to stabilize the fluctuations of real GDP. How significant are these automatic stabilizers? Consider the 1990–1991 recession. Real GDP in 1989 was above potential GDP. But by late 1990 and 1991, real GDP was dropping below potential GDP. As this happened, government spending went up and taxes went down.

The magnitude of these effects is quite large and can be seen by looking back at Figure 15.1. The difference between proposed and actual taxes and spending in the 1991 budget provides an estimate of the effect of the recession on taxes and spending. Tax revenue was $116 billion less than proposed before the recession. Thus, taxes were automatically reduced by this amount. However, spending was $91 billion more than proposed before the recession. Thus, spending rose by $91 billion in response to the recession. The combined effect of a $116 billion reduction in taxes and a $91 billion increase in spending is huge, and the timing was just about perfect. Since tax receipts went down in the recession and transfer payments went up, people's consumption was at a level higher than it would otherwise be. These automatic changes in tax revenues and government spending tended to stabilize the economy and probably made the recession less severe than it would have been. These changes did not completely offset other factors, however, because there still was a recession.

## The Discretion versus Rules Debate for Fiscal Policy

**fiscal policy rule:** a description of how the instruments of policy regularly respond to the state of the economy. Automatic stabilizers are an example of a fiscal policy rule.

For many years economists have debated the usefulness of discretionary and automatic fiscal policy. Automatic fiscal policy is an example of a fiscal policy rule. A **fiscal policy rule** describes how the instruments of fiscal policy respond to the state of the economy. Thus, the debate is sometimes called the "discretion versus rules" debate.

The case for discretionary fiscal policy was made by President Kennedy's Council of Economic Advisers, which included Walter Heller and Nobel Prize–winning economist James Tobin. Proponents of discretionary fiscal policy argue that the automatic stabilizers would not be large or well-timed enough to bring the economy out of a recession quickly. Critics of discretionary policy, such as Milton Friedman, another Nobel Prize winner, emphasize that the effect of policy is uncertain and that there are long lags in the impact of policy. By the time spending increases and taxes are cut, a recession could be over; if so, the policy would only lead to an inflationary boom. Three types of lags are particularly problematic for discretionary fiscal policy: a *recognition lag,* the time between the need for the policy and the recognition of the need; an *implementation lag,* the time between the recognition of the need for the policy and its implementation; and an *impact lag,* the time between the implementation of the policy and its impact on real GDP.

Although lags and uncertainty continue to contribute to the discretion versus rules debate, other issues have also become central. Many economists feel policy rules are desirable because of their stability and reliability. A fiscal policy rule emphasizing the automatic stabilizers might make government plans to reduce the deficit more believable. Countercyclical fiscal policy raises the deficit during recessions. With discretionary policy, there is no guarantee that the deficit will decline after the recession. With an automatic policy rule, there is an expectation that the deficit will decline after the recession is over.

Since the end of the 1980s, there have been few discretionary fiscal policy actions to counter recessions or booms in the United States or Europe. For the most part, discretionary actions have not occurred because of high budget deficits and public concerns about the governments that caused these deficits in the first place.

## Review

▶ Countercyclical fiscal policy is undertaken by governments to reduce economic fluctuations. The aim is to keep real GDP closer to potential GDP.

▶ Two types of countercyclical fiscal policy are (1) discretionary policy, such as the Kennedy-Johnson tax cut, the 1968 tax surcharge, and the Reagan 1982 tax cut; and (2) automatic stabilizers, such as unemployment insurance, social security, and changes in tax revenues.

# ECONOMIC IMPACT OF THE BUDGET DEFICIT

What is the impact of the budget deficit on the economy? Because the budget deficit is equal to the difference between spending and taxes, the impact of the deficit is best understood by looking at the impact of spending and taxes, as we did in the previous section.

## Short-Run and Long-Run Impact of the Deficit

Suppose the budget deficit increases because government purchases rise. Then the impact on the economy is precisely the same as our previous analysis of an increase in government purchases. The analysis of fiscal policy predicts that an increase in the budget deficit due to an increase in government purchases will cause real GDP to rise above potential GDP in the short run. Also, an increase in the budget deficit through a decrease in taxes will cause real GDP to rise temporarily above potential GDP.

In the long run, however, real GDP would return to potential GDP. If the increase in the deficit is caused by an increase in government purchases, investment and net exports would be lower as a share of GDP and interest rates would be higher. The higher interest rate and lower investment are the main harm of a long-lasting budget deficit. Moreover, the increase in government purchases would raise imports both because income rises and because the higher interest rate raises the exchange rate. The higher exchange rate would cause exports to fall. With imports rising and exports falling, net exports would decline, which means that the international trade deficit would be higher as a result of the increased budget deficit.

What if the budget deficit rises because of a cut in taxes? By raising disposable income, a cut in taxes will cause consumption to rise. Thus, in the long run the sum of investment and net exports will be lower as a share of GDP. Again, lower investment means lower long-term real GDP growth.

### Ricardian Equivalence

Economists disagree on the long-run effects of a deficit due to a cut in taxes, however. Some economists argue that a decrease in taxes will not permanently increase consumption. According to this view, people realize that the lower taxes will mean a higher budget deficit and, therefore, higher debt and higher interest payments by the government in the future. With higher interest payments in the future, people will figure that their future taxes, or at least their children's taxes, will be higher than they otherwise would be. Forward-looking consumers, therefore, may not increase their consumption because they realize they will have to pay more in taxes in the future. If they are concerned about their children, they will figure that they need to pass more on to the next generation because the burden of the future deficit on their children has been increased.

The view that increases in the budget deficit through tax cuts will not affect consumption or the other components of GDP is called **Ricardian equivalence** after the nineteenth-century economist David Ricardo. Robert Barro, an economist at Harvard University, has done the most significant theoretical and empirical research in support of Ricardian equivalence. Many economists, however, including Martin Feldstein, also of Harvard University, do not find the evidence in support of Ricardian equivalence convincing. They think that an increase in the budget deficit through tax cuts will raise consumption and lower investment in the long run.

In any case, there is little disagreement among economists that an increase in the deficit as a share of GDP through higher government purchases will have a long-run impact of lower private investment.

### The Burden of the Debt

Our discussion of Ricardian equivalence has focused on the higher debt that future generations incur as a result of the tax cut. The higher debt means that interest payments become an increased expenditure requirement of government. The federal budget, as shown in Table 15.1, already has a large portion of expenditures going to interest payments on the debt. Future interest payments represent a *burden of the debt* on future generations. If Ricardian equivalence holds, however, then an increase in the debt is not a burden on future generations because their parents or grandparents would have passed on additional inheritance to offset the burden.

### Overall Assessment

If we sum up the economic arguments about the deficit, we see that the main long-run harmful effect is due to a reduction of private investment in the economy. This effect is likely to arise if the deficit persists for a long time and if it is due to an increase in government purchases; the harmful effect is also likely to arise if the deficit is due to a decline in tax revenues, though there is more disagreement about the effects of a change in tax revenue than a change in government purchases.

A reduction in investment is harmful to the economy because it lowers the growth of the capital stock and thereby lowers the growth of productivity. Lower productivity growth means a lower standard of living in the future.

## Credible Deficit Reduction Plans

Because of the harmful long-term effects of the deficit, many economists feel that lowering the deficit is a good idea. But just as an increase in the deficit can raise real GDP in the short run, a decrease in the deficit can reduce real GDP below potential GDP in the short run. Thus, even though there is a long-term benefit from deficit reduction, there is possible short-term harm. Is there any way this harm can be reduced?

In recent years economists have searched for ways to lessen the short-run impact of the budget deficit reductions on the economy. The idea of *rational expec-*

**Ricardian equivalence:** the view that a change in taxes today will not affect consumption because people recognize that their, or their children's, future tax burden will change in an opposite direction.

**rational expectations assumption:** the assumption that people forecast the future no better or no worse than economic forecasters. (Ch. 12) *tations* has helped in the search. The idea of rational expectations is that people, like economic forecasters, try to figure out what government actions will be. People also take these expectations of government actions into account in their personal decisions. Government policymakers have **credibility** if their announcements about future government actions are believable to people. If people's expectations are rational, then credibility can greatly influence how a change in the budget deficit affects the economy.

**credibility:** the believability of the government's intentions to carry out stated policies.

For example, if the government announces in advance its intention to reduce the deficit over a number of years in the future, and if the government's announcement is credible, then the negative short-run impact of the deficit reduction on the economy might be greatly reduced. Why?

We know that in the long run, the reduction in the budget deficit will lower interest rates. Thus, if the government announces plans to reduce the budget deficit in the future, people will expect that interest rates will decline in the future; this expectation of a future decline in interest rates may lower current interest rates.

### Interest Rates and Expectations

Expectations of future declines in interest rates lower current interest rates because people have a choice between buying long-term bonds and short-term bonds. Consider the choice between a longer-term government bond with a maturity of 2 years and a shorter-term government bond that lasts 1 year. The choice is shown in Table 15.4. When you are deciding to buy the 2-year bond, your alternative is to buy the short-term bond. Rather than a 2-year bond, you could buy a 1-year bond and then buy another 1-year bond next year. The average interest rate over the two-year period should be about the same as the interest rate on the 2-year bond. Otherwise, no one would buy the bond with the lower average interest rate. If you expect interest rates to rise sharply next year, you will not buy the 2-year bond unless the current interest rate is higher. The interest rates on long-term bonds are thus affected by expectations of future interest rates. If people expect future interest rates to rise, then the interest rates on long-term bonds rise. If people expect future interest rates to fall, then interest rates on long-term bonds fall. The same analysis applies to 5-, 10-, or even 30-year bonds as well as to 2-year bonds.

The table shows the average interest rate for two alternatives:

▶ A 2-year bond is held for 2 years and pays the current long-term interest rate of $R$ percent each year.

▶ A 1-year bond is held for 1 year and pays the current short-term interest rate of 5 percent; another 1-year bond is bought at the end of the first year with an *expected* interest rate of $r$ percent.

| Type of Bond | Interest Rate in First Year | Interest Rate in Second Year | Average Interest Rate |
|---|---|---|---|
| Long term (2 years) | $R$ | $R$ | $R$ |
| Short term (1 year) | 5 | r | $\dfrac{5 + r}{2}$ |

**TABLE 15.4**
**Effect of a Change in Expected Future Interest Rates**

The average interest rate should be the same on the two so that

$$R = \frac{5 + r}{2}$$

Hence, if the expected future short-term interest rate ($r$) rises, so does the current long-term interest rate ($R$).

# Using Economics to Explain a Rise in Long-Term Interest Rates

When faced with a large budget deficit, the government may hope that expectations of a credible multiyear plan of deficit reduction will lower interest rates. In Germany the reverse effect occurred in late 1989 and proved how powerful the expectations effect can be.

In 1989 it became more and more apparent that West Germany and East Germany would unite into one country. But as the inevitability of this event dawned on people, so did the likelihood that the German budget deficit would increase sharply. Unification would require large government expenditures, and it was unlikely that tax increases would be sufficient. Hence, by late 1989 people began to anticipate a large increase in the German budget deficit. The most credible thing anyone could say about German fiscal policy was that the budget deficit would increase.

This anticipation caused German long-term interest rates to jump sharply (see figure). People expected higher interest rates down the road, and this caused interest rates to rise immediately in the bond market.

Because financial capital flows easily across the Atlantic, interest rates in the United States also rose in late 1989 and early 1990. In this case, the expectations proved remarkably accurate. The German budget shifted from a small surplus to a large deficit in one year.

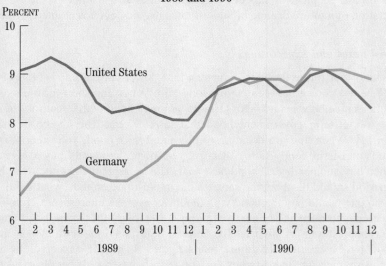

**Long-Term Interest Rates in the United States and Germany; 1989 and 1990**

*Source:* Organization for Economic Cooperation and Development.

Now, suppose that the government announces a credible deficit reduction plan to take place over a 10-year period. People who buy and sell bonds will reason that future short-term interest rates will be lower as a result of the lower budget deficit. If they expect future interest rates to be lower, then the current long-term interest rate on bonds will decline. Now, long-term interest rates as well as short-term interest rates affect investment decisions. Hence, the lower long-term interest rates will reduce borrowing costs, and firms will begin to invest more. Note that the increase in investment is occurring in the short run, not only in the medium run and the long run, because interest rates have declined in the short run.

In the ideal case, the increased investment and net exports would just offset the decline in government purchases in the short run, and there would be no negative effect on real GDP. However, the ideal case is very hard to realize because it depends on the government announcements being very credible and on people adjusting their expectations to take account of the announcements. Moreover, the

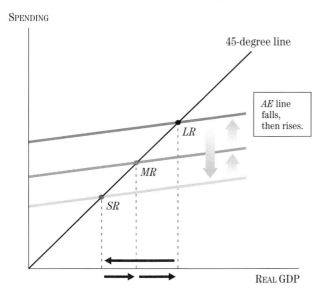

**Case of Little Credibility**

SPENDING

45-degree line

*AE* line
falls,
then rises.

*LR*

*MR*

*SR*

REAL GDP

| | $Y$ | $C$ | $I$ | $X$ | $G$ | $R$ |
|---|---|---|---|---|---|---|
| *SR* | ↓ | ↓ | ↔ | ↑ | ↓ | ↔ |
| *LR* | ↔ | ↑ | ↑ | ↑ | ↓ | ↓ |

The interest rate ($R$) does not decline immediately.

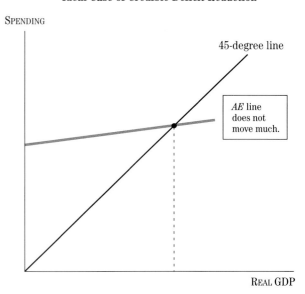

**Ideal Case of Credible Deficit Reduction**

SPENDING

45-degree line

*AE* line
does not
move much.

REAL GDP

| | $Y$ | $C$ | $I$ | $X$ | $G$ | $R$ |
|---|---|---|---|---|---|---|
| *SR* | ↔ | ↑ | ↑ | ↑ | ↓ | ↓ |
| *LR* | ↔ | ↑ | ↑ | ↑ | ↓ | ↓ |

Short-run output effects are mitigated by an
immediate decline in the interest rate ($R$).

speed by which firms increase their investment must exactly match the speed of reduction in government purchases. Also, even if real GDP is unaffected, there may be different effects in different regions of the country because the lower government purchases and the increased investment would not necessarily occur in the same place.

Figure 15.10 illustrates the difference between such a credible deficit reduction plan and the more standard type of deficit reduction. The panel on the left is the standard case of deficit reduction through a cut in purchases that we have already analyzed. The panel on the right is the case of a credible deficit reduction. On the right, the aggregate expenditure (*AE*) line does not move much; the lower government purchases are offset by increased investment through the decline in interest rates. The tables illustrate the key interest rate difference in the two cases. On the left, the interest rate does not decline in the short run; hence, investment stays put. On the right, the interest rate falls in the short run because people foresee the interest rate declining in the long run and, immediately, current interest rates fall.

**FIGURE 15.10**
**Benefits of Credible Budget Deficit Reduction**
On the left, the budget deficit is reduced but the plan has no credibility. Interest rates do not change in the short run. On the right, a reduction in the interest rate in anticipation of budget deficit reduction stimulates investment and offsets the decline in government purchases.

## The Structural versus the Cyclical Deficit

We noted earlier that taxes and spending change automatically in recessions and booms. These automatic changes affect the budget deficit, so in order to analyze the deficit it is important to try to separate out these automatic effects. The *structural, or full-employment, deficit* was designed for this purpose. The definition of **structural deficit** is the answer to the question, "What would the deficit be if real GDP equaled potential GDP?" Economists use the term *full-employment deficit* because full employment occurs when real GDP equals potential GDP; that is, the unemployment rate equals the natural rate, or the "full employment" unemployment rate.

Figure 15.11 introduces a graph to help explain the structural deficit. On the horizontal axis is real GDP. On the vertical axis is the budget deficit. The budget is balanced when the deficit is zero, which is marked by a horizontal line in the diagram. The region above zero represents a situation where taxes are less than spending and the government has a deficit. The region below zero is a situation where the government budget is in surplus. On the horizontal axis, letters *A, B,* and *C* represent three different levels of real GDP.

The downward-sloping line in Figure 15.11 says that as real GDP rises, the budget deficit gets smaller. More real GDP means a smaller deficit. Why? The automatic stabilizers are the reason. When real GDP rises, taxes rise, and spending on transfer programs falls. Because the deficit is the difference between spending and taxes, the deficit gets smaller. Conversely, when real GDP falls, tax receipts decline and spending on transfer programs increases, so the deficit rises. The downward-sloping line in Figure 15.11 pertains to a particular set of government programs and tax laws. A change in these programs or laws would *shift* the line. For example, an increase in tax rates would shift the line down.

Figure 15.12, a similar diagram, shows potential GDP and real GDP in 1991, a recession year when real GDP was below potential GDP. Imagine raising real GDP

**structural deficit:** the level of the government budget deficit under the scenario where real GDP is equal to potential GDP; also called the full-employment deficit.

**FIGURE 15.11**
**The Effect of Real GDP on the Deficit**
The deficit equals spending minus taxes. When real GDP falls, the deficit rises because spending rises and tax receipts fall. When real GDP rises, the deficit falls. When real GDP is at point *A,* there is a deficit; at point *B* the budget is balanced; and at point *C* there is a budget surplus (negative deficit).

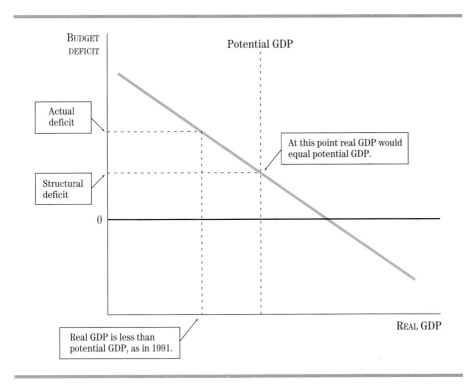

BUDGET DEFICIT

Potential GDP

Actual deficit

At this point real GDP would equal potential GDP.

Structural deficit

0

Real GDP is less than potential GDP, as in 1991.

REAL GDP

**FIGURE 15.12**
**The Structural Deficit versus the Actual Deficit in a Recession Year**
The deficit that would occur when real GDP is equal to potential GDP is called the structural deficit, as shown in the figure. The actual deficit rises above the structural deficit when real GDP falls below potential GDP, such as in 1991, a recession year.

up to potential GDP. We would predict that the deficit would go down, because tax receipts would rise as the economy grew and transfer payments would go down with fewer people unemployed, fewer people retiring, and fewer people on welfare. As we move to the right in the diagram, the deficit gets smaller. The structural deficit occurs when real GDP equals potential GDP.

The structural deficit provides a way to separate out cyclical changes in the budget caused by cyclical changes in the economy. The **cyclical deficit** is defined as the difference between the actual deficit and the structural deficit.

**cyclical deficit:** the difference between the actual deficit and the structural deficit.

Figure 15.12 says that even if the U.S. economy were at full employment, there would still have been a deficit in 1991. Reducing the structural deficit would require changes in government programs to reduce spending or changes in the tax law to increase tax revenue. Such changes in government programs or the tax laws would shift the negatively sloped line down to give budget balance at full employment.

## Review

▶ The impact of a reduction in the deficit on the economy is best analyzed by looking at what happens to taxes and spending. A reduction in the deficit will temporarily reduce real GDP though, in the long run, real GDP returns to potential.

▶ A credible deficit reduction plan will result in smaller reductions in real GDP if interest rates fall in anticipation of the plan.

▶ The structural deficit adjusts the actual deficit for cyclical changes in the economy.

# BUDGET REFORMS

Frustration with many failed attempts by the U.S. government to reduce the structural budget deficit to zero has led to proposals to reform the process under which the Congress and the president determine the budget.

The most widely discussed and popular proposal is the *balanced budget amendment to the U.S. Constitution.* Such an amendment has been voted on by Congress several times but has yet to pass. The amendment would require that the budget be balanced, much like the requirement for many state and local governments. The main advantage of the balanced budget amendment is that, if the law were adhered to, the budget deficit would be eliminated and the good long-term growth effects of a balanced budget would be reaped. However, there is some doubt that such a law could be enforced. What would the penalty be if the budget was not balanced? Another problem with a balanced budget amendment is that it would not permit the deficit to expand in a recession as part of the automatic stabilizers. Hence, recessions could be worse. Some versions of the balanced budget amendment focus only on keeping government spending within a percentage of GDP, allowing taxes to decline temporarily in a recession even if the deficit would rise. Others have escape clauses if there is a recession.

"In a compromise move to cut the budget, Congress and the president agreed to move the decimal one point to the left."

Another process reform gives the president more power to control spending. Starting in 1997, a new law authorized the president of the United States to veto separate items of legislation; this is called *line-item veto* authority. Under previous law the president could veto spending bills but not specific items in these bills. For the first time in U.S. history, President Clinton exercised the line-item veto in August 1997 by vetoing several spending and tax items in the 1997 budget agreement. The line-item veto is likely to be challenged in the courts, and it will take several years to assess the impact of this new law.

Other process reforms apply to the political system. Saying no to spending or yes to taxes is difficult for elected politicians who want to be reelected. *Term limits,* under which politicians could only serve for two or three terms, might make it easier for politicians to vote to cut spending on a program in their area. Alternatively, limiting political contributions from groups that have vested interests in government programs might make it easier for politicians to vote to limit the growth of such programs.

## Review

▶ The balanced budget amendment to the U.S. Constitution, the line-item veto, and term limits are three reforms that could reduce the budget deficit.

▶ The line-item veto was given to the president in 1997, but the balanced budget amendment has failed in Congress several times.

# CONCLUSION

Because the government is such a large player in the economy, its fiscal actions on spending, taxing, and borrowing exert a powerful influence on real GDP and employment. Such actions can cause real GDP to depart from potential GDP and can alter the long-term growth rate of potential GDP.

A first principle of fiscal policy, therefore, is that government not take actions that would harm the economy. Avoiding erratic changes in fiscal policy, making sure that taxes are not increased during recessions, and keeping budget deficits low when real GDP is equal to potential GDP are all part of this first principle. By running persistently large budget deficits in the 1980s and 1990s, fiscal policy in most countries has violated this first principle. Hence, budget reform aimed at reducing the budget deficit has been a high priority for fiscal policy. Changes in the way budget decisions are made—from balanced budget amendments to line-item vetoes—are possible reforms that have been suggested.

A second principle is that fiscal policy can be used to help smooth the economic fluctuations in the economy. Tax cuts and spending increases during recessions can help offset the declines in demand that cause recessions. Conversely, tax increases and spending cuts during booms can help offset forces leading to inflation in the economy.

There is debate among economists about whether the government is capable of taking discretionary actions with these effects. Policy lags and uncertainty make discretionary fiscal policy difficult. There is little disagreement, however, about the importance of automatic stabilizers under which tax and spending actions occur automatically without legislation. Automatic stabilizers cause the deficit to rise in recessions and fall during booms.

Another part of government policy that has powerful effects on the economy is monetary policy. We take up monetary policy in the next chapter.

# KEY POINTS

**1.** Fiscal policy consists of the government's plans for spending, taxes, and borrowing to finance the deficit.

**2.** The government's budget is the primary document of fiscal policy. It gives the priorities for spending and taxes. In the United States, the president must submit a budget proposal to Congress.

**3.** Most industrial countries have had large deficits in the 1990s.

**4.** Because the Congress modifies the proposals and because of unanticipated events, the actual budget differs considerably from the proposed budget.

**5.** Changes in spending and taxes can move real GDP away from potential GDP in the short run. But in the long run, real GDP returns to potential GDP.

**6.** Discretionary changes in taxes and spending can be used to keep real GDP near potential GDP, but this requires excellent timing and flexibility. Lags and uncertainty make discretionary policy difficult.

**7.** The automatic stabilizers are an important part of fiscal policy. They are essentially a policy rule in which tax revenues automatically decline in recessions and rise in booms. Transfer payments move in the reverse direction.

**8.** A decrease in the budget deficit is likely to reduce real GDP in the short run. In the long run, real GDP returns to potential GDP, but investment and net exports are a larger share of GDP.

**9.** There is general agreement among economists about the effects of changes in the deficit due to changes in government purchases. In the case where the deficit is changed by changing taxes, economists who believe in Ricardian equivalence argue that the effects are small or zero in the long run.

**10.** A credible plan to reduce the budget deficit can reduce long-term interest rates and thereby counter the negative effects on real GDP even in the short run.

**11.** Budget reforms that aim to reduce the structural deficit should aim to preserve the automatic stabilizers. This will enable fiscal policy to play an important stabilization role as it moves to a zero structural budget deficit.

# KEY TERMS

| | | |
|---|---|---|
| fiscal policy | federal debt | automatic stabilizer |
| federal budget | bond | fiscal policy rule |
| balanced budget | debt to GDP ratio | Ricardian equivalence |
| budget surplus | countercyclical policy | credibility |
| budget deficit | discretionary fiscal policy | structural deficit |
| budget cycle | progressive tax | cyclical deficit |

# QUESTIONS FOR REVIEW

**1.** Why is the actual budget deficit always different from the president's proposed deficit?

**2.** How does the government's debt differ from the government's budget deficit?

**3.** What are the differences between the short-run impact of a change in (a) purchases, (b) taxes, and (c) transfer payments?

**4.** Why is the long-run effect of a cut in government spending on investment less controversial than the effect of an increase in taxes?

**5.** What is Ricardian equivalence?

**6.** Why might interest rates fall when a credible program of budget deficit reduction is announced?

**7.** What is the difference between the structural deficit and the actual deficit?

**8.** What are the automatic stabilizers, and how do they help mitigate economic fluctuations?

**9.** What fiscal policy reform is needed in many countries?

**10.** Why has budget deficit reduction proved so difficult for so many countries?

# PROBLEMS

**1.** Use a diagram with inflation on the vertical axis and real GDP on the horizontal axis to show the short-run, medium-run, and long-run effects of an increase in the budget deficit on the inflation rate and real GDP. Show how the aggregate demand/inflation curve and the price adjustment line shift over time.

**2.** Suppose you have the following data on projected and actual figures for the U.S. budget for 2001 (in billions of dollars):

| | Projected Budget | Actual Budget |
|---|---|---|
| Taxes | 2,150 | 2,100 |
| Expenditures | 2,250 | 2,400 |

a) What was the projected budget deficit? What was the actual budget deficit? Why did this happen?
b) If the government debt is $3,400 billion at the end of 2000, what is the debt at the end of 2001?

c) If GDP is $9,000 billion in 2001, what is the debt to GDP ratio? How does this compare to the debt to GDP ratio for 1992? (*Hint:* See Figures 15.3 and 15.4.)

**3.** Suppose the president of the United States promises to implement a program that reduces discretionary government spending in order to eliminate the budget deficit in five years. Progress is made for several years, but in the fourth year, there is a huge increase in oil prices. Output falls and the deficit rises. In the next election, the president's challenger campaigns on the apparent broken promise. Suppose you are advising the president during the reelection campaign. What should the president say? Write your advice in a half-page memo.

**4.** Suppose the economy is currently $100 billion below potential GDP, and the government wants to pursue discretionary fiscal policy to speed the recovery.

a) Show this situation using the aggregate demand/inflation curve. Indicate the effect of an increase in government purchases.

b) What are the long-run benefits to *not* increasing government purchases as a proportion of real GDP? (*Hint:* Think about the long-run growth model in Chapter 9.)

5. The federal budget deficit for the United States rose from about 3 percent of GDP in 1990 to about 5 percent of GDP in 1991.

a) Explain why at least part of this increase in the deficit occurred because of the recession in 1991.

b) Suppose real GDP was equal to potential GDP in 1990 and below potential GDP in 1991. Sketch a diagram that shows the responsiveness of the deficit to GDP and show the structural deficit. How large a share of GDP is the structural deficit?

c) Is it good or bad for the economy that the deficit increased as a result of the recession?

6. Examine the following hypothetical data (in billions of dollars):

| Year | Budget Deficit | Government Debt as of Jan. 1 | GDP |
|------|------|------|------|
| 1996 | 100 | 1,000 | 4,000 |
| 1997 | 150 | 1,100 | 4,200 |
| 1998 | — | — | 4,800 |
| 1999 | 200 | 1,400 | 5,400 |

a) Fill in the missing values in the preceding table.

b) What is the percentage change in debt and GDP from 1997 to 1998?

c) What is the percentage change in the debt and GDP from 1998 to 1999?

d) Calculate the debt to GDP ratio for each year. How does this ratio change over time? Why?

7. Explain how a credible plan to decrease government expenditures ameliorates the downturn in the economy caused by the decrease in aggregate expenditures. Illustrate your answer with the aggregate expenditure curve.

8. Suppose that you are advising the prime minister of a country with budget deficit problems. You know that reducing the budget deficit will hurt production and employment in the short run but will be beneficial for the economy in the long run. The finance minister has a reputation of running large budget deficits and has little credibility. How would you recommend minimizing the negative short-run effects without compromising the budget deficit reduction? Explain.

9. State whether each of the following is true or false and explain your answer.

a) It is not possible to "grow out of" the government debt.

b) If the economy is already at potential GDP, then any increase in G will be inflationary.

c) It is possible to eliminate the deficit without eliminating the debt.

10. Suppose the government deficit is 3 percent of real GDP now, but economists say that the structural deficit is 2 percent.

a) Is real GDP currently above or below potential GDP? Why? Draw the diagram showing this situation.

b) In your diagram, show the situation where real GDP increases.

c) Draw the situation where there is a budgetary reform so that the structural deficit is zero. Does this mean that the current deficit goes to zero?

11. The Japanese government had a structural budget surplus in the late 1980s and real GDP was above potential GDP.

a) Draw this situation in a diagram like Figure 15.12.

b) Suppose Japanese citizens demand that their government get rid of the government surplus. Show what happens using the aggregate demand/inflation curve and the price adjustment line.

c) If the Japanese government has a credible, permanent increase in G, how does this affect the change in Japanese interest rates?

12. Suppose that real GDP is below potential GDP, and the Council of Economic Advisers is trying to evaluate various proposals for fiscal stimulus. They are uncertain about whether the multiplier is 1.7 or 2.5.

a) Draw the aggregate expenditure diagram for this situation. What is the slope of the aggregate expenditure line in each case?

b) Suppose the economic advisers decide the multiplier is 1.7, and they decide an increase in G of $50 billion would bring real GDP to potential GDP. Draw this in your diagram. If they are correct about the value of the multiplier, by how much does real GDP rise?

c) Suppose the Congress takes immediate action on the increase in G. If the multiplier is actually 2.5, by how much will they overshoot their target of potential GDP? Show this with the aggregate expenditure curve.

# Monetary Policy

Monetary policy refers to the entirety of actions taken by the central bank that affect the money supply and thereby interest rates, exchange rates, inflation, unemployment, and real GDP. Monetary policy is a powerful force affecting our lives. Pivotal national events have been convincingly attributed to it, including the Great Depression of the 1930s, the Great Inflation of the 1970s, and the long back-to-back expansions of the 1980s and 1990s.

We showed in Chapters 13 and 14 why monetary policy affects real GDP. By taking actions that raise or lower interest rates, the central bank can affect investment, net exports, and consumption in the short run. It thus can cause the departure of real GDP from potential GDP during booms and recessions. Moreover, the way the central bank responds to developments in the econ-omy influences the speed at which real GDP returns to potential GDP during recoveries from recessions. Ultimately, monetary policy determines the rate of inflation; it thereby affects productivity and the growth of potential GDP in the long run.

In this chapter, we look at the independence of central banks and the rationale for this independence. We also show that people's demand for money depends on the interest rate, and we examine *how* central banks raise or lower interest rates in the short run by changing the money supply. Finally, we consider a number of alternative monetary policies, including simply keeping money growth constant. As with fiscal policy, there is disagreement among economists over monetary policy, and we will examine the reasons for this disagreement.

# CENTRAL BANK INDEPENDENCE

The most important feature of a central bank, whether it is the Fed in the United States, the Bank of England in the United Kingdom, the Bundesbank in Germany, or the Bank of Japan in Japan, is the degree of independence the law gives it from the government.

The officials of the Fed are appointed by the president of the United States to long terms that may span several different governments; thus the term of the chair of the Fed does not coincide with the political terms of the president of the United States. For example, Paul Volcker served through most of the Reagan years, even though he was appointed by President Carter. Alan Greenspan served under Presidents Reagan, Bush, and Clinton. (The five Fed chairs who served during the past 40 years are shown below.) Therefore, like Supreme Court justices in the United States, Fed officials develop an independence.

Although it is difficult to measure independence objectively, the Fed seems to have more independence than the Bank of Japan and less independence than the Bundesbank. In 1997 the British Parliament gave the Bank of England greater independence; before 1997 the Bank of England had less independence than the Fed, but now it appears to have more. The advantage of **central bank independence** is that it prevents governments in power from using monetary policy in ways that appear beneficial in the short run but that harm the economy in the long run.

**central bank independence:** a description of the legal authority of central banks to make decisions on monetary policy with little interference by the government in power.

## Short-Run Gain versus Long-Run Pain

We showed in Chapter 14 that a change in monetary policy can temporarily raise real GDP above potential GDP in the short run but that only inflation will be higher in the long run. Such a change in monetary policy toward higher inflation would first entail a reduction in interest rates and would shift the aggregate demand/inflation (*ADI*) curve to the right, as shown in Figure 16.1. Real GDP would rise along with investment, consumption, and net exports; unemployment would fall. In the short run, there would be no effect on inflation because of the slowness of firms to change their price decisions. The economic gain of such a temporary economic boom might help in a reelection, or it might raise the popularity needed to push legislation for new programs through the political system. However, the economic

William McChesney
Martin
1951–1969

Arthur Burns
1969–1978

G. William Miller
1978–1979

Paul Volcker
1979–1987

Alan Greenspan
1987–

**FIGURE 16.1**
**Short-Run Gain and Long-Run Pain from a Change in Monetary Policy**

The Fed can temporarily stimulate the economy in the short run—real GDP rises above potential GDP. But in the long run the inflation rate is higher and this is harmful to the economy.

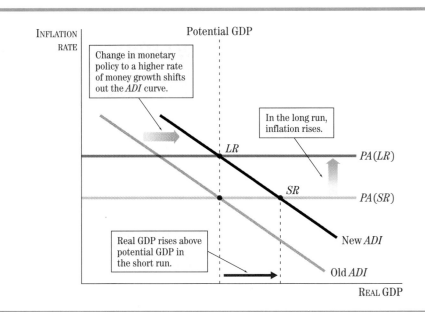

pain—higher inflation in the long run, also shown in Figure 16.1—would not be seen until after the election or after the legislation is passed.

Thus, there is a natural tendency toward higher inflation in the political system. If the government in power had complete control over the decisions of the central bank, it could take actions to make the economy look good in the short run for political purposes and not worry that it might look bad in the long run. Removing the central bank from the direct control of the government reduces this politically induced bias toward higher inflation because it is then more difficult for the government to get the central bank to take such actions. In fact, Figure 16.2 shows that central banks with more independence tend to have lower inflation performance.

**FIGURE 16.2**
**Central Bank Independence and Inflation**

The scatter plot shows that average inflation rates tend to be negatively related to the independence of central banks. The independence of the central bank is calculated by studying the laws of each country, including the length of the term of office of the head of the central bank (a longer term means more independence) and restrictions on the central bank lending to the government.

*Source:* Data from Alex Cukierman, *Central Bank Strategy, Credibility, and Independence* (Cambridge, Mass.: MIT Press, 1992).

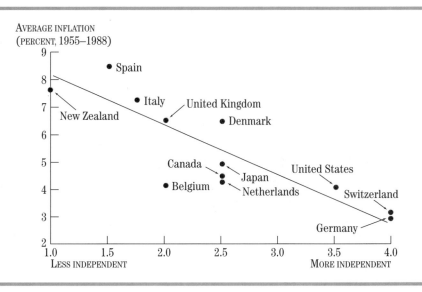

## The Political Business Cycle

The **political business cycle** is the tendency of governments to use economic policy to cause an economic boom just before an election and then let the economy slow down right after the election. Because both fiscal and monetary policy raise real GDP above potential GDP in the short run, a political business cycle can be caused by either monetary or fiscal policy. Many economic and political studies have shown that the chances of an incumbent being reelected are increased greatly if the economy is doing well, as it always seems to in a boom. After the election, inflation could rise and cause a bust, but that would be long before the next election. By the time of the next election, policy could again be used to cause a boom, and the cycle is repeated.

Research in the 1970s by William Nordhaus of Yale University uncovered some evidence of a political business cycle in the United States. For example, some feel that the boom in the economy before the 1972 election may have been due to a monetary policy change pushing real GDP above potential GDP. On the other hand, the U.S. economy was near a recession in the 1980 and 1992 elections, the exact opposite of a political business cycle. Thus, the evidence of a political business cycle in the United States is no longer strong. In any case, political business cycles are harmful to the economy and especially to those who suffer from the higher inflation and unemployment at the end of the cycle. Preventing political business cycles is another reason for having a central bank that has some independence from the government in power.

**political business cycle:** a business cycle resulting from politicians' use of fiscal or monetary policy to affect the outcome of an election.

## Time Inconsistency

The temptation of governments to use monetary policy for short-run gains despite the long-run costs is difficult to resist. Recent research has shown that even governments that aim solely to improve the well-being of the average citizen will say they want low inflation but then stimulate the economy to lower unemployment, fully aware of the inflationary consequences.

This temptation is known as **time inconsistency** because governments say they want low inflation but are later inconsistent by following policies that lead to higher inflation. They act like a teacher who tells the class there will be an exam to get the students to study, but then on the day of the exam, announces the exam is canceled. The students are happy to miss the exam and the teacher does not have to grade it. Everyone appears to be better off in the short run.

**time inconsistency:** the situation in which policymakers have the incentive to announce one economic policy but then change that policy after citizens have acted on the initial, stated policy.

However, just as the teacher who cancels the exam will lose credibility with future classes, the central bank that tries the inconsistent policy will lose credibility. People will assume that the central bank will actually raise inflation even if it says it is aiming for low inflation. Credibility benefits monetary policy, as we show later in the chapter, and the costs of a loss of credibility are great.

## Government Borrowing from the Central Bank

There is yet another reason for the central bank to have a certain amount of independence from the government in power. If the government, rather than the central bank, had the ability to control the money supply, then the government might simply decide to print money to pay for its expenditures. The resulting increase in inflation could be large and harmful. For example, during the Revolutionary War, the American colonies printed paper money to pay for the war expenditures. The result was a huge inflation.

It is, of course, not unusual for governments to spend more than they receive in the form of tax revenue. We saw in the previous chapter that many industrialized countries have budget deficits and thus must borrow. But suppose the government could not borrow, perhaps because people were worried about political instability. During a war, for example, people might not want to lend to the government, worrying that the government would lose the war and would not pay back its borrowing. Similarly, political instability made it difficult for the newly elected government of Russia to borrow in the 1990s. In such a situation, if the government has control of the central bank it can simply instruct the central bank to print the money to pay for its deficit. If the deficit was large the inflation would be severe. Consider, for example, what would have happened if the U.S. central bank issued $236 billion in currency to make up for the difference between spending and taxes in the United States in 1993. This would have been a very large increase in the money supply in the United States and would have caused a horrible inflation. It would have increased the U.S. monetary base—currency plus bank reserves—from $386 billion to $622 billion, or about 61 percent in one year.

There are more subtle ways that a central bank with little independence can succumb to the needs of government finance. During World War II in the United States, the Fed agreed as part of the war effort to hold interest rates low in order to keep the interest rates on the government debt down. After World War II the Fed was able to remove itself from this agreement because of its independence; it recognized that holding interest rates too low would eventually lead to inflation.

The ramification of a central bank fully financing a huge government budget deficit is always inflation. That is why the inflation rate was so high in Russia and Brazil in the early 1990s. These cases illustrate another reason for central bank independence: to avoid the temptations to use the central bank to finance the government deficit and thereby cause inflation.

The importance of central bank independence has been stressed by many economists. Over 170 years ago, the great British economist David Ricardo described his idea of an ideal central bank:

It is said that Government could not be safely entrusted with the power of issuing paper money; that it would most certainly abuse it. . . . There would, I confess, be great danger of this if the Government—that is to say the ministers—were themselves to be entrusted with the power of issuing paper money. But I propose to place this trust in the hands of Commissioners, not removable from their official situation but by a vote of one or both houses of Parliament. I propose also to prevent all intercourse between these Commissioners and the ministers, by forbidding every species of money transaction between them. The Commissioners should never, on any pretence, lend money to Government, nor be in the slightest degree under its control or influence.[1]

## Possible Abuses of Independence

Central bank independence is no guarantee against monetary policy mistakes, however, and it could even lead to more mistakes. In principle, an independent central bank could cause more inflation than a central bank under control of the government. For example, those in charge of the central bank could—after they are appointed—succumb to arguments that high inflation is not so harmful after all. Or, at the other extreme, those in charge of the central bank could become so focused

### Secrets of the Temple

This 1987 book raised questions about the independence of the Fed chair. By emphasizing the mystique of the Fed, the book attracted much popular attention. The picture on the cover is of the board table with several governors discussing monetary policy.

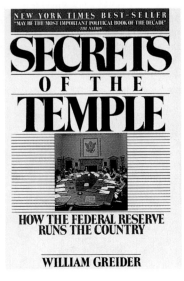

1. David Ricardo, *Plan for a National Bank,* 1824, pp. 10–11.

on inflation that they could be blinded to the effects of monetary policy on real GDP and employment and could either cause a recession or make an existing recession deeper or longer. Thus, a disadvantage of central bank independence is that it can be taken too far.

Whether independent or not, central banks need to be held *accountable* for their actions. If those in charge of the central bank do not perform their job well, it is appropriate that they not be reappointed. When the central bank of New Zealand was given greater independence in the late 1980s, its accountability was formalized very explicitly: If the head of the central bank does not fulfill low inflation goals agreed to in advance, the head is fired. But the central bank has independence in determining how to achieve these goals. This greater independence and accountability led to lower inflation in New Zealand. In fact, if you look back at Figure 16.2, you will see New Zealand *before* central bank independence; since independence, it has moved down and to the right toward lower inflation.

## Review

▶ Central bank independence removes the central bank from short-run political pressures to lower interest rates, when doing so would ultimately raise inflation.

▶ Independent central banks need to be held accountable for their actions.

▶ Countries with more independent central banks have tended to have lower inflation than countries with less independent central banks.

# MONEY DEMAND, MONEY SUPPLY, AND THE INTEREST RATE

Now that we have explored the rationale for the independence of Fed decisions, let's examine how the Fed carries out these decisions. If the Fed decides to raise interest rates, what action does it take to bring about this rise?

We will show how the interest rate is determined in a money market that consists of money demand and money supply. The Fed changes the interest rate by changing the money supply. To see how this works, we must first describe money demand and show that it depends on the interest rate.

### Money Demand

**Money demand** is defined as a relationship between the interest rate and the quantity of money people are willing to hold at any given interest rate. As shown in Figure 16.3, the amount of money demanded is negatively related to the interest rate. One reason people hold money is to carry out transactions: buying and selling goods. Figure 16.3 shows that people will hold less money if the interest rate is high. That is, a higher interest rate reduces the amount of money people will want to carry around in their wallets or hold in their checking accounts. Conversely, a

**money demand:** a relationship between the interest rate and the quantity of money that people are willing to hold at any given interest rate.

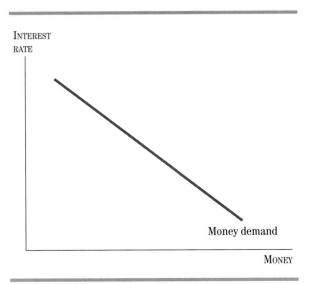

INTEREST RATE

Money demand

MONEY

**FIGURE 16.3**
**The Demand for Money**

The interest rate is the opportunity cost of holding money. Higher interest rates on Treasury bills or other interest-bearing assets raise the opportunity cost of holding money and lower the quantity of money demanded.

lower interest rate will increase the amount of money people will want to hold. Why is money demand negatively related to the interest rate?

Remember that money (currency plus checking deposits) is only part of the wealth of most individuals. People usually hold some of their wealth in financial assets that pay interest. For example, some people hold securities, such as Treasury bills, as an alternative to money. If you bought Treasury bills in 1993, they would pay 3 percent interest; in 1996, they paid 5 percent interest. Holding money is different from holding Treasury bills because currency does not pay interest and checking deposits pay low, or no, interest. If you hold all your money in the form of cash in your wallet, clearly you do not gain any interest. Thus, an individual's decision to hold money is best viewed as an alternative to holding some other financial asset such as a Treasury bill. If you hold money, you get little or no interest; if you hold one of the alternatives, you earn interest.

The interest rate on the vertical axis in Figure 16.3 is the average interest rate on these other interest-bearing assets that people hold as alternatives to money. Now, if the interest rate on these alternatives rises, people will want to put more funds in those alternatives and hold less as money. If they hold the funds as currency, they get no interest on the funds. If they hold the funds in a checking account, they may get a small amount of interest but certainly less interest than would be gained on other securities. There is a lower quantity of money demanded at higher interest rates because putting the funds in interest-bearing securities becomes more attractive compared to keeping the funds in a wallet or purse.

In other words, the interest rate on the alternatives to holding money is the *opportunity cost* of holding money. When the opportunity cost increases, people hold less money. When the opportunity cost decreases, people hold more money.

Figure 16.3 represents money demand in the economy as a whole. The curve is obtained by adding up the money demanded by all the individuals in the economy at each interest rate. The money held by businesses—in cash registers or in checking accounts—should also be added in.

## Money Supply

The Fed, of course, has no direct control over how much money as an individual you hold in your wallet or checking account, but it does control the supply of money in the whole economy. It does this by changing the monetary base—currency plus bank reserves, as we showed in Chapter 10. It changes the monetary base by either buying bonds or selling bonds.

On any given day the Fed buys and sells billions of dollars of government bonds. When the Fed buys government bonds, it has to pay for them with something. It pays for them with bank reserves—the deposits banks have with the Fed. For example, if the Fed wants to buy bonds held by Citibank, it says, "We want $1 billion worth of bonds, and we will pay for them by increasing Citibank's account with us by $1 billion." This is an electronic transaction. Citibank's deposits at the Fed (reserves) have increased by $1 billion and the Fed gets the bonds. They have exchanged bank reserves for the bonds. Now, the *monetary base* equals

**monetary base:** currency plus reserves. (Ch. 10)

currency plus reserves. By increasing reserves, the Fed increases the monetary base. Hence, *by buying bonds, the Fed increases the monetary base. By selling bonds, the Fed decreases the monetary base.* Buying and selling bonds is called an **open market operation.** The term *open market operation* is used because the market is open to anyone.

The *money multiplier,* as we studied in Chapter 10, provides a link between the money supply ($M$) and the monetary base ($MB$). The money multiplier is given by:

**open market operation:** the buying and selling of bonds by the central bank.

$$\frac{M}{MB} = \frac{1 + k}{r + k}$$

where $r$ is the required reserve ratio and $k$ is the currency to deposit ratio. Suppose $r$ is .1 and the amount of currency people desire to hold as a fraction of deposits $k$ is .2; then the money multiplier is $(1 + .2)/(.1 + .2) = 4$. Then an increase in the monetary base ($MB$) of $1 billion leads to increases in the money supply ($M$) of $4 billion.

Suppose the Fed buys bonds; this increases the monetary base, and according to the money multiplier the money supply in the economy increases. Similarly, if it sells bonds, it decreases the money supply.

Do not confuse the money multiplier with the government purchases multiplier described in Chapter 12. The government purchases multiplier tells us that an increase in government purchases of goods and services increases real GDP in the short run by a multiple of the increase in government purchases. The money multiplier has nothing to do with government purchases. The money multiplier tells us that an increase in the monetary base will increase the money supply by a multiple of the increase in the monetary base.

## The Determination of the Interest Rate

We have now shown that money demand is determined by people in the economy deciding how much of their wealth to hold as money, and the money supply depends on the Fed. Now we put the two together to determine the interest rate, just as we combine the demand and supply for any good to determine the price. The quantity of money demanded must equal the quantity of money supplied. If the Fed supplies $300 billion in money, then people must hold that amount of money—no more and no less.

The interest rate brings the quantity of money demanded into equality with the quantity of money supplied. This is shown in Figure 16.4. The axes are the same as Figure 16.3, with the interest rate on the vertical axis and the quantity of money on the horizontal axis. We have added a vertical line to represent the money supply, as determined by the Fed. Observe how the interest rate plays the role of the price in this supply and demand diagram. There is only one place where this money supply line intersects the money demand curve. This intersection determines the interest rate in the money market, just as the intersection of the supply and demand curve for peanuts determines the price of peanuts in a peanut market. If the quantity of money supplied were above the quantity of money demanded, then people would put their excess money in interest-bearing accounts, driving down the interest rate on those accounts; the interest rate would fall. If the quantity of money supplied were below the quantity of money demanded, the interest rate would rise. There is only one value of the interest rate for which the money demand curve intersects the money supply line.

**FIGURE 16.4**
**The Interest Rate and the Supply and Demand for Money**
The interest rate in the money market is determined at the intersection of the money demand curve and the money supply line.

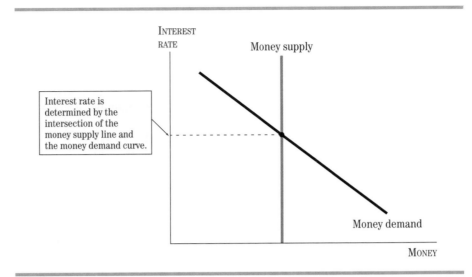

# Review

▶ The demand for money depends inversely on the interest rate. A higher interest rate means a larger opportunity cost of holding money and therefore a lower amount of money demanded. Lower interest rates increase the amount of money demanded.

▶ The money supply is determined by the Fed. By buying bonds, the Fed increases the money supply.

By selling bonds, the Fed decreases the money supply.

▶ The interest rate is determined at the point where the money demand curve intersects the money supply line.

# FED POLICY ACTIONS

We can now use the money demand and money supply diagram to show how the Fed affects the interest rate by changing the money supply.

## Open Market Operations and Changes in the Federal Funds Rate

Let us describe what might happen on a typical day in the New York bond market to see how the Fed changes the interest rate. Suppose the Federal Open Market Committee (FOMC), the group at the Fed responsible for monetary policy, votes to lower the short-term interest rate by ¼ of a percentage point.

The situation facing the Fed is shown in the left panel of Figure 16.5, which shows money demand and money supply. To lower the interest rate the Fed must

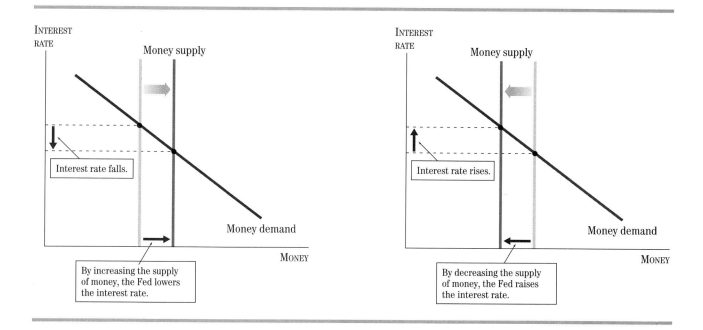

increase the money supply. This is shown in the diagram by shifting out the money supply line. At the higher money supply, there is a new intersection of the money supply and money demand curves. At this intersection, the interest rate is lower, which is exactly what the Fed wants.

In order to increase the money supply the Fed knows that, according to the money multiplier, it must increase the monetary base. In sum, if the Fed wants to lower the interest rate, it needs to increase the monetary base, and we know that this means it must buy bonds in the bond market.

Thus, the Fed buys the bonds from some bank, perhaps Citibank. The Fed pays for the bonds by increasing the amount of funds in Citibank's account so that bank reserves rise. With the rise in reserves we know that the monetary base rises, the money supply increases, and the interest rate falls; in our example the interest rate falls by ¼ percentage point.

The interest rate the Fed looks at in order to make sure that its actions are having the intended effect is called the *federal funds rate,* which is the short-term interest rate that banks charge each other on overnight loans. This interest rate is related to all other interest rates in the economy. (See Figure 16.6.) In particular, the federal funds rate is very closely related to interest rates on Treasury bills and other alternatives to holding money. The federal funds rate is also closely related to interest rates on bank loans, whether the loans are for construction, automobiles, or mortgages.

If the Fed wanted to raise the short-term interest rate, it would take action in precisely the opposite direction. It would sell bonds, which would lower bank reserves, lower the monetary base, lower the money supply, and raise interest rates. This case is illustrated in the panel on the right of Figure 16.5, which shows the money supply declining and the interest rate rising.

**FIGURE 16.5**

**The Fed Can Change the Interest Rate by Changing the Money Supply**

The Fed lowers the interest rate by increasing the supply of money, as in the graph on the left. The Fed can raise the interest rate by decreasing the supply of money, as in the graph on the right. The Fed changes the money supply by adjusting the monetary base through open market operations.

**FIGURE 16.6**
**Short-Term Interest Rates**
The federal funds rate is the interest rate the Fed focuses on when deliberating about policy. Other short-term interest rates move up and down with the federal funds rate. The rate on prime (low-risk) bank loans is about 3 percentage points above the federal funds rate.

*Source:* Federal Reserve Board.

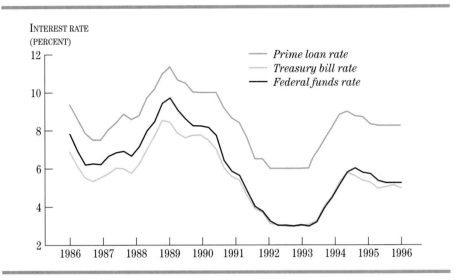

It is very important to remember that when the Fed changes the interest rate, it also changes the money supply. When the Fed lowers the interest rate, for example, it increases reserves, the monetary base, and thus the money supply. If the Fed increases the money supply too much, then inflation will eventually rise. The Fed must consider the impact of its actions on the money supply and on inflation each time it considers raising or lowering interest rates.

## The Monetary Transmission Channel

**monetary transmission channel:** a description of how a change in monetary policy eventually affects real GDP.

The complete sequence of events through which a decision of the central bank to buy bonds changes interest rates and shifts real GDP in the short run is called a **monetary transmission channel.** The monetary transmission channel, from an initial Fed bond purchase to a short-run rise in real GDP, can be summarized as follows:

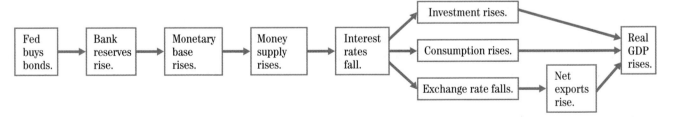

When the Fed buys bonds in the open market, the reserves at banks rise. Because reserves are part of the monetary base, this causes the monetary base to rise. The money multiplier tells us that the money supply is a multiple of the monetary base, so this causes the money supply to rise. In order for people to hold the additional money, the interest rate must fall; this stimulates investment and consumption. Finally, the decline in the interest rate causes the exchange rate to fall, which raises net exports. The increase in investment, consumption, and net exports raises real GDP in the short run. (In the long run, however, as prices adjust, real GDP returns to potential GDP, just as in Figure 16.1.) Remember that this all works in reverse: If the Fed sells bonds, real GDP will fall in the short run.

Economists have investigated the monetary transmission channel in great detail. For example, some economists like to focus on the role of *banks* in the monetary transmission channel. Recall that, as part of the multiplier process, banks expand their loans after an open market purchase. The loans are used to finance investment purchases, such as new equipment, and consumption purchases, such as new automobiles. The increase in loans provided by banks has a direct impact on aggregate spending and on real GDP.

## Other Tools of Monetary Policy

Open market operations are a "tool" that the Fed uses to bring about changes in the money supply and interest rates. The Fed has two other tools it sometimes uses in conducting monetary policy.

### The Discount Rate

The discount rate is one of these tools. The **discount rate** is the rate the Fed charges commercial banks when they borrow from the Fed. To understand why commercial banks borrow from the Fed, we must consider another role for central banks: the role of *lender of the last resort*. During recessions and depressions in the nineteenth and early twentieth centuries, there were frequently "runs" on banks in which people scrambled to withdraw their deposits for fear their bank was going under. Rumors caused runs even on sound banks. By agreeing to lend to banks if they experience a run, the Fed can bolster confidence in the bank. The mere existence of a central bank willing to lend reduces the chance of runs by raising confidence.

When commercial banks borrow from the Fed, economists say they "go to the discount window." Borrowings from the Fed are now very small. The Fed keeps the discount rate just a little below the federal funds rate. Because the discount rate is lower than the federal funds rate, the Fed then must discourage each bank from borrowing too much at the discount window.

### Changes in Reserve Requirements

Another tool of monetary policy is the reserve requirement. Recall that the money multiplier depends on the required reserve ratio ($r$). If the Fed decreases the required reserve ratio—that is, decreases reserve requirements—then the money multiplier rises. For a given monetary base, therefore, a reduction in reserve requirements increases the money supply. Conversely, an increase in reserve requirements lowers the money supply.

In practice, however, the Fed very rarely changes reserve requirements; and when it does so its aim is not to change the money supply, because open market operations are sufficient to achieve any desired change in the money supply. Sometimes the Fed changes reserve requirements to affect the profits at banks. For example, in 1990, the Fed lowered reserve requirements in order to raise profits at banks and thereby reduce the chance that some banks would become insolvent during the 1990–1991 recession. Banks do not receive interest on reserves; thus, lower reserve requirements mean they can make more profits by making more interest-earning loans.

---

**Keeping Track of the Monetary Transmission Channel**

Here is a helpful memory device:

The Fed *Buys* bonds, and real GDP *Booms* in the short run.

The Fed *Sells* bonds, and real GDP *Slumps* in the short run.

**discount rate:** the interest rate that the Fed charges commercial banks when they borrow from the Fed.

In 1990, when the Fed lowered reserve requirements, it also lowered the monetary base so that the money supply was unaffected. In other words, the Fed used one of its other tools—open market operations—to exactly offset the effect of the reserve requirement tool on the money supply.

## Review

▶ The Fed affects the short-term interest rate by changing the money supply. By buying bonds in the open market, the Fed increases the money supply and the interest rate falls. By selling bonds in the open market, the Fed decreases the money supply and the interest rate rises. These purchases and sales are called open market operations.

▶ In addition to open market operations, the Fed has two other tools: the discount rate and reserve requirements. By lowering reserve requirements, the Fed can increase bank profits, because banks do not receive interest on reserves.

## ALTERNATIVE MONETARY POLICIES

We have now shown the actions the Fed must take when it decides to change the interest rate. Recall that the Fed usually decides to change the interest rate when inflation changes. For example, on March 25, 1997, the Fed announced that it was raising the interest rate from 5.25 percent to 5.50 percent because it was concerned that inflation was rising. We studied such a monetary policy response in Chapter 13. In this section we consider alternative ways the Fed might respond to changes in inflation as well as to changes in other variables.

In order to examine alternative Fed policy responses to inflation, look first at Figure 16.7, which shows an aggregate demand/inflation curve and a price adjustment line just as we derived them in Chapter 13. A rise in inflation is shown as an upward shift in the price adjustment line. Recall that the aggregate demand/inflation curve incorporates the Fed policy response to a rise in inflation. When inflation rises, the Fed raises the interest rate, and this tends to reduce real GDP relative to potential GDP in the short run, as shown in Figure 16.7. The decline in real GDP relative to potential GDP then puts downward pressure on inflation.

In Chapter 13 we described this Fed policy in terms of a monetary policy rule in which the Fed increases interest rates when inflation rises and decreases interest rates when inflation falls. That monetary policy rule is shown in Table 13.1 on page 336 and Figure 13.5 on page 337. In this section we show that many alternative monetary policy rules also imply a downward-sloping aggregate demand/inflation curve. However, alternative monetary policy rules imply different *slopes* of the aggregate demand/inflation curve. For example, a monetary policy rule that raises interest rates by more than shown in Table 13.1 will result in a flatter aggregate demand/inflation curve. Why? Because the larger change in the interest rate, for a given increase in inflation, will cause real GDP to decline by a larger amount, as shown for the flatter curve in Figure 16.7.

Now let's show why other monetary policy rules imply downward-sloping aggregate demand/inflation curves, though perhaps with different slopes.

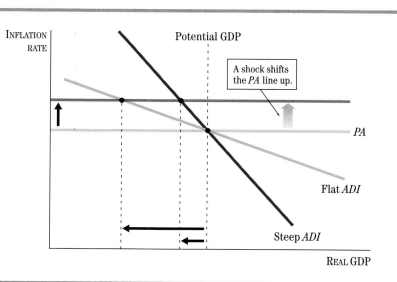

**FIGURE 16.7**
**Alternative Monetary Policies**
When a rise in inflation shifts the *PA* line up, the Fed's actions—incorporated into the *ADI* curve—affect the impact on real GDP. Many different monetary policy rules imply a downward-sloping *ADI* curve. They differ in how steep or flat the curve is.

## The Constant Money Growth Rule

Historical studies by Milton Friedman and Anna Schwartz have led them to argue in favor of a monetary policy that simply holds the growth rate of the money supply constant from year to year. This is called a **constant money growth rule.**

A constant money growth rule would give good inflation performance in the long run. For example, from the quantity equation of money (Chapter 10), if the velocity growth rate is zero and the long-term real GDP growth rate is 3 percent, then setting money growth at 5 percent would keep inflation at 2 percent on average. If the Fed had a *target inflation rate* of 2 percent, then setting money growth at 5 percent would achieve this target over the long run.

### Implications for the Aggregate Demand/Inflation Curve

Even with a constant money growth rule, inflation would not be perfectly stable from year to year. There would be shocks to the economy that would push the inflation rate around. However, with a constant money growth rule, if inflation picked up, whether because of an oil price shock or another shock, then interest rates would rise and real GDP would decline, just as described by the aggregate demand/inflation curve. Why would interest rates rise? With higher inflation, people would find they needed more money to carry out their transactions. For example, if inflation suddenly rose to 100 percent this year, the price level would double and people would need twice as much money. Money demand, as shown in Figure 16.4, would shift up. But with the constant money growth rule the Fed does not increase the money supply by enough to meet the increased demand. Hence, the amount of money demanded would be greater than the amount of money supplied; and, as Figure 16.4 suggests, the interest rate would rise. The higher interest rate would, in turn, reduce investment, consumption, and net exports. Hence, real GDP would fall. In sum, with higher inflation and lower real GDP, we trace out a downward-sloping aggregate demand/inflation curve.

**constant money growth rule:**
a monetary policy in which the central bank keeps money growth constant.

*Example.* According to the quantity equation for money (see Chapter 10):

Inflation rate + real GDP growth = money growth + velocity growth

Thus,

if money growth = 5 percent

velocity growth = 0 percent

real GDP growth = 3 percent

then the inflation rate = 2 percent.

The *slope* of the aggregate demand/inflation curve with a constant money growth rule would depend on how sensitive money demand is to the interest rate. This sensitivity to the interest rate determines how much the interest rate must change to bring the quantity of money demanded into equality with the quantity of money supplied by the Fed. If money demand were not very sensitive to the interest rate, then a big change in the interest rate would be required to bring the quantity of money demanded into equality with the fixed quantity of money supplied. This big change in the interest rate would have a large effect on real GDP and trace out a relatively flat aggregate demand/inflation curve.

### Debates about Constant Money Growth Rules

Monetarists are economists who generally advocate a constant money growth rule. The monetarists argue that the main advantage of a constant money growth rule is that it prevents erratic shifts in monetary policy. We know that such shifts in monetary policy will cause real GDP to fluctuate and can cause boom-bust cycles. In other words, the constant money growth rule is attractive to monetarists because they feel it will do less harm to the economy. They worry about rules in which the Fed staff must decide each week or month how much to adjust the money supply in order to move interest rates around as determined by the FOMC. They agree with most other economists that the best policy is one that keeps the aggregate demand/inflation curve from shifting. They disagree about the best means of keeping it from shifting.

Those who object to the constant money growth rule do not differ with monetarists about the importance of keeping aggregate demand stable—that is, keeping the aggregate demand/inflation curve from shifting. They feel that uncertainty about measuring and defining the money supply will lead to poor performance with a constant money growth rule. In other words, they feel that a constant money growth rule will lead to more and larger shifts in the aggregate demand/inflation curve than would other rules. That is why they recommend the Fed focus more on interest rates, as in the policy rule discussed in Chapter 13.

## Real GDP in the Monetary Policy Rule

Another monetary policy rule is a slight modification of the monetary policy rule described in Chapter 13. It formally adds in real GDP along with inflation as a variable influencing the Fed's interest rate decisions. For this rule, the central bank raises the interest rate when real GDP rises above potential GDP and lowers the interest rate when real GDP falls below potential GDP. Real GDP thus becomes another factor in the monetary policy rule along with the inflation rate.

If the central bank takes actions to raise the interest rate in this way when the economy goes into a boom, then the higher interest rate will slow the growth of real GDP and cut off the boom. Or, if the economy is in a recession, the central bank will reduce the interest rate. In this case, a lower interest rate could help bring about a more rapid recovery.

Table 16.1 shows a numerical example describing this type of policy rule. On the left is the inflation rate. On the top is the percent deviation of real GDP from potential GDP. The entries in the shaded part of the table show the interest rate. For example, the blue entry shows that when inflation is 2 percent and real GDP is equal to potential GDP (the percent deviation of real GDP from potential GDP is zero), the interest rate is 4 percent. When inflation rises to 4 percent, the interest

|  | | Percent Deviation of Real GDP from Potential GDP | | |
| --- | --- | --- | --- | --- |
|  | | −2 | 0 | 2 |
| Inflation Rate (percent) | 0 | .5 | 1 | 2 |
|  | 2 | 3 | 4 | 5 |
|  | 4 | 6 | 7 | 8 |
|  | 6 | 9 | 10 | 11 |
|  | 8 | 12 | 13 | 14 |

(The entries in the shaded area show the interest rate for each inflation rate and real GDP deviation.)

●————————————————

**TABLE 16.1**
**A Numerical Example of Central Bank Interest Rate Policy Reacting to Both Real GDP and Inflation**
(Compare with Table 13.1 on page 336.)

rate rises to 7 percent. Each column of Table 16.1 tells the same story: When inflation rises, the central bank raises the interest rate. Note that the interest rate rises more than inflation rises for every column in Table 16.1, just as in Table 13.1.

Now observe in Table 16.1 that the central bank's response to inflation also depends on what happens to real GDP. If real GDP is falling below potential GDP in a recession, the central bank reduces the interest rate. In other words, when real GDP falls below potential GDP, the central bank lowers the interest rate, and when GDP rises above potential the central bank raises the interest rate.

What are the reasons for the Fed to react to real GDP as well as to inflation in this way? First consider the case of a boom and then the case of a recession.

If the economy goes into a boom and real GDP rises above potential GDP, the Fed would raise the interest rate according to Table 16.1, even if the inflation rate had not started to increase. Such a policy response is sometimes called a **preemptive monetary strike** because the Fed increases the interest rate in anticipation of a rise in inflation, before the inflation rate actually rises. The interest rate response to higher real GDP may be based on an assessment by the Fed that the boom will soon bring higher inflation and, because monetary policy works with a lag, it is better to react sooner rather than later.

If the economy goes into a recession, the rationale for reacting to real GDP is somewhat different. In the case of a recession, the decline of real GDP relative to potential GDP will call for a reduction of the interest rate, according to the policy rule in Table 16.1. The reduction in the interest rate will tend to stimulate real GDP and offset the recession, perhaps leading to a quicker recovery from the recession. Moreover, the decline in real GDP relative to potential GDP may be a signal of lower inflation in the future, another reason for the Fed to lower the interest rate.

In reality the Fed and other central banks appear to react to real GDP as well as to inflation in this way. In other words, Table 16.1 is a more accurate description of central bank behavior than Table 13.1, though Table 13.1 is a close approximation.

The monetary policy rule in Table 16.1 also leads to a downward-sloping aggregate demand/inflation curve, though the curve will be steeper than the simpler policy rule of Table 13.1, in which the Fed reacts only to inflation. Suppose that there is an increase in the inflation rate, as in Figure 16.7. Then the Fed will increase the interest rate and this will tend to reduce real GDP. However, as real GDP declines, the Fed keeps the interest rate below that level given by the policy rule without real GDP. Thus, for this policy rule, the Fed does not increase the interest rate as much for a given increase in inflation and, therefore, real GDP does not decline as much for any increase in inflation; in other words, the aggregate demand/inflation curve is steeper.

**preemptive monetary strike:** a Fed interest rate increase in anticipation of a rise in inflation.

### The Gold Standard

For many years before the Fed was founded, much of the world operated under a
monetary policy that was called the **gold standard.** When on a gold standard in the
late nineteenth and early twentieth centuries, the U.S. Treasury had effective
responsibility for monetary policy. Under the gold standard, the Treasury agreed to
buy and sell gold at a fixed number of dollars per ounce. Also, the law tied the
money supply in the economy to a multiple of the amount of gold at the Treasury.
Such a policy would also tend to generate a downward-sloping aggregate
demand/inflation curve. Why? If, for example, the price of gold began to rise above
the fixed price, perhaps because of a general inflation that raised all prices, then the
Treasury would start to lose gold. People would want to buy gold at the low fixed
price, and the Treasury would have to sell it. But less gold at the Treasury would
reduce the money supply. Thus, interest rates would rise and eventually would
result in a decline in real GDP. Thus, the gold standard can be considered another
example of a monetary policy rule.

The main advantage of a gold standard is that, as long as the relative price of
gold does not change, there would be no inflation. The main disadvantage of a gold
standard is that the relative price of gold could change. For example, when there
were gold discoveries, the price of gold fell, and this led people to sell gold to the
Treasury at the higher price. As the stock of gold at the Treasury rose, the money
supply rose; this caused real GDP to rise in the short run, and eventually inflation
rose. Thus, under the gold standard, changes in the price of gold added to fluctuations in real GDP.

## Review

▶ Many alternative monetary policy rules imply a
downward-sloping aggregate demand/inflation
curve.

▶ The rules differ in how steep the aggregate
demand/inflation curve is and how stable it is.

▶ Reacting to real GDP as well as to inflation allows
the Fed to take preemptive strikes against inflation
and better mitigate recessions.

▶ Monetarists prefer constant growth rate rules because
such rules result in less erratic shifts in policy.

# GAINS FROM CREDIBILITY

Central bank independence and clearly stated procedures for setting the interest
rate, as described thus far in this chapter, are likely to bolster the credibility of monetary policy. What are the advantages of a credible monetary policy? There are two
key advantages. One is a better understanding of Fed policy actions; the other is
less costly disinflations. Let us consider each in turn.

### Interpreting Policy Actions

An advantage of credibility for monetary policy is that the Fed can take actions that
may appear contrary to its goals, but explain what it is doing and be believed. For

# The Fed Chairman Speaks on Principles of Monetary Policy

*Alan Greenspan was appointed to the chair of the Board of Governors of the Federal Reserve System by President Reagan, to a second term by President Bush, and to a third term by President Clinton. As part of the Senate confirmation process, Greenspan testified before the Senate Banking Committee. In doing so he gave a set of general principles of monetary policy that are excerpted here.*

I see the fundamental task of monetary policy as fostering the financial conditions most conducive to the American economy performing at its fullest potential. As I have often noted before, there is every reason to believe that the main contribution the central bank can make to the achievement of this national economic objective over long periods is to promote reasonable price stability. Removing uncertainty about future price levels and eliminating the costs and distortions inevitably involved in coping with inflation will encourage productive investment and saving to raise living standards. Monetary policy is uniquely qualified to address this issue: Inflation is ultimately determined by the provision of liquidity to the economy by the central bank and, except through its effect on inflation, monetary policy has little long-term influence on the growth of capital and the labor force or the increase in productivity, which together determine long-run economic growth.

But a central bank must also recognize that the "long run" is made up of a series of "short runs." Our policies do affect output and employment in the short and intermediate terms, and we must be mindful of these effects. The monetary authority can, and should, lean against prevailing trends, not only when inflation threatens but also when the forces of disinflation seem to be gathering excessive momentum. That is, in fact, what has concerned us in recent months, and we have been taking actions designed to assist in returning the economy to a solid growth path.

However, the Federal Reserve, or any other central bank, must also be conscious of the limits of its capabilities. We can try to provide a backdrop for stable, sustainable growth, but we cannot iron out every fluctuation, and attempts to do so could be counterproductive. What we have learned about monetary policy since the beginnings of the Federal Reserve System is that the longer-term effect of a policy action may be quite different from its initial impact; what we do not know with precision is the size and timing of these effects, especially in the short run. Uncertainty about the near-term twists and turns of the economy, along with the awareness of the potential differences between long- and short-term effects, suggests both flexibility in the conduct of monetary policy and close attention to the longer-term context in conducting day-to-day operations.

*Note how Greenspan touches on many of the issues discussed in this chapter: the difference between the long-run and short-run effects of monetary policy, the goal of price stability, inflation being ultimately determined by liquidity (another word for the money supply), and the uncertainty about the size and timing of the impacts of monetary policy.*

*Source:* Federal Reserve Bulletin, 1991.

example, suppose the Fed sees that the relationship between money and the interest rate is currently going off track. Suppose that there is a shift in money demand, so that at every interest rate people demand more money. Such a shift is illustrated in Figure 16.8. To keep interest rates from changing in such a circumstance, the Fed would have to increase the money supply, as shown in the figure.

If the Fed had little credibility, then people might interpret such an increase in the money supply as an indication that the Fed was going to allow for more inflation. But with credibility the Fed could state its views—that it was increasing the money supply because of a shift in money demand—and people would not worry that the Fed was trying to raise the inflation rate.

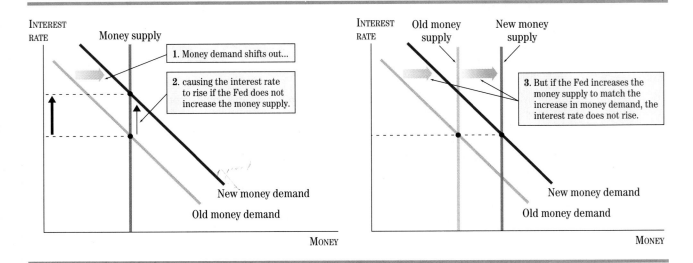

## FIGURE 16.8
### Shift in Money Demand and Fed Responses

The money demand curve shifts out. If the Fed does not increase the money supply, then the interest rate increases. If the Fed has credibility, it can increase the money supply without raising people's expectations of inflation.

## FIGURE 16.9
### Benefits of a Credible Disinflation

In the left graph, the *ADI* curve shifts to the new inflation target rapidly. The economy goes into a recession. In the right graph, the policy shift is announced, is credible, and occurs gradually. In the ideal case, there is little or no growth slowdown.

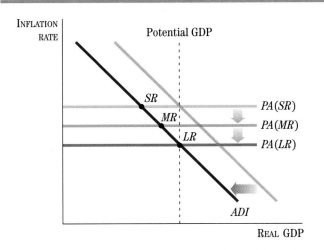

A sudden disinflation with no credibility: A recession occurs as interest rates jump and inflation does not change quickly.

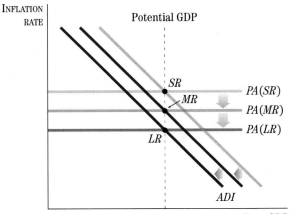

The ideal case of a more credible disinflation: Lower expectations of inflation and a more gradual shift in the *ADI* curve allow inflation to come down with little or no recession.

### Expectations and Credible Disinflation

An important issue for monetary policy is how to reduce the inflation rate when it is too high. We considered this problem of disinflation in Chapter 14. We showed that a recession usually occurs when the Fed tries to reduce the rate of inflation. This is illustrated again in the left panel of Figure 16.9. However, if the Fed announces its disinflation path and is credible, then it is possible for disinflation to occur with a smaller decline in real GDP.

For example, in the right panel of Figure 16.9, the aggregate demand/inflation curve *and* the price adjustment line shift down together. With a credible policy of disinflation, the rate of inflation adjusts down because people expect lower inflation in the future. However, getting expectations of inflation down requires a great deal of credibility. If the Fed does not have much credibility, the disinflation will be as costly as shown in the left panel, regardless of what the Fed says.

## Review

▶ If a central bank has credibility, it can take actions to offset shifts in money demand without adversely affecting inflation expectations.

▶ A credible disinflation has a smaller impact on output and employment than a disinflation that nobody believes will occur.

## CONCLUSION

In this chapter we examined the reasons for central bank independence. We also showed how the Fed's actions to change the money supply affect the interest rate. Several different central bank policies—for example, keeping the growth rate of the money supply constant, or pegging the price of gold—effectively cause the interest rate to increase when inflation rises and to decrease when inflation falls. Thus, a policy rule can occur even without a central bank. Deciding which policy is a good one and how it can be implemented are the major questions about monetary policy.

In the next chapter we consider how monetary policy works in the global economy. We will see, for example, that different policies for exchange rates among countries involved in international trade affect the independence of monetary policy among those countries.

## KEY POINTS

**1.** Monetary policy has a powerful effect on the economy. Large recessions and large inflations have been caused by monetary policy.

**2.** In most modern economies, monetary policy is the responsibility of the central bank.

**3.** Giving the central bank some independence is a way to avoid political business cycles and the temptation to change policy for short-term gain.

**4.** The Fed determines the money supply in the whole economy.

**5.** The demand for money is negatively related to the interest rate.

**6.** The Fed changes the interest rate by changing the supply of money.

**7.** The Fed can mitigate recessions by responding with lower interest rates.

**8.** Modern macroeconomic research suggests that the Fed should follow some kind of a policy rule in order to reduce uncertainty and gain credibility.

**9.** The Fed can reduce the costs of disinflation if it has such credibility.

**10.** The Fed's policy rule is responsive to real GDP as well as to inflation.

# KEY TERMS

central bank independence
political business cycle
time inconsistency
money demand

open market operation
monetary transmission channel
discount rate
constant money growth rule

preemptive monetary strike
gold standard

# QUESTIONS FOR REVIEW

**1.** What are some examples of the powerful effects of monetary policy?

**2.** What are the advantages and disadvantages of central bank independence?

**3.** What did monetary policy amount to before there were central banks?

**4.** Why is the demand for money inversely related to the interest rate?

**5.** What is the opportunity cost of holding money?

**6.** How does the Fed raise the interest rate?

**7.** How does a constant money growth rule determine the target inflation rate?

**8.** Why should real GDP be a variable in the monetary policy rule?

**9.** What are the advantages of a credible disinflation?

# PROBLEMS

**1.** In recommending central banking reforms for Eastern European economies, the *Economic Report of the President, 1990,* p. 202, asserted, "It is widely agreed that the central bank should have a high degree of independence from the central government so that it can resist political pressures to finance government spending with money creation and can pursue the objective of price stability." Explain the reasoning behind this assertion. What are some counterarguments?

**2.** The original Federal Reserve Act of 1913 allowed the secretary of the Treasury to be a member of the Federal Reserve Board, but a later amendment prohibited this. How would such a change affect the conduct of monetary policy?

**3.** Suppose that the currency to deposit ratio ($k$) equals .2 and the monetary base is $300 billion. By how much does the money supply change when the reserve requirement ratio ($r$) is raised from .1 to .2?

**4.** Suppose the Fed wants to raise the federal funds rate. Describe in detail how it accomplishes this policy.

**5.** What is the discount rate? How does it differ from the federal funds rate? Describe how the Fed affects each of these interest rates.

**6.** Suppose there is an increase in money demand at every interest rate. Show this in a diagram. What effect will this have on the interest rate if the Fed does not increase the money supply?

**7.** Suppose there are two countries, identical except for the fact that the central bank of one country lets interest rates rise sharply when inflation rises and the other lets interest rates rise less when inflation rises. Draw the aggregate demand/inflation curve for each country. What are the benefits and the drawbacks of each country's policy?

**8.** During the early 1990s in Japan, there was deflation and real GDP was below potential GDP.

　a) Draw a diagram showing the situation where there is deflation at potential GDP.

　b) Suppose the Japanese central bank decides it must reinflate and sets a target inflation rate of 2 percent. How does it accomplish this? Show the short-, medium-, and long-run effects.

　c) Is it possible that the central bank can have a fully credible reinflation? What are the benefits of immediate increases in the inflation rate?

9. Suppose that a government has a very bad credit rating (for example, there is serious default risk on the part of the government) and cannot sell bonds to finance its budget deficit. The only way it can finance the deficit is by issuing new money. As the deficit increases, what happens to inflation?

10. Suppose the velocity of money is constant, the growth rate of potential GDP is 2 percent per year, and the Fed's inflation target is initially 4 percent.

   a) The Fed then increases its inflation target to 6 percent per year. Using the quantity equation of money in growth rates, calculate the growth rate of money both before the Fed changes its target and in the long run, after it changes its target.

   b) Suppose, instead, that the Fed increases inflation to 10 percent, and the increase in uncertainty in the economy causes potential GDP to grow by 1 percent. What is the growth rate of money in the long run now?

11. Using the aggregate demand/inflation curve and the price adjustment line, show how real GDP would change over time if the Fed targeted a lower inflation rate and there was no change in fiscal policy. Suppose that real GDP was equal to potential GDP at the time of the change. Describe what happens to real GDP, investment, consumption, and net exports in the short run, medium run, and long run. Explain the role of interest rates and inflation in the adjustment of the economy.

12. Real GDP, consumption, and investment in the United States all declined from 1990 to 1991 and increased in 1992.

   a) Using an aggregate demand/inflation curve and a price adjustment line, show how a change in monetary policy in 1991 could explain these developments.

   b) Using a diagram with a monetary policy rule, describe what would happen to the interest rate and inflation in the short run (1991), the medium run (1992), and the long run according to the explanation in part (a) of this problem.

   c) Net exports increased from 1990 to 1991. Is the explanation in part (a) consistent with this development? If not, what other factors may have explained the behavior of net exports?

# International Finance

Countries are closely linked by trade. It is a rare day when we do not use or consume something made in another part of the world. In fact, advances in telecommunications and transportation and the removal of government restrictions on trade are transforming the world into one interconnected global market rather than separate national markets. Most commodity markets—including oil, copper, and wheat—are already world markets.

Trade between countries also requires another kind of market: the foreign exchange market, where one can obtain currency from another country in order to buy goods made in that country. The foreign currency market is itself a world market. Any time, day or night, the market in foreign currencies is open somewhere in the world. When the market closes for the day in Tokyo, it is just opening in London. When it closes in London, it is just opening in San Francisco. When the market closes in San

Francisco, it is about to open in Tokyo again. The foreign currency market is huge. Foreign currency trading is more than forty times the amount of goods trading in the world.

In this chapter we show how trade imbalances, in which exports are not equal to imports, are a normal part of world trade, but that such trade imbalances require that the people in one country lend funds to people in other countries. We then examine how the exchange rate—the price of foreign currency—is determined in the global market in foreign currencies. Finally, we look at what happens when two or more countries decide to fix the exchange rate between their currencies.

The subject matter of this chapter is called *international finance* because it focuses on how trade deficits are financed and how international financial markets in foreign currencies function.

# BALANCE OF TRADE AROUND THE WORLD

Net exports are defined as exports less imports. Another term for net exports is the trade balance. When net exports are negative, we say there is a trade deficit. If net exports are positive, there is a trade surplus. Some countries have trade surpluses, and some have trade deficits. However, the world as a whole has neither a trade deficit nor a trade surplus. Exports equal imports for the whole world.

## The Trade Deficit

As shown in the top panel of Figure 17.1, the U.S. trade deficit grew rapidly in the 1980s. It then shrank rapidly in the late 1980s before starting to rise again. Because the world as a whole can have no deficit, countries outside the United States had a

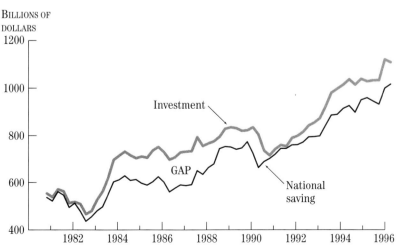

**FIGURE 17.1**
**The Trade Deficit and the Investment-Saving Gap**
In the 1980s, the trade deficit in the United States rose. It narrowed in the late 1980s and then widened again. Observe that these swings in the trade deficit are closely associated with the gap between investment and saving.

*Source:* U.S. Department of Commerce.

425

reverse pattern: The rest of the world's trade surplus with the United States grew rapidly in the 1980s, declined rapidly in the late 1980s, and rose in the 1990s.

Why did these large swings occur? Sometimes trade barriers—*tariffs* and *quotas* in other countries—are offered as the reason for the United States trade deficit. But this clearly makes no sense as an explanation for the changes in the trade deficit in the 1980s and 1990s. For example, Europe, whose trade account with the United States moved from surplus to deficit and back to surplus again during this period, did not change its trade barriers.

The lower panel of Figure 17.1 provides a better explanation. It shows the pattern of (1) investment in new factories and equipment in the United States, and (2) saving by individuals, businesses, and governments in the United States. Although the levels of both investment and saving were increasing, the *gap* between them grew dramatically in the 1980s. The gap then diminished in the early 1990s before widening again. During the 1980s and again in the 1990s, investment rose very rapidly in the United States as investors took advantage of good profit opportunities to build new plants and invest in new machinery. But at the same time the amount of saving that Americans were doing did not increase as rapidly. Thus, a gap grew between the level of investment and the level of saving.

Observe the close relationship between the investment-saving gap and the trade deficit in Figure 17.1. When the investment-saving gap rose, the trade deficit got bigger. When the investment-saving gap fell, the trade deficit got smaller. This close connection is not a coincidence. When the people of a country invest more in new factories and equipment than they save, they have to import more from abroad than they export. The excess of imports over exports (the trade deficit) goes to fill the gap between investment and saving. Another way to state this association between the investment-saving gap and the trade deficit is through an equation: *Saving minus investment equals net exports.* For example, in 1996, saving was $1,017 billion and investment was $1,116 billion; the difference, −$99 billion, equaled net exports; in other words there was a trade deficit of $99 billion in 1996.

The gap between investment and saving is thus at the heart of the large trade deficits in the 1980s and again in the 1990s. As long as the United States is an attractive place to invest and U.S. saving is insufficient to provide for that investment, trade deficits are inevitable.

*Example:* Let
$S$ = saving,
$I$ = investment,
$X$ = net exports,
then $S - I = X$.
If $S = 1,017$ and
$I = 1,116$, then
$X = -99$.

## Both Merchandise Trade and Services Trade Are Important

**merchandise trade:** trade in goods that have physical form, such as oil, wheat, or computers.

**services trade:** trade in services, or things that do not have a physical form, such as consulting or telecommunications.

Both exports and imports can be divided into merchandise and services. **Merchandise trade** includes goods such as trucks, oil, televisions, wheat, textiles, and shoes. **Services trade** includes airplane passenger service, legal services, education, banking services, telephone services, business consulting services, and construction services. Although both merchandise and services are exported and imported, it is easier to imagine merchandise being shipped from one country to another. Examples of U.S. services exports would include an American telecommunications consultant going to Saudi Arabia to give assistance in using a new air traffic control system, or a Japanese graduate student in physics in the United States paying tuition and fees for room and board. Examples of U.S. services imports would include an American traveling on the French *Concorde,* or Apple Computer hiring a German lawyer for assistance in protecting its trademark.

Services trade is more difficult to measure than merchandise trade because the goods do not physically pass through customs booths at ports of entry. In recent years efforts to collect data on services have improved our understanding of the size and importance of services trade.

The **merchandise trade balance** is the difference between merchandise exports and merchandise imports. If merchandise exports are greater than merchandise imports, there is a merchandise trade surplus; if merchandise exports are less than merchandise imports, there is a merchandise trade deficit. Similarly, the **services trade balance** is the difference between services exports and services imports. Adding the services trade balance and merchandise trade balance together gives the total trade balance shown in the upper graph in Figure 17.1.

### The U.S. Merchandise Trade Deficit

There has been a large U.S. merchandise trade deficit since the early 1980s. In 1996 the deficit was $186 billion. The merchandise trade balance is the most frequently reported trade statistic in the United States and in other countries. The merchandise data are easier to understand, and there is a tradition of looking at merchandise trade. Hence, many press reports still focus on the merchandise trade deficit. However, because of the growing importance of services, the merchandise trade deficit is too narrow a measure of a country's trade performance. Countries can gain as much in jobs and income from exporting services as they can gain from exporting merchandise.

### The U.S. Services Trade Surplus

The behavior of services trade is much different from merchandise trade in the United States. The United States has been running a surplus in services trade in recent years. As of 1996, the services trade surplus was $87 billion. The United States exported $238 billion of services in 1996 and imported $151 billion. Adding this services trade surplus to the merchandise trade deficit gives a radically different picture of the U.S. trade deficit. Without services, the trade deficit would have been $186 billion in 1996; with services, the trade deficit was about one-half as large—$99 billion.

Why is there a services trade surplus? A possible explanation is that the United States has a *comparative advantage* in the production of services. U.S. productivity in services is much higher than in other countries. Productivity in telecommunications services is greater in the United States than in Japan and Germany. Productivity in banking services is 50 percent greater in the United States than in the United Kingdom.

## The Balance of Payments

Payments made from one country to another can take place for many reasons: Imports into the United States from Europe, for example, require payments to Europeans by Americans, and exports from the United States to Europe require payments by Europeans to Americans. But there are also transfer payments from foreign workers to family members at home, interest payments on loans, and payments of profits by foreign-owned firms. The **balance of payments** account keeps track of all these payments; it is a record of all the transactions between one country and the rest of the world. The balance of payments has two parts: the current account and the capital account.

---

**merchandise trade balance:** the value of merchandise exports minus the value of merchandise imports.

*Example:* For 1996 in billions of dollars:

| | |
|---|---|
| Merchandise exports | 609 |
| Merchandise imports | −795 |
| Merchandise trade balance | −186 |

**services trade balance:** the value of services exports minus the value of services imports.

*Example:* For 1996 in billions of dollars:

| | |
|---|---|
| Services exports | 238 |
| Services imports | −151 |
| Services trade balance | 87 |

**comparative advantage:** a situation in which a person or country can produce one good more efficiently than another good in comparison with another person or country. (Ch. 2)

**balance of payments:** the record of all the transactions between a country and the rest of the world; it includes information on the value of trade in goods and services as well as transfer payments.

### The Current Account

The *current account* is a measure of all the payments made for currently produced goods and services plus *nontrade flows* of funds between a country and the rest of the world. All nontrade flows are lumped together in two categories: (1) interest, profits, and wages earned by the residents of another country, and (2) transfer payments received by the residents of another country.

In describing these two nontrade flows, we will look at Table 17.1, which shows the relationship between the *merchandise trade balance,* the *total (merchandise plus services) trade balance,* and the *current account balance* in the United States in 1996.

The first category of nontrade flows consists of interest payments, profits, and wages earned by businesses operating and people working in other countries. For example, if you live in Chicago and happen to have a deposit at a bank in London, your interest earnings on the bank deposit are a flow of funds from the United Kingdom to the United States. Another example is Blockbuster Video, headquartered in Ft. Lauderdale, Florida, which owns video rental stores in Australia (and many other countries); the profits earned in the Australian stores represent a flow of funds from Australia to the United States. This category of flows is called **factor income** because it represents earnings for a factor of production: for example, the store where Blockbuster videos are rented.

Factor income can either be paid or received by U.S. residents. If an American firm owns a business affiliate in Latin America or Europe, the interest payments and profits that the U.S. residents earn from the affiliate are called *receipt of factor income.* If a Japanese firm owns a business affiliate in the United States, the interest and profits that the affiliate pays to Japanese residents are *payment of factor income.* The difference between receipts of factor income and payments of factor income is called **net factor income from abroad.** Net factor income from abroad is one of the two items that must be added to the trade balance to get the current account balance.

As shown in Table 17.1, the United States received less factor income from abroad than it paid abroad in 1996; net factor income from abroad was −$9 billion. In other words, interest payments, profits, and wages of U.S. businesses and workers abroad were less than interest payments, profits, and wages of foreign affiliates and foreign workers in the United States. In 1996, receipts of factor income in the United States were $223 billion; payments of factor income were $232 billion.

The second category of nontrade flows consists of **international transfer payments,** which are humanitarian or military aid paid to other countries. International

**factor income:** earnings for a factor of production including wages and profits.

**net factor income from abroad:** the difference between receipts of factor income from foreign countries and payments of factor income to foreigners.

*Example:* For 1996, in billions of dollars:

| Receipt of factor income | 223 |
| Payment of factor income | −232 |
| Net factor income from abroad: | −9 |

**international transfer payments:** payments across international borders in the form of grants, remittances, and aid.

**TABLE 17.1
Measures of the U.S. International Trade, 1996**
(billions of dollars, surplus or deficit [−])

|  | 1996 |
|---|---|
| Merchandise trade balance | −186 |
| *Plus* services trade balance | 87 |
| *Equals* total trade balance (net exports) | −99 |
| *Plus* net factor income from abroad | −9 |
| *Plus* net transfers from abroad | −39 |
| *Equals* current account balance | −147 |

Nontrade flows: net factor income from abroad, net transfers from abroad

*Source:* U.S. Department of Commerce.

# Desert Storm and the Current Account

Table 17.1 shows that net transfers to the United States were negative in 1996. That is the usual situation. Transfer payments made by foreigners to the United States have been much smaller than transfers made by the United States to foreigners for most of the last 70 years. The difference was largest as a share of GDP in the years immediately following World War II. Then, the Marshall Plan and other foreign assistance programs had the United States transferring abroad about 1.5 percent of GDP per year for several years as grants and technical assistance went to help rebuild Japan, Germany, and the rest of Europe. Since then the United States has continued to transfer more abroad in humanitarian and military aid than it has received from abroad. In a typical year the number is much smaller than during the Marshall Plan years—it was ½ percent of GDP in 1996.

However, 1991 was an exception. In 1991 the United States received more funds from foreign countries than it paid out to foreign countries. How did this happen? The U.S. military operation against Iraq—Desert Storm—was the reason. Other countries transferred funds to the United States as reimbursement for the U.S. military operation. Most of these funds came from Japan and Germany. The large receipt of payments was for expenses associated with conducting the air strikes, maintaining the civil defense systems, and sending the ground troops to drive the Iraqi forces from Kuwait.

The amount of funds transferred was large enough to have a very noticeable effect on the U.S. current account. As shown in Figure 17.2 (on page 430), the current account went into surplus in 1991. The year before, 1990, the current account was in deficit; the year after, 1992, it had returned to a deficit. The swing in the current account was largely due to these one-time transfers.

---

transfer payments can go both ways; **net transfers from abroad** are the difference between transfers received in the United States and transfer payments made by the United States. In 1996, net transfers from abroad in the United States were negative, as they are in most years because the United States gives more humanitarian and military aid than it receives. An important exception occurred during the 1991 military operation to drive Iraq from Kuwait. (See the box "Desert Storm and the Current Account.")

If we add net factor incomes from abroad and net transfers from abroad to the trade balance we get the **current account balance.** When the current account balance is negative, as in Table 17.1, we say there is a current account deficit. The behavior of the trade balance (net exports) and the current account balance has been fairly similar in recent years because the fluctuations in the trade deficit have been huge compared with fluctuations in net factor income or net transfers (see Figure 17.2).

**net transfers from abroad:** the difference between transfer payments received and transfer payments made to other countries.

**current account balance:** the value of exports minus the value of imports plus net factor income from abroad plus net transfers from abroad.

## The Capital Account

A current account deficit in the United States means that Americans received fewer payments than they made to other countries. That is, payments to the United States for exports plus factor payments and transfer payments to the United States were less than payments by Americans for imports plus factor payments and transfer payments to other countries. If Americans receive less than they pay, then they must borrow from abroad, or equivalently, foreigners must increase their net assets in the

**FIGURE 17.2**

**The Trade Deficit and the Current Account Deficit**

The trade balance and the current account balance differ by two "non-trade" items: net factor payments from abroad and net transfers from abroad. In most recent years the United States has had both a trade deficit and a current account deficit; both deficits tend to move together because changes in net factor income and transfers are usually relatively small. (1991 was an exception.)

*Source:* U.S. Department of Commerce (quarterly data).

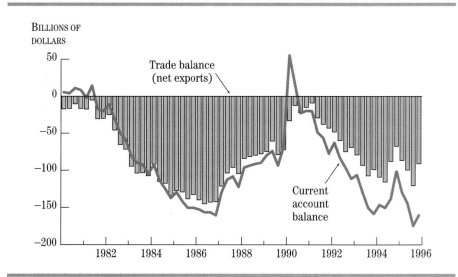

United States. In other words, if the current account deficit is $147 billion, foreigners must have made loans to Americans or bought assets in America for a net total of $147 billion.

The **capital account** measures these changes in loans and assets. For example, if the U.S. current account were in deficit by $100 billion, then the capital account would show an increase in foreign assets in the United States (net of an increase in U.S. assets in other countries) of $100 billion. If the United States were owed, say, $300 billion by foreigners, then the United States would now be owed $200 billion. If the United States already owed foreigners a net $500 billion, then it would now owe $600 billion. U.S. indebtedness to foreigners would go up by $100 billion because of the deficit. Thus, if the capital account is measured correctly, the net increase in foreign loans and foreign-owned assets in the capital account should equal the current account deficit.

Figure 17.3 shows what has happened to the capital account and net U.S. indebtedness in recent years. It shows that the value of assets held in the United States by foreigners is growing, as is the value of assets held in other countries by U.S. residents. But foreign assets in the United States have been growing faster than U.S. assets held abroad. The difference between U.S. assets held abroad and foreign assets held in the United States is **net foreign assets.** Net foreign assets have declined from a positive value in the mid-1980s to a negative value in the mid-1990s. In other words, we might say that the United States shifted from a *net creditor* country to a *net debtor* country, as it borrowed from abroad year after year.

Although the change in net foreign assets each year should be exactly equal to the current account, there are errors and omissions in counting the assets. Generally, however, when the current account is in deficit, America's net foreign asset position declines. When the current account is in surplus, the net asset position increases.

Many people have expressed concern about the United States becoming a net debtor country, as shown in Figure 17.3. But the decline in the net foreign asset

**capital account:** the part of the international accounts of a country that keeps track of the change in domestic assets owned by foreigners and foreign assets owned by citizens.

**net foreign assets:** the difference between citizens' net assets held abroad and net assets in the domestic country held by foreigners.

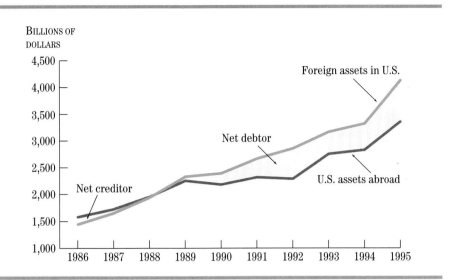

**FIGURE 17.3**
**The Capital Account**
Each year that the current account is in deficit, foreign assets in the United States grow by more than U.S. assets abroad. The capital account keeps track of these assets.
*Source:* U.S. Department of Commerce.

position may simply mean that the United States has more attractive investment opportunities than its citizens want to save up for and buy. In the late nineteenth century, the United States also had huge current account deficits. At that time, investing in U.S. railroads was viewed as an attractive opportunity for British investors. Thanks to that foreign investment, the railroads were built and many Americans prospered.

## Bilateral Surpluses and Deficits

The **bilateral trade balance** is the trade surplus or deficit between *two* countries. That is, the bilateral trade balance of country A with country B equals the exports of country A to country B minus the imports of country A from country B. The U.S. bilateral trade balance with several countries is shown in Table 17.2. Note that the United States has a very large bilateral trade deficit with Japan.

Bilateral trade flow between countries depends on many factors. Consider, for example, the colonial period of American history. The trade across the Atlantic, sometimes called the "triangular trade flow" in the history books, represented the export of manufactured goods from England to America, the export of molasses

**bilateral trade balance:** the value of imports less the value of exports between two countries.

|  | Exports | Imports | Surplus or Deficit (−) |
|---|---|---|---|
| Australia | 10 | 3 | 7 |
| Canada | 128 | 148 | −20 |
| Western Europe | 132 | 147 | −15 |
| Japan | 63 | 124 | −61 |

*Source: Economic Report of the President, 1997.*

**TABLE 17.2**
**Bilateral Trade Between the United States and Several Other Countries in 1995**
(billions of dollars)

from America to the Caribbean, and the export of manufactured rum from the Caribbean to England. All these regions had huge bilateral trade deficits, but the deficits reflected the comparative advantage of England for manufacturing, America for agriculture, and the Caribbean for distilling.

More recently, many political figures in the United States pointed to the bilateral deficit between the United States and Japan as a sign of barriers to trade in Japan. Some people have even suggested taking actions to achieve balance of bilateral trade between the United States and Japan. Such actions would be a mistake for the United States or any other country. In the case of Japan, the large bilateral trade deficit with the United States occurs partly because Japan must import raw materials such as oil from the Middle East and other parts of the world. In order to obtain the funds to pay for the imported raw materials, Japan must export goods to other parts of the world. The United States, being such a large market, is an area ripe for importing goods from Japan. Thus, one reason the United States has a large bilateral trade deficit with Japan simply reflects Japan's need to import goods from other areas of the world.

Bilateral trade deficits are not indicators of how well a country is doing economically, or whether it is being affected by unfair trade practices in other countries. It is the nature of international trade that bilateral deficits and surpluses exist. Think of a personal example. Most people run a bilateral trade deficit with their grocery store. They buy goods from the store but do not sell goods to the store. This is perfectly natural and no one would even think to comment on it. Yet a bilateral trade deficit between countries is exactly the same. Americans buy more goods from Japan than the Japanese buy from Americans, just as you buy more from your grocer than you sell to your grocer.

## Sectoral Deficits

**sectoral trade balance:** the value of exports less the value of imports in a particular sector or industry.

Also receiving political attention is the **sectoral trade balance,** the trade surplus or deficit in certain industries or sectors of the economy, such as automobiles, petroleum, and electronics. For example, one often hears that the United States not only has a bilateral deficit with Japan but also a deficit in the automobile sector.

The United States also has a deficit in the coffee industry, where it exports very little, clearly not having a comparative advantage. Making basketball and tennis shoes is labor intensive. Not surprisingly, therefore, the United States has a deficit in footwear, resulting from the import of shoes produced in countries with less expensive labor.

But other industries are in surplus, such as the pharmaceutical industry. The United States has a strong comparative advantage in pharmaceuticals because of high research and development expenditures, so it is not surprising that it has a large surplus in pharmaceuticals with other countries. The United States also has a large surplus in aircraft. The surplus in the services sector is also noteworthy. The U.S. surplus in business, professional, and technical consulting is about the same size as the U.S. deficit in footwear.

Sectoral deficits, like bilateral deficits, are influenced by comparative advantage. The United States currently has a comparative advantage in pharmaceuticals but not in shoes. Therefore, it has a sectoral trade deficit in footwear and a trade surplus in pharmaceuticals. Changes in the technology of shoe production and pharmaceuticals could change this comparative advantage in the future.

## Review

▶ The gap between saving and investment determines whether there is a trade surplus or a trade deficit.

▶ The U.S. surplus in services reduced the trade deficit by about one-half in 1996.

▶ The current account includes two nontrade flows— net factor incomes and net transfers—as well as the trade account.

▶ The capital account measures purchases and sales of assets. In the 1980s the United States moved from a net creditor to a net debtor position.

▶ Bilateral deficits between countries and sectoral deficits for different types of goods are determined by comparative advantage.

# EXCHANGE RATE DETERMINATION

When goods and services are traded across national boundaries, the buyer from one country must obtain the currency of the other country. For example, to buy a Braun coffeemaker manufactured in Germany, a U.S. retail store like Wal-Mart must pay in German marks. The German workers who produce the coffeemaker will want to be paid in marks because this is what they use to buy food and other goods in Germany. Thus, Wal-Mart must exchange its dollars for marks. The exchange rate, as we noted in Chapter 2, is the price of one currency in terms of another. On April 7, 1997, for example, the mark/dollar exchange rate was 1.71 marks per dollar. But it is not only trade in goods and services that results in the need for exchange of currencies. If you want to put some funds in a German bank account to use in a business you are opening in Germany, then you will also need to exchange your dollars for marks. What determines the exchange rate?

Like any price, the price between two currencies depends on demand and supply. If the demand for dollars goes up, then the price of dollars in terms of foreign currency will rise. For example, if the demand for dollars goes up, the dollar may rise from 1.71 marks per dollar to 2 marks per dollar, or from 100 yen per dollar to 130 yen per dollar. In practice, however, it is virtually impossible to determine the slopes and positions of supply and demand curves for foreign currency and to use them to predict exchange rates. Thousands of currency traders who are interested in obtaining foreign currency—not only to buy foreign goods but also to hold it to earn a higher interest rate, or to speculate—affect supply and demand. Hence, the supply and demand curves shift around by a large amount as expectations and interest rates change.

Nevertheless, the supply and demand model has implications that economists use to help analyze and predict the exchange rate. Two implications are that exchange rates reflect (1) purchasing power parity in the long run, and (2) interest rate differentials in the short run.

## Purchasing Power Parity (PPP)

If transport costs are low and people are not prevented from buying whatever they want, the same commodity in two countries will sell for about the same amount; this is called the **law of one price.** The notion that exchange rates are determined so

**law of one price:** the notion that, with low transportation costs and no trade barriers, the same commodity is sold for the same price in two different countries when measured in the same currency.

**purchasing power parity:** the theory that exchange rates are determined in such a way that the prices of goods in different countries are the same when measured in the same currency.

**tradable goods:** goods for which transportation costs are not prohibitive.

that the price for the same commodity is the same around the world is sometimes called **purchasing power parity.** It provides us with a way to determine the exchange rate.

### Tradable Goods

Consider first a situation where the cost of transporting a good is very low compared to the value of the good. Goods that can be traded without prohibitive transport costs are called **tradable goods.**

An example of a tradable good is a very expensive bottle of French wine—say, a 1978 Chateau Lafite-Rothschild, which costs about $825 for a 12-bottle case in San Francisco. That same type of wine costs 482 British pounds a case in London. Suppose the exchange rate between the British pound and the U.S. dollar is 1.7 dollars per pound. If you want to know how many dollars it would take to buy the case of wine in London, you simply multiply 482 pounds by 1.7 dollars per pound and get $819 for the dollar equivalent for the wine in London. That is about the same as the $825 a case in San Francisco. The difference is less than transport cost for a case of wine, which is probably about $20 dollars. In other words, the dollar price of the wine, whether it is purchased in San Francisco for $825 or in London for $819, is comparable.

In this example, purchasing power parity works quite well. If purchasing power parity did not hold closely for tradable goods, people would either buy or sell wine in London and ship the wine to San Francisco in order to make a nice profit. This would shift either supply or demand until purchasing power parity held. Hence, the exchange rate is such that the price of the wine in the two countries is almost the same.

### Nontradable Goods

What about goods that are not tradable? Here purchasing power parity does not work well. Suppose, for example, you tried to ship a McDonalds' Big Mac purchased in the United States across the ocean. It would not be pleasant to eat. Even if you used an airplane, it would be stale and decayed by the time it arrived at its destination. The transport costs in this case are prohibitive, and purchasing power parity does not usually hold. For example, a Big Mac in Germany cost 4.90 marks in April 1997 and at the same time cost $2.42 in the United States. An exchange rate of 1.71 marks per dollar makes the Big Mac cost $2.86 in Germany. (Divide 4.90 marks by 1.71 marks per dollar and the answer is $2.86.) The $2.86 Big Mac in Germany is 20 percent more than the $2.42 Big Mac in the United States. Thus the exchange rate between the mark and the dollar is not given by purchasing power parity, according to the Big Mac. The purchasing power parity level works out to be 2.02 marks per dollar, because dividing 4.90 marks by 2.02 marks per dollar is about $2.42, the price in the United States.

### Explaining Exchange Rates with PPP in Practice

How well does PPP work in explaining exchange rates if we use prices for both tradable goods and nontradable goods; that is, if we look at the price level for the whole economy? Not very well over short periods of time or for small changes in the price; but statistical studies of purchasing power parity show that it works very well in the long run or for large price changes.

The *Economist* magazine has popularized the idea of using the Big Mac to track purchasing power parity. Note the similarity between the PPP calculations in the text and this recent article on Big Mac PPP. Read the article and try to explain why the Big Mac is "not a perfect measure."

*Source of article: Economist,* April 12, 1997, p. 71. © 1997 The Economist Newspaper Group, Inc. Reprinted with permission. Further reproduction prohibited.

# Big MacCurrencies

## Can hamburgers provide hot tips about exchange rates?

. . . The Big Mac index is based upon the theory of purchasing-power parity (PPP)—the notion that a dollar should buy the same amount in all countries. In the long run, argue PPP fans, currencies should move towards the rate which equalises the prices of an identical basket of goods in each country. Our "basket" is a McDonald's Big Mac, which is now produced in over 100 countries. The Big Mac PPP is the exchange rate that would leave hamburgers costing the same in America as abroad. Comparing actual exchange rates with PPP provides one indication of whether a currency is under- or over-valued. . . .

The first column in the table shows local-currency prices of a Big Mac; the second converts them into dollars. The average American price (including tax) is $2.42. China is the place for bargain hunters: a Beijing Big Mac costs only $1.16. At the other extreme, Big Mac fans pay a beefy $4.02 in Switzerland. In other words, the yuan is the most undervalued currency (by 52%), the Swiss franc the most overvalued (by 66%).

The third column calculates big Mac PPPs. For example, dividing the German price by the American one gives a dollar PPP of DM2.02. The actual rate on April 7th was DM1.71, implying that the D-mark is 18% overvalued against the dollar. But over the past two years the dollar has risen nearer to its PPP against most currencies. The yen is now close to its PPP of ¥121. Two years ago the Big Mac index suggested that it was 100% overvalued against the dollar.

Some critics find these conclusions hard to swallow. Yes, we admit it, the Big Mac is not a perfect measure. Price differences may be distorted by trade barriers on beef, sales taxes, or large variations in the cost of non-traded inputs such as rents. All the same, the index tends to come up with PPP estimates that are similar to those based on more sophisticated methods.

Moreover, research by Robert Cumby, an economist at Georgetown University, suggests that a currency's deviation from Big Mac PPP can be a useful predictor of exchange rates. Over the past year, the Big Mac index has correctly predicted the direction of exchange-rate movements for eight of 12 currencies of large industrial economies. Of the seven currencies which changed by more than 10%, the Big Mac standard got the direction right in six cases. Better than some highly-paid currency forecasters. Investors who turned up their noses at the Big Mac index should now be feeling cheesed off.

### The hamburger standard

| | Big Mac prices | | Implied PPP* of the dollar | Actual $ exchange rate 7/4/97 | Local currency under(−)/over(+) valuation,† % |
|---|---|---|---|---|---|
| | In local currency | In dollars | | | |
| United States‡ | $2.42 | 2.42 | — | — | — |
| Argentina | Peso2.50 | 2.50 | 1.03 | 1.00 | +3 |
| Australia | A$2.50 | 1.94 | 1.03 | 1.29 | −20 |
| Austria | Sch34.00 | 2.82 | 14.0 | 12.0 | +17 |
| Belgium | BFr109 | 3.09 | 45.0 | 35.3 | +28 |
| Brazil | Real2.97 | 2.81 | 1.23 | 1.06 | +16 |
| Britain | ‡1.81 | 2.95 | 1.34†† | 1.63††. | +22 |
| Canada | C$2.88 | 2.07 | 1.19 | 1.39 | −14 |
| Chile | Peso1,200 | 2.88 | 496 | 417 | +19 |
| China | Yuan9.70 | 1.16 | 4.01 | 8.33 | −52 |
| Czech Republic | CKr53.0 | 1.81 | 21.9 | 29.2 | −25 |
| Denmark | DKr25.75 | 3.95 | 10.6 | 6.52 | +63 |
| France | FFr17.5 | 3.04 | 7.23 | 5.76 | +26 |
| Germany | DM4.90 | 2.86 | 2.02 | 1.71 | +18 |
| Hong Kong | HK$9.90 | 1.28 | 4.09 | 7.75 | −47 |
| Hungary | Forint271 | 1.52 | 112 | 178 | −37 |
| Israel | Shekel11.5 | 3.40 | 4.75 | 3.38 | +40 |
| Italy | Lire4,600 | 2.73 | 1,901 | 1,683 | +13 |
| Japan | ¥294 | 2.34 | 121 | 126 | −3 |
| Malaysia | M$3.87 | 1.55 | 1.60 | 2.50 | −36 |
| Mexico | Peso14.9 | 1.89 | 6.16 | 7.90 | −22 |
| Netherlands | Fl5.45 | 2.83 | 2.25 | 1.92 | +17 |
| New Zealand | NZ$3.25 | 2.24 | 1.34 | 1.45 | −7 |
| Poland | Zloty4.30 | 1.39 | 1.78 | 3.10 | −43 |
| Russia | Rouble11,000 | 1.92 | 4,545 | 5,739 | −21 |
| Singapore | S$3.00 | 2.08 | 1.24 | 1.44 | −14 |
| South Africa | Rand7.80 | 1.76 | 3.22 | 4.43 | −27 |
| South Korea | Won2,300 | 2.57 | 950 | 894 | +6 |
| Spain | Pta375 | 2.60 | 155 | 144 | +7 |
| Sweden | SKr26.0 | 3.37 | 10.7 | 7.72 | +39 |
| Switzerland | SFr5.90 | 4.02 | 2.44 | 1.47 | +66 |
| Taiwan | NT$68.0 | 2.47 | 28.1 | 27.6 | +2 |
| Thailand | Baht46.7 | 1.79 | 19.3 | 26.1 | −26 |

*Purchasing-power parity; local price divided by price in the United States.   †Against dollar
‡Average of New York, Chicago, San Francisco and Atlanta   ††Dollars per pound
*Source:* McDonald's

**FIGURE 17.4**
**Purchasing Power Parity,**
**1975–1995**

As predicted by purchasing power parity, the U.S. dollar has appreciated against countries with high inflation (France, Italy, the U.K.) and depreciated against countries with low inflation (Japan, Germany).

*Source: Economic Report of the President, 1997.*

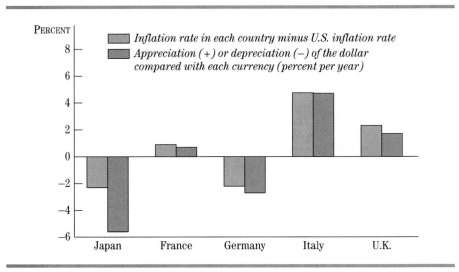

To see that *PPP* works well over long periods of time, it is helpful to introduce some notation. Let *P* be the price level in the United States and *P\** the price level in Germany. Then the purchasing power exchange rate (*E*) would be given by $E \times P = P^*$. For example, if the price level in the United States is $10 and the price level in Germany is 30 marks, then the purchasing power exchange rate is 3 marks per dollar because $E \times P = (3 \times 10) = 30$ when $E = 3$. Now suppose that there is more inflation in the United States than in Germany so that *P* rises to $15 and *P\** stays constant; then according to purchasing power parity, *E* must fall from 3 marks per dollar to 2 marks per dollar so that $E \times P = (2 \times 15)$ stays equal to *P\**. Thus, the inflation in the United States will be matched by a depreciation of the dollar.

Such an association between inflation and the change in the exchange rate is exactly what happens over long periods, as shown in Figure 17.4. This figure shows (1) the inflation rate in several large countries compared to the United States, and (2) the change in the exchange rates of those different countries compared to the United States. For example, over this period from 1975 to 1995 the inflation rate in Italy was higher than in the United States. Over the same period of time the dollar appreciated relative to the lira, the Italian currency. The United Kingdom also had a higher inflation rate than the United States, and the dollar appreciated relative to the pound. Japan and Germany, on the other hand, had inflation rates that were on average lower than in the United States, and, as purchasing power parity would predict, the dollar depreciated relative to the yen and mark. Purchasing power parity works well in explaining exchange rates over this time span.

**real exchange rate:** a measure of the exchange rate between two currencies that adjusts for differences in inflation levels in the two countries.

One can adjust the exchange rate for inflation to get the **real exchange rate.** The change in the real exchange rate is given by the change in the actual exchange rate minus the difference in the inflation rates in the two countries. For example, over the 20-year period from 1975 to 1995, the dollar appreciated against the lira by about 4.7 percent per year. Over that same 20-year period, as shown in Figure 17.4, the inflation rate in Italy was 4.7 percent higher than in the United States (10.0 in Italy and 5.3 in the United States). Thus, the change in the real exchange rate is the change in the actual exchange rate (4.7 percent) minus the difference in the inflation rates (4.7 percent), which equals 0 percent. In other words, the real exchange rate between the dollar and the lira was unchanged. The entire 4.7 percent per year appreciation of the dollar was due to prices in Italy rising 4.7 percent per year faster than prices in the United States.

To summarize, if two countries have widely different inflation rates, the country with the lower inflation rate will have a currency that tends to appreciate over time relative to the country with the higher inflation rate. In this sense, the purchasing power parity theory works well. Over shorter periods of time, the purchasing power parity theory, however, does not work very well. For example, in the mid-1980s the U.S. dollar was much higher than could be explained by purchasing power parity. In the early 1990s, it was lower than purchasing power parity. What explains these deviations from PPP?

## The Interest Rate: A Reason for Deviations from PPP

The most important reason for deviations of the exchange rate from purchasing power parity in the short run is the interest rate.

International investors operating in the global foreign exchange market decide where to place their funds to get the highest return. The capital they invest is highly mobile. The movement of funds around the world to receive the highest return creates a link between the interest rate and the exchange rate that can explain the departures from purchasing power parity.

For example, if the interest rate in the United States rises relative to interest rates abroad, then the U.S. dollar is more attractive to international investors. For an investor deciding whether to put funds in a bank in the United States or in Japan, a rise in the U.S. interest rate compared to Japan makes the United States more attractive, and this raises the price of the dollar. Similarly, if the U.S. interest rate falls relative to Japan's, the dollar will depreciate relative to the yen as international investors move their funds from the United States to Japan.

The chart in the margin shows how interest rates are correlated with the exchange rate. The rise of the dollar relative to other countries in the early 1980s and its subsequent decline in the late 1980s is highly correlated with the interest rate differential. In the early 1980s, interest rates in the United States rose relative to other countries, and then in the mid-1980s, interest rates in the United States declined relative to other countries.

# Review

▶ Purchasing power parity is a useful theory of exchange rates for tradable goods, for periods of high inflation, or for long periods of time.

▶ Short-run deviations from purchasing power parity are explained by interest rates. When the interest rate rises in the United States relative to another country, the exchange rate rises.

▶ The relationship between the interest rate and the exchange rate occurs because capital is very mobile around the world. Investors playing the global foreign exchange market shift their funds in response to interest rate differentials.

# FIXED EXCHANGE RATE SYSTEMS

Throughout history, governments have chosen many times to use economic policy to influence the exchange rate. In the early nineteenth century, Britain adopted a gold standard under which the government pegged the price of gold at a fixed price of about 4 British pounds per ounce. The United States joined the gold standard in 1879, agreeing to buy and sell gold at about $20 an ounce. Because *both* currencies were tied to gold, the relative prices of the two currencies were tied together, at about $5 per pound at this time. If the exchange rate moved away from $5 per pound to, say, $4, gold traders could buy gold in London at $16 an ounce and sell gold in the United States at $20 an ounce. Such an easy profit could not last, and the exchange rate would quickly move back to $5 per British pound.

## International Gold Standard

**fixed exchange rate system:** a system of international exchange rates in which the countries agree to maintain a predetermined value of their currencies in terms of other currencies.

When two or more countries are on a gold standard, the exchange rate between the countries is, therefore, fixed. A system like the international gold standard, where government actions prevent changes in the value of one currency compared to another, is called a **fixed exchange rate system.** In the case of the gold standard, the exchange rates were implicitly fixed because each country kept its exchange rate as close as possible to some particular price of gold. Note that when governments fix the price of gold, they do not set the price by decree, as with government price ceilings or floors discussed in Chapter 3. People are free to buy and sell gold and the price is determined in the gold market, but the government adjusts the supply of gold so that the government purchase price is the equilibrium price.

The gold standard keeps the price of currencies constant in terms of gold. One can also imagine a system without gold in which the countries agreed to peg their exchange rates to each other. For example, the French might agree to buy and sell French francs in exchange for German marks at a set exchange rate. That also is a fixed exchange rate system.

## The Bretton Woods System

**Bretton Woods system:** the international monetary system put in place after World War II; it was based on fixed exchange rates. Infrequent adjustments of the exchange rates were permitted and did occur under the Bretton Woods System.

**flexible exchange rate system:** an international monetary system in which exchange rates are determined in foreign exchange markets and governments do not agree to fix them.

From the end of World War II through the early 1970s, the world's largest economies were linked in a fixed exchange system called the **Bretton Woods system.** As World War II was drawing to a close, a conference was held in Bretton Woods, New Hampshire, to decide on a good exchange rate system for the world economy. John Maynard Keynes was one of the theoreticians present at the conference. The key ingredient of the system was that exchange rates were to be fixed. In certain rare circumstances, provisions were made for decreases in the exchange rate (devaluations) or increases in the exchange rate (revaluations) of the currencies.

The Bretton Woods system lasted for about 25 years before it fell apart in the early 1970s. It was replaced by a **flexible exchange rate system,** whereby governments did not try to fix the value of their currencies in any particular way. Figure 17.5 shows the exchange rate between the German mark and the dollar and between the French franc and the dollar for the period that includes the Bretton Woods fixed exchange rate system and the subsequent flexible exchange rate system. The chart clearly shows that exchange rates were much more volatile in the flexible exchange rate period. Several changes in the exchange rates during the fixed exchange rate period are visible in Figure 17.5: two devaluations of the franc in the late 1950s, and one revaluation of the mark in the early 1960s.

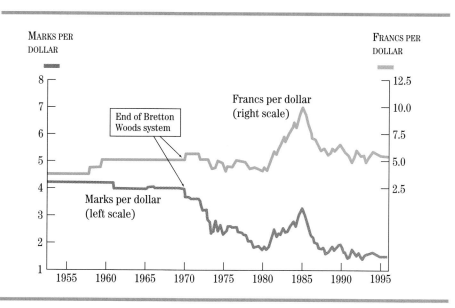

**FIGURE 17.5**

**Francs and Marks per Dollar**

These exchange rates and others have fluctuated since the end of the Bretton Woods fixed exchange rate system. From the mid-1980s through the 1990s, the fluctuations have been smaller.

*Source:* International Monetary Fund.

## The European Monetary System

Within the overall flexible exchange rate system, the countries of Europe have attempted to fix their exchange rates among each other while jointly having flexible exchange rates with the rest of the world; this European system of fixed exchange rates is called the **European monetary system.** Through this exchange rate system, the value, for example, of the French franc in terms of the German mark could not change much. Figure 17.6 shows the behavior of the French franc relative to the mark. Notice that the franc and the mark did not have a significant change in relative value for most of the 1990s.

**European monetary system:** a system of exchange rates in which European currencies are fixed relative to each other but are flexible against the dollar, the yen, and other currencies.

**FIGURE 17.6**

**Exchange Rates in Europe**

The French franc fluctuated little against the German mark until the 1970s, when the Bretton Woods system fell apart. In the 1970s and early 1980s, the franc depreciated against the mark, as Germany had relatively low inflation. In the late 1980s and 1990s, France and Germany fixed their exchange rates against each other.

*Source:* International Monetary Fund.

During the 1990s several European countries made plans to convert the European monetary system from a fixed exchange rate system with several currencies into a system where there is only a single currency. The single currency would be called the *euro,* which would eventually replace francs, marks, and the currencies of other countries that joined in. With a single currency, the exchange rate is effectively fixed for all time because there are no national currencies.

## Review

▶ Governments have frequently fixed the exchange rate between currencies. In these fixed exchange rate systems, the government agrees to buy and sell gold or currencies in the market at a given price.

▶ Examples of fixed exchange rate systems are the international gold standard, the Bretton Woods system, and the European monetary system.

# FIXED EXCHANGE RATES AND INTERNATIONAL INDEPENDENCE

A fixed exchange rate system has implications for economic policy. In this section we will first show that with a fixed exchange rate system, interest rates in different countries cannot be independent of each other. We will then look at some of the reasons why countries chose to fix exchange rates.

### Loss of International Monetary Independence

Suppose the United States decides to set up or join a fixed exchange rate system with Japan and Europe. Suppose also that after the United States joins the system, a deep recession occurs in the United States, and policymakers look to a reduction in interest rates in the United States to help stimulate the economy. Such a reduction in interest rates, according to the exchange rate theory, will tend to lower the value of the dollar relative to other currencies. But if the dollar were fixed to the currencies of other countries, as it would be in a fixed exchange rate system, such a decline in the dollar would not be possible. Hence, if exchange rates were fixed, lower interest rates in the United States relative to interest rates in other countries would not be possible. There is a loss of **international monetary independence** because interest rates in the United States cannot change.

**international monetary independence:** the idea that a flexible exchange rate system gives a country the ability to have much different interest rates than other countries.

A real-life example of the conflict between fixed exchange rates and interest rate changes arose in Europe in the latter part of 1992. At that time, interest rates were rising in Germany because the German inflation rate was rising. But policy makers in Britain, which was facing hard economic times, did not want their interest rates to rise as German interest rates rose. The British faced a decision—either they could keep their interest rates near Germany's and, therefore, raise their interest rates, or they could let their interest rates fall. In the latter case, their exchange rate would depreciate. For much of 1991 and 1992, the British kept their exchange rate stable and that required a rise in British interest rates. But by the end of 1992, increasingly poor conditions in Britain forced the British to devalue and to leave the European monetary system. Then interest rates in Britain could fall.

## Interventions in the Exchange Market

Why wasn't it possible for the British government to go into the exchange market and buy and sell foreign exchange and thereby prevent these changes in the exchange rate? For example, if the British government purchased pounds it would increase the demand for pounds and thereby raise the pound exchange rate. Thus, if the high interest rates in Germany were reducing the value of the British pound, why couldn't the British government buy pounds to offset these pressures? Such buying and selling of foreign currency by governments is called **exchange market intervention.** Such intervention does occur, and it can affect the exchange rate for short periods of time. However, the world currency markets are so huge and fast moving that even governments do not have funds to affect the exchange rate for long by buying and selling foreign exchange.

**exchange market intervention:** purchases and sales of foreign currency by a government in exchange markets with the intention to affect the exchange rate.

If there is a substantial interest rate advantage in favor of one currency, funds will flow into that currency, driving up the value; exchange market intervention by governments cannot do much about it. Empirical studies have shown that exchange market intervention—if it is not matched by a change in interest rates by the central bank—can have only small effects on the exchange rate.

## Reducing Exchange Rate Risk

If fixed exchange rates lead to a loss of international monetary independence, then why do countries form fixed exchange rate systems? One reason to adopt a fixed exchange rate system is that exchange rate volatility can interfere with trade. This is certainly one of the reasons the European countries set up the European monetary system. Firms may not develop long-term relations and contacts in other countries if they are worried about big changes in the exchange rate.

Innovations in financial markets in the 1970s and 1980s have made it easier for companies to **hedge,** or protect against, the risks associated with exchange rate volatility. The futures market in foreign currencies at the Chicago Mercantile Exchange is an example of one of these innovations. In a **futures market** one buys or sells a good for future delivery. There are futures markets for many items, including wheat, orange juice, and crude oil as well as French francs, German marks, and Japanese yen. Futures markets make it possible to ensure against changes in the exchange rate. The following example shows how.

**hedge:** to reduce risk, usually by buying a futures contract to guarantee a price several months in the future.

**futures market:** a market that deals in commodities to be delivered in the future.

Consider the case of the mark/dollar exchange rate. One can buy a contract in the futures market through which one agrees to sell marks for dollars at some future date at a guaranteed price. It is thus possible for a company—like Mattel, the toy manufacturer—to hedge the revenue it might receive when it exports toys to Germany by taking out a futures contract in the Chicago Mercantile Exchange. Mattel can guarantee a price in dollars on those toys even if the mark/dollar exchange rate changes dramatically. By locking in a fixed dollar price in the futures market, firms can hedge the exchange rate risk.

For example, Mattel's "price point" for one of its Masters of the Universe toys, Skeletor, is $3; this is the price it needs to make a profit selling this toy. Suppose that Mattel is currently manufacturing Skeletor toys and expects to sell these in

**Foreign Currency Futures Advertisement**

This is an advertisement for the futures market in exchange rates in Chicago. It mentions U.S. exporters of toys to Germany but also applies to U.S. exporters of other goods to other countries. The advertisement aims to entice exporters to use a market to hedge their risk.

Germany in about six months. It expects to sell each toy for 5 marks in Germany, and the exchange rate is currently $.62 per mark. Thus, the dollar price is $3.10; Mattel can make a profit because $3.10 is greater than $3.00. But suppose the mark falls to $.40. Then Mattel's dollar price falls to 5 marks times $.40, or $2.00, and Mattel has a losing operation on its hands. If Mattel hedges with a futures contract and locks in an exchange rate six months from now of $.61 per mark, then it ensures a profit because $5 \times (.61) = \$3.05$. Thus, futures markets in exchange rates can reduce the risk and uncertainty associated with exchange rate fluctuations.

## Review

▷ A fixed exchange rate system means a loss of international monetary independence for countries in the system.

▷ Flexible exchange rates may cause uncertainty and reduce trade, but the development of futures markets in currencies can reduce the exchange rate risk and uncertainty.

## CONCLUSION

This chapter focused on international trade flows and exchange rates. We have seen that the overall trade deficit, or trade surplus, can ultimately be traced to imbalances in national saving and investment. These imbalances and the resulting deficits and surpluses are not necessarily bad. If the investment opportunities in a country are greater than the saving of the people in the country—as in the railroad construction in America in the 1880s and 1890s—there will be a trade deficit, and foreigners provide the funds for investment by lending or buying real estate or shares in business enterprises. If the people of a country desire to save more than they invest in capital in the country—as in Japan in the 1980s and 1990s—they will lend or buy real estate or shares of businesses in other countries. None of this is bad. Indeed, the excess of saving over investment in relatively advanced countries can help spread the benefits of growth to developing countries.

However, if government policy acts to provide disincentives to save or invest, the resulting trade deficit can indeed be a serious concern. For example, a large and persistent government budget deficit that reduces a country's saving would lead to a trade deficit and be a cause for concern. A government policy that adds risk or creates disincentives to invest and thereby causes a trade surplus would also be a bad policy. But these policies are bad more because of the distortions to saving and investment they create than because of the trade deficit itself.

Bilateral deficits and sectoral deficits are also not necessarily a problem that needs to be addressed by policy. Such deficits are part of the normal operation of international trade between countries; they may be telling us that the international economy is working well, not poorly.

What about the exchange rate? What are the key ideas we have learned about the price of one currency in terms of another? First, a smoothly working foreign exchange market is essential for international trade. Because countries have different currencies, it is necessary to buy or sell foreign exchange when purchasing goods or services in other countries. Second, foreign exchange traders constantly move funds from one country to another electronically to get the highest rate of return. The amount of trading in the foreign exchange market is, therefore, huge; much more foreign exchange is traded each day than the value of the goods and services that are exported or imported. Third, exchange rates are determined by purchasing power parity and interest rates.

There are two basic approaches countries can take to the exchange rate, while not interfering with the freedom of buyers and sellers to obtain foreign exchange. They can agree to fix the exchange rate to another country's exchange rate, in which case the international currency market forces the country to lose its monetary independence—as was illustrated when British interest rates were held up by Germany in 1992. Or they can let their exchange rate be flexible, in which case interest rates can move independently. Both approaches have been tried many times throughout history. Currently the United States and Japan follow a flexible exchange rate system, while the countries within Europe have tried to use a fixed exchange rate system. Because of lack of agreement about what is the best approach, and because of changing circumstances, it is likely that we will continue to see flux in the choice of exchange rate systems.

# KEY POINTS

**1.** Improvements in telecommunications and transportation and the removal of restrictions on trade are making the world economy more integrated.

**2.** The world as a whole cannot have a trade surplus or a trade deficit. As individual countries save more or less than they invest, overall trade deficits and surpluses are created.

**3.** Because of the importance of services, the merchandise trade deficit is much too narrow a measure of the deficit.

**4.** Bilateral deficits and sectoral deficits are influenced by comparative advantage.

**5.** The current account is the broadest measure of a country's balance with other countries.

**6.** The capital account measures changes in the net foreign asset position of a country.

**7.** Purchasing power parity explains exchange rates very well when goods are tradable, when inflation differences are high, or over a long period of time.

**8.** Interest rate differentials explain much of the short-term exchange rate movements.

**9.** Because capital flows freely around the world, interest rates are tied together for countries in a fixed exchange rate system.

**10.** However, fixed exchange rates can reduce uncertainty.

# KEY TERMS

| | | |
|---|---|---|
| merchandise trade | current account balance | fixed exchange rate system |
| services trade | capital account | Bretton Woods system |
| merchandise trade balance | net foreign assets | flexible exchange rate system |
| services trade balance | bilateral trade balance | European monetary system |
| balance of payments | sectoral trade balance | international monetary independence |
| factor income | law of one price | exchange market intervention |
| net factor income from abroad | purchasing power parity | hedge |
| international transfer payments | tradable goods | futures market |
| net transfers from abroad | real exchange rate | |

# QUESTIONS FOR REVIEW

**1.** Why can't the world have a trade surplus or deficit?

**2.** Why is the investment-saving gap so closely related to the trade deficit?

**3.** What is wrong with the merchandise trade deficit as a measure of trade imbalance?

**4.** What is the difference between net exports and the current account deficit?

**5.** Why has the net foreign asset position of the United States moved from positive to negative?

**6.** Of what use is purchasing power parity as a theory of the exchange rate?

**7.** Why is there a loss of international independence when countries join a fixed exchange rate system?

**8.** How can futures markets be used to hedge risk?

**9.** What is the difference between the Bretton Woods system and the European monetary system?

# PROBLEMS

**1.** Calculate the trade deficit or surplus for the following data in billions of dollars:

| Year | 1998 | 2002 |
|---|---|---|
| National saving | 950 | 1,170 |
| Investment | 1,000 | 1,300 |

a) Has the deficit increased or decreased over this time period? Give some possible explanations.

b) Suppose net factor income and net transfers from abroad are zero. Is capital flowing into or out of the country in these years?

**2.** Transport costs relative to the value of most products have been falling throughout the history of world trade. How has this affected the validity of purchasing power parity? Suppose many countries impose trade taxes on goods going in or out of the country. How will this affect purchasing power parity?

**3.** The price of a fresh loaf of French bread in Paris is 5 francs, while the price of a fresh loaf of French bread (same quality) in San Francisco is $2. The price of gold is 2,000 francs per ounce in Paris, and the price of gold in San Fran-

cisco is $400 per ounce. What is your estimate of the exchange rate between dollars and francs? (State your answer in francs per dollar.) Explain your answer.

**4.** You are the chief financial officer of an American computer company. Your company wants to export computers to Great Britain, and market analysts predict that the systems could be sold at £2,000 each. At the current exchange rate of $1.50 for each pound, the company would make a 10 percent profit, which is considered normal for the industry. The marketing department plans to start selling the computers one year from now.

a) How can you, as chief financial officer, eliminate the exchange rate risk? Explain your answer.

b) Suppose you took the appropriate measures to eliminate the exchange rate risk, and at the moment of sale of the computers, the exchange rate is $2 per pound. Was your decision good or not? Why?

**5.** "It is possible to use purchasing power parity to explain appreciations or depreciations of the exchange rates because of inflation. Inflation in the home country minus inflation in the foreign country equals the decrease in the exchange rate when measured in terms of foreign currency per unit of home currency." Is this statement correct? Explain.

6. The consumer price index (CPI) in Italy was 60 in 1980 and 180 in 1992. The CPI in Japan was 80 in 1980 and 120 in 1992. The Italian-Japanese exchange rate was 4 lira per yen in 1980. If purchasing power parity held in 1980, what would purchasing power theory predict for the exchange rate in 1992?

7. Why would a European country want to drop out of the fixed exchange rate system? Why might the country want to join the fixed exchange rate system?

8. Compare and contrast the following:
a) merchandise trade balance and services trade balance
b) bilateral trade balance and sectoral trade balance
c) net factor income from abroad and net transfers from abroad
d) a fixed exchange rate system and a rent control system

# 18

# Macroeconomic Debates

Current theories of economic fluctuations and economic growth were developed from knowledge accumulated over many years. Practicing economists in business and government, including those who work at central banks like the Federal Reserve, draw on these theories when they analyze the economy and make policy decisions.

Macroeconomic theory, however, is by no means stagnant. Indeed, like many of our theories of the physical world—from explanations of how genes in our bodies work to theories of why black holes exist in outer space—macroeconomic theories change over time. Macroeconomic theories may change because a major economic event—such as the Great Depression of the 1930s or the Great Inflation of the 1970s—may reveal problems with a prevailing theory. Some economists may then propose new ideas challenging the prevailing theory. Defenders of the prevailing theory respond. Debate ensues. Eventually, the prevailing theory is usually modified.

There are also heated debates over the implementation of macroeconomic policy. Even economists who have the same basic view of how the macroeconomy works may disagree about the way the theories should be applied to solve current problems. A dispute about rules versus discretion, a difficulty in distinguishing short-term economic fluctuations from long-term economic growth, or an uncertainty about timing are examples of the many debates already mentioned in this book.

The purpose of this chapter is to review these debates and to place them in historical perspective. We look at the schools of thought that developed from the 1930s through the 1960s, including the work of John Maynard Keynes and the Keynesian school, the work of Milton Friedman and the monetarist school, and the work of Robert Solow and those in the neoclassical growth school. We also describe research from the 1970s through the present, including the new classical school, the new Keynesian school, the real business cycle school, and the supply side school. Figure 18.1 provides a visual summary of the schools. Although the theory of economic growth and fluctuations we have described in this book draws on all these schools, in this chapter we concentrate on which ideas come from which schools and on the key differences between the schools.

Much of the debate among macroeconomists has been about whether discretionary fiscal policy can be a useful way to reduce the harm from recessions. Discretionary fiscal policy was once the hallmark of Keynesian

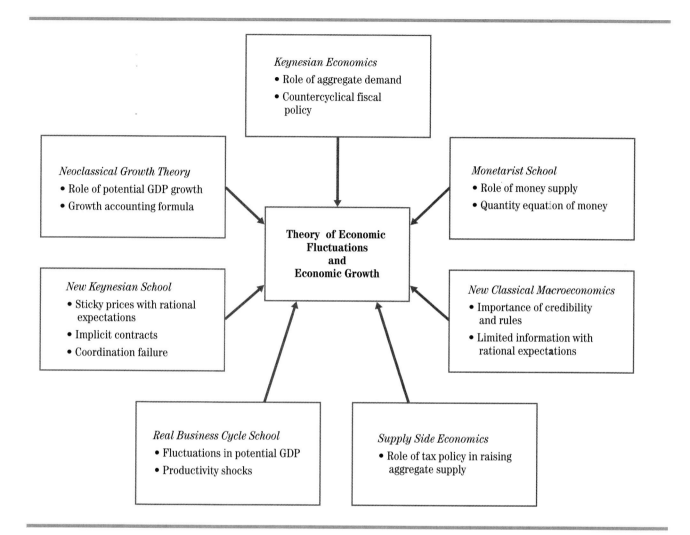

**FIGURE 18.1**

**Spheres of Influence in Macroeconomic Thought**

Different schools of thought have influenced the development of macroeconomics. Keynesian economics, the monetarist school, and neoclassical growth theory developed between the 1930s and the 1960s. New classical macroeconomics, the new Keynesian school, the real business cycle school, and supply side economics represent more recent developments. There has been—and still is—heated debate and controversy among the different groups.

economics. These policy debates have continued. In this chapter we therefore also look at the debates about the discretionary fiscal policy proposals made by Republican President Bush in 1992 and by Democratic President Clinton in 1993 to help speed the recovery from the 1990–1991 recession. Recessions have not disappeared from the economic landscape, and by looking at what was done in this recent recession, we can gain insight to alternative approaches to dealing with the effects of the next one.

# SCHOOLS OF THOUGHT IN MACROECONOMICS

A large number of economic researchers have contributed to each school of thought summarized in Figure 18.1. For each school of thought, several key ideas or terms are also listed in the figure. Many of these key ideas are now incorporated into the theory of economic growth and fluctuations, and have been introduced in previous chapters of this book. Although learning about such a large number of schools of thought may seem like a daunting task, our goal here is to categorize and trace the history of these ideas rather than to explain them afresh.

## Developments from the 1930s Through the 1960s

A good starting point for discussing the different schools of thought in macroeconomics is the economic research that emerged during and immediately after the Great Depression of the 1930s. This catastrophic world event helped cause a major shakeup in economic thinking—the **Keynesian revolution**—that eventually affected all economists, and thus their textbooks, their models, and their public policy advice. It was not until 40 years later, in the early 1970s, that a comparable change in the field of macroeconomics occurred.

### Keynesian Economics

**Keynesian revolution:** a change in macroeconomic thinking, shaped by the Great Depression and the work of John Maynard Keynes, leading to a greater consideration of demand-side policies.

**Keynesian school:** a school of macroeconomic thought concerned with pursuing demand-side macroeconomic policies—primarily fiscal policies working through the multiplier—to reduce unemployment and encourage economic growth.

The publication in 1936 of John Maynard Keynes's book *The General Theory of Employment, Interest and Money* marks the beginning of the **Keynesian school** of macroeconomics. Current Keynesian economists include James Tobin of Yale University and Paul Samuelson of the Massachusetts Institute of Technology.

Keynes wrote the *General Theory* at a time when high unemployment and low production were causing severe distress in the world economy. Keynes's ideas had great appeal because they seemed to explain this catastrophe and to provide a way to end it. Keynes made a break with most previous economists by arguing that the level of total output or production in the economy was determined by aggregate demand: that is, by the total spending of consumers, businesses, government, and foreigners. Increases in government spending would raise aggregate demand and reduce unemployment, according to Keynes. Hence, the usefulness of countercyclical fiscal policy was explained by Keynes's theory.

The term *macroeconomics* as distinct from *microeconomics* arose during the early days of the Keynesian revolution, but it is incorrect to say that economists before Keynes had not worked on macroeconomic issues. The Scottish philosopher David Hume wrote a brilliant essay, "On Money," way back in 1752, which described the short-run impact of an increase in money, including a brief description of the slow adjustment of prices and the multiplier process. Adam Smith wrote about economic growth as well as the role of money in the economy. Many of the debates between Malthus and Ricardo were over macroeconomic issues: Using modern terminology, Malthus argued that deficient aggregate demand could bring real GDP below potential GDP, while Ricardo disagreed, arguing that supply will create its own demand—a principle called *Say's Law* after the French economist J. B. Say, who wrote about it—keeping real GDP equal to potential GDP.

However, these macroeconomic discussions had taken place more than 100 years before the Great Depression. Alfred Marshall, one of Keynes's teachers and author of the great microeconomic treatise *Principles of Economics,* wrote about macroeconomics, but it was clearly less of a priority for him. He chose to publish his macroeconomic book, *Money, Credit and Commerce,* very late in life (he was over 80 years old), and his macroeconomic theory was never as fully articulated as his microeconomic theory. Irving Fisher writing in the United States and Knut Wicksell writing in Sweden also worked on macroeconomic issues, focusing mainly on monetary policy issues.

Despite the work of Marshall, Fisher, and Wicksell, it is clear that macroeconomic issues had receded to the back burner for many economists and that the prevailing economic theories were inadequate to give a convincing or helpful explanation for the Great Depression. Keynes referred to this prevailing theory—"the atmosphere in which I was brought up"—as "the classical theory" and emphasized that he was making a transition away from that theory. Although historians of economic thought distinguish between the classical school of Smith and Ricardo and the neoclassical school of Marshall and his followers, Keynes used the term *classical* to mean "orthodox," referring to the prevailing theory at the time he wrote, including that of Marshall and Marshall's followers.

Keynes wrote little about inflation in the *General Theory,* though he did address inflation in his earlier writings in the 1920s. His analysis in the *General Theory* also deemphasized aggregate supply, or what we have called potential GDP in this book. Keynes also placed little emphasis on monetary policy, though in the *General Theory* he developed the idea that the demand for money depends on the interest rate. Many of Keynes's followers paid even less attention to inflation, aggregate supply, and monetary policy. Keynes's lack of attention to aggregate supply and inflation can almost certainly be explained by the conditions of his time: Real GDP was far below potential GDP, and inflation was a remote concern. Nevertheless, Keynes's inattention to aggregate supply, to inflation, and to monetary policy would be the cause of the most damaging attacks on Keynesian economics in later years.

Despite the criticism, Keynes's ideas have had a lasting effect on much of modern macroeconomics. By the late 1940s, Keynesian ideas were incorporated into introductory economics textbooks, such as the 1948 book by Paul Samuelson; by the 1950s, Keynesian economics had been incorporated into macroeconomic forecasting models. Finally, Keynesian economics was brought formally into national policymaking during the 1960s through the work of James Tobin and other members of President Kennedy's Council of Economic Advisers. In particular, the 1962 *Economic Report of the President* presented the arguments for the Keynesian view in a public policy context.

Key ideas traceable to Keynes's work include the theory that declines in real GDP during recessions are movements of real GDP below potential GDP due to *changes in aggregate demand.* Also attributable to Keynes is the use of the government spending multiplier to show the size of the impact on real GDP of a change in government purchases.

### The Monetarist School

Milton Friedman mounted the earliest and most substantive attacks on Keynesian economics. In the 1950s, Friedman's work on the permanent income hypothesis of consumption was motivated by concerns that the Keynesian marginal propensity to consume and the multiplier were not stable. Friedman's permanent income hypothesis showed that the marginal propensity to consume was unlikely to be stable because people based their consumption more on their permanent income than on their actual income.

Friedman's criticism of the Keynesians' lack of attention to the effects of the money supply and to the power of monetary policy became the source of vociferous debates in macroeconomics in the 1960s. The **monetarist school,** for which Friedman's and Anna Schwartz's work on monetary history provided the foundation, argued that monetary policy was a powerful force—indeed, more powerful than fiscal policy. Friedman and Schwartz showed that declines in money growth were responsible for the prolonged duration of the Great Depression.

A long series of "radio," or "AM/FM," debates between the monetarists and the Keynesians ensued. (The debates were not broadcast over the radio; the term derives from the initials of the main protagonists in the debates, Albert Ando and Franco Modigliani [AM], versus Milton Friedman and David Meiselman [FM]). The main issue was whether changes in the money supply (the monetarist view) or changes in government spending (the Keynesian view) mattered more for changes in real GDP. The FM team argued the case for the money supply and offered proof in the form of empirical verification of the quantity equation of money. The AM team argued the case for government spending and offered proof in the form of empirical verification of the government spending multiplier. Today this debate seems rather pointless to many macroeconomists, because it is clear that aggregate demand can change because of both monetary policy *and* fiscal policy. Indeed, this is true of the theories of economic fluctuations presented in this book. However, before the debate monetary policy played only a small role in most Keynesian economic models; after the debate it played a much bigger role, so in this sense the monetarist criticism had a lasting influence on economic knowledge.

A second part of the monetarist attack on Keynesian economics was its criticism of the idea of a long-run tradeoff between inflation and unemployment that seemed to exist in most Keynesian models. Although Milton Friedman was one of the key figures in this debate, a nonmonetarist economist, Edmund Phelps of Columbia University, developed a similar criticism. In any case the idea that there is no long-run tradeoff between inflation and unemployment has now become part of the accepted assumption of most macroeconomists.

### The Neoclassical Growth School

**monetarist school:** a school of macroeconomic thought that holds that changes in the money supply are the primary cause of fluctuations in real GDP and the ultimate cause of inflation.

**neoclassical growth school:** an approach to macroeconomics that uses the aggregate production function and the growth accounting formula in describing long-term growth, emphasizing aggregate supply rather than aggregate demand.

While the battles between the monetarists and the Keynesians were heating up in the 1950s, another significant development in macroeconomics was beginning. This was the development of the **neoclassical growth school.** Robert Solow's 1956 paper entitled "A Model of Growth" was one of the first key works of the neoclassical growth school. At the time, this development received much less publicity than either Keynesian economics or monetarist economics, perhaps because it applied to the long run rather than to the short run, and long-run issues frequently get less public attention than short-run issues. The term *neoclassical* applies to this school because the framework for analysis is much like that used by neoclassical economists such as Alfred Marshall. Solow's *growth accounting formula* and the production function that underlies potential GDP are the heart of the neoclassical growth model. As stated by Solow, "The aggregate production function is only a little less legitimate a concept than, say, the aggregate consumption function, and for some kinds of long-run macro-models it is almost as indispensable as the latter is for the short-run."[1]

Despite its initial lack of attention, neoclassical growth theory has had a profound influence on modern macroeconomics. Most importantly it brought aggregate supply—that is, the production function and the growth of potential GDP—back into macroeconomics. Together, the monetarist school and the neoclassical growth school re-emphasized the three ingredients—inflation, money, and the growth of potential GDP—that were ignored by those Keynesians who had let aggregate demand and fiscal policy completely dominate macroeconomic theory and policy.

The neoclassical growth school also brought basic microeconomic principles, such as the notion of an equilibrium price and the importance of relative prices, into macroeconomics; these principles were frequently missing from the simple Keynesian theories. The emphasis of neoclassical growth theory on technology is more visible than ever in modern macroeconomics; growth economists such as Paul Romer of Stanford University have built new models of the technology process, examining what motivates the owners of "invention factories," as we discussed in the chapter "Technology and Economic Growth."

## Developments from the 1970s Through the Present

By the mid-1970s—40 years after the start of the Keynesian revolution—signs of another dramatic change in macroeconomic thinking began to appear. These changes are referred to as the **rational expectations revolution,** and they may eventually turn out to be as dramatic in their impact as the Keynesian revolution. Rational expectations—the idea that people look ahead to the future using all available information—is central to this change in thinking in much the same way that the multiplier or the marginal propensity to consume (MPC) was central to the Keynesian revolution. However, just as the Keynesian revolution went well beyond the MPC and the multiplier, the rational expectations revolution went well beyond expectations.

**rational expectations revolution:** a change in macroeconomic thinking during the 1970s based on the assumption that people make rational, forward-looking decisions using all the information available to them.

There is no single treatise such as Keynes's *General Theory* that outlines the rational expectations approach. Much of the research on it is contained in articles published in economics journals by a number of economists. Most representative perhaps are the papers written by a number of researchers in the 1970s and collected in a 1981 book entitled *Rational Expectations and Econometric Practice*, edited by Robert Lucas and Thomas Sargent. Like Keynes's *General Theory,* the papers in this collection were addressed to other professional economists, not to the general public; they make for no easier reading than Keynes's classic.

The rational expectations revolution began as part of an effort to be more explicit about the ideas put forth by Edmund Phelps and Milton Friedman in their

---

1. R. M. Solow, "Technical Change and the Aggregate Production Function," *Review of Economics and Statistics,* Vol. 39, 1957, p. 312.

analysis of the tradeoff between inflation and unemployment (or the departures of real GDP from potential GDP). Expectations of inflation was the key mechanism that both Phelps and Friedman had used to show why there was no long-run trade-off: Only the difference between inflation and expectations of inflation could affect the unemployment rate in the Phelps-Friedman theory. Hence, a permanent increase in inflation would raise people's expectations of inflation and thus leave unemployment unchanged in the long run.

But Phelps and Friedman were less specific about the short-run tradeoff. To be more explicit, economists needed to be more specific about what determined expectations. They used the rational expectations assumption to do so.

The rational expectations assumption itself has had a profound effect on macroeconomics. The important idea that budget deficit reduction might have only a small short-run negative impact was discovered as a result of using rational expectations in macroeconomics. For example, if people try to anticipate government actions (that is, if they have rational expectations), then when the government announces in advance a program to reduce the budget deficit, interest rates will fall and tend to offset the short-run negative impacts of budget deficit reduction.

### New Classical Macroeconomics

One type of macroeconomic analysis with rational expectations assumes that prices are perfectly flexible. In the case where prices are perfectly flexible, the rational expectations assumption has another implication: Changes in monetary policy, if anticipated in advance, have no short-run effect on real GDP. This result is known as the **policy ineffectiveness proposition** and has been stressed by a school of economists called the **new classical school** (not to be confused with the similar-sounding neoclassical school!). Robert Barro of Harvard University, for example, has argued that only unanticipated changes in monetary policy cause changes in real GDP.

**policy ineffectiveness proposition:** the proposition that anticipated monetary policy will have no effect on the economy.

**new classical school:** a school of macroeconomics that holds that prices are perfectly flexible, expectations are rational, and therefore anticipated monetary policy will have no effect on the economy.

The policy ineffectiveness proposition can be illustrated with a supply curve for an individual firm, as shown in Figure 18.2. The price of the good that the firm sells is on the vertical axis, while the quantity supplied by the firm is on the horizontal axis. The relevant price for the firm's supply decision is the *relative price:* the price measured relative to all other goods and services in the economy. The firm will increase the quantity supplied if the price of the good rises relative to the price the firm perceives as prevailing in the economy. On the other hand, if the firm's price rises and the prices of all other goods also rise, then no relative price change will occur and the firms will not adjust the quantity supplied.

If prices are perfectly flexible, an increase in the money supply will immediately raise all prices in the economy. However, because of imperfect information the individual firm will not usually be aware that all other prices in the economy are changing. Thus, if the individual firm does not know that the money supply has increased (because the Fed did not announce the increase) then the firm will see only its own price rising. The firm guesses that the overall price does not rise, or at least does not rise as much as the individual firm's price rises. Thus, an unanticipated increase in the money supply will cause the firm to increase the quantity supplied. With other firms doing the same thing, real GDP will increase in the economy as a whole.

However, suppose that the central bank announces that it will increase the money supply. Then, when firms see their own prices rising, they will assume it is

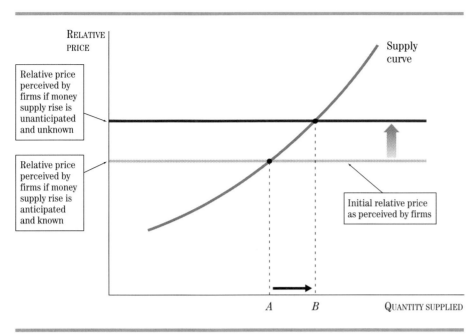

**FIGURE 18.2**
**New Classical View of the Effects of Unanticipated versus Anticipated Increases in the Money Supply**

If the central bank increases the money supply and all prices are flexible, then all prices will rise. However, if the increase in the money supply is unanticipated and unknown, then firms do not realize that all prices rise. Firms think that only their own prices rise; they are fooled into thinking that there is a relative price increase. Hence, they increase the quantity supplied from point *A* to point *B*. However, if the money supply increase is anticipated and known, then firms are not fooled into thinking there is a relative price increase; firms know all prices have risen and keep their quantity supplied at point *A*.

because all prices in the economy are rising. With no change in the relative price, they will, therefore, not change the quantity supplied. Hence, there will be no change in production. Thus, an anticipated change in the money supply has no effect on real GDP, which is the policy ineffectiveness proposition.

### The New Keynesian School

The policy ineffectiveness proposition requires that prices be perfectly flexible. Another school of economics that grew out of the rational expectations revolution is called the **new Keynesian school.** A distinguishing feature of this school is that prices are assumed to be sticky, or slowly adjusting, rather than perfectly flexible. Stanley Fischer of MIT and Jo Anna Gray of the University of Oregon are two of the early contributors to this school, which, like the new classical school, began in the 1970s.

Thus, unlike the new classical models, anticipated monetary policy affects real GDP in the short run in the new Keynesian models. Much research of economists in the new Keynesian school has been devoted to explaining why prices are sticky.

One of the main contributions of the new Keynesian school has been to provide a way to combine the important aspects of the rational expectations revolution—including the important phenomena of credibility, time inconsistency, and policy rules—with a macroeconomic framework that includes the effects of aggregate demand, inflation, monetary policy, and potential GDP growth.

Another development sometimes associated with the new Keynesian school is the idea that the fluctuations in the economy are due to **coordination failure.** A coordination failure arises in circumstances where people's actions depend on what they expect other people will do. If you are running a firm and you expect business

**new Keynesian school:** a school of macroeconomics that holds that prices are sticky and expectations are rational to explain the effect of monetary and fiscal policy.

**coordination failure:** a situation where, because their actions are interdependent, people fail to act in a manner that is mutually beneficial.

to be good, then you will hire more workers and expand production. If you expect business to be bad, then you do not expand production. Thus, there are two possibilities: People expect bad times and, because of this expectation, times turn out to be bad—this is the case of coordination failure—or people expect good times and, because of this expectation, times turn out to be good. If people could agree to coordinate their production, then coordination failure, or bad times, might be eliminated. John Bryant of Rice University has been researching the possibility that periods of deficient aggregate demand might be due to coordination failures.

### The Real Business Cycle School

**real business cycle school:** a group of economists who believe that shifts in potential GDP, largely due to changes in technology, are the primary cause of economic fluctuations.

Another outgrowth of the rational expectations revolution is the **real business cycle school.** The real business cycle school views the fluctuations in real GDP as due to fluctuations in potential GDP. Most typically it assumes the changes in potential GDP to be due to technological change in the production function. In terms of the growth accounting formula, therefore, the source of economic fluctuations is in the technological contribution to growth.

Finn Kydland of Carnegie Mellon University and Edward Prescott of the University of Minnesota are two of the originators of the real business cycle school, which has attracted many economists in recent years. An important contribution of the real business cycle school has been to focus the attention of macroeconomists more on the supply side of the economy. Clearly it is not correct to assume that all the fluctuations in real GDP are due to fluctuations of real GDP around potential GDP. The real business cycle school has provided a method for explaining the other sources of fluctuations in real GDP.

### Supply Side Economics

**supply side economics:** the branch of economics that emphasizes that reducing marginal tax rates on investments and labor will increase aggregate supply, thereby stimulating the macroeconomy.

Like Keynesian economics and monetarist economics, supply side economics is almost a household term, widely discussed in recent years and appearing in many general-usage dictionaries. **Supply side economics** refers to the idea that by cutting taxes or reforming the tax system, the growth rate of aggregate supply, or potential GDP, can be increased.

Few economists would disagree that taxes affect incentives. But they disagree strongly over how large the effects are likely to be. In principle, there is an affinity between supply side economics and the real business cycle school because both emphasize the supply side of the economy, or potential GDP.

## Macroeconomic Theory at the Turn of the Century

During the 1990s, economists came to use a catchy terminology when referring to the different schools of thought. They divided up economists into two broad camps: (1) the *freshwater* camp, including economists of the real business cycle school and the new classical school, many of whom happened to be located in the central regions of the United States (Great Lakes, Mississippi River), and (2) the *saltwater* camp, including economists of the new Keynesian school, many of whom happened to be located in either the eastern or western regions of the United States.

By the late 1990s a consensus of the two camps seemed to be developing. That consensus combined the sticky prices and implicit contracts of the saltwater camp with the careful treatment of information, policy rules, and equilibrium of the fresh-water camp. The consensus is represented by the papers collected in a book called the *Handbook of Macroeconomics*, a summary of modern macroeconomics written by many active researchers. The consensus is also evident in the rational expectations models with sticky prices used at the Federal Reserve Board, the International Monetary Fund, and other institutions with macroeconomic policy responsibility. But whether or not there is a consensus, if history is any guide to the future, macroeconomic debates will continue in the years ahead.

## Review

▶ In examining developments in modern macroeconomics, it is helpful to focus on two periods: (1) the 1930s to the 1960s, which began with the Keynesian revolution and includes the work of the monetarist school and the neoclassical growth school; and (2) the 1970s to the 1990s, which began with the rational expectations revolution and includes

the work of the new classical school, the new Keynesian school, the real business cycle school, and the supply side school.

▶ The recent history of macroeconomic thought is one of heated debates in which the prevailing view gradually changes over time.

# DEBATES ABOUT MACROECONOMIC POLICY

Having examined some of the debates about macroeconomic theory, let us look at the debates about policy. Consider the actions proposed by Presidents Bush and Clinton to help speed recovery from the 1990–1991 recession.

## The Bush Fiscal Package

Table 18.1 summarizes President Bush's macroeconomic policy proposals, made in January 1992. The first proposal was to speed up government purchases. This meant that laws that had already been passed to build or improve roads or bridges would be implemented more quickly. As a result of this speedup, government purchases were to rise by $10 billion in the first six months of 1992.

Shift $10 billion in government purchases from the future into present.

Reduce the amount of tax withheld in the present.

Enact an investment tax credit (called an allowance) to encourage investment in 1992 and 1993 rather than in later years.

Reduce the capital gains tax.

**TABLE 18.1**
**Key Parts of the Bush Stimulus Proposal**

What would be the impact on the economy? The $10 billion increase in spending is only a small fraction of a percent of real GDP for one year. Hence, even with multiplier effects on consumption, this alone would not have had a big effect on the recovery, but it was some stimulus.

The second proposal was to decrease temporarily the amount of income taxes withheld by the government. Individuals who work must pay income taxes equal to a percentage of each paycheck to the government. This withholding of taxes is the way most income taxes are paid in the United States. On the average throughout the economy, taxes are overwithheld. For the year 1992, approximately $25 billion was to be refunded to taxpayers in April 1993. The Bush proposal was to reduce this withholding and help stimulate the economy in 1992. This meant that people would get more money during the year and less money in their refund the following year. Because this tax change was temporary, it was expected to have a fairly small effect on the economy. The effect would certainly be smaller than a permanent tax cut of this magnitude and probably even smaller than a temporary tax cut that was not completely offset by a higher tax the following year.

**investment tax credit:** a reduction in taxes for firms that buy new investment goods that is proportional to the expenditures on the good.

**capital gains tax:** a tax on the increase in the value of an asset.

How much additional consumption would there be if all of the $25 billion was received as income in 1992? Suppose that the marginal propensity to consume out of income is .6. The change in withholding would clearly have a smaller marginal propensity to consume (MPC), but how much smaller we do not know. Perhaps .3 would be a good guess. If you multiply .3 by $25 billion you get $7.5 billion. This is probably a reasonable guess of how much extra consumption would occur as a result of this kind of tax cut. People would have less withheld, their paychecks would be a little larger, and they could spend more. That would amount to less than a small fraction of a percent of real GDP. By adding both the speedup of construction spending and the delay in tax receipts, the effect is still less than ½ of a percent of real GDP.

The remaining parts of the Bush package required legislation that the Congress would have to pass. The **investment tax credit** meant that firms could reduce their taxes if they invested and purchased new investment goods in 1992. For example, a small business could get a tax break if it bought a delivery truck during 1992 rather than the following year. That would give firms an incentive to invest and stimulate demand in the economy.

Another part of the proposal requiring legislation was the capital gains tax reduction. The **capital gains tax** is a tax on the appreciation of assets. If you invest in a stock and its value increases, say by $100, you pay a tax on that capital gain. The Bush administration proposed that the tax be reduced. The aim was to stimulate investment and to help the economy by increasing aggregate demand in the short run and productive capacity in the long run.

The proposal to reduce the capital gains tax was controversial. Opponents of the reduction said that it was a giveaway to the rich. They argued that only 1 percent of the population gets two-thirds of the gains from the cut in capital gains tax. But proponents gave figures showing that 60 percent of the people who get the capital gains tax break earn less than $50,000 per year.

*"Do you blame the previous administration, the present administration or future administrations?"*

### *Debates about the Bush Proposals*

As it turned out, none of the Bush stimulus proposals were enacted into law. Some lawmakers argued that the economy was already recovering. Others argued against the capital gains tax cut. The Congress voted positively on an alternative package with many of the president's proposals, but the package also included a tax increase, which President Bush said he would veto and did veto. His veto was sustained, so there was no stimulus package.

The only part of the stimulus proposals that actually took place were those that could be done without legislation—the adjustment of withholding and the speedup of purchases.

## The Clinton Fiscal Package

After President Clinton was elected in November 1992, he also developed a stimulus program. His economic advisers recommended a large fiscal stimulus to help speed up the recovery from the 1991–1992 recession. The program is summarized in Table 18.2.

Note the similarities between the two proposals. The increase in government spending, the investment tax credit, and the reduction in the capital gains tax (though for a limited set of investments) were also on the Bush stimulus list. However, all the components of the Clinton proposal required congressional action.

### *Debate about the Clinton Proposals*

Like the Bush proposals, the Clinton proposals received much criticism and were not enacted by Congress. The problem in this case was that the proposals would have increased the budget deficit. During this period, the concerns of many economists and the public had shifted to reducing the deficit rather than taking actions to stimulate the economy. Although the Democrats had a majority in both houses of Congress, some Democrats did not like the president's stimulus package because it would increase the deficit, so the plan failed. Because the package did not have an administrative component that could be put in place without legislation, there was no stimulus program at all.

## Lessons

What can be learned from the failed Bush and Clinton discretionary stimulus proposals? Both cases illustrate some of the problems associated with implementing macroeconomic policy. First, there is a big difference between proposing a policy and enacting a policy, even when the president and both houses of Congress belong to the same party. Second, the examples illustrate that lags in getting discretionary

---

Increase government spending by $16 billion on items ranging from infrastructure to immunization programs.

Establish an incremental investment tax credit—to be temporary except for small firms.

Reduce the capital gains tax for investments in certain small companies held for five years or more.

**TABLE 18.2**
**Key Parts of the Clinton Stimulus Proposal**

policies enacted mean that they will most likely be too late to have the desired effect. In retrospect, even if the Clinton stimulus program had been enacted it would have been put in place in 1994. By 1996, data indicated that the economy was very close to full employment in 1994 and not in need of a fiscal stimulus.

Perhaps the most important lesson from this period is that both discretionary proposals were very small in comparison with the automatic stabilizer effects of fiscal policy. The budget deficit grew along with the unemployment rate in 1990 and 1991, just as it did in the 1981–1982 recession and all other recessions. The increase in the cyclical deficit was more than 2 percent of GDP, and it was well timed. The automatic stabilizers provided a substantial degree of fiscal stimulus to the economy, much larger than either of the discretionary action programs proposed.

Fortunately, the economy recovered from the 1990–1991 recession, and the expansion after this recession has been one of the longest in U.S. history. But when the next recession strikes there will undoubtedly be calls for the president to put forth another stimulus package. In doing so the delays in enactment and the power of the automatic stabilizers should be kept in mind.

## Review

▶ Both President Bush and President Clinton proposed discretionary short-term stimulus packages to speed the recovery from the 1990–1991 recession. Both packages were vociferously debated.

▶ In the end, both proposals were defeated by Congress, though for much different reasons. Both illustrate the great difficulties of using discretionary fiscal policy to reduce the fluctuations in the economy.

▶ In retrospect the automatic stabilizers had a much larger impact than either of the proposals would have had.

## CONCLUSION

Newspaper articles and television programs frequently focus on current macroeconomic events—the threat of inflation, the reason for a recession, a president's budget plan, the Fed's interest rate strategy. As this chapter has shown, there are different schools of thought, and even those with the same views have debates about how to implement macroeconomic policy. It seems difficult to tell who is right in any particular instance. Hence, whether you are a casual observer, a concerned voter, or, like most of us, greatly affected by these events, you must make your own judgment.

This chapter has endeavored to provide you with some historical perspective on the different schools of thought so that you can form your own views about current policy problems. Recent case studies, such as the debates over macroeconomic policy discussed in this chapter, are useful for this purpose, but even now as you finish this chapter there are other interesting and important cases evolving. Try out your skills by reading and thinking about one of these—whether it is the next Fed interest rate decision, the next State of the Union address, a proposed reform of tax and budget policy, or simply the "informed opinion" about the macroeconomy from an economic expert.

# KEY POINTS

**1.** Examining different schools of thought and case studies of macroeconomic policy decision-making provides a perspective on the relative importance of different debates and controversies.

**2.** The Keynesian revolution began in the 1930s. It emphasized the importance of aggregate demand and the role of fiscal policy in stabilizing aggregate demand.

**3.** The monetarist school criticized Keynesians for deemphasizing money and for the idea that there was a long-run tradeoff between inflation and unemployment.

**4.** Research on the neoclassical growth model focused attention on aggregate supply and the growth of potential GDP.

**5.** The rational expectations revolution started in the 1970s and brought increased attention to policy credibility,

time inconsistency, monetary independence, and policy rules.

**6.** The new classical school assumes that prices are perfectly flexible, leading to the policy ineffectiveness proposition.

**7.** The new Keynesian school incorporated sticky prices into models with rational expectations and explored the underlying reasons for sticky prices and wages.

**8.** The real business cycle school has shown that fluctuations in potential GDP may be a significant part of economic fluctuations.

**9.** Experience with discretionary policy in the 1990s was not favorable. Two fiscal packages proposed by two presidents were not enacted, leaving countercyclical policy to the automatic stabilizers.

# KEY TERMS

Keynesian revolution
Keynesian school
monetarist school
neoclassical growth school
rational expectations revolution

policy ineffectiveness proposition
new classical school
new Keynesian school
coordination failure
real business cycle school

supply side economics
investment tax credit
capital gains tax

# QUESTIONS FOR REVIEW

**1.** What economic event gave impetus to the Keynesian revolution?

**2.** What did Keynes mean by "the classical theory"?

**3.** What was the Keynesian-monetarist debate?

**4.** What was the impact of neoclassical growth theory on Keynesian economics?

**5.** What is the rational expectations revolution?

**6.** What is the policy ineffectiveness proposition?

**7.** What is the contribution of the real business cycle school to theories of economic fluctuations?

**8.** What was similar and different about the Bush and Clinton short-run stimulus plans? Why did both plans fail to pass Congress?

# PROBLEMS

**1.** Contrast the Keynesian revolution of the 1930s with the rational expectations revolution of the 1970s, describing the contributions and schools of thought associated with each.

**2.** What was the impact of the AM/FM debates on the theory of economic fluctuations?

**3.** Explain why an anticipated *decrease* in the money supply would not affect real GDP if prices were perfectly flexible.

**4.** Compare and contrast new classical macroeconomics with the new Keynesian school.

**5.** Provide two explanations for the 1990–1991 recession, one based on real business cycles and the other based on

the assumption that real GDP departed from a steadily growing potential GDP.

**6.** What are some examples of fiscal policy actions that do not require legislation? Divide your answers into discretionary and automatic actions.

**7.** Suppose it is the year 2002, and the economy is just coming out of the 2001–2002 recession. There is pressure on the president to do something to help the recovery. Remember that there is a presidential election in the year 2004. Based on the experience of President Bush in 1992 and President Clinton in 1993, what would you recommend?

# 19

# Economic Growth Around the World

Macroeconomics provides a pretty good framework for studying the steady upward climb of real GDP over time. In particular, the theory of economic growth tells us how technology and capital have provided workers with the means to raise their productivity and thereby achieve the modern miracle of economic growth.

Yet there is something disquieting about the theory when we look at all the facts. True, technological change can explain a good part of the economic growth miracle, but why exactly did improvements in technology suddenly start in the late 1700s in Europe? Moreover, as we compare living standards around the world, it is clear that people in some countries are much better off than people in other countries. Why has the theory applied so unevenly to different countries around the world, with some growing rapidly and some stuck in poverty, not growing at all? What will determine whether economic growth in the twenty-first century will be as great as the last two centuries or as terrible as the millennia before that?

In this chapter we look for answers to these crucial questions about the initial impetus to economic growth in the advanced countries, about the uneven patterns of economic growth in different countries, and about the prospects of future economic growth throughout the world. All the questions are interrelated and, surprisingly, they seem to have similar answers. We begin our quest for the answers by looking at patterns of growth in different parts of the world.

# CATCHING UP OR NOT?

If technological advances can spread easily—as seems reasonable with modern communications—and if capital and labor have diminishing returns, then poorer regions with low productivity and, therefore, low income per capita will tend to catch up to richer regions by growing more rapidly. Why?

If the spread of new technology is not difficult, then we would expect regions with lower productivity to adopt the more advanced technology of other regions to raise their productivity. For example, the spread of technology appears to be easy in the states in the United States. Individual states have access to the same technology. People in all the states watch the same television networks, have access to the same national newspapers or wire services, and can read the same textbooks. Similar colleges and universities exist in all the states.

Diminishing returns would also tend to cause poor regions to catch up to the rich. Consider a relatively poor region where both capital per worker and output per worker are low. Imagine several hundred workers constructing a road with only rudimentary tools, such as picks, shovels, and perhaps jackhammers. With such low levels of capital, the returns to increasing the amount of capital would be very high. Diminishing returns to capital would not have set in. The addition of a few trucks and some earthmoving equipment to the construction project would bring huge returns in higher output. Regions with relatively low levels of capital per worker would, therefore, attract a great amount of investment; capital per worker would grow rapidly. The growth accounting formula tells us that output per worker grows rapidly when capital per worker grows rapidly. Thus, output per hour of work would grow rapidly in poorer regions where capital per worker is low.

A rich region where the capital per worker is high, however, would gain relatively little from additional capital per worker because diminishing returns have set in. Such a region would attract little investment and the growth rate of capital would be lower; the growth of output would also be lower.

Thus, economic growth theory predicts that regions with low productivity will grow relatively more rapidly than regions that are at the leading edge of technology and where the ratios of capital to labor are high. Regions with low productivity will tend to catch up to the more advanced regions by adopting existing technology and attracting capital.

Figure 19.1 illustrates this catch-up phenomenon. It shows the level of productivity on the horizontal axis and the growth rate of productivity on the vertical axis. The downward-sloping line is the **catch-up line.** A country or region on the upper left-hand part of the line is poor—with low productivity and, therefore, low income per capita—but growing rapidly. A country at the lower right-hand part of the line is rich—with high productivity and, therefore, high income per capita—but growth is relatively less rapid. That the catch-up line exists and is downward-sloping is a prediction of growth theory.

## Catch-up Within the United States

Figure 19.2 examines how well the catch-up line works for the states within the United States. This picture presents the data on real income per capita and the growth rates of real income per capita for each of the states. Because productivity

**Growth accounting formula:**

$$\text{Growth rate of real GDP per hour of work} = $$

$$\frac{1}{3}\left(\begin{array}{c}\text{growth rate of capital} \\ \text{per hour of work}\end{array}\right)$$

$$+\left(\begin{array}{c}\text{growth rate of} \\ \text{technology}\end{array}\right)$$

**catch-up line:** the downward-sloping relation between the level of productivity and growth of productivity predicted by growth theory.

**FIGURE 19.1**
**The Catch-up Line**
Growth theory with spreading technology and diminishing returns to capital and labor predicts that regions with lower productivity will have higher growth rates of productivity. The catch-up line illustrates this prediction. Because productivity is so closely related to income per capita, the catch-up line can also describe a relationship between income per capita and the growth rate of income per capita.

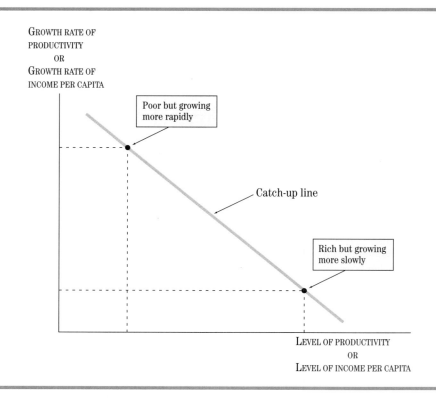

and real income per capita move closely together, we can examine the accuracy of the catch-up line with the real income per capita data. (Again, the adjective *real* means that the income data are adjusted for inflation.) Real income per capita in 1880 is on the horizontal axis, and the growth rate of real income per capita from 1880 to 1980 is on the vertical axis. Each point on the scatter diagram represents a state, and a few of the states are labeled. If you pick a state (observe Nevada, for example, down and to the right), you can read its growth rate by looking over to the left scale, and you can read its 1880 income per capita level by looking down to the horizontal scale.

The diagram clearly shows a tendency for states with low real income per capita in 1880 to have high growth rates. The state observations fall remarkably near a catch-up line. Southern states like Florida and Texas are in the high-growth group. On the other hand, in states that had a relatively high income per capita in 1880, income per capita grew relatively slowly. This group includes California and Nevada.

Thus, the theory of growth works quite well in explaining the relative differences in growth rates in the states of the United States. Where technological know-how is comparable, there is a tendency for relatively poor regions to grow more rapidly than relatively rich regions.

## Catch-up in the Advanced Countries

What if we apply the same thinking to different countries? After all, communication is now global. Figure 19.3 is another scatter diagram with growth rate and income per capita combinations. It is like Figure 19.2 except that it plots real

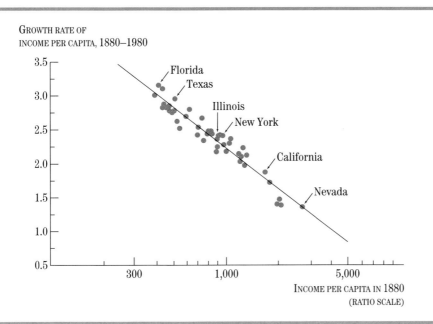

**FIGURE 19.2**
**Evidence of Catch-up Within the United States**

In the United States, those states that had low real income per capita 100 years ago grew relatively rapidly compared to states that had high income per capita. The poor states tended to catch up to the richer states. A catch-up line is drawn through the dots.

*Source: Historical Statistics of the United States: Colonial Times to 1970,* U.S. Department of Commerce, and *State Personal Income,* U.S. Department of Commerce, 1989.

income per capita in 1960 against growth in real income per capita from 1960 to 1990 for several advanced countries. These incomes are measured in U.S. dollars using the purchasing power parity method of comparing different countries discussed in Chapter 6.

Observe in Figure 19.3 that the richer countries, such as the United States, grew less rapidly. In contrast, relatively less rich countries, such as Greece, Portugal, Spain, and Italy, grew more rapidly. Canada and France are somewhere in

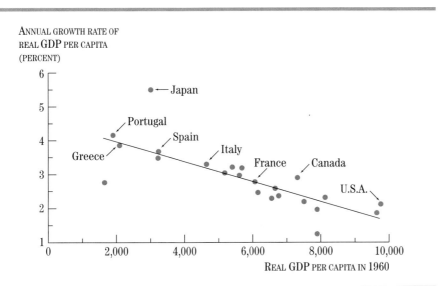

**FIGURE 19.3**
**Evidence of Catch-up in More Advanced Countries, 1960–1990**

For the advanced countries shown in the diagram, income per capita growth has been more rapid for those that started from a lower level of income per capita. Thus, there has been catching up, as shown by the catch-up line drawn through the points.

*Source:* International Comparison Project administered by the United Nations, World Bank, and International Monetary Fund. The data for 1960 are measured in 1985 dollars.

"According to figures released today, last month's gains in productivity were completely negated by this month's gains in counterproductivity."

between. These countries tend to display the catch-up behavior predicted by the growth theory. Apparently, technological advances are spreading and capital-labor ratios are rising more rapidly in countries where they are low and returns to capital are high. So far our look at the evidence confirms the predictions of growth theory.

### Catch-up in the Whole World

However, so far we have not looked beyond the most advanced countries. Figure 19.4 shows a broader group of countries that includes not only the more advanced countries in Figure 19.3 but also countries that are still developing. It is apparent that there is little tendency for this larger group of countries to fall along a catch-up line. There may even be a decline in growth, with many poorer countries falling further behind over time.

The countries with very low growth rates, such as Bangladesh and Ethiopia, are also the countries with very low income per capita. On the other hand, many countries with higher growth rates had a much higher income per capita. Singapore and Hong Kong had higher growth rates even though their income per capita was above Sri Lanka and Ethiopia.

Comparing countries like Singapore and South Korea with countries like Bangladesh and Sri Lanka is striking. South Korea and Singapore had about the same real income per capita as Sri Lanka and Bangladesh in 1960, but South Korea and Singapore surged ahead with a more rapid growth rate over the last 30 years, leaving Bangladesh and Sri Lanka behind. But this is not the exception. Contrary to the predictions of the economic growth theory, which says that technological advances should spread and capital per hour of work should rise from low levels, Figure 19.4 shows little tendency for relatively poor countries to grow relatively rapidly. It appears that something has been preventing either the spread and the adoption of new technology or the increase in investment needed to raise capital-labor ratios. We examine possible explanations as this chapter proceeds.

**FIGURE 19.4**
**Lack of Catch-up for Developing Countries, 1960–1990**

Unlike the states in the United States or the advanced countries, there has been little tendency for poor countries to grow more rapidly than rich countries. The gap between rich and poor has not closed.

*Source:* International Comparison Project administered by the United Nations, World Bank, and International Monetary Fund. The data for 1960 are measured in 1985 dollars.

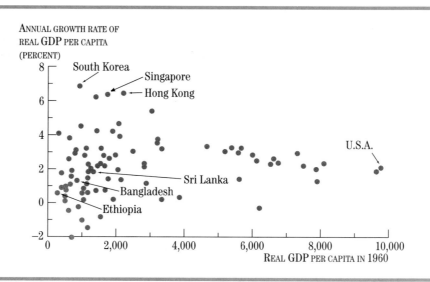

## Review

▶ Economic growth theory predicts that poorer regions tend to catch up to richer ones. The flow of technology around the world and investment in new capital bring this about.

▶ Data for the states in the United States or for the more advanced countries show that such catch-up exists and is quite strong.

▶ However, there has been little evidence of catch-up in the world as a whole. Many of the poor countries have fallen even further behind the developed countries, while other poor countries, in particular those in east Asia, have grown very rapidly.

# ECONOMIC DEVELOPMENT

Aside from raising questions about economic growth theory, the lack of catch-up evidenced in Figure 19.4 describes a disturbing situation. There are huge disparities in world income distribution, and billions of people in low-income countries lack the necessities those in high-income countries frequently take for granted.

## Billions Still in Poverty

The richest countries in the world, with more than $10,000 income per capita, account for about 700 million people. The United States, with 250 million people, is among the richest, along with Japan and most of Western Europe. Another 600 million people live in countries that have an income per capita between $5,000 and $10,000. But the vast majority—about three-fourths of the world's people—live in countries with an income per capita of less than $5,000 per year. This is below the poverty level in advanced countries. Income per capita in South Korea, Venezuela, and Malaysia is only about one-third that of the United States. In China and Sri Lanka it is only one-eighth that of the United States. Income per capita for Ethiopia is a mere 2 percent of that in the United States.

Low income per capita is a serious economic problem, but the implications go well beyond economics. Large differences in income per capita and vast amounts of poverty can lead to war, revolution, or regional conflicts. Will these differences persist? Or is the lack of catch-up that has left so many behind a thing of the past?

## Geographical Patterns

Figure 19.5 shows the location of the relatively rich and the relatively poor countries around the world. Notice that the higher-income countries tend to be in the northern part of the world. An exception to this rule is the relatively high income per capita in Australia and New Zealand. Aside from these exceptions, income disparity appears to have a geographical pattern—the North being relatively rich and the South relatively poor. Often people use the term **North-South problem** to describe world income disparities.

But whether it is North versus South or not, there do appear to be large contiguous regions where many rich or many poor countries are located together. The original increase in economic growth that occurred at the time of the Industrial

**North-South problem:** refers to the geographic dispersion of incomes: Northern countries tend to be relatively rich, and southern ones tend to be relatively poor.

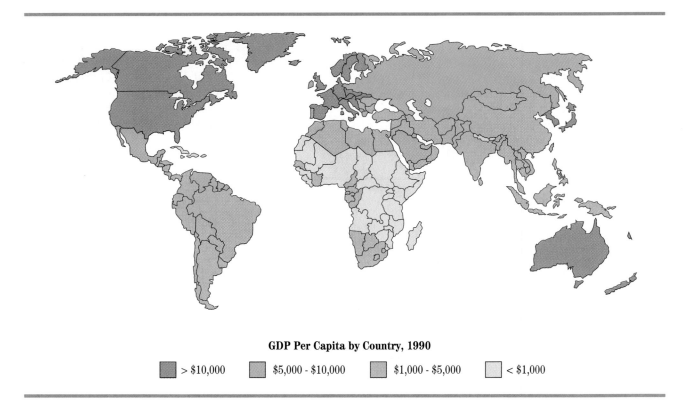

**GDP Per Capita by Country, 1990**

▇ > $10,000     ▇ $5,000 - $10,000     ▇ $1,000 - $5,000     ☐ < $1,000

---

**FIGURE 19.5**
**Rich and Poor Countries Around the World**

The highest-income regions tend to be located in North America, Europe, Japan, Australia, and the Middle East.

*Source:* International Comparison Project administered by the United Nations, World Bank, and International Monetary Fund.

**economic development:**
the process of growth by which countries raise incomes per capita and become industrialized; also refers to the branch of economics that studies this process.

**developing country:** a country that is poor by world standards in terms of real GDP per capita.

**industrialized country:** a country with a large industrial base that is relatively well off by world standards in terms of real GDP per capita.

Revolution started in northwestern Europe—England, France, and Germany. It then spread to America, which industrialized rapidly in the nineteenth and twentieth centuries. It also spread to Japan during the late-nineteenth-century Meiji Restoration, one of the main purposes of which was to import Western technology into the Japanese economy.

## Terminology of Economic Development

**Economic development** is the branch of economics that endeavors to explain why poor countries do not develop faster and to find policies to help them develop faster. Economists who specialize in economic development frequently are experts on the problems experienced by particular countries—such as a poor educational system, political repression, droughts, or poor distribution of food. The term **developing country** describes those countries that are relatively poor, and the term **industrialized country** describes the advanced or relatively well-off countries. Sometimes the term *less-developed country* (LDC) is used rather than *developing country*. There are also terms to distinguish between different developing countries. **Newly industrialized countries** such as Korea and Hong Kong are relatively poor countries that are growing rapidly. **Countries in transition** are relatively poor countries, such as Russia and Poland, that are moving from central planning to market economies.

Table 19.1 shows the shares of world GDP produced by the three classifications of countries: industrialized countries, developing countries, and countries in transition. Thus, this table looks at aggregate income (which equals GDP) rather than at income per capita. Over 50 percent of world GDP comes from the industrialized countries.

| WORLD | 100.00 |
|---|---|
| **Industrialized Countries** | **54.6** |
| Major industrialized countries | 46.8 |
| United States | 21.2 |
| Japan | 8.4 |
| Germany | 5.0 |
| France | 3.6 |
| Italy | 3.4 |
| United Kingdom | 3.3 |
| Canada | 1.9 |
| Other industrialized countries | 7.8 |
| **Developing Countries** | **40.1** |
| By region | |
| Africa | 3.3 |
| Asia | 23.1 |
| Middle East and Europe | 4.8 |
| Western Hemisphere | 8.9 |
| **Countries in Transition** | **5.3** |
| Former Soviet Union | 3.3 |
| Central Europe | 2.0 |

**TABLE 19.1**
**Shares of World GDP**

*Source: World Economic Outlook,* May 1995, p. 113. By permission of International Monetary Fund.

Most striking is the nearly 23 percent share of world GDP in Asia outside of Japan. This large share is due to the newly industrialized countries and to China. China's GDP is already larger than Japan's. Although income per capita is less, China is already a major force in the world economy.

Economic development economists working at universities, the World Bank, the International Monetary Fund, the United Nations, and of course in the developing countries themselves focus their research on reasons why poor countries have grown so slowly. We now proceed to examine these reasons and, in doing so, we will touch on some of the central issues of economic development. Our examination will consider the two key determinants of increasing productivity—improvements in technology and higher capital per worker. We consider technology in the next section and then go on to consider capital in the following sections.

**newly industrialized country:** a country that is growing rapidly and quickly developing its industrial base.

**country in transition:** a country that is transforming from a centrally planned economy to a market economy.

# Review

▶ The slow productivity growth in poor countries has resulted in extreme income inequality around the world. The growth miracle has spread to parts of the world, but productivity in many developing countries of the world has remained low.

▶ With a few exceptions most of the rich countries are in the northern regions of the globe and most of the poor countries are in the southern regions, thus giving rise to the term *North-South problem.*

▶ About 75 percent of the world's population lives in countries with less than $5,000 income per capita.

# OBSTACLES TO THE SPREAD OF TECHNOLOGY

We have now observed two essential facts about economic growth. First, a large and persistent growth wave began for the first time in human history about 200 years ago; this growth wave raised income per capita in some countries to many times that experienced throughout human history. Second, economic growth did not spread throughout much of the world, leaving people in many countries hardly better off than their ancestors. Could these two facts be linked? Could they have the same explanation? A number of ideas have been put forth to explain the increase in economic growth in the late 1700s, and some of these may help explain why growth has not accelerated in many developing countries.

## Reduction in Restrictions in the Eighteenth and Nineteenth Centuries

Some economists and historians have pointed to developments in science as the explanation of the rapid increase in economic growth in Europe in the 1700s. But if that is the explanation, why did the Industrial Revolution not begin in China or in the Islamic nations, where scientific knowledge was far more advanced than in Europe? Others note the importance of natural resources, but these were available in many other countries where there was no Industrial Revolution and, since the mid-nineteenth century, growth in Japan has been high, yet Japan has almost no natural resources. Still others have focused on exploitation, slavery, colonialism, and imperialism, but these evils existed long before the Industrial Revolution.

What, then, is the reason for this increase in economic growth we associate with the Industrial Revolution? Historians of capitalist development from Karl Marx to Joseph Schumpeter have stressed that for the first time in human history, entrepreneurs in the 1700s were gaining the freedom to start business enterprises. Economic historian Angus Maddison shows in his book, *Phases of Capitalist Development,* that the Dutch were the first to lead in productivity, with the British and then the United States soon catching up. He also shows that in the 1700s many Dutch farmers owned their land, that there was a small, weak feudal nobility, and that potential power was in the hands of entrepreneurs. Hence there was greater freedom to produce and sell manufactured and agricultural products. By the late 1700s and early 1800s, similar conditions existed in the United Kingdom and the United States. Firms could ship their products to market and hire workers without political restrictions.

Moreover, these firms now were able to earn as much as they could by selling whatever they wanted at whatever price the market determined. They began to invent and develop new products that were most beneficial to individuals. The business enterprises could keep the profits. Profits were no longer confiscated by the nobles or kings. Individual property rights—including the right to earn and keep profits—were being established and recognized in the courts.

Karl Marx, one of the most knowledgeable historians of the Industrial Revolution, saw earlier than many others that the unleashing of business enterprises and entrepreneurs was the key to economic growth. He credited the business and entrepreneurial class—what he called the bourgeois class—with the creation of more wealth than was created in all of history.

In sum, the sudden increase in technology and productivity may have occurred when it did because of the increased freedom that entrepreneurs had to start businesses, to invent and apply new ideas, and to develop products for the mass of humanity where the large markets existed.

## Remaining Restrictions in Developing Countries

If true, this explanation that the economic growth surge in the late 1700s and 1800s was caused by the removal of restrictions on business enterprises may have lessons for economic development. In many developing countries in this century, there have been heavy restrictions on businesses and a poor definition of individual property rights.

Good examples of these restrictions have been documented in the research of economist Hernando De Soto, who specializes in the economy of Peru. De Soto showed that there is a tremendous amount of regulation in the developing countries. This regulation is so costly that a huge informal economy has emerged. The **informal economy** consists of large numbers of illegal businesses that can avoid the regulations. Remarkably, 61 percent of employment in Peru is in the informal, unregulated, illegal sector of the economy. In the city of Lima, around 33 percent of the houses are built in this informal sector. About 71,000 illegal vendors dominate retail trade, and 93 percent of urban transportation is in the informal sector.

**informal economy:** the portion of an economy characterized by illegal, unregulated businesses.

This large informal sector exists because the costs of setting up a legal business are high. It takes 32 months—filling out forms, waiting for approval, getting permission from several agencies—for a person to start a retail business. It takes six years and 11 months to start a housing construction firm. Hence, it is essentially prohibitive for someone to try to start a small business in the legal sector. Therefore, the informal sector grows.

Why does it matter if the informal sector is large? How does this impede development? Precisely because the sector is informal. It lacks basic laws of property rights and contracts. These laws cannot be enforced in a sector that is outside the law. Bringing new inventions to market requires the security of private property so that one can capture the benefits from taking risks. Otherwise the earnings from the innovation might be taken away by the government or by firms that copy the idea illegally. For example, if a business in the informal sector finds that another firm reneges on a contract to deliver a product, then that firm has no right to use the courts to enforce the contract because the business itself is illegal.

Some economists feel that such restrictions are at the heart of poor economic development. The explanation given earlier for why the Industrial Revolution occurred in the Western countries seems to pinpoint a key reason why developing countries cannot achieve high growth rates. In Europe in the 1700s, a new freedom for businesses to operate in the emerging market economy led to new products and technology. These same types of freedoms and reliance on the market could raise the economic growth rate in the developing countries around the world today.

Perhaps the most pervasive form of restriction on entrepreneurs existed in the centrally planned economies of the former Soviet Union, central Europe, and China. The persistent differences in income per capita between the former East Germany and West Germany is evidence that such restrictions have been important in preventing low-income countries from catching up. As restrictions on the market have been removed, economic growth has increased rapidly in China and other countries of east Asia, such as Vietnam.

Many forecast continued rapid growth in China and the other emerging market economies well into the twenty-first century; if this occurs, a re-examination of the catch-up line 40 years from now for the whole world may show a much better fit for the countries of the world, perhaps as good as in Figures 19.2 and 19.3.

### Human Capital

In order for existing technology to be adopted—whether in the form of innovative organizational structures of firms or as new products—it is necessary to have well-trained and highly skilled workers. For example, it is hard to make use of sophisticated computers to increase productivity when there are few skilled computer programmers.

Recall that human capital refers to the education and training of workers. Low investment in human capital is a serious obstacle to increasing productivity because it hampers the ability of countries that are behind to use new technology.

In fact, economists have found that differences in human capital in different countries can explain why some countries have been more successful at catching up than others. The developing countries that have been catching up most rapidly—in particular the newly industrialized countries like South Korea, Hong Kong, Taiwan, and Singapore—have strong educational systems in grade school and high school. This demonstrates the enormous importance of human capital for raising productivity.

## Review

▶ The removal of restrictions on private enterprise may have been the key factor unleashing the growth of productivity at the time of the Industrial Revolution. Similar restrictions in developing countries may have tended to stifle development in recent years.

▶ An educated work force is also needed to adopt technology. Better-educated and more highly skilled workers—those with human capital—can also use available capital more efficiently.

# OBSTACLES TO RAISING CAPITAL PER WORKER

In addition to obstacles to the spread and adoption of new technology, there are obstacles to the increase in capital per worker that can prevent poor countries from catching up.

### High Population Growth

In order for the capital to labor ratio to increase, it is necessary to invest in new capital. However, the amount of investment in new capital must be larger than the increase in labor, otherwise capital would increase by less than labor and the ratio of capital to labor—the factor influencing productivity—would fall. Thus, high population growth raises the amount of investment needed to increase, or even maintain, a level of capital per worker. High population growth rates can, therefore, slow down the increase in capital per worker.

Population growth rates have declined substantially in countries where income per capita has risen to high levels, such as Europe, Japan, and the United States. Economic analysis of the determinants of population indicates that the high income per capita and resulting greater life expectancy may be the reason for the decline in population growth. When countries reach a level of income per capita where people can survive into their old age without the support of many children, or where there is a greater chance of children reaching working age, people choose to have fewer children. Hence, higher income per capita in developing countries would probably reduce population growth in these countries.

## Insufficient National Saving

Capital accumulation requires investment, which requires saving. National saving equals investment plus net exports. National saving is the sum of *private saving* and *government saving*. In some developing countries where income per capita is barely above subsistence levels, the level of private saving—people's income less their consumption—is low. Government saving—tax receipts less expenditures—is also often low, perhaps because there is little income to tax and because governments have trouble controlling expenditures. Figure 19.6 shows the very low saving rates in the poorest countries of Africa and south Asia compared with the highest-saving countries.

For a poor country, it is natural for national saving to be less than investment and thus for imports to be greater than exports (net exports less than zero). In other words, a poor country naturally looks to net exports—that is, to foreign investment from abroad—as a source of capital formation for economic growth.

## The Lack of Foreign Investment in Developing Countries

Investment from abroad can come in the form of **foreign direct investment,** such as when the U.S. firm Gap Inc. opens a store in Mexico. Technically, when a foreign firm invests in more than 10 percent of the ownership of a business in another country, that investment is defined as direct investment.

Foreign investment also occurs when foreigners buy smaller percentages (less than 10 percent) of firms in developing economies. For example, foreign investment in Mexico takes place when a German buys newly offered common stock in a Mexican firm. In that case, the foreign investment from abroad is defined as **portfolio investment,** that is, less than 10 percent of ownership in a company.

Another way investment can flow in from abroad is through borrowing. Firms in developing economies or their governments can borrow from commercial banks, such as the Bank of America, Dai-Ichi Kangyo, or Crédit Lyonnais. Sometimes the governments of developing economies obtain loans directly from the governments of industrialized economies. Borrowing can also occur from government-sponsored international financial institutions, such as the International Monetary Fund (IMF) and the World Bank.

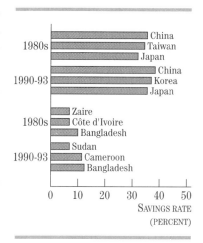

**FIGURE 19.6**
**The Highest and Lowest Saving Countries**
Very low national saving rates in poor countries impede capital accumulation and growth.

*Source: World Economic Outlook,* May 1995. By permission of International Monetary Fund.

National saving =
    investment + net exports
$$S = I + X$$

**foreign direct investment:** investment by a foreign entity of at least a 10 percent direct ownership share in a firm.

**portfolio investment:** investment by a foreign entity of less than a 10 percent ownership share in a firm.

# Using Economics to Explain an Inadequacy of World Saving

Twice a year the International Monetary Fund (IMF) publishes a report—*World Economic Outlook*—on economic growth around the world. In the 1990s this report repeatedly expressed concern about the inadequacy of world saving, worrying that saving is insufficient for economic growth in the developing economies.

In particular, in May 1995 the IMF noted the following pertinent facts about saving rates and interest rates (because the IMF focuses on the whole world, it reports "world" saving rates and "world" interest rates, which are simply averages for all countries of the world):

|                              | 1973–1980 | 1981–1994 |
|------------------------------|-----------|-----------|
| World real interest rate     | 1/2       | 5         |
| World saving rate (percent)  | 25        | 23        |

The table shows that the interest rate is higher and the saving rate is lower in recent periods (the 1980s and 1990s) compared with earlier periods (the 1970s). Noting that "saving has to equal investment," the IMF concluded that "with current real interest rates high . . . there is at least prima facie evidence for a saving adequacy problem."

How did the IMF arrive at this conclusion? Is it warranted? How does the IMF know that the decline in saving is not due to a downward shift in investment demand in developing countries?

Let's examine the IMF's reasoning with the saving-investment diagram introduced in Chapter 8 and shown below. The world interest rate is measured on the vertical axis and world saving or investment as a share of world GDP is on the horizontal axis. Recall that, along the green saving curve, the saving rate rises as the interest rate rises because a higher interest rate gives people a greater incentive to save. Recall also that, along the purple investment curve, the investment rate declines as the interest rate rises because a higher interest rate discourages businesses from investing in plant and equipment. For the whole world, net exports must be zero, so that the world investment rate must equal the world saving rate; hence, the equilibrium interest rate is found at the intersection of the two curves. (Unlike Figure 8.12, we can conveniently ignore net exports in the analysis because $X = 0$.)

The interest rate/saving rate observations noted by the IMF are shown in the diagram. Observe that these observations can be explained by a leftward shift of the world saving rate in the direction of lower world saving. Such a shift *raises* the equilibrium interest rate and lowers the equilibrium amount of investment. In contrast, a shift in the world investment curve toward lower investment, perhaps because of a decline in investment demand in developing countries, *does not* raise the equilibrium interest rate. Hence, by using the interest rate/saving rate observations to identify a shift in the world saving curve, the IMF is correct to conclude that world saving is inadequate in the 1990s, at least compared with the 1970s.

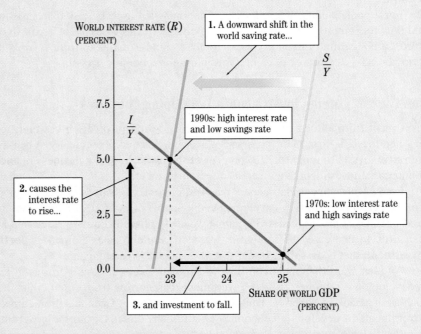

*Source: World Economic Outlook,* May 1995. By permission of International Monetary Fund.

### Loans from International Financial Institutions

The **International Monetary Fund (IMF)** and the **World Bank** were established after World War II as part of a major reform of the international monetary system. Both institutions make loans to the developing economies. They serve as intermediaries, channeling funds from the industrialized countries to the developing countries. The IMF also makes loans to economies in transition, such as Poland and the former Soviet Union.

The IMF tries to help countries implement difficult economic reforms. Frequently it tries to induce the countries to make the reforms by making the loans conditional on the reforms; this is the idea of **conditionality.** Under conditionality, the IMF gives loans to countries only if the countries take on economic reform—such as eliminating price controls or privatizing firms. This conditionality is viewed as a way to encourage reforms that are difficult to undertake because of the various vested interests in each country.

The World Bank, which was originally set up to make loans to developing countries and thereby increase capital accumulation, actually consists of three different agencies. The first is the International Bank for Reconstruction and Development (IBRD). The second is the International Development Association (IDA), which specifically makes loans to the least well-off countries (the poorest of the poor, like Bangladesh), with the expectation that these loans have a lower probability of being repaid. Third is the International Finance Corporation (IFC), which makes loans to business firms.

Most of the loans of the IBRD and the IDA are for specific projects—such as the projects to build a $100 million dam for irrigation in Brazil and a $153 million highway in Poland. Some of the loans from the World Bank are for more general purposes, much as the IMF loans are, and these loans are conditional, as the IMF loans are, on good economic reform.

### Where Is the Saving Coming From?

Despite the existence of these channels by which capital can flow to developing economies, there is a serious question whether the industrialized economies are saving enough to provide the increased capital. When an individual country saves more than it invests at home, it makes foreign investment abroad. A country can invest more than it saves by borrowing from abroad. In the whole world economy, saving must equal investment because (as of this writing) there seems to be no one in outer space to borrow from.

Figure 19.7 shows the percent of saving *supplied* to the world by countries with large trade surpluses and the percent of saving *used* by countries with large trade deficits during the early 1990s. The supply of Japanese saving to the rest of the world is very large; in fact, Japan is by far the largest supplier of capital to the world. In contrast, the United States and several other industrialized countries are users of capital.

**International Monetary Fund (IMF):** an international agency, established after World War II, designed to help countries with balance of payments problems and to ensure the smooth functioning of the international monetary system.

**World Bank:** an international agency, established after World War II, designed to promote the economic development of poorer countries through lending channeled from industrialized countries.

**conditionality:** stipulations on loans to countries from the International Monetary Fund that certain policy prescriptions, such as price reforms or reducing government budget deficits, must be met to receive funds.

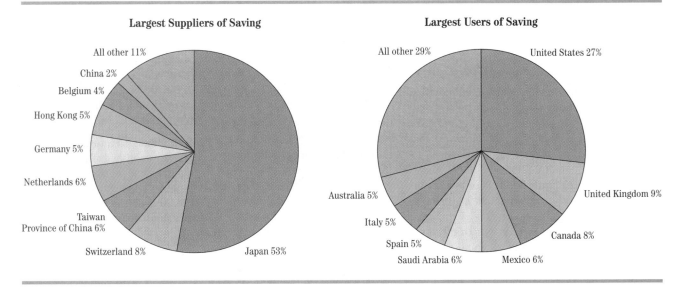

**FIGURE 19.7**
**Suppliers and Users of Saving, 1989–1993**
Japan is the largest supplier of saving, with its trade surplus, whereas the United States is the largest single user, with its trade deficit.

*Source: World Economic Outlook,* May 1995. By permission of International Monetary Fund.

## Review

▶ High rates of population growth and low national saving are two of the obstacles to raising capital per worker in developing economies.

▶ The International Monetary Fund makes loans to developing countries. The loans are frequently conditional on an economic reform program.

▶ The World Bank makes loans mainly for specific projects. It consists of the International Bank for Reconstruction and Development, the International Development Association, and the International Finance Corporation.

# INWARD-LOOKING VERSUS OUTWARD-LOOKING ECONOMIC POLICIES

One of the problems that developing countries face in trying to improve their growth rate is how to integrate their economies with the world economy. The basic question is whether they should encourage international trade with other countries or focus more on producing goods that substitute for international trade. There are two approaches.

In one approach, called the **import substitution strategy,** the developing country attempts to replace products that are imported from industrialized countries with products produced at home. This strategy tends to be inward-looking; laws

**import substitution strategy:** a trade policy designed to encourage local firms to produce goods that are normally imported into the country.

limiting imports coming from abroad are passed, and these are supplemented by subsidies to domestic industries. Taxes on imports—tariffs—are high. Firms may lobby their government to maintain or increase the subsidies or the tariffs which protect the firms from competition; such special interest lobbying is called *rent-seeking* by economists. An important example of this type of import substitution is the development of the steel industry in Brazil in the 1950s. The Brazilian government put tariffs on the import of foreign steel so that the Brazilian steel industry would have less competition.

An alternative way to increase growth is the **export-led strategy.** Under this strategy, the government of the developing country encourages international trade by expanding exports. Hence, the strategy tends to be outward-looking. Growth occurs through the manufacture and sale of products to other countries—shoes to America, black and white televisions to Europe, automobile tires to Japan. The aim of export-led growth is to increase trade rather than reduce trade. Although many countries that have followed export-led strategies have also had high tariffs on some commodities, such as agricultural goods, their strategies have been much more outward-looking than those of the import-substitution countries.

**export-led strategy:** the government's encouragement of the economy's development by establishing an open trade policy and increasing exports.

Table 19.2 shows the difference in economic growth in countries that have tried the import-substitution strategy compared to those that have tried the export-led growth strategy.

The table compares four countries: Brazil, Colombia, South Korea, and Tunisia (all developing countries) over a 23-year period. Brazil switched from an import-substitution strategy to an export-led growth strategy and saw increased economic growth. By the 1970s, economic growth in Brazil was in double digits, much higher than in the 1950s and early 1960s. The change was also dramatic in Colombia. The most dramatic is South Korea. The Korean success story, which began in the 1970s, seems related to the switch from an import-substitution strategy to one relying on trade and export growth. The same basic phenomenon is apparent in Tunisia as well as many other countries.

This experience indicates that a better strategy for increasing economic growth is to be outward-looking rather than inward-looking. A country's chance of catching up is greatly increased if it can adopt technology and use investment from abroad. By engaging in international trade, countries are able to learn more about technologies in other countries. For example, as South Korea's exports of electronic

| Country | Period | Trade Strategy | Growth Rate |
|---|---|---|---|
| Brazil | 1955–1960 | Import substitution | 6.9 |
| Brazil | 1960–1965 | Import substitution | 4.2 |
| Brazil | 1965–1970 | Export-led | 7.6 |
| Brazil | 1970–1976 | Export-led | 10.6 |
| Colombia | 1955–1960 | Import substitution | 4.6 |
| Colombia | 1960–1965 | Import substitution | 1.9 |
| Colombia | 1970–1976 | Export-led | 6.5 |
| South Korea | 1953–1960 | Import substitution | 5.2 |
| South Korea | 1960–1965 | Export-led | 6.5 |
| South Korea | 1970–1976 | Export-led | 10.3 |
| Tunisia | 1960–1970 | Import substitution | 4.6 |
| Tunisia | 1970–1976 | Export-led | 9.4 |

**TABLE 19.2**
**Growth Rates for Different Trade Strategies in Four Countries, 1953–1976**
(real GDP growth rate in percent per year)

equipment grew, the Koreans learned more about technology for producing electronic goods.

More countries appear to be changing their policies from inward-looking to outward-looking based on this experience. Mexico, for example, lowered its restrictions on imports in the mid-1980s and joined the United States and Canada in a free trade area in the 1990s. This approach to fewer restrictions on international markets parallels the developments that are removing restrictions on markets within the former centrally planned countries from Poland to China.

## Review

▶ There are two alternative international strategies for developing economies: One is inward-looking, the other outward-looking.

▶ Import substitution replaces imports by domestic production: It limits imported goods and is inward-looking.

▶ Export-led growth tries to expand exports of manufactured products (textiles, shoes, clothing). It is outward-looking.

▶ The evidence shows that the export-led strategy works better; this is what would be predicted from economic growth theory.

## CONCLUSION

In this chapter we have shown how productivity has increased in many countries because of higher capital per worker and technological change. In some countries there has been a convergence of productivity, with the poorer countries moving closer to the richer countries. However, for many developing countries, productivity has not been catching up and income per capita remains very low.

Among the possible explanations for the lack of catch-up are obstacles to the spread of technology, such as government restrictions on entrepreneurs and a shortage of human capital, and obstacles to higher capital per worker, such as low saving rates and low foreign investment. The removal of similar obstacles in Western Europe in the eighteenth century may have been the reason for the Industrial Revolution. Their removal today may result in another great growth wave in the developing economies.

In fact, there are already signs of the removal of such obstacles to economic growth. The movement from central planning to market systems in China, Vietnam, the countries of Eastern Europe and the former Soviet Union, and the greater reliance on markets in Latin America are examples. There are also signs of a resulting growth wave; growth in China and other countries of Asia has been particularly rapid as government restrictions on markets have been removed.

In the absence of retrenchments or setbacks from ethnic and military conflicts, we may see higher productivity growth in the poorer countries in the future than we have seen in the past. If so, the economic landscape of the world will be transformed.

Suppose, for example, that real GDP in the industrialized countries grows at a 2.5 percent pace for the next 50 years; this is higher than the 2 percent average rate of the 1990s. Suppose also that real GDP in all the other countries of the world grows at 5 percent per year; this is lower than the 6 percent pace of the developing Asian countries during the 1990s. With these growth rates, the countries we now classify as developing or in transition would produce 75 percent of world GDP in the year 2050; the countries we now classify as industrialized would produce 25 percent, a complete about-face from the current situation. This, of course, is an example, not a forecast, but it hints at some of the amazing possibilities for the future.

# KEY POINTS

**1.** Economic growth theory pinpoints capital accumulation and technological change as the two key ingredients of productivity growth. In a world without obstacles to the spread of technology or to investment in new capital, growth theory predicts that poor regions will catch up to rich regions.

**2.** Catch-up has occurred in the states of the United States and among the industrialized countries but is distressingly absent from the developing countries.

**3.** Low incomes and poverty have persisted for the vast majority of the world's population while other countries get richer.

**4.** Insufficient capital accumulation in the poor countries, due to high population growth, low saving rates, or insufficient capital flows from the advanced countries, may have been part of the problem.

**5.** Higher population growth requires more investment in order to raise capital per worker.

**6.** Some countries may have poor growth performance because of restrictions on markets and the lack of property rights. The lifting of those restrictions in Europe in the 1700s was a cause of the economic growth associated with the Industrial Revolution.

**7.** The removal of such restrictions may be a key to increased productivity and economic development.

**8.** Insufficient investment in human capital is another reason for low productivity growth in some countries.

**9.** Outward-looking economic policies that encourage the spread of technology and investment have worked better than inward-looking economic policies, as a comparison of different countries shows.

**10.** In many countries today, including Eastern Europe, Russia, Latin America, and China, there is great potential for higher economic growth as the market system is being encouraged and restrictions on entrepreneurs are being removed.

**11.** Another great growth wave would change the economic landscape of the whole world.

# KEY TERMS

| | | |
|---|---|---|
| catch-up line | newly industrialized country | International Monetary Fund (IMF) |
| North-South problem | country in transition | World Bank |
| economic development | informal economy | conditionality |
| developing country | foreign direct investment | import substitution strategy |
| industrialized country | portfolio investment | export-led strategy |

# QUESTIONS FOR REVIEW

**1.** Why does economic growth theory predict that productivity and real income per capita will grow relatively more rapidly in poor countries?

**2.** Why is catch-up observed among the industrialized economies but not for the whole world?

**3.** Why is the identity that investment plus net exports equals saving important for understanding the flow of capital around the world?

**4.** What is the difference between foreign direct investment and portfolio investment?

5. Why is human capital important for the spread of technology?

6. What is the significance of conditionality for IMF loans?

7. What do government restrictions on entrepreneurs have to do with economic growth?

8. What harm does an informal economy cause?

9. Why does export-led growth appear to work better than import substitution?

# PROBLEMS

1. Complete the following table assuming that the rate of growth of real GDP per capita stays constant. (*Hint:* see the appendix to Chapter 5.)

| Country/ Region | Real GDP per Capita in 1999 | Growth of Real GDP per Capita, 1999–2099 (annual percentage change) | Projected Real GDP per Capita in 2099 |
|---|---|---|---|
| United States | $32,000 | 1.5 | ——— |
| China | $ 3,400 | 7.5 | ——— |

2. What would be the effect of a decrease in the Japanese saving rate on the growth rate of developing countries? Why?

3. The rule of 72 gives the approximate doubling time of a variable if you know its rate of growth. For example, if the population of a country is 200 million and the rate of growth of the population is 2 percent per year, then it will take approximately 35 years for the country's population to reach 400 million. (See the appendix to Chapter 5 for a derivation.) Suppose real income per capita does not grow at all in the United States in the future. Suppose that the per capita growth rate is 4 percent per year in China. About how long will it take for China to catch up with the United States? What is likely to happen to the growth rates before this period of time passes? Use the per capita income data in problem 1.

4. Suppose a developing country does not allow foreign investment to flow into the country and, at the same time, it has a very low saving rate. Use the fact that saving equals investment and the growth accounting formula to explain why this country will have difficulty catching up with industrialized countries. What else can it do to improve its productivity if it does not allow capital in from outside the country?

5. Developed countries have shown that Malthus was wrong to ignore capital and technology, but he also ignored the possibility that people would have fewer children.

a) Examine the growth accounting formula to explain how a reduction in the growth rate of labor affects the growth rate of productivity. Assume that the proportion of the population that is in the labor force is constant.

b) In developing countries, people sometimes view children as a way to ensure that they have support in their old age. How will this attitude affect the growth rate of income per capita?

6. The states of the United States have moved toward each other in real income per capita over the past 100 years, but the countries of the world have not. What are the differences between state borders and country borders that might explain this problem?

7. Most developing countries have low saving rates and governments that run budget deficits. What will be required for such countries to have large increases in their capital stocks? What will happen if industrialized countries' saving rates decline as well? How does this affect the developing countries' prospects for catching up?

8. Which of the following will increase the likelihood of poor countries catching up to rich countries, and which will decrease the likelihood? Explain.

a) Industrialized countries do not allow their technology to be bought or leased by firms in developing countries.

b) Industrialized countries increase the conditional aid that is available for developing countries.

c) Worldwide saving rates fall.

d) Countries place high tariffs on importation of goods.

e) The legal system of developing countries is improved to protect the rights of entrepreneurs.

f) Governments in developing countries make use of their international aid to buy armaments from developed countries.

g) Investment in human capital increases in the developing countries.

9. Plot on a scatter diagram the data for the Asian countries that appears at the top of the next page. Does there appear to be a catch-up line in the scatter diagram?

| Country | Per Capita Real GDP in 1965 (1984 U.S. dollars) | Average Annual Rate of Growth from 1965 to 1985 (%) |
|---|---|---|
| Thailand | 360 | 4.0 |
| Pakistan | 210 | 2.4 |
| Philippines | 380 | 1.9 |
| China | 110 | 5.1 |
| Malaysia | 330 | 4.3 |
| Indonesia | 190 | 4.6 |

**10.** The International Monetary Fund (IMF) estimated that a decline in the world saving rate by 1 percentage point, due to a decline in Japanese saving, would increase the world interest rate by about 75 basis points.[1] Using a diagram like the one in the box on page 472, explain the reasoning behind the IMF's estimate. How large an interest rate rise would you predict from the diagram in the box?

1. *World Economic Outlook,* International Monetary Fund, May 1995, p. 88.

# 20

# Emerging Market Economies

There is perhaps no greater economic policy challenge and opportunity around the world today than the emergence of market economies. The tearing down of the Berlin Wall, the end of central planning in East Germany, and the unification of Germany are stirring symbols of this emergence. So is the end of central planning in Russia, the countries of central and Eastern Europe, and countries in the Transcaucasian and central Asian regions, such as Armenia, Georgia, and Mongolia. The emergence of market economies is also seen in China and Vietnam. A common feature of these countries is that a major transition is occurring—a transition from a *command economy,* or a centrally planned economy in which the government sets prices and decides *what, how,* and *for whom* goods should be produced, to a *market economy* that is based much more on markets and freely determined prices, in which most of these decisions are left to individuals.

Similar attempts to reduce government restrictions on markets are occurring in many other countries in Latin America and Asia. Although these economies were not formerly centrally planned, international and domestic trade was tightly restricted, and major parts of the economies were government owned. In recent years, Argentina, Chile, Mexico, and India have either reduced

government control of large segments of their economies or encouraged closer ties with market economies around the world, or both. Mexico recently joined a free trade agreement with the United States and Canada, while Chile and other countries of Latin America are anxious to join.

Table 20.1 provides a list of countries designated by *Economist* magazine as emerging market economies; clearly the list goes well beyond the former centrally planned economies. Even though the *Economist*'s list is not comprehensive (neither Mongolia, Ukraine, nor Vietnam are included), it demonstrates that the phenomenon of emerging markets is very widespread.

Although the long-run goals of the emerging market economies are to raise economic growth and improve living standards, the short-run problems of moving from a centrally planned economy to a market economy are particularly difficult. In fact, economic growth has faltered in some countries that are trying to make a transition from central planning to a market economy, especially in central and Eastern Europe and the former Soviet Union. People of these countries have shown signs of frustration and impatience with the transition.

In this chapter we take a special look at those emerging market economies that are making a transition from

**TABLE 20.1**

**Emerging Market Economies as Defined by the *Economist***

| | Population (millions) | | Population (millions) | | Population (millions) |
|---|---|---|---|---|---|
| China | 1,260 | Thailand | 64 | Portugal | 11 |
| Hong Kong | 6 | Argentina | 36 | South Africa | 51 |
| India | 1,018 | Brazil | 170 | Turkey | 70 |
| Indonesia | 219 | Chile | 15 | Czech Republic | 11 |
| Malaysia | 22 | Colombia | 39 | Hungary | 10 |
| Philippines | 82 | Mexico | 103 | Poland | 40 |
| Singapore | 3 | Venezuela | 23 | Russia | 151 |
| South Korea | 48 | Greece | 11 | TOTAL | 3,491 |
| Taiwan | 22 | Israel | 6 | | |

*Source:* Population figures are projections for the year 2000 from the *Statistical Abstract of the United States, 1995,* pp. 845–846.

central planning. To understand what is happening now, we need to look back at what economic life was like under central planning. We first show how central planning grew out of the communist revolutions that were induced by the Marxist criticism of market economies. We then examine the aim of market reforms, alternative approaches to reform, and the experience of several economies during the transition.

> **command economy:** an economy in which the government determines prices and production; also called a centrally planned economy. (Ch. 1)

> **market economy:** an economy characterized by freely determined prices and the free exchange of goods and services in markets. (Ch. 1)

# CENTRALLY PLANNED ECONOMIES

With few exceptions, such as the North Korean economy, centrally planned economies no longer exist. But there are important economic lessons to be learned from the experience of the many countries that tried central planning during the twentieth century. A well-known expert on the ideas underlying communism, socialism, and the market economy, Robert Heilbroner, summarizes the lessons this way: "The Soviet Union, China and Eastern Europe have given us the clearest possible proof that capitalism organizes the material affairs of humankind more satisfactorily than socialism."[1]

A socialist economy, also called **socialism,** is an economic system in which the government owns the capital—factories, stores, farms, and equipment—and decisions about production and employment are made by those who run the government as part of a central plan for the economy. In contrast, in a market economy, also called **capitalism,** individuals own the capital, and decisions about production and

> **socialism:** an economic system in which the government owns and controls all the capital and makes decisions about prices and quantities as part of a central plan.

> **capitalism:** an economic system based on a market economy in which capital is individually owned, and production and employment decisions are decentralized.

1. See Robert Heilbroner, "The Triumph of Capitalism," *The New Yorker,* January 1993, pp. 98–109.

**communism:** an economic system in which all capital is collectively owned.

employment are decentralized and made by many individuals buying and selling goods in markets. The term **communism** refers to a theoretical situation where all the people of a country *collectively* own the capital and the land without direct government ownership. Those who advocated communism viewed collective ownership by the people as a long-term goal: A socialist economy would evolve into communism with the government gradually withering away. However, today most economists and historians use the word *communism,* to mean the same thing as *socialism,* as defined here.

Not all socialist economies are the same; there are different degrees of government ownership and centralization. For example, in some socialist economies, farmers could sell a portion of their agricultural output and use the proceeds to buy farm equipment or even consumer goods. Similarly, not all market economies are the same; in most market economies, the government owns the public infrastructure capital and is involved in the production of education, health services, and other goods. The degree of government involvement differs from market economy to market economy. For example, a much larger fraction of medical care is produced by the government in the United Kingdom than is produced by the government in the United States.

However, in reality the differences between socialist economies as a group and market economies as a group are much larger than the differences between the economies within each group. In other words, there is a "night-and-day" distinction between centrally planned economies with government ownership of firms that do not have to compete and market economies with private ownership of firms that do have to compete. To understand this distinction, we need to examine how centrally planned economies worked.

## Central Planning in the Soviet Union

V. I. Lenin and the Bolshevik party (also known as the Communist party) gained control of the government of Russia in the October Revolution of 1917. At this time, the Russian economy was much less developed than most of Western Europe. GDP per capita in Russia was less than one-third that of the United Kingdom or the United States. The economy was mostly agricultural. Although large-scale manufacturing industries were growing, they were still much smaller than those in Germany, the United Kingdom, or the United States. For more than 1,000 years, before the communists gained control, Russia had been ruled by tsars, who held enormous power and resisted economic and political change.

For those reasons, the Russian people were dissatisfied with both their economy and their political system. Lenin and the Bolsheviks seized the opportunity, forcing through a completely new economic system. Most significantly, Lenin decreed that private firms would be taken over by the government, a process called **nationalization.** The Bolsheviks immediately nationalized the banking system, and by mid-1918, a massive nationalization of large- and small-scale industry was under way. Although the alleged reason for the Bolshevik takeover was to give workers control of the economy, Lenin soon rejected worker control. He argued that people like himself were needed to run the economy on behalf of the workers. He began controlling production from the center, appointing administrators to run each industry from offices in Moscow. In doing so he laid the foundation of a command economy—through which government *diktats,* or commands, rather than prices and decentralized markets, would determine what was produced. In 1921, **Gosplan,** the state planning commission, was established. In 1922 the Communist party

**nationalization:** the taking over of private firms by the government.

**Gosplan:** the planning agency of the former Soviet Union.

# Karl Marx, 1818–1883

**BORN:**
Trier, Germany, 1818

**EDUCATION:**
University of Bonn, 1835
University of Berlin, 1836–1841
University of Jena, doctorate in philosophy, 1841

**JOBS:**
Editor, freelance journalist, Cologne, Paris, Brussels, 1842–1848
Independent study, freelance journalist, London 1849–1883

**MAJOR PUBLICATIONS:**
*Communist Manifesto* (with Friedrich Engels), 1848; *Das Kapital,* 1867
(Vol. I); Russian translation, 1868; English translation, 1886

What led to the rejection of markets and the acceptance of socialism in Russia, China, and Eastern Europe in the twentieth century? Although personal ambition, war, and political repression were factors, the economic writings of Karl Marx in the nineteenth century played a key role.

Karl Marx was an economist and social philosopher, but he was also an eloquent journalist and polemicist. Most of his work as an economist was spent analyzing capitalism. His most famous prediction was that capitalism would eventually die of its own internal contradictions.

Marx originally went to college to study law, but he soon was drawn to the writings of the philosopher Hegel, who characterized history as a struggle between conflicting forces; each idea (thesis) generated its opposite (antithesis), which it then had to contend with until a new thesis (synthesis) was created. This Hegelian view provided Marx with a framework to study the historical development of capitalism.

Marx soon became an outspoken critic of the existing economic and political system in Europe. He spent much of his adult life in London, studying and writing in the archives of the British Museum. Marx eked out a modest living—his wife and children struggling at the brink of poverty—through his journalistic writings and through financial assistance from his long-time friend and collaborator, Friedrich Engels.

Marx's polemical writings were influential. The widely read and often-quoted *Communist Manifesto* was a short pamphlet written in 1848 by Marx and Engels. It was nothing less than a stirring call for a revolution:

*A specter is haunting Europe—the specter of communism. . . . Let the ruling classes tremble at a Communist revolution. The proletarians have nothing to lose but their chains. They have a world to win. Working men of all countries, unite!*

Surprisingly, perhaps, Marx and Engels found much to admire in capitalism. They wrote that the *bourgeoisie—* the class that owned or ran the business firms

*. . . has accomplished wonders far surpassing the Egyptian pyramids, Roman aqueducts, and Gothic cathedrals. . . . [D]uring its rule of scarcely one hundred years, [it] has created more massive and more colossal productive forces than have all preceding generations together.*

It is in Marx's economic writings—longer and more ponderous—that his detailed criticism of capitalism is found. In particular, his treatise *Das Kapital* aimed to show why Adam Smith and David Ricardo were wrong in their praise of the market economy. For example, referring to Smith's idea that workers would benefit from increased labor productivity due to the division of labor or to more machinery, Marx wrote in *Das Kapital:*

*Adam Smith, by a fundamentally perverted analysis, arrives at [this] absurd conclusion. . . . In truth, Adam Smith breaks his investigation off, just where its difficulties begin.*

Marx argued instead that increases in labor productivity would not benefit workers; capitalists, trying to maintain their profits, would keep workers' wages from rising. But history shows that wages increased by huge amounts in the 150 years since Marx wrote.

Although socialism may have originally seemed like an attractive alternative to the market system, socialism's own severe problems eventually became obvious. Surprisingly, however, Marx wrote almost nothing about how a socialist economy would work. His writings focused entirely on capitalism.

*Sources of quotes:* Karl Marx and Friedrich Engels, *Communist Manifesto,* 1848, in *Essential Works of Marxism,* ed. A. P. Mendel (New York: Bantam Books, 1961), pp. 1, 44, and 16–17; Karl Marx, *Capital: A Critique of Political Economy* (New York: Modern Library, 1906), p. 647.

established the Soviet Union, incorporating Ukraine and other countries along with Russia into one large command economy.

At the very start, the experiment in central planning was unsuccessful. Production fell and inflation rose dramatically. Much of the blame for the early lack of success could be placed on the civil war between the communists (the Reds) and the anticommunists (the Whites). Moreover, Lenin had little guidance on how to set up a socialist economy. Karl Marx, whose analysis of capitalism provided the intellectual support for the communist revolution, wrote virtually nothing about how a socialist economy or central planning would work (see the box on Karl Marx). In any case, the early 1920s saw a retreat from central planning and a partial reinstatement of the market economy under Lenin's New Economic Policy. But with Lenin's death in 1924 and Joseph Stalin becoming leader of the Communist party's in 1928, central planning was reinstated with even more force than previously.

### The Five-Year Plans

The goal of catching up with Western Europe and the United States came quickly to dominate Stalin's thinking about the economy. Catching up required raising the level of investment in factories and industrial equipment, increasing labor hours, and shifting workers out of agriculture into industry. Stalin wanted to do this rapidly and on a massive scale. To do so he needed to raise investment in heavy industry and reduce consumption. He saw a command economy as the only way to accomplish his goal.

**five-year plan:** a document that stated production goals for the entire Soviet economy for the succeeding five years.

Stalin, therefore, gave Gosplan much more authority to run the economy from the center. In 1928 Gosplan issued a **five-year plan** stipulating production goals for the entire economy. This five-year plan turned out to be the first of a succession of many more five-year plans, and the methods of central planning that would last for 60 years were put in place. Gosplan, under command of the Communist party leaders, controlled production not only for Russia but for the entire Soviet Union, which was spread over eleven time zones and covered one-sixth of the world's land area.

**state enterprise:** an organization, analogous to a firm in a market economy, that is owned and controlled by the government.

Production of most goods took place at **state enterprises**—organizations similar in function to business firms in market economies but owned and controlled by the government. Stalin also virtually abolished private property in agriculture in the Soviet Union. He created **collectivized farms,** through which the government took ownership of most farmland, farm equipment, and livestock.

**collectivized farm:** a farm in a planned economy that is in theory collectively owned by peasants, but controlled by the government.

By setting **production targets** for millions of products throughout the Soviet Union, Gosplan tried to control what and how much should be produced at each state enterprise and collectivized farm. Through this method Stalin was successful in raising the level of investment and reducing people's consumption and thereby rapidly expanding the number of machines and factories devoted to manufacturing. In order to make sure that the labor force was sufficient for this rapid industrialization, the communist government also placed restrictions on workers. For example, new graduates were assigned jobs in different parts of the country, and restrictions on moving to and living in certain areas made it difficult for workers to change jobs if they wanted to.

**production target:** a goal set for the production of goods and services in a planned economy.

### Centrally Controlled Prices

Prices for individual goods were also set at the center, but Gosplan rarely set these prices at levels that would equate the quantity supplied with the quantity demanded. Shortages were typical. Food prices were set very low, resulting in food shortages.

The managers of state enterprises frequently found themselves having to wait for parts or inputs to production. At other times they produced an excess supply that no one could use. To be sure, when shortages got very severe, markets would develop: Enterprise managers in desperate need of materials would offer side payments, or bribes, to other managers or workers to get the materials. These markets operated outside of the normal central planning process and were called *gray* or *black markets*. Some economists feel that these markets enabled central planning to function by reducing crucial shortages.

Recall from Chapter 2 that prices have three roles: They transmit information, coordinate actions by providing incentives, and affect the distribution of income. In a market economy, a change in demand or supply causes a change in the price, which transmits information throughout the economy. Such changes in prices were thwarted by central planning. Central planners simply did not have enough information to know how to change the prices. Thus, the information transmission role of prices did not exist.

The coordination role of prices was deemphasized, although the central planners recognized that prices affected incentives. The managers of the state enterprises were given rewards for hitting production targets, but the rewards were not designed in a way that encouraged efficient management practices. To poke fun at Gosplan, a famous cartoon showed a picture of a nail factory producing *one* large but useless 500-ton nail in order to meet the factory's production target for 500 tons of nails. There were also few rewards for inventing new products or even for finding more efficient ways to produce the existing products. State enterprises thus became very inefficient. Competition between enterprises was discouraged, and production became highly concentrated in a few firms in each industry.

Gosplan did not ignore the role of prices in affecting the distribution of income. Prices were held low on most staple items and high on the few consumer durable items that were produced. By setting prices this way, Gosplan tried to make the distribution of goods and services more equal. But income distribution was by no means egalitarian under central planning. Communist party officials and enterprise managers were given extra payments in the form of better housing, transportation, and the opportunity to shop in stores that contained consumer goods unavailable to ordinary consumers. Because virtually all prices were set by the government, there was no measured inflation, although with prices set too low for many products the economy was frequently in a condition of shortage. The central bank (Gosbank) was the only bank in the country. It provided loans to state enterprises and collectivized farms in the amounts Gosplan instructed. Gosbank also issued currency (rubles) and accepted deposits from consumers.

Gosplan did not have to worry much about taxes because it could set the price of everything. For example, to finance the production of military goods, the central planners could set the price of inputs to defense production low and the price of defense goods high. They could also simply order increased production of military goods and reduced production of some other goods.

## Trade Between the Soviet Union and Eastern Europe

After World War II when communist governments were installed in Poland, Hungary, Czechoslovakia, East Germany, Romania, and Bulgaria, Soviet-style central planning was extended to each of the countries of Eastern Europe. How did international trade take place between the Soviet Union and its close neighbors in the Soviet bloc?

Trade among these countries and the Soviet Union took place through a trading organization called the *Council for Mutual Economic Assistance.* The trade did not take place at world market prices. For example, the Soviet Union, rich in energy resources such as oil and natural gas, would supply energy to the Eastern European countries at prices well below the market prices prevailing throughout the world. The prices were established through political negotiations between the governments, which undoubtedly involved noneconomic considerations such as the placement of military troops and weapons. In exchange for the low-priced energy, the Eastern European countries would provide manufactured goods, though those were of a lesser quality than similar goods produced in the West. Prices for trade between the countries of Eastern Europe were similarly negotiated. Thus, neither domestic nor international trade between the centrally planned economies was market based.

## Technological Change and the Quality of Goods

By most accounts Stalin's forced investment and forced labor strategy did increase economic growth in the 1930s in the Soviet Union. In the years after World War II both the Soviet Union and Eastern Europe grew rapidly. However, it eventually became apparent that great inefficiencies associated with central planning were starting to offset the high levels of investment and labor force participation. The growth of technology began to slow down. Investment rates and labor force participation rates had reached their limits, and technology growth was lagging seriously. Environmental pollution was severe in cities such as Warsaw and Bucharest.

State-owned retail shops had few consumer goods, and those they had were of very poor quality. Long lines were evident at stores, especially those selling anything special, such as candy bars or gasoline. The availability of goods was also poor.

One of the apparent puzzles about central planning was its success in certain areas. The space exploration achievements of the Soviet Union, for example, were outstanding enough for the United States to get involved in the space race. They were the source of President Kennedy's goal of a manned flight to the moon.

One explanation for this success was that an enormous amount of resources were put into defense production. Just as East German athletes dominated the Olympics because of all the resources that went into their training, a centrally planned economy could excel at certain things. Students with talents useful for defense production—mathematics, science, and engineering—were given excellent training in the Soviet Union. Even inefficiency can be offset by enough resources. Moreover, as mentioned previously, economists found that managers in defense production had ways to go outside the central planning system, essentially using gray markets to obtain parts or equipment in short supply. Such markets were tolerated more frequently in the defense industry than in consumer goods industries.

## From Perestroika to the End of the Soviet Union

Pressures to reform the central planning system began in the 1960s and 1970s and gained momentum in the 1980s. In 1985, Mikhail Gorbachev became the leader of the Communist party. To deal with the problems of inefficiency, poor quality, and slow technology growth, he tried to change central planning in a process called **perestroika,** which translates as "restructuring." Perestroika changes were put into the twelfth five-year plan, formulated in 1985. For example, enterprise managers were to be made more accountable for their actions through worker and public criti-

**perestroika:** the restructuring of the Soviet economy by reforming the central planning process.

cism. By 1989, however, it was clear that perestroika was doing little to raise economic growth. Economists complained perestroika was piecemeal because it continued to rely on the central planning process to set prices. An alternative plan, called the Shatalin Plan, after one of Gorbachev's advisers, would have used the market much more. However, it was rejected by Gorbachev because it would have initiated a transition to a market economy and thereby done away with central planning.

But perestroika started a process that would not easily be stopped. The open criticism of the central planning process made it acceptable to criticize the political authorities. Soon people in Eastern Europe were criticizing their own governments and their close ties with the Soviet Union. Gorbachev decided to "let go" of the Eastern European countries in 1989, and by 1990 the republics of the Soviet Union also wanted their freedom. Gradually the Russian Republic began to take over the responsibility for the Soviet Union. After an aborted military coup in 1991, Gorbachev resigned and the Soviet Union ceased to exist. Boris Yeltsin, the president of Russia, disbanded central planning and began to follow a more comprehensive series of reforms aimed at creating a market economy. Yeltsin's own reforms have also been opposed, and a political struggle will determine how successful Russia is in implementing the reforms.

## Soviet-Style Central Planning in China

The Chinese communists under Mao Zedong gained control of China in 1949. Mao's goals were similar to those of the Soviet Union—to rapidly industrialize. In fact, Mao originally viewed the Soviet Union as an economic model. He imported Soviet-style central planning to China. Under Mao and the Communist party, most economic production was controlled by the central government, just as in the Soviet Union. In the 1950s, growth was rapid due to heavy investment.

Starting in 1958, Mao began the "Great Leap Forward," which briefly raised economic growth by promoting a warlike work effort throughout the country calling for a massive expansion of production. But the Great Leap Forward could raise economic growth for only a short period. The communist spirit was not enough to make people work hard year after year. The Great Leap Forward ended in a huge decline in production.

A misguided attempt to revive the spirit of the communist revolution took place during the Cultural Revolution in the late 1960s. But the Cultural Revolution ended up severely hurting the Chinese economy. Productive managers and technicians were forced to leave their jobs and do manual labor. Universities were closed. By the late 1970s it was also clear that economic reform was necessary in China, a subject we will return to later in the chapter.

# Review

▶ Central control of the economy began in Russia soon after the Bolsheviks rose to power. Central planning grew and dominated the Soviet economy under Stalin in the 1920s and 1930s and spread to Eastern Europe and China after World War II.

▶ Although the high investment and high labor force participation led to strong growth initially, central planning eventually broke down. Inefficiency, poor-quality goods, and slow growth of technology were the most obvious problems.

# ALTERNATIVE PATHS TO A MARKET ECONOMY

How does a country change from central planning to a market economy? Recall that the first action of the Communists in Russia was to abolish private property rights and nationalize industry. One of the most difficult parts of reform has been to reverse this step, restoring private ownership and privatizing state enterprises.

## The Goals of Reform

Defining the goals of reform is simple; getting there is what is difficult. The goals are simply the essential ingredients of a market economy, as defined in Chapter 2. To summarize, these are:

▶ *Freely determined prices* evolving out of decentralized markets rather than prices controlled by government.

▶ *Property rights and incentives,* which the Hungarian economist Janos Kornai argues in his book *The Road to a Free Economy* are the most important and frequently underemphasized part of a market economy: Decentralizing decisions without prices providing incentives through property rights will not create efficiency.

▶ *Competitive markets* so that the price system leads to an efficient allocation of goods, labor, and capital.

▶ *Freedom to trade at home and abroad,* which is needed in order to achieve the efficiencies associated with comparative advantage and economies of scale.

▶ *A role for government* in establishing a policy that keeps inflation in check and that efficiently collects taxes to pay for public goods and provides a social safety net.

▶ *A role for nongovernment organizations,* because in a market economy many transactions occur within organizations—as, for example, when an entrepreneur sets up a new firm to market a new product.

There is general agreement that any successful transition from central planning to a market economy must achieve these features of a market economy. A legal system specifying property rights and enforcing contracts must be set up. A banking and currency system must be established. A system of tax collection must be put in place. As is true of many areas of economics, however, there is disagreement about the speed of the transition.

## Shock Therapy or Gradualism?

**shock therapy:** the abrupt introduction of free markets in a formerly centrally planned economy.

**gradualism:** the slow phasing-in of free market reforms.

A major question about the transition to a market economy is how fast it should be. The two basic alternatives are **shock therapy** and **gradualism.** Under shock therapy, or the *big bang* approach, all the elements of the market economy are put in place at once. Under gradualism, the reforms are phased in slowly.

One of the most remarkable aspects of the transition from central planning in the countries of Eastern Europe was the strong commitment to move to market economies on the part of government policymakers and the general public at the start of the reforms in 1989 and 1990. Most officials went out of their way to emphasize that they were not looking for a third way and to recognize the need to move to a Western-style market-based economic system in order to raise living standards.

Such positive attitudes about reform were part of the motivation behind shock therapy. Those in favor of a shock-therapy approach argue that such positive attitudes are probably temporary, creating a brief window of opportunity for reform. The enthusiasm for reform may diminish if, as is likely, the reforms do not bring noticeable improvements quickly. Thus, rather than see the reform movement aborted in midstream, it is better to sweep through the reforms quickly. This was one of the arguments for the shock-therapy approach that was used in Poland.

Another argument in favor of shock therapy is that all the elements of reform are interrelated. Making state enterprises private without competition, for example, could make things worse. And freeing up the price of energy products will reduce the government subsidy needed to finance the energy-producing enterprises. This will reduce the government budget deficit. Also, removing trade barriers and establishing a sound currency will be a guide to what the process should be as the free price system gropes for a new set of relative prices.

The arguments against shock therapy are that people require time to adjust to new circumstances. Enterprises producing medical supplies in Moscow might be used to getting cotton from central Asia, but if free trade makes it more attractive for central Asia to sell cotton in Japan, then production in Moscow will be disrupted.

Even though the production of low-quality black and white television sets in Warsaw is inefficient compared with imports from Malaysia, it might be better to move gradually to free trade. This would give the firms time to move into some other business and the workers time to find other jobs. The arguments against shock therapy are similar to the arguments against a fast disinflation strategy or against an immediate reduction in tariff barriers.

## Review

▶ The goals of a transition to a market economy are much easier to state than to achieve; the goals can be defined in terms of the key ingredients of a market economy.

▶ Shock therapy and gradualism are two different paths to a market-based economy.

## ECONOMIC REFORM IN PRACTICE

What has been the experience of those countries trying to make a transition from central planning to a market-based economy? Table 20.2 presents data on real GDP growth in the formerly centrally planned economies of central and Eastern Europe and the former Soviet Union. A quick glance at this table shows how difficult the transition has been. Although these countries had slow economic growth under communism, the period of transition has seen deep recession. In some countries the

| | Real GDP Growth (percent) | |
| --- | --- | --- |
| | 1992 | 1994 |
| Central and Eastern Europe | | |
| Albania | −9.7 | 7.4 |
| Estonia | −21.6 | 6.0 |
| Hungary | −4.3 | 2.6 |
| Latvia | −35.2 | 2.0 |
| Lithuania | −56.6 | 1.5 |
| Poland | 2.6 | 6.0 |
| Romania | −10.1 | 3.4 |
| Ukraine | −17.0 | −23.0 |
| Russia | −19.0 | −15.0 |
| Caucasus and Central Asia | | |
| Azerbaijan | −22.1 | −21.9 |
| Georgia | −42.7 | −10.0 |
| Kazakhstan | −14.0 | −25.0 |
| Tajikistan | −30.0 | −16.3 |
| Uzbekistan | −11.1 | −2.6 |

*Source: World Economic Outlook,* May 1995. By permission of International Monetary Fund.

decline in real GDP has been nearly as large as the decline in real GDP during the Great Depression in the United States. There are significant signs of improvement in the countries of central and Eastern Europe, except for Ukraine. But Russia and many of the central Asian countries continue to suffer transition problems.

To understand the problems of transition, we must look more carefully at the countries undertaking the transitions. Consider two countries—Poland and China—that have been undergoing a transition for several years and that have achieved positive economic growth.

## Reforms in Poland

Poland was the first country in Eastern Europe to start a transition to a market economy. The Polish program has typified the shock-therapy approach.

Four months after the reform program was put in place in Poland, there were many visible signs of its effects, including a decline in inflation and a reduction of shortages. Inflation, which averaged 420 percent in 1989 and 1990, had fallen to 25 percent by 1992, but the adjustment costs, as evidenced by large declines in production and employment, were painful. Real GDP declined by 12 percent in 1990 and another 7 percent in 1991. However, by 1992 real GDP had stopped falling and showed a small increase. By 1994 economic growth was 6 percent, as shown in Table 20.2.

The Polish stabilization program made use of several policy initiatives. Government expenditures and the budget deficit were reduced sharply, largely through a reduction in government subsidies to state enterprises and a halting of public infrastructure investment. Most prices were deregulated at once and were left to be determined by state enterprises or private firms. Coal prices increased significantly, but internal transportation prices and rents remained low. Wage growth was controlled by government guidelines.

The result of these policies was a substantial decline in demand. There was also a reduction in shortages—the lines of people waiting to be served in butcher shops disappeared, for example. This reduction was brought on partly by the decline in demand, but also because free prices began to bring the quantity supplied into equality with the quantity demanded. Goods started appearing on the shelves, and firms could get intermediate inputs without long delays. Imported consumer goods, most noticeably fruit and vegetables, were more available. The trade account went into surplus in 1990 with exports increasing rapidly and imports declining rapidly.

At the start of the reform program, employment declined surprisingly little despite the large declines in production. The unemployment rate increased only to about 2 percent of the work force in the first few months of the program, but then unemployment increased sharply. Many workers were laid off because the state enterprises needed to reduce wage costs in order to avoid losses as the demand for their products dropped.

In order for a market economy to take root, it is necessary that existing state enterprises be privatized, a process called **privatization,** and that new private firms be able to start up. Moreover, private investment from abroad provides technological know-how. Privatization helps provide managers with the incentive to allocate resources efficiently and increase productivity.

**privatization:** the process of converting a government enterprise into a privately owned enterprise.

The Polish government submitted a privatization bill to the Parliament after the economic reforms began in 1990, but it moved slowly because of extensive debates. The main controversial issue was over who owned the state enterprises that were being sold. Hence, privatization was one part of the Polish reform program that was gradual.

A useful assessment of the Polish economic reforms comes from the person who implemented them firsthand on a day-to-day basis. Leszek Balcerowicz, who was the Polish finance minister in charge of the reforms, put it this way in 1993:

Even successful economic reforms generate some dissatisfaction. Such reforms transform hidden unemployment into open unemployment and produce shifts in the relative pay and prestige of many groups. New entrepreneurs, managers, lawyers, accountants, etc., are on the way up and—as a result—some powerful groups such as miners are on the way down. Not everybody can make a direct use of radically enlarged economic freedom, and those who can't often look with envy at the new ingroups.

But it is a mistake to reject the radical economic reforms simply because they produce these side effects. Postponing difficult steps is even more costly and risky socially, as a look at Ukraine or Russia shows. Radical reforms, as distinct from muddling through, also produce economic dynamism. Despite inherited hyperinflation and shortages, Poland has had a positive rate of growth since late 1991, and this year it is going to be the fastest growing country in Europe. Poland's decline in aggregate consumption in 1990–91 was by far the smallest among the Central and Eastern European countries.[2]

## Reforms in China

Market-based reforms began in China earlier than in the former Soviet Union. The first reforms were in the agriculture sector. By the late 1970s, the Chinese government was leasing land back to individual farmers in order to give them more incentive to produce. The reform resulted in a huge increase in the growth rate of farm

2. From, "Why the Leftists Won the Polish Election, " from *The Wall Street Journal,* September 28, 1993, Section A, p. 10.

output. Agriculture production grew by 3 percent per year from 1952 to 1978; from 1978 (when the reforms began) to 1981, the growth rate was about 6 percent per year. Moreover, the increased efficiency in agriculture has increased the supply of labor in the industrial sector.

By the mid-1980s, about the same time as perestroika was starting in the Soviet Union, economic reforms were already spreading beyond the farm sector. Individual state enterprises were first given more discretion to experiment with new products and to use the profits generated from those products. As in the case of agriculture, industrial enterprises were leased to the managers, who could then keep part of the profits. As a result of these reforms, real GDP growth increased rapidly. Economic growth averaged a remarkably rapid 9.6 percent per year from 1987 to 1994. During the 1990s real GDP was falling in Russia.

China also reduced restrictions on foreign trade. In fact, much of China's growth has come from producing goods for foreign trade. Exports grew even more rapidly than real GDP. However, reform of exchange rates and monetary policy came much later in China. Free exchange of the local currency in terms of foreign currency was fully established only in 1993. And by the early 1990s, inflation was starting to become a problem in China. The inflation rate reached 22 percent in 1994.

To summarize, the overall reform in China has been much more gradual than in Poland. But economists continue to debate whether the gradual reform is better or worse than shock therapy.

## Review

▶ Poland took the lead in major economic reform in Eastern Europe. Its reform program is the prototype of shock therapy.

▶ The transition has been hard on the Polish economy. However, real GDP growth started increasing in 1992 and reached 6 percent in 1994. Institutions have been put in place that will help foster the market economy in the future.

▶ China started its market-based reforms in the late 1970s by selling off a large amount of land to the farmers. Controls on state enterprises have been lifted more gradually.

# ECONOMIC FREEDOM AND POLITICAL FREEDOM

Free markets and political freedom are not the same thing. Free markets, or economic freedom, allow people to engage freely in trade without restriction. Political freedom allows people to engage in free speech or to vote for their political representatives without restriction.

In principle a society can have political freedom without economic freedom—people could vote for central planning and price controls. Or a society could have economic freedom without political freedom: A dictator could allow people to trade without restrictions. Economists and political scientists have long debated whether there is a tendency for political freedom and economic freedom to exist together.

In abolishing private property and establishing central planning it is clear that Lenin and Stalin placed severe restrictions on people's political freedom. Indeed, millions who refused to go along with Stalin's program were imprisoned or executed. Thus, as practiced, socialism stifled both economic and political freedom. By abolishing private property it eliminated one of the key ingredients of a free market economy. But by abolishing democracy where it existed, or preventing its establishment through totalitarian dictatorship, it also restricted political freedom.

Central planning as practiced in the Soviet Union, China, and Eastern Europe resulted in a great loss of economic freedom along with a great loss of political freedom. Central planning was run by dictatorships. In order to carry out the collectivization of agriculture and forced investment and labor strategy of the 1930s the Soviet government had to imprison or execute many people. And the effort to restore a market economy and end central planning in Russia and Eastern Europe has been associated with an increase in democracy and political freedom.

However, the association of political and economic restrictions under communism does not prove that economic freedom and political freedom are necessarily connected. Throughout history there are examples where economic freedom has increased while political freedom has been repressed and vice versa. Many refer to China in the late 1980s as an example: A highly publicized and televised confrontation between dissident students and the government in Beijing indicated that the move toward free markets was not necessarily a move to political freedom.

## Review

▶ The relationship between political freedom and economic freedom has long been of interest to economists and political scientists.

▶ History has shown that there is no causal relationship between democracy and free markets. There is, however, a close relationship between economic progress and political freedom. Most countries today with high real GDP per capita are also democracies with few restrictions on political freedom.

# CONCLUSION

It was the economic failure of central planning and strict state control that led to socialism's demise. The failure of the centrally planned economy in East Germany in comparison with the success of the market economy in West Germany was as close as the real world ever gets to a controlled experiment. But if the emerging market economies do not deliver economic success for the people of these regions—a success that will be as obvious as was the failure of socialism—it is likely that there will be more changes, perhaps for the worse. And the success or failure of the market reforms in one country strongly influences what goes on elsewhere. Policymakers in Latin American countries say that the spirit of economic and political reform in those countries was stimulated by the "revolution of 1989" in Eastern Europe.

As we have seen in this chapter, the countries that are attempting a transition to a market economy have a difficult task before them. There have been setbacks, and there are likely to be more. The people of the United States, Japan, and Europe have a historic opportunity to participate and support the emerging market economies through developing links, investing, and providing technical cooperation, assistance, and advice. They have much to gain if the transition is successful.

# KEY POINTS

**1.** The term *emerging market economies* usually refers to both former centrally planned economies making the transition to market economies and to developing economies that have recently increased privatization and reduced restrictions on trade.

**2.** Central planning and state control grew out of the communist revolutions under Lenin in Russia in 1917 and under Mao in China in 1949. Central planning was extended to central and Eastern Europe after World War II. At communism's height, over one-third of the world's population lived in centrally planned economies.

**3.** By mounting an intellectual criticism of the classical economists' model, Marx spearheaded the communist revolutions that eventually led to central planning.

**4.** Most centrally planned economies grew rapidly in their early stages due to heavy investment, but eventually productivity growth slowed down sharply and even declined.

**5.** The transition from central planning to a free market economy is much more difficult than the reverse transition. The road from socialism to free markets will be long, with the gains perhaps not noticeable for many years.

**6.** There are two different approaches to transition: shock therapy and gradualism.

# KEY TERMS

| | | |
|---|---|---|
| socialism | five-year plan | shock therapy |
| capitalism | state enterprise | gradualism |
| communism | collectivized farms | privatization |
| nationalization | production targets | |
| Gosplan | perestroika | |

# QUESTIONS FOR REVIEW

**1.** When did central planning begin, and why?

**2.** What led to dissatisfaction with central planning and the end of socialism in Russia?

**3.** What comparison of countries is most useful for demonstrating the inefficiencies of central planning?

**4.** What are the six goals of an economic reform program?

**5.** What is the difference between shock therapy and

gradualism in the transition to a market economy?

**6.** What political argument favors shock therapy?

**7.** In what sense was the Polish reform program shock therapy, and in what sense was it more gradual?

**8.** Describe the difference between economic freedom and political freedom.

# PROBLEMS

**1.** In 1960 Mao Zedong wrote, "The whole Socialist camp headed by the Soviet Union . . . now accounts for nearly 40 percent of the world's . . . gross industrial output . . . and it will not be long before it surpasses the gross industrial output of all the capitalist countries put together." Explain

why such a statement was believable at the time, and why the prediction turned out to be so inaccurate.

**2.** Why was central planning successful in increasing real GDP growth for a while? Why did real GDP growth eventually falter under central planning?

**3.** Design a gradual program for transition from central planning to a market-based economy. Explain how the basic features of a market economy will be achieved. Defend your plan against a proposal for a shock-therapy approach.

**4.** Explain why it may be easier to move from a market economy with private property to a command-and-control economy without private property than the other way around. Give a real-world example to prove your point.

**5.** Describe Gosplan's role during the period of central planning in the former Soviet Union.

**6.** Has Poland or China had an easier time with the transition from central planning? Why do you think this is the case?

**7.** "Economic freedom and political freedom necessarily go together." Is this statement valid? Explain.

**8.** Could state-owned firms be made to operate as if they were private firms? For example, suppose that the managers of the state enterprises were instructed to maximize profits with prices and wages set by the central planners. According to the Hungarian economist Janos Kornai, the answer to this question is no. In *The Road to a Free Economy,* he writes, "It is futile to expect a state-owned unit to behave as if it were privately owned." Provide an argument supporting Kornai's view. Be sure to mention the role of prices as well as the role of private property and incentives.

**9.** Compare and contrast how the three key questions—*how, what,* and *for whom* goods and services should be produced—are dealt with in a centrally planned economy versus in a market economy.

**10.** Comment on the validity of the following statement made by Fareed Zakaria in the *New York Times Book Review* on March 30, 1997. Support your answer with historical examples and economic reasoning: "Capitalism was and is a destructive and revolutionary phenomenon. It leveled European feudalism and aristocracy, then proceeded, in this century, to destroy statism, both fascist and communist. It has created a dynamic, materialistic, and dominating global culture with an aspiring middle class at its helm."

# 21

# The Gains from International Trade

On July 4, 1993, an explosion in a Sumitomo Chemical factory in Japan sent the price of computer memory chips soaring by 50 percent all over the world. Why? This factory made 65 percent of the world's supply of a special epoxy used to seal computer memory chips in their cases. When investigative reporters asked why the market was so concentrated at one firm, they found that the company was a low-cost producer; despite the small demand for this epoxy in Japan or in any one country, by producing for the world market, this factory could specialize, invest heavily in research, and achieve low-cost production. Such concentration and specialization are not unusual. The computer firm Intel dominates the world market for the computer memory chip, the brain of the PC. Another Japanese firm, Kyocera, supplies 70 percent of the market for the ceramic that surrounds the memory chip. In fact, inside the typical PC are parts of materials made in scores of different countries.

Later on that same day in the United States, Americans celebrated Independence Day. Many listened to tapes and CDs on electronic equipment made in Malaysia. Others played tennis wearing Nike shoes made in Korea or went swimming in Ocean Pacific swimsuits made in Sri Lanka. Still others looked at their Casio digital watches made in Mexico to be sure they would not miss the fireworks. A few even drove to the celebration in German cars. In the meantime, the people in other countries who had made the products Americans imported—such as the Malaysians, Koreans, Sri Lankans, Mexicans, and Germans—were buying American products: Caterpillar tractors, Motorola cellular phones, Microsoft Windows, Boeing 747s, and Merck pharmaceuticals to remove parasites from livestock or treat heart attacks.

These examples demonstrate two important reasons why people benefit from international trade. First, international trade allows firms such as Sumitomo Chemical and Intel to reduce costs by selling products to larger markets throughout the world. Second, international trade allows different countries to specialize in producing what they are relatively efficient at producing, such as pharmaceuticals in the United States and digital watches in Mexico.

This chapter explores the reasons for these gains from trade. After discussing some of the differences between international trade and within-country trade, we examine the arguments Adam Smith originally made in favor of international trade. We then develop models that economists use to study and measure the gains from international trade.

# TRADE AND SOVEREIGNTY

**International trade** is trade between people or firms in different countries. Trade between people in Seattle and Vancouver, Canada, is international trade, whereas trade between Seattle and Anchorage is trade within a country. Thus, international trade is just another kind of economic interaction; it is subject to the same basic economic principles as trade between people in the same country.

**international trade:** trade between people or firms in different countries.

**commerce clause:** the clause in the U.S. Constitution that prohibits restraint of trade between states.

## Sovereign National Governments

International trade differs from trade in domestic markets, however, because countries are governed by their own laws and sovereign national governments. Sovereign national governments frequently place restrictions on trade between countries that they do not place on trade within countries. For example, the Texas legislature cannot prohibit the import of Florida oranges into Texas. The **commerce clause** of the U.S. Constitution forbids such restraint of trade between states. But the United States is a sovereign government. It can restrict or put taxes on the import of oranges from Brazil. Similarly, Japan can restrict the import of rice, and Australia can put taxes on the import of Japanese automobiles. The United States can also restrict the export of goods such as high-technology computers if it fears other countries may use the computers for military purposes. Many countries also have immigration laws that limit the movement of people between countries but not within countries.

Because each country has its own sovereign national government, intervention in the international economy—for good or for bad—may require international negotiation when policy actions taken in one country affect another country. Negotiations between governments may go beyond economics to areas such as national security. Dealing simultaneously with both economic and related noneconomic issues makes international economic policy challenging and interesting.

## Recent Trends in International Trade

International trade has grown much faster than trade within countries in recent years. Figure 21.1 shows the trade in goods and services between countries for all countries in the world as a percent of world GDP. International trade has doubled as a proportion of world GDP during the last 30 or so years. Why has international trade grown so rapidly? There are two main reasons.

First, the cost of transportation and communication has been reduced dramatically. Air travel, telephone, and computer linkages have declined in price relative to

**FIGURE 21.1**
**Rapidly Expanding International Trade**
International trade has increased faster than GDP in the last 30 or so years as trade restrictions and the cost of transportation and communications have gone down. International trade is measured as the sum of exports of all countries. The graph shows international trade as a percent of world GDP.

INTERNATIONAL TRADE AS A PERCENT OF WORLD GDP

other goods and services. The cost of air travel fell to 11 cents per mile in 1990 from 68 cents per mile in 1930, while the cost of a three-minute phone call from New York to London fell to $3 in 1990 from $245 in 1930 (adjusting the 1930 prices for general inflation).

Second, and perhaps even more important, government restrictions on trade between countries have come down. Western European countries are integrating into a single market. Canada, Mexico, and the United States have agreed to integrate their economies into a free trade area, where the term *free* indicates the elimination of restrictions on trade. Previously closed economies have opened themselves to world trade through major political and economic reforms. The formerly closed economies in Eastern Europe, Russia, and China, for example, are anxious to join the world trading system. Export-oriented countries in Asia are growing rapidly, and governments in South America such as Argentina and Chile are opening their economies to competition and foreign trade.

These countries are making these changes in an effort to help people. But why does international trade help them? Let's now consider that question.

## Review

▶ The basic principles of economics apply to international trade between countries just as they apply to domestic trade within countries.

▶ A greater tendency for governments to interfere with trade between countries, national sovereignty, and restrictions on immigration are reasons

international trade must be given special treatment by economists and economics textbooks.

▶ International trade has grown rapidly in recent years, most likely because of reduced transportation costs and lower government barriers to trade.

# THE ATTACK ON MERCANTILISM

**mercantilism:** the notion, popular in the 1700s, that the wealth of a nation was based on how much it could export in excess of its imports, and thereby accumulate precious metals.

**export:** the sale of goods and services abroad.

**import:** the purchase of goods and services from abroad.

**net exports:** the value of goods and services sold abroad minus the value of goods and services bought from the rest of the world; exports minus imports.

Adam Smith was one of the first economists to show why the people of a country benefit from trade with other countries. International trade issues are woven throughout Smith's 1776 *Wealth of Nations,* and he devoted special chapters to international trade. Although the world and economics have changed substantially since the time of Adam Smith, many of his points still hold and are worth knowing.

The prevailing economic wisdom at the time Smith wrote his book was **mercantilism,** which held that countries would grow wealthy by accumulating gold and silver. They would do so by *exporting*—selling goods and services abroad—as much as possible, and by *importing*—buying goods and services abroad—as little as possible. In other words, a mercantilist policy tries to maximize **exports** minus **imports**—or what is called **net exports,** or the foreign trade balance. With exports greater than imports, so the mercantilist argument went, foreigners would have to pay the country gold and silver, which the country could then accumulate.

Adam Smith attacked mercantilism and, in contrast, put forth the revolutionary idea that the wealth of a nation depends on the incomes of the people in the country and what they are able to consume, not on the gold and silver held by the monarchs and nobles. According to Smith, imports rather than exports are the purpose of trade; imports of goods and services rather than the accumulation of gold and silver improve people's standard of living. The only reason to export is to pay for imports. Imposing **tariffs,** or taxes on imports, to limit imports for the purpose of accumulating gold and silver serves only to impoverish a nation. "It is not by the importation of gold and silver, that the discovery of America has enriched Europe," he wrote. "By the abundance of the American mines, those metals have become cheaper. A service of plate can now be purchased for about a third [of what] it would have cost in the fifteenth century."[1] Instead of the tariffs advocated by the mercantilists, Smith proposed a policy of **free trade**—the elimination of tariffs on imports. Smith put forth four specific reasons why a country could gain from trade: (1) mutual gains from voluntary exchange of existing goods, (2) increased competition, (3) the division of labor, and (4) better use of skills and resources in different countries. We briefly summarize all four and develop the last two in more detail in the remainder of the chapter.

**tariff:** a tax on imports.

**free trade:** a complete lack of restrictions on international trade.

## Mutual Gains from Voluntary Exchange of Existing Goods

We have emphasized that when two people voluntarily exchange existing goods, they mutually gain, even though there is no increase in the amount of goods in the economy. People benefit from voluntary exchange by reaching a preferred combination of the different goods than before trade. Adam Smith emphasized this mutual benefit and argued that it applies just as well to people in different countries as to people in the same country.

But the gains from trade go beyond the benefits of exchanging existing goods. Trade can increase the amount of goods by making production more efficient.

## Increased Competition

International trade makes the home market more competitive. This lowers prices. In Smith's words, "By restraining, either by high duties, or by absolute prohibitions, the importation of such goods from foreign countries as can be produced at home, the monopoly of the home market is more or less secured to the domestic industry . . ."[2]

Adam Smith's analysis of the competition effects of international trade applies very well to modern times. We see evidence of trade spurring on competition in many industries, from automobiles to steel to telecommunications. Competition from abroad helped improve the quality and reduce the price of cars in the United States. It also helped reduce the price and improve the quality of telephones and beef in Japan.

## The Division of Labor

Smith identified the division of labor as a key reason for trade. The division of labor reduces costs since each worker can specialize and develop expertise in a certain area. But the division of labor requires that the market for the good be large. There is much less opportunity for the division of labor in an automobile firm producing 1,000 cars than in one producing 1,000,000 cars.

In other words, the size of the market is key to Smith's idea of the division of labor, and, with international trade, the markets can be larger. In fact, the title of one chapter in the *Wealth of Nations* is "That the division of labour is limited by the

1. Adam Smith, *Wealth of Nations* (New York: Modern Library, 1994), p. 476.
2. Ibid., p. 481.

extent of the market." In this chapter, Smith showed how international trade would increase the size of the market and allow for a greater division of labor. He argued, for example, that the nations along the shores of the Mediterranean Sea developed because of the ease of navigation on relatively calm waters. Trade with other nations over a vast area allowed for much larger markets.

### Better Use of Skills and Resources in Different Countries

A fourth part of Smith's analysis of the gain from trade focused on the differences between countries. Smith argued that countries can gain from trade if they export things that they are good at producing and import things that other countries are good at producing. For example, the United States and Colombia can gain from trade if the United States produces wheat, which it can produce more cheaply than Colombia, and Colombia produces coffee, which it can produce more cheaply than the United States.

Smith supported this view with commonsense analogies: "It is the maxim of every prudent master of a family, never to attempt to make at home what it will cost him more to make than to buy." Or, "The taylor does not attempt to make his own shoes, but buys them from the shoemaker."[3]

Although correct as far as it goes, Smith's analysis of international differences did not go far enough. It was not until David Ricardo developed the theory of comparative advantage in 1817 that it was clear that the tailor could gain from trading with the shoemaker even if the tailor could produce both clothes and shoes better than the shoemaker. We examine comparative advantage in the next section and show that it is a powerful argument for international trade that goes well beyond examples like coffee and wheat.

## Review

▶ The mercantilists argued that a country could grow wealthy by exporting more than it imports and thereby accumulating gold and silver. Adam Smith argued that rather than gold and silver, it is people's consumption of goods and services that makes a country wealthy.

▶ He proposed a policy of free trade rather than the high tariffs advocated by the mercantilists. He gave four reasons why there would be gains from trade: mutual benefits from exchanging existing goods, increased competition, lower costs through the division of labor, and better use of skills and resources in different countries.

## COMPARATIVE ADVANTAGE

David Ricardo's theory of comparative advantage shows how a country can improve the income of its citizens by allowing them to trade with people in other countries, even if the people of the country are less efficient at producing all items.

3. Ibid., p. 485.

The United States, for example, may be more efficient than Korea in the production of both pharmaceutical goods and electronic goods. Even so, it may make sense for the United States to trade with Korea.

## A Simple Example of Comparative Advantage

Consider first a parable to convey the general idea of comparative advantage. Rose is a highly skilled computer programmer who writes computer-assisted drawing programs. Rose owns a small firm that sells her programs to architects. She hires an experienced salesman, Sam, to contact the architects and sell her software. Thus, Rose specializes in programming, and Sam specializes in sales.

Let us complicate the story. Rose is a friendly, outgoing person and, because she knows her product better than Sam does, she is better at sales than Sam. We say that Rose has an **absolute advantage** over Sam in both programming and sales because she is better at both jobs. But it still makes sense for Rose to hire Sam because her efficiency at programming compared to Sam's is greater than her efficiency at sales compared to Sam's. We say that Rose has a *comparative advantage* over Sam in programming rather than in sales. If Rose sold her programs, then she would have to sacrifice her programming time, and her profits would fall. Thus, even though Rose is better at both programming and sales, she hires Sam to do the selling so she can program full time.

All this seems sensible. However, there is one additional part of the terminology that may at first seem confusing but is important. We said that Rose has the comparative advantage in programming, not in sales. But who does have the comparative advantage in sales? Sam does. Even though Sam is less efficient at both sales and programming, we say he has a comparative advantage in sales because, compared with Rose, he does relatively better at sales than he does at programming. A person cannot have a comparative advantage in both of only two activities.

**absolute advantage:** a situation in which a person or country is more efficient at producing a good in comparison with another person or country.

**comparative advantage:** a situation in which a person or country can produce one good more efficiently than another good in comparison with another person or country. (Ch. 2)

### *Opportunity Cost, Relative Efficiency, and Comparative Advantage*

The idea of comparative advantage can also be explained in terms of *opportunity cost.* The opportunity cost of Rose or Sam spending more time selling is that she or he can produce fewer programs. Similarly, the opportunity cost of Rose or Sam spending more time writing programs is that she or he can make fewer sales.

Observe that, in the example, Sam has a lower opportunity cost of spending his time selling than Rose does; thus, it makes sense for Sam to do the selling rather than Rose. In contrast, Rose has a lower opportunity cost of spending her time writing computer programs than Sam does; thus, it makes sense for Rose to write computer programs rather than Sam.

Opportunity costs give us a way to define comparative advantage: A person with a lower opportunity cost of producing a good than another person has a comparative advantage in that good. Thus, Rose has a comparative advantage in computer programming, and Sam has a comparative advantage in sales.

Comparative advantage can also be explained in terms of relative efficiency: A person who is relatively more efficient at producing good X than good Y compared to another person has a comparative advantage in good X. Thus, again, we see that Rose has a comparative advantage in computer programming because she is relatively more efficient at producing computer programs than making sales compared to Sam.

**opportunity cost:** the value of the next-best foregone alternative that was not chosen because something else was chosen. (Ch. 2)

### From People to Countries

Why is this story about Rose and Sam a parable? Because we can think of Rose and Sam as two countries that differ in efficiency at producing one product versus another. In the parable, Rose has a comparative advantage over Sam in programming, and Sam has a comparative advantage over Rose in sales. In general, *country A has a comparative advantage over country B in the production of a good if the opportunity cost of producing the good in country A is less than in country B,* or alternatively but equivalently stated, *if country A can produce the good relatively more efficiently than other goods compared to country B.* Thus, if you understand the Rose and Sam story, you should have no problems with the American and Korean story, which we now examine in more detail.

## Trade Between Countries: Pharmaceuticals and Electronics

Consider the following two goods: (1) pharmaceutical goods—vaccines, antibiotics, antidepressants, analgesics, and treatments for high blood pressure or cholesterol; and (2) electronic goods—TV sets, boom boxes, portable stereos, electronic keyboards, and compact disk players. Different skills are required for the production of pharmaceuticals and electronic goods. Pharmaceutical production requires investment, knowledge of chemistry and biology, and the marketing of products where doctors make most of the choices. Producing electronic goods requires investment, knowledge of electrical engineering and microcircuitry, and the marketing of goods where consumers make most of the choices.

Table 21.1 provides an example of productivity differences in the production of pharmaceutical goods and electronic goods in two different countries, the United States and Korea. Productivity is measured by the amount of each good that can be produced by a worker per day of work. To be specific, let us suppose that the pharmaceutical goods are vaccines measured in vials, that the electronic goods are TV sets measured in numbers of TV sets, and that labor is the only factor of production in making vaccines and TV sets. The theory of comparative advantage does not depend on any of these assumptions, but they make the exposition much easier.

According to Table 21.1, in the United States it takes a worker one day of work to produce 6 vials of vaccines or 3 TV sets. In Korea one worker can produce 1 vial of vaccine or 2 TV sets. Thus, the United States is more productive than Korea in both vaccines and TV sets. We say that a country has an *absolute advantage* over another country in the production of a good if it is more efficient at producing that good. In this example, the United States has an absolute advantage in both vaccine and TV set production.

**TABLE 21.1**
**Pharmaceutical and Electronic Goods Productivity in the United States and Korea**
(hypothetical example)

| | Output per Day of Work | |
| --- | --- | --- |
| | Pharmaceutical Goods (vials of vaccine) | Electronic Goods (number of TV sets) |
| United States | 6 | 3 |
| Korea | 1 | 2 |

However, the United States has a comparative advantage over Korea in the production of vaccines rather than TV sets. To see this, note that a worker in the United States can produce 6 times as many vials of vaccine as a worker in Korea but only 1.5 times more TV sets. In other words, the United States is relatively more efficient in vaccines than in TV sets compared with Korea. Korea, being able to produce TV sets relatively more efficiently than vaccines compared to the United States, has a comparative advantage in TV sets.

Observe also how opportunity costs determine who has the comparative advantage. To produce 3 more TV sets, the United States must sacrifice 6 vials of vaccine; in other words, *in the United States the opportunity cost of 1 more TV set is 2 vials of vaccine*. In Korea, to produce 2 more TV sets, the Koreans must sacrifice 1 vial of vaccine; in other words, *in Korea, the opportunity cost of 1 more TV set is only ½ vial of vaccine*. Thus, we see that the opportunity cost of producing TV sets in Korea is lower than in the United States. By examining opportunity costs, we again see that Korea has a comparative advantage in TV sets.

**Electronics versus Pharmaceuticals**

In the hypothetical example used in this chapter, Korea has a comparative advantage in electronics and the United States has a comparative advantage in pharmaceuticals. Thus, with trade between Korea and the United States, electronic goods will be produced in Korea, as shown in the left-hand photo, and pharmaceutical goods will be produced in the United States, as shown in the right-hand photo.

### An American Worker's View

Because labor productivity in both goods is higher in the United States than in Korea, wages are higher in the United States than in Korea in the example. Now think about the situation from the point of view of American workers who are paid more than Korean workers. They might wonder how they can compete with Korea. The Korean workers' wages seem very low compared to theirs. It doesn't seem fair. But as we will see, comparative advantage implies that American workers can gain from trade with the Koreans.

### A Korean Worker's View

It is useful to think about Table 21.1 from the perspective of a Korean worker as well as a U.S. worker. From the Korean perspective, it might be noted that Korean workers are less productive in both electronic goods and pharmaceutical goods. Korean workers might wonder how they can ever compete with the United States, which looks like a productive powerhouse. The U.S. workers are more productive in both types of goods. Again, it doesn't seem fair. As we will see, however, the Koreans can also gain from trade with the Americans.

## The Relative Price of Pharmaceutical Goods and Electronic Goods

To measure how much the Koreans and Americans can gain from trade we need to consider the *relative price* of pharmaceutical goods and electronic goods in Korea and the United States. The relative price describes how many pharmaceutical goods can be traded for electronic goods and, therefore, how much each country can gain from trade. For example, suppose the price of TV sets is $200 and the price of a vial of vaccine is $100. Then 2 vials of vaccine cost the same as 1 TV set; we say the relative price is 2 vials of vaccine per TV set. The next few paragraphs show how to determine the relative price from data on the costs of production.

### Relative Price Without Trade

First, let us find the relative price with no trade between the countries. The relative price of two goods should depend on the relative costs of production. A good for which the cost of producing an additional quantity is relatively low will have a relatively low price.

Consider the United States. In this example, a day of work can produce either 6 vials of vaccine or 3 TV sets. With labor as the only factor of production, 6 vials of vaccine cost the same to produce as 3 TV sets; that is, 2 vials of vaccine cost the same to produce as 1 TV set. Therefore, the relative price should be 2 vials of vaccine per TV set.

Now consider Korea. Electronic goods should have a relatively low price in Korea because they are relatively cheap to produce. A day of work can produce either 1 vial of vaccine or 2 TV sets; thus 1 vial of vaccine costs the same to produce as 2 TV sets in Korea. Therefore, the relative price is ½ vial of vaccine per TV set.

### Relative Price with Trade

Now consider what happens when both countries trade without government restrictions. If transportation costs are negligible and markets are competitive, then the price of a good must be the same whether it is in the United States or Korea. Why? Because any difference in price would quickly be eliminated by trade; if the price of TV sets is much less in Korea than in the United States, then traders would buy TV sets in Korea and sell them in the United States and make a profit; by doing so, however, they reduce the supply of TV sets in Korea and increase the supply in the United States. This would drive up the price in Korea and drive down the price in the United States until the price of TV sets in the two countries was the same. Thus, with trade, the price of vaccines and the price of TV sets will converge to the same levels in both countries. The relative price will therefore converge to the same value in both countries.

If the relative price is going to be the same in both countries, then we know the price must be somewhere between the price in each country before trade. That is, the price must be between 2 vials of vaccine per TV set (the U.S. relative price) and ½ vial of vaccine per TV set (the Korean relative price). We do not know exactly

**Another example of relative prices:**
Price of Phish concert = $45
Price of Phish T-shirt = $15
Relative price = 3 T-shirts per concert

| | United States | Korea |
|---|---|---|
| Relative price before trade: | 2 vials of vaccine per TV set | ½ vial of vaccine per TV set |
| Relative price range after trade: | Between ½ and 2 | Between ½ and 2 |
| Relative price assumption: | 1 | 1 |

**TABLE 21.2**
**The Relative Price**
The relative price must be the same in both countries with trade (vials of vaccine per TV set).

where the price will fall in between ½ and 2. It depends on the *demand* for vaccines and TV sets in Korea and the United States. Let us assume that the relative price is 1 vial of vaccine per TV set after trade, which is between ½ and 2 and a nice, easy number for making computations. The calculation of the price with trade is summarized in Table 21.2.

The relative price of vaccines and TV sets after trade—which we have assumed to be 1 vial per TV set—is called the *terms of trade*. In general, the **terms of trade** for a country are given by the quantity of imported goods that it can obtain per unit of exported goods. As we will see, Korea will be exporting TV sets and importing vaccines, while the United States will be exporting vaccines and importing TV sets.

**terms of trade:** quantity of imported goods a country can obtain in exchange for a unit of exported goods.

## Comparative Advantage and Gains from Trade

What are the **gains from trade** due to comparative advantage? First, consider some examples.

**gains from trade:** improvements in income, production, or satisfaction owing to the exchange of goods or services.

### One Country's Gain

Suppose that 10 American workers move out of electronics production and begin producing pharmaceuticals. We know from Table 21.1 that these 10 American workers can produce 60 vials of vaccine per day. Formerly, the 10 American workers were producing 30 TV sets per day. But their 60 vials of vaccine can be traded for TV sets produced in Korea. With the relative price of 1 vial per TV set, Americans will be able to exchange these 60 vials of vaccine for 60 TV sets. Thus, Americans gain 30 more TV sets by moving 10 more workers into vaccine production. This gain from trade is summarized in Table 21.3.

### The Other Country's Gain

The same thing can happen in Korea. A Korean manufacturer can hire 30 workers who were formerly working in vaccine production to now produce TV sets. Vaccine production declines by 30 vials, but TV production increases by 60 TV sets. These 60 TV sets can be traded with Americans for 60 vials of vaccine. The reduction in the production of vaccine of 30 vials results in an import of vaccine of 60 vials; thus, the gain from trade is 30 vials of vaccine. The Koreans, by moving workers out of vaccine production and into TV set production, are getting more vaccine. This gain from trade for Korea is summarized in Table 21.3. Observe that the exports of TV sets from Korea equal the imports of TV sets to the United States.

**TABLE 21.3**
**Changing Production and Gaining from Trade in the United States and Korea**

**United States**

|  | Change in Production | Amount Traded | Net Gain from Trade |
|---|---|---|---|
| Vaccines | Up 60 vials | Export 60 vials | 0 |
| TV Sets | Down 30 sets | Import 60 sets | 30 sets |

**Korea**

|  | Change in Production | Amount Traded | Net Gain from Trade |
|---|---|---|---|
| Vaccines | Down 30 vials | Import 60 vials | 30 vials |
| TV Sets | Up 60 sets | Export 60 sets | 0 |

### *Just Like a New Technique*

International trade is like the discovery of a new idea or technique that makes workers more productive. It is as if workers in the United States figure out how to produce more TV sets with the same amount of effort. Their trick is that they actually produce vaccines that are then traded for the TV sets. Like any other new technique, international trade improves the well-being of Americans. International trade also improves the well-being of the Koreans; it is as if they discovered a new technique, too.

## Graphical Illustration of the Gains from Trade

The gains from trade due to comparative advantage can also be illustrated graphically with production possibilities curves, as shown in Figure 21.2. There are two graphs in the figure—one for the United States and the other for Korea. In both graphs the horizontal axis has the number of TV sets and the vertical axis has the number of vials of vaccine produced.

### *Production Possibilities Curves Without Trade*

The solid purple lines in the two graphs show the production possibilities curves for vaccines and TV sets in the United States and in Korea before trade. To derive them we assume, for illustrative purposes, that there are 10,000 workers in the United States and 30,000 workers in Korea who can make either vaccines or TV sets.

If all the available workers in the United States produce vaccines, then total production will be 60,000 vials of vaccine (6 × 10,000) and zero TV sets. Alternatively, if 5,000 workers produce vaccines in the United States and 5,000 workers produce TV sets, then total production will be 30,000 vials of vaccine (6 × 5,000) and 15,000 TV sets (3 × 5,000). The solid line in the graph on the left of Figure 21.2 shows these possibilities and all other possibilities for producing vaccines and TV sets. It is the production possibilities curve without trade.

Korea's production possibilities curve without trade is shown by the solid purple line in the graph on the right of Figure 21.2. For example, if all 30,000 Korean workers produce TV sets, a total of 60,000 TV sets can be produced (2 × 30,000). This and other possibilities are on the curve.

**United States**

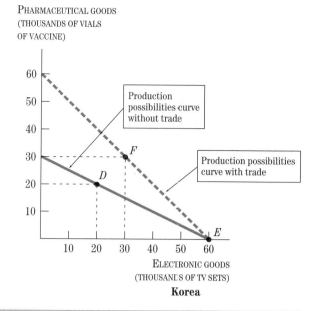

**Korea**

The slopes of the two production possibility curves without trade in Figure 21.2 show how many vials of vaccine can be transformed into TV sets in Korea and the United States. The production possibilities curve for the United States is steeper than for Korea because an increase in production of 1 TV set reduces vaccine production by 2 vials in the United States but by only ½ vial in Korea. The slope of the production possibilities curve is the opportunity cost; the opportunity cost of producing TV sets in the United States is higher than it is in Korea.

### Production Possibilities Curves with Trade

The dashed purple lines in the two graphs in Figure 21.2 show the different combinations of vaccine and TV sets available in Korea and the United States when there is trade between the two countries at a relative price of 1 vial of vaccine for 1 TV set. These dashed lines are labeled "production possibilities curve with trade" to contrast them with the "production possibilities curve without trade" label on the solid line. The diagram shows that the production possibilities curves with trade are shifted out compared with the curves without trade.

To see how the production possibilities curve with trade is derived, consider how the United States could move from point *A* to point *C* in Figure 21.2. At point *A* Americans produce and consume without trade 15,000 TV sets and 30,000 vials of vaccine by having 5,000 workers in each industry. Now suppose all U.S. workers move out of TV set production into vaccine production, shifting U.S. production to zero TV sets and 60,000 vials of vaccine, as shown by point *B*. Then by trading some of the vaccine, Americans can obtain TV sets. As they trade more vaccine away, they move down the production possibilities curve with trade: 1 less vial of vaccine means 1 more TV set along the curve. If they move to point *C* in the diagram, they have traded 30,000 vials for 30,000 TV sets. Americans now have

**FIGURE 21.2**
**Comparative Advantage**

The production possibilities curves show electronic goods production (TV sets) versus pharmaceutical production (vaccines) in Korea and the United States. On the left, Americans are better off with trade because the production possibilities curve shifts out with trade; thus, with trade, Americans can reach a point like *C* rather than *A*. The gains from trade due to comparative advantage are shown by the distance between the two production possibilities curves—one with trade and the other without trade. On the right, Koreans are also better off because their production possibilities curve shifts out; thus, Koreans can reach point *F*, which is better than point *D*. To reach this outcome, Americans specialize in producing at point *B* and Koreans specialize in producing at point *E*.

30,000 TV sets and are left with 30,000 vials of vaccine. By producing more vaccine, the Americans get to purchase more TV sets. The distance from point *A* (before trade) to point *C* (after trade) in Figure 21.2 is the gain from trade: 15,000 more TV sets.

It would be possible, of course, to choose any other point on the production possibilities curve with trade. If Americans prefer more TV sets and fewer vaccines, they could move down along that dashed line, trading more of their vaccine for more TV sets. In general, the production possibilities curve *with* trade is further out than the production possibilities curve *without* trade, indicating the gain from trade.

Observe that the slope of the production possibilities curve with trade is given by the relative price: the number of vials of vaccine that can be obtained for a TV set. When the relative price is 1 vial per TV set, the slope is $-1$ because 1 less vial gives 1 more TV set. If the relative price were $\frac{1}{2}$ vial per TV set, then the production possibilities curve with trade would be flatter.

The gains to Korea from trade are illustrated in the right-hand graph of Figure 21.2. For example, at point *D*, without trade, Koreans produce 20,000 TV sets with 10,000 workers and, with the remaining 20,000 workers, produce 20,000 vials of vaccine. With trade, they shift all production into TV sets, as at point *E* on the right graph. Then they trade the TV sets for vaccine. Such trade allows more consumption of vaccine in Korea. At point *F* in the right diagram the Koreans could consume 30,000 vials of vaccine and 30,000 TV sets, which is 10,000 more of each than before trade at point *D*. As in the case of the United States, the production possibilities curve shifts out with trade, and the size of the shift represents the gain from trade.

This example of Americans and Koreans consuming more than they were before trade illustrates the *principle of comparative advantage: By specializing in producing products in which they have a comparative advantage, countries can increase the amount of goods available for consumption.* Trade increases the amount of production in the world; it shifts out the production possibilities curves.

### Increasing Opportunity Costs: Incomplete Specialization

One of the special assumptions in the example we have used to illustrate the theory of comparative advantage in Table 21.3 and Figure 21.2 is that opportunity costs are constant rather than increasing. It is because of this assumption that the production possibilities curves without trade in Figure 21.2 are straight lines rather than the bowed-out lines that we studied in Chapter 2. With increasing opportunity costs, the curves would be bowed out.

The straight-line production possibilities curves are the reason for complete specialization, with Korea producing no vaccines and the United States producing no TV sets. If there were increasing opportunity costs, as in the more typical example of the production possibilities curve, then complete specialization would not occur. Why? With increasing opportunity costs, as more and more workers are moved into the production of vaccines in the United States, the opportunity cost of producing more vaccine will rise. And as workers are moved out of vaccine production in Korea, the opportunity cost of vaccine production in Korea will fall. At some point the U.S. opportunity cost of vaccine production may rise to equal Korea's, at which point further specialization in vaccine production would cease in the United States. Thus, with increasing opportunity costs and bowed-out production possibilities curves there will most likely be incomplete specialization. But the principle of comparative advantage is not changed by increasing opportunity costs. By specializing to some degree in the goods they have a comparative advantage in, countries can increase world production. There are still substantial gains from trade, whether between Rose and Sam or between America and Korea.

## Review

▶ Comparative advantage shows that a country can gain from trade even if it is more efficient at producing every product than another country. A country has a comparative advantage in a product if it is relatively more efficient at producing that product than the other country.

▶ The theory of comparative advantage predicts that there are gains from trade from increasing production

in the good a country has a comparative advantage in and reducing production of the other good. By exporting the good it has a comparative advantage in, a country can increase consumption of both goods.

▶ Comparative advantage is like a new technology in which the country effectively produces more by having some goods produced in another country.

# REASONS FOR COMPARATIVE ADVANTAGE

What determines a country's comparative advantage? There are some obvious answers. For example, Central America has a comparative advantage over North America in producing tropical fruit because of weather conditions: Bananas will not grow in Kansas or Nebraska outside of greenhouses.

In most cases, however, comparative advantage does not result from differences in climate and natural resources. More frequently, comparative advantage is due to decisions by individuals, by firms, or by the government in a given country. For example, a comparative advantage of the United States in pharmaceuticals might be due to investment in research and in physical and human capital in the areas of chemistry and biology. An enormous amount of research goes into developing technological know-how to produce pharmaceutical products.

In Korea, on the other hand, there may be less capital available for such huge expenditures on research in the pharmaceutical area. A Korean comparative advantage in electronic goods might be due to a large, well-trained work force that is well suited to electronics and small-scale assembly. For example, the excellent math and technical training in Korean high schools may provide a large labor force for the electronics industry.

## Dynamic Comparative Advantage

Comparative advantages can change over time. In fact, the United States did have a comparative advantage in TV sets in the 1950s and early 1960s before the countries of east Asia developed skills and knowledge in these areas. A country may have a comparative advantage in a good it has recently developed, but then technology spreads to other countries, which develop the comparative advantage, and the first country goes on to something else.

Perhaps the United States's comparative advantage in pharmaceuticals will go to other countries in the future, and the United States will develop a comparative

**dynamic comparative advantage:** changes in comparative advantage over time from investment in physical and human capital and in technology.

advantage in other, yet unforeseen areas. The term **dynamic comparative advantage** describes changes in comparative advantage over time because of investment in physical and human capital and in technology.

## Factor Abundance of Countries and Factor Intensity of Industries

To illustrate the importance of capital for comparative advantage, imagine a world in which all comparative advantage can be explained through differences between countries in the amount of physical capital that workers have to work with. It is such a world that is described by the Heckscher-Ohlin model, named after the two Swedish economists, Eli Heckscher and Bertil Ohlin, who developed it. Ohlin won a Nobel Prize for his work in international economics. The Heckscher-Ohlin model provides a particular explanation for comparative advantage.

Here is how comparative advantage develops in such a model. Suppose America has a higher level of capital per worker than Korea. In other words, America is **capital abundant** compared to Korea, and—what amounts to the same thing—Korea is **labor abundant** compared to America. We noted how pharmaceutical production uses more capital per worker than electronics production; in other words, pharmaceutical production is relatively **capital intensive,** while electronics production is relatively **labor intensive.** Hence, it makes sense that the United States has a comparative advantage in pharmaceuticals: The United States is relatively capital abundant, and pharmaceuticals are relatively capital intensive. On the other hand, Korea has a comparative advantage in electronics because Korea is relatively labor abundant, and electronics are relatively labor intensive. Thus, the Heckscher-Ohlin model predicts that if a country has a relative abundance of a factor (labor or capital), it will have a comparative advantage in those goods that require a greater amount of that factor.

**capital abundant:** a higher level of capital per worker in one country relative to another.

**labor abundant:** a lower level of capital per worker in one country relative to another.

**capital intensive:** production that uses a relatively high level of capital per worker.

**labor intensive:** production that uses a relatively low level of capital per worker.

### The Leontief Paradox

Of course, the relative amount of physical capital compared to labor cannot explain all of comparative advantage: Human capital and research are also important. In fact, the economist Wassily Leontief (who also won a Nobel Prize) showed in a famous paper in 1953 that the United States tended to export goods that are more labor intensive than the goods it imports. At the time Leontief's paper was published, this finding was taken as a major puzzle because, by most measures, the United States had been a relatively capital-abundant country. His finding is still called the **Leontief paradox.**

**Leontief paradox:** the inconsistency that Wassily Leontief found between the data on U.S. trade and the Heckscher-Ohlin model.

However, it turned out that U.S. exports require more human capital—worker education and training—and more research than U.S. imports. For example, scientists and engineers were found to be more important in producing U.S. exports than they were in producing U.S. imports. And research and development expenditures were found to be more important in U.S. exports than in U.S. imports. Including these other factors helped explain the Leontief paradox because the United States had a relative abundance in these research and human capital factors.

### Factor-Price Equalization

An important implication of the Heckscher-Ohlin model is that trade will tend to bring factor prices (the price of labor and the price of capital) into equality in different countries. In other words, if the comparative advantage between Korea and the

United States was due only to differences in relative capital and labor abundance, then trade would tend to increase real wages in Korea and lower real wages in the United States.

More generally, trade tends to increase demand for the factor that is relatively abundant in a country and decrease demand for the factor that is relatively scarce. This raises the price of the relatively abundant factor and lowers the price of the relatively scarce factor. Suppose the United States is more capital abundant than Korea and has a comparative advantage in pharmaceuticals, which are more capital intensive than electronics. Then with trade, the price of capital would rise relative to the price of labor in the United States. The intuition behind this prediction—which is called **factor-price equalization**—is that demand for labor (the relatively scarce factor) shifts down with trade as the United States increases production of pharmaceuticals and reduces its production of electronic goods. On the other hand, the demand for capital (the relatively abundant factor) shifts up with trade. Although there is no immigration, it is as if foreign workers compete with workers in the labor-scarce country and bid down the wage. Because technology also influences wages and productivity, it has been hard to detect such movements in wages. Wages in the developed world with high productivity due to high levels of technology remain well above wages in the less-developed world with low productivity due to low levels of technology.

In other words, changes in technology can offset the effects of factor-price equalization on wages. If trade raises technological know-how sufficiently, then no one has to suffer from greater trade. In our example of comparative advantage, American workers are paid more than Korean workers both before and after trade; that is because their overall level of productivity is higher. Workers in countries with higher productivity will be paid more than workers with lower productivity even in countries that trade.

Factor-price equalization can explain another phenomenon: growing wage disparity in the United States during the past 25 years in which the wages of high-skilled workers have risen relative to the wages of less-skilled workers. The United States is relatively abundant in high-skilled workers and developing countries are relatively abundant in low-skilled workers. Thus high-skilled workers' wages should rise and low-skilled workers' wages should fall in the United States, according to factor-price equalization. In this application of factor-price equalization, the two factors are high-skilled workers and low-skilled workers.

In the next section, we show that there are gains in efficiency and lower cost from trade that can benefit all workers.

**factor-price equalization:** the equalization of the price of labor and the price of capital across countries when they are engaging in free trade.

# Review

▶ Comparative advantage changes over time and depends on the actions of individuals in a country. Comparative advantage is determined partly by physical and human capital and partly by technology in the country relative to other countries. It is not solely bestowed on the country through natural resources or a good climate. Thus, comparative advantage is a dynamic concept.

▶ International trade will tend to equalize wages in different countries. Technological differences, however, can keep wages high in high-productivity countries. The greater dispersion of wages in the developed countries in recent years may be partially due to international trade. Nevertheless, if trade increases productivity, wages can rise for all workers.

# GAINS FROM EXPANDED MARKETS

In the introduction to this chapter and in the discussion of Adam Smith's writings, we stressed the gains from trade that come from larger-sized markets. Having discussed the principle of comparative advantage, we now examine this other source of the gains from trade.

## An Example of Gains from Trade Through Expanded Markets

Let us start with a simple example. Consider two countries such as the United States and Germany that are similar in resources, capital, and skilled labor. Suppose there is a market in Germany and the United States for two medical diagnostic products—magnetic resonance imaging (MRI) machines and ultrasound scanners. Suppose the technology for producing each type of diagnostic device is the same in each country. We assume that the technology is identical because we want to show that trade will take place without differences between the countries.

Figure 21.3 illustrates the situation. Without trade, both Germany and the United States produce 1,000 MRIs and 1,000 ultrasound scanners. This amount of production meets the demand in the two separate markets. The cost per unit of producing each MRI unit is $300,000, while the cost per unit of producing each ultrasound scanner is $200,000. Again, these costs are the same in each country.

### *Effects of a Larger Market*

Now suppose that the two countries trade. Observe in Figure 21.3—and this is very important—that the *cost per unit* of producing MRIs and ultrasound scanners *declines as more are produced.* Trade increases the size of the market for each product. In this example the market is twice as large with trade than without it: 2,000 MRIs rather than 1,000 and 2,000 ultrasound scanners rather than 1,000. The production of MRIs in the United States can expand, while the production of ultrasound scanners in the United States can contract. Similarly, the production of ultrasound scanners in Germany can expand, and the production of MRIs in Germany can contract. By specializing production of MRIs in the United States, the cost per unit of MRIs declines to $150,000. Similarly, the cost per unit of ultrasound scanners declines to $150,000. The United States exports MRIs to Germany so that the number of MRIs in Germany can be the same as without trade, and Germany exports ultrasound scanners to the United States. The gain from trade is the reduction in cost per unit. This gain from trade has occurred without any differences in the efficiency of production between each country.

Note that we could have set up the example differently. We could have had Germany specializing in MRIs and the United States specializing in ultrasound scanner production. Then the United States would have exported ultrasound scanners and Germany would have exported MRIs. But the gains from trade would have been exactly the same. Unlike the comparative advantage motive for trade, the expanded markets motive cannot alone predict what the direction of trade will be.

### *Intraindustry Trade versus Interindustry Trade*

MRIs and ultrasound scanners are similar products; they are considered to be in the same industry, the medical diagnostic equipment industry. Thus, the trade between

**United States**

Production: 1,000 MRI units
Cost: $300,000 per unit

Production: 1,000 ultrasound units
Cost: $200,000 per unit

No Trade

**Germany**

Production: 1,000 MRI units
Cost: $300,000 per unit

Production: 1,000 ultrasound units
Cost: $200,000 per unit

**United States**

Production: 2,000 MRI units
Cost: $150,000 per unit

U.S. exports 1,000 MRI units to Germany.

Germany exports 1,000 ultrasound units to U.S.

**Germany**

Production: 2,000 ultrasound units
Cost: $150,000 per unit

**FIGURE 21.3**
**Gains from Global Markets**
In this example, the technology of producing magnetic resonance imaging (MRI) machines and ultrasound scanners is assumed to be the same in the United States and Germany. In the top panel, with no trade between the United States and Germany, the quantity produced is low in each country and the cost per unit is high. With trade, the U.S. firm increases its production of MRIs and exports to Germany; the German firm increases its production of ultrasound scanners and exports to the United States. As a result, cost per unit comes down significantly.

Germany and the United States in MRIs and ultrasound scanners is called **intraindustry trade,** which means trade in goods in the same industry.

In contrast, the trade that took place in the example of comparative advantage was **interindustry trade,** because vaccines and TV sets are in different industries. In that example, the exports of vaccines from the United States greatly exceed imports of vaccines, producing a U.S. industry trade surplus in vaccines. Imports of TV sets into the United States are much greater than exports of TV sets, producing a U.S. industry trade deficit in TV sets.

These examples convey an important message about international trade. Trade due to comparative advantage tends to be interindustry, and trade due to expanded markets tends to be intraindustry. In reality, a huge amount of international trade is intraindustry trade. This indicates that creating larger markets is an important motive for trade.

**intraindustry trade:** trade between countries in goods from the same or similar industries.

**interindustry trade:** trade between countries in goods from different industries.

## Measuring the Gains from Expanded Markets

The medical equipment example illustrates how larger markets can reduce costs. To fully describe the gains to trade from larger markets, we need to consider a model.

# Talking Points on the Gains from Trade

Modern-day advocates of freer trade frequently emphasize that larger markets generate gains for consumers. To promote trade agreements in the 1990s, people who worked for Presidents Bush and Clinton made speeches and held meetings with members of Congress and many other interested groups. Many of their "talking points"—short phrases circulated around the administration that people can easily remember and repeat—focused on the gains from trade through larger markets. Examples of actual talking points used are:

▶   *The further integration of North American manufacturing facilities and the resulting product rationalizations would increase trade and the competitiveness of U.S. producers.*

▶   *U.S. companies operating in both Mexico and the United States will be able to reduce costs through product rationalization. They will no longer have to make the same vehicle, or the same parts for those vehicles, in two countries.*

▶   *Removal of internal distortions and economies of scale would enhance the international competitiveness of the North American automotive industry.*

Observe how close these talking points are to the model illustrated in Figure 21.4. The term *economies of scale* refers to the decline in cost per unit. *Product rationalization* refers to locating production in fewer factories in order to reduce cost per unit. (*Internal distortions* means that trade barriers had caused factories to be too small.)

The application of economics to gains from international trade due to larger markets is referred to as "new trade theory" because much of the research took place in the last 15 years. As the talking points indicate, the theory is already being used in practice.

### A Relationship Between Cost per Unit and the Number of Firms

Let us first establish the principle exemplified in the medical equipment example: As the number of firms in a market of a given size increases, the cost per unit at each firm increases because each firm produces less. This is shown in the four graphs on the left of Figure 21.4, where four identical firms are shown. With one firm in the market, cost per unit is $10, but cost per unit rises to $30 when four firms are in the market.

Next observe the situation in the four graphs on the right of Figure 21.4. These graphs represent the same four firms, but now the size of the market is larger. By comparing the graphs on the left (smaller market) with those on the right (larger market) we see that an increase in the size of the market reduces cost per unit at each firm, holding the number of firms constant in the industry. For example, when there is one firm in the market, cost per unit is $5 for the larger market compared with $10 for the smaller market. Or with four firms, cost per unit is $25 for the larger market compared with $30 for the smaller market. Compare the little tables in Figure 21.4. As the market increases in size, each firm produces at a lower cost per unit.

Figure 21.5 summarizes the information in Figure 21.4. It shows the positive relationship between the number of firms in the market, shown on the horizontal axis, and the cost per unit at each firm. As the figure indicates, more firms mean a higher cost per unit at each firm. (Be careful to note that the horizontal axis in Figure 21.5 is the *number* of firms in a given *market,* not the quantity produced by a given firm.) When the size of the market increases, the relationship between the number of firms in the market and the cost per unit shifts down, as shown in Figure 21.5. In other words, as the market increases in size, cost per unit declines at each firm if the number of firms does not change.

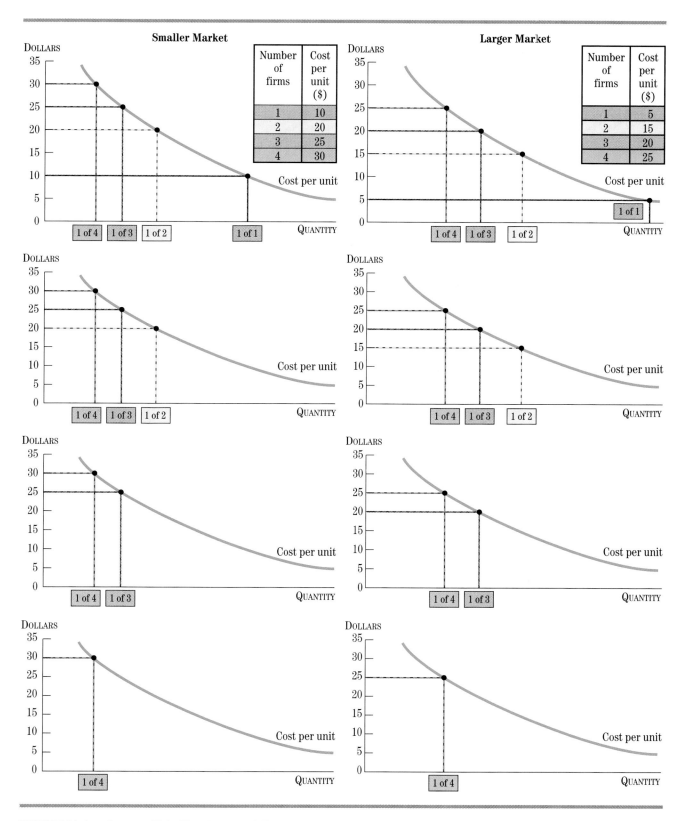

**FIGURE 21.4     Cost per Unit: The Number of Firms and Market Size**

**FIGURE 21.5**
**The Relationship Between Cost
per Unit and the Number of Firms**

The first four points on each curve
are plotted from the two tables in
Figure 17.4 for 1 to 4 firms; the
other points can be similarly
obtained. Each curve shows how
cost per unit at each firm rises as
the number of firms increases in a
market of a given size. The curve
shifts down when the size of the
market increases.

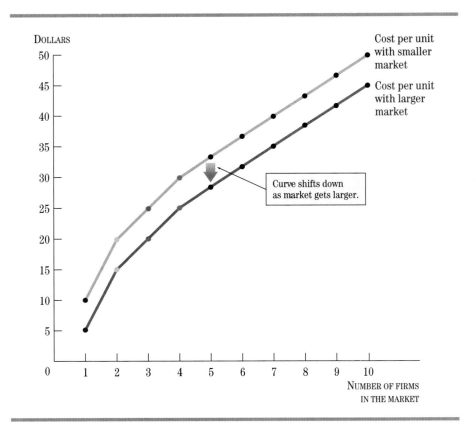

### A Relationship Between the Price and the Number of Firms

A general feature of most markets is that as the number of firms in the market
increases, the price at each firm declines. More firms make the market more competitive. Thus, there is a relationship between the price and the number of firms, as shown
in Figure 21.6. As in Figure 21.5, the number of firms is on the horizontal axis. The
curve in Figure 21.6 is downward-sloping because more firms mean a lower price.

### Equilibrium Price and Number of Firms

In the long run as firms either enter or exit an industry, price will tend to equal cost
per unit. If the price for each unit were greater than the cost per unit, then there
would be a profit opportunity for new firms; the number of firms in the industry
would rise. If the price were less than the cost per unit, then firms would exit the
industry. Only when price equals cost per unit is there a long-run equilibrium.
Because price equals cost per unit, the curves in Figures 21.5 and 21.6 can be combined to determine the price and the number of firms in long-run equilibrium. As
shown in Figure 21.7, there is a long-run equilibrium in the industry when the
downward-sloping line for Figure 21.6 intersects the upward-sloping line (for the
smaller market) from Figure 21.5. At this point, price equals cost per unit.

Corresponding to this long-run equilibrium is an equilibrium number of firms.
More firms would lower the price below cost per unit, causing firms to leave the

**FIGURE 21.6**
**The Relationship Between the
Price and the Number of Firms**

As the number of firms increases,
the market price declines. This
curve summarizes this relationship.

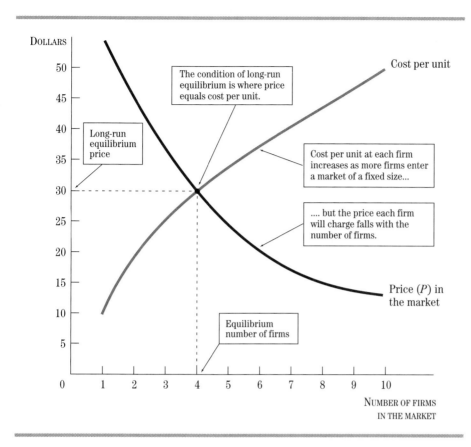

**FIGURE 21.7**

**Long-Run Equilibrium Number of Firms and Cost per Unit**

A condition for long-run equilibrium is that price equals cost per unit. In this diagram this condition is shown at the intersection of the two curves.

industry; fewer firms would raise price above cost per unit, attracting new firms to the industry. Figure 21.7 shows how the possibility of entry and exit results in a long-run equilibrium with price equal to cost per unit.

### Increasing the Size of the Market

Now let us see how the industry equilibrium changes when the size of the market increases due to international trade. In Figure 21.8, we show how an increase in the size of the market, due perhaps to the creation of a free trade area, reduces the price and increases the number of firms. The curve showing the cost per unit of each firm shifts down and out as the market expands; that is, for each number of firms the cost per unit declines for each firm. This brings about a new intersection and a long-run equilibrium at a lower price. Moreover, the increase in the number of firms suggests that there will be more product variety, which is another part of the gain from trade.

### The North American Automobile Market

The gains from trade due to larger markets arise in many real-world examples. Trade in cars between Canada and the United States now occurs even though

**FIGURE 21.8**
**Gains from Trade Due to Larger Markets**

When trade occurs, the market increases from the size of the market in one country to the combined size of the market in two or more countries. This larger market shifts the upward-sloping line down because cost per unit for each firm is lower when the market is bigger. In the long-run equilibrium at the intersection of the two new curves the price is lower and there are more firms. With more firms, there is more variety. Lower price and more variety are the gains from trade.

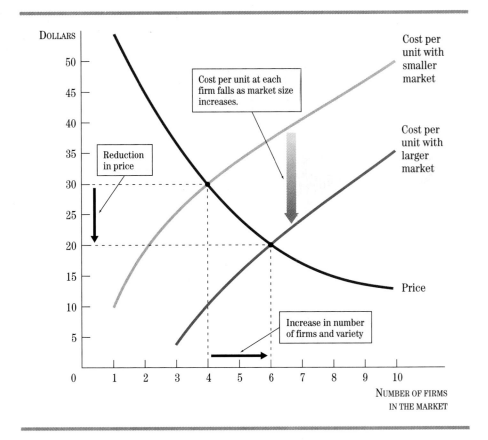

neither country has an obvious comparative advantage. Before 1964 trade in cars between Canada and the United States was restricted. Canadian factories thus had to limit their production to the Canadian market. This kept costs per unit high. When free trade in cars was permitted, the production in Canadian factories increased, and the Canadian factories began to export cars to the United States. By producing more cars, cost per unit declined. The term **new trade theory** refers to the models of international trade that emphasize the size of the market, and its effect on cost per unit.

**new trade theory:** models of international trade in which cost per unit declines as the international market grows.

# Review

▶  Lowering costs per unit through the division of labor requires large markets. International trade creates large markets.

▶  A graphical model can be used to explain the gains from international trade; the model shows that a larger market reduces prices.

# David Ricardo, 1772–1823

**BORN:**
London, 1772

**EDUCATION:**
Never attended college

**JOBS:**
Stockbroker, 1786–1815
Member of Parliament, 1819–1823

**MAJOR PUBLICATIONS:**
*The High Price of Bullion*, 1810; *On the Principles of Political Economy and Taxation*, 1817; *A Plan for a National Bank*, 1824

David Ricardo did not go to college. Instead, he went to work as a stockbroker at age 14 and eventually accumulated a vast fortune, including a beautiful country estate. Although Ricardo did not get interested in economics until he was 27, did not write on economics until he was 37, and then died young at age 51, he became one of the most influential economists of all time.

Ricardo continued the tradition of Adam Smith. In fact, he got interested in economics after reading Smith's *Wealth of Nations* during a vacation. But Ricardo greatly extended and improved on Smith's theories and made them more precise. Along with Smith and Robert Malthus—who was Ricardo's close friend but frequent intellectual opponent—Ricardo is considered by historians to be in the classical school, which argued for laissez-faire, free trade, and competitive markets in 18th- and 19th-century Britain.

Ricardo grappled with three of the most important policy issues in economics: inflation, taxes, and international trade. Both his first book, published in 1810, and his last book, published the year after his death, focused on inflation and what the government should do to keep inflation low.

Taxes were the subject of about one-third of the chapters of his major economics treatise, *On the Principles of Political Economy and Taxation*. In analyzing the effects of taxes—whether on corn, rent, land, gold, houses, profits, or wages—Ricardo emphasized how taxes affected people's incentives, and in particular the incentive to save for the future. He wrote:

*There are no taxes which have not a tendency to lessen the power to accumulate. . . . It should be the policy of governments . . . never to lay such taxes as will inevitably fall on capital; since by so doing, they impair the funds for the maintenance of labour, and thereby diminish the future production of the country.*

But perhaps Ricardo's most famous contribution is to international trade—in particular, his theory of comparative advantage. Ricardo used this theory to argue for repeal of the restrictions on agricultural imports known as the corn laws. Although he had a seat in the Parliament from which to argue his free trade position, it was not until 20 years after his death that the corn laws were repealed.

Ricardo's theory of comparative advantage is a good example of how he improved on the work of Adam Smith. Here is how Ricardo described comparative advantage in 1817:

*Under a system of perfectly free commerce, each country naturally devotes its capital and labour to such employments as are most beneficial to each. . . . It will appear then, that a country possessing very considerable advantages in machinery and skill, and which may therefore be enabled to manufacture commodities with much less labour than her neighbors, may, in return for such commodities, import a portion of the corn required for its consumption, even if its land were more fertile, and corn could be grown with less labour than in the country from which it was imported. Two men can both make shoes and hats, and one is superior to the other in both employments; but in making hats, he can only exceed his competitor by one-fifth or 20 per cent., and in making shoes he can excel him by one-third or 33 per cent.;—will it not be for the interest of both, that the superior man should employ himself exclusively in making shoes, and the inferior man in making hats?*

Ricardo then went on to compare his more powerful comparative advantage result with Adam Smith's simple examples where each country had an absolute advantage over the other in producing one good versus another good.

*Source of quotes:* David Ricardo, *On the Principles of Political Economy and Taxation*, 1817, pp. 136, 152–153, in *The Works and Correspondence of David Ricardo*, ed. Piero Sraffa (Cambridge University Press, 1962).

# THE TRANSITION TO FREE TRADE

We have now seen how opening economies to international trade results in changes in production; TV sets and ultrasound scanner production in the United States declined as a result of opening the U.S. economy to trade in our examples. When one industry shrinks as a result of the removal of restrictions on trade, the cost of adjustment in the short run may be quite large, even if other industries grow. The problems of making a transition to free trade therefore deserve special examination, even if the gains from free trade unambiguously benefit all in the long run.

Although it is certainly possible for more workers in the United States to produce pharmaceuticals and for fewer workers to produce TV sets, those who lose their jobs in electronics, even temporarily, suffer. In the short run, it is difficult to retrain workers. Workers who are laid off as the electronics industry shrinks cannot move easily to the pharmaceutical industry. Many have to retire early. Retraining is possible, but it takes time and is difficult for older workers.

## Phaseout of Trade Restrictions

**phaseout:** the gradual reduction of a government regulation or trade barrier.

These human costs of adjustment are a reason for a slow phaseout of trade barriers. **Phaseout** means that trade barriers are reduced a little bit each year. A slow phaseout of trade barriers was part of the North American Free Trade Agreement between Canada, Mexico, and the United States. It called for a phaseout period of 10 to 15 years depending on the product. For example, some tariffs were scheduled to be cut by 25 percent in the first year, 50 percent after 5 years, and 100 percent after 10 years. The purpose of the slow phaseout was to allow production to shift from one industry to another slowly. The intention was to adjust the work force through attrition as workers normally retired.

## Trade Adjustment Assistance

**trade adjustment assistance:** transfer payments made to workers who will be hurt by the move to free trade.

Costs of transition are also the reason many people recommend **trade adjustment assistance,** which refers to transfer payments to workers who happen to be hurt because of a move to free trade. Unemployment insurance and other existing transfer programs might go a long way toward providing such assistance. However, because society as a whole benefits from free trade, some increased resources can be used to help the workers who bear the brunt of the adjustment. In other words, the extra income that can be obtained by trade may be used to ease the adjustment.

Transition costs are not a reason to avoid free trade. They are a reason to phase out the restrictions on trade gradually and to provide trade adjustment assistance to workers as needed.

# Review

▶ Although free trade increases the well-being of a country's citizens, there may be a transition period during which some people lose their jobs and suffer a loss of income.

▶ Phasing out trade restrictions slowly and providing trade adjustment assistance eases the burden of this transition.

# CONCLUSION

In this chapter, we have focused on the economic gains to the citizens of a country from international trade. We have mentioned four reasons for such gains: the mutual benefits from voluntary exchange, reduction in market power from greater competition, comparative advantage, and larger markets which reduce costs per unit. All four reasons apply to trade within a country as well as to international trade. Most of the chapter was spent showing how to measure the gains due to comparative advantage and larger markets.

In the next chapter, we will consider government policy toward international trade. In concluding this chapter, it is important to point out that the benefits of international trade go well beyond economic gains.

International trade sometimes puts competitive pressure on governments to deliver better policies. Within the United States, competition between states can make regulatory and tax policies more efficient. Similarly, competition can make regulatory policies in countries more efficient.

International trade can also improve international relations. Trade enables Americans to learn more about Southeast Asians or Europeans or Latin Americans. This improves understanding and reduces the possibilities for international conflict. Developing international trade with Russia and the other countries of the former Soviet Union might even reduce the possibility of another cold war or new international conflict in the future. If many people have an economic stake in a relationship, they will not like a military action that threatens that relationship.

International trade is, unfortunately, sometimes viewed as a war between countries. As the 1990s began, many worried about other countries, in particular Japan, catching up to the United States in income per capita. By the mid-1990s, this view changed radically as the Japanese economy faltered. But international trade is not a zero-sum game. If Japan grows more rapidly again, this need not have any detrimental effect on the well-being of Americans. Rather, international trade results in net gains for the citizens of both countries.

# KEY POINTS

**1.** The principles of economics can be used to analyze international trade just as they can be used to analyze trade within a country.

**2.** International trade is different from within-country trade because national governments can place restrictions on the trade of goods and services between countries and on immigration.

**3.** According to the principle of comparative advantage, countries that specialize in producing goods that they have a comparative advantage in can increase world production and raise consumption in their own country.

**4.** The gains from trade due to comparative advantage can be shown graphically by shifting out the production possibilities curve.

**5.** Comparative advantage is a dynamic concept. If people in one country improve their skills or develop low-cost production methods through research, they will alter the comparative advantage.

**6.** If differences in the relative abundance of capital and labor are the reason for differences in comparative advantage, then international trade will tend to equalize real wages.

**7.** Lower cost per unit in larger markets is another key reason for gains from trade.

**8.** When the size of the market increases, cost per unit declines, there are more firms, and there is greater variety of products.

**9.** Opening an economy to trade by reducing trade barriers usually entails short-term adjustment costs for some workers, even though the long-term effects are beneficial. A slow phaseout of trade restrictions and trade adjustment assistance can reduce the harm from this adjustment.

**10.** The gains from international trade extend beyond economics to improving the operation of government and improving international relations. International trade is not a zero-sum game where one country wins only if another loses.

# KEY TERMS

| | | |
|---|---|---|
| international trade | absolute advantage | Leontief paradox |
| commerce clause | terms of trade | factor-price equalization |
| mercantilism | gains from trade | intraindustry trade |
| exports | dynamic comparative advantage | interindustry trade |
| imports | capital abundant | new trade theory |
| net exports | labor abundant | phaseout |
| tariff | capital intensive | trade adjustment assistance |
| free trade | labor intensive | |

# QUESTIONS FOR REVIEW

**1.** What is the difference between absolute advantage and comparative advantage?

**2.** If the relative price of two goods is 4 in one country and 6 in another country before trade, in what range will the relative price be after trade?

**3.** What is the difference between the production possibilities curve before trade and after trade?

**4.** In what sense is comparative advantage a dynamic concept?

**5.** Why does trade take place even if one country does not have an absolute advantage over another?

**6.** Why might costs per unit decline when the market increases in size?

**7.** What is the difference between interindustry trade and intraindustry trade?

**8.** What explains the Leontief paradox?

**9.** Why are trade restrictions frequently phased out slowly?

**10.** What are four reasons for economic gains from trade?

# PROBLEMS

**1.** Suppose the production of corn and cantaloupes per unit of labor in the United States and Mexico is as follows:

| | Corn | Cantaloupes |
|---|---|---|
| United States | 5 ears | 1 melon |
| Mexico | 1 ear | 1 melon |

a) Which country has a comparative advantage in corn production?

b) With free trade between the United States and Mexico, is it possible for 3 ears of corn to be worth the same as 1 melon? Explain.

c) Suppose that with free trade the price is 3 ears per melon. Suppose that the United States and Mexico both have 1 billion worker-hours that can be devoted to either corn production or cantaloupe production. Draw production possibilities curves between corn and cantaloupe production in the two countries with and without trade.

d) Is it possible for government policies in either the United States or Mexico to alter the comparative advantage? Explain and give two examples.

**2.** In the North American Free Trade Agreement between Canada, Mexico, and the United States, the phaseouts are slowest for American cantaloupes and Mexican corn. Explain the rationale for these phaseouts. Doesn't problem 1 say there is a gain from removing the barriers?

**3.** Suppose there are two goods, wheat and clothing, and two countries, the United States and Brazil, in the world. The production of wheat and clothing requires only labor. In the United States it takes 1 unit of labor to produce 4 bushels of wheat and 1 unit of labor to produce 2 items of clothing. In Brazil it takes 1 unit of labor to produce 1 bushel of wheat and 1 unit of labor to produce 1 item of clothing.

a) Suppose the United States has 100 units of labor and Brazil has 120. Draw the production possibilities curve for each country without trade. Which country has the absolute advantage in each good? Indicate each country's comparative advantage.

b) In what range would the world trading price ratio lie when these countries open up to free trade? Will both countries be better off? Why? Show this on your diagram.

**4.** Suppose France has 250 units of labor and Belgium has 100 units of labor. In France, 1 unit of labor can produce 1 shirt or 3 bottles of wine. In Belgium, 2 units of labor can produce 1 shirt or 3 bottles of wine. Draw the production possibilities curve for each country. If these countries open up to trade, what will happen? Why?

**5.** What is meant by factor-price equalization? Both opponents and supporters of the North American Free Trade Agreement used this theory to argue their positions. Explain how this is possible.

**6.** "Trade adjustment assistance is necessary for any government agreement that opens up trade." Comment.

**7.** Comparative advantage explains interindustry trade in different goods between countries. How do economists explain intraindustry trade, that is, trade in the same industry between countries? Why might people in the United States want to buy German cars, and Germans want to buy cars from the United States?

**8.** Suppose there are two countries, initially not trading with each other. Will prices fall when the two countries open up trade between them? Use both the comparative advantage and the expanded market models of trade to explain how prices will change.

**9.** Suppose an economics professor can type 15 pages in an hour or write half an economics lecture in an hour. Will she ever have a reason to hire an assistant who can type 10 pages per hour? Use the idea of comparative advantage to explain.

**10.** "Developing countries should exploit their own comparative advantage and quit trying to invest in physical and human capital to develop high-tech industries." Comment.

**11.** Suppose that each firm in an industry has total costs of production as follows:

| Quantity of Output | Total Costs ($) |
| --- | --- |
| 1 | 100 |
| 2 | 104 |
| 3 | 109 |
| 4 | 116 |
| 5 | 125 |
| 6 | 136 |
| 7 | 149 |
| 8 | 164 |
| 9 | 181 |
| 10 | 200 |
| 11 | 221 |
| 12 | 244 |

Suppose that the quantity demanded in the market is 6 units and that demand is perfectly inelastic.

a) Compute cost per unit for each firm in the industry for the cases when there are 2, 3, and 6 firms in the industry. Plot the relationship between cost per unit and the number of firms, with cost per unit on the vertical axis and number of firms on the horizontal axis.

b) Now suppose demand shifts out to 12 units because of an expansion of trade but is still perfectly inelastic. Find and plot cost per unit as in part (a) and compare the two plots.

**12.** How does the relative abundance of factors of production affect comparative advantage? Suppose you found that imports to the United States from Mexico were mainly goods, such as cement, that require much capital compared to labor, and that exports from the United States to Mexico were mainly goods, such as computer software, that require much labor compared to capital. Would your finding constitute evidence against the theory of comparative advantage?

**13.** The mercantilists advised that government always try to run trade surpluses (where exports are greater than imports) and avoid trade deficits (where exports are less than imports). What was Adam Smith's argument against this advice? Does his advice still apply today?

**14.** The following relationship between price, cost per unit, and the number of firms describes an industry in a single country.

| Number of Firms | Cost per Unit ($) | Price ($) |
| --- | --- | --- |
| 1 | 10 | 90 |
| 2 | 20 | 80 |
| 3 | 30 | 70 |
| 4 | 40 | 60 |
| 5 | 50 | 50 |
| 6 | 60 | 46 |
| 7 | 70 | 43 |
| 8 | 80 | 40 |
| 9 | 90 | 38 |
| 10 | 100 | 36 |

a) Graph (1) the relationship between cost per unit and the number of firms, and (2) the relationship between price and the number of firms. Why does one slope up and the other slope down?

b) Find the long-run equilibrium price and number of firms.

c) Now suppose the country opens its borders to trade with other countries; as a result the relationship between cost per unit and the number of firms becomes as follows:

| Number of Firms | Cost per Unit ($) |
| --- | --- |
| 1 | 5 |
| 2 | 10 |
| 3 | 15 |
| 4 | 20 |
| 5 | 25 |
| 6 | 30 |
| 7 | 35 |
| 8 | 40 |
| 9 | 45 |
| 10 | 50 |

Find the new long-run equilibrium price and number of firms.

d) What are the gains from expanding the market through the reduction in trade barriers?

# 22

# International Trade Policy

Each year the U.S. government publishes a list hundreds of pages long, detailing the most significant restrictions that other governments place on international trade. The list includes Australia's 25 percent tariff on cars; Brazil's 70 percent tariff on motorcycles; France's ban on imports of U.S. poultry; India's 70 percent tariff on chocolate; Japan's restrictions on rice imports; Russia's 30 percent tariff on aircraft; and on and on.

The European countries and Japan publish their own long lists of restrictions the U.S. government places on international trade. These include import restrictions on textiles, apparel, cheese, ice cream, sugar syrup, cotton, and peanuts; the prohibition on foreign-made ships participating in U.S. coastal shipping; and on and on. Clearly, despite significant progress in trade agreements over the last 50 years, the world is still far from free trade. Why do we have a world with many trade barriers? The answer lies in politics as much as in economics.

In the United States, trade policy has changed course many times during the twentieth century as the political climate changed. Tariffs declined during the first part of the century, a trend that lasted until World War I. Then, soon after World War I, tariffs began to rise again, reaching record levels and causing economic damage during the Great Depression of the 1930s. Policy then changed direction yet again, with tariffs declining in the 1940s. This trend continued during the years after World War II, with the United States leading a multilateral effort to reduce barriers to trade around the world.

Trade policy has veered in other directions over the last 25 years, with greater emphasis placed on regional trade; the free trade agreement of the United States, Canada, and Mexico to cut tariffs among them to zero (NAFTA) is one example of this shift. New types of barriers to trade, such as voluntary agreements between countries to manage the volume of trade, have multiplied. At the same time, populist politicians such as Pat Buchanan and Ross Perot gained large followings by protesting free trade. As the twenty-first century begins, many worry that a powerful political movement demanding higher trade barriers could arise again.

This chapter considers both the economics and the politics of international trade policy. It examines the impact of the trade barriers that currently exist, the gains that could occur from eliminating them, the arguments given in favor of them, and the various policies that might be taken to reduce them.

# THE EFFECTS OF TRADE RESTRICTIONS

Governments use many methods to restrict international trade. Policies that restrict trade are called **protectionist policies** because the restrictions usually protect industries from foreign imports. In addition to reducing imports, these policies raise prices, as we show next.

**protectionist policy:** a policy that restricts trade to protect domestic producers.

## Tariffs

The oldest and most common method for a government to restrict trade is the *tariff,* a tax on goods imported into a country. The higher the tariff, the more trade is restricted. An **ad valorem tariff** is a tax equal to a certain percentage of the value of the good. For example, a 15 percent tariff on the value of goods imported is an ad valorem tariff. If $100,000 worth of goods are imported, the tariff revenue is $15,000. A **specific tariff** is a tax on the quantity sold, such as 50 cents for each kilogram of zinc.

**ad valorem tariff:** a tax on imports evaluated as a percentage of the value of the import.

**specific tariff:** a tax on imports that is proportional to the number of units or items imported.

The economic effects of a tariff are illustrated in Figure 22.1. We consider a particular good—automobiles, for example—that is exported from one country (Japan, for example) and imported by another country (the United States, for example). There is an *import demand curve* and an *export supply curve* shown in Figure 22.1. The **import demand curve** gives the quantity of imported goods that will be demanded at each price. The import demand curve shows that a higher price for imported goods will reduce the quantity of the goods demanded. A higher price on Nissans and Toyotas, for example, will lead to a smaller quantity of Nissans and Toyotas demanded by Americans. Like the standard demand curve, the import demand curve is downward-sloping.

**import demand curve:** a curve showing the quantity of imports demanded at various prices.

The **export supply curve** gives the quantity of exports that foreign firms are willing to sell at each price. In the case of Nissans and Toyotas, the export supply curve gives the quantity of Toyotas and Nissans that Japanese producers are willing to sell in the United States. The supply curve is upward-sloping because foreign producers are willing to supply more cars when the price is higher, just like an ordinary supply curve.

**export supply curve:** a curve showing the quantity of exports supplied at various prices.

In equilibrium, for any single type of good, the quantity of exports supplied must equal the quantity of imports demanded. Thus, the intersection of the export supply curve and import demand curve gives the amount imported into the country and the price.

When the government imposes a tariff, the supply curve shifts up, as shown in Figure 22.1. The tariff increases the marginal cost of supplying cars to the United

**FIGURE 22.1**
**The Effects of a Tariff**
A tariff shifts the export supply curve up by the amount of the tariff. Thus, the price paid for imports by consumers rises and the quantity imported declines. The price increase (upward-pointing black arrow) is less than the tariff (upward-pointing blue arrow). The revenue to the government is shown by the shaded area; it is the tariff times the amount imported.

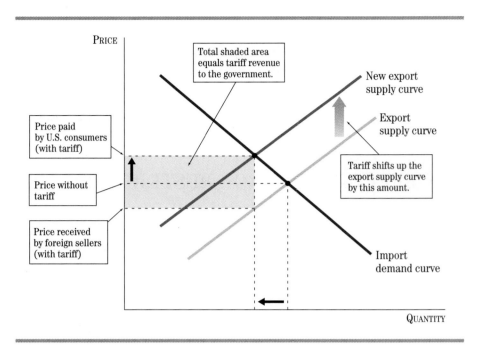

States. The amount of the tariff in dollars is the amount by which the supply curve shifts up; it is given by the length of the blue arrow in Figure 22.1.

The tariff changes the intersection of the export supply curve and the import demand curve. At the new equilibrium, a lower quantity is imported at a higher price. The price paid for cars by consumers rises, but the increase in the price is less than the tariff. In Figure 22.1, the black arrow shows the price increase. The blue arrow is longer than the upward-pointing black arrow along the vertical axis, which shows the tariff increase. The size of the price increase depends on the slopes of the demand curve and the supply curve.

The price received by suppliers equals the price paid by consumers less the tariff that must be paid to the government. Observe that the price received by the sellers declines due to the tariff.

The amount of revenue that the government collects is given by the quantity imported times the tariff, which is indicated by the shaded rectangle in Figure 22.1. For example, if the tariff is $1,000 per car and 1 million cars are imported, the revenue is $1 billion. Tariff revenues are called *duties* and are collected by customs.

The tariff also has an effect on U.S. car producers. Because the tariff reduces imports from abroad and raises their price, the demand for cars produced by import-competing companies in the United States—General Motors, Ford, or Chrysler—increases. This increase in demand will raise the price of U.S. cars. Thus, consumers pay more for both imported cars and domestically produced cars.

## Quotas

**quota:** an upper limit on the quantity of a good that may be imported or sold.

Another method of government restriction of international trade is called a **quota.** A quota sets a limit, a maximum, on the amount of a given good that can be

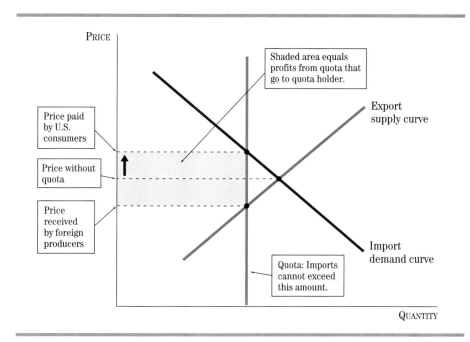

Price

Shaded area equals profits from quota that go to quota holder.

Export supply curve

Price paid by U.S. consumers

Price without quota

Price received by foreign producers

Import demand curve

Quota: Imports cannot exceed this amount.

Quantity

**FIGURE 22.2**
**The Effects of a Quota**
A quota can be set to allow the same quantity of imports as a tariff. The quota in this figure and the tariff in Figure 22.1 allow the same quantity of imports into the country. The price increase is the same for the quota and the tariff. But, in the case of a quota, the revenue goes to quota holders, not to the U.S. government.

imported. The United States has quotas on the import of ice cream, sugar, cotton, peanuts, and other commodities. Foreigners can supply only a limited amount to the United States.

The economic effect of a quota is illustrated in Figure 22.2. The export supply curve and the import demand curve are identical to Figure 22.1. The quota, the maximum that foreign firms can export to the United States, is indicated in Figure 22.2 by the solid purple vertical line labeled "quota." Exporters cannot supply more cars than the quota and, therefore, American consumers cannot buy more than this amount. We have chosen the quota amount to equal the quantity imported with the tariff in Figure 22.1. This shows that the government can achieve, if it wants to, the same effects on the quantity imported using a quota or a tariff. Moreover, the price increase in Figure 22.2, represented by the black arrow along the vertical axis, is the same as the price increase in Figure 22.1. Viewed from the domestic market, therefore, a quota and a tariff are equivalent: If the quota is set to allow in the same quantity of imports as the tariff, then the price increase will be the same. Consumers pay more for imports in both cases, and the demand for domestically produced goods that are substitutes for imports will increase. The price of domestically produced cars would also increase if there were a quota on foreign cars.

Then what is the difference in the effects of a tariff and a quota? Unlike a tariff, no revenue goes to the government with a quota. The difference between the price that the foreign suppliers get and the higher price that the consumers pay goes to the holders of the quota—the ones who are allowed to import into the country. Frequently foreign countries hold the quotas. The revenue the quota holders get is indicated by the shaded rectangle in Figure 22.2. It is equal to the quantity imported times the difference between the price paid by the consumers and the price received by the producers. The size of that rectangle is identical to the size of the rectangle showing the revenue paid to the government in the case of the tariff in Figure 22.1.

## Voluntary Restraint Agreements (VRAs)

**voluntary restraint agreement
(VRA):** a country's self-imposed
government restriction on exports
to a particular country.

A relatively new alternative to tariffs and quotas is the **voluntary restraint agreement (VRA).** These restraints are similar to quotas except that one country, such as the United States, asks another country to "volunteer" to restrict its firms' exports to the United States. Although a tariff or a quota must be passed by Congress, VRAs can be negotiated by the president without Congress approving.

The United States negotiated VRAs with Japan for automobiles in the early 1980s. The Japanese government agreed to limit the number of automobiles Japanese firms exported to the United States to 2.8 million. There are also VRAs on machine tools and textiles exported to the United States. These voluntary agreements usually occur because of pressure that one country, such as the United States, exerts on the other country. Hence, they are not actually voluntary. For example, a foreign government might agree to a VRA because the other country may be about to impose steep tariffs. Or there may be diplomatic pressures unrelated to economics that one country can use to pressure another country into the so-called voluntary actions.

What is the economic effect of a VRA? Figure 22.3 examines the impact. The supply and demand curves are identical to those in Figures 22.1 and 22.2. The amount of the VRA chosen for illustration is the same as the quota in Figure 22.2 and the resulting quantity from the tariff in Figure 22.1. This shows that the effect of the VRA on price and quantity can be made identical to the quota and the tariff. Consumers pay more under tariffs, quotas, or VRAs. The difference between VRAs and quotas is the recipient of the equivalent of the tariff revenue. In the case of the VRA, these revenues go to the foreign firms. As firms reduce their production, the price rises, and their profits rise. Thus, what would have been tariff revenue to the U.S. government in the case of a U.S. tariff becomes increased profits for foreign firms in the case of a VRA.

**FIGURE 22.3**
**The Effects of a Voluntary
Restraint Agreement (VRA)**

The effects are just like the quota in Figure 22.2 except the revenue goes to foreign firms rather than quota holders. Because of the VRA, the foreign firms act as if they are in a cartel to restrict output and raise prices.

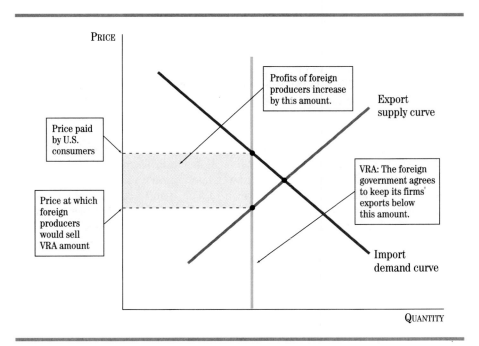

Studies show that the VRAs used in the United States in the 1980s for automobiles did lead to a higher price and additional revenue to the Japanese automobile producers. The price of Japanese cars sold in the United States rose by about $1,000, and the increase in demand for U.S. cars led to their price increasing by about $1,400 for the average car.

## Voluntary Import Expansion (VIE)

A new type of intervention by the government in foreign trade is the **voluntary import expansion (VIE).** With VIEs, a government agrees to have its firms expand their imports of foreign goods from another country. For example, the United States arranged for a VIE with Japan in semiconductors in 1986 and renewed it in 1991. Under this agreement, the Japanese government was to see to it that Japanese firms purchased foreign semiconductors in the amount of at least 20 percent of the Japanese market for semiconductors. The rationale given by the U.S. government was that Japanese firms had a preference for Japanese semiconductors, though the Japanese government denied it. To offset this preference, the U.S. government asked the Japanese government to volunteer to increase U.S. imports.

**voluntary import expansion (VIE):** a government agreement to expand imports from a particular country.

A VIE may seem rather benign; after all, trade is apparently being increased, not decreased. Although there is not a consensus among economists about the effects of VIEs, some economists estimate the effects on U.S. consumers to be much like that of VRAs or quotas. Consider a VIE with Japan in which the Japanese agree to import more U.S. cars. Suppose the Japanese government gets Japanese rental car companies to buy more U.S. automobiles. The "voluntary" increase in demand for U.S. cars in Japan causes an increase in the price of U.S. cars in Japan. This is likely to raise the price of Japanese cars in Japan as well.

Now consider what happens in the United States. The higher price of cars in Japan reduces the number of Japanese cars Japanese firms will want to export to the United States. As illustrated in Figure 22.4, this upward shift in the export supply curve will raise the price of cars in the U.S. market. Thus, a VIE has effects similar to a VRA, quota, or tariff.

The reason there is not a consensus about the effect of VIEs on U.S. consumer prices is that some economic analysts estimate that the price of cars in Japan will not rise. In their view, the Japanese are discriminating against foreign products, and offsetting the discrimination by government action will not raise prices.

## Trade Barriers Related to Domestic Policies

Other government policies can restrict international trade even if their main purpose is related to domestic policy. Quality and performance standards, for example, may be biased against foreign products. The standards may have a good purpose, such as safety or compatibility with other products, but frequently they do not. Consider the Canadian plywood standards for building construction, which keep out U.S. plywood. The Canadians argue that the standards are needed to satisfy building requirements in Canada, but Americans argue that plywood that does not meet the Canadian standards works just as well. A safety restriction against American-made baseball bats in Japan during the 1980s is another example. Most Americans viewed the bats as perfectly safe and viewed the Japanese safety standard as a restriction on trade.

Standards, therefore, are a tricky problem because governments can argue that they are for the purpose of improving performance in their own country. The U.S.

**FIGURE 22.4**
**The Effects of a Voluntary Import Expansion (VIE)**
With a VIE, the export supply curve is likely to shift up if the price foreign producers receive in their home market (not shown on this diagram) rises when there is an expansion in demand due to the VIE. The upward shift in the export supply curve raises the price of cars in the United States.

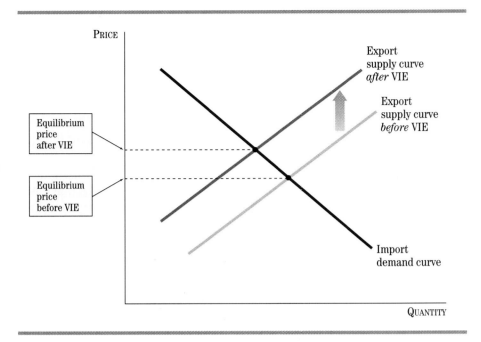

Food and Drug Administration does not allow untested drugs into the United States even though foreign governments deem them safe. The FDA argues that the restriction is necessary to protect consumers, but foreign governments view it as a trade restriction. Such a standard does seem like a trade barrier, but in reality it is a matter of dispute.

Another domestic policy that affects trade policy is government procurement, the process by which governments buy goods and services. If government procurement policy has a bias against foreign products, then it is considered a restriction on trade. For example, the U.S. government has a "Buy American" policy that gives a slight edge to American suppliers of goods and services. Federal employees must try to travel on domestic airlines even when traveling abroad. The government of Japan has had a policy of only buying Japanese supercomputers.

Any government procurement policy that is biased against lower-priced foreign goods in favor of more expensive domestic goods will either require higher taxes or will raise prices for the consumers of government services. Such a policy is like other trade restrictions.

# Review

▶ The most common ways for government to restrict foreign trade are tariffs and quotas. Voluntary restraint agreements and voluntary import expansions have become more popular in recent years.

▶ Tariffs and quotas have the same effect on price and quantity. They differ in who gets the tariff revenue.

▶ Many government standards and regulations aimed at domestic trade affect international trade. They present a tricky problem for trade policy.

# THE HISTORY OF TRADE RESTRICTIONS

As stated earlier, tariffs are the oldest form of trade restriction. Throughout history, governments have used tariffs to raise revenue. **Revenue tariffs,** whose main purpose is raising revenue, were by far the most significant source of federal revenue in the United States before the income tax was enacted in 1917 (see Figure 22.5). Revenue tariffs are still common in less-developed countries because they are easy for the government to collect as the goods come through a port or one of a few checkpoints.

## U.S. Tariffs

Tariffs are a big part of U.S. history. Even before the United States was a country, a tariff on tea imported into the colonies led to the Boston Tea Party. One of the first acts of the U.S. Congress placed tariffs on imports. Figure 22.6 summarizes the history of tariffs in the United States since the early 1800s.

### *From the Tariff of Abominations to Smoot-Hawley*

Tariffs were high throughout much of U.S. history, rarely getting below 20 percent in the nineteenth century. In addition to raising revenue, these tariffs had the purpose of reducing imports of manufactured goods. The tariffs offered protection to manufacturers in the North but raised prices for consumers. Since the South was mainly agricultural and a consumer of manufactured goods, there was a constant dispute between the North and the South over these tariffs.

The highest of these tariffs was nicknamed the "tariff of abominations." This tariff, passed in 1828, brought the average tariff level in the United States to over 60 percent. The tariff made purchases of farm equipment much more expensive in the southern states. It almost led to a civil war before the actual Civil War as the southern states threatened to secede. However, because the tariff was so high, it was soon repealed, and for the next 10 years tariffs were relatively low by nineteenth-century standards.

The most devastating increase in tariffs in U.S. history occurred during the Great Depression. The **Smoot-Hawley tariff** of 1930 raised average tariffs to 59 percent. Congress and President Hoover apparently hoped that raising tariffs would help stimulate U.S. production and offset the Great Depression. But the increase had precisely the opposite effect. Other countries retaliated by raising their tariffs on U.S. goods. Each country tried to beat the others with higher tariffs, a phenomenon known as a **trade war.** The Smoot-Hawley tariff had terrible consequences. Figure 22.7 is a dramatic illustration of the decline in trade that occurred at the time of these tariff increases during the Great Depression. The Smoot-Hawley tariff made the Great Depression worse than it would have otherwise been.

### *From the Reciprocal Trade Agreement Act to GATT*

The only good thing about the Smoot-Hawley tariff was that it demonstrated to the whole world how harmful tariffs can be. In order to achieve lower tariffs, the Congress passed and President Roosevelt signed the **Reciprocal Trade Agreement Act** in 1934. This act was probably the most significant event in the history of U.S. trade policy. It authorized the president to cut U.S. tariffs by up to 50 percent if other countries would cut their tariffs on a reciprocating basis. The reciprocal trade

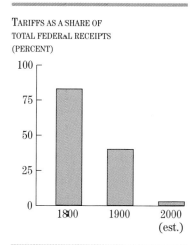

TARIFFS AS A SHARE OF TOTAL FEDERAL RECEIPTS (PERCENT)

**FIGURE 22.5**
**Tariffs as a Share of Total Federal Revenue**
The first tariff, passed in 1789, represented nearly all of the federal government's revenue; 200 years later, tariff revenues were only about 1 percent of the total.

*Source: Historical Statistics of the United States, Colonial Times to 1957, series Y 259–260 and Budget of the U.S. Government, 1993.*

**revenue tariff:** an import tax whose main purpose is to provide revenue to the government.

**Smoot-Hawley tariff:** a set of tariffs imposed in 1930 that raised the average tariff level to 59 percent by 1932.

**trade war:** a conflict among nations over trade policies caused by imposition of protectionist policies on the part of one country and subsequent retaliatory actions by other countries.

**Reciprocal Trade Agreement Act:** passed in 1934 by the U.S. Congress, it allowed cuts in tariff rates based on similar cuts in tariff rates in European countries.

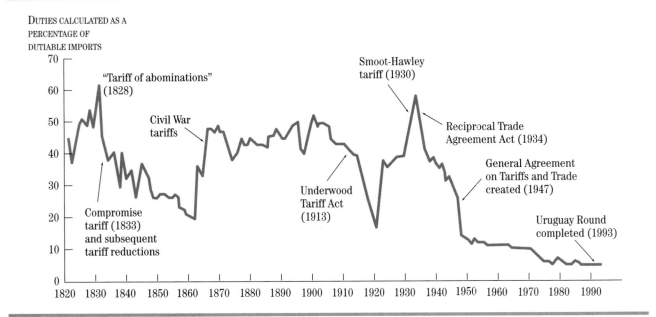

DUTIES CALCULATED AS A
PERCENTAGE OF
DUTIABLE IMPORTS

**FIGURE 22.6**
**History of Tariffs in the United States**

The chart shows the ratio of tariff revenues to the value of imports subject to tariffs measured as a percentage. This percentage is a measure of the average tariff excluding goods not subject to any tariff.

*Source: Historical Statistics of the United States, Colonial Times to 1970* and *Statistical Abstract of the United States,* 1993, Table 1353.

**General Agreement on Tariffs and Trade (GATT):** an international treaty and organization designed to promote mutual reductions in tariffs and other trade barriers among countries.

**antidumping duty:** a tariff imposed on a country as a penalty for dumping goods.

**dumping:** the selling of goods by foreign firms at a price below average cost or below the price in the domestic country.

agreements resulted in a remarkable reduction in tariffs. By the end of World War II the average tariff level was down from a peak of 59 percent under Smoot-Hawley to 25 percent. The successful approach to tariff reduction under the Reciprocal Trade Agreement Act was made permanent in 1947 with the creation of a new international organization, the **General Agreement on Tariffs and Trade (GATT).** GATT was set up to continue the process of tariff reduction. During the half century since the end of World War II, tariffs have continued to decline on a reciprocating basis. By 1992 the average U.S. tariff level was down to 5.2 percent.

### Antidumping Duties

No history of U.S. tariffs would be complete without a discussion of antidumping duties. **Antidumping duties** are tariffs put on foreign firms as a penalty for dumping. When a firm sells products in another country at prices below average cost or below the price in the home country, it is called **dumping.** Dumping can occur for many reasons. For example, the firm might want to sell at a lower price in the foreign market, where the demand is more elastic, than in the home market, where it is less elastic. If so, consumers in the foreign market benefit. But some people argue that dumping is a way for foreign firms to drive domestic firms out of business and thereby gain market share and market power. In any case, in the United States and other countries, dumping is illegal; the penalty is a high tariff—the antidumping duty—on the good that is being dumped.

Many economists are concerned that antidumping duties, or even the threat of such duties, are serious restrictions on trade. They reduce imports and raise consumer prices. Moreover, they are frequently used for protectionist purposes. Firms in industries that desire additional protection can file dumping charges and request that tariffs be raised. Frequently, they are successful. Thus, an important issue for the future is how to reduce the use of antidumping duties for restricting trade.

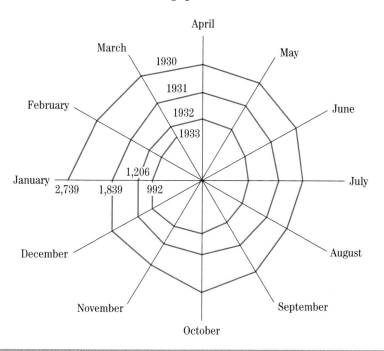

**Contracting Spiral of World Trade**

**FIGURE 22.7**
**Decline in World Trade During the Great Depression**
This circular graph, used by Charles Kindleberger of MIT, illustrates how world trade collapsed after tariffs increased during the Great Depression. The distance from the middle of the graph to the point in each spoke is the amount of trade (in millions of dollars) during each month. A time-series graph could show the same information but would look less dramatic.

*Source:* From Charles Kindleberger, *The World in Depression, 1929–39* (Berkeley: University of California Press, 1973). Data reprinted by permission from League of Nations, *Monthly Bulletin of Statistics,* February 1934.

### The Rise of Nontariff Barriers

As tariffs were being reduced in the post–World War II period, a conflicting trend began to emerge. Some of the other methods to restrict trade—called **nontariff barriers** to trade—grew in popularity. Nontariff barriers include anything from quotas to quality standards aimed at reducing the import of foreign products. Nontariff barriers may have arisen as a replacement for tariffs in response to political pressure for protection of certain industries.

**nontariff barrier:** any government action other than a tariff that reduces imports, such as a quota or a standard.

  The Multifiber Agreement (MFA) is an example. It grew from a small VRA program into a complex worldwide system of VRAs designed to limit the imports of textiles and apparel into the United States and Europe. The MFA limits imports of thousands of products, from men's and women's shirts to swimsuits. Reducing such nontariff barriers—whether in textiles or agriculture—is a major objective of trade policy today.

## How Large Are the Gains from Reducing Trade Restrictions?

Restrictions on trade raise prices and reduce the quantity of products available to consumers. Estimates made in the late 1980s indicate that the gain from removing these restrictions could be as large as $60 billion per year.

  To get a better understanding of the gains, consider three of the many goods and services that might be affected: textiles, cars, and sugar. The textile and apparel MFA is estimated to have cost consumers $11 billion in 1987, although domestic producers gained $4 billion. The net loss is thus $7 billion. VRAs on Japanese automobiles are estimated to have cost American consumers $5.8 billion in 1984, while

U.S. producers gained $2.6 billion; the net loss was thus $3.2 billion. Quotas on sugar imports were estimated to have cost American consumers $1.9 billion in 1987, while the gain to producers was $1 billion; the net loss was $.9 billion.

### The Political Economy of Protectionist Pressures

These calculations of the gains from trade as well as the brief review of U.S. tariff history help explain why restrictions on trade that harm the overall economy continue to exist. Firms and workers in industries protected by import restrictions benefit from these restrictions. For example, the producers gain about $4 billion in textiles and $1 billion in sugar. Thus, removing protection has losers as well as winners within a country even though the winners benefit more than the losers are hurt.

In most cases, the people who benefit from protection are few and the people who lose are many. Individual firms or workers in textiles benefit from protection by thousands of dollars a year, while each consumer may lose hundreds of dollars a year. Thus, those who benefit from protection lobby their representatives heavily, while those who lose from protection are more diffuse and have less power.

## Review

▶ Tariffs have been used by governments to raise revenue long before income taxes were invented.

▶ Tariffs have also been used for protectionist purposes in several important instances in U.S. history. Manufacturing firms in the North were protected by tariffs at the expense of consumers of manufactured goods, many of whom were in the South.

▶ The Smoot-Hawley tariff of the 1930s was one of the most harmful in U.S. history. It led to a trade war in which other countries raised tariffs in retaliation.

▶ Tariffs have come down since the 1930s. However, in recent years, nontariff barriers to trade have gone up.

▶ Although tariffs are now low on average by historical standards, tariffs and nontariff barriers still cost American consumers billions of dollars each year.

# ARGUMENTS FOR TRADE BARRIERS

It appears that many trade barriers exist because of the political power of the interest groups that demand them. But aren't there any good economic rationales for trade barriers? Are trade barriers ever beneficial to the economy as a whole? Let's examine some arguments that say they are.

### Restricting Supply and Strategic Trade Policy

If the firms in one country produce much of the world's supply of a good, then the country can gain by restricting trade. By restricting the amount that the firms supply to the world, the country can raise the world price and the firms' profits. In fact, this is precisely what oil exporting countries do. Even the whole country may benefit if some of the extra profits are taxed away.

This argument in favor of trade restrictions is an old one. However, it has two serious problems. First, it invites retaliation. Other countries may raise their tariffs in response. If one retaliation invites another retaliation, then a trade war might be started. Second, restricting trade to increase domestic firms' profits is a beggar-thy-neighbor policy because one country gains only at the expense of other countries.

In recent years more sophisticated versions of this rationale for trade restrictions have appeared. A **strategic trade policy** is a set of actions—subsidies or tax credits—that aims to encourage large firms to start up in a particular country. If those firms are able to capture most of the world market, then the policy of restricting supply and raising prices becomes a possibility. Strategic trade policy gets its name from the strategic interaction between governments that arises when they endeavor to subsidize firms. Here is how such strategic interaction arises.

**strategic trade policy:** a set of government actions designed to encourage large firms to locate or start up in that country.

Suppose European governments subsidize the production of a new aircraft at the European firm Airbus. By doing so, they may prevent a U.S. firm, perhaps Boeing, from producing the aircraft. Why? The world market might not be large enough for two aircraft of the same type. In other words, with two firms cost per unit may be greater than the expected purchase price of the aircraft. With only one firm producing, cost per unit might be lower.

If the subsidy is successful in keeping Boeing out, the eventual profits at the European firm may be greater than the subsidy. However, there is a risk to Europe. Boeing could produce the aircraft anyway, perhaps thinking that cost per unit will be low enough even with two aircraft of the same type. Then the profits in Europe would not cover the subsidy. Thus, Europe must try to guess what Boeing will do. The problem gets more complicated if the U.S. government gets involved and threatens to subsidize Boeing. Because of such strategic behavior, the European subsidy policy could fail as the United States retaliates with its own subsidy. Aside from being a beggar-thy-neighbor policy, strategic trade policy is difficult to carry out because of the strategic behavior.

## The Infant Industry Argument

One of the earliest statements of the **infant industry argument** in favor of trade restrictions was put forth by Alexander Hamilton in 1791 in his *Report on Manufactures*. Hamilton argued that manufacturing firms in the newly created United States should be protected from imports. Once the industries were established, they could compete with foreign imports. But as they got started, they needed protection until they reached a certain scale.

**infant industry argument:** the view that a new industry may be helped by protectionist policies.

A danger with the infant industry argument is that the protection may last long after it was initially justified. In Latin America, for example, infant industry arguments were used to justify import protection in the 1950s. However, these barriers to trade lasted long after any kind of a reasonable infant industry argument could be made.

## The National Security Argument

A nation's security is another argument for trade restrictions. The national security argument is that there are certain goods, such as special metals, computers, ships, or aircraft, the country needs to be able to produce in time of war. If it does not have an industry that produces them, it could be at a severe disadvantage.

However, national security arguments can be used by firms seeking protection from foreign imports. Japanese rice farmers, for example, made national security arguments for protection from rice imports. In fact, the rice restriction has little to do with national security because rice can be imported from many different countries. In the United States, the textile industry has argued on national security grounds that it needs protection because it provides military uniforms made from U.S. textiles.

It is important to examine whether there are alternatives to trade restrictions before applying the national security argument and restricting trade. For example, rather than restricting rice imports, the Japanese could store a large amount of rice in case of a war emergency. Or the United States could store millions of extra uniforms rather than restrict textile imports if one really thought that uniforms were a national security issue. In fact, the United States does have stockpiles of many rare minerals and metals needed for national defense production.

## Retaliation Threats

Threatening other countries or retaliating against them when they have trade restrictions is another possible reason to deviate from free trade. If the United States threatens the Japanese by saying it will close U.S. markets, then it may encourage Japan to open its markets to the United States. Thus, by retaliating or threatening, there is a possibility of increasing international trade around the world.

However, the retaliation argument can also be used by those seeking protection. Those in the United States who are most vocal about retaliation against other countries are frequently those who want to protect an industry. Many economists worry about threats of retaliation because they fear that other countries will respond with further retaliation, and a trade war will occur.

## What If Other Countries Subsidize Their Firms?

If foreign governments subsidize their firms' exports, does this justify U.S. government subsidies to U.S. firms to help them compete against the foreign firms?

Foreign subsidies to foreign producers are a particularly difficult issue. On the one hand, if foreign subsidies lower the price of U.S. imports, then U.S. consumers benefit. If Europe wants to use taxpayer funds to subsidize aircraft manufacturers, then why not enjoy the lower-cost aircraft? On the other hand, foreign subsidies enable industries to thrive more for political reasons than economic ones. From a global perspective, such government intervention should be avoided since it hurts consumers.

## Unfair Competition from the Sun?

Firms seeking protection frequently complain about "unfair competition" from other countries. In a famous satire of such complaints, a French economist, Frédéric Bastiat, wrote about candlemakers complaining about a foreign rival—the sun! The candlemakers in Bastiat's satire petitioned French legislators to pass a law requiring the closing of all windows, dormers, skylights, shutters, curtains, and blinds to protect them from this competition. Though written more than 150 years ago, the behavior Bastiat described seems to apply to many modern producers who seek protection from competition.

## Review

▶ An old rationale for trade restrictions is to raise the price of exports. But reducing supply through trade restrictions is a beggar-thy-neighbor policy that is likely to result in retaliation.

▶ National security, infant industry, and retaliation are other arguments in favor of trade restrictions. Each has the possibility of being used by protectionists.

# HOW TO REDUCE TRADE BARRIERS

Viewed in their entirety, the economic arguments against trade restrictions seem to overwhelm the economic arguments in favor of trade restrictions. The economic arguments in favor of free trade have been in existence for over 200 years. The recommendation of early economists such as Adam Smith and David Ricardo was simple: Develop a policy to reduce trade barriers.

However, it was not until many years after Smith and Ricardo wrote that their recommendations were translated into a practical trade policy. Then, as now, political pressures favoring protection made the repeal of trade barriers difficult, as well as hazardous to political careers. (See the box "The End of the Corn Laws.") Today, a carefully formulated trade policy can include a variety of approaches.

### Unilateral Disarmament

One approach to removing trade barriers in a country is simply to remove them unilaterally. Making an analogy with the arms race, we call this policy **unilateral disarmament.** When a country unilaterally reduces its arms, it does so without getting anything in arms reduction from other countries. With unilateral disarmament in trade policy, a country reduces its trade barriers without other countries also reducing their trade barriers. Unilateral disarmament is what Smith and Ricardo recommended for England.

**unilateral disarmament:** in trade policy, the removal of trade barriers by one country without reciprocal action on the part of other countries.

It is difficult to achieve unilateral disarmament today. Consider, for example, the Trade-Enhancement Initiative started in 1990 to reduce American and European barriers to imports from the emerging democracies in Eastern Europe. Despite powerful arguments from economists that such reduction would spur the development of market economies in these areas, little reduction in trade barriers occurred as a result of this initiative. Strong protests from clothing manufacturers in the United States and dairy product manufacturers in Europe prevented any significant increase of the amount of Polish men's suits or Hungarian cheese allowed to be imported.

As the example shows, the difficulty of unilateral disarmament is that some individuals are hurt, if only temporarily, and it is hard to compensate them. The workers and producers in the textile industry benefit from the restriction on Polish suits; the removal of the barriers is a significant cost to them even if it is outweighed by gains to society. Of those who gain, each gains only a little. Of those who lose, each loses a lot. The political pressures they exert are significant. As a result, unilateral disarmament is rarely successful in the developed countries today as a means of reducing trade barriers.

# Using Economics to Explain the End of the Corn Laws

Corn laws, recorded back as far as the twelfth century, restricted imports of grains, including wheat, rye, and barley, into England. Adam Smith devoted an entire chapter of his 1776 *Wealth of Nations* to the corn laws, arguing that "the praises which have been bestowed upon the law . . . are altogether unmerited."* But legislation introduced in 1791 raised the grain import tariff even further. The corn laws were unpopular with everyone except the landowners and farmers.

The Anti-Corn League, founded in 1839 by Richard Cobden, was the most significant pressure group in nineteenth-century England. The Anti-Corn League used the arguments of Smith and Ricardo that the corn laws were an economic disaster and a moral tragedy: The laws impoverished and even starved the working class, constrained the growth of manufacturing, and

provided government support to the wealthy. The catalyst was the Irish potato famine of 1845, which raised agricultural prices even further.

Robert Peel, the Tory prime minister from 1841 to 1846, was reform minded. He introduced currency reform and reduced tariffs on many goods after reintroducing the income tax. Until 1845 he was against repeal of the corn laws, primarily because of strong support for them from landowners in the Tory party. But under pressure from Cobden and the Anti-Corn League, he changed his position after the potato famine and argued for the repeal of the corn laws.

In February 1846, Peel introduced a package of measures abolishing duties on imported corn over a three-year period. Only a minority of his party supported him, but the package passed. The split in the

Tory party ended Peel's career, and the party did not win an election until the emergence of the new Conservative party in 1868, when Benjamin Disraeli was elected.

The repeal of the corn laws and other protectionist measures ushered in the free trade era in England. The economist-philosopher John Stuart Mill's *Principles of Political Economy* was published in 1848 and became the handbook of free markets for nearly 50 years: "Laisserfaire, in short, should be the general practice: every departure from it, unless required by some great good, is a certain evil."†

*Adam Smith, *Wealth of Nations* (New York: Modern Library, 1994), p. 560.

†John Stuart Mill, *Principles of Political Economy,* 1848, p. 950, in *Reprints of Economic Classics,* ed. Augustus M. Kelley (New York: Bookseller, 1965).

## Multilateral Negotiations

**multilateral negotiation:** simultaneous tariff reductions on the part of many countries.

An alternative to unilateral disarmament is **multilateral negotiation,** which involves simultaneous tariff reductions among many countries. The main example of the multilateral approach is the General Agreement on Tariffs and Trade (GATT). With multilateral negotiations, opposing political interests can cancel each other out. For example, import-competing domestic industries that will be hurt by the reduction of trade barriers, such as textiles in the United States or agriculture in Europe and Japan, can be countered by export interests that will gain from the reduction in trade barriers. Since consumers will gain, they are also a potential counter to protectionism, but they are too diffuse to make a difference, as we just discussed. With multilateral negotiations, interested exporters who gain from the reduction in barriers will push the political process to get the reductions.

Multilateral negotiations also balance international interests. For example, to get less-developed countries to remove their barriers on imports of financial and telecommunications services, the United States had to agree to remove agricultural trade barriers in the United States.

### The Uruguay Round

Multilateral trade negotiations under GATT have taken place in a series of negotiating rounds, each of which lasts several years. During each round, the countries try to come to agreement on a list of tariff reductions and the removal of other trade restrictions. There have been eight rounds of negotiations since GATT was established in 1947. The most recent was the **Uruguay Round,** named after the country where the first negotiations occurred in 1986. After many years, the Uruguay Round negotiations ended in 1993. An important innovation of the Uruguay Round was that it created a new multilateral organization, called the **World Trade Organization (WTO),** to settle disputes between countries about unfair trade policies.

**Uruguay Round:** the most recent round of negotiations on the General Agreement on Tariffs and Trade, begun in 1986 in Uruguay.

**World Trade Organization (WTO):** an international organization that can mediate trade disputes.

The reduction in tariffs through multilateral negotiations under GATT has been dramatic. Tariffs are expected to go below 3 percent on average in the United States with the implementation of the Uruguay Round agreement. Recall that this compares with nearly 60 percent in the mid-1930s.

### Most-Favored Nation Policy

Multilateral negotiations are almost always conducted on a **most-favored nation (MFN)** basis. MFN means that when the United States or any other country reduces its tariffs under GATT, it reduces them for virtually everyone. Today, if a country is not granted MFN status, the United States imposes Smoot-Hawley–level tariffs on the country. For example, concern about human rights in China led some to argue that the United States should remove MFN status for China. Doing so would have raised tariffs on Chinese imports to about 60 percent.

**most-favored nation (MFN):** the principle by which all countries involved in GATT negotiations receive the same tariff rates as the country with the lowest negotiated tariff rates.

## Regional Trading Areas

Creating regional trading areas is an increasingly popular approach to reducing trade barriers. For example, in 1988 a free trade agreement between the United States and Canada called for removal of all trade restrictions between those two countries. The North American Free Trade Agreement (NAFTA) will reduce tariffs to zero between Canada, the United States, and Mexico. An even wider free trade area is proposed for the whole Western Hemisphere.

Regional trading areas have some advantages over multilateral approaches. First, fewer countries are involved, so the negotiations are easier. Second, regional political factors can help offset protectionist pressures. For example, the political goal of European unity helped establish grassroots support to reduce trade barriers among the countries of Europe. More recently, the countries of Europe have formed a single market with even fewer restrictions on trade.

### Trade Diversion versus Trade Creation

But there are disadvantages of regional trading areas in comparison with multilateral reductions in trade barriers under GATT. **Trade diversion** is one disadvantage. Trade is diverted when low-cost firms from countries outside the trading area are replaced by high-cost firms within the trading area. For example, as a result of NAFTA, producers of electronic equipment in Southeast Asia will have to pay a U.S. tariff, while producers of the same equipment in Mexico will not have to pay

**trade diversion:** the shifting of trade away from the low-cost producer toward a higher-cost producer because of a reduction in trade barriers with the country of the higher-cost producer.

**trade creation:** the increase in trade due to a decrease in trade barriers.

the tariff. As a result, some production will shift from Southeast Asia to Mexico; that is viewed as a trade diversion from what might otherwise be a low-cost producer. The hope is that **trade creation**—the increase in trade due to the lower tariffs between the countries—outweighs trade diversion.

### *Free Trade Areas versus Customs Unions*

**free trade area (FTA):** an area that has no trade barriers between the countries in the area.

**customs union:** a free trade area with a common external tariff.

There is an important difference between two types of regional trading areas: **free trade areas (FTAs)** and **customs unions.** In both, barriers to trade between countries in the area or the union are removed. But external tariffs are treated differently: Under a customs union, such as the European Union (EU), external tariffs are the same for all countries. For example, semiconductor tariffs are exactly the same in France, Germany, and the other members of the EU. Under a free trade area, external tariffs can differ for the different countries in the free trade area. For example, the United States's external tariffs on textiles are higher than Mexico's. These differences in external tariffs under an FTA cause complications because a good could be shipped into the country with the low tariff and then moved within the FTA to the country with the high tariff. To prevent such external tariff avoidance, **domestic content restrictions** must be incorporated into the agreement. These restrictions say that in order to qualify for the zero tariffs between the countries, a certain fraction of the product must be made within the FTA. For example, under NAFTA, the majority of parts in television sets and automobiles must be manufactured in Canada, Mexico, or the United States in order for the television or car to qualify for a zero tariff.

**domestic content restriction:** a requirement that a fraction of the product must be produced within the area to qualify for zero tariffs between the countries in the free trade area.

## Managed Trade

**managed trade:** a situation in which a government takes actions to promote or restrict trade in certain goods, usually by setting targets for exports or imports.

Trade policymakers and news reporters frequently use the term **managed trade** to refer to the actions of government agencies to affect trade by persuading firms to buy or sell larger or smaller quantities of goods in other countries. The term means different things to different people. Most frequently, managed trade includes the VRAs and VIEs discussed earlier in the chapter. The semiconductor agreement between Japan and the United States is an example of managed trade. Managed trade actions like VRAs and VIEs stipulate certain numerical targets for exports or imports. The numerical target is usually stated as a percent of the market that must be imported or exported. For example, the semiconductor VIE called for imports equal to 20 percent of the Japanese market.

Some economic analysts in the United States argue that managed trade has the purpose of avoiding trade barriers such as tariffs or quotas. They believe managed trade is needed because governments intervene in the market in other countries. Managed trade is the way things are, they argue, and the U.S. government needs to face up to it. But others argue—and this is the more typical view among economists—that there are alternatives to managed trade that work better to improve economic efficiency. Many economists argue that managed trade is actually a form of trade barrier. For example, if a country should want to promote a certain economic activity—say, semiconductor production—then rather than requiring that foreigners buy that product, the government can provide tax credits or direct research subsidies. This is more transparent and does not have the side effect of raising U.S. consumer prices.

## Review

▶ There are many different approaches to removing restrictions on international trade, including unilateral disarmament, multilateral negotiations under GATT, and regional trading areas—FTAs and custom unions.

▶ Managed trade—such as voluntary import expansions—is put forth as a way to increase rather than restrict trade. But many economists argue that it is an intervention in the market that can be handled in better ways.

# CONCLUSION

Very few economists disagree with the proposition that tariffs and quotas usually reduce the general economic well-being of a society. In fact, polls of economists show that they disagree less on this proposition than virtually any other in economics, except perhaps the similar proposition that government price controls reduce economic well-being. This unanimity among economists was reflected in the debate over the North American Free Trade Agreement in 1993 in the United States. Every living Nobel Prize–winning economist endorsed the agreement to eliminate tariffs and quotas among Canada, Mexico, and the United States.

This chapter has shown that despite this unanimity, many restrictions on international trade still exist. True, there have been substantial reductions in tariffs in the last 50 years, and the recently completed Uruguay Round and North American Free Trade Agreement promise to continue this reduction in tariffs. But the use of nontariff barriers and antidumping laws has yet to show signs of diminishing. Trade disputes between the United States and Japan over domestic economic policies and particular products have worried some economists, who fear that a trade war with escalating trade restrictions could occur.

The need for cooperation in the formulation of trade policies is likely to increase rather than decrease in the future. The challenge is to develop a means for conducting international trade policy in a world in which many sovereign governments, each of which is free to formulate its own policy, coexist.

# KEY POINTS

**1.** Despite the economic arguments put forth in support of free trade, there are still plenty of restrictions on trade in the world.

**2.** Tariffs and quotas are the two main forms of restricting international trade. They are equivalent in their effects on prices and imports.

**3.** Tariffs were originally a major source of government revenue but are relatively insignificant sources of revenue today.

**4.** Quotas do not generate any revenue for the government. The quota holders get all the revenue.

**5.** Voluntary export restraints are much like quotas except they can be negotiated without an act of Congress, and the revenue usually goes to the foreign producer in the form of increased profits.

**6.** Strategic trade, national security, and infant industry are arguments put forth in support of trade barriers. In most cases, they are overwhelmed by the arguments in favor of reduced trade barriers.

**7.** Eliminating restrictions on trade unilaterally is difficult because of the harm done to those who are protected by the restrictions.

**8.** Regional trading areas and multilateral tariff reductions endeavor to reduce trade barriers by balancing export interests against import-competing interests.

**9.** Free trade areas and customs unions both create trade and divert trade.

**10.** Quantitative estimates of the gains from eliminating trade barriers are large in the United States and even larger for the world as a whole.

# KEY TERMS

protectionist policy
ad valorem tariff
specific tariff
import demand curve
export supply curve
quota
voluntary restraint agreement (VRA)
voluntary import expansion (VIE)
revenue tariffs
Smoot-Hawley tariff

trade war
Reciprocal Trade Agreement Act
General Agreement on Tariffs and
  Trade (GATT)
antidumping duties
dumping
nontariff barriers
strategic trade policy
infant industry argument
unilateral disarmament

multilateral negotiation
Uruguay Round
World Trade Organization (WTO)
most-favored nation (MFN)
trade diversion
trade creation
free trade area (FTA)
customs union
domestic content restrictions
managed trade

# QUESTIONS FOR REVIEW

**1.** In what sense are a tariff and a quota equivalent?

**2.** Why might a tariff raise the price of the imported product by less than the amount of the tariff?

**3.** How does a voluntary restraint agreement encourage the restriction of supply in the foreign country?

**4.** What are some examples of government standards and government procurement being used as trade barriers?

**5.** Why is unilateral disarmament a difficult way to reduce trade barriers?

**6.** How do multilateral negotiations or regional trading areas make the reduction of trade barriers easier politically?

**7.** Why might a free trade area cause trade diversion?

**8.** What is the infant industry argument in favor of trade protection?

**9.** What are the disadvantages of using retaliation in trade policy?

**10.** How large are the gains from reducing trade barriers?

# PROBLEMS

**1.** Estimates show that voluntary export restraints through which the government of Japan restricted automobile exports to the United States in the mid-1980s raised the price of Japanese cars in the United States by about $1,000. Sketch a diagram to show how this occurred and briefly explain the price increase.

**2.** Suppose the United States can produce steel domestically at $20,000 a ton, while Mexico can produce it at $15,000 and Brazil at $10,000. Assume the United States, Brazil, and Mexico currently impose a tariff of 60 percent on foreign steel. Given these assumptions, who produces the steel Americans consume? Would it be beneficial for the United States to form an economic union with Mexico if they keep the same tariff on Brazilian steel? Why?

**3.** Suppose the U.S. government decides to cut the quantity of textile imports in half by using quotas. Draw a diagram to illustrate this policy. Who benefits and who loses from this policy?

**4.** During the 1970s, several oil-producing countries restricted their exports of oil. What is the economic rationale for this restriction on trade? Why is it called a beggar-thy-neighbor policy?

**5.** "Maintaining a large trade surplus improves consumer welfare." Comment.

**6.** Suppose the U.S. government has decided for national security reasons that it must reduce the quantity of machine tools imported. What is the rationale? How can the United

States accomplish this goal? Which policy would you recommend? Why?

**7.** The United States imports lumber from Canada. Draw an export supply, import demand diagram to analyze this situation. Suppose Canada gives a new export subsidy to its lumber industry. What will happen to the price and quantity in the United States? Is the United States better off? Why does the United States government complain when foreign governments subsidize their export industries?

**8.** "Import tariffs are a blunt instrument for protecting industries. It would be better to try to support productivity improvements in these industries." Comment.

**9.** Suppose French wine suddenly becomes popular in the United States. How does this affect the price and quantity of imports of French wine? Suppose the U.S. wine industry lobbies for protection. If the government imposes a tariff in order to restore the original quantity of imports, what will happen to the price of French wine in the United States? Show how much tariff revenue the government will collect.

**10.** Suppose the United States decides to withdraw most-favored nation treatment from China. What would happen to the price and quantity of U.S. imports from China? Use a diagram to explain your answer.

# Glossary

**absolute advantage** a situation in which a person or country is more efficient at producing a good in comparison with another person or country. (21)

**ad valorem tariff** a tax on imports evaluated as a percentage of the value of the import. (22)

**aggregate demand** the total demand for goods and services by consumers, businesses, government, and foreigners. (5)

**aggregate demand/inflation (*ADI*) curve** a line showing a negative relationship between inflation and the aggregate quantity of goods and services demanded at that inflation rate. (13)

**aggregate expenditure line** the relation between the sum of the four components of spending ($C + I + G + X$) and aggregate income. (11)

**aggregate hours** the total number of hours worked by all workers in the economy in a given period of time. (7)

**aggregate income** the total income received by all factors of production in the economy; also simply called "income." (11)

**aggregate supply** the total value of all goods and services produced in the economy by the available supply of capital, labor, and technology (also called potential GDP). (5)

**antidumping duty** a tariff imposed on a country as a penalty for dumping goods. (22)

**asset** something of value owned by a person or a firm. (10)

**automatic stabilizers** automatic tax and spending changes that occur over the course of the business cycle that tend to stabilize the fluctuations in real GDP. (15)

**balance of payments** the record of all the transactions between a country and the rest of the world; it includes information on the value of trade in goods and services as well as transfer payments. (17)

**balanced budget** a budget for which tax revenues equal spending. (15)

**balanced budget multiplier** the ratio of the change in real GDP to a change in government purchases when the change in government purchases is matched by an equivalent change in taxes. (12)

**bank** a firm that channels funds from savers to investors by accepting deposits and making loans. (10)

**barter** trade in goods or services without the use of money. (10)

**baseline** the path of an economic variable that would occur without the policy change under consideration. (14)

**bilateral trade balance** the value of imports less the value of exports between two countries. (17)

**Board of Governors of the Federal Reserve System** the seven member governing board of the central bank of the United States. (10)

**bond** a financial contract that stipulates a specific repayment of principal plus interest on a loan at a given date in the future. (15)

**bond** a promise by a firm or government to pay a certain amount of money to the bondholder on a fixed date in the future. (10)

**boom** unusually rapid increases in real GDP; frequently used to refer to the period when real GDP is greater than potential GDP. (14)

**boom-bust cycle** a business cycle caused by a monetary policy in which interest rates are initially too low, causing a boom, and there is a subsequent increase in interest rates, which causes a recession. (14)

**Bretton Woods system** the international monetary system put in place after World War II; it was based on fixed exchange rates. Infrequent adjustments of the exchange rates were permitted and did occur under the Bretton Woods system. (17)

**budget cycle** the more than two-year process in which the federal budget is proposed, modified, enacted, and implemented. (15)

**budget deficit** the amount by which government spending exceeds tax revenues. (15)

**budget surplus** the amount by which tax revenues exceed spending. (15)

**business cycles** short-term fluctuations in real GDP and employment. (5)

**business fixed investment** investment by firms in physical capital, such as factories and equipment. (6)

**capital** the factories, improvements to cultivated land, machinery and other tools, equipment, and structures used to produce goods and services. (1, 5, 8)

**capital abundant** a higher level of capital per worker in one country relative to another. (21)

**capital account** the part of the international accounts of a country that keeps track of the change in domestic assets owned by foreigners and foreign assets owned by citizens. (17)

**capital gains tax**   a tax on the increase in the value of an asset. (18)

**capital income**   the sum of profits, rental payments, and interest payments. (6)

**capital intensive**   production that uses a relatively high level of capital per worker. (21)

**capital-saving technological change**   a technological innovation that reduces the amount of capital needed to produce a given amount of output with a given amount of labor. (9)

**capitalism**   an economic system based on a market economy in which capital is individually owned, and production and employment decisions are decentralized. (20)

**Cartesian coordinate system**   a graphing system in which ordered pairs of numbers are represented on a plane by the distances from a point to two perpendicular lines, called axes. (1ap)

**catch-up line**   the downward-sloping relation between the level of productivity and growth of productivity predicted by growth theory. (19)

**causation**   a relation of cause and effect between variables in which one variable is a determinant of another variable. (1)

**central bank**   the government institution that controls monetary policy in most countries. (10, 16)

**central bank independence**   a description of the legal authority of central banks to make decisions on monetary policy with little interference by the government in power. (16)

*ceteris paribus*   all other things being equal; refers to holding all other variables constant or keeping all other things the same when one variable is changed. (1)

**chain weighted price index**   a price index using a changing basket of goods and services computed just as real GDP is computed, usually mentioned as a measure of inflation. (6)

**checking deposit**   an account at a financial institution on which checks can be written; also called checkable deposit. (10)

**choice**   a selection among alternative goods, services, or actions. (2)

**coincidence of wants**   a condition required for exchange in a nonmonetary system; to accomplish a trade, it is necessary to find someone who has what you want and also wants what you have. (10)

**collectivized farm**   a farm in a planned economy that is in theory collectively owned by peasants, but controlled by the government. (20)

**command economy**   an economy in which the government determines prices and production; also called a centrally planned economy. (1, 20)

**commerce clause**   the clause in the U.S. Constitution that prohibits restraint of trade between states. (21)

**commodity money**   a good used as money that has some intrinsic value in a nonmonetary use. (10)

**communism**   an economic system in which all capital is collectively owned. (20)

**comparative advantage**   a situation in which a person or country can produce one good more efficiently than another good in comparison with another person or country. (2, 17, 22)

**complement**   a good that is usually consumed or used together with another good. (3)

**conditional forecast**   a prediction that depends on assumed values for government purchases, taxes, or some other variable that affects the forecast. (11)

**conditionality**   stipulations on loans to countries from the International Monetary Fund that certain policy prescriptions, such as price reforms or reducing government budget deficits, must be met to receive funds. (19)

**constant money growth rule**   a monetary policy in which the central bank keeps money growth constant. (16)

**consumer price index (CPI)**   a price index equal to the current price of a fixed market basket of consumer goods and services in a base year. (6)

**consumption**   purchases of final goods and services by individuals. (6)

**consumption function**   the positive relationship between consumption and income. (11)

**consumption share**   the proportion of GDP that is used for consumption; equals consumption divided by GDP, or $C/Y$. (8)

**consumption smoothing**   the idea that, although their incomes fluctuate, people try to stabilize consumption spending from year to year. (12)

**controlled experiments**   empirical tests of theories in a controlled setting in which particular effects can be isolated. (1)

**coordination failure**   a situation where, because their actions are interdependent, people fail to act in a manner that is mutually beneficial. (18)

**correlation**   the degree to which economic variables are observed to move together: If they move in the same direction, there is positive correlation; if they move in opposite directions, there is negative correlation. (1)

**Council of Economic Advisers**   a three-member group of economists appointed by the president of the United States to analyze the economy and make recommendations about economic policy. (1)

**countercyclical policy**   a policy designed to offset the fluctuations in the business cycle. (15)

**country in transition**   a country that is transforming from a centrally planned economy to a market economy. (19)

**credibility** the believability of the government's intentions to carry out stated policies. (15)

**cross-price elasticity of demand** the percentage change in the quantity demanded of one good divided by the percentage change in the price of another good. (4)

**crowding out** the decline in private investment owing to an increase in government purchases. (8)

**currency** money in its physical form: coin and paper money. (10)

**currency to deposit ratio** the proportion of currency that people in the economy want to hold relative to their deposits; it equals currency divided by deposits. (10)

**current account balance** the value of exports minus the value of imports plus net factor income from abroad plus net transfers from abroad. (17)

**Current Population Survey** a monthly survey of a sample of U.S. households done by the U.S. Census Bureau; it measures employment, unemployment, the labor force, and other characteristics of the U.S. population. (7)

**customs union** a free trade area with a common external tariff. (22)

**cyclical deficit** the difference between the actual deficit and the structural deficit. (15)

**cyclical unemployment** unemployment due to a recession, when the rate of unemployment is above the natural rate of unemployment. (7)

**debt to GDP ratio** the total amount of outstanding loans the federal government owes divided by nominal GDP. (15)

**deflation** a decrease in the overall price level, or a negative inflation rate. (14)

**demand** a relationship between price and quantity demanded. (3)

**demand curve** a graph of demand showing the downward-sloping relationship between price and quantity demanded. (3)

**demand schedule** a tabular presentation of demand showing the price and quantity demanded for a particular good, all else being equal. (3)

**demand shock** a shift in one of the components of aggregate demand that leads to a shift in the aggregate demand/inflation curve. (14)

**depreciation** the decrease in an asset's value over time; for capital, it is the amount by which physical capital wears out over a given period of time. (6)

**developing country** a country that is poor by world standards in terms of real GDP per capita. (19)

**diffusion** the spreading of an innovation throughout the economy. (9)

**diminishing returns** a situation in which successive increases in the use of an input, holding other inputs constant, will eventually cause a decline in the additional production derived from one more unit of that input. (9)

**discount rate** the interest rate that the Fed charges commercial banks when they borrow from the Fed. (16)

**discretionary fiscal policy** changes in tax or spending policy requiring legislative or administrative action by the president or Congress. (15)

**disinflation** a reduction in the inflation rate. (14)

**disposable income** income that households have to spend after taxes have been paid and transfers from the government have been received. (11)

**division of labor** dividing work into different tasks with groups of workers specializing in each task. (2, 9)

**domestic content restriction** a requirement that a fraction of the product must be produced within the area to qualify for zero tariffs between the countries in the free trade area. (22)

**dual scale** a graph that uses time on the horizontal axis and different scales on left and right vertical axes to compare the movements in two variables over time. (1ap)

**dumping** the selling of goods by foreign firms at a price below average cost or below the price in the domestic country. (22)

**dynamic comparative advantage** changes in comparative advantage over time from investment in physical and human capital and in technology. (21)

**economic development** the process of growth by which countries raise incomes per capita and become industrialized; also refers to the branch of economics that studies this process. (19)

**economic fluctuations** swings in real GDP that lead to deviations of the economy from its long-term growth trend. (5)

**economic growth** an upward trend in real GDP, reflecting expansion in the economy over time; it can be represented as an outward shift in the production possibilities curve. (2, 5)

**economic history** the study of economic events and the collection of economic observations from the past. (1)

**economic interaction** exchanges of goods and services between people. (2)

**economic model** an explanation of how the economy or part of the economy works. (1)

**economic variable** any economic measure that can vary over a range of values. (1)

**efficiency wage** a wage higher than that which would equate quantity supplied and quantity demanded set by employers in order to increase worker efficiency, for example, by decreasing shirking by workers. (7)

**elastic demand**   demand for which price elasticity is greater than 1. (4)

**employment-to-population ratio**   the ratio (usually expressed as a percentage) of employed workers to the working-age population. (7)

**equilibrium interest rate**   the interest rate that equates the sum of consumption, investment, and net export shares to the share of GDP available for nongovernment use. (8)

**equilibrium price**   the price at which quantity supplied equals quantity demanded. (3)

**equilibrium quantity**   the quantity traded at the equilibrium price. (3)

**European monetary system**   a system of exchange rates in which European currencies are fixed relative to each other but are flexible against the dollar, the yen, and other currencies. (17)

**exchange market intervention**   purchases and sales of foreign currency by a government in exchange markets with the intention to affect the exchange rate. (17)

**exchange rate**   the price of one currency in terms of another. (2)

**expansion**   the period between the trough of a recession and the next peak, consisting of a general rise in output and employment. (5)

**experimental economics**   a branch of economics that uses laboratory experiments to analyze economic behavior. (1)

**export supply curve**   a curve showing the quantity of exports supplied at various prices. (22)

**export-led strategy**   the government's encouragement of the economy's development by establishing an open trade policy and increasing exports. (19)

**export**   the sale of goods and services abroad. (20 )

**exports**   the total value of the goods and services that people in one country sell to people in other countries. (6)

**factor income**   earnings for a factor of production including wages and profits. (17)

**factor-price equalization**   the equalization of the price of labor and the price of capital across countries when they are engaging in free trade. (21)

**federal budget**   a summary of the federal government's proposals for spending, taxes, and the deficit. (15)

**federal debt**   the total amount of outstanding loans owed by the federal government. (15)

**federal funds rate**   the interest rate on overnight loans between banks that the Federal Reserve influences by changing the supply of funds (bank reserves) in the market. (13)

**Federal Open Market Committee (FOMC)**   the committee, consisting of the seven members of the Board of Governors and the twelve presidents of the Fed district banks, that meets about eight times per year to decide monetary policy; only five of the presidents vote at any one time. (10)

**Federal Reserve System (the Fed)**   the central bank of the United States, which oversees the creation of money in the United States. (10)

**final good**   a new good that undergoes no further processing before it is sold to consumers. (6)

**financial intermediary**   a firm that channels funds from savers to investors by accepting deposits and making loans. (10)

**fiscal policy**   the government's plans for spending, for taxes, and for borrowing. (15)

**fiscal policy rule**   a description of how the instruments of policy regularly respond to the state of the economy. Automatic stabilizers are an example of a fiscal policy rule. (15)

**five-year plan**   a document that stated production goals for the entire Soviet economy for the succeeding five years. (20)

**fixed exchange rate system**   a system of international exchange rates in which the countries agree to maintain a predetermined value of their currencies in terms of other currencies. (17)

**flexible exchange rate system**   an international monetary system in which exchange rates are determined in foreign exchange markets and governments do not agree to fix them. (17)

**flexible price assumption**   an assumption that prices adjust instantaneously in response to a change in supply or demand. (11)

**forecast**   a prediction of an economic variable such as real GDP. (11)

**foreign direct investment**   investment by a foreign entity of at least a 10 percent direct ownership share in the firm. (19)

**45-degree line**   the line showing that aggregate expenditure equals aggregate income. (11)

**forward-looking consumption model**   a model that explains consumer behavior by assuming people anticipate future income when deciding on consumption spending today. (12)

**free trade**   a complete lack of restrictions on international trade. (21)

**free trade area (FTA)**   an area that has no trade barriers between the countries in the area. (21)

**freely determined price**   a price that is determined by the individuals and firms interacting in markets. (2)

**frictional unemployment**   short-term unemployment arising from normal turnover in the labor market, such as when people change occupations or locations, or are new entrants. (7)

**futures market**  a market that deals in commodities to be delivered in the future. (17)

**gains from trade**  improvements in income, production, or satisfaction owing to the exchange of goods or services. (2, 21)

**GDP deflator**  nominal GDP divided by real GDP; it measures the level of prices of goods and services included in real GDP relative to a given base year. (6)

**General Agreement on Tariffs and Trade (GATT)**  an international treaty and organization designed to promote mutual reductions in tariffs and other trade barriers among countries. (22)

**gold standard**  a monetary standard in which the value of money is linked to gold. (10, 16)

**Gosplan**  the planning agency of the former Soviet Union. (20)

**government failure**  a situation in which the government makes things worse than the market, even though there may be market failure. (2)

**government procurement**  the process by which governments buy goods and services. (22)

**government purchases**  purchases by federal, state, and local governments of new goods and services. (6)

**government purchases share**  the proportion of GDP that is used for government purchases; equals government purchases divided by GDP, or *G/Y*. (8)

**gradualism**  the slow phasing-in of free market reforms. (20)

**gross domestic product (GDP)**  a measure of the value of all the goods and services newly produced in an economy during a specified period of time. (1)

**gross investment**  the total amount of investment, including that which goes to replacing worn out capital. (6)

**growth accounting formula**  an equation that states that the growth rate of real GDP per hour of work equals capital's share of income times the growth rate of capital per hour of work plus the growth rate of technology. (9)

**hedge**  to reduce risk, usually by buying a futures contract to guarantee a price several months in the future. (17)

**human capital**  a person's accumulated knowledge and skills. (9)

**implicit contract**  an informal agreement between a firm and its customers or between a firm and its employees. (11)

**import**  the purchase of goods and services from abroad. (21)

**import demand curve**  a curve showing the quantity of imports demanded at various prices. (22)

**import substitution strategy**  a trade policy designed to encourage local firms to produce goods that are normally imported into the country. (19)

**imports**  the total value of the goods and services that people in one country buy from people in other countries. (6)

**incentive**  a device that motivates people to take action, usually so as to increase economic efficiency. (2)

**income elasticity of demand**  the percentage change in quantity demanded of one good divided by the percentage change in income. (4)

**increasing opportunity cost**  a situation in which producing more of one good requires giving up producing an increasing amount of another good. (2)

**indirect business taxes**  taxes, such as sales taxes, that are levied on products when they are sold. (6)

**industrialized country**  a country with a large industrial base that is relatively well off by world standards in terms of real GDP per capita. (19)

**inelastic demand**  demand for which the price elasticity is less than 1. (4)

**infant industry argument**  the view that a new industry may be encouraged by protectionist policies. (22)

**inferior good**  a good for which demand decreases when income rises and increases when income falls. (3)

**inflation**  an increase in the overall price level. (1)

**inflation rate**  the percentage increase in the overall price level over a given period of time, usually one year. (1, 5)

**informal economy**  the portion of an economy characterized by illegal, unregulated businesses. (19)

**innovation**  applications of new knowledge in a way that creates new products or significantly changes old ones. (9)

**inputs or factors of production**  labor, capital, and other resources used in the production of goods and services. (1)

**insider**  a person who already works for a firm and has some influence over wage and hiring policy. (7)

**intellectual property laws**  laws that protect ownership rights over ideas and inventions; includes patent laws, copyright laws, and trademark laws. (9)

**interest rate**  the amount received per dollar loaned per year, usually expressed as a percentage (e.g., 6 percent) of the loan. (5)

**interindustry trade**  trade between countries in goods from different industries. (21)

**intermediate good**  a good that undergoes further processing before it is sold to consumers. (6)

**International Monetary Fund (IMF)**  an international agency, established after World War II, designed to help countries with balance of payments problems and to ensure the smooth functioning of the international monetary system. (19)

**international monetary independence** the idea that a flexible exchange rate system gives a country the ability to have much different interest rates than other countries. (17)

**international trade** exchange of goods and services between people or firms in different nations. (2, 21)

**international transfer payments** payments across international borders in the form of grants, remittances, and aid. (17)

**intraindustry trade** trade between countries in goods from the same or similar industries. (21)

**invention** a discovery of new knowledge. (9)

**inventory investment** a change in the stock of inventories from one date to another. (6)

**investment** purchases of final goods by firms plus purchases of newly produced residences by households. (6, 8)

**investment-saving gap** the difference between the level of investment and the level of saving in the economy. (17)

**investment share** the proportion of GDP that is used for investment; equals investment divided by GDP or *I/Y*. (8)

**investment tax credit** a reduction in taxes for firms that buy new investment goods that is proportional to the expenditures on the good. (18)

**iron law of wages** the prediction that wages will always tend to equal the subsistence level. (9)

**job leavers** people who are unemployed because they quit their previous job. (7)

**job losers** people who are unemployed because they lost their previous job. (7)

**job rationing** a reason for unemployment in which the quantity of labor supplied is greater than the quantity demanded because the real wage is too high. (7)

**job search** a reason for unemployment in which uncertainty in the labor market and workers' limited information requires people to spend time searching for a job. (7)

**job vacancies** positions that firms are trying to fill, but for which they have yet to find suitable workers. (7)

**Keynesian revolution** a change in macroeconomic thinking, shaped by the Great Depression and the work of John Maynard Keynes, leading to a greater consideration of demand-side policies. (18)

**Keynesian school** a school of macroeconomic thought concerned with pursuing demand-side macroeconomic policies—primarily fiscal policies working through the multiplier—to reduce unemployment and encourage economic growth. (18)

**labor** the number of hours people work in producing goods and services. (1, 5)

**labor abundant** a lower level of capital per worker in one country relative to another. (21)

**labor demand curve** a downward-sloping relationship showing the quantity of labor firms are willing to hire at each wage. (7)

**labor force** all those who are either employed or unemployed. (7)

**labor force participation rate** the ratio (usually expressed as a percentage) of people in the labor force to the working-age population. (7)

**labor income** the sum of wages, salaries, and fringe benefits paid to workers. (6)

**labor intensive** production that uses a relatively low level of capital per worker. (21)

**labor productivity** output per hour of work. (5)

**labor-saving technological change** a technological innovation that reduces the amount of labor needed to produce a given amount of output with a given amount of capital. (9)

**labor supply curve** the relationship showing the quantity of labor workers are willing to supply at each wage. (7)

**law of demand** the tendency for the quantity demanded of a good in a market to decline as its price rises. (3)

**law of one price** the notion that, with low transportation costs and no trade barriers, the same commodity is sold for the same price in two different countries when measured in the same currency. (17)

**law of supply** the tendency for the quantity supplied of a good in a market to increase as its price rises. (3)

**learning by doing** a situation in which workers become more proficient by doing a particular task many times. (9)

**Leontief paradox** the inconsistency that Wassily Leontief found between the data on U.S. trade and the Heckscher-Ohlin model. (21)

**liability** something of value a person or firm owes to someone else. (10)

**life-cycle model** a type of forward-looking consumption model that assumes that people base their consumption decisions on their expected lifetime income rather than on their current income. (12)

**limited information** a situation in which firms have incomplete knowledge about some market conditions, such as whether a change in demand for their product is temporary or permanent or whether the change is due to a recession or boom in the whole economy. (11)

**linear** a situation in which a curve is straight, with a constant slope. (1ap)

**liquidity constraint** the situation in which people cannot borrow to smooth their consumption spending when their income is low. (12)

**loan** an interest-bearing asset to the bank that lends money to an individual or firm. (10)

**M1** currency plus checking deposits plus travelers checks. (10)

**M2** M1 plus savings, time, and limited checking deposits. (10)

**macroeconomics** the branch of economics that examines the workings and problems of the economy as a whole— economic growth, inflation, unemployment, and economic fluctuations. (1)

**Malthusian equilibrium** a situation in which production equals the subsistence level of output because population adjusts based on consumption of food. (9)

**managed trade** a situation in which a government takes actions to promote or restrict trade in certain goods, usually by setting targets for exports or imports. (22)

**marginal propensity to consume (MPC)** the slope of the consumption function, showing the change in consumption that is due to a given change in income. (11)

**marginal propensity to import (MPI)** the change in imports because of a given change in income. (12)

**marginal propensity to save (MPS)** the change in saving due to a given change in income; MPS = 1 − marginal propensity to consume (MPC). (12)

**market** an arrangement by which economic exchanges between people take place. (1, 2)

**market economy** an economy characterized by freely determined prices and the free exchange of goods and services in markets. (1, 20)

**market equilibrium** the situation in which the price is equal to the equilibrium price and the quantity traded equals the equilibrium quantity. (3)

**market failure** any situation in which the market does not lead to an efficient economic outcome and in which there is a potential role for government. (2)

**medium of exchange** an item that is generally accepted as a means of payment for goods and services. (2, 10)

**mercantilism** the notion, popular in the 1700s, that the wealth of a nation was based on how much it could export in excess of its imports, and thereby accumulate precious metals. (21)

**merchandise trade** trade in goods that have physical form, such as oil, wheat, or computers. (17)

**merchandise trade balance** the value of merchandise exports minus the value of merchandise imports. (17)

**microeconomics** the branch of economics that examines individual decision-making at firms and households and the way they interact in specific industries and markets. (1)

**minimum wage** a wage per hour below which it is illegal to pay workers. (3, 7)

**mixed economy** a market economy in which the government plays a very large role. (1)

**monetarist school** a school of macroeconomic thought that holds that changes in the money supply are the primary cause of fluctuations in real GDP and the ultimate cause of inflation. (18)

**monetary base** currency plus reserves. (10, 16)

**monetary policy rule** a description of how much the interest rate or other instruments of monetary policy respond to inflation or other measures of the state of the economy. (13)

**monetary transmission channel** a description of how a change in monetary policy eventually affects real GDP. (16)

**money** that part of a person's wealth that can be readily used for transactions; money also serves as a store of value and a unit of account. (10)

**money demand** a relationship between the interest rate and the quantity of money that people are willing to hold at any given interest rate. (16)

**money multiplier** the multiple by which the money supply changes due to a change in the monetary base. (10)

**money supply** the sum of currency (coin and paper money) held by the public and deposits at banks. (10)

**most-favored nation (MFN)** the principle by which all countries involved in GATT negotiations receive the same tariff rates as the country with the lowest negotiated tariff rates. (22)

**movement along the curve** a situation in which a change in the variable on one axis causes a change in the variable on the other axis, but maintains the position of the curve. (1ap)

**multilateral negotiation** simultaneous tariff reductions on the part of many countries. (22)

**multilateral trade** trade among more than two persons or nations. (2)

**multiplier** the ratio of the change in real GDP to the shift in the aggregate expenditure line. (12)

**national income** the sum of labor income and capital income. (6)

**national income and product accounts** official government tabulation of the components of GDP and aggregate income. (6)

**national saving** aggregate income minus consumption minus government purchases. (6)

**national saving rate** the proportion of GDP that is saved, neither consumed nor spent on government purchases;

equals national saving (*S*) divided by GDP, or *S/Y*. It also equals 1 minus the consumption share minus the government purchases share of GDP. (8)

**nationalization** the taking over of private firms by the government. (20)

**natural unemployment rate** the unemployment rate that exists in normal times when there is neither a recession nor a boom and real GDP is equal to potential GDP. (7, 11)

**negative slope** a slope of a curve that is less than zero, representing a negative or inverse relationship between two variables. (1ap)

**negatively related** a situation in which an increase in one variable is associated with a decrease in another variable; also called *inversely related*. (1)

**neoclassical growth school** an approach to macroeconomics that uses the aggregate production function and the growth accounting formula in describing long-term growth, emphasizing aggregate supply rather than aggregate demand. (18)

**net exports** the value of goods and services sold abroad minus the value of goods and services bought from the rest of the world; exports minus imports. (6, 21)

**net exports share** the proportion of GDP that is equal to net exports; equals net exports divided by GDP, or *X/Y*. (8)

**net factor income from abroad** the difference between receipts of factor income from foreign countries and payments of factor income to foreigners. (17)

**net foreign assets** the difference between citizens' net assets held abroad and net assets in the domestic country held by foreigners. (17)

**net investment** gross investment minus depreciation. (6)

**net transfers from abroad** the difference between transfer payments received and transfer payments made to other countries. (17)

**new classical school** a school of macroeconomics that holds that prices are perfectly flexible, expectations are rational, and therefore anticipated monetary policy will have no effect on the economy. (18)

**new entrants** people who are unemployed because they just entered the labor force and are still looking for work. (7)

**new Keynesian school** a school of macroeconomics that holds that prices are sticky and expectations are rational to explain the effect of monetary and fiscal policy. (18)

**new trade theory** models of international trade in which cost per unit declines as the international market grows. (21)

**newly industrialized country** a country that is growing rapidly and quickly developing its industrial base. (19)

**nominal GDP** gross domestic product without any correction for inflation; the same as GDP; the value of all goods and services newly produced in a country during some period of time, usually a year. (6)

**nominal interest rate** the interest rate uncorrected for inflation. (5)

**nominal rigidities** inflexibilities in wages and prices. (11)

**nonexcludability** the situation in which no one can be prevented from consuming a good. (9)

**nonrivalry** the situation in which more people can consume a good without reducing the amount available for others to consume. (9)

**nontariff barrier** any government action other than a tariff that reduces imports, such as a quota or a standard. (22)

**normal good** a good for which demand increases when income rises and decreases when income falls. (3)

**normative economics** economic analysis that makes recommendations about economic policy. (1)

**North-South problem** refers to the geographic dispersion of incomes: Northern countries tend to be relatively rich, and southern ones tend to be relatively poor. (19)

**open-market operation** the buying and selling of bonds by the central bank. (16)

**opportunity cost** the value of the next-best foregone alternative that was not chosen because something else was chosen. (2)

**organization** a human structure, such as a family, firm, government, or college, through which people may exchange goods and services. (2)

**outsider** someone who is not working for a particular firm, making it difficult for him or her to get a job with that firm although he or she is willing to work for a lower wage. (7)

**overall price level** an average of the prices of all goods and services with greater weight given to items on which more is spent. (1)

**paper money** currency made of paper that has no intrinsic value. (10)

**part-time worker** someone who works between 1 and 34 hours per week. (7)

**patent** a grant giving an inventor exclusive rights to use an invention for 17 years. (9)

**peak** the highest point in real GDP before a recession. (5)

**perestroika** the restructuring of the Soviet economy by reforming the central planning process. (20)

**perfectly elastic demand** demand for which the price elasticity is infinite, indicating an infinite response to a change in the price and therefore a horizontal demand curve. (4)

**perfectly elastic supply**    supply for which the price elasticity is infinite, indicating an infinite response of quantity supplied to a change in price and thereby a horizontal supply curve. (4)

**perfectly inelastic demand**    demand for which the price elasticity is zero, indicating no response to a change in price and therefore a vertical demand curve. (4)

**perfectly inelastic supply**    supply for which the price elasticity is zero, indicating no response of quantity supplied to a change in price and thereby a vertical supply curve. (4)

**permanent income model**    a type of forward-looking consumption model that assumes that people distinguish between temporary changes in their income and permanent changes in their income; the permanent changes have a larger effect on consumption. (12)

**personal income**    income paid directly to individuals; includes labor income, transfer payments, and the part of capital income that is paid out to individuals. (6)

**phaseout**    the gradual reduction of a government regulation or trade barrier. (21)

**Phillips curve**    a downward-sloping relationship between inflation and unemployment; originally found by A. W. Phillips in data from the late 1800s and early 1900s. (10)

**policy ineffectiveness proposition**    the proposition that anticipated monetary policy will have no effect on the economy. (18)

**political business cycle**    a business cycle resulting from politicians' use of fiscal or monetary policy to affect the outcome of an election. (16)

**portfolio investment**    investment by a foreign entity of less than a 10 percent ownership share in the firm. (19)

**positive economics**    economic analysis that explains what happens in the economy and why, without making recommendations about economic policy. (1)

**positive slope**    a slope of a curve that is greater than zero, representing a positive or direct relationship between two variables. (1ap)

**positively related**    a situation in which an increase in one variable is associated with an increase in another variable; also called *directly related*. (1)

**potential GDP**    the economy's long-term growth trend for real GDP determined by the available supply of capital, labor, and technology. Real GDP fluctuates above and below potential GDP. (5, 11)

**preemptive monetary strike**    a Fed interest rate increase in anticipation of a rise in inflation. (16)

**price**    refers to a particular good and is defined as the amount of money or other goods that one must pay to obtain the good. (3)

**price adjustment (*PA*) line**    a flat line showing the level of inflation in the economy at a given point in time. It shifts up when real GDP is greater than potential GDP, and it shifts down when real GDP is less than potential GDP; it also shifts when expectations of inflation or raw materials prices change. (13)

**price ceiling**    a government price control that sets the maximum allowable price for a good. (3)

**price control**    a government law or regulation that sets or limits the price to be charged for a particular good. (3)

**price elasticity of demand**    the percentage change in the quantity demanded of a good divided by the percentage change in the price of that good. (4)

**price elasticity of supply**    the percentage change in quantity supplied divided by the percentage change in price. (4)

**price floor**    a government price control that sets the minimum allowable price for a good. (3)

**price level**    the average level of prices in the economy. (6)

**price shock**    a change in the price of a key commodity such as oil, usually because of a shortage, that causes a shift in the price adjustment line; also sometimes called a supply shock. (14)

**privatization**    the process of converting a government enterprise into a privately owned enterprise. (20)

**production function**    the relationship that describes output as a function of labor, capital, and technology. (5)

**production possibilities**    alternative combinations of production of various goods that are possible, given the economy's resources. (2)

**production possibilities curve**    a curve showing the maximum combinations of production of two goods that are possible, given the economy's resources. (2)

**production target**    a goal set for the production of goods and services in a planned economy. (20)

**productivity curve**    a relationship stating the output per hour of work for each amount of capital per hour of work in the economy. (9ap)

**progressive tax**    a tax for which the amount of an individual's taxes rises as a proportion of income as the person's income increases. (15)

**property rights**    rights over the use, sale, and proceeds from a good or resource. (2)

**protectionist policy**    a policy that restricts trade to protect domestic producers. (22)

**public infrastructure investment**    purchases of capital by government for use as public goods, which add to the productive capacity of the economy. (8)

**purchasing power parity**    the theory that exchange rates are determined in such a way that the prices of goods in different countries are the same when measured in the same currency. (17)

**purchasing power parity exchange rate**   an exchange rate such that the prices of similar goods in different countries are the same when measured in the same currency. (6)

**quantity demanded**   the amount of a good that people want to buy at a given price. (3)

**quantity equation of money**   the equation relating the price level and real GDP to the quantity of money and the velocity of money: The quantity of money times its velocity equals the price level times real GDP; in terms of growth rates it states that money growth plus velocity growth equals inflation plus real GDP growth. (10)

**quantity supplied**   the amount of a good that firms are willing to sell at a given price. (3)

**quota**   a governmental limit on the quantity of a particular good sold or imported. (3, 22)

**rational expectations assumption**   the assumption that people forecast the future no better or no worse than economic forecasters. (12, 15)

**rational expectations revolution**   a change in macroeconomic thinking during the 1970s based on the assumption that people make rational, forward-looking decisions using all the information available to them. (18)

**real business cycle school**   a group of economists who believe that shifts in potential GDP, largely due to changes in technology, are the primary cause of economic fluctuations. (18)

**real business cycle theory**   a theory of macroeconomics that stresses that shifts in potential GDP are a primary cause of fluctuations in real GDP; the shifts in potential GDP are usually caused by changes in technology. (11, 14)

**real exchange rate**   a measure of the exchange rate between two currencies that adjusts for differences in inflation levels in the two countries. (17)

**real gross domestic product (real GDP)**   a measure of the value of all the goods and services newly produced in a country during some period of time, adjusted for inflation. (1, 5, 6)

**real interest rate**   the interest rate minus the expected rate of inflation; it adjusts the nominal interest rate for inflation. (5)

**real wage**   the wage or price of labor adjusted for inflation; in contrast, the nominal wage has not been adjusted for inflation. (7)

**recession**   a decline in real GDP that lasts for at least six months. (5)

**Reciprocal Trade Agreement Act**   passed in 1934 by the U.S. Congress, it allowed cuts in tariff rates based on similar cuts in tariff rates in European countries. (22)

**recovery**   the early part of an economic expansion, immediately after the trough of the recession. (5)

**reinflation**   an increase in the inflation rate caused by a change in monetary policy. (14)

**relative price**   the price of a particular good compared to the price of other goods. (1)

**relatively elastic**   a situation in which the elasticity of one good is greater than the elasticity of another good. (4)

**rent control**   a government price control that sets the maximum allowable rent on a house or apartment. (3)

**rent-seeking**   behavior on the part of firms or individuals intended to preserve or obtain rights, privileges, or licenses through which above-normal profits (economic profits greater than zero) can be earned. (19)

**required reserve ratio**   the fraction of a bank's deposits that it is required to hold at the Fed. (10)

**research and development (R & D)**   activities designed to further scientific knowledge and develop new products. (9)

**reserves**   deposits that commercial banks hold at the Fed. (10)

**residential investment**   purchases of new houses and apartment buildings. (6)

**revenue tariff**   an import tax whose main purpose is to provide revenue to the government. (22)

**Ricardian equivalence**   the view that a change in taxes today will not affect consumption because people recognize that their, or their children's, future tax burden will change in an opposite direction. (15)

**savings deposit**   an account at a financial institution that is very liquid but generally cannot be easily used for transactions. (10)

**scarcity**   the situation in which the quantity of resources is insufficient to meet all wants. (2)

**scatter plot**   a graph in which points in a Cartesian coordinate system represent the values of two variables. (1ap)

**seasonal unemployment**   unemployment that varies with the seasons of the year due to seasonal fluctuations in supply or demand for labor. (7)

**sectoral trade balance**   the value of exports less the value of imports in a particular sector or industry. (17)

**services trade**   trade in services, or things that do not have a physical form, such as consulting or telecommunications. (17)

**services trade balance**   the value of services exports minus the value of services imports. (17)

**shift of the curve** a change in the position of a curve usually caused by a change in a variable not represented on either axis. (1ap)

**shock therapy** the abrupt introduction of free markets in a formerly centrally planned economy. (20)

**shortage** the situation in which quantity demanded is greater than quantity supplied. (3)

**slope** refers to a curve and is defined as the change in the variable on the vertical axis divided by the change in the variable on the horizontal axis. (1ap)

**Smoot-Hawley tariff** a set of tariffs imposed in 1930 that raised the average tariff level to 59 percent by 1932. (22)

**socialism** an economic system in which the government owns and controls all the capital and makes decisions about prices and quantities as part of a central plan. (20)

**specialization** the situation in which a resource, such as labor, concentrates and develops efficiency at a particular task. (2)

**specific tariff** a tax on imports that is proportional to the number of units or items imported. (22)

**spending balance** the level of income or real GDP at which the 45-degree line and the aggregate expenditure line cross; also called equilibrium income. (11)

**stagflation** the situation in which high inflation and high unemployment occur simultaneously. (14)

**state enterprise** an organization, analogous to a firm in a market economy, that is owned and controlled by the government. (20)

**statistical discrepancy** the discrepancy between calculations of GDP using the spending approach and the income approach due to unreported data or errors in data collection. (6)

**sticky price assumption** an assumption that prices do not move quickly in response to a change in supply or demand; the assumption is used in the theory of economic fluctuations. (11)

**store of value** something that will allow purchasing power to be carried from one period to the next. (10)

**strategic trade policy** a set of government actions designed to encourage large firms to locate or start up in that country. (22)

**structural deficit** the level of the government budget deficit under the scenario where real GDP is equal to potential GDP; also called the full-employment deficit. (15)

**structural unemployment** long-term unemployment due to structural problems such as poor skills or longer term changes in demand or insufficient work incentives. (7)

**subsistence line** a line representing the minimum amount of production the population needs to survive or subsist. (9)

**substitute** a good that has many of the same characteristics and can be used in place of another good. (3)

**supply** a relationship between price and quantity supplied. (3)

**supply curve** a graph of supply showing the upward-sloping relationship between price and quantity supplied. (3)

**supply schedule** a tabular presentation of supply showing the price and quantity supplied of a particular good, all else being equal. (3)

**supply side economics** the branch of economics that emphasizes that reducing marginal tax rates on investments and labor will increase aggregate supply, thereby stimulating the macroeconomy. (18)

**surplus** the situation in which quantity supplied is greater than quantity demanded. (3)

**target inflation rate** the central bank's goal for the average rate of inflation over the long run. (13)

**tariff** a tax on imports. (21)

**tax rate** the percentage of income or the value of a good paid to the government in the form of taxes. (12)

**tax revenue** the total amount the government receives in the form of taxes; equals the tax rate times income (also simply called taxes). (12)

**technological change** improvement in technology over time. (9)

**technology** anything that raises the amount of output that can be produced with a given level of capital and labor. (5, 9)

**terms of trade** quantity of imported goods a country can obtain in exchange for a unit of exported goods. (20)

**time deposit** an account at a financial institution that requires that the money be left in the account for a specified period of time. (10)

**time inconsistency** the situation in which policymakers have the incentive to announce one economic policy but then change that policy after citizens have acted on the initial, stated policy. (16)

**time-series graph** a graph that plots a variable over time, usually with time on the horizontal axis. (1ap)

**tradable goods** goods for which transportation costs are not prohibitive. (17)

**trade adjustment assistance** transfer payments made to workers who will be hurt by the move to free trade. (21)

**trade balance** the value of exports minus the value of imports. (6)

**trade creation** the increase in trade due to a decrease in trade barriers. (22)

**trade diversion**   the shifting of trade away from the low-cost producer toward a higher-cost producer because of a reduction in trade barriers with the country of the higher-cost producer. (22)

**trade war**   a conflict among nations over trade policies caused by imposition of protectionist policies on the part of one country and subsequent retaliatory actions by other countries. (22)

**transaction cost**   the cost of buying or selling in a market including search, bargaining, and writing contracts. (2)

**transfer price**   a price that one department of an organization must pay to receive goods or services from another department in the same organization. (2)

**trough**   the lowest point of real GDP at the end of a recession. (5)

**twin deficits**   a term referring to a situation in which a government budget deficit and an international trade deficit occur simultaneously. (12)

**unemployment rate**   the ratio (usually expressed as a percentage) of unemployed workers to the labor force. (5, 7)

**unilateral disarmament**   in trade policy, the removal of trade barriers by one country without reciprocal action on the part of other countries. (22)

**unit elastic demand**   demand for which price elasticity equals 1. (4)

**unit of account**   a standard unit in which prices can be quoted and values of goods can be compared. (10)

**unit-free measure**   a measure that does not depend on a unit of measurement. (4)

**Uruguay Round**   the most recent round of negotiations on the General Agreement on Tariffs and Trade, begun in 1986 in Uruguay. (22)

**value added**   the value of the firm's production minus the value of the intermediate goods used in production. (6)

**velocity**   a measure of how fast money is turned over in the economy: Velocity equals nominal GDP divided by the money supply. (10)

**voluntary import expansion (VIE)**   a government agreement to expand imports from a particular country. (22)

**voluntary restraint agreement (VRA)**   a country's self-imposed government restriction on exports to a particular country. (22)

**working-age population**   persons over 16 years of age who are not in an institution such as a jail or hospital. (7)

**World Bank**   an international agency, established after World War II, designed to promote the economic development of poorer countries through lending channeled from industrialized countries. (19)

**World Trade Organization (WTO)**   an international organization that can mediate trade disputes. (22)

# INDEX

Note: Page numbers followed by n indicate footnotes.

PHOTO CREDITS *(continued from page iv)*

**Chapter 4:** p. 104, Raphael Caillarde/Gamma Liaison; p. 106, The Granger Collection. **Chapter 5:** p. 127 (left), Andrew Sacks/Tony Stone Wide World; p. 127 (middle), Joe Caputo/Gamma Liaison; p. 127 (right), C. J. Pickerell/The Image Works. **Chapter 6:** p. 141, Sobel Klonsky/The Image Bank; p. 147, Mark Antman/The Image Works. **Chapter 7:** p. 177 (left), Brent Jones/Stock Boston; p. 177 (middle), Mark Richards/Photo Edit; p. 177 (right), Anveal Vokra/The Picture Cube. **Chapter 8:** p. 196 (left), The Bettmann Archive; p. 196 (middle), The Bettmann Archive; p. 196 (right), Eric A. Weissmann/Stock Boston. **Chapter 9:** p. 222 (left), The Granger Collection; p. 222 (middle), The Granger Collection; p. 222 (right), Ed Lano/The Picture Cube; p. 226, The Bettmann Archive; p. 234 (left), The Bettmann Archive; p. 234 (right), Peter Menzel/Stock Boston. **Chapter 10:** p. 249 (top), The Granger Collection; p. 249 (bottom), The Bettmann Archive; p. 265, The Bettmann Archive; p. 266, The Bettmann Archive. **Chapter 11:** p. 280, Jack Spratt/The Image Works. **Chapter 12:** p. 313, The Bettmann Archive; p. 320 (top), Eric Sander/Gamma Liaison; p. 320 (bottom left), Bob Daemmrich/The Image Works; p. 320 (bottom right), Bob Daemmrich/The Image Works. **Chapter 16:** p. 403 (left), The Bettmann Archive; p. 403 (second from left), James Andanson/Sygma; p. 403 (center), John Coleman/Sygma; p. 403 (second from right), R. Maiman/Sygma; p. 403 (right), Jeffrey Markowitz/Sygma. **Chapter 17:** p. 442, Courtesy of Chicago Mercantile Exchange. **Chapter 20:** p. 483, The Bettmann Archive. **Chapter 21:** p. 503 (left), Nathan Benn/Stock Boston; p. 503 (right), Bill Galley/Stock Boston; p. 519, The Bettmann Archive.

CARTOON CREDITS

**Chapter 1:** p. 21, P. Steiner. Cartoonists and Writers Syndicate. **Chapter 3:** p. 79, Toos. Cartoonists and Writers Syndicate. **Chapter 5:** p. 128, Sidney Harris. Cartoonists and Writers Syndicate. **Chapter 6:** p. 137, Sidney Harris. Cartoonists and Writers Syndicate. **Chapter 8:** p. 202, Raeside. Cartoonists and Writers Syndicate. **Chapter 9:** p. 233, Sidney Harris. Cartoonists and Writers Syndicate. **Chapter 11:** p, 281, © 1994 Robert Mankoff from the Cartoon Bank, Inc. **Chapter 12:** p. 329, TOLES copyright Buffalo News. Reprinted with permission of Universal Press Syndicate. All rights reserved. **Chapter 14:** p. 354, Courtesy of Vikram Madan. **Chapter 15:** p. 398, With permission from Singer Media Corporation, San Clemente, California 92673. **Chapter 18:** p. 450, Sidney Harris. Cartoonists and Writers Syndicate; p. 456, With permission from Singer Media Corporation, San Clemente, California 92673. **Chapter 19:** p. 464, © 1994 Robert Mankoff from the Cartoon Bank, Inc. **Chapter 20:** p. 489, Pat Bagley. Courtesy of Salt Lake Tribune. **Chapter 21:** p. 502, Jeff Stahler. Reprinted by permission of NEA, Inc.